EDWINA MOUNTBATTEN

Edwina Mountbatten

A Life of Her Own

*

JANET
MORGAN

HarperCollins
An Imprint of HarperCollins*Publishers*

First published in 1991
by HarperCollins Publishers,
77–85 Fulham Palace Road,
Hammersmith, London W6 8JB

9 8 7 6 5 4 3 2 1

BRITISH LIBRARY CATALOGUING IN PUBLICATION DATA

Morgan, Janet
Edwina Mountbatten: a life of her own.
1. Great Britain. Welfare Work. Mountbatten, Edwina
Mountbatten, Countess, 1901–1960
I. Title
361.924

ISBN 0 00 217597 5

Photoset in Linotron Palatino by
Rowland Phototypesetting Ltd,
Bury St Edmunds, Suffolk
Printed and bound in Great Britain by
HarperCollins Book Manufacturing, Glasgow

For my father –
and for Robert

Contents

List of Illustrations   *page* ix

1 The Expert's Expert   1

2 Sir Ernest Acquires a Grand-daughter   16

3 Too Good to be True   27

4 Wilfrid Loses a Wife   39

5 The Intruder   49

6 Edwina's Education   65

7 Two Deaths in a Fortnight   80

8 Too Many Suitors   95

9 An Indian Morning   107

10 A Fashionable Wedding   122

11 Meeting the World   136

12 A Divine Little Daughter   151

13 Faster and Faster   167

14 Infidelity   179

15 Constant Dramas   200

16 The Treaty   208

17 Various Trials   221

18 The Perfect Companion   233

19 Lost Horizon   250

20 Mobilization   264

21 The Warrior and the Healer   286

22 The Bombshell   311

23 Edwina Inspects   335

24 Deliverance   355

25 Diminuendo   370

26 The Last Vicereine   382

27 Torn Apart   413

28 Breaking Her Silence   423

29 Poetry and Philosophy   450

30 Leave-taking   473

    Acknowledgements   483

    Index   487

List of Illustrations

facing page

Sir Ernest Cassel
Wilhelmina Cassel ('Auntie Grannie')
Maudie Ashley, Mary and Edwina
Wilfrid Ashley   22

Villa Cassel
Broadlands (*Crown copyright*)   23

Molly Ashley
Edwina   54

The Links School
Alde House   55

Edwina
Dickie Mountbatten   118

The wedding of the year (*Illustrated London News*)   119

Mary Pickford, Douglas Fairbanks, Edwina and Dickie
Edwina's pearls
Nice and Friendly (*The Bodley Head*)   150

Edwina and Laddie Sanford
Edwina and Jeanie Norton at the *Express* switchboard   151

Adsdean
Nada and Georgie Milford Haven, Dickie
Dickie's Mother, 'Aunt Victoria'   214

Peter Murphy, Edwina and Sophie Tucker
Larry Gray and Edwina   215

Marjorie and Edwina
Yola, Edwina and Anti Szapary
Bunny Phillips
Yola Letellier   246

Edwina, Pamela and Patricia   *facing page* 247

Edwina in uniform (*Illustrated London News*)   374

Edwina's war Years:
sorting knitted garments; visiting hospitals;
the Mountbatten family; with the troops   375

Vicereine (*Fox Photos*)   406

Dickie and Edwina with the Maharajah of Bikaner
Edwina and Gandhi (*Associated Press*)
Edwina and Nehru   407

*Unless otherwise specified, all pictures
come from the Broadlands Archive*

CHAPTER ONE

The Expert's Expert

Whenever Edwina Mountbatten did something especially shocking or original, people would observe that she was, after all, only partly English. They were thinking of her grandfather, Sir Ernest Cassel, the connection, it was said, that explained everything. Up to a point, they were right.

Sir Ernest was larger than life, in every way substantial. He had travelled everywhere and spoke many languages, including those of numbers and money. He made industries move and shook entire countries out of lethargy. He acquired houses and apartments, filling them with ornate and expensive objects. He founded hospitals and schools. His fortune was colossal and he was immensely generous. His figure was ample and his acquaintance vast, for Cassel knew everybody in politics, finance and society.

He was a complex man, a foreigner who became a fixture in British life, a cosmopolitan who wanted to belong to England. He remained detached, an outsider looking in, an insider looking out. Cassel was German by birth and also in temperament, almost a caricature of one of his good, bourgeois countrymen, for he was meticulous, efficient, extremely polite, fatalistic, reflective and anxious about his health. A sentimental man, he always remembered anniversaries. He was interested in sunbathing, fresh air and Nature cures and regularly mortified his flesh at Continental spas. Men and women liked him, children most of all.

He began quietly, being born into a moderately prosperous Jewish family, descended from sensible, thrifty people who had lived and worked for the past three hundred years in an unexotic part of Germany. Ernest, who was born in 1852, was the youngest of the three children of Amalia and Jacob Cassel, who had a modest banking business in Cologne. All Ernest's ancestors on his father's side seem to have known how to manage money; the first recorded Cassel, Joseph, was from 1688 financial adviser to the Archbishop of Cologne, the Prince Elector. Joseph's son was Purveyor to the Court and his son held the lease on the Elector's mint at Bonn. Other Cassels, related by profession and possibly by blood, served in similar posts elsewhere in Germany. One of these was Loeb Benedict Cassel, who settled in Hesse, a place to which this story will return.

Ernest, his brother Max and his sister Wilhelmina had a comfortable, if firmly regulated, childhood. Ernest was not just quick and subtle. He was also a romantic, who played the violin, hoping at one time that he might become a professional musician. Although Jacob did not encourage this, he by no means forced his son to choose a business career but offered him instead the choice of becoming a professional chess player, for Ernest was so good at the game that he could follow twelve different boards at once, murmuring his advice into two dozen ears. Ernest did not, however, choose chess. At fourteen he decided to leave school, showing his aptitude for psychological bargaining by holding a valuable piece of porcelain out of the window and threatening to drop it unless he got his way. He won his point – and thereupon apprenticed himself to the local bank, originally Dutch, of J. W. Eltzbacher, which specialized in financing large industrial concerns and foreign business, including the development of the new railways and industries spreading over the Rhineland. This was astute. Already Ernest was breaking away from the parochial, patterned life of the family bank, the synagogue and his relations. Two years later he left home altogether and, nearly seventeen, set off for England with a bag of clothes and his violin. He had come to seek his fortune; soon he was to find, increase and spend it. In time Edwina would inherit a large proportion of these Cassel millions. She would also receive and learn from her grandfather many of the instincts and skills by which the millions were amassed.

Ernest quickly found a job with a firm of grain merchants in Liverpool. They must have been impressed, for they paid him two pounds a week. Having tasted England and improved his English, he moved on to Paris, as a clerk with the Anglo-Egyptian Bank. There he met what every keen young person most requires: a patron. Conscious of his own energies and ambitions, looking for a way to break into worldly circles, Cassel found his impresario in an associate of the Paris bank, the adroit and influential Baron Moritz de Hirsch. Hirsch and Cassel took to each other. They were both natural travellers, at home anywhere. They were both individualists. Both knew when to keep

2

secrets and when to speak. Most important, the older and the younger man had the same attitude towards money: for them it was a dynamic force, a current that could run everywhere, ignoring geography and language, moving across political and national boundaries. For a financial wizard like Hirsch, money was not a commodity in itself but a means to many sorts of end – which on the way produced more money. In Cassel, Hirsch recognized genius.

Cassel stayed only a few months in Paris, for the outbreak of the Franco-Prussian war in 1870 meant that as a German subject he had to leave France. In that short time, however, he had taken two important steps: meeting Hirsch and making his first foray into Anglo-Egyptian business. Now he returned to London, where he heard that Louis Bischoffsheim, of the financial house of Bischoffsheim and Goldschmidt, was looking for a confidential clerk. It was thought that Cassel got the job because, unlike applicants who sent in elaborate letters recommending themselves, he simply said:

> Dear Sirs,
>
> I apply for the position in your office and refer you to my former chiefs, Messrs Eltzbacher, Cologne.
>
> Yours sincerely,
> Ernest Cassel.

The effect of his business-like letter must none the less have been reinforced by the fact that Hirsch, who spoke for Cassel, was Bischoffsheim's brother-in-law, and Goldschmidt Cassel's cousin.

Ernest quickly became a friend of the Bischoffsheim family. 'Mrs Bisch' liked him, which was important. Cassel was now nineteen, with energy and appetite to rush about the world for Bischoffsheim and Goldschmidt, but sufficient discretion to be trusted with delicate business. He quickly became indispensable, rescuing a firm in Constantinople, negotiating complex loans in South America, settling an unfortunate engagement in Nicaragua. At twenty-two he was made manager of the bank, with a handsome salary to add to the commission on his successful ventures. He had begun at two hundred and fifty pounds a year. Now, it is said, he was offered 'five', that is, five hundred. 'You mean five thousand, Mr Bischoffsheim,' Cassel replied, and got it.

Ernest was busy and successful. Hirsch had launched him into society and the Bischoffsheims treated him as a son. Cassel's immediate family was shrinking. In 1874 his mother Amalia died and the next year he lost both his father and his brother Max. Ernest at least had his sister to look after, for Wilhelmina had divorced her husband – he was said by the family to have run off with a circus rider – and was left with two young children, Felix and Anna. Jacob's estate amounted to four or five thousand pounds, to be halved between Ernest and his sister, but Ernest was now sufficiently well-established to be able to settle the legacy on Wilhelmina.

Who knows whether Cassel was lonely? He was making a place for himself in England, putting down roots deliberately but with genuine enthusiasm. This needed intelligence and application, for the English upper and upper-middle classes were tribes with special rules and conventions, while the aristocracy lived in a rarefied world of its own. A good many of the English people he was getting to know were unimaginative, sporting, anti-Semitic and suspicious of artists and foreigners. To be clever was a handicap. To be rich was useful but not sufficient. You had to join in, which required patience and stamina.

Ernest did join in. He rented houses and gave card parties and racing parties; he hunted and, although at first he fell off his horse, he persisted. He organized shooting parties and provided lavish picnics. To those who could not come, he sent pheasants, partridges and venison. He kept quiet about his visits to museums, his friend-ships with painters, musicians, theatrical people. Gradually he was accepted. Cassel had come from nowhere but he was arriving, at a great pace.

In 1878 he married. His wife, Annette, was a Scot, the daughter of Robert Thompson Maxwell, of Croft House, near Darlington. Ernest took two more steps towards respectability: he became a British subject and bought a house in Bayswater. Annette's marriage to Cassel was happy but brief. Within three years she contracted tuberculosis and, despite the best medical help that could be bought, she died. There are no photographs of her; Ernest kept no letters. Two bequests remained. The first was spiritual. Annette was a Catholic convert and, as she died, she begged Ernest to become a Catholic too, so that they might meet in the after-life. He kept his promise: a non-practising Jew, he became a non-practising Catholic, although most of his friends never knew it. Annette's second legacy was a daughter, Maudie, their only child. From the time of his wife's death, it was in Maudie that Ernest placed his trust and hope. Maudie was Edwina's mother.

The Expert's Expert

Who was to look after Maudie, supervise the nurses and governesses and run Ernest's household? The answer was obvious: Wilhelmina. She now came to live with her brother in London, bringing Felix and Anna. Wilhelmina dropped her former husband's surname, Schoenbrunn, reverting to her maiden name of Cassel. This might have been confusing but Mrs Cassel was so much herself and became so well-known and well-loved, that only the most ignorant newcomer momentarily mistook her for Ernest's wife. She was called Bobbie by their friends – and eventually, by Edwina, 'Auntie-Grannie'.

For her first ten years Maudie – her full name was Amalia Mary Maud – lived mostly at 2 Orme Square, the house in Bayswater, with her father, aunt and cousins. In the holidays Ernest took houses in the country and at the seaside; he insisted on ozone (recently discovered) and good air. He liked to have Maudie with him but, for times when they were parted, he had made for himself a small double-headed bronze medallion, the size of a sixpence, with her likeness on one side and his own upon the other. It was a financier's idea; thus he could always keep her in his pocket. Ernest liked children. He was kind and playful and was to remain so to the end of his life. Mrs Cassel's children's children were to remember Great-Uncle Ernest in his old age, chatting affectionately as he solemnly walked up and down the terrace steps for exercise, promising them whatever toys they wanted, if they were good. For Ernest was also exacting. His manners were formal, his standards high, and he required the same diligence and punctiliousness from his household, especially from Maudie. In some respects she satisfied him. She was bright, good at languages – she spoke and wrote fluent French, German and Italian – and she had her father's quick judgement. She was to grow up into an excellent bridge player and, liking mild risk, an enthusiastic gambler at roulette and at the races. Maudie was, on the other hand, dreamy, lazy, easily flattered. Ernest tried not to spoil her. He was anxious that his little girl should not grow up into a bored young woman. He was also afraid that without a strict regime she might over-tire herself and fade away, as Annette had done. So Maudie's diet was carefully controlled, her hours of work and play and her bedtimes planned. Apart from her cousins, who were anyway some years older, she did not mix much with other children. Her father was often abroad; when he came home, he scrutinized the work she had done in the schoolroom, the brightness of her eyes and the colour in her cheeks. Later, when Maudie's husband complained that she danced too much, entertained too many people, was never at home, she excused herself by reminding him of her rigorously ordered childhood, for which, she explained, she was now compensating.

In her early years, however, any wilfulness was suppressed. Maudie was loving and dutiful. She was taught to praise God, respect the dead and honour her father and her aunt. She was educated at home, for there were few schools for girls from such families. Her upbringing in Bayswater was much as it might have been in Cologne; the English bourgeoisie was less introspective than those whom Queen Victoria called 'our German cousins' but in other respects it was very similar.

Maudie was a sweet-natured, pretty, friendly child, polite to visitors, whose numbers grew as her father's standing and success increased. His touch seemed unerring; from 1880 onwards his international activities and his fortune steadily expanded. He invested in Mexico, America and Sweden, in railways, mines and steel. Cassel's closest associate was the American financier Jacob Schiff, whom he first met on a visit to New York in the late 1870s, to discuss the reconstruction of the Erie railroad company. By 1880 Schiff and Cassel were writing to each other every week, with domestic as well as business news. They shared a love of the Swiss Alps and it was there, in the autumn of 1890, that their devotion became complete. The two families were exploring the lower ranges of Mont Blanc when Frieda, Schiff's daughter, fell into a crevasse. Cassel unhesitatingly leapt into the chasm to save her. Frieda's fractured shoulder healed in time; the affection between Schiff and Cassel was now unbreakable.

The professional collaboration between Cassel and Schiff flourished so well that in 1884 Cassel, now an independent force, loosened his ties with Bischoffsheim and Goldschmidt. He had never become a partner, preferring to work for a salary and a share of the profits of his undertakings on the firm's behalf. Now he resigned as manager, although he continued to keep an office at the bank's premises in Throgmorton Street. As it was, Cassel spent a great deal of time travelling abroad. In the mid to late 1880s he arranged loans for the governments of Egypt, Brazil, Argentina, Uruguay and China; he was in iron, copper, railways, arms and shipping.

Cassel's growing wealth increased his influence. He was cultivated by kings, presidents and politicians. Their advisers sought his advice. Cassel not only provided the capital that was needed as one country after another embarked on its industrial revolution; he also helped these princes and ministers with their personal investments. Having shored up their finances, he helped them fill the hours of leisure in which they could then indulge. They were grateful for his assistance and his hospitality – and for his tact. He did not seek to humble the powerful or to outshine the glamorous. Cassel was a discreet enabler.

And how he entertained. By 1889 the house in Orme Square was too small, not least because, as well as collecting guests, Cassel had begun to acquire objects: fine paintings, French and English furniture, Dresden china, Renaissance bronzes, English silver, Chinese jade. In 1889 he moved from Bayswater to 48 Grosvenor Square in Mayfair. He also anchored himself more firmly in the country, and by 1896 he was racing horses he had bred himself. Cassel was enthusiastic and competitive. The best private trainers taught him about bloodstock and told him which animals to buy, so that he advanced steadily in the lists of winning owners, until at last he stood next to the Duke of Portland and Leopold de Rothschild. He had to wait nearly twenty years until the Committee of the Jockey Club elected him as a member but, if Cassel cared, he did not show it. Some said that he was excluded for so long because he was thought to be less interested in bloodlines and horseflesh than in using his fortune to associate with grandees. Others maintained that Cassel was kept out because he was a Jew; worse, a Jewish financier. It would not have helped if they had known that he had been transformed into a Catholic. Cassel's enemies thought in stereotypes and he fitted into more than one. He was not just a foreigner but, professionally and socially, a speculator, who was making something out of nothing. Old-fashioned society, insular and conformist, still regarded plutocrats like Cassel as interlopers. The higher Cassel rose, the keener his critics were to topple him.

He had almost reached the pinnacle. At a race meeting he met the next and grandest of those friends with whom he was to develop a mutually beneficial connection. The first had been Hirsch, the second Schiff. The third was the Prince of Wales, the future King Edward VII. The two men quickly took to one another. They looked alike; both were stocky, with neat pointed beards. There were deeper resemblances. They were both adventurers, each in his own way ignoring the constraints of late Victorian society. The Prince belonged to a fast set of smart people, who dined, drank and gambled with an enthusiasm that Queen Victoria and her circle thought imprudent;

the liaisons of the Prince's friends were notorious. Cassel was not daring in that way but, compared with most of his colleagues in the financial and business world, he was a risk-taker on a grand scale. It was Cassel who backed the inventors and manufacturers who were developing new processes, new tools, new materials, Cassel who moved in where other investors feared to tread: into railways, the London Underground, gold and diamond mines, sugar-beet cultivation, steel mills, irrigation schemes.

In another way, too, Cassel and the Prince of Wales were similar. Each sat at the centre of an intricate web, spreading out from London across Europe and the world. For Edward, this was his vast constellation of royal relations, whose weddings and funerals he attended and with whom he swapped photographs at Christmas. Cassel's network was one of financial and industrial collaborators, with whom he negotiated and exchanged telegrams and instruments of credit. Yet each was isolated, the Prince by his peculiar position, largely symbolic, in which he enjoyed little power or even information, Cassel because he was a clever foreigner, generous with his hospitality but reticent about himself. He remained firmly planted alongside his sensible sister, with Mrs Bisch for an ally, and various women in whom he could confide. His great and increasing wealth defined him and set him apart.

Thus the Prince and Cassel were different from most of those among whom they dined, drank and played bridge. They were drawn together. The Prince was the ideal client, Cassel the perfect adviser. Edward could not manage his finances and in any case his position prevented him from speculating on his own account. Cassel took over the direction of the Prince's affairs. Their mutual respect and affection increased; it was eventually to have an important bearing on Edwina's life.

As Cassel's fortune, access and acquaintance grew, doors were opened for Maudie, who was now allowed to walk through them, since in 1897 she had come out and could at last pay visits on her own. That is, with a lady's maid and, as chaperone, Mrs Cassel or Mrs Bisch. Maudie was plump with a tiny waist, made tinier by the complex engineering beneath her clothes. She had long pale brown hair, not put up but worn in a thick plait tied with ribbons. At eighteen she was entering a well-upholstered world of large houses, conservatories and ballrooms, full of people who made her feel shy.

The Expert's Expert

She soon gained confidence. Maudie liked music and painting, she was intelligent and well-read in four languages – she particularly liked the wistful, impressionistic poetry of Théophile Gautier – and she soon picked up the sort of conversation that would help her survive at dinner. She saw how others dressed and became elegant herself; Cassel supplied the funds. She had smart dresses and furs; her jewels were kept in a box made like a chariot, of silver, with a puple velvet lining. Her travelling hatbox was 'a marvel'; as it held a dozen huge hats it must have resembled a coffin. Her sitting-room was decorated in aquamarine, a grey-green Corot its greatest treasure. She was a good dancer, a skilful bridge player, and she could sketch. She made friends easily; the older women mothered her and, though charming, innocent and capable of enjoying herself, she behaved sensibly with admiring men. As the only daughter of a very rich father, Maudie had to beware of fortune-hunters; in any case, she was a romantic. Mrs Cassel and Mrs Bisch kept watch, deftly piloting their charge and her convoy of hatboxes and parasols and trunks.

Maudie was looking for the perfect husband. She was encouraged by one friend in particular, Sarojini Chattopadhyay, whom she had met during a holiday in Coblenz in 1896. Sarojini, the daughter of a wealthy and distinguished Indian family, was intense, rhapsodic, frank about her feelings and desires. 'Marry for love', she declared. This, she sternly warned her protégée, was the only way to find true happiness. Although Maudie had nothing like Sarojini's strength of character, she promised to make up her mind for herself. She would be methodical and on no account would she be rushed into a decision. Throughout successive summers, autumns and springs, in 1897, 1898 and 1899, she appeared at dances and parties, looking about her, a progress that Sarojini followed as the 'society papers' arrived, weeks out of date, in India.

Much of Maudie's exploration took place at other peoples' houses in the country, each of which she conscientiously photographed. These places were without exception enormous: Eastwell, a turreted pile with steps down to an artificial lake; Lowther Castle, the flag flying among crenallated towers. At Gopsall, Atherstone, the Curzons were among the guests, with Lord Howe, Lord Chesterfield and Edward Sassoon. She was at Chatsworth, at Penn House and The Priory, Reigate. At last, at Little Dalby Hall, Melton Mowbray, a house with fretted balconies and dozens of chimneys, Maudie decided that she had fallen in love. His name was Hanbury Tracy and he asked if he might speak to her father. Alas, Ernest did not approve and at the beginning of November the desolate suitor left England for California. Maudie kept her admirer's letters, tied up in kitchen string with a love-knot. She did not grieve for long; Hanbury Tracy was soon to be displaced. Until that time, however, Maudie's relations with her father were scratchy. She longed to be independent and said so.

Meanwhile Cassel went from strength to strength. In 1899 he at last acquired his own place in the country, Moulton Paddocks, near Newmarket, a large, ivy-covered, pedimented house, that grew larger every six or seven years as Cassel built on more, keeping pace with his rivals and colleagues in the City: Sir Julius Wernher, Alfred Beit, Baron Ferdinand de Rothschild, Nathan de Rothschild and Baron Meyer de Rothschild (who *was* a member of the Jockey Club). All millionaires, who wanted solid and splendid shrines, they embarked on an orgy of construction, extension and embellishment – at Luton Hoo, in Park Lane, at Waddesdon, Tring and Mentmore. At Moulton Cassel put in stabling for fifty horses. He also moved his London office to Old Broad Street, where his employees included Winston Churchill's brother, Jack, whose father, Lord Randolph, was an old friend. At one time Cassel almost found himself employing both the young Churchills. If Winston continued to fail his military examinations, his father declared, he would put him into business; Lord Randolph was one of those who saw the City as a refuge for those too stupid for the Army.

Cassel was powerful, prosperous and famous. His Swedish interests had been consolidated into a company with a capital of nearly a million pounds; he had put up two million pounds to build the Aswan dam and the Assyut barrage on the Nile; he raised funds to construct railways in America and Mexico. Some said that in London Cassel was respected for an achievement closer to the hearts of bellicose Englishmen, the acquisition for Vickers of the Maxim Gun and Ammunition Company. For years he underwrote the company's chief financial issues and, assisted by the Foreign Office, made sure when he could that the purchase of arms from Vickers was a condition of his loans to foreign governments. In 1899 he was knighted. According to the Queen, who gave the knighthood to him, the honour was for his work in Egypt. Others said it was for putting the British munitions

The Expert's Expert

industry on a sound footing. Whatever the reason, Sir Ernest had now arrived. Wits who had seen Oscar Wilde's play now spoke of 'The Importance of Being Sir Ernest'.

Maudie blossomed too. She had spells of lassitude, when she would languish on a sofa, composing short stories that went no further than the first paragraph. (For example: 'The tale of the rainbow trout. What makes a summer's day? . . . the buzzing, the droning and piping of all the little insects' etc.) On the whole, however, she was full of energy, to Sir Ernest's relief, since he watched her health even more closely than his own. He had asked Queen Victoria's doctor, Sir William Broadbent, for the secret of a long and healthy life; Sir William gave the unexceptionable prescription: Peace and Fresh Air. From 1890, therefore, when Maudie was eleven, Sir Ernest took her almost every year to the Alps. It was to the Riederfurka, a small hotel 2100 metres up on the Riederalp in Switzerland, that Maudie was brought to mend her unhappy heart. Among the guests in August 1900 were Sir Philip de Laszlo, the fashionable portrait-painter, Richid Saadi Bey, the Turkish diplomat, and Mr Evelyn Ashley and his wife Lady Alice, who had both been there the year before. This time the Ashleys brought with them Evelyn's son Wilfrid, who had been invalided home with fever from the Boer War.

Maudie had first met Wilfrid in May 1899, when she had stayed at Milburn, near Esher in Surrey. He was much older, thirty-three to her twenty. He had been to Harrow, Magdalen College, Oxford, and to Sandhurst, and after that he had spent nine years in the Grenadier Guards. Wilfrid was good-looking; women habitually described him as the handsomest man they had ever seen. His hair shone, his moustache was neat, he had a noble brow, fine eyebrows and a slender, well-shaped nose. Beneath the moustache, however, the mouth was weak; the liquid eyes were not far-seeing. This elegant creature could not have been more unlike Maudie's father. That, perhaps, was part of the attraction.

Wilfrid had passed the greater part of his life among men: at school and university, at his military academy, in the Guards. He was good at doing the things men did, principally fishing and shooting, but with women he was not at ease. He charmed them, they liked him, but so far there had always been something lacking. Maudie Cassel was different. She was not a great beauty but she was attractive, with her 'dark-fair' hair, grey-green eyes and white transparent skin. She

11

was young, light-hearted and uncomplicated, with the mysterious and formidable figure of her father as a foil.

Sir Ernest was completely unlike Evelyn Ashley. Wilfrid's father was gentle, fine-drawn, unambitious. Indeed, the two families were wholly dissimilar. The Cassel stem was a stout, straightforward growth, its offshoots, in so far as they were known, energetic and true. Wilfrid's ancestry was just the opposite. His family tree had grown high and wide, bearing vivid blossoms and vigorous mutations. His great-grandmother's brother had been the Second Viscount Melbourne, Queen Victoria's Prime Minister, 'Lord M.'. That great-grandmother's second husband was the Queen's rakish Foreign Secretary, Lord Palmerston. Wilfrid's grandmother was Emily Cowper, wife of the seventh Earl of Shaftesbury, the philanthropist, who had worked for the protection of women and children, factory workers and chimney-sweeps, campaigned for the abolition of slavery, the protection of lunatics, the regulation of mines and the care of animals. (He is commemorated by the statue of Eros at Piccadilly Circus.) Of Shaftesbury's ancestors, one had introduced the cultivation of the cabbage into England, another the Habeas Corpus Act. Evelyn, Wilfrid's father, had been a barrister and held office in Gladstone's Liberal Cabinet. Lady Alice was Evelyn's second wife; his first, a descendant of the Indian princess Pocahontas, had died in the first year of their marriage, leaving a son, Wilfrid. It was a heady mix.

Some six months after Maudie first met Wilfrid at Milburn he had been sent out to South Africa, in command of a battalion. In the spring of 1900 he came home, haggard, exhausted, feverish, prone to headaches and depression, with pains in his back and legs. He was welcomed as a hero, although his months in battle had hardly been successful. Wilfrid's parents had taken him to the Continent to recover his strength and now, miserable and uncertain about his future, he arrived at the Riederfurka.

Weeks passed, until one afternoon, while Wilfrid helped Maudie across the rocks, he asked her to marry him. She said yes, as he handed her over an awkward piece of ground, and, when they were safely on the other side, said no. Wilfrid kissed her and insisted. Maudie said yes again. On their return Laszlo observed that Maudie looked slightly pink. Neither Maudie nor Wilfrid told their secret. Wilfrid did not dare speak to Sir Ernest; Maudie did not tell Wilhelmina.

The Expert's Expert

On 29 August Wilfrid had to return to England; his sick leave was up, and he was expected to rejoin his regiment at Aldershot. Unusually, Maudie was left to speak to her father; Wilfrid sent a telegram, wishing her luck, from the post office at the hamlet in the bottom of the valley. His second communication, a letter written from the station buffet at Lausanne, was already nostalgic: 'Today I am paying rather in the shape of rheumatics for sitting out yesterday in the rain but oh my own it *was* worth it. At least *I* thought so. This old African fever does make the bones ache . . .'

Wilfrid's first mission on staggering off the train at Victoria was to order a diamond ring at Tiffany's. He was a little uncertain: 'too big a stone looks pretentious. I fancy this is rather on the small side . . . but we will see . . . A small hand can't stand a large stone you know . . .' Already Wilfrid was revealing himself to be a worrier. He liked to be at least half an hour early for trains, he refused to go into stuffy station restaurants. He fretted about the best place to have a photograph taken for Maudie. Should he be done in Aldershot? 'Don't please say "yes" as I do want to be made handsome in London.'

As soon as Wilfrid had gone, Maudie approached her father. Sir Ernest must have been surprised that Wilfrid had not asked to speak to him directly but Maudie explained that, just as Sir Ernest's agreement was needed on the one side, so the Ashleys' approval was needed on the other. She and Wilfrid were acting, in effect, as negotiators on behalf of two equally important principals. If Sir Ernest had doubts, or if he conveyed them to Maudie, she did not pass them on to Wilfrid. Sir Ernest was sad to be losing his daughter, although, as Mrs Cassel reminded him, it had always been inevitable. He tried to put a good face on it. As Maudie told Wilfrid: 'he was so nice and affectionate to me the last few days, although we neither of us touched upon the future. He is so devoted I am afraid he feels the fact of my willingly leaving him dreadfully . . . I feel an ungrateful mule.'

Sir Ernest was possessive and Maudie had been beginning to feel the burden of it. One of Wilfrid's attractions was that he offered what seemed to be a more normal way of life: 'Putting money aside', Wilfrid wrote, '(that means something but by no means everything) you have not had nearly so good a time as most girls . . . As you have not been strong you have missed many pleasures such as hunting, balls etc and above all I fancy [you have had] no one to confide in. Darling

. . . I will try oh so hard to share your worries and sorrows'. Maudie agreed with all this, apart from protesting at being called a girl: 'I beg your pardon', said Wilfrid, 'woman'.

Sir Ernest at least considered Wilfrid a suitable match, although he wondered whether Maudie's new life would be as secure and comfortable as that to which she had been used. There was land, certainly, and there were houses. Wilfrid would not inherit a title but the Ashley name was old and honourable. He might make a profession for himself, although there had so far been no sign of it. Maudie would have a handsome marriage settlement from her father – but what income did Wilfrid enjoy? Could he support her? On this last point Sir Ernest's forebodings were justified.

Maudie, left on an alp with her French and German novels, soon had the engagement ring to remind her of her new status. The diamond was not considered too small: 'They chaff me about it and say I stick my finger out to be admired which is perhaps true'. This distraction had disadvantages: 'played poker last night and needless to say after the arrival of the darling ring I lost every hand . . . I think it would be advisable to look up in *Vanity Fair* the chapter on how to live on nothing a year'. She longed to be reunited with Wilfrid; her loose, generous handwriting and almost complete lack of punctuation made her letters seem particularly frenzied. 'I feel sentimental tonight', she confessed. 'I suppose the German instinct has got the upper hand in my nature.'

Wilfrid, back in Aldershot, was more down-to-earth. What were Maudie's habits when it came to catching trains? Was she early or late arriving at railway stations? What about newspapers? ('You know my love for *The Times*'.) More important even than these details was the question of her marriage settlement: 'Tomorrow I go up to see your Father in the City at 4 p.m.. I have heard again from my Father and I don't think there will be any hitches. He will give me about what I mentioned to you at the Rieder and I don't see how he can do much more without stinting himself and the property. A landed property has so many outgoings compared with other forms of income. I hope your Father will understand.'

'So don't worry, dear', Wilfrid assured her, trying to sound protective. Years later, when Dickie Mountbatten was being tiresome, he too would scatter a few 'dears' in his letters to Edwina. Neither Wilfrid nor Dickie, both affectionate but emotionally obtuse, realized how clearly their wives saw through them. Not that Wilfrid was completely prosaic. He wanted Maudie as fervently as she longed for him. 'I wish', he replied to one of her wilder letters, 'the scene behind the door you saw in your dream could happen *now*, except the maid appearing'. Like Maudie, he needed reassurance: 'Dearest, you are not tired of me yet are you and you will stick to me, won't you?'

All lovers are much the same.

CHAPTER TWO

Sir Ernest Acquires a Grand-daughter

So Maudie Cassel became Mrs Ashley – but first there were formalities to go through. Wilfrid's family approved of the engagement, although his father caused Maudie some anxiety by taking his time to write to Sir Ernest. 'Pure forgetfulness', Wilfrid assured her. Her lover could be self-centred, too. On Wilfrid's birthday, while Maudie was still abroad, he wrote her an unpromising letter, congratulating himself on having found a nice girl who would make him happy. Even in play this was revealing; perhaps Wilfrid was drunk? He did admit that he had some imperfections, setting himself to learn French from a children's book Maudie had sent, while she tried to study political economy, to be able to talk to her future father-in-law. For the next hurdle was the visit Maudie, Mrs Cassel and Sir Ernest were to pay to the Ashleys in October. Maudie did not want their engagement to be announced until after the inspection; Wilfrid's family had written kind and welcoming letters but she wished to see for herself that they blessed the match. Wilfrid, on the other hand, longed to tell the world – or to be able to tell his friends before the world told them.

The visit took place, the news was published, letters poured in, along with advice. One friend directed Maudie to *A Word to Wives*: '. . . The husband, when you know how to treat him, is not a wholly bad creature . . . on the contrary, when well looked after and managed with tact, he makes a pleasant companion, useful commodity, good father and altogether a great addition to the household.' Maudie copied this out, with a significant slip, not 'useful commodity' but 'useful dependent'.

Maudie and Wilfrid were married on 4 January 1901, at St George's, Hanover Square. Her dress came from Lucy Wallace, who had attracted much attention by the wedding-gown she had made for her sister, the romantic novelist Elinor Glyn. The Prince of Wales was a

Sir Ernest Acquires a Grand-daughter

witness and the reception was at 48 Grovenor Square, where the guests could admire the display of presents: china, glass, silver for the table, jewels for Maudie. Sir Ernest had produced various mementoes: a diamond tiara with an extra piece to form a necklace, an emerald and diamond necklace, ingenious pieces of emerald and diamond jewellery that could be dismantled to provide bracelets and brooches. It was not only Maudie that Sir Ernest was giving away: in anticipation of the marriage he had already made a discreet contribution to the Prince of Wales' Hospital Fund for London and now he offered some two hundred thousand pounds, also anonymously, to a charity selected by the Prince, who tactfully suggested that a sanatorium should be built for tuberculosis patients, in memory of Maudie's mother. Edward was unfortunately more prescient than he knew.

The first part of the honeymoon was spent at Milburn, where Maudie and Wilfrid had first met, and from there they went on to Egypt. To console himself, Sir Ernest left for India to stay with the Viceroy and the Maharajah of Jaipur. He returned in time for his annual spring visit to the south of France, where Maudie and Wilfrid were now installed, and to the news that Maudie was expecting a baby. She and Wilfrid were greatly relieved; they were so eager for a child that, even in the first three months of their marriage, Maudie had told Winston Churchill how miserable she was at her failure to conceive. Now he was one of the first to hear.

In late April Maudie and Wilfrid came back to England. They had found a house in Bruton Street, No. 32, which Sir Ernest bought for them. Wilfrid had done much of the searching – 'Portland Place too far off'; 'Norfolk Street pitch dark' – and now he looked for furniture and fussed about servants, complaining to Maudie how time-consuming it all was and enjoying every detail.

They had plenty of leisure. Although the South African War dragged on, Wilfrid had leave to stay in England, to enable him to help his father manage the family estate. Broadlands, the Ashleys' house in Hampshire, was not like the intimidating residences in which Maudie had often stayed. The original part of the house exemplified the best eighteenth-century taste, for it had been planned and decorated by William Kent and Henry Holland and the airy rooms had much fine plasterwork, delicately painted, by Joseph Rose the Elder, who had worked for Robert Adam. The house stood on the banks of the River

Test; Maudie was particularly fond of the gardens, where the grass ran down to the river. The lawns were banked and curved as if by nature, with carefully placed trees and, in spring, drifts of bulbs. An ugly Victorian wing had been added to one side of the house but the main part was square and formal, its pillars and porticoes giving it the appearance of a temple. Maudie photographed and sketched house, gardens and the surrounding park, encircling her pictures with wreaths of leaves and flowers, framing them with painted ribbons and rosettes, an echo of the plaster patterns on the ceilings, walls, doorways and chimney-pieces.

Maudie certainly did not allow the fact that she was expecting a baby to prevent her from enjoying the gaieties Wilfrid had promised. There were family visits: to Sir Ernest at Moulton Paddocks and Mrs Bisch at Stanmore, to help her entertain Waldorf Astor and Lord and Lady Brougham and Vaux. Together, this time, Maudie and Wilfrid went on to other houses: to the Caernarvons at Highclere Castle, the Devonshires at Chatsworth, to Glynde in Sussex and, when autumn came, Classiebawn Castle, Evelyn Ashley's estate in Ireland. At last, in October, while Wilfrid was shooting, Maudie rested and at the end of November the baby was born. Maudie and Wilfrid had a daughter; more important, Sir Ernest had a grand-daughter.

The infant began life with a narrow escape. She was christened in Romsey Abbey, with the Countess of Shaftesbury and Mrs Cassel as godmothers, and as godfather the King, for Queen Victoria had died shortly after Maudie's marriage and the Prince of Wales was now Edward VII. He wanted the baby to be called Edwardina; fortunately, Maudie prevailed. The baby was christened Edwina Cynthia Annette. The King, who was not annoyed by the omission of one syllable, presented the infant with a silver mug; her father gave her a pearl necklace.

There was little for Maudie to do with a tiny baby, except see her and pet her from time to time. Nursemaids looked after Edwina's immediate needs, bringing her out for airings. The baby was regularly photographed: in her pearls, looking surprised; in a robe encrusted with lace, with bare feet and remarkably long toes; in a smocked cotton gown and kid shoes, playing with a box of toy monkeys. In a packet of tissue paper Maudie kept locks of Edwina's hair, first cut when she was two months old. Pale gold at first, the tiny curls gradually turned darker. Like Wilfrid's hair, Edwina's was soft and fine.

The baby was a treasure, put away until she should become more interesting. She was hardly missed, for Maudie and Wilfrid were wrapped up in each other and Sir Ernest occupied with business, which prospered mightily. He had so managed matters that the new King was able to ascend the throne unencumbered by debt, to the astonishment of many of his cronies. In 1902 Cassel had his reward when the King made him a member of his Privy Council. The courtiers were taken aback when Sir Ernest, who so exactly fitted their picture of a Jewish capitalist, asked to take the Privy Councillor's oath upon the Bible. They were less surprised at the honour the King had shown his friend, for Cassel was indispensable to Edward, who saw him often, confided in him always and bombarded him daily with inde-cipherable notes instructing him to buy, sell, or rearrange his shares. 'Peace is signed', the King told Cassel in June 1902, as his Ministers put the Boer War behind them. 'Consols are sure to go up tomorrow. Could you not make a large investment for me?' Cassel accompanied the King to Biarritz, to Cowes; he became known as 'Windsor Cassel'. He knew how to soothe and humour his client: 'Dearest girlie,' he wrote to Maudie, from HM Yacht *Victoria and Albert*, 'the King is rather pleased with me because I made one or two mistakes in bridge . . .'

Sir Ernest's house in Grosvenor Square was now too small to hold his collections or accommodate his dinner parties. In 1905 he bought Brook House in Park Lane, an enormous pile built in the 1850s by Dudley Coutts Marjoribanks and now sold by his son, Lord Tweed-mouth, with many of its treasures: panels painted by Fragonard and Boucher with clouds and flowers, marble and plaster chimney-pieces by Canova and Wedgwood, pictures and china, carpets and furniture. Brook House was already magnificent. Thomas Wyatt, the architect, had given it five floors, including a vast top storey, with a balconied *piano nobile* overlooking Brook Street and Park Lane. In the adjoining garden a stream bubbled among mulberry trees and here there was a dining-room in a two-storey pavilion, with an arched loggia and domed turrets at each corner, like a miniature Turkish palace parked alongside a larger one.

These splendours did not satisfy Sir Ernest. 'He seems on the spend', Wilfrid said in awe. For three years Cassel adapted and adorned the house; Wilfrid and Maudie, Mrs Cassel and Mrs Bisch, any friend whose attention he could snatch, were taken to see Sir Benjamin Baker's models of the new interior. 'What a palace they are building', wrote Wilfrid, amazed. 'He will be ruined.' The works were certainly ambitious. There were six kitchens and several hydraulic lifts, including an extra-strong one for luggage. Twelve bathrooms opened out of as many bedrooms and one cabinet housed a cavernous Turkish bath. Sir Ernest was also one of the first subscribers to the London telephone system, the 'electric speaking tube'. The whole house, including the kitchens, was lined with Italian marble, except for the dining-room, panelled in oak, and the library, whose walls, floor and furniture were of golden-brown cherry-wood, with cherry-wood bookshelves decorated with black Wedgwood cameos depicting famous authors. The entrance was of lapis lazuli and green-veined marble; the main hall, grand staircase and first-floor gallery were lined with eight hundred tons of white marble, brought from the Michelangelo quarry at Sarravezza. Sir Ernest decreed that the only patch of colour visitors were to see as they climbed the staircase was to be provided by a portrait of the King. This proved to be a mistake. Suddenly confronted by the royal picture, Cassel's guests automatically straightened and slipped upon the marble. Such disorder upset Sir Ernest's perfect composition; he abandoned his dramatic scheme and covered the stairs with a thick crimson carpet. Looking-glass lined the doors, which reflected the Corinthian pillars supporting the tiers of galleries, rising upwards to a great glassed-over dome. Sir Ernest had been impressed by the illuminations at the St Louis Exhibition. Now he reproduced their effect, fitting electric torches into hundreds of antique bronze lamps, brought from Rome, to light the grand staircase and the arches of the dining-room, whose ceiling was thirty feet high. In 1908 Sir Ernest moved in. His guests were dumbstruck; no one could ever remember anything but the hall and staircase, so dazzled were they when they arrived and when they left.

Brook House in its glory was an opera house, in which Sir Ernest arranged the stage, conducted the orchestra, worked the lights. Maudie and Wilfrid had parts to play. Marriage had not removed Maudie from her father's orbit, which was indeed so all-embracing that this would have been difficult. She and Wilfrid had their own establishment and their own friends but they went to most of Cassel's parties, he attended theirs, and many of the same guests came to both. Maudie was no longer an innocent observer. She had become a confident young married woman, at ease with everyone from Winston Churchill to Wickham Steed, *The Times* correspondent in Vienna, from Mrs Keppel, the King's mistress, to the author and composer Ethel Smyth. The house in Bruton Street was too small to allow Maudie to entertain many people at a time – and there was no room for guests to stay – but a stream of visitors came in and out all day, causing Wilfrid to complain that it was rather hard never to have his wife to himself. It was at Bruton Street, not Brook House, that Eleonora Duse acted at a party in 1904, the only time she did so at a private residence. J. Forbes Robertson, the actor-manager, was a friend; Sir John Fisher, later First Lord of the Admiralty, would drop in on 'Mrs Maudie' for a private chat before dinner. Like her father, Maudie kept up with every sort of person: Campbell-Bannerman, the Liberal Leader in the Commons, was as welcome as the Duke of Devonshire; Sarojini Chattopadhyay as close a confidante as Vittoria Colonna, Princess Teano, the descendant of an old English house which had intermarried with the family of the hereditary Prince-Assistants to the Pope. Maudie corresponded with all of them; her letters, though brief, were always timely and amusing.

Maudie had quickly learnt her role; Wilfrid waited disconsolately in the wings. He longed to go into Parliament, where many friends and relatives awaited him. Maudie had promised to supply the funds, although she wished that Wilfrid had been a Liberal rather than a Conservative. At last, in late 1903, he heard of a possible constituency in Lancashire. '*This is strictly between you and me* . . .' he wrote excitedly to Maudie. '[The] President of the local Conservative Association wants to talk matters over with me. I have written to our respective Fathers to ask permission to stand . . .' The constituency was Blackpool, then held by a Conservative Member who intended to retire. But the Member could not go, for the Party was split on the question of Free Trade and its managers unwilling to risk a by-election. In 1904 Maudie appealed to the Prime Minister, asking for five minutes in which to explain the problem. Mr Balfour saw her but even Maudie's eloquence could not win him over. Wilfrid was in a difficult position. He could not cultivate his prospective constituents without seeming presumptuous. If, on the other hand, he stayed away, they might accuse him of neglect. He and Maudie found a middle way. She subscribed to Lancashire charities and appeared occasionally at local fêtes, and Wilfrid paid brief but regular visits to Blackpool, between shooting and fishing engagements. Maudie even swallowed her objections and joined the Ladies' Grand Council of the Primrose League. In the summer of 1904 the Ashleys took a house in the constituency, The Knowle, and daringly gave a garden party. It was a success, to Wilfrid and Maudie's relief.

The next year, Wilfrid was bolder. He decided to spend several weeks at The Knowle, conferring with his agent and wooing the voters, while Maudie went off to the Alps with her father. It was hard. Each continued to be passionately attracted to the other; every separation, however brief, was regarded as an interruption to their continuing honeymoon. Reluctantly but stoically, they parted, Wilfrid for Blackpool, Maudie for Switzerland, to another Cassel establishment. For in 1901, while the Ashleys were away on their honeymoon, Sir Ernest had acquired part of the Alps for himself, a site in the mountains above Moerel, at exactly the same height as the Riederfurka. There he had built a Swiss version of Brook House, a huge, sedate, twenty-five-roomed cottage, its wooden shutters, ledges and balconies artfully fretted with cut-outs and curlicues. A tower and pinnacles reared above the trees, the whole edifice being confidently topped by two weather-vanes and a Swiss flag.

For much of the summer Maudie was on the alp, Wilfrid at The Knowle, with Edwina, now four and a half, for company. A small boy, Nigel Pilcher, was produced as a playmate, with Mrs Harris, Edwina's nurse, as supervisor. She could not keep them out of Wilfrid's room, especially in the morning, when they liked to watch him shaving. In August Edwina was brought to Classiebawn Castle, where she found her cousin Dermot Pakenham. Every day the two children played on the sands; they became inseparable, which was just as well, since Wilfrid was preoccupied with the estate – marking trees for cutting, arranging new plantations – and with going out after teal and shoveller on the lake. Although he liked being at Classiebawn, he could not relax. Each day there was some new anxiety. First it was lumbago. Then it was money. Letter after letter to Maudie fussed about bills, accounts and the price of stock. There were so many calls on Wilfrid's pocket: 'Don't spend more than you can help as I am jolly well broke and no more money comes in till October 1st . . .' How he wished Maudie were home. He sent white heather 'as a love token' and marked his letters with crosses and circles: 'Do you know what these mean?' He swore that they should not be parted again. 'Let us

Sir Ernest Cassel

Mrs Cassel (Auntie Grannie)

Maudie, Mary and Edwina

Wilfrid Ashley

Villa Cassel

Broadlands

by all means go to India. I care not where I go as long as it is with you.'

The idea that Maudie and Wilfrid might go to India had been planted some time before by Sarojini, who had married and was now Sarojini Naidu. What an adventure it would be to visit India with Wilfrid, to see Sarojini and her family. Her daughter Padmaja, 'a little elf . . . with exquisite eyes and an inordinate love of fine clothes', was only a year older than Edwina. The scheme did not come off – but fifty years later Edwina and Padmaja were to meet at last and look each other over.

India would not have suited Wilfrid, nor he India. In any case, he now found himself preparing for a general election, for at the end of 1905 the Government fell. Polling was in January 1906. Although the Conservatives were defeated, Wilfrid's seat was safe and he took his place on the Opposition benches. Maudie was delighted, Sir Ernest almost more so. He came in full fig, with all his decorations, to the Opening of Parliament, where, as Wilfrid recorded, he was greatly honoured by the King, 'who gave him a place close to the Throne where only Foreign Ambassadors stand, the first time anyone had been there except Diplomats'. But, as the King recognized, Sir Ernest was the epitome of diplomacy.

At first Wilfrid was disappointed with the House of Commons: 'Perhaps my views will change. I trust so – but at present I call this place a fraud – a waste of time and deadly dull'. By March he had begun to feel at home and, 'at last', he told Maudie, 'I have done something!!! I have put down a question with reference to the Trawlers' Grievances at Fleetwood. I do not expect that the Government will expire in consequence but it will look well in the Local Press'. Wilfrid had begun his long trek in the footsteps of the Seventh Earl.

Meanwhile, in the autumn of 1905, Maudie conceived a second child. This pregnancy was more difficult. Sir William Broadbent recommended a warmer climate, so in February she was packed off with Mrs Cassel to Biarritz. Edwina, who had last seen her mother intermittently in November and December, was now sent to Brighton with her nurse, where Sir Ernest visited her, and, according to her father, was delighted to find she had become 'very assertive'. 'I rather doubt if this is a good thing', Wilfrid added gloomily. He wanted peace and quiet. Parliamentary life wore him out. Mrs Bisch invited him to dinner to make sure he was eating properly but it was Maudie for whom he pined. Without her, Wilfrid could take no important decisions. He was looking for a footman for their London house, hunting for a larger place in Blackpool, hesitating over the price of the new motor. '. . . a 40 HP chassis costs £1050. Say we get it for £1000, extras £1300 . . .' Could they run to it? 'I shall wait till you come over . . . you can tackle these people better than I can.'

Sir Ernest's anxieties were all for Maudie. He did not go so far as to exhibit a sympathetic pregnancy but, when his daughter was too weak to come downstairs, he felt shaky. 'How curious! My legs are famine stricken. There must be heredity in this.' He had, admittedly, been fasting on fresh fruit, boiled fowl and water, with little noticeable success. Sir Ernest tried to deny himself but how could he refuse the lavish dishes and good wines he set before the King and Mrs Keppel, before the Duke of Devonshire, Mrs Ronnie Greville, Mr Balfour, and Mrs Bisch? There was nothing for it but to escape to France, where the spring sun would allow him to shed his fur-lined overcoat and, with luck, the extra flesh that cushioned him against the London winter. 'We will have a high old time at Biarritz', Cassel promised Maudie – and himself. By the time he got there, Maudie was stronger and enjoying little outings in the motor. At the end of April she came home.

Not to London, which was thought too noisy, too dirty, too full of people eager to call, but to Stanmore, ten miles from the city, where Mrs Bisch lived at The Warren House, her country oasis. There on 22 July the baby arrived, a girl, christened Ruth Mary Clarice but known first as Mary and later, by her own wish, more grandly as Maria. It was not an easy birth and the infant was so weak that an incubator was rushed to Stanmore from London. Mary was to grow up into a pretty, self-centred fantasizer, who competed with her elder sister by behaving melodramatically and constructing elaborate myths about herself. Her fables, which she entirely believed, were to begin at the beginning, with her account of her own arrival, for she had been born, she declared, a full two months prematurely. Only Maudie's presence of mind in walking up the road to The Warren House, Mary said, had saved her mother and herself. This was nonsense.

Edwina was pleased to have a new sister. She liked looking after small, delicate creatures, although until now these had been animals rather than humans – rabbits, puppies and kittens. Mary's birth also

24

meant that, for a month at least, Edwina saw more of her mother, for Maudie remained quietly at Stanmore. In mid-August, when Edwina was sent off to her Irish cousins, Maudie remained at The Warren House, supervising the purchase of The Grove, a house with a small farm, almost next door, for which Sir Ernest had provided the funds. Wilfrid was away for much of the late summer, stalking, shooting and fishing with Cabinet ministers in Scotland, and, despite the heroic railway journeys he made backwards and forwards every ten days or so, he and Maudie were mostly apart. She wrote each day, letters that said virtually nothing about the baby but a great deal about Wilfrid's rheumatism, which flourished in the Scotch mist.

Edwina's life was now a mixture of strict routine and sudden shifts. She had regular meals, regular baths, regular hours of getting up and going to bed; she was dressed in the correct clothes for the nursery, the drawing-room, for going out and coming in. Her daily life was as much of a performance, on a smaller scale, as that of her father and mother and their friends. In other respects she had a choppy, shapeless childhood, with no boundaries and few anchors. The child was transported from one temporary stopping-place to another. Maudie and Wilfrid would not have her at Bruton Street, for there was little to do with a five-year-old in London, so she was parked with Mrs Bisch and Mrs Cassel at The Warren House. The Shaftesburys' house, St Giles, was another refuge. A huge place, built of rosy brick and stone, with tall windows, it stood like a cathedral in a great park of long grasses and fine trees. There Edwina had two cousins who were almost the same age as herself, Lady Dorothy and Lady Mary Ashley-Cooper.

On the Cassel side Edwina had as yet only one near contemporary, for Felix, Mrs Cassel's son, now in his mid-thirties, was still a bachelor. Mrs Cassel's other child, Anna, had married two years before Maudie. Cousin Anna and her husband, Colonel Jenkins, had one daughter, Marjorie, eighteen months older than Edwina, and as their house, Wherwell Priory, was only twelve miles from Broadlands, Edwina and Marjorie often played together and, later, shared each other's governesses, Edwina's Mademoiselle and Marjorie's Fräulein. Wherwell, which Sir Ernest first rented and then bought for his niece, was a charming house, less austere than Broadlands. The Test ran alongside, in one place underneath the house, so that the gardens were always green and leafy. Marjorie, who lived for dogs and ponies, fishing and riding, was amazed that Edwina wanted dolls as well. She privately thought her younger cousin rather too good to be true.

When The Grove was finished, Edwina spent part of each spring and winter there but even that house was more like a base camp than home, a place from which she set off to visit other people. Her parents were always arriving or departing; it is not surprising that Edwina grew up into a restless traveller. It was in Sir Ernest that the rootless child found one fixed and stable feature. He had not been able to keep Maudie for himself but Edwina's affection was all available. She was intelligent, pretty and strong; her grandfather liked to know where she was and what she was doing. He saw that she was fond of animals, so he supplied kittens, puppies, rabbits and, more, asked after them. He gave Edwina her first pony and, as important, watched her learn to ride it. No one else paid Edwina as much attention.

Sir Ernest made Edwina feel secure. About her parents, however, there was something fleeting and ambiguous. Edwina saw little of them and less of them together. When the House of Commons was sitting, Wilfrid was in London, Maudie at Stanmore. When the House rose, Wilfrid was away shooting and fishing; if Maudie accompanied him to his constituency or to stay with friends, Edwina remained behind with Mary. When Maudie and Wilfrid were in the same place at the same time, they were almost exclusively preoccupied with themselves and with each other. Edwina was learning to fend for herself.

CHAPTER THREE

Too Good to be True

E dwina's parents were well matched. Everyone thought so; they thought it themselves. In character, however, they were unalike, Maudie being quicker, brighter and more observant than Wilfrid, who was meticulous, formal and dull. Like all obsessives, Wilfrid was acutely aware of the passage of time. In fact he had years before him but for Maudie, drifting through the seasons, the days were running out. She had never entirely recovered her health after Mary's birth in the early summer. Throughout the winter of 1906 Wilfrid, Sir Ernest, Mrs Cassel and Mrs Bisch tried to see that she did not overtax herself but by Christmas she was no stronger, although she was more than ever amorous, excited, eager for company and for travel. Her feverish impatience increased Sir Ernest's anxiety: what he dreaded was TB, a deceitful, merciless disease, whose symptoms he knew; as patients grew weaker, their appetite for life increased. While their energy and stamina drained away, they became hectic and restless. This, to her father's watchful eye, seemed to be happening to Maudie.

In the New Year of 1907, therefore, Sir Ernest took his daughter and son-in-law to Egypt, their first visit since 1901, although, as Maudie wrote in her notes of the trip, 'Wilfrid . . . in spite of six years of married bliss pretends that we are still honeymooning . . .' They went out in the SS *Marmora*, finding on board the King's brother, Prince Arthur, Duke of Connaught, his Duchess, and their daughter, Princess Patricia. The Duke, who had fought in the Egyptian war in 1882 and was now Inspector-General of the Forces, was making one of his regular tours. All six got on splendidly, which was a good thing for the sea was choppy and the boat shook violently.

From their base, the Mena House Hotel, in its garden of roses, magnolias and oleanders, looking out towards the Pyramids, Sir Ernest and his party travelled on to the enormous reservoir he had funded, a great basin, contained by the dam holding back eighty miles of the Nile. Then he took the Ashleys to see the temple at Luxor, before they returned to Cairo for some society. 'There are lots of nice men in Egypt,' wrote Maudie enthusiastically, after a series of dances and dinners. Wilfrid, alas, was not among them, for he had gone to hunt gazelle. As usual, he found things unsatisfactory: 'all right except for a headache . . . sun very hot . . . tents none too cool'. From Cairo, where he bought some odds and ends from the Museum's surplus stock, he caught the boat-train home, 'a d. . . . ble time . . . rough sea – rain – cold'. At least he found some fellow MPs on board: 'All Conservatives', he assured his wife.

Companionable Tories were all very well but the person Wilfrid really wanted was Maudie. From Alexandria she and her father had sailed to Naples, hurrying through, for Sir Ernest wanted to be in Biarritz in good time to prepare for a visit from the King, who was coming to stay at a house Cassel had taken, the Villa Eugénie, built by Napoleon III for the Empress. At first Maudie was delighted to be back in France with her friend Alice Keppel but as day succeeded day she began to rebel. They were there six weeks, the entire time being devoted to amusing the King. 'We are his servants quite as much as the housemaid or the butler', Maudie said indignantly. It was unbearably tedious. Mrs Keppel, used to the deadly royal routine, knew how to pretend to be enjoying herself and while they were abroad and among friends she had the consolation of being treated as the King's official consort. Maudie, displaced from the centre of Sir Ernest's attention and bored to tears, could not stand it. She pleaded for relief. Edwina was sent for. She came with Mademoiselle Minart, her French governess, but there was nothing for her to do but be photographed with the King and her grandfather, given violet cachous from Mrs Keppel's reticule, and allowed to play with a large fox-terrier, whose collar was engraved with the reminder: 'I am Caesar, the King's dog.' The fuss over Edwina's arrival, and, a week or two later, her departure, restored Maudie to some prominence – but only temporarily.

The Mediterranean spring none the less did Maudie good, and she returned to London feeling stronger. She needed all her energy, for she and Wilfrid were invited everywhere, not just by those whom Sir Ernest so assiduously entertained and who now returned his hospitality, but by the Ashleys' own circle of rich and fashionable people. It would be pleasant to think that Edwina occasionally saw her mother dressing for these parties, that she tried on Maudie's tiny silk shoes or played with her brushes, that she was given a dab of face powder or, if she had been exceptionally good, invited to drape herself in her mother's rope of thirty-five perfectly matched pearls, to balance on her own curls the bandeau with the diamond flight of swallows or to examine the emerald, ruby and diamond brooches, in the shape of flowers, fishes and peacocks. It did not occur to Maudie to play in this way. She rarely went to the schoolroom or the nursery and Edwina and Mary were not permitted to come to their parents' quarters. 'Surprised at 7.30 by Edwina in her dressing-gown', Wilfrid had reported to Maudie in 1905, when Edwina was four: 'a practice not to be encouraged'. This was not unusual in families like the Ashleys', accustomed to handing their children over to nurses, nannies and governesses. Parents who took trouble with their children – the Desboroughs, for example, and the Wyndhams – were considered odd. So young herself, so caught up in her own programme of engagements, Maudie was in any case too immature to be able to forget herself and look at life from a six-year-old's point of view. Her relationship with her elder daughter was affectionate and respectful. There was no spontaneity, no rumpling, no springing of surprises, teasing only of the most grave and, to a child, baffling sort. Maudie, who had hardly known her own mother, had no idea how to be a mother to Edwina.

To an outsider, Edwina's childhood may have seemed secure and comfortable. In fact it was unsatisfactory and incomplete. Consider, for example, her sixth, seventh and eighth years, 1907, 1908 and 1909. She spent little time with her parents. In July 1907, while Maudie and Wilfrid were at parties in London and in the country, Edwina stayed with her grandfather at the Villa Cassel. Her name, in shaky capitals, appears in the visitors' book, standing bravely among the spidery signatures of Sir Ernest's other guests, all at least fifty years older than herself. In August she was taken by her father to Classiebawn, where there were cousins near her own age, while Maudie, recovering from the Season, was at Stanmore or staying with friends in Hampshire and Sussex. In September, when Edwina returned to The Grove, Wilfrid was hunting elk in Sweden and Maudie buying clothes in Paris. Wilfrid was in Scotland in October, shooting birds, while Maudie loyally stood in for him at Blackpool. 'A useful invention,' she told Wilfrid, 'would be a Patent Bazaar Opener.' Edwina remained at

The Grove in November and December but for a good part of that time her parents were at Broadlands, watching over Wilfrid's father, Evelyn, who had collapsed, rallied, and then, in late November, died.

The next two years were much the same. One moment of intimacy was an expedition Edwina made with her father in February 1909. While Mary was having her hair cut, Wilfrid told Maudie, 'Edwina paraded on foot up and down Bond Street this morning with me *alone*.' Another treat had come at the end of 1908, when Edwina celebrated her seventh birthday by having tea with her mother. This was all the more delightful because Maudie, too frail to get up, allowed Edwina to sit at a specially decorated birthday table in her bedroom. These two reunions were sufficiently unusual to be remarked upon by Wilfrid and Maudie, in letters in which they also spoke with surprise of how friendly Edwina seemed to be, as one might talk of a neglected relation who has none the less remained loyal to the family.

These were not the only occasions on which Edwina and one or other parent were together. They were, however, among the few on which she received the undistracted attention of either her father or her mother. Wilfrid, who always found plenty to fret about, was a poor hand at hiding his preoccupations, even from a child. This was, admittedly, a particularly difficult time: his father's death had brought endless anxieties and complications over the running of the Broadlands estate. As a temporary expedient Wilfrid closed the house altogether for almost a year but even that reduced the outgoings only marginally. The Bruton Street house was let in the spring of 1908 and the following year The Grove. Wilfrid shuffled his borrowings but, as he told Maudie, money vanished like melting snow. Stock owned by his father turned out to be worth only seven hundred pounds. The worst year was 1908, when bills fell due for work at Broadlands and The Grove; it seemed that the Ashleys might not be able to afford a spring holiday on their own. They agonized over alternatives. Not Biarritz, they decided; Maudie said she would not be 'mixed up with that lot again'. With discreet help from Mrs Cassel, they made their way to the Riviera, which Maudie liked so much that, when Wilfrid returned to England, she stayed on.

Sir Ernest was devastated when he learnt that Maudie would not be coming to Biarritz. She and Wilfrid had not dared to explain quite how rocky their finances were, although Maudie had twice tentatively begun a discussion, taking courage from Sir Ernest's reiterated promises to help if they found themselves in difficulty. It was not until the end of 1910 that, pressed by Wilfrid, she told her father the full awfulness of their position. Sir Ernest gave her his reactions in a dignified, tender letter. 'Child of mine . . . it will be a real pleasure for me to help you out of troubles which are not of your making . . . Do not worry about finance.' It was signed: 'with all my heart, Papa'.

Wilfrid's anxiety was not lost on Edwina. At the beginning of 1909 he had advised her to open a savings account at the Post Office, into which she had put nine of the ten pounds Sir Ernest had given her for Christmas. When Sir Ernest made his next ten-pound contribution, Wilfrid reported to Maudie that, 'in chaff I said at luncheon, "Edwina. I am hard up. Will you give me some?" She said nothing at the time but afterwards, when we were alone, she said, "Daddy, if you really want it, you may have it all"'. This, he thought, showed Edwina's sweet and unselfish nature. What others see is a tactful child. Edwina knew that her father had no money because he told her so himself. She understood, too, that her mother was her father's banker. Several months after the savings account had been opened, Edwina had written secretly on the subject to Maudie, 'quite by myself, and no one is going to read it . . . you do not mind if there are some mistakes do you'. She was already thinking of future outlays: 'You know,' she wrote, going straight to the point, 'I have not got any money at all. I would like to give something to Mary and to Minette for Xtmas, but she must not know it, will you tell me what to give her, because she will not tell me what, so would you send me a little money dear Mama.' The more Edwina considered the question, the more, like her father, she panicked: 'I should like to give you something for Xtmas, dear Mama, but what, I must think hard. I will give Grand Papa the photo you sent me, but what should I give to Auntie Bobbie. . . .' Wilfrid's influence is plain.

Edwina was now writing regularly to her mother, who remained elusive. In 1908 Maudie spent part of the spring and autumn in Paris, in June she was in London with Wilfrid and in July at Moulton Paddocks helping Sir Ernest entertain the King. January and February 1909 she passed in Egypt, where Wilfrid joined her for several weeks, March and April found her in the South of France. Wilfrid came to her there once Parliament had risen and in May they returned to London, to give what had become an annual party for the Connaughts. Both Maudie and Wilfrid were in Scotland for the early part of July and August, Edwina now being at the Villa Cassel with her cousin Marjorie and Sir Ernest. For a fortnight at the end of August Edwina's path at last crossed Maudie's when she was taken to Biarritz for a fortnight to see her mother, who was on her way to Aix-les-Bains with Wilfrid. He had decided that the strain of parliamentary life entitled him to a cure.

Edwina returned to England in September; her mother remained in France, moved briefly to Switzerland for a reunion with Wilfrid at the Villa Cassel, and then went with him to Paris to buy clothes. Maudie did not come home for Christmas. Instead, she returned to Egypt; Wilfrid went out for the New Year. In 1908 and 1909, therefore, Edwina seems to have seen her mother, or to have been in the same house, villa or hotel, for altogether no more than twelve weeks. It hardly seems fair that, when Edwina went to stay for a few days in January 1909 with Maudie's old friend Violet de Trafford, Wilfrid should have exclaimed, 'What a gad-about she is'. Mary did not try to hide the fact that she missed her mother, telling everyone she met that: 'Mummie gone in motor car' and, later, 'Mummie gone in boat', based on information she had from her nurse. Edwina, older, quieter and more practical, simply asked Father Christmas at the end of 1908 for 'some pretty maps of Europe and England'.

Maudie, so much an absentee, never learnt to make a companion of her daughter. Her letters to Edwina were all wrong. The drawings were charming – pictures of cows and pigs from the Agricultural Show at Blackpool, or of a donkey at Aswan – but Maudie found it difficult to write in a way a child could understand. Grouse shooting in Scotland was, she told Edwina, 'not quite my line'. When her daughter lost a tooth, Maudie observed, as she might have done to one of her own friends, 'You must look like an old hag'. The postcard she sent from Scotland, 'A Highland Washing', was off-colour and well off the mark: a coy picture of a small boy, naked except for tam and sporran, thoughtfully sponging himself beside a loch.

Wilfrid invited Edwina to laugh at him, in situations she could envisage. 'Poor Daddy is going to have 24 hot baths', he wrote from Aix-les-Bains, 'and he has to stay here 24 days to take them. Won't he be clean when he has finished!!!' Maudie made one or two efforts at letters like that but, again, she hit the wrong note. Edwina was invited to pity and protect her mother: 'here is a picture of a dachshund', Maudie wrote 'which I wanted to buy but Daddy would not let me'. Such messages were better than nothing, however, and one at least was inspiring. This was a letter Maudie sent from Aswan in early 1909, describing the games on the banks of the Nile. 'There are no children here', it began, 'except black ones with round tummies and very little clothes on'. (No children, that is, whose names Maudie knew.) 'They play about on the sands and when they feel hot they just jump into the water and splash about.' Some weeks later, feeling hot herself, Edwina hopped into the Test at Broadlands, enticing Mary in after her. They were rescued by the new gardener's boy, who was immediately promoted.

Although she could speak, read, and write four languages, Maudie was tongue-tied when it came to communicating with her daughter. She seemed unable to construct the simplest enquiries or requests, never asking about Edwina's pony or suggesting that she practise her exercises on the piano or work at her French. If Maudie was interested in what Edwina was doing, she did not show it. Many of her letters were so unspecific that they read like extracts from a sentimental manual for the well-behaved child: 'Be kind to Daddy. You must give him lots of your love. That is what people want most in this world.' No wonder Edwina had no clear picture of her mother. It was fitting that, from her trip to Monte Carlo with Wilfrid in 1909, Maudie should send her daughter a sketch of their *wagon-lit*, curtains closed. Beneath the drawing she had written: 'You can't see me because I'm asleep inside'. Mama was indeed caught up in her own dream.

In some respects Maudie was not unworldly. Wilfrid left much business in her hands and she kept detailed notes of their income and expenditure; she was not careless with money, as the General Manager of the Ritz Hotel discovered each year during the negotiations over the arrangements for the party for the Connaughts. Maudie's account-ing was meticulous but, once assured that she was being correctly charged, she spent happily, at Floris, Liberty, Worth and the National Fur Company, on subscriptions to everything from the Church of England to the Incorporated Society for Psychical Research. There were large resources on which to draw. The credit side of her balance sheets shows the size and variety of her shareholdings, many in companies founded or funded by Sir Ernest: the Egyption Irrigation Company, Buenos Aires Grand Metropolitan Transport, Atchison Topeka, Vickers Maxim, the British Electric Traction Company, Uruguay Five Per Cent, Western Union Telegraph, American Smelters . . . In 1909 her dividends brought her between three and seven hundred pounds a month, quite enough for purchases from Tiffany, Cartier, and Bumpus the bookshop, and to enable her to write to Wilfrid, 'Here is the cheque to make you happy'.

Wilfrid's happiness was Maudie's keenest wish. It is not too much to say that they were mutually obsessed. Every reunion in Paris, Biarritz or Cairo was the occasion for another honeymoon – they called it that themselves. Wilfrid warned Maudie that passion drove her temperature up but neither could resist. Their marriage was not cursed by too much proximity: 'We see too little of each other', Maudie told Wilfrid, 'but you are busy and I am lazy'. At least, she wrote in 1908, 'it is good to feel that after 7 years you should really still care to be with me and alone!' For when Sir Ernest and Mrs Cassel were not with them, Maudie and Wilfrid did think of themselves as being alone, a devoted couple, whose household happened to include two small girls. This threw Edwina upon her own resources, more so because she saw few other children. If Edwina had been brought up in London, she could have gone to a dancing class or to music lessons where she would have made friends of her own age. Wilfrid did his best. While they still had the Bruton Street house, he once or twice had Edwina fetched from Stanmore so that she could go to a fancy-dress party or out to tea, but, without Maudie to make arrangements and negotiate with other mothers, he was hardly able to return these invitations.

When The Grove was let after Evelyn Ashley's death and Edwina and Mary moved to Broadlands, they depended on each other for company. Edwina shared some lessons with Cousin Marjorie in the schoolroom at Broadlands or at Wherwell but even this was like studying with a sister. Her circle was tiny: Dermot and Joan, her Pakenham cousins, lived in Ireland, so she saw them only when Wilfrid took her to Classiebawn; her Ashley-Cooper cousins rarely came to Broadlands and Edwina did not visit St Giles more than once or twice a fortnight. Robert and Henry Everett, the sons of Wilfrid's agent, were sometimes asked to tea, but Edwina was not yet old enough to go off with them to explore the woods and fields at Broadlands. Until she was nine, Edwina had only two regular companions: Marjorie and Mary.

Does a child miss what she does not know she lacks? Edwina was strong and healthy. She ate well, slept well, liked her lessons and

Too Good to be True

enjoyed her walks and rides. Unlike Mary, she did not throw tan-
trums, sulk or become over-excited. When Edwina was good, she was
very, very good. As she showed when she offered Wilfrid all her
money, she could talk like a child in a textbook. This was understandable, for she had been given little scope for exploring everyday
relationships. Her father and mother appeared only intermittently,
their attention focused largely on each other; her grandfather, Mrs
Cassel, Mrs Bisch, Mrs Jenkins, and Uncle Felix were benevolent
deities. Mademoiselle Minart was not a strong character; judging by
her letters to Maudie, she was amiable and respectful, a guardian for
Edwina but hardly a guide. It is scarcely surprising that Edwina was
self-contained. She played less with children than with dolls and
animals – her pets now included a pair of Chinese kittens, half black,
half mouse. 'A doll, not to big and not to small', suggested Edwina,
aged seven, in a letter to Father Christmas, left in the chimney in
Maudie's sitting-room at Broadlands, 'and some nice toys for my little
sister Mary'. Maudie was hopeless at choosing the right presents.
Unprompted, she could think only of things she would have wanted
herself: 'a very pretty Assouan shawl and a pair of bedroom slippers,
white embroidered in gold and I fear a little large for you'. She sent
exotic sweetmeats, which Wilfrid and Sir Ernest liked but not Edwina,
and sets of matching hairbrushes, remembering that once, after a rare
expedition to her mother's bedroom, Edwina had asked for 'a nice
silver brush for my dressing tabel'.

It was a prosaic childhood, spent among kind but unimaginative
grown-ups. Aunt Alice took Edwina to the children's services in St
Paul's; Mrs Cassel dispensed chocolates and peppermints. Sir Ernest
tried hardest. In the summer of 1909 he carried Edwina and Marjorie
off to the Villa Cassel, where he did his best to amuse them, to the
point of throwing routine aside and arranging, one glorious morning,
a *breakfast* picnic. It was at the Villa that Marjorie learnt how sickeningly
good Edwina could be. The two girls, who had annoyed Sir Ernest,
were scolded and punished. 'I'm glad that's over', observed Marjorie.
'Now I can forget about it.' 'Oh no', said Edwina. 'I always think
about it for a long time afterwards'. Marjorie was enraged at this
mixture of piety and disloyalty.

Sir Ernest was not irritated for long. 'I love having the chicks here',
he told Maudie. 'They are having a high old time . . . Edwina is sweet
and full of life and spirits'. It was good for him to be distracted, if

35

only briefly, for he had overworked and felt 'dead tired'. One leg had swollen; to ease it, he wore special trousers, with slits over the knees for targeted sunbathing.

Cassel was now sixty. He still looked for new ventures in new territories, although unlike many rich men he was not tempted into Fleet Street. In 1907 he refused to buy *The Times*, and in 1908 to invest in the *Daily Express*, saying firmly to Wilfrid, who had been used as an intermediary, 'I *never* invest in newspapers'. A pragmatist *par excellence*, he kept friends on all sides; he could not have done so had he been a Press Lord. Cassel preferred to spend his fortune on medicine and education; in 1907 he gave £10,000 to the Imperial College of Science and Technology.

In all his comings and goings Cassel thought constantly of Maudie. He continued to worry about her health. In the summer of 1909, fortified by her Egyptian trip at the beginning of the year and her visit to Monte Carlo with Wilfrid at Easter, she had seemed well. While Mary was at the seaside with her nurse and Edwina in Switzerland, Maudie and Wilfrid took off for Scotland and some strenuous country house visiting. In late August, leaving Wilfrid in the north to play golf and shoot, she joined Sir Ernest at Biarritz. Here she began to feel the strain of the recent weeks' entertainment – late nights, dancing, cards. Now she was put to bed at nine o'clock, after a day spent lying quietly among pine trees. She had so much massage, she said, that her skin must be as soft as a baby's – but there was no Wilfrid to tell her so.

Maudie did not return to England for her husband's birthday in September. Instead she sent bouquets of roses. She was still weak and her skin unnaturally flushed. She longed to leave Biarritz. Everyone there, she said, was suffering from 'advanced nerves'. At last she was removed to Switzerland where Wilfrid joined her at the Villa Cassel, bringing her back in late September to Paris for fittings for her spring wardrobe. Having installed her at Sir Ernest's apartment in the rue du Cirque, Wilfrid made his way back to London. Maudie did not bring her dresses home. Her hectic colour would not subside and Sir Ernest asked his cousin Julius Goldschmidt to arrange for her to see the best French doctor, who diagnosed 'tubercular trouble arising from the glands' and recommended that a surgeon collapse a lung. Fortunately Maudie escaped a full-scale pneumothorax. What she needed, according to the experts in Paris, was a strict diet and a warm climate. Wilfrid rushed back to France to escort Maudie to Marseilles, where he put her on the boat to Port Said and miserably made his way back to London, his only consolation two boxes of crystallized plums. Ill and lonely, Maudie and her maid set off for Egypt, in a dirty boat infested with earwigs. She paved the decks with gold, she said, to get an edible meal.

Maudie was installed in the Mena House Hotel in as much comfort as Cassel could contrive. He took three floors, so that she should be disturbed neither from above nor below. One by one her female relations came out: Mrs Cassel, Cousin Anna, Mrs Bisch. This year Edwina did not celebrate her birthday with her mother, although Maudie sent a jewel box and another silver brush. 'I did miss you so much, darling Mama', Edwina wrote, 'though I had a very pretty table I loved the one you got me ready last year. I had no party but I had a big cake with nice surprises'. It poured with rain at Broadlands, in Stanmore and in London. Sir Ernest did his best to distract Edwina and Mary, sending books and new pets and laying out sovereigns. Wilfrid was so worried about Maudie that he made himself ill and had to move into Brook House to be properly looked after. Maudie fretted on his behalf, making him promise to tell the cook to give him porridge.

Edwina knew that her mother was weak and ill and her father wretchedly anxious. Each day she expected better news. 'When Mama is strong again', 'When Mama is home again': those were her horizons. Well-meaning Mademoiselle Minart indicated to Edwina that her mother's indisposition had a special cause. Maudie's last serious illness had followed Mary's birth; perhaps another child was on the way. 'And after all', Edwina had told Father Christmas, 'bring us a little Baby Brother'. But no one said anything. Instead of explanations, she was given treats. They could not fill the void. Although Edwina and Mary had seen little of Maudie when she had been at home, the grown-ups' long faces did not let them forget her absence. Edwina fixed her hopes on the successive anniversaries that were so dear to the Cassel household. Surely Mama would be home for 18 December? Invitations were carefully written out:

> Edwina and Mary Ashley request the pleasure of their Father's company, to tea in the Head Room at 5 o'clock on the occasion of their Mamie's birthday. RSVP

But Maudie did not miraculously appear among the group that assembled in the Head Room, under the glass-eyed stares of the elk,

Edwina Mountbatten

stags, deer and other animals, shot, decapitated and displayed by successive generations of Wilfrid's family. Wilfrid had to be in London but Cousin Anna tried to make things festive: 'Darling Mama', Edwina wrote, 'we had a very nice little party for you'. Marjorie came, with the Everett boys, and Mary and Edwina made sure Maudie was remembered. 'There was a cake and you were at one end of the table. After, we had cheers for you and games'.

There was always Christmas – but that turned out to be a double disappointment. Sir Ernest had asked them all to Moulton Paddocks but, when Wilfrid decided to go out to Maudie in Egypt, taking Mrs Cassel, the plan was changed and Sir Ernest joined the children at Broadlands. There was a decorated tree and Maudie had sent presents: a pin-cushion for Edwina to match her brushes. Sir Ernest could not endure the chilly house and sodden park. He took the children to stay at Brook House and sent them to the pantomime, 'Pinkie and the Fairies' and 'Aladdin'.

'Auntie Bisch' carried Edwina down to Stanmore, where the cook taught her to make sweets. 'I am sending you some Toffe', she told Maudie. 'It is very good and when I'll see you again we shall make you some every week.' Edwina's letters became more wistful: 'I asked Father Christmas . . . that you might be quite strong and' – again – 'that we should like a little baby boy'. Someone mentioned in Edwina's hearing that a woman friend was going to Biarritz in the spring: 'I hope she won't see you before me'.

A baby boy was the last thing Maudie could be expected to produce, for Doctor Beauchamp, sent out from England, believed that she was afflicted by 'an infection from the womb', for which he recommended a scrape. He refused to operate unless a female relation was nearby; that was why Mrs Cassel had come out to Egypt with Wilfrid at Christmas. Wilfrid was glad of her company, for he was sick with worry. In her letters Maudie had tried to reassure him but her hand was shaky and she could write only in pencil. Although she hid her fears from Wilfrid, she was now preparing loving messages for him to read after her death. She was sure she would not see out the year.

CHAPTER FOUR

Wilfrid Loses a Wife

In the first eight years of Edwina's childhood she lived a shifting, unsystematic existence, spent in half a dozen places, with half a dozen relations mothering her. She had much to make her feel secure: the solid forms of Sir Ernest and Mrs Cassel; vast, over-heated, over-furnished houses. Her clothes were scaled-down replicas of an adult's wardrobe, substantial garments of plaid, velvet and wool, trimmed with fur and bolstered underneath by layers of cotton. When she travelled, it was in motor cars built like tanks, with padded upholstery and huge goggle lamps, and in railway carriages panelled in mahogany. She had regular lessons with patient Minette and her own timetable of duties: tidying the schoolroom, cleaning the animals, although she knew little of the day-to-day routine of the households in which she lived for, apart from rare visits to the kitchen to make toffee, she scarcely saw anything of the machinery worked by house-keepers and butlers, bootboys and chambermaids, chauffeurs and gardeners. Her friends were few but close; her relations took care not to spoil her but anniversaries were made festive. Although her father was jumpy about money, none of the family was in want and Grand-papa's way of living was thoroughly opulent. The grown-ups com-plained about their health but, except for darling Mama, they were robust, even, in some cases, portly. Beneath the small girl's feet, the ground seemed firm.

In 1910 everything fell into disarray. Lessons became irregular and scrappy; Edwina's father and grandfather, aunts and cousins travelled even more frantically than before; plans were changed at the last minute; her mother seemed unlikely ever to come home. Sir Ernest, on whose sagacity they all relied, became for once distracted, weary and depressed. No wonder: as the year unfolded, he was assailed from every direction.

Cassel was beside himself with worry about Maudie, fearing that, once she gave in, her decline was certain. As soon as Christmas was over, he hurried to Egypt to relieve Wilfrid. Her husband's recent visit had helped Maudie to rally. She could now eat a little – although it was impossible to face some of the dishes with which the Egyptian cook tried to tempt her, 'a lamb roast whole' for instance, 'with its head on, *à l'Arabe*'. She lay on her balcony in the winter sun, longing for news of home. The *Daily Mail* was sent out to her and she begged Wilfrid for cuttings from other newspapers, so that she could read about their friends – not just society gossip but political news as well, for the country was in the middle of a crisis. It was this that had taken Wilfrid home. At the end of November the House of Lords had thrown out Lloyd George's Budget. The Lords' action had been declared unconstitutional and there was to be a general election in January. Wilfrid was as keen as mustard, especially since his opponent, Hodgkinson, was, he said indignantly, more a Socialist than a Liberal.

Wilfrid was so excited that Maudie begged him not to over-exert himself. Would he, to please her, take two grams of quinine every day, double that if he felt very tired? 'It is an excellent tonic and you will want all the strength you can get'. Wilfrid kept his seat. The Liberals remained in power, however, although their majority over the Conservatives was so slender – two seats only – that to get any legislation through they needed the support of Labour Members and the Irish Nationalists. It looked as if there might be a second general election. The corridors buzzed. Hundreds of speeches were made. Wilfrid adored it – and he did not worry about expenses, having persuaded Maudie to spend some money due to her from American shares. His only sadness was that politics kept him from his wife; but these events, he reminded her, might affect his whole future life. Missing her desperately, he crept into her empty bed at Bruton Street and wrote to her from there.

Edwina had not returned to Broadlands after Christmas. While her father was electioneering in Blackpool, she and her governess had made a long visit to Mrs Bischoffsheim, still in mourning for her husband, who had died two years before. Everyone thought Edwina's company was exactly what Mrs Bisch needed and everyone was right. Whenever it seemed appropriate, which was often, Edwina would fling her arms around her hostess and, addressing her through the crape, tell her how much she loved her. 'You are so kind', she proclaimed, 'that it is silly not to call you *Auntie* Bisch now'. Later in life Edwina was to be famous for always knowing exactly the right thing to say; some wondered how much of her conversation was calculated to please. So it is interesting to read what Mrs Bisch wrote to Maudie at the end of Edwina's visit: 'I knew she was a dear but I had no idea how fascinating she is in her ways and what charm she puts into her manner, not only because it comes naturally to her but she does it consciously, because she knows the impression she wishes to produce.' At nine years old, Mrs Bisch reported, Edwina made conversation like a grown-up person: 'Wilfrid will tell you the message – quite spontaneous of course – she gave him for you last night . . . perfect as regards affection, idea and expression . . .' Numbed by grief though she was, the old lady still had a sharp eye. Marjorie was right. Edwina was a goody-goody.

In February Edwina returned to Bruton Street. Grandmama Alice took her to church and Mademoiselle Minart saw to her lessons. By now Edwina could read in German, write in French and conjugate verbs in both. A 'nice and tiny piano' had been installed in her mother's boudoir, on which she practised: 'I find I have forgotten a lot but I'll soon pick it up'. The pony Sir Ernest had given her was brought to London, so she could ride in Hyde Park, and there on the Row she made some friends. Having, she thought, outgrown her toys, she gave them to Mary: 'My caravan and music cart – we are having great fun with them'. Edwina mothered Mary; indeed, she had begun to mother Maudie, in letters that were protective and encouraging. 'I love the card you wrote yourself', Edwina had said at Christmas. 'It is so sweet'. Where Maudie's vague scrawls were immature, Edwina's regular bulletins, with 'many sweet kisses', 'many kind messages', were efficient, effective and, as Mrs Bisch had noticed, almost adult.

The election over, Wilfrid, accompanied by Cousin Anna, hurried out to Egypt to see how Maudie was. Still too weak to come home, she was nevertheless much better and now she had jettisoned her walking-sticks she could once more throw herself into Wilfrid's arms. Patients with TB were notoriously passionate – 'Do you ever see', doctors said, 'a phthisical icicle?' – and Cousin Anna must have felt superfluous. Edwina sent three pressed primroses from Broadlands: 'The Spring is coming, be quick and get strong again . . . we will make a pretty corner for you in the garden, the one you like best'. Maudie wrote a postcard, 'the first since months. All were happy to see it and to know you were better'. Edwina poured out her news. She was reading *Pauvre Blaise*, she had bought two German books.

Edwina Mountbatten

There were seventeen lambs at the farm at The Grove and 'the prettiest little calf . . . I gave it the name of Roussette, Mère Barberin's cow in *Sans Famille*.' She was filling a basket with little vegetables for Mary's goat and doing needlework for Mrs Cassel's birthday. 'I wish I could come with Cousin Anna. I could tell you much more than I can write.' Edwina was bursting with energy and, according to Mademoiselle Minart, with questions. She asked repeatedly how the lambs appeared and why. Minette was not sure what to say: 'des questions se multiplient', she told Maudie, 'la curiosité s'éveille'. Edwina was at an awkward age. She had begun to understand that there was some interesting process here but Minette did not want to shock her with explanations. When would 'bien chère Madame' be home to deal with this?

At Easter Edwina stayed with Marjorie at Wherwell: 'We are having an egg hunt today . . . no real hare has come to my room like it did last year but Auntie Bisch sent me a tiny one in an egg'. There was a painted egg from Auntie-Grannie and Edwina gave Mary another filled with toys. At luncheon she and Marjorie were allowed to drink Mrs Cassel's health in soda water, 'and yours of course', she assured Maudie, and on Easter Day they came downstairs for dinner. Mrs Cassel also noticed that Edwina was old enough to need her teeth stopping. That done, Edwina, Sir Ernest and Mrs Cassel left for Biarritz.

Once installed in the Villa Eugénie, Edwina saw more of Auntie-Grannie than of Grandpapa. He was pursued by business: 'even here', he told Maudie, 'so that I have to do a lot of thinking and even more telegraphing'. There were other preoccupations. The King was there, in a party that included Mrs Keppel and Winston Churchill, now Home Secretary. The King teased Cassel for plotting with Churchill but the older and the younger man had much to conspire about. Like Churchill, Cassel was anxious about the power of Germany, not just her growing international influence but also the ever-increasing size of her navy. For two years Sir Ernest had hoped that the German and British Governments might agree on a way of rearming more slowly. In 1908 he had started discussions behind the scenes with Albert Ballin, head of the Hamburg-Amerika Shipping Company in Germany and a friend of the Emperor, who knew that Cassel was a friend of the King. Edward VII was the Emperor's uncle but their personal relations were prickly. Ballin and Cassel believed that jointly they might not only bring the two potentates together but that they might also be able to initiate discussions between Admiral Tirpitz, the architect of Germany's naval programme, and Maudie's admirer, Sir John Fisher, the First Sea Lord.

From mid-1908 to mid-1909 Cassel and Ballin met and corresponded, not only speaking but also negotiating for the two Admirals and their two Majesties. When the German and British Foreign Offices heard of the conversations in the autumn of 1909, they were understandably furious. Ambassadors do not like non-professionals meddling in policy-making and the German Ambassador in London and the British Ambassador in Berlin were no exception. Ballin and Cassel were to stop talking at once. The door was closed – for the time being. Cassel did not let things rest. He continued to discuss the issue with powerful political friends, Liberal and Conservative, and in Churchill he had an especially attentive ear. Sir Ernest wanted a firm understanding and a definite ratio between the navies of both powers – but the diplomats seemed to make less headway than the amateurs had been doing before their knuckles were rapped. Cassel thought war was brewing and that short-sighted, arrogant men were failing to prevent it. All this was on his mind as he tried to entertain the King at Biarritz. That, too, was an uphill struggle, for Edward was plainly unwell. His cough was worse and he found breathing an effort. Sir Ernest's world was disintegrating all about him.

By the beginning of May the whole family was back in England. Wilfrid's arrival seemed to have accelerated Maudie's recovery and, tired of the Pyramids and hungry for Broadlands' green lawns, she had tossed aside her novels and insisted on going home. As soon as Sir Ernest was back, she sent a bouquet to mark the arrival of spring. 'I hope you have missed the old father just a little', he wrote, and put a sprig of lily of the valley in his coat. Not all the news was good. The next day Sir Ernest was due to see the King, who had now collapsed entirely. 'I shall not give in', he had told a visitor, but he was quite unfit to carry out any of the week's royal programme. 'There is grave ground for anxiety', Sir Ernest told Maudie, 'but', making a nice distinction, 'no reason to despair'.

At eleven o'clock on Friday morning, 6 May, the Palace telephoned Brook House to say the appointment was put off. Half an hour later an equerry rang again: it had been reinstated. Cassel was asked to go to the King at once but to let him speak as little as possible. Sir Ernest hurried round to the Palace. First he was taken up to see the Queen, who asked warmly after Maudie, and then her daughter Victoria came in, also anxious for news. The Prince of Wales, whom Cassel met on the stairs, wanted full details of Maudie's illness; Cassel had to be short, for there was their own invalid to see. The King was in his sitting-room; his doctor, Sir James Reid, later told Cassel that His Majesty had been determined to dress for his visitor and that he could not stop him, although he had talked him out of having a bath. The King rose from his chair to shake hands, looking worn with pain. His speech was indistinct but Cassel was touched by his hesitant smile as he too spoke of Maudie. 'I am very seedy', he told Cassel, 'but I wanted to see you'. They talked a little business until Cassel thought he should ask leave to go, for fear of tiring his friend. Before he left, Cassel gave the King an envelope containing £10,000 in banknotes.

Sir Ernest was only slightly reassured. 'I can't imagine that his case is as bad as the doctors make out', he wrote to Maudie. 'If only he would reserve his strength'. That night the King died. Years before he had given Mrs Keppel a letter, asking her to be with him at the end. Queen Alexandra sent for her and both women were with him as he expired.

Sir Ernest had lost one of his oldest friends. Some thought he had also lost his influence – but he was not excluded. The new King was disinclined to cut off one of his father's dearest companions. Indeed, one of the first letters George V sent on his thickly black-bordered writing-paper was an affectionate line to 'My dear Cassel'. The King did his best to look on the bright side: 'Perhaps', he wrote consolingly, 'the remembrance that you were one of the last to see him . . . will be a sad satisfaction to you'. Sir Ernest also endeared himself by behaving well over the £10,000 he had left with the dying Edward VII. After the funeral, the King's Private Secretary had returned the banknotes to Cassel with a letter to say that he presumed they belonged to him, rather than being the result of some speculation. Cassel called at the Palace and tactfully explained that the sum represented a regular payment of interest on one of the King's investments and that he wished to return it, which he did. Nothing more was said.

Sir Ernest did not lose his access to the Palace. When the official mourning was over, King George came to Moulton Paddocks to shoot and from time to time he asked Cassel for advice on nuances of foreign policy as well as on finance. Relations were more formal – there were no chats at the bridge table, between races at Newmarket, or on the terrace at the Villa Eugénie – but, if Cassel wanted a word, it was always arranged. He was in any case a friend of Queen Alexandra. When the late King's widow had recovered from her immediate prostration, she wrote herself to thank Sir Ernest for the dozens of flowers he had sent in her husband's memory and in December and at successive Christmases she gave him small mementoes: links, a watch, a photograph frame, an inkstand, with a sad message written among the sprigs of holly on each label: 'This was the King's'. Mrs Keppel, too, remained a friend, of whom Sir Ernest saw more than he did of the Queen. He occasionally lent her his apartment in the rue du Cirque and she often stayed with Mrs Cassel. It was seven years, however, before she could be persuaded to return to Biarritz.

It is generally said that the First World War closed the Edwardian age – lavish, sybaritic, marked by great gulfs between classes and by enormous disparities of wealth. In fact, the beginning of the end arrived when the old King died, and Cassel knew it. Sir Ernest had been a dazzling star in the Edwardian constellation. He was not extinguished when King Edward was removed but from that time his light did not burn as vigorously. At the end of 1910 he gave up active business on his own account, investing two hundred thousand pounds in the London banking house of Saemy Japhet & Co. Cassel was growing old.

His mind remained clear, his judgement shrewd – but his heart was not in business. The King had gone and, keener even than that blow, Maudie was slipping away. She had stayed at The Grove for a fortnight, lying on a day-bed in the garden, where Edwina was allowed to come to read to her in the afternoons. In late May Maudie was moved to Broadlands and all through June she was well enough to see a trickle of visitors, among them Winston Churchill. 'To be with you is just perfect', sighed Wilfrid, obliged to leave his wife for a short burst of bazaar-opening, another general election being in the offing. From the woods at Broadlands Maudie sent him spring violets, which he pressed and kept in his pocket-book. The children did not stay with their mother but followed their father to Blackpool, where they could have breezy air and games on the sand: 'By the Sea I think of Thee' said Mary's postcard to 'Darling Mamie'. From there the girls went on to Moulton Paddocks, to try to entertain Grandpapa Ernest, who was restless and elusive. 'Even when it's pouring', Edwina reported, 'he's up on the estate at eight o'clock'. Maudie feared that her daughters might be living too heady a life; Edwina reassured her. They did play with cards, she admitted, but only for Mary's favourite game of building castles; at home she had been allowed to use nothing more corrupting than old photographs. Other diversions, Edwina explained, were also designed only for her little sister's pleasure: 'You know we don't dance a regular Menuet, but all sorts of dances, just to amuse Mary'. In any case, Edwina added, '. . . very soon I shall be 9 years old. Don't you think I am an old girl?' Furthermore, 'Are you thinking it over for my pocket money?'

The pocket money was settled at two pounds eight shillings a year, plus six shillings from Mrs Cassel. In other respects, however, Maudie did not agree that Edwina was 'an old girl'. Mrs Cassel and Minette were asked to make sure that she went to bed at the proper time. To tire her out, Minette took Edwina for long walks across the estate and her pony, Sambo, was sent over to Moulton from Broadlands.

The children spent a happy summer. 'I can see now', wrote Edwina, 'that you are getting stronger, you can draw and write long letters again, which I love so much.' She and Mary did not know that Maudie was growing weaker. All summer she remained at Broadlands, lying day and night in a hut in the garden. She hated the still air of the sickroom, preferring to be among the lawns, the river and the roses that grew against the harmonious pink brick walls of the stables and the dairy. Her milk, from a special herd of Friesians, was carefully pasteurized and she was fed the most delicate and nourishing foods.

So that the children would not be too astonished, Maudie wrote a line explaining these strange living arrangements: 'I am in my new home', said a brief postcard, 'I call it a rabbit hutch'. Edwina was fascinated. 'What a lovely day it is for you to be in the garden. I should love to be with you and read to you *The Enchanted Castle* as I did when you came home from Egypt.' The grown-ups tried to make light of the change: 'How much you will have grown all this time in bed', Edwina observed. 'Minette thinks "an inch for each month".' She was hopeful: 'it would be nice for you and me if you were here, perhaps you will come soon . . .' Maudie did not come to Moulton.

In September Edwina and Mary returned to Broadlands. Their mother's rabbit hutch was not the only novelty, for Sir Ernest had sent Maudie a Pekinese – Fo Fo – to cheer her up. Edwina had reservations. 'He seemed very nice,' she agreed, 'but I hope he doesn't bite'. She was right. Fo Fo had to be tied to Maudie's bedpost to keep him out of trouble. Now the children could see how frail their mother was. To cheer them up – and blow away any germs they might have attracted – Wilfrid took them to Cleethorpes in October, and installed them in an hotel. 'Such nasty weather', Edwina reported. 'Cold, rain and wind.'

Rather than returning to Broadlands, Edwina and Mary were next taken to Wherwell, where they spent all November and much of December, and from there, on Edwina's ninth birthday, Mademoiselle Minart sent Maudie a bulletin. Minette was proud of her charge. Edwina had grown tall and strong, she had excellent manners and worked hard at her studies. She had been rather spoilt: Sir Ernest and Mrs Cassel had come for her birthday and Mrs Jenkins had arranged a party. But she was sad that she could not see her mother or give her a hug. On one of their walks Edwina had suddenly complained of the silence at Wherwell – 'I like the noise in the town much better'– and had begun to hum little songs to distract herself. This was not good. Minette did not like to see Edwina feeling so cut off. Could they not come back to Broadlands, if only for a day or two? They needed more books and toys and bien chère Madame would hardly be disturbed. A little visit from the children might even do her good – and Minette had just the dish to tempt her appetite: delicious quince butter with home-made wafers. Could they not come?

Maudie had scarcely enough strength to write Edwina a line for her birthday. She sent presents ('my pretty clothes brushes', Edwina said tactfully) and money for the savings bank, but she did not ask for her daughter. Edwina wondered whether she was being kept away because she had done something wrong. She begged Minette to say that she had been good. Could she and Minette not come? Edwina would not be a nuisance: 'I wanted to be with you only a little while.'

Edwina could not consult her father, who was in the north again, defending his seat in the second election of 1910. This, on top of everything else, made Wilfrid frantic, exhausted and more fussy than ever. He drove Sir Ernest to distraction.

Winter was coming. Broadlands was too cold for Maudie but she was not strong enough for another journey to Egypt. Sir Ernest had her brought to Bruton Street, where he surrounded her with nurses. The election over – the result was much the same as before – Wilfrid joined Maudie in London for Christmas, eating her dinner as well as his own, and delighting the day nurse, who thought her patient's appetite had miraculously returned. Maudie was allowed to see a few friends but there was still no reunion with the children. From Wherwell they had gone to Moulton Paddocks, where they stayed until the end of January. Sir Ernest's Christmas presents to Maudie were jewels and a cheque for £5000, a godsend to Wilfrid, who wanted to improve the cottages at Broadlands. But necklaces were no use to Maudie now; all she needed, she said, were a few nightgowns. Edwina wrote a brave letter. For almost as long as she could remember her mother had spent her days in bed or on a sofa, but now: 'I know you are better. In my dream last night I have seen you quite dressed'.

Sir Ernest and Mrs Cassel came back to London in late January. Maudie insisted that Wilfrid should have his shooting but, after trying it once or twice, he could not bear to leave her. Edwina and Mary were taken from Newmarket to Bournemouth, to the Canford Cliffs Hotel (telegraphic address: Salubritas). On 5 February, while they were away, Maudie died. The funeral was at Romsey Abbey; the children were not there. Maudie was buried in the family vault in the cemetery on the hill above Broadlands. On the same morning there were memorial services in Blackpool and in St George's, Hanover Square; newspapers from Preston to Cairo listed the mourners, good, great, fashionable and royal, and described every detail: the wreaths from King George and the Kaiser; messages from all quarters, from the Khedive to the Blackpool Tradesmen's Association.

On her own and Mary's behalf Edwina wrote a bleak letter to her father: 'I am so very sorry darling Mama left us all so suddenly and for ever, I wanted to kiss her only once and now I didn't, but it is very nice to think her spirit will always be with me'. Kindly Minette had done her best; had Maudie not been called away so quickly, Minette explained, of course she would have seen the children. But Edwina was heartbroken. She had wanted so much to see Mama . . . 'and now I didn't'.

CHAPTER FIVE

The Intruder

Three months before she died Maudie had rewritten her will, confirming that all she had was to go to Wilfrid, 'to do with what he thinks best'. Her witness was Ellen Harrison, Mrs Cassel's chief nurse, secretary and housekeeper, who had been seconded to look after Maudie. Maudie's note was unnecessary, except as a last expression of trust in her husband. The disposition of her stocks and shares, of her joint share in the houses Sir Ernest had bought, of her possessions – all had been arranged long before. Everything was indeed bequeathed to Wilfrid and, eventually, to Edwina and Mary. Maudie's jewels were sent to Collingwood for valuation: two tiaras, a diamond trefoil and one of gold leaves and flowers; two diamond bandeaux; four pearl necklaces, one of six rows, three with diamonds; nine necklaces of emeralds, amethysts, platinum, diamonds, of all shapes and sizes; nineteen bracelets of rubies, diamonds, sapphires, pearls; pendants, brooches, rings and earrings; and a list of 'sundries': watches, buttons, hatpins, waist clasps and buckles; hairpins, vanity cases, sunshade handles (one pink quartz, one gold with 'Maudie' in diamonds); manicure sets, scent bottles, salts bottles, a pencil case of silver seed pearls and, pathetically, a pendant in the shape of the Egyptian key of life. Most of these had been presents from Sir Ernest. In time Edwina and Mary would have them.

Wilfrid kept his wife's violets, faded now, and a St Christopher medallion that had been her mother's, which Maudie had given him two weeks before she died. She also left Wilfrid a letter, written in December 1909, to be opened after her death, the last of the long love-letters she had so often given him, but this time including various specific requests. She hoped that he would continue his political career; in fact it was unthinkable that Wilfrid would have considered abandoning it, however devastated he was. Next, she thought that 'for the sake of Broadlands' he should marry again, an idea that appalled Wilfrid, for the time being. As for the children, Maudie sensibly asked that they should not be brought up to have a horror of death. Wilfrid should talk of her and let them think she was watching over them, 'as', – here Maudie hedged a little – 'I shall certainly try to'. Minette should not be kept on for more than a year. Wilfrid should tell Edwina of Maudie's horror of women with 'advanced ideas' and prevent her from becoming a suffragette. Here he was to succeed only partially.

Maudie sent her fond love to dear Papa – 'We have always loved if we have not always understood one another' – and asked forgiveness for being impatient with Mrs Cassel, in whose lap she had once been cuddled to sleep. And that – with a list of bequests to nurses and maids, and a request that Auntie Bobbie should have the heart-shaped diamond ring and bracelet, and Vittoria, Violet de Trafford, Mrs Bisch and Marjorie other souvenirs – was that.

Wilfrid tried to immerse himself in politics. He mooched about the House of Commons, where Balfour took pity on him and made him a Whip, and from Fridays to Mondays he sought refuge at his friends' houses in the country. But Sir Ernest refused all invitations, sending his regrets on writing-paper bordered half an inch in black. He had Wilfrid to breakfast at Brook House but otherwise he entertained no one. Cassel was inconsolable. From the day Maudie died until the day of his own death the alcove at the top of the great staircase at Brook House was filled with lilies of the valley, obtained with tremendous difficulty and expense. There too Sir Ernest placed a bust of Maudie, more lilies wreathed about the marble figure.

Cassel took on himself the duty of choosing mementoes for Maudie's friends, for his bewildered son-in-law was inclined to send the wrong things from Bruton Street. 'It was not what I meant', wrote Sir Ernest, '. . . the filligree work was meant for the children . . .' He had another task, to deal with appeals for money. From far and wide people wrote to ask if they might show their sympathy by begging him for a cheque. Cassel had already decided what he would do in Maudie's memory. Fifty thousand pounds was to be shared among King Edward VII's Hospital Fund and hospitals in Hampshire and Blackpool. This was a substantial sum. He also arranged for the establishment, in memory of the late King, of a foundation to help distressed British people in Germany and Germans in Britain, launching it with a gift of £210,000. A further £30,000 went to a fund for workmen in Swedish mines. The following year, 1912, Cassel gave

The Intruder

£10,000 to the Deaconesses' Hospital in Alexandria and in 1913 £50,000 for the relief of the sick and needy in his birthplace, Cologne, with another £20,000 for the King Edward VII Sanatorium he had founded in 1902. Arranging these benefactions gave Cassel an occupation, although it did little to assuage his grief.

It could not last for ever. Towards the end of 1911 Sir Ernest was shaken out of his retreat from the world by new approaches from his colleague Albert Ballin. Winston Churchill had now become First Lord of the Admiralty, an appointment that offered another chance at peacemaking. Encouraged by Churchill and Lloyd George, the Chancellor of the Exchequer, who wanted to save money on rearmament, the Foreign Secretary sent Cassel on a reconnoitring expedition to Germany. In late January 1912 Cassel spent two days with Ballin in Berlin, where they saw the Chancellor and the Emperor, from whom Cassel brought back friendly messages. At the beginning of February, Haldane, the Secretary of State for War and a fluent German speaker, set off for Berlin, taking Cassel with him. Three years before, the German Chancellor had objected to Ballin and Cassel's private diplomacy; he had not changed his view. The mission was a failure.

Sir Ernest had begun to revive. A year after Maudie's death he still could not bear to visit Broadlands but in the spring of 1912 he started buying houses again, always a good sign. The first was Six Mile Bottom, a large estate near Newmarket, which he acquired not so much for the house, an unpleasing villa close to the road, as for the shooting, which was good. Next, in 1913, he bought a property in Bournemouth, to share with his sister, Mrs Cassel, who liked that part of the coast. This house, Branksome Dene, became a second home for Edwina and Mary. Mrs Cassel was a plump old lady, suffering from breathlessness and trouble with her legs, happy to live a quiet life among her potted palms and *petit point*. Cousin Anna, Sir Ernest's niece, now acted as his hostess in London during the week; from Fridays to Mondays he entertained guests at Branksome, outside the racing and shooting seasons, which he continued to spend at Moulton.

When the weekend parties were large, Sir Ernest would send extra servants down from London; such a change from Brook House, they thought, for Branksome Dene was all chintz and white paintwork, and the sea breeze blew through the fresh cotton curtains. Sir Ernest's theatrical, musical and artistic friends came to see him at

Bournemouth, the seaside being more to their taste than Newmarket. Burne-Jones offered to look for pictures to decorate the two new houses, a Gainsborough and a Romney being among his first finds, and Sir Guy Laking, Keeper of the London Museum, bid on Cassel's behalf for furniture at Christie's. The painter, Alma-Tadema, was a friend and among Sir Ernest's guests at Branksome were E. F. Benson, the novelist, and Beerbohm Tree and Forbes Robertson, the actor-managers.

So, in different surroundings, Cassel began to entertain once more. He was subdued – but he had never been loud. To emphasize a point, he became even quieter, and flintily polite. His attentiveness was legendary, his concentration phenomenal. It unnerved those with whom he negotiated. Saemy Japhet thought Cassel the best listener he had ever met; Edwina inherited this skill.

The first year after Maudie's death was strange for Edwina and Mary. Life was in some ways exactly as it had always been, in others quite changed. Mademoiselle Minart had been replaced by Mademoiselle Jenny, but lessons were more or less the same, an undemanding two or three hours a day, in which Edwina copied poetry and did simple calculations, read and wrote in German and French, pottered through elementary history and geography. The animals still needed attention, piano practice had to be kept up. There was more church, and, from time to time, a solemn visit to the cemetery. The children's lives had a steadier routine. Edwina and Mary did not go to London; Broadlands became the centre of their lives. Edwina's world became smaller, quieter, more manageable. She and Mary no longer found themselves suddenly transported to Stanmore, Cleethorpes, Moulton, Wherwell. For three years they had lived among adults who were on edge, hoping, doubting, waiting for a crisis. Now that the worst had happened, leaving everyone exhausted, ordinary life seemed an anti-climax.

Being so young and unused to loss, it was hard for Edwina to understand and accommodate her reactions to her mother's death, which went deep. Both children felt deserted and rejected. Mary, at six, was visibly disturbed. Always volatile, she became stormy, wilful and unco-operative. Sir Ernest and Wilfrid spoke darkly of 'Mary's little ways'; only Edwina could control her. On Mary, however, the impact of Maudie's defection was at least immediate and obvious. In Edwina's case, the effects were more insidious. A conscientious child, she felt responsible for what had happened, without knowing that she did. Would the outcome have been different if she had been able to see her mother, to read to her, and 'go about a little in the garden'? What else should she have said or done, or might she have said and done better? Maudie's departure, so sudden and final, was bound to leave a question mark.

Edwina was more anxious than ever to do her duty. Her exercise books, never untidy, became even neater; every photograph in her album was meticulously labelled; given a diary, she filled each page with a complete record of the day's events. She was polite, considerate and appreciative – other children must have found her unbearable. She fussed over Mary, read to her, played with her, made sure she had her sunhat on. Edwina's protectiveness towards Mary and Mary's dependence on Edwina were fixed from that moment.

Edwina's ultra-dutiful behaviour was in part an instinctive reaction to Maudie's death, a natural expiation and precaution. There were other reasons. The death of her mother, so long the centre of attention, had left a vacuum. Would all eyes now be on Edwina, her father's consolation, her sister's guardian, her grandfather's hope? She was in danger of becoming self-important. Although Wilfrid and Sir Ernest were in a state of shock, Mrs Cassel and Cousin Anna knew what was needed: a firm, breezy, intelligent governess. In September 1912 she arrived. This was Laura Devéria, whose influence was miraculous.

The family had already begun to cheer up, rallied by an ambitious expedition Sir Ernest had arranged. Encouraged by Ballin, he chartered a ship from the Hamburg-Amerika line - not a yacht but a 4907-ton, twin-screw steamer – with a crew of a hundred and fifty. The *Ypyranga* was fitted up with armchairs, deckchairs and bridge tables, staffed with the family's own nurses and governesses and Sir Ernest's chef, equipped with special biscuits, mineral waters, chocolate and champagne, enough to last its occupants for weeks. Edwina, Mary and Marjorie were kitted out in floppy white skirts, edged with navy, and dashing sailor hats. Some of Sir Ernest's guests came for the whole voyage, others joined or left at various ports. Wilfrid, whose rheumatism bothered him, got off in Italy and took himself home to Bath. Sir Ernest recommended radium: 'It tastes like water and I am assured it cannot do any possible harm to anybody'. From Norway Wilfrid got a postcard from Edwina, who was ecstatic: 'Now we are at Green Harbour, Spitzbergen. We have just landed and it smells terribly of Whales'. She had been given a camera and enthusiastically snapped expanses of sea, empty fjords and indistinguishable stretches of the Scandinavian coast. She also managed to lose the uncomfortable plate the dentist had put on her teeth. It had jumped out of her mouth, she said, and fallen into the sea. The cruise raised Sir Ernest's spirits to such an extent that when it was over he at last felt able to look in at the Villa Cassel for a week or two.

The children did not go with him but home to Branksome, where they found Miss Devéria. Edwina photographed her new governess sitting on the sands and striding through the gardens, her calf-length skirt and loose jacket looking wonderfully practical and dashing, her hatbrim turned back to show a laughing, open face. Mademoiselle Jenny blossomed under the influence of her new colleague. The firmly-buttoned, well-starched, corseted nurses remained – Nurse Harrison, Nurse Ollard, Nurse Fritze and Nurse Cullum – to look after Auntie-Grannie and keep an eye on Edwina and Mary, but a blast of fresh air had blown into the children's lives. Lessons were less amateurish. Mademoiselle Jenny and Miss Devéria were thorough, so that later, when Edwina went to school, she was able to hold her own. She was introduced to serious books – Kipling and, later, Shelley, Browning and Tennyson – and taken to concerts; she was at last told something about Sir Ernest's pictures and about the political questions which so interested her father, her grandfather and their visitors.

Bit by bit the children calmed down. There was one small drama, when Mary fell ill in the spring of 1913. The doctor diagnosed appendicitis and she was operated on at Brook House, Sir Ernest standing anxiously by. Edwina came to London to be with her and when Mary was strong enough Sir Ernest rewarded her for being brave by taking the girls to a military tournament. The marches and mock battles were exciting but they reminded Cassel of his nightmare: war. He smelt trouble. It was coming nearer – but not yet close enough to cut him off from the part of the Continent he liked best, the mountains and meadows in the high country where France, Italy and Switzerland converge.

In late July a large party set off for the Villa Cassel – Sir Ernest, Cousin Anna and Marjorie, Edwina, Mary, Miss Devéria, Mademoiselle Jenny, and Mrs Cassel, who for the first time could not stand the altitude and had to be sent down the mountain to the best hotel in Vevey. Exercise and the thin air sharpened appetites for the

54

Molly

Edwina

The Links School

Alde House

The Intruder

lavish teas that were set out each afternoon on the verandah, which was protected from the hot sun by wide, striped awnings, unrolled with a crank at exactly the same time each morning. In the evening, when the sun suddenly disappeared behind the mountains, the children did not beg to stay up and play cards; exhausted, they slept like stones.

It was their last summer in Switzerland for many years. Early in 1914 Ballin and Cassel tried to arrange a meeting between Admiral Tirpitz and Churchill at the German Naval Review at Kiel in June but the idea became bogged down in a swamp of protocol and eventually sank out of sight. By August Britain was at war with Germany. Tension had been rising for months but, when the crisis came after the assassination of Archduke Franz Ferdinand at Sarajevo, British Ministers were taken unawares. Distracted by domestic problems, labour unrest, the battle over Irish Home Rule, they turned away from foreign troubles and, in that little space, the wave that had been building for so long at last reared up and toppled over. In the last hours of peace, some influential people kept their heads. Churchill did not dither, nor his new First Sea Lord, Prince Louis of Battenberg. A great concentration of ships had been assembled in mid-July in a trial mobilization and now, on his own initiative, Prince Louis ordered that they should not disperse. The Navy was ready. Cassel was prepared. He had known for years that war was coming and had done what he could to prevent it.

Now there was a great upheaval in Edwina's life, just as she had begun to settle down. It was not the Kaiser who caused it but her father, or, rather, her father's new wife. This was the Hon. Mrs Lionel Forbes-Sempill, Molly, whom Wilfrid and Maudie had first met in 1910, at the house of the Chairman of the Primrose League. Molly Forbes-Sempill had parted from her husband, a Commander in the Navy – people said that each had been unfaithful to the other – and in the spring of 1914 she was waiting for the final stages of her divorce. In July Edwina and Mary were at Broadstairs, at Mrs Owen's breezy boarding house, Overblow, with Miss Devéria and Nurse Cullum. When they returned to Broadlands, Wilfrid told them that Molly was coming to live with them; when she came, they did not like her.

On August 12th Molly's divorce proceedings were completed and on the 28th she and Wilfrid were married. For their honeymoon, they took a motor tour, for which Molly wore a flat hat, a six-foot pink chiffon scarf floating out behind. Cassel had been introduced to Molly shortly after the engagement was announced. He sent her a wedding present, with a brief, formal letter. Sir Ernest had ceased to mourn his own wife's death only when he began to mourn that of his daughter but Wilfrid was made of weaker stuff. He had been lonely, most acutely when he was among married friends – and a wife was useful in the constituency. Maudie had told him that 'for the sake of Broadlands' he should marry again and Molly, whose sister was the wife of Hamar Greenwood, a Liberal MP, seemed to understand the nature of political responsibility and the demands it imposed. If Wilfrid had qualms, he rationalized them away. Molly's arrival at Broadlands coincided, appropriately, with the beginning of the Great War.

She started with a handicap. It was not easy to step into the shoes of delicate, amusing, charming Maudie, whom many friends had loved and for whom every one had felt sorry, from the hoariest Emperor to Mademoiselle Minart, from the grooms at Broadlands to the Egyptian cook at the Mena House. One of Molly's mistakes was that she appeared to be trying to do so, and too quickly. Even before she and Wilfrid were married, she had explained how she intended to redecorate the rooms at Broadlands and now she swiftly stripped away the wallcoverings of faded brocade, startling the children and the staff. Her scheme was an improvement but her ruthlessness was dreadful. Molly was bossy, convinced that her own ideas were right. People shuddered when she came into their drawing-rooms because she would immediately suggest how they should rearrange the furniture. Perhaps things had chugged along rather too easily at Broadlands. Aunt Alice and Papa Evelyn had been sweet-tempered and kind; Maudie had spent too little time there, most of it as an invalid, to make a great mark on the housekeeping arrangements. All now changed. Molly was a dragon, breathing fire and smoke upon staff, family and guests. Visitors were warned that, on arrival, they should ring the bell no more than once: 'the servants are well-trained'. The children were sent to bed at half past six, 'to be out of the way', their stepmother said, in their hearing. One more example is enough. Wilfrid invited a friend to fish. It was too wet for the river and so the visitor came home at lunch-time, disrupting Molly's routine. When he appeared in the dining-room, he was ordered to eat his sandwiches in the hall, where his damp clothes could do no damage. It was not a joke. Molly had simply put her own arrangements first. She did not mean to make her guests – and everyone else – uncomfortable. But she did and Edwina, who was hospitable, was upset.

Molly did not appreciate that she was treading on eggshells. If she did, she laboriously crunched them underfoot. Marjorie was shocked by one episode. The children were about to get into a train with their stepmother and her friend, the writer and explorer, Rosita Forbes, when Molly announced that, although she and Mrs Forbes were travelling first-class, third was good enough for Edwina and Mary. Mrs Forbes insisted that they should all travel together and paid the difference. Edwina, being proud, felt hurt and embarrassed. Molly had shown herself to be not only unkind but heedless of her own dignity and that of anyone else. She was especially insensitive towards children, who one way and another took their revenge. At tea-time, when Edwina and Mary came into the drawing-room, Molly poured out their milk. They were supposed to tell her when the cup was full, but Edwina never did and the milk invariably overflowed. She had willing allies in her cousins, Marjorie and the daughters of Cousin Felix, now Judge Advocate General, and Cousin Helen, whom he had married in 1908. In one spectacular gesture, Josefine Cassel made a bleeding head out of *papier mâché* and put it in Molly's bed.

Molly was pretentious. At dances, after the war, she would hold her right arm above her head, waving an ostrich feather fan. Although she was handsome, this looked ridiculous. Another affectation was to ask the children to call her 'Madre'; when they did, they could not manage to give the impression she wanted. It made her sound improbable, like a character in Italian opera.

It was useful to have a wicked stepmother as a target for the deflection of bitterness and rage. Like a widower in a fairy tale, Wilfrid weakly let a virago into the house and then took himself off into the woods, leaving his two little girls to battle things out with the intruder. If Molly wanted to woo Edwina and Mary, she did not go about it cleverly – but then she was not clever. If, on the other hand, she wished to supply them with a first-class cruel stepmother, she exceeded all expectations.

Her first move was to sack Laura Devéria. Mary was now old enough to be taught with Edwina, and the governess had charge of them both. Molly did not approve of Miss Devéria's uncensorious ways; not did she wish to compete for her stepdaughters' attention, affection and respect. Keenly conscious of her own status, Molly found Miss Devéria unnerving. So Laura left. Sir Ernest and Auntie-Grannie were sad, Edwina and Mary sadder still. Molly had usurped not one throne, but two.

The children were now taught by Miss Atwood, competent and friendly but dull in comparison with her predecessor. They were resentful and Mary was particularly naughty. Molly felt they conspired against her and, when Marjorie came to stay, that it was three against one. (She was right.) Wilfrid was trying to raise and train a battalion in Liverpool. He was edgy and anxious to set off to France to fight, but the more jumpy he grew, the more troublesome his sciatica became, and he feared he would never get there. Molly complained that Broadlands was impossible to run with so many male staff away at the war, so for Christmas the children went to Sir Ernest and Auntie-Grannie at Branksome. Mrs Cassel was delighted to have them, although she was almost dropping with tiredness, for she had been organizing nursing for the wounded men who were beginning to stream home across the Channel.

At this point the children had only the haziest notion of what the war was about. They knew that their father and Colonel Jenkins, Marjorie's father, were organizing soldiers and that the older brothers of their friends were going to France. But they knew nothing of invasion scares, nor of the ghastly muddles on French battlefields. No one told them about the anti-German hysteria simmering in England, particularly in London, which by the end of 1915 hit their own family. Sir Ernest was the victim. He had done nothing that could be construed as disloyal to his adopted country; indeed, his was one of the largest subscriptions to the War Loan. He was so trusted by the Government that in September 1915 he was asked, unofficially, to accompany Lord Reading on a secret mission to New York, where after a month's discussion the Americans offered the Allies a vital loan of half a million dollars. As soon as Cassel returned, he was attacked. His German birth and German name made him an obvious target; his detractors turned all the evidence of his patriotism against him. He was, they said, too friendly with all sides, the go-between who had conversations with the German Emperor. He was neither properly British nor properly German. His religious beliefs were equivocal; he had been sworn in with the Catholic members of the new King's Privy Council and yet his origins were obviously Jewish. The rumour got about that on the roof of Brook House he had a specially designed wireless set, to keep in touch with Germany.

Cassel knew he had highly placed enemies – although he may not have known that in 1910, when the Prime Minister and the Foreign Secretary had made a list of three hundred prospective new peers, in case they had to pack the Lords with supporters, his name was not among those of his fellow City magnates. All those who had a grudge, who resented or disliked him, could now sow doubt in fertile ground. Wilfrid had warned his father-in-law. In early May, when lurid stories were being spread of German atrocities, he had advised Sir Ernest to demonstrate his loyalty to the Allies by condemning the enemy's methods of waging war. Cassel thanked Wilfrid but remained silent:'I have the greatest objection to giving way to popular clamour . . . The fact that others have done so is no reason for my following their course'. He went only as far as giving an interview to the Editor of the *Chicago Daily News*, to encourage support for the Allies in America; perhaps, he told Wilfrid, the text would be cabled to the London papers. If it was, it did not prevent an anti-Cassel drive. Sir George Mackgill laid information against both Cassel and Sir Edgar Speyer, another financier, Chairman of the London Underground and a friend of Asquith, citing the British Nationality and Status of Aliens Act, passed the year before, and calling upon them to show by what right, being of German birth, they had retained their membership of the Privy Council. The case was heard by three judges in a Court presided over by Lord Reading, Cassel's friend and recent companion on the mission to America. The Court found in favour of Sir Ernest and Sir Edgar; their friends, ashamed, wrote warm letters of support. Sir Edgar resigned his Privy Councillorship and left for America; Cassel did not budge. His view of human nature was never rose-coloured but, understandably, he was hurt. His humiliation was minor, however, compared with that which the First Sea Lord had undergone a year earlier. Prince Louis of Battenberg had felt impelled to resign, in view of the innuendo in the popular press against 'the Germhun' and insinuations from professional rivals that he should do the decent thing and go. It was weeks before Edwina heard about the outcry against her grandfather, unlike Dickie Mountbatten, who learnt the news of his father's destruction straightaway and wept over it. But when Edwina was told what had happened, she was angry and, like Dickie, never forgot it.

While all this was going on, Wilfrid and Molly were at the Ritz in London, pampering Wilfrid's rheumatism and waiting to see whether he was to go to France with a reserve battalion. The children had spent a happy summer with Miss Atwood at Classiebawn, shrimping, exploring, picking sea-pinks. Wilfrid and Molly had been in Buxton, taking a cure. All the girls' letters were to their father, sending 'very large kisses' and their love, coolly, to Madre. Edwina wrote in clear, precise German; Molly, who did not understand it, complained that her stepdaughter's handwriting was difficult to read. Edwina then wrote in French. Molly was annoyed, especially when Mary did the same, managing her letters, she said, 'sans demande riain a Mlle Atwood ou Edwina', erratic French but a brave effort.

Mary said she was trying to be good but she did not try hard enough for Molly, who decided that she should go away to school. This was Molly's second strike. On 23 January 1916 the sisters spent a melancholy Sunday together, their last, they thought, until Easter, cleaning the animals, packing parcels for prisoners of war and listening to a dull sermon from the local vicar. After lunch they trailed round the garden and the stables, where Mary said goodbye to the horses and her birds, played a few miserable games of cards and went sadly to bed. Edwina tried to cheer things up by letting her pet mice out for a run.

Half a day later the children discovered, to their intense delight, that Molly could not command the universe. When they went to Victoria to find the school train, Mary holding tight to Edwina's hand, they learnt that measles had broken out among the pupils. 'Mary of course could not go', Edwina wrote triumphantly in her diary. They made the most of this reprieve, joyfully riding round Yew Tree Copse and Badger's Path, playing the gramophone and Matador, their second-best game, Halma, the top favourite, being packed in Mary's trunk.

Three days later Mary and Miss Atwood set off again. Edwina and Mary were determined that their alliance would survive Molly's tactic of divide and rule. Edwina persuaded Cook to let her make peppermint creams, caramels and chocolate toffee to send to Mary at Eastbourne; she weeded Mary's garden and planted it with forget-me-nots – appropriate, if rash at the end of a soggy January. Mary wrote long letters about her school, which she liked, and Edwina sent equally long replies. Luckily Molly spent most of her time in London or in Blackpool with Wilfrid, who had stayed only briefly in France, since Molly had decided that his sciatica disqualified him from active warfare and that he should come home. When Molly was at Broadlands, Edwina saw her only between tea and dinner, when they played cribbage, Halma or draughts. Winter was lonely without her sister. Every weekday morning, including Saturdays, Edwina did lessons with Miss Atwood until eleven, when she was sent out to ride, walk or bicycle, sometimes going as far as Romsey post office to see to her savings account. After lunch in the schoolroom she rested, before another hour of lessons until tea, which she had either in the schoolroom or, if Molly wanted her, downstairs. Then there were card and board games: Bezique, Newmarket, 'Progressive Old Maid' and, on special occasions, bridge, followed by more lessons and supper. Edwina knitted scarves for soldiers while Miss Atwood made lace on a cushion, the click of her bobbins as soothing as the ticking of a clock. Every night before she went to bed, the child sought out old Mrs Turner, the former housekeeper, who had first come to Broadlands in 1866 and now lived in retirement at the top of the house. These evening chats were even more comforting than Miss Atwood's final tucking-in. Edwina read a great deal: *L'Aiguille Creuse*, 'full of awful murders', *A Study in Scarlet*, *Dombey and Son*, her face so close to the page that Miss Atwood took her to an oculist, who discovered that her huge blue eyes were short-sighted. Edwina hated her spectacles, discarding them whenever she could. Over the years her eyesight – and headaches – got worse.

Edwina was healthy and energetic, loving each minute out of doors. She rode whenever it was fine and adored jumping ditches and bars. When Mary was at home, Edwina had followed the hounds with her in the waggonette but now she took part in the hunt, revelling in runs with the Hursley Hounds. She liked to sit in the stables, talking to Worsfold the groom about the habits of partridges, pheasants and horses. On Sundays there were no lessons. Pious visitors took Edwina to church for morning service, which she would later describe irreverently to Mary. This was also the day for cleaning the animals: Darby and Joan, the mice, and their nine offspring, and the dogs, Pip, Popsy and Pekoe. There was little to be done for Crumps, the tortoise, except to photograph him – or her; the most demanding of the pets were a

Edwina Mountbatten

baby jay, abandoned by its parents, and Goldie, a golden pheasant which Sir Ernest had given her. Looking after the animals was a pleasure; whenever Edwina felt particularly depressed or excited, she cleaned the mice.

She was orderly by nature. Having taught herself two-finger typing, she spent weeks cataloguing the books in the schoolroom. Her piano music was tidily arranged; her garden and Mary's regularly weeded. In the diary Marjorie gave her for her birthday in 1915, Edwina carefully made a list of key dates: everyone's birthday, including Miss Devéria's, and the dates of various people's engagements, marriages, and disengagements. She listed jobs to be done – 'Water flowers'; 'See about M. A.'s present' – checking them off with a triumphant 'Done', a habit she kept all her life. Edwina's accounts were as meticulous as her mother's had been. On the debit side: Church 2d; Seed 3d; Prisoners 8d; Nibs 6d; Sweets 6d. She bought her own knitting wool; drops, bows and Jeyes Fluid for the animals; and luxuries like Pine Essence and Pot Pourri. Each week she gave Worsfold sixpence, rising to eightpence, for helping to groom her pony. Under 'credits' she put her four shillings a week pocket money and, when she saw Grandpapa or Auntie-Grannie, 'Tip': one pound or one guinea. Each month Edwina made up the balance and noted Cash in Hand. In her diary she recorded the names of all visitors to Broadlands, their times of arrival, the weight of the fish they caught, the number of birds they shot, if any, and their times of departure: 'Dover 7.43'. She amended the list of charges for telegrams when the rates were altered in March and entered in 'the Remembrancer' the serial number of her wrist-watch, her glove measurement (small, six and a half) and the size of her boots (five), though not her weight, about which she was self-conscious, for Wilfrid cruelly called her 'Fatsy'. Edwina was tall, if plump, eager, exact and anxious. At night, according to Marjorie, who sometimes shared her room, she ground her teeth.

When Mary had been away a month, Edwina had her own, grisly adventure. On one foot the fourth toe bruised easily and an expert, Dr Jackson Clark, proposed complete amputation of the part above the top joint. At the end of February Edwina was installed in a London nursing home, with Miss Atwood in lodgings next door. It was ghastly. The chloroform made Edwina sick, the operation was agony. Dr Clark she thought *'horrible*, the nurses worse'. The Home was not like home; a patient in the next room played the piano and a baby

The Intruder

howled all night. Papa and Madre came and played Halma. Edwina's salvation was Grandpapa, who brought grapes and chocolates, easy needlework and materials for making lavender sachets. After three days, Edwina was allowed to leave, her foot wrapped in cotton wool and held fast with splints. Now there was no riding, nor even walking. Rather than returning to Broadlands, she and Miss Atwood stayed at The Grove. Sir Ernest, Auntie-Grannie, Uncle Felix and Aunt Helen tried to make things pleasant, taking Edwina to tea at Fuller's or Gorringe's after her appointments with the hated Dr Clark. It was ages before she could hobble, in hideous surgical boots. Molly felt neglected. 'She is having some sort of "cure" for 3 weeks', Edwina wrote derisively to Mary, 'and is not allowed to walk about and has to lie on the sofa all day'. Edwina's nurse was replaced by one for Molly.

The torment came to an end. In April Mary came home from school, straight to The Grove. 'A glorious time', said Edwina, although Mary celebrated by eating too many cakes and making herself sick. After frantic shopping – Harrods, Debenham and Freebody, Swears and Wells, more teas at Gorringe's – interspersed with lunch at Brook House with Grandpapa and in South Audley Street with Mrs Bisch, Edwina and Mary escaped to Branksome for Auntie-Grannie's Easter party. Apart from a visit to the dentist, the only local hazard, they had a blissful ten days, walking with Grandpapa, playing piquet with Mrs Keppel, racing on the beach.

Mary went back to school, the parting eased by a morning at the zoo. Edwina returned to Broadlands, where all the spring and summer pleasures waited. She picked primroses and violets in the woods and rode in the early morning and evening. Marjorie came over from Wherwell to play duets, climb trees and raid birds' nests. Mary had said that Edwina might play with her child-sized motor, a present from Sir Ernest, but she preferred tennis and croquet and bicycling down the hill in the park with Jack and Bobbie Everett, and games of Blind Man's Buff, Hide and Seek, and French and English. Edwina sat and read by the river, fished and caught nothing. It pleased her to record in her diary that Molly caught nothing either. Wilfrid was more successful; his salmon and trout were used to feed visiting Generals. Some of the guests called on Edwina in the schoolroom and when Grandpapa stayed she was allowed, at his request, to come downstairs for dinner.

Edwina Mountbatten

There was one blot. Cousin Harry, Evelyn Ashley's son from his second marriage, was with his regiment in France. To Edwina Harry was a romantic figure. She was keenly interested in love and marriage, as fourteen-year-old girls often are, and in why Harry had broken off his engagement before he had gone away to fight. Edwina had written regularly to him; Harry, who was fond of her, wrote back. On 9 May she learnt that he had been wounded. Grandmama Alice left for France the next day and found her son in the hospital at Étaples. Days passed before she could report that he was out of danger.

Edwina now took notice of current events, partly, perhaps largely, because of Harry. She compiled a 'History of the War', cutting out articles from *The Times*, which she bought with her pocket money. The Classiebawn connection gave her an interest in affairs in Ireland, and she made special notes in her diary of the capture of Sir Roger Casement and the events that followed. Edwina struggled beside General Townshend in the siege of Kut, she wrote pages on the Battle of Jutland, listing British ships and the numbers of men lost. She made special mention of the sinking of the *Hampshire* in June, with Kitchener aboard: at Romsey there was '. . . a most lovely service, lots of soldiers played hymns and the Last Post and the organist played Chopin's Funeral March'. Edwina looked for Zeppelins, seeing only an airship that had been forced to ditch, and listened eagerly to first-hand accounts of life at the front. The Monds, who lived nearby at Melchett, had turned part of their house into a hospital and on one memorable afternoon Mary, Nora and Henry Mond took Edwina for a picnic in the New Forest with a wounded officer who plied her with strawberries and taught her to smoke cigarettes. Then Molly dropped another bombshell. In July Edwina learnt that she too was to go away to school.

CHAPTER SIX

Edwina's Education

Edwina was knocked sideways. The spring and early summer had been so happy, although, looking back, there had been omens. In May the mice had died and Goldie, the golden pheasant, had followed shortly after. Crumps the tortoise had expired; Edwina buried him under the mulberry tree, festooning her room with purple lilac as a sign of mourning. Molly had obviously been planning something. There had been the sequence of visits to the dentist, the doctor and the oculist and, a glaring clue, to Harrods, to be fitted for a matching coat and skirt. Wilfrid announced the news before dinner on 3 July, a black date, immediately added to Edwina's calendar of wartime disasters. He explained that he and Molly felt that Edwina had too few companions, 'but of course', she wrote in her diary, 'the long and short of it was that Madre wanted to get rid of me and Miss A. – the pig!!'

Edwina did not agree that she was too much on her own. She missed Mary but she had a good many friends, not only Marjorie and the Shaftesburys, but others whose parents were neighbours at Broadlands and The Grove: Mary Mond, the Malmesburys, the Everett boys, Lavender and Diana Sloane-Stanley, Rosalind Benson and Lois Sturt, Rosemary Hall-Walker, Rosemary Rees and Joan Foster, who had given Edwina an amber necklace after the operation on her toe. Edwina disliked the daughters of Molly's and Wilfrid's friends on principle – 'a most uninteresting child', was one entry in her diary – but she was capable of choosing her own allies. 'Not enough companionship': how could they fob her off with that? During the next twenty-four hours Edwina complained to everyone at Broadlands – in the kitchen, the pantry, the housekeeper's room, the garden, the stables, the farm and the estate office. She commiserated with Miss Atwood, who would have to look for another place, and confided in Jackie the jay, in his summer cage behind the geraniums. 'Feeling very sick about it', Edwina said, but at least Wilfrid and Madre left her alone and went off to London: 'the Lord be praised for the departure of the latter'.

Another day – and Edwina had not only resigned herself to Molly's scheme but had almost begun to look forward to it. Term did not start until the end of September so she would have all summer to say goodbye to the house, the garden and the animals. There was some good news. The school Molly had chosen for Mary was so fashionable that, when fashion changed, it was snuffed out. Mary and Edwina were to go to the same school, The Links, where together they could make the best of their exile. As a start, Edwina took the dogs to Romsey to be photographed and, in a positive mood, gave the parrot a bath. There were still two and a half months before she need even think about packing.

It was a wonderful summer. Harry came home in a wheelchair, irritating Molly, who was afraid that it would crush the edges of the lawn. Edwina played tennis and ferocious croquet every afternoon and, when she could, in the evenings as well. The Congregational School had its summer treat in the park at Broadlands, moving for tea to the Abbey when it came on to rain, since Molly did not want wet children near the house. The Baptists were luckier; the sun shone all afternoon and hundreds of people turned up for sports and merry-go-rounds. Mary came home in time for her birthday and, as Grandpapa had given her a bicycle, she and Edwina were able to explore the lanes together. They took books and their tea to the river bank and went boating with the Everetts. Once a week they drove over to Wherwell to play with Marjorie, fish and punt and to help with the arrangements for a War Economy Demonstration: three hundred people came for exhibitions of Economical Cooking and Laundry.

In September Miss Atwood, Mary, Marjorie and Edwina moved to Moulton Paddocks for the last fortnight of the holidays. On the second night there was a Zeppelin raid over Newmarket. Everyone slept through it and Edwina was furious. Grandpapa, Auntie-Grannie and Cousin Anna were full of ideas: a 'dress up' tea (Edwina was a Chinaman); tennis in the Winter Garden when it rained; concerts on the Electric Piano after breakfast. The children cycled to the racing stables to see Sir Ernest's horses; they practised galloping on the Heath, Mary on Jumbo and Edwina on Titmouse. Edwina and Marjorie were allowed to shoot – Grandpapa took them out after partridges – and all three girls stayed up for dinner and bridge in the evening. There

66

Edwina's Education

was clock golf and croquet, tea on the verandah and toffee-making in the kitchen, a visit to Cambridge to look at the colleges.

It could not last. A quick excursion to London for last-minute essentials – a ghastly tie, handkerchiefs, vests and black stockings – one more visit to the dentist in Bournemouth. Edwina finished typing the Book Catalogue, picked a box of mushrooms for Auntie-Grannie, had her last game of tennis with the Everetts and her last duet with Marjorie, fitted on her horrible school uniform and visited 'darling Mummie's grave'. She and Mary endured a final hated hair-washing and on 26 September, sped on their way by Grandpapa, who gave them lunch at Brook House and a guinea each, they joined the train for Eastbourne: '37 girls in school. Very excited'.

The Links was run by Miss Jane Potts, who had been governess to Queen Victoria's grand-daughter, Princess Alice. Behind her back the girls called her 'Potty'; face to face, she made them tremble. At the beginning of each day one privileged girl was asked to stand on a chair and do up the row of tiny buttons that marched down the back of the headmistress's dress, 'Hooking Miss Potts' being the reward for diligent work. In the evening the older pupils assembled in the drawing-room to hear selected items from the newspapers and after-wards a poor victim played airs on the piano: 'Awful time', Edwina thought, 'and we always have to bow on leaving . . .' The drawing-room was light and sunny, with a large bay window looking on to the garden, pale painted walls and billowing floor-length muslin curtains. Miss Potts surrounded herself with books, photographs and flowering plants; two dozen girls could be accommodated on an assortment of chairs and cushions, with others sitting on a hairy hearthrug. The school had been put together from one very large house and several smaller ones, in which the girls slept and did their prep. Rooms were shared, two pupils in each, and twice a week the bigger girls bathed the little ones. Bedrooms and studies were simply furnished, like Edwina and Mary's schoolroom and bedrooms at home. Elsewhere, in the hall, dining-room and sitting-room, the place was welcoming. Banisters, floors and furniture were highly polished, the stairs carpeted with Axminster, radiators – the house was well-heated – disguised with ornate brass grilles. There were ornaments, pictures and flowers; The Links was not spartan.

Edwina was not unhappy, although she had never been thrown in with so many other girls at once, gangling girls, puddingy girls, all looking their worst in shapeless white blouses, sack-like gymslips and hats like Tommies' helmets. This was her introduction to communal living. Edwina shared a room with Mary, as she had done at home until she was twelve, and some of her friends were also at The Links – Diana Sloane-Stanley was one. She soon added others: Margaret Lindsay, Marjorie Chinnery-Haldane, Syssyllt Franklen and Nancy Reiss. Edwina's first difficulty was that, having always been taught at her own pace, she had no idea how hard she would find schoolwork. She had studied by herself, with her own governess; only when she had shared lessons with Marjorie had there been someone with whom to compete. She was not used to discussing problems in a group nor to a system of marking in which her performance was measured against an average. Replying to questions in front of other people was a challenge; so was playing before an unfamiliar music master, said to be strict. What was wanted in an essay? What would examinations be like?

Edwina found she could cope. In French and German she shot to the top of her class. Mr Gaba, the German master, wheeled her in, along with Violet Quicke, the head girl, for a special lesson in front of Miss Potts. This gave Edwina confidence – and she had another boost from the music master, Mr Samuel, on whom she developed a crush: 'very nice lesson, though somewhat stormy in the middle'. Botany was more than manageable – she got 71 out of 100 in the end-of-term examination – and so was European and English History. Despite her assiduous reading of *The Times*, she did not shine in Current Events, where she found the lectures dull, although she did get 75 out of 100 for an essay on 'The Rights and Wrongs of Socialism'.

Just as the school uniform, with its striped neckties, copied that worn at a boys' school, so the curriculum at The Links was a watered-down version of the lessons the girls' brothers were learning elsewhere. The English Literature course took in Tennyson, Kipling (*Bridge Guard in the Karoo*, *The Law of the Jungle*) and the tamer bits of Robert Service, with a leavening of Shelley, Keats and Rupert Brooke. The girls were encouraged to copy out hearty admonitions, like this from Theodore Roosevelt: 'When you play, play hard – when you work, don't play at all', and maxims from Virgil, Thomas Carlyle and la Rochefoucauld. In their own essays, however, they were expected to be ladylike: a tutor carefully struck out a reference to 'the impurity of love and the mania of religious ecstasy' in Edwina's summary of *Idylls of the King*.

The teaching was competent, if unimaginative. Every so often the girls were warned that an inspector would be coming from Oxford, 'to listen to all the lessons', Edwina said, 'listen to us practising, watch us have meals and even look round our rooms and drawers . . . a perfectly awful ordeal'. They did hours of prep, before tea, before dinner, sometimes before breakfast, but the content was milk and water: no Latin, no Greek, only a little arithmetic. The most rigorous test of memory was learning the Collects, for those who like Edwina were preparing for confirmation. Sewing, singing and elocution made up the rest. In the summer English schoolgirls played cricket, as schoolboys did, and Edwina was in the first eleven. But the play was ladylike and interspersed with gentle games of tennis. In autumn and winter the mixture was the same: roller-skating and dancing – foxtrots, marches and the valse – punctuated each day by lethal bursts of lacrosse.

Edwina adored lacrosse, 'the most ripping game'. So it was, if your opponent thwacked you with her stick. 'Mary got hit on the nose'; 'poor Esme got hurt and we had to stop rather suddenly'. Edwina wrote enthusiastically to Auntie-Grannie, who sent her a 'Crosse' of her own for her birthday. She was competitive; in lacrosse she played Point, marking and racing forward with the ball. She was full of energy. At home she had spent at least half the day out of doors; here, fed on stodge, she missed fresh air and exercise. Although the grounds were large, walking round them in crocodile was no more than conversation on the move; roller-skating took place indoors. Edwina was delighted to hurtle over muddy playing fields and, on days when a mistress felt energetic, to go for six-mile walks over the Downs or for 'a good blow by the sea'.

Edwina and Mary were not miserable at The Links. Although they were two forms apart, the school was small, so they felt they had each other, along with many friends and plenty of fun. Miss Potts arranged regular outings to bazaars, where the girls could buy cakes, and to entertainments in Eastbourne. They were taken to concerts to hear amateur performers – their own Mr Samuel, the piano master, and Mr Reed, who taught the violin, playing Chopin and Bach – and professional musicians: 'Daisy Kennedy', Edwina reported, 'and Benno Moisewitch, perfectly heavenly'. On wet afternoons they were allowed to play card games; in the evenings there were lantern-slide lectures and once there was a conjuror. Old girls came to stay the night; one was Cynthia Curzon, another Edith Barker, who recited, 'not very well', Edwina thought, 'but it was a change'. There was sea-bathing in summer, skating and snowballing in winter. Once a week sweets were distributed and on her birthday each girl had a party. For Edwina's fifteenth birthday, in the middle of her first term, Auntie-Grannie sent a cake, not knowing that the school cook had made another. Papa's present caused a sensation: 'a darling little gold brooch with a fox's head in diamonds with ruby eyes on it'. It arrived early, 'as Madre had mistaken the date'.

Visitors were encouraged to come at weekends. Marjorie and Cousin Anna brought provisions for a picnic on the Downs, Auntie-Grannie took Mary and Edwina for tea at an hotel at Beachy Head, and at half-term Miss Atwood carried them off to Devonshire Park to hear the orchestra and eat a great tea. To Mary and Edwina's amazement Molly came down to take them out to lunch at the Grand: 'such fun and we munched chocolates'.

The first term passed quickly until, suddenly, after examinations and a performance by 'The Links Tragicks', trunks were repacked for the Christmas holidays. Miss Atwood met Edwina and Mary from the train, whistled them round Knightsbridge and into Harrods for lunch, and took them down to Broadlands, for a reunion with the animals and the staff, although not with Wilfrid and Molly, who were still in London. At Christmas everyone went to Branksome. The girls talked incessantly of school. Marjorie found this tedious but cheerfully agreed to get a lacrosse stick to play with Mary and Edwina. Holidays seemed more fun against the background of school and, anyway, these were particularly happy ones, with crackers and presents distributed in Mrs Cassel's Christmas ceremony of bestowal, 'the Bescherung'. Special expeditions and treats were sandwiched between duty visits to church and to the Shaftesbury Society's Home for Crippled Children. Grandpapa, Cousin Anna and Cousin Teddy, Marjorie's father, took Marjorie, Mary and Edwina to *The Sleeping Beauty* and there were sorties to Bournemouth for shopping and races along the beach. Sir Ernest's Christmas present to Edwina was a beautiful jade bangle and a diamond and emerald pendant. He was fond of red-headed Mary but it was his elder grand-daughter who filled Maudie's place in his heart.

Edwina's Education

Edwina remained at The Links for two years, until the end of the war. Some people have implied that she was unhappy. No so. In the first year Edwina had a new challenge, which she seized. In the second she was not so much miserable as bored, like Syssyllt and Margaret Lindsay, who was now head girl. Edwina did not like silly rules: no letter-writing except on Sundays, for example. She loathed being told to do certain things at stated hours, especially those she had done endless times before. Some have suggested that her position was awkward because it was known that she would inherit her grandfather's millions, and that the other girls therefore expected her to put gold sovereigns into the offertory plate and to be lavish with presents and sweets. This was not the case. No one knew how Sir Ernest might dispose of his fortune; since the beginning of the war he had given nearly half a million pounds to charities for wounded servicemen and their families and, if past behaviour were a guide, he might eventually give all he owned to hospitals. Edwina was not at this time pursued by the press; she was still an obscure schoolgirl. At The Links there was little opportunity for extravagance or display; sweets were rationed and at the beginning of term the girls handed their money to Miss Potts for safe keeping. Each week a small amount was given back for essential purchases and the church collection, so that Edwina could not have donated more than others. Like everyone else, she hoped that her allowance would be augmented by tips from visiting relations but she would have been thought mad to have given those away. There was talk when Wilfrid's showy birthday present arrived, or when a relation turned up in a smart motor, but those were only nine-day wonders. Edwina and Mary were sufficiently intelligent to know what they could safely discuss and what not; not, perhaps, the Villa Cassel or Biarritz, but certainly ponies, governesses and telephones, for most of the girls at The Links came from families that were wealthy, if not on the Cassel scale. Edwina noticed the conventions and conformed.

Was she teased, as some have suggested, because her grandfather had a Jewish name? This would have been likely at a boys' school; girls who wanted to be unpleasant found other sorts of ammunition. In any case, Edwina and Mary were Ashleys. In so far as it was known, their history made them popular – dead mother, wicked stepmother. Was it true that Edwina was derided because her grandfather had been persecuted at the beginning of the war? No. The girls

71

could be catty about trivia but on that sort of question they were more sympathetic than boys and in any case The Links was too small a place for unsubstantiated rumour to flourish for long.

Edwina did not have a horrid time at The Links. She simply grew out of the place. Anxious always to be learning or experiencing something new, she soon exhausted its resources. She was in the cricket and tennis teams and had mastered every accomplishment from shorthand to music. She expressed herself clearly in handwriting that was mature; a letter she wrote to her father in May 1918 is in the hand she kept to the end of her life. In that letter, Edwina pointed out that she had now spent three terms in the fifth form, the highest in the school: 'I do wish I could leave soon, anyhow at the end of next term, when I should be 17 . . . I could always go on with certain subjects, *particularly music*'. Edwina had always thought of herself as Marjorie's contemporary; her cousin was now eighteen and a half and enjoying grown-up entertainments. But what was to be done with Edwina? Europe was still unsettled after the Great War and no one her family knew would be travelling until late spring or summer at the earliest. Auntie-Grannie was too old to take Edwina abroad, Cousin Anna preoccupied with Marjorie, and Molly did not want to be lumbered with her stepdaughter. Edwina must mark time. But how? Her French and German were already better than good; so were her music, her drawing and her knowledge of English literature. Syssyllt Franklen, Peggy du Buisson and Eileen Douglas-Pennant were going on to Alde House at Aldeburgh. It was decided that Edwina should go with them.

In November 1919 Mary returned to The Links alone. It was Edwina who ensured that she was looked after on the train from Southampton West to Eastbourne, together with her luggage, key to trunk, health certificates and ticket, who equipped her with stamps and writing-paper and, once term had started, sent her chocolate, in official-looking envelopes to escape Potty's sharp eyes. Mary missed her protector: 'all the mistresses get dreadfully at me now you are gone'. Each week she briefed Edwina in schoolgirl slang on the doings of the 'old birds' and the 'topping matches'. Now Mary was fourteen she called herself 'Maria'; Edwina was 'darling Dweenie' or, affectionately, 'you lucky hound'. Even as Maria, Mary was neither as confident nor as independent as Edwina had been at the same age. She was hopeless at schoolwork, getting zero for mathematics even after a year's coaching. Mary looked constantly to her sister for advice. She begged for Edwina's photograph and for some of their mother's letters; Edwina got these past Miss Potts as well, along with a Cricket Scoring Book.

Meanwhile, Edwina and Syssyllt braced themselves for Aldeburgh. As schools for finishing young ladies are generally reckoned, Alde House was untypical. It called itself a Domestic Science Training College, its aim being to instil the rudiments of competent housekeeping into batches of twenty girls at a time. The place was run by Mrs Hervey, a stout, smiling woman in flowing black garments. The house was equally solid, which was as well. Icy winds blew in from the Suffolk coast, across overgrown gardens and an empty fountain, for in the last two years of the war the grounds had suffered, as able-bodied men had gone to fight and flowerbeds had been dug up for vegetables. The house was run with the minimum of staff, the students themselves doing turns at cooking, cleaning and laundering. Baths had to be taken in a separate annexe. Edwina's photograph album has a snapshot of her, dressed in boots and fur-collared coat, draped with towels, making her way beneath leafless trees, along the path to the bathing quarters.

The College was a halfway house. The students, no longer girls, were not quite women. They were encouraged to join the Girl Guides and put into khaki tunics with stiff leather belts and wide-brimmed felt hats, of the sort Wilfrid would have worn in the Boer War. On other days they were taught how to put up their hair and pose languidly for photographs. There was a fair amount of dressing-up. For her turn as housekeeper, Edwina was kitted out in gloves and an intimidating hat, with an important handbag. On afternoon walks the girls carried enormous fur muffs, as if they had already become respectable, omnicompetent married women who ran their houses impeccably and tyrannized the grocer. For classes they were dressed in all-enveloping ankle-length cotton gowns, aprons and ludicrous mob-caps. No real kitchenmaid could have done any scrubbing while managing these impractical garments and, indeed, photographs of Mrs Hervey and her apprentices look distinctly Marie Antoinettish.

The girls were taught to peel potatoes, boil eggs, make beds, remove stains and bring up the shine on a table. Edwina did not dislike practical work, if it was useful. At The Links she had enjoyed the Red Cross lessons; now she took her turn as scullion, although she was, not surprisingly, happier as housekeeper – ordering meals, paying wages, getting in stores. She was efficient and convincing, so much so that she was one of two students to represent Alde House at a Domestic Science display in London in July, 'to show', she told Wilfrid, 'that Private schools are just as good and quite up to the standard of the Public ones'. Edwina learnt how long domestic jobs should take and how far supplies might be stretched. She acquired a keen eye for sloppiness and waste. But after she left Alde House she was never known to use broom or saucepan and all her life she hated having to discuss housekeeping or servants. That, too, was a legacy of her time with Mrs Hervey.

At Alde House Edwina discovered that she could put together a team. Well-organized herself, she began to organize others. Her first target was her family. Edwina and Syssyllt wanted to go abroad and meet new people, that is, young men. The war was well over and Mrs Hervey had confirmed the peace by throwing the gardens of Alde House open to the public and staging a pageant, in which Edwina, in white and carrying red roses and a Union Jack, stood for England.

For Edwina this was also a private celebration, her pleas having been heard. Her grandfather had agreed that she should have a spell on the Continent – France or Italy, he thought – and had said that he would pay for it. No doubt a suitable lady could be found to chaperone her: Marjorie's former governess, perhaps? Edwina was overjoyed. She longed to be sufficiently far out of range to be able to do as she liked, at least until the family heard about it. 'Heavenly', she told Wilfrid, suggesting that it would be good for his health if he came too, since she knew that Molly would never let him.

Sir Ernest was almost as excited as Edwina. He wrote to friends, telegraphed hotels, organized bank drafts in the necessary currencies. 'Most of the time, if not all', he declared, 'will be spent at Rome.' No detail escaped him. 'Has Molly made any arrangements for Edwina's outfit?' he asked Wilfrid. On 25 October Edwina set off. Her original scheme had been modified. Syssyllt could not leave England until December, so Marjorie was to come for the first part of the tour, solving two problems at once, for she and the Earl of Brecknock had told their respective parents that they had an understanding and both families, thinking the pair too young to announce an engagement, wished to separate them, if only temporarily. Edwina was glad that Marjorie would be travelling with her. Her cousin had already come out and they might be invited together to grown-up dances and amusements.

But Sir Ernest was firm. Edwina would not come out until the following spring: until then she was to be a girl inspecting art and culture, not a young woman appraising possible husbands. Though officially out, for the time being Marjorie must come in again. This looked grim. Their chaperone, moreover, was not to be Marjorie's former governess, whom they could manage, but the devout and conscientious Miss Cranston, secretary to Lady Zia Wernher, daughter-in-law of Sir Ernest's friend, Sir Julius Wernher. 'Miss Cranston is a dear', Edwina assured her father, when she first met her chaperone. ('Call me Jane.') In fact, she found Miss Cranston irritating. Battle lines were formed.

A further inhibition was the presence of Sir Ernest, who with Marjorie's father, Cousin Teddy, accompanied Edwina and Marjorie on the first part of their journey. There were advantages to 'travelling with Grandpapa'. Edwina's first night of comparative freedom was spent at the Ritz in Paris. She and Marjorie had a suite, 'a darling little sitting room and a bathroom each so we feel most grand'. They shared a large bedroom, more fun, since they could chat all night, although Edwina was amazed at Marjorie's clutter. Repacking everything would be daunting, she thought, and as they had no maid they would have to tackle it themselves. Marjorie found Edwina very prim. When breakfast was brought Edwina was so shocked to see a man walking into the bedroom that she dived beneath the sheets. This shyness did not last.

Sir Ernest's programme had three objects: Shopping, Culture and Society. The shopping began magnificently, with the selection of an early birthday present for Edwina: a fur coat, 'mole, with a very smart lining', for a Roman winter might be chilly. Sir Ernest was not simply being solicitous. Edwina had emerged from the schoolroom and now he wanted her to learn to buy her clothes in Paris, as her mother had done. By the time Edwina left for Rome she was equipped with soft silk blouses, the smoothest gloves, a fur wrap, new jewels and various becoming hats.

Next, culture. On their first day in Paris the girls were marched into the Louvre to see Sir Ernest's favourite pictures. Edwina gazed respectfully at the works of Raphael and Leonardo da Vinci: 'perfectly wonderful', she said at what she thought were the right moments.

They were taken to the theatre and the opera, to Nôtre Dame and the Sainte Chapelle, and on Sunday to a service at the Madeleine, where Edwina and Marjorie began to giggle. They pretended that the incense was making them sneeze, 'so', Edwina tactfully explained, 'we didn't enjoy it as much as we might have'.

Introducing the girls to French society was easy, for Sir Ernest had many friends in Paris. Some lived among fine collections of paintings and furniture – if not on the Brook House scale – so that visiting could be combined with the inspection of more art. Monsieur May, for instance, gave a large luncheon party in his apartment in the Faubourg St Honoré, where every room was hung with pictures. At Dampierre were the Duc and Duchesse de Luynes, in a moated chateau with grand state rooms: 'rather over-decorated', sniffed Edwina, but she liked the Van Dycks and Nattiers. At Versailles Sir Ernest knew no one on whom they might call, so the party had to be content with seeing over the gardens and the Palace, including the table on which the Peace Treaty had been signed, a nice conclusion to Edwina's 'History of the War'.

Although Sir Ernest had hired a motor they were lucky to leave their base camp at all. 'The Ritz is full of people we know', Edwina told Wilfrid. Friends of the Cassels, friends of the Ashleys and the Jenkinses, friends of friends – a flock of migratory birds passing through Paris, as they did every year at the same season. Each evening friends and acquaintances bowed and beamed across the dining-room. Edwina loved it: 'we're always very gay'. The waiters were charming, the orchestra was co-operative. Edwina and Marjorie asked for ragtime and, although Sir Ernest found it a strain, he did not object. Edwina was miles from the first step on a downward path, or so Sir Ernest thought. His protégées had behaved amirably. They had been neither mischievous nor headstrong, apart, that is, from insisting that they be allowed to ascend to the top of the Eiffel Tower – and even then they had been escorted by Cousin Teddy.

After a week Sir Ernest had to leave. Miss Cranston now appeared, a well-meaning but ineffectual substitute, to escort Edwina and Marjorie on the Train de Luxe for Rome. Cousin Teddy came too. After a nineteen-hour journey, they installed themselves in the Palace Hotel in a suite of rooms on the fourth floor. Edwina and Marjorie offered the sunnier bedrooms to Cousin Teddy and Miss Cranston, thereby ensuring that their own quarters were separated from their

Edwina's Education

chaperone's by a large sitting-room. Within two days they had acquired a piano, a maid and an Italian teacher, Signora Poce.

Satisfied that all was in order, Cousin Teddy returned to London, leaving Miss Cranston in charge. Judging by Edwina's letters home, their chaperone had an easy time. The two girls made the most respectable friends, their interests were serious, their amusements decorous. They had been given an introduction to the formidable Mrs Strong, of the British School in Rome, who now gave a tea party in their honour. Mrs Strong knew everyone in Rome, 'all kinds of charming people', Edwina assured her father. Exactly those, in fact, of whom Wilfrid and Molly would approve: the Marchese Miscattelli, 'who is very musical and gets up concerts at his own house', the Conte and Contessa Lovatelli, 'both very clever'; Miss Buchanan, the British Ambassador's daughter; Baron and Baroness Bonde, 'so nice and the latter a friend of Mummie's'.

These new acquaintances were anxious to entertain them: 'You see we are quite gay and full of engagements'. The Marchese Miscattelli had promised a concert; Mrs Strong would see to galleries, gardens, churches and ruins. By the end of the first month, Edwina had reported on and photographed the Colosseum, the Sistine Chapel, the Capitol and the Forum, 'too interesting for words', the roads to Marino Albano and Frascati, 'darling old towns', the Arches of Titus, Constantine and Septimus Severus. What with piano lessons from Signor Bustini of the Academy, Signora Poce's Italian lessons, 'little tea parties in our sitting room', and riding on the Campagna on hired horses, Grandpapa and Wilfrid would appreciate that there was hardly a moment to spare.

That was not the whole story. Edwina said nothing of Captain Mott, with his cleft chin and neat moustache, or Mr Scott, so sleek that his hair looked like boot-polish thinly applied to his perfectly-shaped head. Still more attractive were the Italians: Galeazzo Manzi-Fe, olive-skinned, with brooding dark eyes; Folco Malaspira, in his uniform of high-buttoned jacket, well-cut breeches and tight, high boots; Ricardo, a magnificent duke, by whom Edwina was utterly dazzled. (It was the cloak that did it, she told her daughters years later.) Miss Cranston found it impossible to discourage these marvellous young men. The Contessas, Marcheses and Baronesses were no help, for Edwina and Marjorie had fallen in with a set of young, high-spirited women whom they preferred as chaperones: Elena Cugnoni, Constance Malaspira and her sister, frank, expressive, openly affectionate, their eyes sparkling with fun. Edwina and Marjorie were swept away on a torrent of mellifluous Italian. Even the weather conspired against Miss Cranston. Bright, clear and crisp, it lured her charges out of drawing-rooms and museums, into the Flower Market, away in an open-topped motor to Tivoli, to the Acqua Santa to play golf, to hunt at Centocelle. Edwina, Marjorie and their companions galloped over the Campagna, picnicked on the grass, sat in restaurants talking for hours over wine and cigarettes.

There was no time for writing home. 'The posts from here are getting worse and worse', Edwina explained, 'some of our letters have gone completely astray'. Miss Cranston's desperate reports were, however, successfully getting through to London. When Marjorie came home before Christmas, Sir Ernest interrogated her. Marjorie kept her head, making much of the polite tea parties and the Italian lessons. Edwina could not be expected to spend all her time with older people, talking English in overheated palazzos. Surely it was better for her Italian to practise conversation with companions of her own age? Would Sir Ernest begrudge her a little golf, a daily ride? He had forbidden evening parties, it was true, but not simple picnics in the midday sun. Sir Ernest was placated. Marjorie breathed again.

Sir Ernest was shrewd. He adored Edwina, not least because she was as adventurous as he himself had been at the same age. There was probably some truth in Miss Cranston's flustered accounts. It would have been surprising if such a chaperone had been able to control his strong-minded, high-spirited grand-daughter. So far Edwina did not appear to have embarrassed herself or other people. Her reputation was intact – and her new friends sounded interesting. Syssyllt Franklen was going out to join her; perhaps this would be a good moment for Mrs Strong to wade in with another burst of art and culture.

The sightseeing began again. No sooner had Syssyllt unpacked than she and Edwina were hurried off to a succession of villas and gardens, all most wonderful, Edwina observed, but quite unlike the ordered opulence of Brook House and Moulton Paddocks: 'everything falling to ruins . . . why the owners don't keep their place in repair I can't imagine'. Mrs Strong's armoury was inexhaustible; she knew every famous picture and sculpture in every obscure chapel. Edwina and Syssyllt – even Miss Cranston – reeled with exhaustion. But like

Edwina's Education

Napoleon, Mrs Strong was defeated by the winter. A week after Syssyllt's arrival, she and Edwina secured a Christmas truce.

Having assured Mrs Strong that they could manage on their own, Syssyllt and Edwina bought a tree, decorated their sitting-room, ordered supplies and alerted their friends, Elena, 'Folchetto', the Malaspira sisters, Manzi-Fe, Ricardo, Mott and Scott. In they trooped, sitting on the table, perching on the balcony rails, crowding in front of the camera, bringing new admirers, Angelo and Leporelli, proposing new extravagances. 'We are going to have a very English Christmas', Edwina told her father, mentioning the tree. Wilfrid was not interested. Molly wanted him to take her motoring on the Continent and he was preoccupied with that.

At Branksome Dene Sir Ernest and Mrs Cassel wondered what Edwina was doing. They were comforted by her letters. Every page spoke of some ennobling sight: Michelangelo, Guido Reni. They did not see her photograph album, which now had fewer pictures of ruins. Instead, there were photographs of 'Wee MacGregor', the smallest caddy at the golf course, of Folco's carefully tailored legs, seen from behind as he lined up a shot, of Syssyllt, looking sultry, and Edwina, more slyly beautiful with every picture. Her plumpness was falling away, Elena and Constance had shown her how to drape her furs and loosen her jackets. She quickened in the presence of admiring men. Sir Ernest had intended his grand-daughter's Italian trip to be educative – and it was. Edwina had learnt how to make herself comfortable in foreign hotels, how to give orders to proud assistants in smart shops, to chefs and waiters, how to flirt and listen to compliments, and how to dissemble. She had discovered that it was pleasant to do exactly what she wanted, especially if it was risky. She had picked up a lot of racy Italian. Above all, Marjorie always said, it was during her visit to Italy that Edwina discovered men.

CHAPTER SEVEN

Two Deaths in a Fortnight

W hat next? When Edwina came home, Molly was unwelcoming, Wilfrid busy. Sir Ernest announced that she must stay at Brook House and in May, when she came out, she would be launched from there. He would bear the expense, a relief to her father, who was finding Broadlands a drain.

It is a romantic picture: the beautiful eighteen-year-old girl, sole companion of her grandfather, an ageing multi-millionaire, the two of them rattling round in an enormous mansion, part museum, part mausoleum. Romantic and wrong. Brook House was neither gloomy nor empty. The servants alone made a crowd: the chef, with four assistants; the housekeeper, with a band of housemaids, one kept permanently in the still-room, washing flower vases. Sir Ernest had a valet, Edwina her maid, Weller, sister to the Weller who looked after Queen Mary. The butler's department consisted of himself and four footmen in livery, although since the beginning of the First World War they no longer went into powdered hair during the London season. When Margaret Lindsay saw how the manservants were arrayed, she was amazed. Her father was the Premier Earl of Scotland and, she said, we never dressed the men up like that. There were three chauffeurs, an oddman for other jobs, and a house electrician, with helper, to look after Sir Ernest's illuminations.

Top of the tree was Stella Underhill, who had come to Brook House in 1913. She supervised the staff, paid their wages and looked after the accounts. It was her job to check the housebooks; she had to know the meaning of each entry, in case Sir Ernest sent for the ledgers. Miss Underhill knew how Brook House should be run. It was she who had suggested during the war that five housemaids would do, instead of seven; when the housekeeper disagreed and was given notice, Miss Underhill had recommended the head housemaid, Mrs Lankester, as her successor. Sir Ernest respected Miss Underhill's judgement; only she could persuade him to alter his habits. Luncheon and dinner were always served in the two-storey dining-room, even when Sir Ernest was alone, but during the war it was impossible to get enough coal for the huge fireplace. Miss Underhill spoke to Sir Ernest, who obediently moved into a smaller room, small enough, that is, to hold no more than ten people. He went further: having vacated the dining-room, Sir Ernest also removed one of the four Van Dycks that hung on its walls. The picture was sold to an American collector and a Murillo put up instead. Miss Underhill disapproved. The Murillo looked wrong. She made no objection to its subject or its style; it was, she said, too small. At the end of the war, Sir Ernest learnt that the American had died. The Van Dyck came back.

Edwina had not been brought to Brook House to oversee Sir Ernest's household. She was too young and inexperienced, despite the dress rehearsals she had gone through at Alde House. The management of Brook House, and of Sir Ernest, required a deft, sophisticated hand – and Miss Underhill was already in charge. She had originally been recruited by Mrs Cassel to look after the housekeeping, everything else – correspondence, travel arrangements, philanthropy – being dealt with by the five clerks Sir Ernest kept at an office in Green Street, one of whom came round each morning to sit in the Secretary's room at Brook House to await instructions. The war changed that as well, as one by one the men were called up. Miss Underhill moved into the Secretary's room and took over the letters and files. The war ended, the men returned and found Miss Underhill in occupation. Thereafter they stayed in Green Street.

Backstage, Brook House hummed with life. Nor were the servants exclusively preoccupied with looking after each other. Throughout the war Sir Ernest had never ceased to entertain. The show went on, its scale and extravagance slightly diminished, for, as Miss Underhill pointed out, the servants must recognize that for the war's duration they should not expect to live as comfortably as before. By the spring of 1920, however, when Edwina arrived, the house was lively again and the staff had recovered their pre-war panache. The chef concocted exotic dishes, with plain food for Sir Ernest, who still worried about his weight. The housekeeper wired elaborate arrangements of flowers, including the eighteen dozen carnations sent up each week from Moulton. Miss Underhill instructed the butler, who instructed the footmen, to withdraw the appropriate china, silver and glass from

81

their cabinets and to extract the more valuable pieces from the strong-room in the basement. Edwina had little to do but admire. Sir Ernest was the impresario, Miss Underhill stage manager. He produced the lists of guests, she prepared the table plans, set out strictly according to precedence. When Sir Ernest wanted some special effect, he would alter the placing; if and only if Miss Underhill agreed, she would type out a final draft. Miss Underhill herself set out the place cards at each seat in the dining-room. Edwina was not allowed to help, even in emergencies. There were no emergencies. On dinner-party nights, Miss Underhill would stay late at Brook House, in case a guest dropped out at the last minute and the seating had to be rearranged. She remained on duty until, at half past eight, the guests went into the dining-room. There Sir Ernest presided. Mrs Cassel, his hostess before the war, had now retired to Branksome, where she spent the greater part of the day in bed, and her daughter had succeeded her. This was hard on Cousin Anna, who had to come up to London from Wherwell even when she had guests of her own. Sir Ernest intended Edwina to take her place.

First Edwina had to be formally introduced to grown-up society. She was to be presented at Court in May, giving two months to prepare her for what would be a stiff competition. The dozen young women who would emerge as the season's most interesting would be judged according to three criteria: connections; prospects; and beauty. Two out of three would do. Intelligence helped but was neither necessary nor sufficient. Edwina was a promising candidate; her looks, however, needed work. Wilfrid had given his daughter her wide mouth, level brows and large well-spaced eyes but, next to her girlfriends, she looked mannish, with her strong features and closely bound hair. Moreover, despite Edwina's apprenticeship in Paris and Rome, her wardrobe was largely that of a schoolgirl. Now work began in earnest. Blouses and skirts gave way to jackets and dresses, pleated and draped, with dropped waists. She bought hats that shaded her face and ordered quantities of shoes with low curved heels. Sir Ernest provided jewels and a foxfur wrap, complete with head. All bills were sent to him. Brook House buzzed. Dressmakers arrived with tape-measures and pins; messengers delivered hatboxes, shoeboxes, gloveboxes. Edwina's friends came to see her preparations and admire her rooms. They need not have been afraid of disturbing Sir Ernest, who liked the young people, noisier than Maudie and her friends, but respectful. His grand-daughter was the most interesting and unpredictable project he had ever had.

Edwina was launched in the first week of May, with a ball at Brook House, shared with Marjorie. Miss Ashley's introduction to society was also marked by breathless accounts in every newspaper. Sycophantic and knowing, the gossip writers charted her progress: dinner at this house, a dance at the next, evening after evening for eight weeks. Edwina was tireless. She did not need the lists in the newspapers to help her recall the names of her hosts and fellow-guests, although without her spectacles their faces had looked indistinct. The press cuttings told Edwina that she was enjoying an easy triumph, attracting dancing partners and supper partners in shoals, and that she always knew the right thing to say and the most appropriate person to whom to say it. This was not the case. These formal dinners and grand dances were unlike the family parties Edwina was used to and between her departure from Alde House and her arrival in Park Lane she had been given no opportunity to learn the ropes. Molly had done nothing to ease the transition from schoolroom to drawing-room, the Italian interlude had given Edwina zest but no polish. Mrs Jenkins, who steered Edwina through this testing time, found her shyer and more awkward than Marjorie had been the year before. One person who noticed it was Sybil Cholmondeley, the daughter of Aline de Rothschild and Sir Ernest's friend Sir Edward Sassoon. At a party given by her brother, Sir Philip Sassoon, at his house in Park Lane, Lady Cholmondeley found Edwina sitting alone on a sofa. Her rescuer never forgot the look of relief on the young girl's face as she rose from the spot where she had been marooned.

In time, Edwina came to be considered one of the most interesting of the season's debutantes. People were not put off by the embarrassing label, 'Richest Heiress', pinned on her by the press, and her new friends soon discovered that she danced well, talked enthusiastically and listened attentively. Most important, she had stamina. In late June she looked as lively as she had done in May, if not livelier, for she was encouraged by success. There was one flaw, her lack of freedom. At eighteen and a half Edwina wanted to go where she liked, do what she wished, and, although Cousin Anna was a tolerant chaperone, her charge felt over-protected and hedged in. The jungle was full of eyes: mothers and aunts, watching at luncheons, tea parties and balls, ready to pounce. Edwina had less liberty than she had enjoyed in Rome. Private conversation with a man was possible only if she were dancing with him or sitting next to him at dinner. Even then she was observed. Her girlfriends could come to Sir Ernest's house and she could go to theirs, but on such expeditions, or forays to Bond Street to shop, she was accompanied by her maid. Young ladies did not wander about on their own, with no escort to help them manage their parcels, protect them from raindrops, hand them in and out of motors and ensure that they were not accosted by people who had not been introduced.

Home ground, however, was thought secure and the country safer than town. Edwina found, as Maudie had done twenty-five years before, that her best chance of slipping away was when she stayed with her friends for tennis and croquet, sailing, shooting, fishing and golf. Her hosts were not so foolish as to believe that fresh air and strenuous exercise would leave the young people with no energy for flirtation. On the contrary, a balanced mixture of outdoor pursuits, indoor games, good food and comfortable sofas was believed to be the best recipe for matchmaking. In parks and woods, on the river and the moors, supervision was less strict, for no outsiders had been invited. There were only eligible young men, alluring young women, hopeful relations and benevolent hosts, attended by a flock of servants, all eyes and ears.

As spring gave way to summer, Edwina began a succession of visits. In July she was at Polesden Lacey, where Mrs Ronnie Greville had a party that included the King's second son, Prince Albert. Mrs Greville was hospitable and rich; her money came from brewing. She was also indiscreet, except about the royal family, whom she revered. Short, stout and not a beauty – Edwina called her 'wee Maggie', but not, of course, to her face – she was also very kind. At Polesden Edwina was snapped up by Grace Vanderbilt and carried off to Nuneham Courtenay, which her parents, General and Mrs Vanderbilt, of the American railway and shipping family, had taken for the summer. In August she was at Cowes, staying with the Barings at Nubia House and watching the racing from the Vanderbilts' yacht, *Sheela*. In August she was in Scotland at Balcarres, until at last she came home to Moulton Paddocks and Branksome for a reunion with Grandpapa, Auntie-Grannie, Cousin Anna and Mary. How serene Sir Ernest looked, as he sat with his sister, his niece, and his old friend Mrs Joshua, in comfortable wicker chairs, newspapers and footstools handy, rugs within reach in case it should turn chilly. Edwina brought photographs of the friends with whom she had spent the past two months, assembling, parting and regrouping at one house or another: Grace Vanderbilt, Poppy Baring, James Stuart, Dick Hermon, John Lascelles, Billy Jolliffe, Colin Davidson, Audrey James. They posed in tennis clothes, yachting clothes and, as Maudie's friends would not have dreamt of doing, in bathrobes and rubber bathing caps. Unlike her mother at the same age, Edwina did not stand ramrod straight before the camera; she drooped, in a fashionable concave posture.

Sir Ernest was delighted that Edwina was in demand – he also wanted her himself. Brook House had been closed for the summer but in the autumn he had arranged a shoot, to which two of the King's sons had been invited. Edwina acted as her grandfather's hostess: 'an extremely mad and hilarious party', she told Wilfrid, 'Prince Bertie and Prince Henry behaving worse than anyone!' Sir Harry Stonor, Groom-in-Waiting to the King, came too, with Randolph Wilson, who taught Edwina to drive the Owen Magnetic Car, built like a battleship, and Charlie Rhys, with whose parents Edwina had stayed at Dynevor Castle in Wales. (One evening Charlie had asked Edwina to marry him. She intended to say yes but at breakfast she decided he looked like a frog, and changed her mind.) At Moulton Edwina was so busy keeping everyone – and herself – amused that she had no time to try on the bridesmaid's dress she was to wear at Marjorie's wedding the following week. When the Princes left Sir Ernest wanted her to help prepare to receive the Tsarevich. It is surprising that Marjorie had a second to fit her wedding gear, for she was shooting as well. On 19 October she was married to the Earl of Brecknock, at St Margaret's, Westminster, with Edwina and Mary among her attendants and Charlie Rhys as best man. Two days after the wedding Edwina was off to shoot at Marsh Court, followed by a visit to St Giles for two dances and a shoot. Sir Ernest's hostess at Brook House? She was hardly there at all.

Sad news now came from New York. Sir Ernest's old friend Schiff was seriously ill; indeed, Cassel himself had been feeling increasingly seedy. His doctor had prescribed a stay at the best hotel on the Riviera, where the climate was soft and balmy. Sir Ernest left London in late October and at the end of November Edwina joined him in Monte Carlo. Her grandfather's spirits had improved. Every morning he dutifully inhaled the sea air from his balcony and in the afternoons he strolled along the terrace, Mrs Joshua on one arm and Mrs Rosenheim on the other. From time to time he discarded his overcoat; Edwina sat hatless on her balcony. The waves sparkled, the sun shone and Sir Ernest encouraged her to enjoy herself.

This was difficult; not because her duties were extensive, her chief responsibility being to help Sir Ernest entertain guests at luncheon and dinner, taking the ladies away when it was time to withdraw. The trouble was that everyone was so old and the pace so stately. Mrs Rosenheim was a sweet-faced widow in crape and a veil, Mrs Joshua in her fifties. Lord Northcliffe was an invalid. Harry Stonor had seen better days with King Edward VII, in whose memory he still wore his trousers creased up the sides, rather than front and back. (It was said that his pyjamas were also ironed that way.) Richid Saadi Bey had been a friend of Edwina's mother. Sir John Simon had already been Attorney General and Home Secretary. Lord Beaverbrook, though only forty, was so powerful that he seemed old as well. Compared with Edwina's recently-acquired friends, her grandfather's set was antediluvian. Conversation was hard work.

It became harder at Christmas, when Wilfrid and Molly arrived. Edwina tried to be polite to her stepmother, who was simultaneously ingratiating and critical. At least Wilfrid and Molly were not staying in the same hotel; in a neatly-executed joint manoeuvre Sir Ernest and Edwina had persuaded them that another one was cheaper. Edwina spent much of her time and all her superfluous energy on the golf course at Mont Agel, with Nell Joshua, whom she had always liked. They shared a suite and formed an alliance, escaping to shop and parade in the town. Sir Ernest ruled that Edwina and Nell were not to go about unaccompanied and summoned Miss Cranston. Having recovered from her ordeal in Rome, she now applied herself to the hopeless task of trying to catch Edwina's shadow.

At the end of 1920 word came of Schiff's death in New York. Sir Ernest had lost his oldest friend. He was miserable and complained that Monte Carlo was crowded and in early January he and Edwina moved to the Hotel Regina at Cimiez, near Nice, where they were joined by Cousin Anna and Mr and Mrs Winston Churchill. Marjorie and her husband came out, dramatically lowering the average age of the party. Sir Ernest had decided that he liked the Riviera almost as much as Biarritz. King Leopold of the Belgians had a solid and

Two Deaths in a Fortnight

imposing villa, which Cassel thought he might buy. He did, for two and a quarter million francs. He could not move in – though well situated, the Villa des Cèdres was dilapidated – but finding a project completed his cure.

In March Sir Ernest returned to Brook House and Edwina's official duties began, for his interest in life had revived and invitations were fired off all over London. He was eager to discuss business, politics and the progress of his latest charitable fund, a trust he had established in 1919 to mark the fiftieth anniversary of his arrival in England. A quarter of a million pounds had been set aside to found a hospital for the treatment of nervous disorders. Another half million was provided for adult education. Distinguished people came to Brook House but it is wishful thinking to conjure up a picture of Edwina delighting statesmen, philosophers and philanthropists with intelligent questions. She was bored to tears. Miss Underhill knew it. The girl won her over by thoughtfully offering her Sir Ernest's unused opera tickets. (He had two of the best seats in the stalls at Covent Garden.) Now Edwina begged Miss Underhill to alter the seating plans, so that she need not sit next to the most important guests. She was not interested in higher education for women but in the latest gramophone records, prospects for Wimbledon, the fashionable length for hair. Edwina had a 'Greek coiffure', curled tresses over her ears and a bun at the nape of her neck, but she suspected that this was beginning to date. She was anxious about her hemline, seven inches from the ground, and on the long side. Alas, the table plans could not be changed.

Edwina fell back on the strategy she had learnt in Rome. She could not shirk her grandfather's formal luncheons and dinners but at other times she contrived to be absent. It was impossible for her to go to restaurants or private supper clubs in the evening – someone would be sure to inform Sir Ernest – but she discovered small cafés for intimate lunches – a favourite was in Conduit Street, far enough from Park Lane to be safe. Friends with motors were a godsend. Edwina learnt to be imprecise, letting it be assumed that she was with Marjorie, for now that his great-niece was married, Sir Ernest thought her a suitable chaperone. Edwina was equally vague when Marjorie asked what she was doing. This was unfair, since Marjorie rightly felt that she should know where Edwina was, and with whom, in case there was an accident.

Edwina Mountbatten

She was relieved when Edwina left London for parties in the country. In May she stayed with the Glentanars to fish and caught her first salmon – two in one day. In early July she was at Bisham Abbey, in a party that included Elizabeth Bowes-Lyon and Prince Albert, now Duke of York, before joining Sir Ernest at Cap Ferrat, where he was supervising the rebuilding of the Villa des Cèdres. 'Edwina is made much of here', he told Mrs Schiff, 'rather too much, I think', but he was proud that she was a success and sorry to see her leave at the end of the month.

From France Edwina went to the Barings at Nubia House, in a party for Cowes. Princess Mary brought the severe straw hat she had worn in 1920, so firmly anchored with hatpins that even during a game of tennis it did not budge. There was the same cycle of parties, aboard and ashore, with the same group of people: the Portals, the Vanderbilts, the Mainwarings. A strong breeze whipped the sea. On the great yachts, *Sabrina*, *Valdora*, *Venetia*, the guests steadied themselves, gritted their teeth and smiled valiantly at the camera. The more uncomfortable they were, the more certain they could be that they were really enjoying themselves.

There were some surprises. The Vanderbilts had a different yacht, bigger and sleeker than the last. This year they also had a new guest, Dickie Mountbatten, who had missed Cowes the year before. From March to October he had been with his cousin, the Prince of Wales, on a voyage in *Renown* to Australia and New Zealand. Mountbatten talked endlessly about the royal tour, for while the Prince had been bored and homesick, hating the fuss and formalities of the trip, Dickie had delighted in his role of confidant. There had been much to confide: the Prince had pined for Freda Dudley Ward, to whom he had been attached for the past three years, and Mountbatten had consulted the Prince about Audrey James, whom he had pursued after seeing her photograph in the *Tatler* in the autumn of 1919. Audrey was the daughter of Mrs Willie James, whom the late King Edward had admired. Audrey was wide-eyed, with a sweetly curved mouth and chin, but she had £4000 a year and dozens of adorers. A week after they had been introduced, Dickie had kissed her and found himself engaged. When he returned from the tour in *Renown*, she had cooled. 'I wouldn't have her back', he told a friend, 'if she came and implored me . . . even if she did change her mind again, I should live in constant dread of the same thing happening'. Self-preservation was crucial.

Two Deaths in a Fortnight

'Also I *was* too young to really think of getting married'. Audrey looked elsewhere and found Dudley Coats, from the wealthy cotton family, whose sisters, Mabel and Betty, were friends of Edwina. By the time Dickie and Edwina met at Cowes in 1921, his heart had mended. Mrs Vanderbilt hoped he would give it to her daughter. Dickie liked Grace but thought her too direct and her complexion suspiciously rosy.

Edwina knew as little of Dickie Mountbatten as he of her, although his friend Peter Murphy had said that she was the most interesting girl to have come out in 1920. During Edwina's first season Dickie had been away in *Renown* and they had met only once, at Mrs Vanderbilt's ball at Claridge's in October, shortly after Dickie's return. Edwina gave him one dance. Nor had she seen him at the houses where she had stayed in the autumn, winter and spring. At the end of 1920 Dickie had been doing a sub-lieutenant's course at Portsmouth and in the late spring of 1921 he had been given command of a platoon of naval stokers and sent to Liverpool, to help the Army deal with striking coal-miners. For Dickie Mountbatten had a profession. At twelve and three-quarters he had gone from his preparatory school, Locker's Park, to the Royal Naval College at Osborne and three years later to Dartmouth, with a final spell at Keyham, the Navy's engineering college. To his fury he was just too young for the Battle of Jutland, the last important naval confrontation of the Great War. Worse, his cousin Prince Albert had seen it all from a gun-turret on HMS *Collingwood*.

Dickie still hoped for action when, as a junior midshipman, the lowest of the low, he joined Beatty's flagship, *Lion*, in July 1916. But five months later his elder brother Georgie had been transferred to *Lion* and, since the Admiralty preferred not to let brothers serve in the same ship, Dickie was moved to *Queen Elizabeth*, the flagship of the Grand Fleet, based at Scapa Flow. Here his duties were routine; his war at sea was spent on patrol, a tedious life, exacting only because it was hard to stay alert. There were occasional excitements: while Edwina learnt to play lacrosse at The Links, Dickie, in *Lion*, was missed by three torpedoes. From *Queen Elizabeth* he was sent for two months to the submarine *K6*; in 1918 he did a torpedo course in HMS *Trimble* at Portsmouth and in July of that year, while Edwina was manoeuvring to leave school, Dickie was visiting the trenches in France, an experience which confirmed his view that he was better off in the Navy. In October he at last tasted real responsibility. Now a sub-lieutenant, he joined *P31*, an escort and anti-submarine vessel. But the war was over; as a friend warned him, 'we are now at sea arseing about the Channel doing bugger all as usual'.

Too late for war, too early for Edwina. While she was scrubbing floors at Alde House, Dickie had first tasted grown-up society. The Admiralty had decided that a short spell at university should be offered to some of the naval cadets whose training had been abbreviated by the war and Dickie had found himself an undergraduate at Christ's College, Cambridge, alongside his cousins, Prince Albert and Prince Henry, who occupied a house just outside the town. Dickie was well equipped to enjoy himself as a student. Unselfconscious and inquisitive, he liked new ideas, especially those expounded by his friend Peter Murphy, who talked politics and culture. At nineteen, the same age as other first-year men, Dickie could sample undergraduate societies without feeling that he had grown beyond them. He discovered debating. Used to working at the double, he did not find it difficult to swot up his notes quickly for a tutorial or to write an essay at the last minute.

After three years in the Navy Dickie was not going to waste time doing things that did not interest him. At the height of his passion for Audrey James, he would drive to London for a dance, tear back to Cambridge for an essay or a lecture, shoot back to London for tea and another dance and, having gone three days and nights without sleep, return to Cambridge. At one of those London parties, Lady Winifred Renshaw's in Portman Square, Dickie saw Edwina again. They did not dance; he was monopolizing Audrey. Not long afterwards, he left England with the Prince of Wales. His time as an undergraduate had been so short that he never tired of it.

Dickie Mountbatten was not only virtually unknown to Edwina but also quite unlike the young men she did know. She had spent the past year with admirers who wore plus-fours, tweed caps and stout shoes; Dickie, keen and trim, always looked as if he were in uniform, as he often was. Other men played tennis, Mountbatten did acrobatics on the court. He was always on the move, turning somersaults on the deck of *Venetia*, shinning up the rigging with his friend Dick Curzon. On a cloudy day with high waves he would put on a rubber cap and a bathing suit and aquaplane on a flat board towed behind a launch. Edwina asked Dickie's sister-in-law, Nada Milford Haven, how old he was: 'your first sign of interest in me', he said later.

Two Deaths in a Fortnight

Dickie was twenty-one, Edwina not yet twenty. They met every-where, at Nubia House, at a charity dance at Cowes, where Edwina cut her other partners for him, and again at Lady Baring's dance. Dickie begged her to come out in the Vanderbilts' yacht; 'I didn't know why . . . couldn't have told you the reason if you'd asked', he wrote, months afterwards, playing the part of an innocent. Edwina knew why. She had seen others succumb, including the self-assured Italian officers she had met in Rome. She declined to look at the moonlight from the Vanderbilts' yacht and, worse, explained that she was spending the day with Paul Hammond, a confident American.

At the end of the week Edwina was to leave the Barings and return to London. Sir Ernest was in France, preparing to start a motor tour, on which he expected Edwina to join him. The Vanderbilts had arranged to take their party for a cruise along the coast of Belgium and Northern France. Mrs Vanderbilt, still trying to make a match for Grace, pressed Dickie to come with them, but he had been asked by Cousin David to stay at his house on Dartmoor. Mrs Vanderbilt understood; an invitation from the Prince of Wales naturally took precedence.

Edwina had agreed to join the Vanderbilts' cruise, thinking that Dickie would be aboard. She telegraphed to Sir Ernest, who was not put out, since he had already had to change his plans. The roads in France were bad and he had decided to motor through the Black Forest instead. Dickie would have been impressed if he had known the precautions Edwina had taken. She had not only sent her telegram to the Villa des Cèdres, knowing Sir Ernest had just left it, but had explained in her wire that, unless she heard from him straightaway, she would assume that he gave his permission. To his horror, Dickie realized that he would be left on shore while *Venetia* sailed on with Edwina. At midnight, at the last party before they all left Cowes, she asked him to come with them on the cruise. It took Dickie until two o'clock in the morning to persuade Mrs Vanderbilt that the Prince's invitation could in fact be set aside.

Plain sailing? Hardly. Dickie found Edwina difficult to fathom. On the first day at sea his hopes were high. The sun shone and she agreed that they should look for a comfortable corner of the quarterdeck. Dickie found a good place, took it for himself and fell asleep; Edwina marched away in a huff. Then she asked him to stop calling her 'Miss Ashley'. She smiled at him but so she did to the other young men on board, Dick Curzon and Colin Davidson. Dickie did not know what to do. Curzon, a dangerous rival, was full of bright ideas; why not change course, he suggested to Mrs Vanderbilt, and drop in on the King and Queen of the Belgians? *Venetia* came in to Ostend, the General telephoned. While their hosts drank tea at the Palace, Edwina and Dickie walked on the beach. Dick Curzon came too. Edwina had bribed her maid to stay behind, not knowing that Dickie had done the same. Dickie found a seaside café, the Omar Khayyam, where they could dance. Mrs Vanderbilt was horrified when she heard how her party had entertained themselves.

Girls were baffling. Dickie did not know how bold to be. Edwina and even the boisterous Grace could be demure; half an hour later their manner would change completely. In Le Touquet, for instance, the girls persuaded the proprietor of a dress shop to unclothe the models in the window, shocking Mountbatten and Curzon, who averted their eyes from the pale rubber flesh. Dickie was none the less encouraged. On the way back to the yacht, he managed to squeeze into the front of the motor, next to Edwina, and put his arm round her, saying that he was making room for the driver. Edwina did not seem to mind. Dickie grew braver. He was hoping for something, he said. Could she guess what it was? Edwina gave nothing away, saying that she supposed that Dickie was longing for the Prince of Wales to ask him to join the royal tour to India. That had indeed been Dickie's dearest wish but now he had another: to be allowed to kiss her. Since he dared not say so, he pretended her guess was right. There were no embraces but at least there was proximity. On their last night in the Channel the sea was calm but Edwina thought she felt seasick and rang for a steward. She was not greatly surprised when Dickie rushed to her cabin; the cure, he explained, was to sleep on deck, so they spent the night camped in the lifeboat. Mrs Vanderbilt was appalled, more so because Grace had slept there too. 'Hoydenish', she called it, but she did not tell Sir Ernest.

After a night crushed up together under the stars it was impossible for Edwina to remain aloof and when Dickie asked whether she would like to meet his parents, who lived near Southampton, she said yes. From Le Touquet he proudly sent a telegram. 'Bringing girl to lunch.' Dickie's father was almost as excited as his son. He set off down the drive at Fishponds to meet the taxi and, when he saw this prize, he was astounded. Edwina was beautiful, intelligent and attentive and by the time Dickie saw her on to the London train that afternoon he was certain that his father and mother approved. Perhaps he was not too young to marry after all.

Dickie's other wish was now granted. The Prince of Wales asked him to come with him on his tour to India and Japan, lasting almost a year. They were to leave in October. Dickie told Edwina his programme for the next six weeks: he was to return to his new ship, HMS *Repulse*, which was going up to Inverness, with Dickie's father on board as the guest of the captain, Dudley Pound. This would be the longest voyage the former First Sea Lord had made since his resignation and Dickie, who adored his father, was looking forward to the cruise. Edwina was joining her grandfather at Baden for the last few days of his motor tour and, when they returned to England, she was to go to the Saviles for the Doncaster races. After that she might be in Scotland at just the time when *Repulse* would be at Inverness.

Dickie made a plan. His cousins David and Bertie would be shooting at Dunrobin in mid-September and he had asked the Duchess of Sutherland if he could come ashore from *Repulse* to join them; 'It would be marvellous luck if you were there then', he told Edwina. He had also heard that Mrs Greville was going to India in the winter and that she would be staying at Viceregal Lodge in Delhi during the Prince's visit. Edwina had said how much she would like to see India; here was her chance, for Lord Reading, the Viceroy, was an old friend of Sir Ernest and Mrs Greville knew and liked Edwina. 'If your Grandparent won't take you, you simply must go with her'.

Dunrobin was easily fixed. The day after Edwina arrived Dickie was ferried over from *Repulse*. When the launch reached the shore, he said goodbye to his father, who was taking the night train from Inverness to London. The Sutherlands' party was huge but Dickie had an excuse to seek out Edwina, since the kindly Duke of York had persuaded Eileen Sutherland to rearrange the list for the tennis tournament so that Dickie and Edwina could be partners. They sat in a bow window to discuss tactics – but the matches were never played. Next morning Dickie was called to the telephone. His father had gone to his club in Piccadilly to meet his wife and younger daughter. He was so shaky that after lunch they sent him to bed. He had died that evening.

Dickie was told on Sunday morning. It was a colossal blow. He spent the day with the Prince of Wales, not liking to ask for Edwina 'in case it might be thought queer'. A destroyer was to take him back to *Repulse* at dawn on Monday morning and as he waited, pacing up and down, he noticed a note from Edwina that had been brought to his room. As it was three o'clock in the morning he could not go to her but he left a letter, asking her to let him know when she was back in London. Two days later, before the funeral, Dickie wrote again. 'Besides David', he assured her, Edwina was the only person he had wanted to see. 'I wonder if you realise how enormously Papa took to you.'

Dickie was not ashamed to ask for comfort. Edwina had said that she might be coming back to London on the 23rd or 24th of September. Could they meet? They would have to be careful, since he was in mourning and she would be unchaperoned, but he hoped they could manage lunch: 'I do know the discreetest little restaurant where no one would ever see us'. Edwina returned sooner than either of them expected. On the same day on which Dickie's letter arrived she heard that her grandfather wanted her in London; she took the next train south. At the station Miss Underhill was waiting to meet her. That evening at six o'clock a footman had found Sir Ernest lying over his desk in the library at Brook House. He was dead.

Not without one final effort. Before he collapsed Sir Ernest had struggled to tear off the collar that seemed to cramp and stifle him. The footman was aghast. He rang, throwing the maids into a panic, for Mrs Lankester was out, Godfrey the butler was out, Jessie Passant, head housemaid, was out. Someone volunteered to tell Miss Underhill, in sole charge at last. She summoned the undertakers and sent for Mrs Cassel, Colonel Ashley, Mrs Jenkins and Sir Felix, none of whom could reach London until the following day. When Edwina reached Brook House, the lights were dimmed and the great doors closed.

CHAPTER EIGHT

Too Many Suitors

S ir Ernest was gone, Miss Underhill remained. Breaking her own rule, she spent the night at Brook House, so that Edwina should not be alone nor the servants leaderless. Like Nature, Miss Underhill abhorred a vacuum. There was nothing for Edwina to do. Engagements were cancelled, decisions deferred, the clocks stopped. Her friends were away. One person only would understand how strange it all was. In the early morning Edwina sent a note to Dickie, who was at York House, asking him to come as soon as he could.

At noon he arrived, and took Edwina, unchaperoned, out of the silent house, into Hyde Park. They walked across the grass among the fallen leaves, talking not just about Sir Ernest and Dickie's father, who had been buried three days earlier, but also about themselves. Shock and fatigue made everything unreal. They were surprised to find themselves talking urgently about the future. Dickie knew what he was doing next – sailing to India with the Prince of Wales – but Edwina was adrift. Where should she go? What should she do? With the wisdom of one who has known death for a week, Dickie told her to keep calm: 'It's not cowardly to deal with things one by one'.

There was an immediate problem, Edwina told him. The Duke of Sutherland had written an embarrassingly flirtatious letter. Dickie was delighted to advise. He drafted an answer and set out a plan of action. He would take Geordie's letter home, re-type it on his own machine, a copy, he said darkly, being 'less incriminating' than the original, and burn everything for her when the correspondence was over. Edwina had found a protector. If she hoped that one confidence would produce another, she was disappointed. Dickie had been dropping hints for a month; in a note he had sent that morning he had dared to send not just 'all my sympathy' but, squeezed in awkwardly as if it were an afterthought, 'and love'. But he was so nervous that he missed Edwina's signals. From York House he wrote another commiserating letter: 'It's so difficult to talk and "sentimentalities" mean nothing when spoken and, if felt, need not be spoken at all.' That was as near as he came to saying, or not saying, what Edwina wanted to hear.

In the afternoon Mrs Cassel arrived from Bournemouth to take charge. There were dozens of letters to answer, including, three times a day, anxious notes from Dickie, who was now with his mother at Fishponds. Sir Ernest's funeral took place at the Catholic church in Farm Street and from there, watched by a sorrowing assembly of black-clad clerks, secretaries, indoor and outdoor servants, lined up in order of precedence, his family took his body on its last journey, to the cemetery at Kensal Green. Next day Dickie returned to London, in case Edwina needed him. The two young people wandered aimlessly about, dodging anyone who might know them, looking for an unoccupied bench in the park, hoping the rain would hold off. At one point they were forced to take cover at Mrs Jack's, from whom Edwina bought her shoes. Improvising quickly, she asked to see the latest model, a hideous creation with double T-straps over the top of the foot and – this pleased Dickie – 'Louis' heels. Dickie was entranced by Edwina's tiny feet. He was completely bewitched and Edwina knew it. Death, like love, makes the blood run faster, and she and Dickie had been assailed by both. Edwina was light-headed. As they passed the Rolls-Royce showroom in Mayfair, she asked Dickie whether, having ordered the shoes, they should not now order a car. Alas, Dickie replied, he could never afford it. Edwina said nothing – yet.

Edwina's family did not know that she was meeting Dickie. They had other preoccupations: chiefly, the contents of Sir Ernest's will. This had been drawn up the year before, in July 1920, based on an outline made just after Edwina had come out. Although Cassel's estate was large and his interests complicated, the arrangements were simple. Friends and relations were to receive substantial annuities, the largest being a sum of thirty thousand pounds for Mrs Cassel. Other bequests went to Sir Ernest's clerks and servants in London and Bournemouth, at Moulton Paddocks, in Switzerland and Paris. Mrs Cassel was asked to select pictures, furniture and plate, as mementoes for relations and friends, including the Asquiths, the Readings, the Churchills, Mrs Keppel, Mrs Schiff and Mrs Bischoffs-heim. The portrait of King Edward VII, and all presents given to Sir Ernest by the King and by Queen Alexandra were to be treated as heirlooms and never sold or given away. Linen, china, glass, furniture and fixtures, pictures, plate, silver and other ornaments were bequeathed to Mrs Cassel for her use, to pass after her death to Edwina. All consumable stores, together with motor cars, horses, saddlery and stable furniture, were to go to Mrs Cassel.

The allocation of the houses themselves was straightforward. Edwina and Mary jointly inherited the Villa Cassel. For the remainder of her life Mrs Cassel was to enjoy the use of Brook House and the stables behind it in Woods Mews. She was also to keep Moulton Paddocks and Branksome Dene. After her death, these properties were to pass to Edwina. The estates at Newmarket – Six Mile Bottom and Hare Park – were to be kept for Mary. Of all the properties, Brook House and its contents had been most precious to Sir Ernest and he gave a long list of directions for their future. These treasures were never to be sold. If Edwina did not survive, and had no living children, they were to go to Mary. If Mary died, and all her children, they passed to Felix. Should Felix die, with all his children, Anna was next in line and, after her, Marjorie, then her children. Sir Ernest's instructions were as precise as if he had been determining the order of succession to the English throne and, indeed, he stipulated that, if his entire family were wiped out, Brook House and everything in it should be offered to whichever sovereign was reigning at the time. If for some inconceivable reason such an offer were refused, the property was to be held in trust for King Edward's Hospital Fund for London. To Sir Ernest, who had been so devoted to the King and to the charities named after him, this was almost as good as keeping Brook House in the family.

He was less possessive about the other houses. If Moulton Paddocks and Branksome Dene were sold, with their furniture, the proceeds were to go to Edwina, as part of her share of his residuary estate. Any sum raised by the sale of Six Mile Bottom and Hare Park was, similarly, to be part of Mary's share. The residuary estate – everything Sir Ernest owned that was not covered by some specific bequest – was in any case huge, amounting, it was believed, to at least seven and a half million pounds.

Sir Ernest had set out in a dozen lines the principles he wished his executors and trustees to follow. His fortune was to be divided into sixty-four parts. Eight sixty-fourths, that is, one eighth, were bequeathed to Anna and her children; sixteen sixty-fourths were to go to Mary, when she came of age; and twenty-five sixty-fourths, by far the largest portion, to Edwina. If Mary should die childless, her share went to Edwina; if Edwina should die, leaving no children, Mary would have Edwina's share. These arrangements meant that Edwina would receive a very large income, although her grandfather, the expert's expert, would not be there to invest it for her. The only guidance Sir Ernest gave from beyond the grave was that her trustees should never place more than a hundred thousand pounds in any single security or investment.

For the time being, however, Edwina had no money. When she came of age in November 1922 she would receive whatever income from her inheritance the trustees thought fit. Only when she married or reached her twenty-eighth birthday, whichever came first, would she be able to enjoy the whole of her income from the trust. Newspapers were describing her as 'The Great Heiress' but Sir Ernest's death meant that even her dress allowance had gone. Wilfrid had long lost the habit of giving her pocket money; her only funds, for tips and anything that could not be bought on account, came from Mrs Cassel. Edwina was suddenly more restricted than she had been for months. Whatever 'The Richest Girl in Britain' did was noticed – and she could afford to do very little.

At least Mrs Cassel did not insist that Edwina should remain at home to mourn Sir Ernest. Edwina had not forgotten that Mrs Greville was going out to India and she had already called on her and steered the conversation round to the subject of the Prince's tour and the character and reputation of the Prince's ADC. Mrs Greville, a great matchmaker, guessed that she was being pumped. She now presented herself at Brook House and proposed to Mrs Cassel that after the funeral Edwina should come for a day or two to her house at Polesden Lacey. Mrs Greville told Edwina that she would also invite Dickie Mountbatten, suggesting that they fix a date to suit them both.

Meanwhile Dickie had consulted his brother Georgie and his wife, Nada. Nada's sister, Zia, was married to Harold Wernher, the son of Sir Julius Wernher, who had financed the development of the South African gold and diamond industries. A friend and colleague of Sir Ernest, Sir Julius had died before the Great War. Prompted by Dickie, Nada invited Edwina to spend the first weekend in October at St George, the Milford Havens' house at Southsea.

Dickie Mountbatten had grown up in a close and openly affectionate family. All his life he was happiest when he could think that his friends and relations were part of a harmonious circle, with himself at its centre. He had made a hero of his brother, admiring his quick, inventive brain, which Georgie applied not so much to his studies as to making life as comfortable as possible: his cabin on the *New Zealand* was rigged up with fans, radiators and automatic tea-making equipment of his own devising. When critics said Georgie was lazy, Dickie explained that, being so capable, his brother had no need to plug away at his work. If Georgie gave a good opinion of Edwina, Dickie could be sure that he had made the right choice. Edwina's verdict on Georgie was equally important. To Dickie, she was now as much a paragon as his brother. Perhaps she would help him with his tennis, golf and shooting; he and the Prince of Wales were taking lessons at the London Shooting School, to try to improve their style. 'I happen to know how brilliant you really are', Dickie told Edwina – and he believed it. He was still in awe of her, despite the vulnerability she had displayed after Sir Ernest's death. If Georgie impressed her, it would help.

Edwina arrived at Southsea on Saturday; on Sunday they were joined by Dickie's mother, the Dowager Marchioness of Milford Haven, formerly Princess Victoria of Hesse, and his older sisters, Alice and Louise, for an expedition to *Renown*, on which Dickie and the Prince of Wales were to sail in less than three weeks' time. Dickie was relieved to see how well Edwina got on with everybody, but he held back, thinking that it would be unfair to declare himself just as he was about to disappear to the other side of the world. Late in the afternoon they found themselves alone in the billiard-room at St George. They were over-excited and exhausted – not surprisingly, after two deaths in a fortnight. Dickie heard himself saying more than he had intended, Edwina fell into his arms, and they both burst into tears.

They decided to say nothing to their families. Edwina was not of age; Dickie was, just, but he was on the point of leaving the country. Neither family was in a fit state to be faced with such an announcement. Keeping their secret was difficult. When Georgie and Nada drove Edwina on to Branksome, Dickie stayed behind, for fear that he might put his arm round her and give everything away. Nada interrogated Dickie; Mrs Cassel questioned Edwina. Marjorie had more than an inkling. Grace Vanderbilt asked Dickie why his eyes moistened when Schubert was played on the piano; Poppy Baring stamped her foot and told him: 'You know what I want to know and I do think you might tell me', Mrs Greville telephoned Edwina about arrangements for the shoot at Polesden Lacey: could Edwina give her Dickie Mountbatten's address? Edwina said she had forgotten it.

If Mrs Cassel noticed that Dickie wrote every day, she said nothing. Dickie's family was not so restrained. Each day he had a letter, each evening there was a self-consciously casual conversation with Edwina on the telephone. Dickie's mother warned him to say nothing to commit himself. Lady Milford Haven was not possessive but she was wise. She was particularly close to her youngest child and Dickie had always been sure of her interest and her backing. 'You know I love you very much, my dear boy', she had written to him, when he moved to boarding-school at the age of nine, 'and it makes no difference in my feelings and thoughts if I am nearer or farther from you – and if you needed me much, I would come to you from anywhere . . .' Throughout his schooldays and his first years in the Navy, Dickie had told his mother all his hopes and fears. Victoria knew that her boy was impulsive, enthusiastic and trusting, anxious to please, easily hurt. She had urged him to distinguish clearly between right and wrong, honesty and cheating, duty and convenience. She taught him to be proud of his family's standards and not to flinch. 'As long as you have done nothing really wrong and to be ashamed of,' she wrote, when he was beaten at school, 'there is no actual disgrace in being "swished".' Dickie had grown up thoughtful, loyal and sweet-tempered. His mother knew that he was immature. He looked it, being as yet unco-ordinated and lanky, with the bony nose and prominent ears of a boy who is still growing. Lady Milford Haven believed that her son was too young to make a well-informed choice. In the aftermath of his father's death, he was vulnerable and his mother was anxious that he should not be pulled hither and thither by another Audrey James.

True, Edwina Ashley seemed more sympathetic than Audrey, less hard and less tricky. Her great disadvantage was that she was, or would be, so immensely wealthy. Dickie's father, the eldest son of Prince Alexander of Hesse, had inherited a comfortable fortune in Germany, and his mother, the daughter of Princess Alice, had received various legacies, including one from her grandmother, Queen Victoria. After the war, however, the German funds were worthless.

Too Many Suitors

Dickie's father had nothing but his naval pay. On this they had maintained themselves, four children and a small household. Dickie would have about £300 a year from dividends. This was not to be sneezed at, being almost as much as his pay – £310 a year – as a junior naval officer, but it was vastly less than the income Edwina would receive when she came of age. The disparity worried Dickie's mother, who did not like the thought that her son might be, or might appear to be, dependent on his wife.

Had she known the story of Edwina's parents' marriage, she would have seen a parallel. Like Wilfrid, Dickie had fallen for a girl with a far larger fortune than his own. Like Maudie, Edwina had chosen someone from a grander family. The Ashley blood was blue, Dickie's royal purple. Its source was the house of Hesse, a small but influential state in Germany, whose rulers were famous for their interest in the arts, tolerance of religious and political dissent, and readiness to despatch their combative citizens to fight in wars and skirmishes started by other people. Dickie's family had a strong Russian connection. His grandfather, Prince Alexander of Hesse, was the Tsar's godson and Alexander's sister had married the Tsarevich. Prince Louis of Battenberg, Dickie's father, was the eldest of five children. One of his brothers married a daughter of Queen Victoria; his cousin, Grand Duke Louis IV, married another, Princess Alice. Young Prince Louis was serious and responsible, with one quirk: he longed to become a sailor, although Hesse was land-locked and the German fleet at that time almost non-existent. Louis pressed his parents to allow him to join the British Navy. They agreed; as they feared, their son did not have an easy time. His contemporaries were hostile, mocking his foreign accent and resenting his royal connections. Being efficient, energetic and good-tempered, however, he was eventually accepted and even liked. In his journey to the top, Prince Louis' connections with the British royal family were as much a hindrance as a help. He was largely self-propelled, with one powerful auxiliary engine – his wife, Princess Victoria, Dickie's mother. She was a daughter of Louis' cousin, Grand Duke Louis IV, and Princess Alice, so that in marrying her, Prince Louis bound even more closely together Queen Victoria's family and the house of Hesse.

Dickie's mother was well-read, level-headed and unstuffy, a perfect ally, and together she and Prince Louis worked at his profession. By 1903, when he became Director of Naval Intelligence in the Admiralty, he was greatly respected, except by diehard traditionalists. When Louis' career crashed in the anti-German clamour of 1914, Victoria steadied him. It was then that King George agreed to anglicize his family name – Queen Victoria's husband, Prince Albert, had been a Saxe-Coburg-Gotha – and had asked those of his German cousins who were British citizens to do likewise. Tecks, Schleswig-Holsteins and Battenbergs were rechristened. Prince Louis and Princess Victoria became the Marquess and Marchioness of Milford Haven, Dickie's brother Georgie Earl of Medina, and Dickie Lord Louis Mountbatten, adding more entries to the complicated crossword-puzzle of his genealogy. Shortly after he had embraced Edwina in the billiard-room, Dickie sent her a bookplate showing his coat of arms, to help her sort things out.

To Edwina the whole pattern was extraordinary and intriguing. Dickie appeared to be related to every European royal family: one uncle had married the sister of the Queen of Italy; a nephew of his grandfather had married a Danish princess. Another uncle had been, temporarily, the Sovereign Prince of Bulgaria. Dickie's mother's family was intertwined with the royal houses of Spain, Greece, Russia, Germany and Sweden, in a web spun largely single-handed by Queen Victoria. Uncles, aunts and cousins had perished in wars, coups and revolutions, most recently, the entire Russian royal family, murdered in 1918, but dozens remained. In comparison, Edwina's own childhood seemed unpopulated.

Dickie's mother sensed this difference. She had lost her own mother when she was a child, and, like Edwina, she had become detached and independent. Would that, reinforced by great wealth, be right for Dickie? Victoria asked Dickie to hold back: 'I am afraid,' he told Edwina, 'that my father's death has rather upset my poor dear Mother's nerves . . . I look to you, darling, to help me in not mentioning anything until after India.' At Polesden Lacey he hovered over her, ready to spring into action if anyone became too familiar. In the evenings, while Edwina played cards, Dickie sat as near as he dared, pretending to read *The Siege of Lucknow*, in preparation for his journey.

The weeks whizzed by. *Renown* sailed on 26 October. The Duke of York and Prince Henry came to see their brother off; Georgie and Nada, Zia, Louise and Lady Milford Haven assembled on the ship to say goodbye. They brought Edwina, tactfully leaving her alone for half an hour with Dickie in his cabin. He had worked out that they would be parted for two hundred and forty-six days and now he gave her a little watch to keep an eye on the time. As the ship sailed, the party on the dockside held back their tears, in case the photographers should be embarrassed. No one laughed at Dickie when he pulled out a telescope and, instead of gazing out to sea and India, trained it on the shore.

It was an eternity. Early that morning, before he joined the ship, Dickie had written Edwina a farewell letter; when it reached her, he said, there would be one fewer day to go. Dickie was acutely sensitive to the ticking of the clock. He had been brought up to be punctual – Princess Victoria made it a rule to be three minutes early for everything – and he hated to lose precious seconds. Connected with this obsession was a passion for detail. Dickie was fanatically well-organized, numbering, cataloguing, categorizing. 'German', said his critics but this gentle mania was a symptom of insecurity. Dickie wanted to be as successful as his father, as clever as Georgie, as punctilious as his mother. He wrote to Edwina every day, crossing off the weeks and months of their separation.

It was appropriate that Dickie should keep the unofficial diary of the Prince's tour, a job he had also done on the earlier visits to New Zealand and Australia. Each night he typed out seven copies, one for himself, one for the record, the others for the Prince, Mama, Bertie, Edwina and Freda Dudley Ward. Dickie wrote as he spoke, frankly and unselfconsciously. All the news of the tour would be in the diary, he told Edwina, so his letters would be only about themselves. He found a surprising amount to say. He was missing her dreadfully; every night he talked to her photograph, although he had to hide it if the Prince or the other ADCs came into his cabin. He was playing Schubert on the gramophone and encouraging the ship's jazz band to learn Edwina's favourite dance-tunes: 'We've got a banjo in now, which makes a lot of difference, and the saxophone has come on enormously.' Not that he was enjoying himself. At Poona there was going to be 'some rotten ball' but he would excuse himself by explaining that he was still in mourning. Every Saturday night at sea, he told her, we drink to 'Sweethearts and Wives': he thought of it as her toast.

Left to herself, Edwina was intent on having fun: 'You feel so much better afterwards.' With her friend Margaret Lindsay, she went to 'very improper plays on the sly'. (One was *The Sign of the Dove*, with

Gladys Cooper). Nada and Georgie took her dancing till three o'clock in the morning, at 'a marvellous place, The Frolics, at the back of Regent Street, very low and quite divine'. Having found Dickie and then, if only temporarily, lost him again, Edwina needed reassurance. By describing the lively time she was having, she made Dickie jealous and worried. His anxiety increased when she told him that the doctor said she had overstrained her heart, 'probably at Dunrobin', and that she was having 'Arsenic Inoculations', adding with deliberate nonchalance that the treatment 'really is quite harmless and doesn't make you feel at all ill, at least not so far'. She spared him nothing: the letter she had received from Paul Hammond, with whom she had gone off in Cowes Week, inviting her to New York; the diamond bracelet from Cartier sent by Geordie Sutherland, which she had regretfully sent back; her 'grand succès' with Lord Fermoy, Henry Howard and Captain Hay at a shoot in Norfolk, where she had 'behaved shockingly'. She enclosed the verses her admirers had written:

> At Blickling the charming Miss Ashley
> Went and put her small foot in it – rashly.
> She said let's play Sardines
> And explained what it means,
> But our hostess considered it ghastly.

It was enough to chill Dickie's blood.

He responded as he was meant to do, reminding Edwina of all they had done together – only a total of three weeks' walking and talking, with a dance or two in the summer, but he made the most of it. He remembered her birthday and described the presents he had chosen for her in Benares: blue and gold stuff, gold brocade for shoes, plus gold shoe-laces, and the same in silver, for Mrs Jack to make up. Although 'I know nothing about ladies' clothes', he was sure she would look divine. In Bombay he bought her a headdress, lacquer bowls and two swords, for he had started to think about the home they would furnish together. He was collecting heads, the tally so far being one pig's head, stuck at Jodhpur, four shikara from Bikaner and a huge black buck from Bharatpur, where he, the Prince and the Maharajah had hunted from the back of a motor car, careering at speed over rough country: 'An excellent advertisement for Rolls'. His previous tour with the Prince had yielded a red deer head and a small skull from New Zealand and three kangaroo tails from Australia, 'so the hall will be a sort of Natural History Museum if you ever let me put any of them up'.

Dickie was so uncomplicated that he failed to see that Edwina might be jealous. His descriptions of pig-sticking, tiger-shooting and paper-chases conducted on horseback were meant to give her a share in the expedition. All the time, he declared, he thought of her, even when engaged in the dangerous business of hunting crocodiles: if only his victim had not tumbled into the water, he would have sent her the skin for a pair of shoes. As for other girls, she had nothing to fear. Only one, the sister of the Commanding Officer of the Viceroy's bodyguard, had caught Dickie's eye, largely, he explained, because she rather resembled Edwina in the way she did her hair, 'only a *slight* likeness', he quickly emphasized: 'darling, don't imagine that I even *vaguely* think that anyone exists who could match you'.

Dickie did not hide the fact that he was enjoying himself, more so than the Prince, who pined for Freda Dudley Ward. One reason for the tour was to try to improve Anglo-Indian relations, which had dived steeply downwards after the Amritsar massacre three years before. The royal party had a cool reception. A ceremony at Allahabad University was boycotted by the students; there and at Benares the streets were empty. There were demonstrations in Madras and at Patiala an onlooker fired twice at the ADCs' car. The Prince believed his visit was helping the nationalists. 'I don't feel I'm doing a scrap of good', he told the King. He moped, punishing himself with violent exercise and a near-starvation diet. Dickie marvelled at his cousin's energy and self-denial: 'I've never seen anybody take so much exercise on so little food, as he only eats biscuits for lunch'. From Rawalpindi the Prince sent his photograph to Freda, to show her the thinness of his legs. He complained incessantly about his parents' failure to understand him. Dickie, who had seen some of the Prince's correspondence, had told his mother that 'his father's letters might be the letters of a Director to his Assistant Manager'. The analogy was apt – but the Prince resented the demands of the family business.

Mountbatten was the perfect companion. Like an eager puppy, he cheered his master up by his readiness to experiment and his determination to enjoy himself: polo, for example, which he first tried at Jodhpur. 'I was very bewildered at first', he told Edwina, not surprisingly, since Frank Messervy, a high-spirited cavalry officer, had explained that the correct way to mount a polo pony was by leaping up on it from behind. When there was no more to say about the misery of separation from Mrs Dudley Ward, the Prince would ask Dickie about the condition of his own heart. Dickie was happy to comply. Before *Renown* had even reached Gibraltar, they had discussed whether Edwina would accept him, should he dare to ask. The hypothetical nature of the question, Dickie assured her, showed that the Prince had not yet divined the truth. For the next three months the Prince dutifully pretended not to have guessed the extent of Dickie's understanding with Edwina.

Edwina was lonely and dreadfully bored. Mrs Cassel was nursing her swollen legs at Branksome and Mrs Jenkins was too busy to be a chaperone. Marjorie had her own preoccupations, Wilfrid and Molly did not wish to be encumbered. Edwina had suggested a trip to America to stay with Grace Vanderbilt but Wilfrid thought that too daring. Edwina next proposed that she should go with Wilfrid and Molly to Italy and Sicily, to Dickie's dismay: 'Too many suitors'. That also fell through.

Mrs Cassel was sympathetic. She declared that she was too old for parties at Brook House but she gave them at Branksome Dene instead. It was she who entertained Georgie and Nada, Marjorie and Brecky, Cousin Felix and Aunt Helen, and who asked Edwina what she would really like to do with herself. Edwina told her story, a confidence expected weeks ago. Mrs Cassel advised Edwina to go to her father, so in mid-December Edwina took herself to Broadlands. Although Wilfrid had not met Dickie, he knew that his family was well-connected. Edwina's mother had been married when she was twenty, so Wilfrid could hardly say that his daughter was too young, and he was in no position to argue against her marrying a man who was likely to have less capital than herself.

Meanwhile Lady Reading had written to her old friend Mrs Cassel, inviting Edwina to come to Delhi in the middle of January, when she would not be so much in mourning. Mrs Cassel told Edwina that she would lend her a hundred pounds for the fare and insisted on equipping her with new hats and dresses. Wilfrid agreed that, if a chaperone could be found, his daughter might go. Edwina took herself to Cook's, asked to see the passenger list and picked out a name. On Christmas Day she sent Dickie an ecstatic cable.

CHAPTER NINE

An Indian Morning

S traight away Dickie began issuing instructions. Edwina would need a lady's topee, 'Henry Heath or Ranken make good ones', and 'lightish glasses which cut out the harmful rays'. She should bring the shoes Mrs Jack had made, and tennis and riding clothes. Viceregal Lodge was well stocked with side-saddles and he had a delicious vision of Edwina in flowing skirt and neat, polished boots. Dickie fussed over the smallest detail, as anxiously as Wilfrid had once done in his letters to Maudie. Dickie, however, was concerned with his correspondent's comfort rather than his own. 'Please be very careful what sort of food you eat and above all what water you drink.' One English girl, staying at a most respectable hotel, had died of cholera within forty-eight hours. 'Soda water – if of an English Brand – is always safe. Other water may give you typhoid.' Even on a cloudy day Edwina should protect her head, especially between nine in the morning and four in the afternoon: 'Get sunstroke once and you never can be sure of yourself again'. He wished she were travelling with an experienced and trustworthy man; since she was not, Dickie gave two special reminders for the journey. Edwina should remember that she was travelling *in*, not *on*, *Moorea*, and she should visit the crater at Aden and look out for the sunsets.

To those who travelled in her, *Moorea* was known as 'The Champion Squeaker'. Edwina joined the ship at Marseilles, missing a dreadful passage through the Bay of Biscay, so turbulent that one elderly passenger died and had to be buried at sea. The journey from Marseilles to Port Said was ghastly and two days passed before Edwina managed to stagger out on deck, leaving Weller, her maid, clinging piteously to the sides of her bunk below. They docked at Aden at 10 p.m., too late for sunsets, but Edwina told her chaperone that there was time to inspect the crater before the ship left again at midnight. The companion she had selected was Mrs Carey Evans, a daughter of Lloyd George and the wife of the Viceroy's personal physician, who was taking her two small children to India. Only eight years older than Edwina, she found her charge intimidating. Now, however, she put her foot down. Aden was full of iniquity, especially at night; danger lurked round every corner. Edwina said she would go with some friends, people her chaperone thought undesirable. Fortunately they decided to stay on board and drink champagne, so Mrs Carey Evans was spared a sleepless night, for, as she said later, 'I couldn't have stopped her if she'd been really determined.'

Edwina was dreadfully bored. Her companion's friends were dull and the entertainment – bridge, poker, a fancy-dress ball – was humdrum. She was sustained only by Dickie's letters, which awaited her at every stop. The nearer she drew to India, the more exhaustively he briefed her. There were lists of the people in the Prince's retinue, with short character sketches of each: de Montmorency, for example, who 'knows a lot about India and little about anything else'; Fruity Metcalfe, 'the nicest fellow we have. Poor, honest, a typical Indian cavalryman'. Dickie included a mass photograph of the Prince's party, with a tracing of each person's head, named and annotated. As the picture was blurred, he said, Edwina might not be able to recognize people's faces but if she memorized the uniforms she would be able to identify everybody when she was first introduced.

Edwina was not short of homework. Dickie also sent lists of the Viceroy's staff, grouped into various useful categories and listed in order of precedence. Edwina was not to be surprised that Dickie himself came 'absolutely last'. Each person had a precedence number: 'As a naval lieutenant mine is 78, as an ADC to the PoW 74, and if I was out here as a member of the family you could take off 70.' Knowing he really came so high, Dickie said, he could 'laugh secretly at all these poor misguided people struggling to go even one place higher . . .' Edwina did not fail to notice how deeply he cared about such things himself.

She was not the only one to receive advice. As soon as she learnt that Edwina was going out to India, Dickie's mother had written him a long and careful letter. For weeks Victoria had suspected what was in her son's mind; now, she told him:

Well, you know all I want is for you to be happy when you marry and therefore to marry only when you are quite sure of yourself and that your love is not only based on the attraction a nice girl has on your rather impulsive heart but that your head has a real share in your choice – for you must remember that even with one's wife one does not remain in that state called 'being in love' so that to be happy another quieter love must follow, based on joint understanding and liking of each other's characters.

Victoria had not forgotten the débâcle over Audrey James. She went on:

Therefore keep yourself in hand and don't hurry matters until you are sure that besides 'being in love' there are other sides to the girl (I think her very nice) which seem to draw you to her. Ask yourself, if she or you were disfigured by an accident, you could still bear to look at each other, and many such questions of the head.

Dickie's mother knew her son's faults. Her closing words were these:

Now enough 'Old hen preaching to a duckling'. Only one more word. Don't discuss yourself up and down. It may bore the girl if she is not built that way, and too much talking only muddles brains.

Dickie told Edwina what Lady Milford Haven had said, in a letter that awaited her when *Moorea* reached Aden. Trying to follow his mother's advice, he none the less filled a couple of pages with his thoughts on the disfigurement question: '. . . I should love you just as much', he concluded, 'and probably take greater care of you than ever'. The 'probably' was at least honest. 'So I have answered Mama's question to my own (and therefore to her) satisfaction'. There was only one outstanding worry, which Dickie's mother had conveyed to Georgie, who had passed it on to Dickie. 'Five minutes conversation would (I feel sure) settle that difficulty – so I will leave that till Delhi'. This was the question of Edwina's fortune.

Colonel Carey Evans was waiting in Bombay and, after tea at the Yacht Club, dinner and a bath, the whole party took the Special Mail to Delhi, the fastest train in India. The Colonel produced another envelope from Dickie, enclosing a letter, a railway timetable in case they missed the Special, and a Hindustani phrase-book, put together for the Prince's entourage, to enable Edwina to summon a bearer, order a whisky and soda, or send for a horse.

She reached Viceregal Lodge at half past one in the morning, after twenty-five hours in the train. Dickie was lodged in the Prince's Pavilion, specially built in the grounds, with the Prince of Wales' feathers, gigantically reproduced in gilded wood, fixed over the entrance. Above these, when the Prince was in residence, the Royal Standard hung limp in the stifling air. Only Dickie shared the pavilion with his cousin, the others being housed in a set of splendid tents, carpeted and furnished with lamps, pictures, sofas and garlands. The tents were both beautiful and comfortable but, although shielded by damp screens, through which a battery of fans directed a stream of air, in the middle of the day they were as hot as ovens. Edwina was fortunate; she was one of two guests housed in Viceregal Lodge, where the walls were thick and the huge rooms dark and cool. The other was Mrs Ronnie Greville, who had a sitting-room the size of a cricket pitch, which she immediately put at Edwina's disposal. Here she and Dickie were reunited.

Edwina was glad that Dickie had briefed her so thoroughly. As the representatives of the King-Emperor and his Queen, the Viceroy and Vicereine were treated with the utmost deference. Strict adherence to protocol was thought more, not less, important so many miles from home and the ritual was more magnificent in Delhi than in London or Balmoral. 'Quite overpowering', Edwina told Mrs Cassel; 'the curtseying and etiquette are awful'. The size and scale of everything made her reel. Viceregal Lodge covered acres, one vast room going on to the next, arched entrances leading to a succession of caverns of marble and inlaid wood. There were scores of servants, graded by caste and function, each so skilled in one particular task – pouring water, ironing, opening doors – that its performance had become an art.

Edwina had never been so solicitously attended. 'I can't tell you how smart and rich one feels here,' she wrote to Mrs Cassel. 'A car whenever you want one. About ten servants for everything; special flowers for each dress etc.' She washed her hands in water where a flower floated; at first light she lay beneath cool, thin sheets, listening to the sound of an Indian early morning: unfamiliar birdsong, subdued laughter, hand-made brooms sweeping the verandahs. No order need be given to the discreetly attentive servants. There were no decisions to take, since each hour was allocated, each function choreographed: printed programmes gave times of arrival and departure, seating plans, hours of meals, nature of dress to be worn, number of guns to be fired in any accompanying salutes. It was as if Edwina had arrived in the middle of a play, on a stage where long ago each actor had learnt his part. The cast was immense, the performance overpoweringly formal and repetitious.

When the Prince arrived, the Viceroy's guests and staff were mustered for an official photograph, in which the ladies, even Mrs Greville in her famous emeralds, were outdazzled by the men. The British officers wore uniforms plated with medals and gold braid, the Indians, sitting cross-legged upon a carpet, were festooned with gold and silver cords, twined, tasselled and looped. They carried turbans on their heads, swords over their knees. There, with jewelled belts and sashes, headdresses marvellous with feathers and precious stones, were the Indian ADCs, their titles as magnificent as their appearance: the Maharaj Kumar of Bikaner, Raja Sir Hari Singh of Kashmir, Nawabzada Hamidullah Khan of Bhopal. Even the four civilian Englishmen, clutching their topees, sported jewelled stockpins and in their buttonholes small bouquets. In the middle sat the Prince of Wales, peering from beneath his protective headgear, lace, braid and decorations entirely covering his jacket, trying to remain alert as the sun moved higher in the sky.

'The Little Prince', as Edwina called him, for he was at least six inches shorter than Dickie, had by now had enough of the tour. He was, Edwina reported, 'quite fed up with . . . the terrific pomp and ceremony': the Inspection of Pensioners; the opening of Kitchener College; the unveiling of the King Edward VII Memorial, in heat so scorching that the Prince felt sick; an enormous State Banquet. 'What they called a tiny dinner party,' Edwina said, 'was one for only eighty people'. On the day after the Prince returned to Delhi, there was a Durbar. Thousands of people came to gaze at the son of the King-Emperor, before the Prince was driven away to a garden party and a fancy-dress dance. As he observed sadly to Edwina, there were still four months to go.

Dickie and Edwina rode together, walked together, visited forts and tombs. In the afternoons they danced to the gramophone in the Prince's private sitting-room, inventing a step of their own, which they practised to a recording of *Kalhua Blues* until the record was worn

111

through. Edwina loyally declined an invitation to hunt so that she could watch Dickie play polo; everyone must have known why, but Dickie still believed that only the Prince and perhaps Mrs Greville had guessed their secret. Hiscock, Dickie's valet, and Weller, Edwina's maid, had drawn their own conclusions, as Dickie realized when he found Hiscock devotedly cleaning Edwina's riding boots and Weller ironing his ties. Mesmerized, the household awaited an announcement.

At last, on 10 February, as Dickie described it afterwards, 'I really did ask you in actual words and . . . you really did say yes.' Next day they gave their news to the Prince, the Readings, Mrs Greville and Lord Cromer, the Chief of Staff, who all pretended to be surprised. 'It was impossible not to tell them', Edwina explained to Mrs Cassel, 'and they have all been too nice about it'. Now the Viceroy and Vicereine awoke from their trance. 'Edwina is in our charge here', Lord Reading wrote to Mrs Cassel, in a panic; 'I am experienced enough to know the importance of conventions and formalities in these matters'. Romance was very well but had Edwina's family really given their approval in advance?

The crucial issue, according to the Viceroy, was the disposition of Edwina's fortune: 'In plain English, Edwina in my opinion brings far more than she gets by the marriage'. Proper discussions should take place before the engagement was formally announced. Sir Ernest would have insisted on this and, now that he was gone, Mrs Cassel and Cousin Felix must look after Edwina's interests. Lord Reading believed that Edwina's fortune should remain securely in her own hands. If the marriage were a success, no harm would be done. If, 'Heaven forbid', it should turn out unhappily, 'or not so happily as we should all wish, she will be in a far better position if she has control of the money'. All this should be settled immediately, for, once the engagement was announced, it would be difficult to stand firm on terms that would protect Edwina. Not that the Viceroy had anything to say against Dickie Mountbatten: 'Lord Louis is good-looking and attractive on first impression but I know too little of him to express an opinion.'

Lord Reading's point was a good one and he put it kindly. Lady Reading, whose letter followed by the next post, was not so subtle, although she wrote in code. 'I am afraid she has definitely made up her mind about him', she told Mrs Cassel. 'I say afraid,' she went on, 'tho' I know nothing against him except that he is too young.' What the Vicereine meant was that she suspected Dickie of being an adventurer. Lady Reading had hoped that Edwina would have cared 'for someone older with more of a career before him'. Or, rather, a career behind him, so that the Readings could be sure it was Edwina's heart and not her wealth that was being wooed.

Mrs Cassel swept aside these doubts. She did not tell the Readings that, when she had agreed to fund Edwina's venture, she had known exactly what its purpose was, but she did assure them that Edwina had since consulted her and that she and Wilfrid both approved of Dickie. Nothing was to be published until Wilfrid, Dickie's mother and the King all formally consented to the match. Having done his duty by Sir Ernest's shade, Lord Reading said no more.

The engagement was the worst-kept secret at Viceregal Lodge; Dickie and Edwina, not Their Excellencies, became the focus of attention. The Prince's staff, the Viceroy's household, guests and servants all felt a pang when the lovers parted, for the Prince was leaving Delhi again, this time for pig-sticking in Patiala. Edwina saw Dickie off on the Royal Train. He hated leaving her. His polo went awry and his only consolation was the *Blue Danube Blues*, which he played interminably on the gramophone, 'dancing all our little special steps round the room by myself . . .'

Edwina did not moon about for long. There was too much to do. She and Dickie had agreed that the time had come to tell their families and friends, although Dickie had impressed on her the importance of saying nothing publicly until the King had given his permission. In the first two days of Dickie's absence, Edwina therefore wrote to forty people, asking for secrecy.

Dickie meanwhile sent a letter to Edwina's father, asking for his consent and apologizing for approaching him by post. He also cabled Georgie, giving him plenipotentiary powers to speak to Colonel Ashley and, when he had secured Wilfrid's formal consent, to approach the King. Edwina was sure that something would go wrong with this stately minuet. 'Please hurry them all up', she begged Mrs Cassel, 'it will be sure to leak out in some way'. It had done so already – and the leak came from a source she and Dickie least expected: the King. As soon as Edwina had accepted him, Dickie had sent Georgie a triumphant signal, announcing: 'All is well. Prepare Mama. Writing families immediately'. Georgie and Nada had been away when the wire arrived and, as it was simply addressed to 'Milford Haven', Dickie's mother opened it, understood at once, and told the King the news when she saw him at Court that evening. The King told the Queen, the Queen told the Princes, the Princes the entourage. Within hours, the news was all over London.

Molly's friends told Molly and Molly told Wilfrid. By the time Dickie's letter arrived, asking for Edwina's hand, her father was in a sulk. Edwina's engagement was already proving more of a nuisance than he would have liked and now, on top of everything, he had been by-passed. Dickie, Georgie and Dickie's mother wrote letters of apology but Wilfrid still complained, making the most of being able to grumble about the King. He absolutely refused to publish a formal announcement, saying that it could just as well wait until Edwina was home at the end of April. This was a blow. As Dickie pointed out, Wilfrid's delaying 'may put the King's back up'.

Edwina did not allow these worries to spoil the rest of her stay. Mrs Greville took her to the jewellers; Sir Edwin Lutyens showed her his plans for New Delhi. She was taken to Fatehpur Sikri, a great, empty city built on a rock overlooking the simmering plain, and to the Taj Mahal and the Fort at Agra, 'travelling in the most lovely Special, with torch bearers all along the line.' Dickie was jealous when Edwina told him about her 'new captives'. One was Lutyens (he gave a dinner party for Edwina, 'with a Tom-Tom band – most weird'), another Lord Cromer, who wrote a sweet letter reflecting on the happiness of married life. She was invited to hunt game in South India by Lord Willingdon, King George's favourite tennis partner, now Governor of Madras. 'I shall write very strong letters to Willingdon and Lutyens', Dickie promised, 'leading innocent flappers astray!' Lord Reading was completely besotted. He took Edwina to hear a debate in the Legislative Assembly and insisted that she come with him to Meerut, first to the Circuit House and then to the races, where he laid on luncheon with strawberries and cream: '. . . not much chance of escape either . . . one hour and forty minutes in the Rolls . . .' The Viceroy was also making what Edwina described as 'frantic efforts' to arrange her passage home. Lady Falmouth and her daughter Pamela were returning in the *Macedonia* on 22 April, before the heat in Delhi became unbearable, and they could escort Edwina back to England. The ship was said to be full but intervention from the top secured better quarters than Edwina could have got for herself: a two-berth cabin on the shady side of the promenade deck. She did not forget this lesson.

Dickie was now in the north, on the last stage of the Indian part of the tour. He watched the clock, counting the months, weeks and days until he and Edwina could be married – although Wilfrid still dithered and the engagement had not yet been announced. At every bazaar Dickie bought useful things for their life together: Kashmiri tablecloths made out of shawls, papier-mâché candelabra, special polo sticks, cheaper than the ones at home, and a game called 'polo on foot', which he was sure Edwina would like. He would have got carpets, prayer rugs and saddle-bags: 'Only my overdraft at the bank stopped me from buying much more.'

Dickie still worried about the huge difference between Edwina's future income and his own. He had been brought up to be careful with shillings and guineas and to accept that he could not live as expensively as Cousin David and his other friends. The prospect of marrying someone who would have access to tens, even hundreds, of thousands was pleasant but unnerving and Dickie wished to assure himself, not just Edwina, that he did not intend to be knocked off course. Edwina did not like discussing money and, remembering Wilfrid's self-deprecating jokes, found talk of it embarrassing. She thought Dickie's fears well-meant but theoretical, for until her marriage she had no access to her fortune and after it she intended to share all she had with her husband.

Dickie, however, wanted everything fair and square – and some decisions would not wait. Edwina had said that he should continue his polo, but did she know how expensive it would be? Then there was the question of servants. Edwina had agreed that Dickie needed a man to look after his clothes. Was that all right? Edwina answered all Dickie's questions, agreed with everything, and privately thought his agonizing sweet but pointless. The most complicated issue was the car. In Delhi Edwina had told Dickie that she would give him a Rolls-Royce as a wedding present. Buying a new one took months, for each car was designed and fitted like a bespoke suit and there was a long waiting list. Then the Prince offered to sell Edwina his own. The Duke of York was roped in to arrange matters with Barkers, the Rolls-Royce coach-builders. Pages of instructions came from Dickie: the car was to be lengthened, Dickie being so much taller, and repainted. Every letter had a list of suggestions. There was the complex matter of registration and licence, all direct descendants of George III or George IV (Dickie, for once, could not remember which) being exempt from taxes on carriages, armorial bearings, dogs and suchlike. They were also excused petrol tax and if a crest were painted on the car no extra licences need be paid. Would Edwina object to the car's being registered in Dickie's name? And would she find out whether the exemption applied to the new Road Fund Licence? And would she see to everything? Edwina was not surprised when Dickie wrote to ask her to arrange for Weller to retrieve a razor strop he had left hanging on a peg on the inside of the bathroom door of No. 2 Tent in the grounds of Viceregal Lodge. He had a spare, he said, so it did not really matter – but Edwina knew that it did.

Just as Dickie tried to find a way of talking to Edwina about money, so he cast about for the right tone of voice in which to express his feelings for her. Delicate and protective letters would suddenly launch into enthusiastic recollections of their kisses and of those bits of Edwina he had been allowed to see: hands, feet, arms as far as the elbows, legs as far as the knees, her face and neck, plus a discreet glimpse of her breasts, which he named, after the First World War campaign medals, Mutt and Jeff. This was a different Dickie from the person Edwina had met at Cowes. She had woken him so suddenly that he was dizzy. No wonder. Like her mother, Edwina was attractive, but with better health, a tougher intelligence and greater willpower. She was as demure as a volcano waiting to erupt. Old men recognized it, young ones sensed it. At twenty, Edwina combined Wilfrid's handsome features and long limbs with Maudie's gentle, flirtatious manner. A strong face and a young body, an appearance and character that seemed to mix feminine and masculine, all made Edwina unusual and exciting. Dickie longed for their reunion.

Faced with a *fait accompli*, Lady Reading had decided to be motherly, so that when Dickie briefly abandoned the Prince before they left India for good, he found himself enthusiastically welcomed at Viceregal Lodge. This was in mid-March. In Delhi the thermometer continued to climb and those who could left for the hills. Dickie and Edwina rode, talked and danced in a shimmering haze. 'Three perfect days', Dickie wrote, 'then three very sad months . . . and then (let's hope) three generations of bliss'. He gave Hiscock a letter for Weller to slip under Edwina's pillow after he had gone; it contained his first – and only – poem.

116

An Indian Morning

Oh female of ridiculous dimensions
Your proclivity for dancing is absurd
Though your terpsichorian effort far surpasses
All the animated annals of the world

Was it his partner or Dickie's head that was spinning?

Edwina did not pine. The Viceroy had promised to send her to the pink city of Jaipur, withdrawn the invitation because he thought the place unsafe for women, and now decided to solve the problem by escorting her himself. The day after Dickie left, they set off. Lady Reading, Sister Meikle, her nurse, and Colonel Carey Evans came too, with a troop of ADCs and servants, for the expedition had become a full-scale shoot. To his amazement Lord Reading got a tiger and, to prove it, insisted that he and Edwina be photographed with the corpse, after Lady Reading had poked at it with her parasol to make sure that it was dead. The tiger hunt was so successful that Edwina dared to ask the Viceroy if they might try pig-sticking. Certainly not, Lord Reading replied. If she came too close to an enraged boar, she might be attacked, and, unlike the men, would have no spear with which to defend herself. This was not good enough for Edwina. Before breakfast she stole off with the ADCs, saw them take five pigs and got back without the Readings knowing. Dickie was aghast when she told him. He admired her spirit but it was dangerous sport. He realized later that this adventure was typical: Edwina liked taking risks and, being competitive, would not be prevented from doing anything he was allowed to do.

Back in Delhi the heat was 'simply grilling'. Edwina had just enough energy to interview the local Rolls-Royce agent, who had brought samples of enamel. 'I chose a rather nice grey', better, she thought, than the colour the Prince had selected for his next car, which she suspected would fade, like curtains. Work on the Rolls was moving quickly, more so than Wilfrid, who had still done nothing about announcing the engagement, although, after more than a month's delay, he had at least sent Dickie a wire, giving his consent.

Now that Dickie had left India, Edwina wanted to be on her way home. Not before she had made one last expedition, a trip in Dickie's footsteps to the North West Frontier and Kashmir. For a day or two it looked as if she would not get there, for there was trouble at the border. In any case, Lady Reading complained, the Viceroy had too much work in Delhi, otherwise they would have escaped long ago to Simla, in the Himalayan foothills, to which staff, servants, clerks, files and reference books shifted every summer. Lord Reading was 'worried to death', Edwina thought, over the possible repercussions of Gandhi's recent arrest, the only reference to politics she made in any of her letters home. She persuaded the Viceroy that Delhi in late March was no place for clear thinking and on those grounds he was at last induced to leave his desk for the hills and, first, for a visit to the Maharajah of Alwar.

The Viceroy's Metre Gauge train was ordered for the Readings, Edwina and their personal servants, the Viceregal Narrow Gauge for the assistants, sixty servants and the luggage. Programmes were printed: 11 p.m. to 4.24 a.m.: Sleep in Siding; 6.45 a.m. to 7 a.m.: Early Tea and Hot Water; 8.30am: Arrival at Maharaj station, 31-Gun Salute. Motors were allocated for the short trip from the Railway Station to Lansdowne Palace, the Viceroy's base at Alwar: Racing Rolls (Police), Daimler (Viceroy), New Rolls (Vicereine), State Rolls (Edwina), Crown Magnetic (Nurse and Surgeon), Touring Rolls (General Crozier), followed by four lorries and an omnibus for the servants and baggage, and, for the shooting expedition, two Sedans, a Packard and a Wolseley. The Viceroy did not travel light.

This caravan was for a three-day visit, two nights being spent at the Maharajah's shooting-box, four times the size of Buckingham Palace, beside a lake in the jungle. Lady Reading, heavily veiled, parasol in one hand and binoculars in the other, took her place in an armchair on the back of an elephant, to accompany her husband into the wild country. Someone wounded a tiger, which fled for miles up near-perpendicular inclines, Edwina and the Maharajah thundering behind on their elephants until the quarry was finally cornered. Edwina was exultant; this was better than hunting with the Hursley Hounds. They celebrated with a State Banquet, music and dancing. The Palace was illuminated, the gardens lit by torches. Edwina exchanged her torn riding clothes for a silk dress and covered her scratched arms with white kid gloves.

The Viceroy's party returned to Delhi for one night, before the long, hot journey to the North West Frontier. The road was filthy and dust lodged in their hair and caked their skin. At Peshawar the country was transformed: 'rather like Scotland', Edwina thought, but with orange blossom in the gardens. Her senses were sharpened by the

Edwina

Dickie

The wedding of the year

crisp air, the altitude, and their proximity to the frontier. There was a keen military vigour to life up here; the Viceroy's party was guarded day and night by fierce sentries, 'three or four deep, armed to the teeth'. Edwina was forbidden to go to the town or the bazaar, where there had been disturbances, but was taken instead to a rifle factory. Lord Reading inspected the Khyber Pass and, having pronounced it safe, agreed to let her go with an armed escort to look over the border into Afghanistan, riding between steep cliffs, through narrow defiles where for centuries there had been bloody ambushes. The place was bleak, shingly and precipitous, the twisting road made Edwina dizzy and she was 'quite ga ga from the sun', but she was enthralled by the long views 'right into Afghanistan and over the Hindu Kush', the sharp feeling of danger, the alertness of her guides. For the first time her letters came alive, as she described the mountains and the winding camel caravan she saw below in the valley: 'miles and miles, donkeys, children, goats, sheep, men, women, with all their worldly belongings, trekking back to Afghanistan . . . I've never seen anything so interesting'. Back at the Fort, the soldiers who had guarded her breathed more easily. Stress and the thin air had made everyone hungry and there, on the roof of the world, they stoked up on scones and chocolate cake, as if they had just returned from a shoot at Balmoral or Dunrobin. Edwina thought it the most wonderful expedition of her life.

Meanwhile more letters had come from Dickie. The Prince wanted to know when they were to be married, for he had offered to be their best man. As Dickie said to Edwina, 'Can't you see him tipping the verger?' All the Prince's brothers wanted to come to the wedding, especially the Duke of York, who had become, by post, very fond of Edwina. 'I wish you would not call me Sir in your letters,' he had said unstuffily, only two months before. 'I would much rather you called me Prince Bertie at all times. Please do this, will you?' *Renown* was now en route from Hong Kong to Yokohama. Poor Fruity was in bandages, for his pony had fallen on him during a polo match in Colombo, but otherwise the Prince's party was in good spirits, although everyone was tired of rubber factories, processions and visits to universities. Even Dickie sometimes wondered 'whether it was right to carry on with the Tour instead of going home with you and getting married at once'. Incidentally, had Edwina considered the question of the Banns? Had she by any chance read the Naval Marriage

Act and was she sure of Dickie's names? (Louis Francis Albert Victor Nicholas.) There was the matter of dress. Dickie had consulted the Prince and various authorities, all of whom agreed that, if the King consented, full dress should be worn. 'Naval weddings are nearly always in uniform,' Dickie explained, 'because it's an old custom and besides the average NO doesn't possess a tail coat . . .' Did Edwina approve? Next, the list of guests. 'I've started and find it a ghastly show'. They had better make separate lists and then compare notes. 'Why not get a note book to take in the *Macedonia* . . . If you put down each person or family and their address you'll find that you'll be kept quite busy.'

Edwina was too preoccupied to think of lists. She had left the Readings, and with Lord Rawlinson, the Commander-in-Chief, had travelled in a Special to Rawalpindi, to join Lady Falmouth and Pamela for a trip to Kashmir. For four days they stayed in Srinagar, a romantic jumble of medieval wooden houses, clustered round lakes and rivers. It was cool – Dickie had advised Edwina to wear tweed and furs – but the town was full of peach, almond and cherry blossom, with clumps of irises growing in every corner and small red and white tulips sprouting from turfy roofs. Three nights were spent at a little bungalow some miles up river, where the women walked and talked while the men hunted bear. A last picnic in deep snow in the mountains, nine thousand feet above Srinagar, and it was time to leave for Rawalpindi, Bombay and home. The drive down to the plain was hot, dusty and sad; the Windhams, Edwina's hosts in Kashmir, learnt on the day she left that their eldest son had been killed pig-sticking in Baroda. Dickie had been right; it was a dangerous game. The temperature was now 110 degrees and huge baths of ice were brought on to the train from 'Pindi to Bombay. Edwina and Pamela removed their dresses and sat in the tubs in their petticoats, which entertained the ADC but scandalized Lady Falmouth, especially when Edwina forgot to put her skirt back on before walking down the train. It was a relief to board *Macedonia*, where the Viceroy's ADC was waiting, laden with flowers and boxes of mangoes, the last of Lord Reading's many kindnesses.

Edwina fell into a deckchair, the coolest and most comfortable place from which to wave goodbye to India – and waited for a Colonel from the Khyber, who happened to be on board, to bring her soda water and pink jelly. She did not know how much of India she was bringing home, for the Viceroy's ADC had decided not to mention that he had also supervised the loading of innumerable tea-chests, containing Dickie's purchases and the heads and skins of the birds and animals he had shot, all labelled for delivery to Brook House.

CHAPTER TEN

A Fashionable Wedding

Time went backwards as *Macedonia* steamed anti-clockwise from east to west. Edwina returned to her old life, well chaperoned, under-occupied. No longer the centre of attention, she sat in the ship's writing-room, trying to make lists of wedding guests and finding it such a chore that at one point she wished she could be married in a registry office at ten o'clock in the morning. After the bright colours, clear light and wide spaces of India, *Macedonia* seemed drab and cramped. The only recreations were bridge and piquet and, until the ship met storms in the Red Sea, brisk walks round the deck. The small, conventional world from which Edwina had briefly escaped was closing in once more.

She endured the dreary days and early nights by thinking of the future. What about beginning their honeymoon with a week in Paris, she asked Dickie, 'going to the most awful places we can find?' Paris, Edwina believed, was where depravity could be got, although she knew next to nothing about it. She could not bear to be classed with the other unmarried innocents on board and, nonchalantly smoking cigarettes, tried bravely to appear older than she was. At Aden she bought sixteen long white ostrich feathers, their fronds like floating silk, of the sort worn by experienced beauties in her mother's day.

Dickie's chief indulgence was to write to Edwina, from Colombo, Kuala Lumpur, Singapore, Hong Kong, Japan. He spent hours working out how long his letters would take, which of Edwina's stops he should aim for, and how many days remained to their reunion, calculated both from the time of writing and the date at which she would be reading each letter. The Prince's postmaster did his best to answer Dickie's questions and by adroit mailing the ardent lover managed to ensure that a packet of correspondence awaited Edwina at every port. Dickie planned well ahead. Knowing that he would not be home until mid-1922, he had brought to India a Russian enamelled egg that had belonged to his aunt, the late Tsarina, to send back to

A Fashionable Wedding

Branksome as an Easter present for Edwina. Immersed in the logistical complexities of getting a registered parcel from Ceylon to arrive in Bournemouth on the right date, he had overlooked the fact that the whole exercise was unnecessary, since Georgie or the Duke of York would have willingly arranged a delivery. Convenience, however, was not the point. Dickie liked a challenge.

By the end of the first week in May, when Dickie had reached Yokohama and Edwina Marseilles, he could at last put on each letter the number of days until their marriage, for the King, prompted by the Duke of York, had suggested that the wedding should take place in the third week of July. He and the Queen had tactfully given a choice of dates, 18, 19 or 20 July, 'to suit Edwina's personal convenience'; she picked the 18th and asked Mrs Cassel to alert the bridesmaids. Wilfrid dug his heels in and refused to announce the engagement, let alone the date of the wedding, until Edwina was home. This was foolish, since there was bound to be another leak. Someone talked – the Prince of Wales was sure it was the King – and suddenly the engagement was OFFICIAL, placarded on newspaper posters all over London, in red letters four feet high, 'side by side', Mrs Cassel reported, 'with the Armstrong Murder Case'.

Dickie was in a fever of excitement. Each day, as he ripped another sheet from his Tear-Off Calendar, he thought of some new detail. The Chapel Royal would be too small, he said, having conferred with the Prince of Wales. Should Edwina not book St Margaret's, Westminster? People were writing to ask what wedding presents they would like; had she made a list? The Prince of Wales had offered a silver Triton, holding up a silver globe engraved in coloured enamel with the routes of the tours the cousins had made together, so Dickie was tracing a chart to be telegraphed to the Goldsmiths and Silversmiths Company. He was also mapping out the future. In Malaya the Prince had caught him buying children's toys: 'one girl and one boy, wouldn't it be divine, darling?' Now that the Battenberg name had been given up and Georgie had become Milford Haven, Dickie and Edwina would 'be practically founding the family of Mountbatten'.

That provoked another train of thought. Dickie wished to do nothing to embarrass this unborn Mountbatten family; 'after all, it's a young name, with nothing against it at present'. He had already told Edwina about his only business venture, a small investment in the Repeating Gramophone Company, of which he was director and

123

his friend Arthur Cotton the manager, chief engineer and salesman. It was unclear what, if anything, the company produced, still less what it sold, but its fortunes were precarious and its future uncertain. Advertising might boost sales but there were no funds. Should Dickie resign? 'If it went bust, people might start running down the Mountbattens'. This was small beer compared with Sir Ernest's sugar mills, iron mines, dams and rolling stock, but Dickie believed there was an expanding market for gramophones and Edwina believed in Dickie. She would pay the advertisers' bills and the company and the Mountbatten name would be safe. Arthur Cotton, much relieved, sent her six months' supply of gramophone needles by the next post.

Dickie was also nervous about the actual mechanics of starting the Mountbatten line: 'Please darling don't get fussed or frightened', he told Edwina, partly to reassure himself. 'I'm a very patient chap, just out to please you . . .' He had been considering where their joint initiation might best take place. Paris would certainly be fun but immediately after the wedding they would want to collapse somewhere not too far from London. There was a set of railway timetables in the library on *Renown* and Dickie had looked up non-stop trains from Paddington; the car could be sent on ahead. He now proposed that they take up 'a marvellous offer' from Cousin David, the loan of Tor Royal, the Prince's house near Plymouth. As its only permanent resident was a caretaker, they would be quite alone, except of course for 'your maid, my man, a cook and one or two housemaids'. Edwina need not worry about finding staff; Dickie already knew a splendid cook who kept a baker's shop on the Isle of Wight. The house, with only twelve main rooms, was 'delightfully small', so they would be quite domestic, and they could ride David's horses over the moor. Dickie would take Edwina to the Naval College at Dartmouth and a further inducement was the proximity of Princetown Jail, where the prison doctor, a friend of the Prince's detective, would show them round. Edwina was doubtless relieved to hear, three letters later, that since Tor Royal was only half-finished, 'David's offer is a wash-out'.

For Edwina had set her heart on Paris, which, since her first visit with Sir Ernest, Marjorie and Cousin Teddy, had represented freedom and sophistication. A reconnoitring expedition now seemed a good idea. Mrs Cassel agreed that Edwina should leave *Macedonia* at Marseilles and travel overland with Weller, stopping off in Paris to inspect summer and autumn fashions before ordering her trousseau.

A Fashionable Wedding

Marjorie would join her there, since Edwina could hardly roam the city on her own. She would also bring money; Edwina had exhausted her funds and when she arrived in Paris she had to borrow from the only person she knew, the manager of the Ritz, who cashed an IOU and considerately suggested that she stay not at his own hotel but more modestly at the Vouillement. 'Such a divine man', Edwina told Dickie, 'so it doesn't matter'. Together the cousins assaulted the smart shops behind the Champs Elysées. Edwina listed her successes: 'A divine dress, a dream, an evening dress, no *two*, and countless other things'. Dickie claimed to be as interested in Edwina's purchases as she had tried to be in his hunting trophies. One detail did catch his eye. Edwina warned him that skirts in Paris *'and*, I believe, in London', were now worn long and that he might never see her legs again. Dickie need not have worried. Hems were to hover between calf and ankle for months yet, before beginning a gradual upward journey to the centre of the knee, which they reached in 1926, remaining there, in Edwina's case, until 1952.

Cast-off admirers were waiting at home, 'various old lovers, as sweet as ever'. Edwina had returned in time for the start of the Season and, after a quiet Whitsuntide with Mrs Cassel at Branksome, she shot back to London for dinners, dances and plays. Brook House had been closed after Sir Ernest's death and would not be opened until the wedding, so Edwina stayed with the Brecknocks, slipping off to dance at Rector's: 'Marjorie was perfectly *furious*'. She assured Dickie that she was being *'very* good' and that her rejected beaux were 'perfectly sweet about our engagement'. Hugh Molyneux, for example, wrote her a manly letter, hoping fiercely that, 'by God, Dickie knows how lucky he is'.

Late nights left Edwina *'much* madder than usual', she said, and Dickie could only hope that his friends and relations were helping her keep her head. He did not realize how light their supervision was. Nada, for one, was a most unsuitable chaperone, for she liked noisy parties, fast driving, frenzied dancing and suggestive stories, and Georgie was too lazy and indulgent to interfere. Harold and Zia Wernher were so respectable that they did not dream that Edwina might be dancing at nightclubs without Dickie to protect her. Faithful Prince Bertie took Edwina aside when he saw her at dances, to talk admiringly of Dickie and the Prince of Wales, but he could not always be on hand to represent his cousin's interests. He did not like to upset his parents, who disapproved of much of Park Lane society and shrank from the very thought of nightclubs.

The unremitting flow of letters from Dickie was another reminder, if Edwina needed one, that she had already given her heart. Tokyo and Kyoto had been raided for furniture for their future home, he said: inlaid wooden puzzle-boxes, water-colours, seven hundred hand-painted place cards for the dinner table, two dozen menu holders, dwarf trees . . . He thought he had enough for a small exhibition. He would prepare tickets stating the origin of each object and have the whole lot sent to Edwina: 'Fishponds is so tiny, they'd swamp the place out'. Such an assortment had never yet been seen at Brook House, even in Sir Ernest's prime.

By now Dickie was tiring of the trip. The geisha parties were like children's entertainments; catching ducks in butterfly-nets was comic but a bore. There were two high points: the first a conducted tour of Japan's newest battleship, the *Mutsu*, which Dickie managed to examine inside and out, for his guides had no idea that the Prince's cousin was a professional sailor and the Japanese Commander, who might have known better, was away. 'As regards Japan from the point of view of a world power', Dickie observed, 'my visit has been an eye-opener.'

The second triumph was also the result of Dickie's curiosity and persistence. The Emperor had presented the Prince and his retinue with handsome Japanese costumes, 'worth over £50!', said Dickie in awe, 'with our family crests worked into them', just the thing for a fancy-dress ball or 'dinner one night at home'. Dickie thought Edwina should have one as well. The purchase took three hours, the display of garments being preceded by cigarettes, Japanese tea, cakes eaten with chopsticks and commemorative photographs. That was not the end of the story. Colonel Yamamoto was asked to write to the Japanese Embassy in London, to arrange for someone to show Edwina how to tie the *obi*; Dickie interviewed an expert, who taught him how Edwina should dress her hair, 'but you needn't worry specially'.

It did not seem strange to Dickie's companions that he should spend the morning in a shop, discussing the symbolism of the Japanese coiffure. The whole party was in a daze, particularly the Prince. Although he tried to be cheerful, encouraging Dickie to talk about wedding arrangements and the parties they would have once they returned to England, their conversations generally ended gloomily. Dickie assured his melancholy cousin that he would always be welcome at Brook House. 'I made him promise that he would never wait to be invited but was just to ring up to ask if we were in and if he could come round at any time of the day'. The *ménage* might go further: 'I also said that he could keep a suit of clothes in my room so if he motored down from hunting he could stop and have a bath and change into his own suit and stay for dinner'. The Prince missed Freda Dudley Ward, Dickie missed Edwina. By the time they got to Suez the two of them were in a frenzy of lovesickness.

Renown arrived at Plymouth on 20 June. Georgie Milford Haven was there to meet her, with the Duke of York. He brought two important communications: the news that the King had agreed that No. 3 uniforms could be worn for the wedding, and a note from Edwina. She and Nada had considered motoring down to Plymouth, 'but,' she told Dickie, 'being extremely squashed by everyone else we refrained'. She also explained that she would not be there to meet the Special Train at Paddington the next day: 'there would be such a crowd'. Edwina was right. Not only the public, but the King and Queen, all their courtiers and most of the Cabinet were waiting on the platform, with a convoy of State carriages in attendance to bring everyone back to Buckingham Palace for a celebration lunch. Dickie enjoyed the fuss; to the Prince it was like travelling to a wake. On the way Dickie waved his cocked hat to Edwina, who was watching the procession from the balcony of Bath House, but they did not meet until the early evening, at Marjorie's house. For the time being, Dickie could stop counting the hours.

Dickie had given Edwina his news in his letters. Now he wanted to talk about his emotions. Edwina preferred to go over their programme. Each reunion, for the next forty years, was to be the same. Their first evening was spent in public, dining and dancing at Claridge's and afterwards at Lady Sondes' dance at the Hyde Park Hotel. The pattern of the Mountbattens' future life was set from that moment: 'alone' meant being surrounded by friends and relations. 'You know I'll always do what you want and go where you want – off duty', Dickie promised, when Edwina outlined the plans people were making to entertain them before their wedding. He would agree to everything, asking only that she leave some evenings when they could dance together. Best of all would be a few nostalgic meals at 'our little restaurant opposite the Rolls shop'; this was wishful thinking. Everyone wanted to see them. Lady Cunard gave a luncheon party, a dinner and two dances, Mrs Corrigan a dance, Mrs Greville a dinner and a dance. They had tea with Mrs Vanderbilt, back in London for the Season, dined and danced at the Devonshires, the Blandfords, Lady Carnarvon's and the house of the Chilean Minister. There was also Princess Mary's costume ball for the London Hospitals. The Prince of Wales was present; asked how he was, he replied tensely, 'Bearing up'.

Luckily neither Edwina nor Dickie was easily fatigued. The first weekend after Dickie's return was spent with Mrs Cassel, who had moved into Forest House at Ham, while Brook House was closed. There Dickie was presented to Mrs Bisch, who immediately arranged a dinner and dance, to which she pressed Dickie to bring the Prince of Wales. Next, Edwina and Dickie lunched with Dickie's mother, who presented her future daughter-in-law with a splendid ruby for Cartier to set as an engagement ring, and asked Edwina to call her 'Aunt Victoria' until they thought of something better, which they never did. Mrs Cassel entertained Dickie's mother and sisters, Alice and Louise, and Alice's children, 'the Greek Princesses', as the infatuated gossip columnists called them. On 25 June, Dickie's twenty-second birthday, she gave a non-stop lunch, tea and dinner party at Ham, at which Dickie was served with slices of Edwina's history by an assortment of people brought up to talk to him: Colonel Jenkins; Philip Sassoon; Mrs Joshua, Sir Ernest's devoted companion; Margaret Lindsay, who remembered Miss Potts's School. Aunt Victoria gave a wary luncheon party for Wilfrid and Molly, and Georgie and Nada were invited to Broadlands, where Nada politely admired the interior decoration and tried not to tease Wilfrid, who was nervous, not unreasonably. Wilfrid and Molly, Dickie and Edwina were invited to dine with the King and Queen at Buckingham Palace; Molly was furious when the engagement was cancelled because of Field Marshal Sir Henry Wilson's assassination the previous afternoon. Harold and Zia Wernher gave a dinner with balalaika music and Mrs Greville assembled a weekend house party at Polesden for Dickie and Edwina, the Brecknocks, the Wernhers, Grace Vanderbilt and Fruity. Edwina also took Dickie to stay at Moulton Paddocks, where he saw the conservatory, the electric piano, the stables and the kitchen where she had once made sweets. He got there just in time. Marjorie's parents had taken the house while the Newmarket races were on and after that the estate was to be sold. Between visits to Broadlands, Branksome, Forest House and Fishponds, Dickie drove with Edwina to Heathfield to see her sister. 'It's always been my ambition to get lost in a girls' school', he said when they met, but, despite this unoriginal opening, he was a hit with Mary. 'Not as good at tennis as Prince Bertie', she observed, but Dickie had at least been county champion at tiddlywinks.

Without a fast car Dickie and Edwina would have been unable to manage their programme: Netley, Portsmouth, Polesden, Ham, London, Broadlands, Newmarket, London, speeding along dusty roads, at forty miles an hour. Every second counted; at Newmarket Dickie watched to see when the King would leave, hurried Edwina out after the fifth race, skilfully positioned the Rolls among the royal convoy and so got up to London in two hours and ten minutes. Edwina wanted to do her share of driving and when she and Marjorie returned from Paris they had practised manoeuvring the Rolls. 'Don't tell the Prince', Edwina said, 'or he'll have a fit as it isn't paid for'. She loved driving and now thought she might get a second car for herself, 'a little Talbot Darracq or an AC', since the Rolls was cumbersome and she had trouble changing gear: 'Appalling', she told Dickie, 'I hope *you* make a noise'. Now the car was his, Dickie had a fine time with Georgie, examining the engine, setting the mileometer and experimenting with the accelerator. Although Dickie and Edwina were both keen to take the wheel, they decided that for long journeys they had better have an experienced chauffeur, not so much for driving as for tidying up after mishaps. The first of these occurred en route to Broadlands, when a tyre burst, 'after only 1000 miles', Dickie indignantly told the manufacturer, '*and* the 1st spare wheel had a faulty valve'. A Mr Rasdill was promptly engaged.

There was also business to complete. Dickie and Wilfrid discussed the marriage settlement, which Cousin Felix then translated into lawyer's prose. Dickie made his will and Georgie witnessed it. New passports were prepared and hastily amended when the King made Dickie a Knight Commander of the Victorian Order two days before the wedding. A valet, Thorogood, was taken on, kitted out and instructed in his new master's special express way of dressing and, to be shipshape for the honeymoon, Dickie had his hair cut and his teeth restopped.

Edwina Mountbatten

This was nothing compared with Edwina's preparations. For days she discussed, ordered, fitted and fitted again the quantities of garments in her trousseau: dresses, sports clothes, hats, shoes and underclothing. There were outfits for the links and tennis court and 'clothes of indoor indolence', as the fashion magazines described the tea gowns made from the Indian fabrics Dickie had brought home. Even Maudie had not been arrayed like this. The most effusive prose was kept for what the columnists circumspectly referred to as 'Miss Ashley's exquisite lingerie'. Her undergarments, made by Savigny and David of Dover Street, were displayed to the press a week before the wedding, which horrified Queen Mary, who had forbidden any description, let alone exhibition, of the underclothing in Princess Mary's trousseau. Pages were given to the triple ninons, crêpes de Chine, batistes and washing satin; to the hand-made laces, hemstitching and drawn-thread work. Nothing like this had been seen before: straight sleeveless nightgowns with transparent tops in a Cook's tour of lace – Valenciennes, Brussels, Point de Paris, Flandres, Milan, Point de Rosaline, Binches, Point d'Angleterre, Point de Venise. Ribbons, wild roses and true lovers' knots were worked in everywhere. There were slips and knickers in startling colours: old rose, deep mauve and yellow ochre, adorned with parchment-coloured lace. Those who called at Dover Street were glad to see that the collection would be properly looked after: each set of undergarments was folded over a large, perfumed satin pad, with an embroidered satin envelope to hide the whole arrangement, perfectly combining modesty and ostentation. Every item was embroidered with a tiny cypher, E and M intertwined in a diamond-shaped frame, although it was unlikely that the maids at Brook House would mix up these frilly cobwebs with other people's laundry.

Dickie's preoccupations were more down to earth. 'By the way', he told Wilfrid, 'I notice that they still have the paveway up in places at the Park Lane end of Brook Street'. Perhaps Colonel Ashley could write to the Clerk of the Borough to hurry up the work: 'I don't like to think even of the ghastly congestion . . . on the 18th, besides the inconvenience to various Crowned Heads'. Wilfrid felt neglected, for Mrs Cassel, who was paying for the wedding, had taken charge of the presents, invitations, arrangements at the church and the reception. He threw himself into traffic management, working so zealously that he was well prepared when, three months later, he was made

A Fashionable Wedding

Parliamentary Secretary to the Ministry of Transport and the Office of Works.

In tackling any great undertaking – an examination, a battle, his approaching marriage – Dickie followed a simple rule. Having reconnoitred the ground and checked his information and supplies, the vital thing, he believed, was to get plenty of sleep. On the three nights before the wedding he dined quietly, went to bed early and rose late. For exercise he walked across the Park with the Princes, David, Bertie, George and Henry, to lunch at Buckingham Palace. Edwina, on the other hand, spun faster and faster, rushing through last-minute fittings, dashing over to Brook House for conferences with Mrs Cassel, squeezing in confidential chats with old friends; 'hectic one', Dickie called her. The day before the wedding was taken up with rehearsals. In the late morning Edwina and Dickie went to St Margaret's to see Catherine Wendell marry Lord Porchester, useful, Dickie said, as 'we picked up some tips'. As a naval officer and a Battenberg, Dickie was used to parades but he thought that Edwina needed coaching in her first star part. He was determined that their own ceremony should be perfectly choreographed, words, music, uniforms, flowers, fanfares all working together, and that Edwina should be sure of every move. Lord Porchester and his bride did not know how keenly they were watched.

Edwina was to have seven bridesmaids: Mary, her cousins Joan Pakenham and Lady Mary Ashley-Cooper, and Dickie's four nieces, Margarita, Theodora, Cecile and Sophie. All had longed to be chosen but now the moment had come their knees turned to water. It was not the drill that made them nervous, for Cousin Dickie was exacting but kind. What alarmed them was their wardrobe, which Edwina had designed. Delphinium blue was the fashionable colour – it also matched Edwina's eyes – and to achieve the right effect the bridesmaids' dresses had been made in layers of blue crêpe and mauve georgette, which hung in folds and, as they strode along, accumulated between their knees. The dresses were tied with sashes of mauve and green shot silk, which kept slipping, since the smaller girls had no waists to speak of and the older ones were obliged to follow fashion and drape the fabric round their hips. Each bridesmaid wore a silver lace cap, with a floppy brim, and, although their green shoes were comfortable, their silver silk stockings could not be prevented from wrinkling round the ankles. Dressing the bridesmaids as flappers was not a good idea.

Edwina Mountbatten

It is not surprising that Edwina's common sense had deserted her. All ideas of proportion had disappeared. Brook House was crammed with wedding presents, Dickie's souvenirs having been temporarily relegated to the cellars and his animal skins sent to the taxidermist. Detectives had been hired to guard the jewellery, displayed in glass cases: a diamond pendant from Queen Alexandra, tiaras and rings from Wilfrid and Mrs Cassel, jewelled brooches, boxes and clocks from Maharajahs, Rajahs and the Aga Khan, silver candlesticks and gold wine-coolers, innumerable pairs of links for Dickie, and a set of onyx and diamond waistcoat buttons from Lady Cunard, for which he unfortunately thanked Mrs Vanderbilt by mistake. Geordie Sutherland sweetly gave Edwina the diamond bracelet she had formerly returned, Mrs Greville sent diamond hair ornaments, links for Dickie, and a silver inkstand and bellpush for Brook House, which did not require them. There were useful presents – shooting sticks, a barograph, a telescope and an aneroid barometer – and holy ones: a cut-glass bottle of Jordan water, for instance, from Dickie's old tutor, the Reverend Lawrence Long. Some were home-made: two pairs of knitted shooting stockings; a lamp with a hand-painted shade from Nada's father, Grand Duke Michael of Russia; and from Mr Asquith a volume of his own *Occasional Addresses*. Other books were nautical: two lives of Nelson, the *Works* of Captain Marryat, and *More Sea Fights of the Great War*. Nurse Harrison scored by choosing Kipling. Close friends, advised by Dickie, gave kit for the honeymoon: maps of Europe from the Brecknocks, of Spain from Freda Dudley Ward and of England, Wales and Scotland from Audrey Coats; travelling rugs, luxuriously fitted dressing-cases, leather cushions, silver picnic kettles, a portable egg-boiler and, from Arthur Cotton, a dance gramophone. Aunt Victoria gave Edwina a tiara with five stars in diamonds and pearls. The Rolls-Royce, Edwina's gift to Dickie, now sported a present from the Wernhers, a mascot of a silver sailor, signalling the call-up sign with red and yellow semaphore flags.

The 18th was drizzly but by midday the crowds outside Brook House were so large that the butler called the police. Edwina and her bridesmaids practised the management of her train, acres of woven silver cloth, covered with antique lace, given by Mrs Cassel. On her head Edwina wore a wreath of orange blossom, mounted on silver wire, a crystal dewdrop fixed to each flower. Her dress had the simplicity that is achieved only by the expenditure of much time and money. Straight, with no acknowledgement of bosom, waist or hips, it fell to her ankles in a sheet of silver, tied halfway down by two sashes embroidered with pearls, diamonds and crystals. Levering the bride into and out of the motor was the most taxing part of the ceremony, the bridesmaids valiantly struggling with her train and their own bouquets of delphiniums and trailing silver ribbon. Edwina carried only a single Madonna lily. St Margaret's was filled with delphiniums, so that Dickie, half closing his eyes, could imagine himself at sea.

'By 3 p.m.', Dickie noted in his diary, 'we were married', and to the music of Mendelssohn's Wedding March he piloted Edwina out of the church and into the world, beneath an arch of swords held by naval officers from *Renown* and *Repulse*. Edwina, who was unpainted, bit her lips to redden them, as she faced the wall of newspaper and cinema photographers. The cheering populace waved paper flags and, when the rain came on, their umbrellas. The bride and groom climbed into Dickie's Rolls, to which a party of sailors attached first an old shoe and then themselves, and, panting and heaving for the newsreel cameras, the men hauled the motor away from the church. Once round the corner, a flag-draped motor lorry took over to pull the Rolls the rest of the way to Park Lane.

At Brook House, Howard Howes, the Court florists, had transformed Sir Ernest's marble staircase into a grove of ten-foot orange trees, hung with fruit, and at the head of the stairs sat Mrs Cassel, in a black poke-bonnet lined with white. Gigantic bronze and white lilies decorated the reception rooms, the hall was lined with delphiniums so tall as to be unnatural, and every spare corner held carnations, in memory of Sir Ernest. Eight hundred guests tried not to knock over these arrangements; this was difficult for those who, like Molly, wore extensive hats. The servants hung over the balconies to get a better view. One housemaid never forgot the apparition of Queen Alexandra, in a gown of blue and gold, with a gold hat sprouting blue ostrich feathers. Dickie made a speech, called Edwina, 'my fiancée', and handed her his sword to cut the cake, so lavishly decorated that it was difficult to know where to begin. The top tier was shaped like a crown, with sugar icing instead of ermine, the whole creation tricked out with miniature anchors, sails and hawsers. Tiny lifebuoys and little lifeboats hung from silver davits, a pessimistic addition. Dickie presented each bridesmaid with a brooch, not naval crowns, as they had feared, but elegant rectangular diamond clips that would come in useful when they were grown up. At last, in a pink dress with a brown cloak, a shower of rose leaves and rice, Edwina left Brook House and, with Dickie at the wheel, they trundled off down Park Lane. The coast being clear, the guests devoured the remains of the cake; some also pocketed its ornaments. Mrs Jenkins was horrified; more so when she found that all the carnations had disappeared as well.

Dickie had estimated that they would need two hours to reach Broadlands, which Molly had offered them for the first part of their honeymoon, but the journey took longer because a fuse kept going in the Rolls and every dozen miles he had to rig up a repair. At one stop they came across a man Dickie had met in India. 'May I introduce, well, I suppose, my wife?' said the bridegroom, turning pink. At Romsey a crowd waited to greet them and, to the sound of cheers and the Abbey bells, they chugged into Broadlands, meeting the last stragglers from a Band of Hope fête that had been held that afternoon in the park. Dinner was waiting, light but nourishing, and a fire was burning in the bedroom.

Both Dickie and Edwina were nervous, not least because they had little idea of what was expected. Nurse Harrison had given Edwina a last-minute biology lesson, but Dickie had only instinct to rely on. They were determined to do things properly: Edwina's lace-trimmed trousseau was a step in that direction, although the mixture of rose-buds and swansdown, mauve and ochre satin, indicated that she was not sure whether to play the sweetheart or the vamp. They were tired; the shades of their relations hovered disconcertingly about the room. Nevertheless, as Dickie recalled on the first anniversary of their marriage: 'We both thought it part of our duty to try . . . weren't we fools!!' He did not wish to distress his bride. Sensibly, they went to sleep, woke early and carried on from there.

It was a curious interlude. The Mountbattens were at Broadlands for what Dickie described later as 'four days of perfect, wonderful bliss', but it was not unadulterated. On the first day Wilfrid and Molly came down by train to open a church fair in the grounds. At least the Ashleys had enough tact not to arrive until the afternoon, which was as well, since Edwina and Dickie stayed in bed until lunchtime. The press infiltrated the fairgoing public and next day surprising pictures appeared in the newspapers, showing the honeymoon couple walking dreamily through the garden with the bride's father alongside, while in the background her stepmother, clutching an exhausted Pekinese, addressed the fairgoers through a microphone. After tea Edwina and Dickie drove the Ashleys to the station, where the Rolls broke down again. On the second day they made their first official visit, to the cinema in Romsey, to see the Pathé Gazette newsfilm of the wedding. Edwina and Dickie were beginning to feel like a couple; seeing themselves together, jerkily immortalized in black and white, confirmed it. The newspapers had cloyingly described the engagement and wedding as a fairy story; Dickie, for whom pictures were worth any number of words, described it as 'a movie script'. Already, after two days of marriage, the Mountbattens' private life and public appearances were becoming one and the same.

CHAPTER ELEVEN

Meeting the World

O ther couples leave the stage after their weddings, to get used to each other and to allow their friends and relations time to adjust. Edwina and Dickie did not retire. Only one day of their honeymoon was spent alone, pottering through the lanes in the Rolls, meeting no one. This was disappointing for, having been the centre of attention, they found it strange to be left to themselves. They called on all those relations who lived within forty miles: Milford Havens, Wernhers, Jenkinses, Aunt Victoria and her friend, Nona Crichton, her former lady-in-waiting. Dickie and Edwina confirmed their marriage by displaying it to others.

Broadlands was not the ideal place to practise being a couple. On the fifth day of their honeymoon the Mountbattens returned to London and that evening took the next step in joint domestic life by giving their first dinner party at Brook House. There were two guests, the Prince and Fruity, who, as bachelors, made their hosts feel more married than ever. Edwina and Dickie had the place more or less to themselves, for Mrs Cassel had tactfully removed herself to Branksome, keeping only a set of rooms for occasional use. With Miss Underhill's help, they interviewed a butler and gave instructions for the arrangement and decoration of their bedrooms, dressing-rooms and bathrooms. This business was fitted into a single day, together with shopping, lunch with Dickie's sisters and nieces, dinner with Wilfrid and the Brecknocks and an expedition to *The Dover Road* with Dickie's Uncle Arthur, Duke of Connaught, a play chosen for its geographic relevance, since this was the route they were taking next morning.

A cluster of relations and friends was at Victoria to see the Mountbattens off, along with the station master and the manager of Thomas Cook. Everyone was gratifyingly deferential: the station master looked after them at Dover, the *commissaire spécial* met them at Calais and the manager of the Ritz received them on the steps of the hotel. Dickie logged these courtesies in his daily diary, with other highlights of the trip: reserved compartments, best cabins, the principal suite at the Ritz. He recognized, however, that all this was not simply a tribute to himself but also to the soundness of Edwina's credit.

Edwina had made Dickie promise that they would see the most startling entertainments Paris could provide. Alas, their three days in the city were pleasantly sedate, for he had no idea where to look for exciting clubs and suggestive revue. On their last evening the Mountbattens dined at the hotel and went to bed early before their departure for Spain. Dickie had spent an entire afternoon planning the route to the south, marking the new road maps, plotting the distance a fully-loaded Rolls-Royce might cover in a day, identifying and booking suitable hotels at every stop. To his amazement, Edwina was annoyed when he told her what a quick and uncomplicated journey he had arranged. She did not like decisions being made on her behalf and, had she been consulted, she would have chosen a meandering route, stopping at random. To please her, Dickie cancelled the reservations.

They set off via Versailles, pausing for a picnic lunch in a quiet road off the N10. Although Edwina felt seedy, she shared the driving; Weller and Rasdill sat in the back among the luggage, Thorogood having gone on by railway to Spain, taking the heavy baggage. The first overnight stop was at Tours. The last Saturday in July, the beginning of the French summer holiday, was no time to be looking for accommodation and the Hôtel Métropole could find only one poky room for the Mountbattens, with makeshift lodgings for the maid and chauffeur in a house nearby. After a cramped night in what Dickie described as 'a so-called double bed', Edwina agreed that in the circumstances it was wiser to telegraph ahead for rooms. Even this system was not foolproof. Dickie found the Hôtel de Londres at Bergerac 'thrilled at our arrival' but the Mountbattens' bedroom was beside the main drain and the hot water boiler exploded in the bathroom. Edwina and Dickie were both sleeping badly. They were jumpy and insecure, convinced that a prowler was trying to get in to steal Edwina's jewels. For the rest of the trip they stayed at grander establishments, in rooms with double doors and high, shuttered windows.

They also kept to the main highway, the lanes being muddy, rutted and full of cows. Each day they tried to beat their own record, speeding down through Biarritz to San Sebastian, towards the mountains and the sea. Six days from Paris and an hour from Santander, Dickie's royal relations awaited them. Through the dust came a procession of cars, no more than half a dozen, for in the holidays only a small retinue of detectives and court officials accompanied King Alfonso and Queen Ena. The King had a fine moustache and wore a flat cap at an angle. He looked rakish, as he meant to. There were kisses and compliments and then he carried Edwina off to his own car, while the Queen got into Dickie's Rolls and the entourage followed politely behind. The Queen was twice related to Dickie's family, her mother, Princess Beatrice, being his mother's aunt and her father his father's brother. Now in her mid-thirties, she was tall and elegant. Edwina got on well with the Queen, who took her shopping and lent her a mantilla, comb and fan for parties, but Alfonso made her feel uncomfortable. When they went motoring, Edwina tried to stay with Dickie, or manoeuvred herself into the same car as the Queen or the two princes.

The other hazard was the bull ring. On the first afternoon the Mountbattens were taken to watch three famous matadors fight at the arena in Santander. They found it hard to stomach: 'the first part with horses', Dickie wrote in his diary, 'is quite revolting'. Three days later they endured a short visit behind the scenes to see the bulls being prepared for the mid-week fight; Edwina felt so ill that afterwards she escaped to bed, missing lunch. The Queen suspected morning sickness and sent for the royal doctor, who became quite flustered when he realized that his distinguished patient had no idea why she was being so thoroughly examined. Dickie was stunned when the doctor took him aside and explained that 'Votre Altesse', as he pleasingly called the English visitor, was not about to become a father.

Alfonso insisted that they see one more bullfight before he left for Deauville. Edwina refused, so Dickie went without her; the King had awarded him the Grand Cross of Isabella the Catholic and he did not wish to seem ungrateful. Luckily he saw and heard little, his eyes and ears being blocked by a raging cold, caught while swimming with Edwina off the rocks. Magdalena, the summer palace, stood on a peninsula that jutted into the Bay of Biscay, and the water was freezing cold – another disappointment, for Edwina had supposed that they would sit on warm sands and scamper in and out of the kindly ocean. There was little to do. Their days were devoted to the princes,

Meeting the World

Alfonsito and poor deaf mute Jaime, and the Duchess of Aosta's boys, two enormous dukes who turned up with their mother. Alfonsito liked being driven at top speed in the Rolls but, after Dickie first squashed an astonished dog and then lurched into a pothole, breaking the front spring, he and Edwina decided it was time to leave. They drove carefully back to Biarritz, managing to upset a cartload of pigs, abandoned the car and Rasdill at the Rolls depot there, and decanted themselves, Weller, Thorogood and the luggage on to the overnight *train de luxe* for Paris.

Dickie's plan was to drive east to Germany, to introduce Edwina to Hesse and his Hessian relations and revisit the castles, palaces and shooting lodges where he had spent the happiest part of his childhood. While they waited for the car, he spread out the maps, taking an hour or two off to shoot up the Eiffel Tower while Edwina looked at hats. Dickie had tried to pick out an attractive route but the journey to the border was grim. The Great War had been fought across this country, inch by inch, and the villages were devastated, the fields ruined, the roads so bad that they bent the luggage grid. Verdun, where the Mountbattens spent the night, was, Dickie said, 'a mass of shambles'.

It was dark when the Mountbattens reached Wolfsgarten, the Grand Duke's summer palace, not far from Darmstadt, where Dickie's Uncle Ernie and his second wife, Aunt Onor, Princess Eleanore of Somslich, lived with their sons George Donatus and Louis, 'Don' and 'Lu'. The beautiful ivy-covered house stood among orchards where the trees were neatly pruned and the grass grew long. The place was large but to Dickie it seemed half its original size, for he had last seen it nine years before, from a child's perspective. The relations, old friends and retainers who were staying there – Baroness von Buxhoevden, former lady-in-waiting to the Tsarina; Georgina von Rotsmann; Dickie's nurse, Sophie Becht – all seemed shrunk, their sweet faces papery, their clothes faded. Many rooms were closed, which did not stop Dickie from inspecting the furniture under the dust sheets. Edwina liked the unpretentiousness of everything. Weeds grew out of the walls of the Rosenhohe, the family mausoleum, and Uncle Ernie drove about Darmstadt in a dilapidated carriage, although, Dickie noted, people still bowed to him in the streets. Heiligenberg Castle, the Battenbergs' country house, was in an even greater state of disrepair. Dickie's father had sold it in 1920 and the new owners had chopped up the rooms and neglected the grounds. Inflation made it hard to keep up standards. Dickie was horrified: 'a box of common chocolate – 20 Marks!' While they were there the currency fell so steeply in value that their sterling funds were almost doubled: Dickie bought furs for Edwina and his sister Louise, an aquamarine pendant and earrings for Edwina, who had her ears pierced in Frankfurt while Dickie was at the bank, and for himself a great prize, a Kodak cine camera with Zeiss lenses, with which he belatedly began a movie record of their trip. The Mountbattens' happiness can be seen in the films that were taken at Wolfsgarten. Don and Lu managed the camera, and the Mountbattens larked about on the lawn in their dressing-gowns, Edwina with her hair loose, Dickie entwined in a bath towel. Edwina was photographed knitting and Dickie turning somersaults; even Uncle Ernie performed for the camera by doing his exercises on a rug spread on the grass.

On one of their expeditions to Frankfurt, Dickie returned to the car to find Peter Murphy leaning against the bonnet. This was the intelligent, amiable, impecunious Irishman who had taken Dickie up at Cambridge, introduced him to books, music and politics, organized his first meeting with Audrey James, urged him to drop her when she hesitated, and encouraged his suit for Edwina. In theory, the Mountbattens were the last people of whom Peter should have approved, for he made a show of being anti-capitalist, anti-imperialist, anti-upper class. Peter was, however, the sort of socialist whose beliefs were inconsistent with his way of living, for he liked luxury and frivolity; it amused him to be a left-wing officer in the Guards. He had returned from his first visit to the Soviet Union, Marjorie said, and complained that the food was bad and that he could not buy smart boots. Peter liked to make a mystery of himself; Irish by birth, he claimed to have no roots. He spoke fluent French, Italian, German and Russian, for he had an excellent ear and could reproduce on the piano any tune he heard at a nightclub. He never said what he was doing, where he had been or where he was going, partly to tease and also to protect himself; Peter was homosexual and it was safer to be vague. Turning up unexpectedly in Hesse was typical.

Dickie and Edwina were delighted to see him. They carried him back to Wolfsgarten, where he sprawled on the grass, told Uncle Ernie amusing stories and played the piano to Aunt Onor after lunch, before disappearing without saying goodbye. It was the perfect end to the Mountbattens' visit, a reminder that the world waited beyond these drowsy estates. Dickie and Edwina turned west and drove back to Paris, where Nada and Georgie were now installed as their guests at the Ritz. No difficulty this time in finding unconventional places to dine and dance. Nada had a nose for peculiar nightclubs, places that appalled Dickie but not his brother, who had a small collection of pornographic photographs at home. Instead of retiring demurely to their rooms after dinner, the Mountbatten party now returned at half past two in the morning, sometimes not until four. Dickie found this wearing; he had looked up the way to the Grand Guignol theatre, which he had last visited in 1919, and was content to drop in there in the evening, watch one or two short and gory melodramas, dance briefly at the Acacia and go back to the Ritz to bed. Edwina liked to move on to Zelli's, for cocktails and more dancing, and to Montmartre after that; Georgie and Nada sometimes stayed out even later. Dickie did not ask where they went. After three days and nights, he was relieved when they staggered back to London.

It was the beginning of September 1922 when the Mountbattens returned to their mooring in Park Lane. No couple seemed more secure, firmly anchored by Edwina's great inheritance, roped in by thick strings of uncles, aunts, brothers, sisters and cousins from both families. There was one uncertainty: Dickie's future. He and Edwina had decided that he should stay in the Navy, 'where I do stand a chance of making a name for myself if I work hard'. But did the Navy want him? A year before, Britain had agreed with the United States, Japan, France and Italy that, to prevent another dangerous and expensive arms race, the size of their fleets should be kept in the existing ratio and no new capital ships built for the next ten years. Moreover, unemployment was climbing steeply and the City, the popular press and the House of Commons had demanded economies – No More Squander Mania – to revive business and the export trade and allow income tax to be reduced. A special committee had been set up, with Sir Eric Geddes as chairman, and in February 1922 it published its recommendations, which included cuts of £21 million in spending on the Navy. In the Budget the proposed reduction in naval expenditure had been halved but these savings were to be made in addition to the economies resulting from the agreement with the American, French, Italian and Japanese Governments. All round, this meant that 350 lieutenants would have to be retired. By the end of 1923 more than half the officers from Dickie's year would have left the Navy.

Edwina Mountbatten

Admiral Chatfield, who had been Captain of Dickie's first ship, *Lion*, was a member of the committee set up to decide who should stay and who should go. Dickie had been Chatfield's 'doggie' – ADC and errand boy – and the Admiral knew that he was not a royal amateur but a determined, energetic and conscientious officer. The fact that Mountbatten had a rich wife, Chatfield said, should not disqualify him from a naval career; the committee had to consider the good of the Service. Mountbatten was permitted to remain.

Dickie's long-term future was safe but now he and Edwina found themselves faced with a more immediate worry. Dickie had taken leave until November, so that they could fit a trip to America into their honeymoon, but it seemed as if the Navy might want him sooner. Greece and Turkey were fighting over territory on the shores of the Mediterranean, including a neutral zone protected by an occupying force of British and French troops. The Turks advanced, the French threatened to withdraw, and the British asked for support from the Empire, which was not forthcoming. By mid-September, a fortnight before the Mountbattens were to sail for New York, the Cabinet expected war. British forces were strengthened at Chanak in the neutral zone and the Navy hovered menacingly off the Dardanelles. Luckily for Dickie, the British Commander-in-Chief delayed action until tempers cooled, with the support of the British High Commissioner in Constantinople, who spun out discussions until a face-saving formula could be concocted. The chief casualty was the Prime Minister, for Lloyd George's handling of the Chanak crisis was the last straw for his increasingly exasperated Conservative partners in the Coalition and at the beginning of October they withdrew their support. Lloyd George resigned, Bonar Law became Prime Minister in his place (chosen mainly, it was said, because he was as little like Lloyd George as anyone could be), and a Conservative Government was formed for the first time for seventeen years. Wilfrid's moment had come. At the end of October he was translated to the Government benches and rewarded for his diligence in the Whips' office with a junior post but a mouthful of a title: Parliamentary Secretary to the Office of Works and the Ministry of Transport. It had been a long apprenticeship.

While the Chanak crisis was at its most tense, Dickie and Edwina were at Dunrobin, fishing and stalking in a party that included the Duke of York, who had temporarily escaped from the tartan-lined cocoon of Balmoral, where the King dined in a kilt to the music of bagpipes. The Mountbattens concentrated on the entertainments that had been so suddenly interrupted the year before: trudging miles after stags in the fine mist, waiting in fast-flowing water for salmon, writing letters on wet mornings and playing poker in the darkening afternoons. Edwina had fitted Dickie out with new guns from Purdey and they had preceded their trip to the north with lessons at the London Shooting School, but the weather was so bad that there was little chance to shine. Dickie got two large stags, Edwina had one chance and missed, and then the fog came down.

A day or two in London, with an evening at *The Cabaret Girl* and dancing at the Frolics Club, retuned them for America. The Mountbattens left on 27 September on the *Majestic*, the biggest passenger ship in the world, in which they occupied one of the largest suites, a bedroom, bathroom, dressing-room, wardrobe-room and sitting-room, all at the price of a single cabin, 'for advertisement's sake, I believe', Dickie noted disingenuously. The Mountbattens did not give their fellow-travellers much to talk about. Edwina, who was seasick, dosed herself with Mothersills and they took most of their meals in their sitting-room, from which Dickie occasionally emerged to look over the bridge and the engine-room and for what he described as 'a companionable yarn' with the officers on dogwatch in the early evening.

This quiet interlude ended on the final day of the voyage. New York expected them and, as the *Majestic* docked, an army of reporters, photographers and movie cameramen raced on to the ship along with the quarantine and customs inspectors. The Mountbattens escaped only by promising to give a press conference later on at Ritz-Carlton, where they were staying. They were a gift to journalists. Columns might be filled, and were, with Dickie's helpful answers to idiotic questions about Edwardian parlour games and British sporting etiquette. If Edwina did not actually say, 'how jolly', when told that Niagara was the place for honeymoon couples, and Dickie did not observe that he kept 'frightfully out of politics', they were supposed to have done so. Had not the Prince of Wales once described baseball as 'deucedly interesting'? As the press and newsreels presented them, Dickie and Edwina were at once fantastic and astoundingly normal. Like ordinary Americans they went to musicals and the movies and watched baseball while eating ice-cream cones and drinking soda

143

pop. In their case, however, Jerome Kern himself took them to the theatre, Douglas Fairbanks and Mary Pickford went with them to the cinema, and at the World Series game the great Babe Ruth shook their hands. 'Titled honeymooners greet our Babe', shrieked the *Buffalo Express* in an ecstatic muddle of snobbery and populism, while the *Globe* reported adoringly that Lady Louis had quickly picked up the correct responses: 'Atta boy, Babe!' and 'Take him out!'

The Mountbattens did their best to be agreeable. Dickie had the eager intelligence of a natural performer. He knew how to deal with small groups of people, defusing tension with a joke, moving things along, and on his tours with the Prince he had learnt to work a crowd. Now he was no longer walking three steps behind his cousin; he and Edwina were the stars. He expanded under the lights. The gawky boy disappeared and was replaced by a confident young man in a double-breasted suit. Edwina's experience of mass admiration was relatively recent. Like many young women, but to an exaggerated degree, she had first found herself the focus of attention at her wedding, where ritual had carried her along and the press, though avid, had been deferential. Here the scrutiny was direct and bold. It might have overwhelmed her but she took her cue from Dickie, who handled himself with increasing professionalism, treating the reporters like impresarios and the public as old friends. Edwina relaxed. She was not upset or inhibited by the stories in the press, for most were silly and none was hostile. Whatever she and Dickie did was applauded as being either perfectly appropriate or tremendously original.

Indeed, for the first time in her life Edwina could feel completely unconstrained. Relations were an ocean away, distant in time as well as space, since they were already ambling through an English afternoon when she and Dickie were beginning each zippy American morning. Their friends were new and up to the minute; in the crisp October air they crackled electrically, like the New York doorknobs that gave off sparks. People were free with introductions and invitations, sending telegrams, messages, flowers and fruit, offering tickets, motor cars and secretarial help, the loan of horses, the use of their houses. Refusals were out of the question, for the Mountbattens' hosts believed that with efficient planning everything could be fitted in, and they were so well-organized that not a minute was wasted. In three days Edwina and Dickie were taken, between luncheon parties and dinners, to two plays, *Shore Leave* and *The Cat and the Canary*, two reviews, the *Ziegfeld Follies* and George White's *Scandals*, slicker and louder than anything available in London, to dance to Paul Whiteman's Big Show Band and to hear jazz at The Tent and The Plantation. Paul Hammond took them to Meadow Brook to see the American polo team beat Argentina; Felix Warburg drove them out to White Plains for riding and swimming. Their days and nights were fully programmed, their hosts relentlessly hospitable.

Dickie had been to America once before, for a brief stop at San Diego with the Prince of Wales; Edwina, never. They were eager to see everything, or all, at least, of which they had heard: New York, Washington and Chicago; Niagara Falls, the Grand Canyon and Hollywood; Florida, the Sunshine State, whose boom was just beginning; and the Far West. This ambitious tour was being arranged for them by a friend of Aunt Victoria's, Colonel Robert M. Thompson, President of the Consolidated Arizona Smelting Company: 'Mama has a lot of money in it'. Colonel Thompson possessed a private railway carriage, the *Boston*, with space for seven guests and the staff: three man-servants, two maids, three attendants and, in case anything should go wrong, an official of the Santa Fe Railroad Company. He had assembled a sizeable party, including his daughter and son-in-law, Mr and Mrs Stephen H. P. Pell, and an American naval officer, Lieutenant Nielson, assigned as ADC to Dickie by the US Navy Department. Freddie Nielson had not been surprised by this appointment, since he was married to the Colonel's niece, Eulalia, who came too. On 7 October the Colonel, a commanding figure with bushy eyebrows and a generous white moustache, loaded his guests on to the train for the first part of the expedition, north towards Canada, west to Chicago and diagonally down to Arizona.

With much hitching and unhitching, the *Boston* was hauled across the country and deposited here and there at places which Colonel Thompson thought the visitors should see, the first being Fort Ticonderoga, built by the French, captured by the British, exchanged back and forth and now owned by the Stephen Pells. The first night was spent there, the next six in the train. Edwina's compartment had a double bed, in which the Mountbattens were rhythmically chanted to sleep as the huge pistons drove the *Boston* forward. During the day they pulled up at obscure stations, to be greeted by small crowds of railway officials and dour Red Indians, waiting to be photographed.

Edwina Mountbatten

The newspapers had positioned their representatives along the route and the reporters found themselves treated to a general-purpose address Dickie had devised, made up of answers to anticipated questions. 'Same thing every time', he told a startled correspondent for the *Chicago Daily News*: 'Easier to do it myself.' In this way the Colonel's party covered several thousand miles, stopping off to drive through the Adirondacks and admire the autumn leaves, brilliant red, sharp yellow and old gold. At Niagara they dressed in oilskins and saw the Falls. They visited power stations, museums, and Colonel Thompson's friends; in Chicago their hostess, Mrs Countiss, was so excited that she forgot to invite her husband.

As the train approached California, West Coast society was mustering. The people of Los Angeles wished to entertain the Mountbattens, the Daughters of the Empire League to give a banquet. All were disappointed, for Dickie and Edwina were in more powerful hands. The Sutherlands had given them an introduction to Charlie Chaplin, who awaited them at Pasadena station with the Fairbanks' Rolls-Royce and a luggage van. Douglas Fairbanks and Mary Pickford were in New York but they had lent the Mountbattens and their companions their large, white, wood-frame house, Pickfair, decorated with awnings, carriage-lamps, bay trees and an ineffectual Virginia creeper, half a mile away from the site of Chaplin's own half-built residence. At first, Dickie said, Colonel Thompson had been 'rather stuffy' about their enjoying the hospitality of movie people, until he saw that here his party could enjoy a few days' privacy. Reporters and cameramen were allowed on to the estate for one session only, in which the Mountbattens and Chaplin were photographed unconvincingly mowing the Fairbanks' lawn, a sight which, they learnt later, had shocked King George and Queen Mary. Fortunately no pictures appeared of Edwina, in turban, high-heeled shoes and Mary Pickford's knee-length black satin bathing costume, teetering on the diving-board over the outdoor swimming pool.

Real monarchs were far away; in Hollywood it was illusion that counted. At the Paramount Studios Cecil B. de Mille showed the Mountbattens the sets for his new film – a nautical scene and an eighteenth-century castle. Dickie was captivated, Edwina puzzled. Why should a dummy ship, pitching and rolling on a pivot, excite her husband as much as *Lion* or *Renown*, or a false ballroom, with cardboard chandeliers, impress him as much as Buckingham Palace?

Meeting the World

Edwina was prosaic, uncomfortable with tricks and effects, unused to fantasy. This was not surprising. In her childhood her imagination had been given little to feed on, apart from an annual trip to the pantomime. She had been brought up by practical, down-to-earth people, their minds, like their houses, filled with three-dimensional stuff, solid furniture whose provenance was known and certified. In Hollywood, Edwina learnt that not everything was what it seemed.

Dickie could not have been more at ease in this artifical world, for he had always been interested in the impressionistic and illusory. From his boyhood he had liked and continued to like puppets, shadow play, conjuring tricks, distorting mirrors, *trompe l'oeil* and dressing-up. For years he had played with miniature theatres and, more recently, moving pictures, and he understood how effects could be contrived by using light, shade and movement and deploying scraps of this and that. These were useful skills; in Dickie's family there was no wealth to help make a show and appearances had to be kept up with what came to hand: crests and coronets, uniforms and titles. No wonder he felt at home. Hollywood, like constitutional monarchy, was sustained by mystique, clever stage management, props and sentiment, everything Dickie was used to, plus technology.

The studios were laboratories, where lenses and shutters, nitrate and celluloid changed script into pictures; meanwhile, in another sort of alchemy, producers, agents and accountants turned fiction into money. The Mountbattens' friends, Fairbanks, Chaplin and Mary Pickford, were entrepreneurs as well as actors; with D. W. Griffith, the producer, they had founded a studio of their own, United Artists, to distribute their films and secure a percentage of the profits. Their newest production was *Robin Hood*. Dickie and Edwina walked through the half-dismantled sets: lath and plaster towers, the remnants of a greensward made of squares of turf, a replica of Sherwood Forest with ferns in pots. The film opened during the Mountbattens' stay and they attended the first performance, representatives of the Old World, blessing its re-creation by the New.

Chaplin now proposed that the party should produce its own movie, shot on location in the Fairbanks' garden. Everyone took part, including the child star, Jackie Coogan, who dropped in for lunch, Colonel Thompson, and Thorogood in the role of a disdainful butler. The film had a working title, *The Hit*, later changed to *Nice and Friendly*, and a rough and ready script. At the centre of the drama was Edwina

147

and her four-foot rope of pearls. She had worn them often throughout the trip, tempting Providence, for they hung almost to her waist and could easily have caught and spilled. Dickie thought they attracted burglars; in the film his premonition was acted out. Villains, that is, the Colonel and his family, hid among the Fairbanks' rosebushes and, having overpowered the hero, played by Dickie, smartly abducted the heroine and her necklace. Order was restored with the intervention of an unheroic-looking tramp, Chaplin, with trick mallet. The plot was unambitious, the cast hopeless. Chaplin's pupils were interested in the mechanics of film-making – Edwina and the Colonel experimented with the make-up box, while Dickie tried out their host's collection of flexible walking-sticks – but as participants they were disastrous, forgetting their moves, missing their cues and constantly looking in the wrong direction. Edwina was wooden and awkward before the camera. She could not forget who she was, not surprisingly, since she had been asked to play herself.

A midnight visit to the studio to see a run-through of the film (Chaplin presented Dickie with a precious souvenir, a rubber hammer) and it was time for the long cross-country journey to the East. Desert gave way to mountains, mountains to swamps and prairies. The Mountbattens were pitched out of their state of suspended animation halfway along the route, with news that in Washington, the first main stop, Dickie was expected to give an address at the Navy League dinner on Navy Day. Since Colonel Thompson was Honorary President of the League, there was no escape. For three days Dickie polished his remarks, trying them out on the British Naval Attaché and the Ambassador when they arrived in Washington. By then Edwina knew the speech by heart: 'Poor Snoopsie', she murmured, as Dickie tried to memorize it. Speechmaking, the Ambassador warned them, was the easy part of the banquet, the worst being the hours of marches and 'Gems from Musical Comedy', through which the guests had to sit. The Ambassador was right.

South to Florida, to fish from the Colonel's Mississippi paddleboat, moored in a coconut grove; back to Washington, celebrating Eulalia's birthday with mah-jong in the parlour car and blindfold golf in the corridors. 'The Colonel is rather tired', Dickie wrote in his diary. One more week of concerts, dinners, lunches and teas; visits to the Naval Academy at Annapolis; to Mrs Maclean, who owned the Hope diamond; to the world-famous oculist, Dr Wilmer, who prescribed new reading glasses for Dickie and clucked over Edwina's myopia. They rode the Colonel's horses, picnicked at George Washington's house, drank tea on the presidential yacht, and called on the President, Warren G. Harding, to make inconsequential conversation. For this meeting the Embassy advised Dickie to wear a top hat and spats. Civilian formal dress did not suit him; as he posed, cane in hand, on the White House steps, he looked distinctly Chaplinesque.

The Washington Season had begun, with bridge parties and small dances for its older members, paper-chases and smaller dances still for the younger set. Dickie and Edwina fled to New York. Here, to the intense irritation of professional party-givers, they spent their time either with the Schiffs and the Warburgs, old family friends, or at strange places with unlikely people. The greatest stir was caused on the first night of their return to New York, when they attended the opening of a new supper club, the Cercle Connu, in the Crystal Room at the Ritz. The evening began with exhibition dancing by the Mountbattens' friend Charlotte Demarest, who on the day of her wedding had gone off instead with Count Zichy, an impoverished Austrian. The Zichys had earned their keep all summer by dancing in a casino at Atlantic City, a resort that New York matrons thought disreputable, and it was generally predicted that the supper club would fail. With the Mountbattens as patrons, it was an instant success.

The last ten days of their stay were more conventional. Months before, Mrs Vanderbilt had insisted that Dickie and Edwina end their tour at 640 Fifth Avenue and, although they knew this was a snare, they were too fond of her to refuse. Here it was impossible to avoid fashionable entertainment: Chaliapin in *Boris Godunov*, tea parties, dances and dinners for fifty people or more, orchestrated either by Mrs Vanderbilt herself or by one of the hostesses with whom she had a treaty of reciprocity. The climax came on 28 November, Edwina's twenty-first birthday, when she was presented with one birthday cake at lunch with the Warburgs, another at tea with the Vanderbilts, and a third at dinner with the Dillinghams, followed by a breakneck ride to a first night at the Globe Theatre, with an escort of speed-cops on motor-bicycles. Edwina and Dickie were beginning to flag. They had been away two months, travelled fifteen thousand miles, done and seen everything, all of it new, from *The Insect Play* to *Rain*. They had discovered make-up and electric massage and how much pleasure

149

could be packed into twenty-four hours. Their hosts kept going to the end, with a last dinner and dance at 640 Fifth Avenue, in honour of Grace Vanderbilt's arrival from England and the Mountbattens' departure. At four o'clock in the morning when Dickie and Edwina staggered into bed, thinking everything was over, Paul Whiteman turned up with his band, to play them out of America, as he had played them in.

Mary Pickford, Douglas Fairbanks,
Edwina and Dickie

Edwina's pearls

Edwina and Charlie Chaplin in *Nice and Friendly*

Edwina with Laddie Sanford

Edwina and Jeanie Norton at the time of the General Strike

CHAPTER TWELVE

A Divine Little Daughter

L aden with movies and jazz records, Dickie and Edwina boarded the *Olympic*, on which Mr Warburg's indefatigable secretary had obtained a large suite at a third of the usual price. The ship was quiet and the Mountbattens caught up on lost sleep, interspersed with games of bridge and mah-jong. Weller fell thankfully into her bunk, too tired even to complain about the sea; Thorogood stoically applied himself to learning how to operate the projector Dickie had acquired for the private cinema he proposed to set up at Brook House.

It was fortunate that the return voyage was out of season, for maid and valet, like their employers, needed time to readjust. Once home, their party would no longer be the chief attraction, or, at any rate, it was not supposed to be. In England the King's relations did not give interviews and, when a *Daily Mirror* reporter and photographer came alongside at Cherbourg, Dickie had to explain that he and Edwina now wanted to avoid publicity. Their home-coming was, if anything, too subdued. No crowd of friends awaited them at Southampton and, although the Rolls was there, it did not transport them to a matinée, a movie or a baseball game but to Broadlands for a chilly breakfast with Molly, who sent them out into a dank November morning. Edwina and Dickie perched uncomfortably on shooting sticks, watching the guns. No one seemed to want to hear about America, so, after three tedious hours, they decamped to Branksome for the night.

Dickie had expected that he would now be sent to HMS *Truant*, a destroyer attached to the Signal School at Portsmouth. When he called at the Admiralty, however, he learnt that he was ordered to Constantinople as a watchkeeper in *Revenge*. Dickie accepted this philosophically, for he had anticipated that assignment in September and felt that in effect he had enjoyed three months' grace. He set off to inquire about railway tickets to Constantinople, going straight to Wilfrid, who was so delighted to show what the Ministry of Transport

151

could do that he quite forgot to be annoyed at being treated like a branch of Cook's.

Edwina was furious. Left on her own she would be miserable. The Admiralty was being perverse and Dickie should object. It was no good: 'the Gods' at the top of the office had decided that Mountbatten needed a turn in a big ship before the Signal Course. Dickie had to join *Revenge* in mid-January, which gave time for a long-drawn-out reunion with his family, now reassembled in England for the first time since the wedding. His sister Alice, her husband and five children had just arrived from the Mediterranean in a gunboat, after an adventure that was hair-raising even for Battenbergs, who were accustomed to war and revolution. The Greek royal family had suffered a run of bad luck. King Constantine, the brother of Alice's husband Andrew, had been deposed and exiled in 1917, recalled to his throne in 1920, and then deposed again by a revolutionary government that had also confined Alice and the children to *Mon Repos*, their beautiful but inaptly-named villa on the island of Corfu. Andrew had been charged with treason and imprisoned in Athens, where he waited to be shot. The Foreign Office considered, took a deep breath and commissioned a former naval attaché in Athens, Commander Talbot, to negotiate with the revolutionaries, who agreed to release Prince Andrew. Since they did not like to be seen giving in to pressure, he was smuggled out of prison and put on board HMS *Calypso*. The rest of the family was collected from Corfu and the whole party brought to London, arriving just as Edwina and Dickie returned from America. Dickie's mother now summoned everyone to Kensington Palace, where she and her unmarried daughter Louise shared a grace-and-favour apartment, to hear Commander Talbot tell his story over the teacups. Dickie was rather envious, this being the sort of exploit he would have liked to have undertaken himself. A week after meeting Commander Talbot, the Mountbattens presented themselves for tea at Buckingham Palace, where, according to Dickie, they found the King 'most affable'. This was a relief, for they had braced themselves for a rebuke. As it was, Dickie said, 'they never even mentioned our stay at Hollywood, which we were supposed to be in trouble about.'

Between family lunch, dinner and tea parties, Dickie assembled his kit. Properly utilized, Edwina's fortune was no longer embarrassing and it was helpful to have ready cash for essentials. When the Rolls-Royce collided with a bus in Knightsbridge, for instance, and had to be sent away for repair, there was no difficulty about ordering a new one. They also purchased a car for Edwina, a two-seater Rolls, the only one of its kind. (The chauffeur-cum-mechanic had to ride behind like a footman in a dickey-seat built into the boot.) Edwina thought it was amusing to have so much spare money: when three different furriers appeared at Brook House with coats for her to see, and she and Dickie could not remember which one they had invited, she bought from them all. Dickie was less carefree. He kept a note of every purchase and, asked what he would like for Christmas, modestly suggested 'various books on British flags and naval battles'. Mrs Cassel gave him the only expensive item on his list, a clock which struck the time by ships' bells, which he had seen in a shop in Cowes. Dickie and Edwina spent the holiday at Branksome, among a great collection of Cassels, Jenkinses and Brecknocks. Even Wilfrid and Molly came, although only for a night. The celebrations were taken seriously: two formal present-giving ceremonies, one for the servants, one for the family, and what Dickie described as 'a great Xmas tree stunt at 5 p.m.'. As his own contribution to the entertainment, he turned one of the saloons into a cinema and showed the entire household his favourite films, two Chaplins, *Nice and Friendly*, and the newsreel of the wedding.

Edwina was restless, bored with tennis on mild December mornings, poker in the evenings and *Mother Goose* at the pantomime. She was still running at American speed and in London she tried to fill each minute, as they had done in New York and Hollywood. Before Christmas she and Dickie had spent every evening at a play, a revue or a nightclub, sometimes, when they were not required to dine and dance at a private house, all three. They had also made a circuit of Mayfair clubs. Dickie and Fruity were honorary members of the Grafton Galleries, which had a Negro band but, even so, was not thought too scandalous, since it closed at 2 a.m. and guests were supposed to dance with their gloves on. Dickie had free membership of the Embassy Club, at the Piccadilly end of Bond Street, where the Prince of Wales, who was normally there on Thursday nights, had his own sofa at a table by the wall. The Duke of York sometimes joined them, with trepidation, for he knew how deeply his parents disapproved of cocktails, jazz and dancing cheek-to-cheek. Edwina had a taste for places that were not smart, like Rectors, in a cellar in the Tottenham Court Road.

Edwina Mountbatten

In New York the Mountbattens had developed a taste for showy revue and intimate cabaret. Dickie, who was impressed by demonstrations of professional skill, liked complicated tunes and clever visual effects, while Edwina never tired of jerky, syncopated dance music, sentimental love songs and the sound of a wailing saxophone. When the Mountbattens took to a performance, they revisited it week after week. They and their friends could spot the smallest alteration in the Co-Optimists revue and *The Cabaret Girl*; Peter Murphy was said to know *Battling Butler* by heart. The proprietors of theatres, restaurants and dancing places were delighted to have such faithful clients, for the patronage of the Prince's companions was valuable and intelligent managers made the most of it. Edwina and her friends had much in common with the actors, dancers and musicians they admired, both sets being bright, smart, pleasure-hungry and nocturnal. It was not unusual to see Dickie and Edwina, the Brecknocks, Georgie and Nada, Peter, Fruity and the Prince eating bacon and eggs with their favourite performers after a show, for their circles overlapped and their interests were much the same.

Although Dickie and Edwina rarely got to bed before three, they remained clear-eyed and lively, in part because they preferred lemonade to cocktails. Dickie rose early, took an egg and the top of a cottage loaf for breakfast and buckled down to work. Edwina slept late. To exclude all sound from her bedroom, the windows giving on to Park Lane were double-glazed and the doors to the landing, an outer and inner set, kept shut until she rang. She lay in sheets of fine linen, a nightmare to launder, for they were threaded with pink ribbon and decorated with silk bows, which had to be removed and replaced each time, and inset with lace, which was soaked in cream to keep its colour. Upon the bed was a swansdown quilt, its pink casing entirely covered with ostrich feathers, so that it seemed to float. The room had been redecorated since the wedding, with wallpaper, curtains and carpet of pale grey, like clouds. Edwina's bathroom, on the other hand, recalled Sir Ernest's robust taste. A vast bath of Italian marble was flanked by an enormous double washstand, on which Edwina invariably left her rings; new housemaids tried them for size. Among the flasks of perfumed oils and jars of cream was one sturdy bottle containing the blackened nerve from Dickie's left front tooth, damaged in a hunting accident in 1920 and recently removed. This was his farewell gift before he left for Constantinople.

A Divine Little Daughter

It was a little party that said goodbye to Dickie at Victoria in the second week of January. Only his mother, his sister Louise and two of his Greek nieces, Margarita and Theodora ('Dolla') came to wave him off, although that was partly because Alice, Andrew, and their other daughters, Cecile and Sophie ('Tiny'), were at the Gare du Nord to wave him in. Various supporters – Edwina, Peter Murphy, Marjorie and Brecky – joined him for the journey. That evening the English party danced at the Pigalle and Zelli's, 'both quite empty and not up to the usual standard', noted Dickie, who now thought himself an expert. Not so deserted, however, that they were entirely on their own and, when Dickie danced with an unknown girl, Edwina was furiously jealous. Dickie was first pleased and then contrite; he did not realize that it was not his partner Edwina resented but *Revenge*, for which he was abandoning her next day. Edwina justified her outburst by explaining that she was suffering from what she euphemistically called 'her affairs', or, as Dickie respectfully put it, 'the "P"', for 'Plague'. He did not know that such a quarrel would occur at every leave-taking; nor did Edwina. This was their first night apart since their marriage.

All was straight by the time Edwina saw Dickie on to the Simplon-Orient Express at the Gare de Lyon, along with 220 kilos of luggage, this being half as much again as the standard allowance. By one o'clock in the morning she felt completely bereft. Dickie's other farewell present, a toy rabbit with the unoriginal name of Bun, was, according to her diary, no consolation: 'Very miserable night'. During the day there was plenty to do but whenever Edwina returned to the hotel, Dickie's absence hit her: 'Very lonely'. He, meanwhile, was bumping towards Constantinople, missing his wife every inch of the way. From Milan he sent a letter and a cable, from Belgrade he tried in vain to despatch a telegram to tell her it was snowing, and, after a desperate search for Yugoslav stamps, finally gave a letter to some naval officers who were travelling in the opposite direction. At Sofia he struggled to obtain the right currency to send another cable and nearly missed the train. Not that there was much to say. His toothache was gone and so was the headache that succeeded it: 'Remind me to tell you something about it'.

Edwina returned to Bournemouth, for she and Dickie had decided that until he knew where he would be posted next it was futile to look for a house. Although there were other guests at Branksome Dene,

155

they were, like their hostess, aged ladies – Melba was the most lively – who spent much of the day knitting and chatting and the evening playing bridge for small stakes, before retiring early. Edwina's chief distraction was a black spaniel, Simon: 'Very sweet but not house trained.' At least she had a companion on her dreary walks along the beach and soon, for the puppy was quick to learn, to sit on the bed while she had breakfast.

Dickie had no time to be bored once he had shifted on to *Revenge*. A hundred men of the fo'c'sle division were directly in his care, plus another sixty in the foremost gun-turret. He tried to learn all he could about his charges, devising for the purpose a special form on which he charted each man's personal and professional history and a description of his appearance. In addition, twenty midshipmen were assigned to him; Dickie not only had to teach them all their seamanship but mother them as well. This suited him perfectly. Within two days he had organized an impromptu sing-song round the piano; after a fortnight he took charge of the Dance Club. He rigged up a court for deck hockey, 'bumble-puppy' and exercise with a medicine ball, laid on boxing matches, football and tug-of-war competitions, took the midshipmen for picnics on the islands in the Marmara Sea, and taught them to play mah-jong.

Alone in his cabin Dickie was homesick. He arranged Edwina's photographs and next day rearranged them, and on the anniversary of their engagement in mid-February he wrote twenty-four pages of reminiscence, going back to the first time they had met. It was so difficult, he said, to be brave and cheerful all the time. He also had trouble suppressing impure thoughts, although they were of the most harmless kind, being no more than visions of Edwina's elegant feet and legs, encased in a pair of soft leather riding boots they had ordered in Paris on their honeymoon. Edwina, who was not alarmed, sent photographs of her knees and asked for two cap ribbons from *Revenge* for garters.

Fortunately Dickie had work to do. If war broke out, he would cable 'Fun has started' – but it would not be amusing. He hoped that he would be ordered to remain with his gunners in the turret, rather than being assigned to the observation post, a particularly dangerous position in the grounds of a smallpox hospital behind the front line of the British trenches. Having explained all this, he assured his wife that 'there was nothing to worry about, darling . . .'

A Divine Little Daughter

At Branksome Edwina had little to do but feel sorry for herself. She returned to Brook House but London, shrouded in thick fog, was more gloomy than the seaside. Laszlo had been commissioned to paint her portrait and now the sittings began; Edwina wore her wedding dress and felt all the more like a deserted bride. When the picture was finished she sent a photograph of it to Dickie. It squinted, he said, so she asked Laszlo to repaint the eyes and took herself to the oculist, who prescribed exercises. This was discouraging and she felt more miserable than ever. The doctor gave her a tonic, X-rayed her heart and told her she was growing stronger all the time. She visited Sir Ernest's grave and saw *If Winter Comes*: 'Very heartrending'.

This mood could not last. January and February were empty months, most people being incarcerated in damp country houses, where they spent four-day weekends entertaining each other. Fruity, the Brecknocks, the Prince of Wales and the Duke of York came to the rescue, carrying Edwina off on the old round: the Co-Optimists revue and *The Cabaret Girl*; dancing at the Berkeley and the Grafton Galleries; the Midnight Follies at the Metropole. One evening, for a change, she took Louise, Margarita and Dolla to Norma Talmadge's new film, *The Eternal Flame*, and afterwards they went back to Brook House and listened to *The Cabaret Girl* on the Electrophone, a one-way loudspeaking telephone that relayed the sound directly from the theatre.

Mornings and afternoons were hardest. Miss Underhill was so efficient that there were few instructions to give and, although Edwina made a point of inspecting the Brook House accounts, it was foolish to do so more than once a week. Sessions with Miss Powell, the manicurist, took up an hour every four days and in mid-February Edwina spent an entire morning having her hair permanently waved, a smelly and painful process, risky too, since it could produce a greenish fuzz. She prudently asked only for a twist behind each ear, a change so modest that it was hard to tell the difference. The days dragged: shopping, the dentist, inspecting a sculptor's studio with Lady Cunard, tea with Miss Devéria, bridge with Mrs Dresselhuys, afternoons at the cinema with Margaret Lindsay, visits to Mary at Heathfield, letters to her husband.

Edwina wrote regularly to Dickie about his relations, for once a week she had lunch at Kensington Palace with Aunt Victoria. The Duke of York's engagement to Lady Elizabeth Bowes-Lyon had been announced in January and he was ecstatically happy. 'About time too', his younger brother said. Prince George was delighted that 'the young duker', as he called his brother, had secured Elizabeth at last. 'She is rather sweet and ought to make him a good wife if she isn't too unselfish and doesn't always give in to him.' Although Prince George spoke so confidently about his brother's fiancée, he knew nothing about women. Edwina tried to keep him amused, taking him to lunch with Lady Cunard and dancing with him at the Embassy, 'strictly incognito', he stipulated, unrealistically. Edwina liked Prince George because he was thoughtful, innocent and an eye-catching substitute for Dickie when the Brecknocks or the Milford Havens took her out in the evening. She bought him socks and ties in Bond Street and enjoyed showing him off. She also explained the mysteries of reproduction. Dickie was not jealous, for he regarded Prince George as a young brother and liked to think of his wife and cousin pottering about together in the Rolls – that is, until he heard rumours of a smash. Frantic wires went from *Revenge*; Edwina's reply: 'All well. Car very little damaged'. They had been lucky. Edwina had driven Prince George down to Guildford on a winter afternoon, to stay with Geordie Sutherland at Sutton Place: 'Please don't be worried, darling . . . Eileen isn't there but there's a large party . . .' A car had swerved across the road, damaging the right side of the Rolls and ripping off the running board. Edwina swore she had dimmed the headlights; the other driver, whose car was wrecked, maintained that he had been dazzled. The insurance company paid what was only the latest of many bills, for two or three times a week Edwina and Martin, her new chauffeur, managed to dent, bump or graze shop-fronts, buses, trams and passing motor cars. The garage lent Edwina another Rolls, which was badly squashed a week later while she was at the dentist.

Dickie had now been away six weeks and Edwina was thoroughly depressed. Nothing could revive her for long, she told him. Dickie was contrite. 'When I think how I used to actually go out shopping separately from you and talk to Admiral Kerr about aeroplanes . . .' He promised to make up for it when he came home: '. . . you must drive the car and everything'.

Edwina was not entirely at a loose end, however, for in every letter Dickie sent a list of errands. Unimpressed by the films that were shown on board *Revenge*, he asked her to get a copy of *Robin Hood* from the Fairbanks' agent in London and to despatch it in a stout tin box with a Bramah Lock: 'See if the Foreign Office messenger could take it – your Daddy could get in touch with them'. Next, she should persuade C. B. Cochran to transcribe the music. The Ship's Band would provide the sound-track, with 'whistling arrow effects' devised by Dickie, who communicated with the projectionist and the band-master through a voice-pipe specially adapted by himself.

Edwina became used to receiving detailed orders. Dickie needed six shirts from Hawes and Curtis, eye lotion, toothwash, writing-paper, socks, collars, his own napkin ring, music for foxtrots, black leather uniform shoes with 'Jeddite' rubber soles. ('The only person to speak to at Peals is *Mr Moore*, personally.') Edwina ticked off each task when it was done. She was to teach Martin and Thorogood to drive both cars ('Make sure they oil the engines'). Martin should have a dust coat or blue Burberry with black crested buttons, less ostentatious than gilt ones, which were unsuitable for wearing in the country. Perhaps the butler, MacGowan, should be instructed to stock the cellar – but only if there were an opportunity of getting good wines and champagnes at a reasonable price. Thorogood should be asked to ensure that Dickie's cheap cabin pictures and collapsible chair were moved from storage in Portsmouth to storage at Devonport, since Commander Joel had written to say that: 'The Signal Course will be a "cert" . . . after this show is over.' And if cables should arrive which Dickie had signed with the one word VENUS, that would mean, he said, that he was missing Edwina terribly. He had adopted this idea, he admitted, from the Prince of Wales, who used the same code at the end of his wires to Freda Dudley Ward. Edwina had only one request. She had been visiting Syssyllt and Audrey, who had just had their first babies, and was eager to have one herself. Dickie was thrilled. 'As soon as you please'.

Revenge came into Plymouth on 5 April. The Mountbattens were reunited at the Grand Hotel – 'too, too marvellous' – and at the end of the week, when Dickie's fortnight's leave began, they hurtled back to London. He was keen to embark on the production of a baby. The most propitious time for conception, the Mountbattens thought, was after dining alone and spending a calm evening together. This was rare. The days were filled with luncheon parties at Claridge's, the Embassy, and Brook House, the nights with dancing to the Savoy Havannah Band, and at the Folies Bergère, a new 'low haunt'. George Gershwin played for them, Tallulah Bankhead had them to parties in her dressing-room. The Mountbattens gave a party of their own to celebrate Dickie's return, 'a tiny dance', as Edwina described it, for fifty people, almost outnumbered by Paul Whiteman's Band.

Dickie had more leave for the Duke of York's wedding. The Mountbattens took their seats in the Abbey, he in a new full-dress uniform, she in black and white with a magpie feather in her hat. No couple looked more decorous but, after the wedding breakfast at Buckingham Palace, they disobeyed instructions, and, instead of staying to see the Duke and Duchess of York off to Polesden Lacey for their honeymoon, slid away to the country so that Dickie could play polo. They made for Trent, Sir Philip Sassoon's house at New Barnet. Dickie was now so obsessed by the game that he became restless if a day passed without practice on one of the ponies Edwina had encouraged him to buy. At weekends he played at Sassoon's country estate, Port Lympne. 'Most divine place', Edwina thought, 'though very oddly decorated inside'. There was an octagonal library, a Moorish courtyard, an enormous swimming pool surrounded by sun terraces. Dickie found it bizarre but restful: 'Quite like a second honeymoon here', he observed, as they conscientiously embraced.

Edwina now began to look for a house near the coast, for Dickie was to stay with *Revenge* until the Signal Course began, and he wanted Edwina and the ponies nearby. In early May she found Maiden Castle House, near Dorchester, a square, substantial brick villa, with eight good bedrooms. The Mountbattens took the place and two housemaids for six weeks, added pictures, cushions, linen and china, imported Weller, MacGowan, Thorogood and Martin, found a cook and kitchen-maid, settled in and invited their friends, in batches. Dickie brought groups of midshipmen home for tea and tennis; to meet Prince George, Grace Vanderbilt, Peter Murphy and Mrs Cassel was, he thought, part of their education. While the Mountbattens were in Dorchester, Brook House was let, to reassure Mrs Cassel, who worried about the rising cost of living, and Dickie, who had been looking at the accounts. In January he and Edwina had spent more than £3,000, 'which is living at a rate of over £36,000 a year or at least £6,000 above our income'. They must do something to lessen the outgoings. At sea he could live quite cheaply but at home they should retrench. Edwina did not take Dickie's warnings seriously but to please Mrs Cassel she agreed to put other people into Brook House while they were out of it. The first tenant was Mrs Vanderbilt.

A Divine Little Daughter

The Mountbattens spent a month in the country until they were summoned to London. Dickie's great-aunt, Princess Helena, whom they had last seen, in lace, gold silk, sables and a brown straw hat, at the Duke of York's wedding breakfast, had expired at the age of seventy-seven. Death, even in someone else's family, brought out the best in Mrs Vanderbilt and, despite the disruption, she welcomed the Mountbattens back into their own quarters at Brook House. There Edwina remained, for on the day of the funeral she felt so peculiar that Dickie agreed that she should risk the King's displeasure by staying at home. While he accompanied his royal relations to Windsor, Edwina sent for Dr Simson, the Queen's obstetrician, who told her she was expecting a baby. 'Good news', Dickie wrote in his diary that night; they had begun to despair. In April he had tried to tackle the problem scientifically by carefully programming Edwina's day: a lazy afternoon, an early and nutritious dinner, a visit to the cinema in Plymouth to see Pola Negri in *Passion*, bed at ten-thirty. Even this had failed to do the trick – but now they could congratulate themselves.

At the beginning of July *Revenge* sailed to Scotland for a month's refit in the naval dockyard at Rosyth. Edwina packed up at Maiden Castle House; paid bills, sent away the servants and joined Mrs Cassel, who was on holiday at Sidmouth. When Dickie was at home her only concession to pregnancy had been to give up tennis. Now she sat knitting tiny garments, the picture of a sailor's wife waiting ashore. Sustaining this role was such an effort that after three days Edwina collapsed with a mixture of neuralgia and migraine. She fled to Philip Sassoon's house in Park Lane; older female friends thought this dangerous but London brought her back to life. Edwina needed non-stop activity: dinner at the Ritz with Peter Murphy, followed by *Dover Street to Dixie*; lunch at Kensington Palace for Louise's birthday; a party at Lords for the second day of the Eton and Harrow cricket match; an afternoon watching polo at Ranelagh with Hannah Gubbay, Philip Sassoon's cousin; *Stop Flirting* with the Brecknocks; lunch at Claridge's with Fruity; shopping; manicure; hairwash; a last dinner and a dash to see *The Lilies of the Field*, before she caught the night sleeper to Edinburgh to join Dickie.

He had negotiated special terms at the Caledonian Hotel: three guineas a day for a suite, with a piano and a day bed, twelve shillings for housing each servant. Dickie was delighted with such economical arrangements: 'However', he told Edwina apologetically, 'I know you dislike these details'. Now she continued her education as a junior officer's wife. For three weeks Edwina hung about, shopping in Princes Street, being fitted for tweeds, drinking tea at McVitie's. The weather was damp and cold. She took Simon for walks in the gardens at Holyrood, had her hair washed, went miserably to the cinema, and begged Margaret Lindsay to come from Balcarres to keep her company.

It was a relief when *Revenge* was ordered back to Devonport for the last part of the refit. While Dickie sailed south, Edwina raced down on the train, spent a night at Brook House with the Vanderbilts, ran over for the weekend to Broadlands, where Molly was giving a dance, and then motored to Cowes with Bobbie Cunningham-Reid, Conservative Member of Parliament for Warrington and Wilfrid's Parliamentary Private Secretary. Edwina ate ices and danced with Paul Hammond, who had come over from America in the Marconi yacht, *Elettra*. She abandoned her regime of sedate walks, regular meals and early nights and when she returned to London, where the Vanderbilts had lent her Brook House while they cruised in *Atlantic*, she danced every night with Hugh Molyneux at the Riviera Club, the Grafton Galleries or the Blue Lagoon. Dickie came home in mid-August on a fortnight's leave. He found Edwina keen to go everywhere and do everything, despite her pregnancy. They saw the shows he had not yet seen and danced at the Riviera with two new friends, Fred Astaire and his sister Adele, stars in Edwina's favourite revue, *Stop Flirting*.

Revenge now returned to Rosyth to take on ammunition before moving from there to the naval base at Invergordon. Edwina and Mary had reserved rooms at the Highland Hotel at Strathpeffer, a few miles from Invergordon. There they found a wire from Dickie to say that his ship had gone up the coast for firing practice and they had better go to Dunrobin and look for him there. They drove on to the Sutherlands, and waited for Dickie to come ashore from *Revenge*. The weather was so bad that it took him two and a half hours to reach the shore and after an hour for tea he had to struggle back again. That was all they saw of him for three days. At last a wire arrived to say *Revenge* was back at Invergordon. Edwina and Mary returned to Strathpeffer. Dickie did his best to be with Edwina, even when it meant leaving the hotel at six to be back on *Revenge* at eight, coming ashore again before lunch and, when he was on night-firing exercises, leaving at nine in the evening. It was impossible to plan and Martin spent hours driving fruitlessly to and from Invergordon, while Edwina and Mary consoled themselves with tea in the Station Hotel at Inverness. Edwina pretended not to mind but she found the uncertainty embarrassing and their brief reunions frustrating. After one night at Dunrobin they parted for another month and Edwina, trying not to feel abandoned, came south.

She distracted herself as best as she could, with a week in Paris, installing Mary at the finishing school run by Madame Ozanne. Back in England, she could not stay still: Lympne, London, Polesden, London, Branksome, London. She wrote faithfully to Dickie but no longer plaintively, for she was growing used to his absences. She missed him in bursts, when she found herself with nothing to do. He wanted her company all the time, wishing that he could take part in her amusements and that she could share what he was doing.

Edwina had started a streaming cold. The aunts and cousins were not surprised, for they thought she was doing far too much. Dickie was able to spend more time with her, as he was now based at Portland while *Revenge* took part in exercises off the south coast. Once again the Mountbattens took Maiden Castle House. Edwina's days were quieter there than in London, although in four weeks she had five sets of people to stay and thirty-two additional guests for lunch or dinner. Dickie tore backwards and forwards to Portland and Plymouth, leaving at five in the morning, returning at half past ten at night, having driven a hundred miles through twisting lanes. As the days passed, Edwina at last became more tranquil, content, between visitors, to do embroidery, while Dickie read aloud or they listened in together to the wireless. In the afternoons, when he had leave, they went shopping for cheap crockery to use in his latest home-made film; Dickie intended to run it backwards, so that smashed china would appear to reconstruct itself and overturned chairs to stand up straight again. For Edwina's twenty-second birthday he gave her what she called 'a divine little all-round diamond ring'; Dickie felt very much married and so, for the moment, did Edwina. With her Christmas present to him, a typewriter, he devotedly brought her address and telephone book up to date.

Dickie hated the thought that he would be away when the baby was born, but in January *Revenge* sailed for exercises in the

Mediterranean. He tried to imagine that Edwina was in his cabin, sustaining the illusion by playing the gramophone, his eyes closed, holding his own hand. It did not help. In an old despatch case he found a list of girls he had met on the first royal tour, some of whom he had 'mildly flirted with in New Zealand and Australia', although, he added sadly, 'as you know I never got very far with any of them'. None was a patch on Edwina. If only he were home.

The builders were now in Brook House, making day and night nurseries out of Sir Ernest's old bedroom and reorganizing the second floor to provide quarters for the baby's nurse, Miss Nisbit, and a children's nurse, Miss Woodard. Mrs Cassel could not decide how much use she wanted to make of the place. She complained that it was too expensive to keep up, what with light, heat, her own staff of servants and the two thousand pounds a year she paid to Sir Ernest's trustees for her share of rates and repairs. She rarely came to London and thought she might as well let the house for a second summer. Edwina did not like this: 'It would probably mean our taking another house in London', she told Dickie, 'which seems futile'. She therefore suggested that Mrs Cassel should turn over Brook House entirely to Dickie and herself: 'We could do just as we liked and use all the rooms', and, since they spent so much anyhow, the extra cost would make little difference. Furthermore, she pointed out, 'there's sure to be a bust up among the servants with two households going, like now'. Trouble below deck was something Dickie was trained to avoid. He agreed that Mrs Cassel should discuss Edwina's scheme with Cousin Felix and set about drawing up a scheme for amalgamating the two households: wages should be standardized, for a start, and MacGowan should look round for a second footman. Tucker, who worked for Mrs Cassel, should be house butler, giving a hand at busy times, 'and should be properly equipped with a blue livery coat and white waistcoat'. ('This will make you laugh at me, won't it, Snoopsie?') Dickie wrote screeds about garaging arrangements and chauffeurs' wages, pensions and laundry, the duties of housemaids and the precise responsibilities of the chef, all of which helped to keep homesickness at bay. Edwina simply directed his suggestions and recommendations to Miss Underhill.

As soon as the new scheme was officially agreed with Sir Ernest's trustees, Edwina moved into Mrs Cassel's former bedroom on the second floor. It was larger and lighter than her own had been, with

A Divine Little Daughter

windows looking over Park Lane and down to Hyde Park Corner. The grained woodwork was pale and unpolished and the furniture painted pink, with Edwina's own embroidered cushions on the day bed. Nada helped arrange pictures and photographs, for she had come to Brook House for the baby's arrival. Aunt Victoria was in and out, Cousin Anna promised to be there for the baby's birth and Margaret Lindsay, Marjorie and Dr Simson looked in each day to see how Edwina was getting on. On 2 February Nurse Nisbit moved in. Edwina was surprised, since she felt the same as usual. Nurse Nisbit tried to slow her down. Matinées and early evening performances at the cinema were all Lady Louis was allowed, with nothing more demanding in the morning than visits from the manicurist and gentle fittings with a specialist in firm elasticated underclothes.

There was still no sign of the baby's arrival. A week passed and Nurse Nisbit had been converted to her employer's way of life. Edwina was out late almost every night. She saw another doctor, who told her not to worry, and gave three large luncheon parties. Dickie was sure the baby was about to emerge; on 14 February he wrote to Edwina to tell her so. He was right. At ten o'clock on the 13th Nurse Nisbit telephoned Dr Simson; Edwina was sure it was a false alarm. As soon as he arrived he gave her chloroform and sent for an anaesthetist, who knocked Edwina out. Two hours later, at half past one on the 14th, the baby was born: 'A divine little daughter', Edwina wrote in her diary, using pencil, so as not to ink the sheets: 'Too thrilling'.

Edwina's ordeal, such as it was, was over; the fuss was just beginning. Cables and flowers were delivered every fifteen minutes; Miss Underhill answered fifty letters on the first morning. Aunt Victoria, Cousin Anna and the Brecknocks peered at the infant – 'Baby *too* sweet', Edwina noted, 'and weighs 7.25lb'. Mrs Cassel sent a gift of an arrow made of rubies, Dickie's mother gave her a bracelet that had been Queen Victoria's, and a messenger produced a St Valentine's Day present from Dickie, a ruby ring he had secretly ordered weeks before. He had heard the news at ten in the morning in a cable from Aunt Victoria. The officers' mess toasted the baby's arrival in champagne, the men drank her health in beer and in the afternoon Dickie and his friends went ashore at Madeira, took a special train on the funicular railway to the island's summit and careered ecstatically down to Funchal in basket toboggans. He spent the evening at the casino, and with his winnings bought 'a tiny tiny rocking chair' and 'the sweetest little frock or whatever it is called'. He was delighted to have a girl, 'so much nicer . . . I feel quite drunk about it'. For once, he actually was.

CHAPTER THIRTEEN

Faster and Faster

T he cause of the excitement was now taken to the nursery, where she was fed, bathed, changed, picked up and put down by Nannie Woodard. Enraptured housemaids peeped into the baby's cradle and twice a day she was exhibited to visitors and then hidden again, as if she were a water-colour that had to be protected from the light. The Prince of Wales, Prince George and Marjorie admired her; Wilfrid, Cousin Felix and Philip Sassoon dangled their pocket watches before her startled eyes. Molly was not among the visitors. She remained in Monte Carlo, languishing on a balcony, doctors in attendance, for she was, she said, much frailer than Edwina. Wilfrid wandered disconsolately in and out of Brook House, longing for the old days with Maudie.

Most of the visitors came to see Edwina, not the baby. Aunt Victoria was an exception. She scrutinized the infant from top to toe: she had long limbs, she reported to Dickie, so there was some hope that she would not develop the solid Battenberg wrists and ankles. Although Dickie had not yet seen so much as a photograph of his daughter, he already thought of her as a person, for whom he was buying presents, making plans, and worrying in case the newspaper headline, 'The Richest Baby', should dog her all her life.

Edwina was more detached. Having described her child, 'lots of hair and the divinest little head imaginable and big blue eyes', she found no more to say. Nannie Woodard took over and Edwina concentrated on her recovery. Electric massage helped and three weeks after the birth Edwina was ready for her first outing, lunch with the Brecknocks and the Duke and Duchess of York. Two days later she was seen, slender but shaky, at the Metropole. On 15 March the baby was despatched to Branksome Dene: 'Too sad, parting', wrote Edwina in her diary, '. . . took Nurse Nisbit to the Movies'.

Now she was her proper size again, Edwina was eager to go to Paris for fittings and a week's excitement with Nada. From there they

167

made their way to Mrs Pulitzer's villa at Antibes. When Edwina arrived at the Château de la Garoupe her hostess immediately sent her to bed. Mrs Pulitzer thought it was childbirth, not nightclubs, that had given her guest dark circles under her eyes and that a week's rest would do her good. In two days Edwina revived. She and Nada were terrified of being bored. The pace quickened, their fellow-visitors became racy and over-excited. People announced that they would not be back for breakfast after dances that lasted until dawn. Mrs Pulitzer's parties became larger and noisier. Telephones rang along the coast, as hosts and guests sought brighter and faster ways of entertaining one another.

The South of France had altered since Sir Ernest had first explored Nice and Cannes with his placid, elderly guests. American millionaires had discovered the Riviera, colonizing old-fashioned hotels and enthusiastically reorganizing the plumbing in the villas they rented in the hills above the sea.

Her grandfather's ghost dispelled, Edwina allowed herself a little gaming at the Casino and the Sporting Club. Each day a fresh consignment of amusing guests was decanted from the Blue Train, new friends, and old friends in new guises. Among these was Paula Gellibrand, one of the most striking debutantes of 1919. Now a model for *Vogue*, she arrived with her husband, the Marquis de Casa Maury, and an immense collection of dresses, modelled on nuns' habits but made from expensive fabrics. Edwina liked Paula, who was irreverent and brittle, and who did not seem to mind when her women friends deserted her for trial spins across the bay in her husband's speedboat. Bobby Casa Maury was Castilian. He had been born in Cuba and educated in England, acquiring on the way an alluring mixture of pride, bravado and beautiful manners. He loved powerful Hispano engines – there was one in his speedboat and one in his motor car – and liked showing off to Edwina. She had never been driven so fast in her life: 'Quite marvellous', she said, 'terrific speed', for Bobby was a racing driver and knew how to accelerate on the corners of twisting coastal roads. By the time she returned to London, Edwina had resolved to buy a Hispano for herself.

That was in April. Dickie came home on leave four days later, was introduced to his daughter and, he said, fell in love with her at once. The christening took place on the 22nd in the Chapel Royal; the baby was named Patricia Edwina Victoria. Nannie Woodard, sensibly dressed in grey flannel, displayed the infant to the official photographer, before handing the lacy bundle to Edwina, swathed in black satin with ermine trimmings that tickled the baby's nose. She kept few photographs and press cuttings of Patricia's birth or christening. Edwina's album for 1924 had dozens of snapshots of her friends, playing tennis, hunting, yachting, winning cups at polo, many of herself, three of Simon, her black spaniel, but only nine of Patricia in the first months of her life. Edwina consigned her daughter to experts, as her own mother had done, until the child had acquired a clearer identity. Dickie's attitude was different. He looked for smiles, analysed every murmur and longed for Patricia to crawl so that he could film her with his movie camera. The proudest of proud fathers, he could hardly bear to leave her.

Dickie was as happy as a lark. The naval review at Gibraltar had gone splendidly; 'independent witnesses', he said, had declared his platoon the smartest. His cabaret team, the Blackbirds, had given two successful shows, in which Dickie's performance with Charlie Chaplin's rubber hammer had convulsed the entire ship's company. Between rehearsals he had invented a new way of fixing positions at sea and drafted a plot for a detective story, which he sent to Agatha Christie, suggesting that she might like to use it as a vehicle for Hercule Poirot. (She did.) Bursting with energy, confidence and self-importance, he charged into London for his Easter leave.

The Mountbattens went everywhere. Edwina applauded Dickie's polo, played golf with him, helped him try out ponies, motor cars and dance steps. They were at all the new movies and plays: *St Joan*, *Collusion* and *The Fake*; they attended the first Court, the Investiture and the State Ball for Cousin Missy and the King of Roumania, who pleased Dickie beyond measure by presenting him with a Grand Cross, 'with a lovely light blue and silver ribbon'. The Mountbattens did everything and, when they were with the Princes or their Hollywood friends, adoring crowds joined in. Douglas Fairbanks and Mary Pickford were in London and, although they stayed at the Royal Carlton Hotel, they spent most of their days and the greater part of their nights with the Mountbattens. Dickie took Douglas to the tailor from whom both he and the Prince of Wales got their clothes and Fairbanks ordered two of the garments the cousins had designed: a backless evening waistcoat, secured by a nautical contrivance of loops and string, and a simplified, 'single-ended' evening bow-tie. These were just the thing for Douglas to wear at the private showing of his new film, *The Thief of Baghdad*, in the ballroom at Brook House, with the Prince of Wales, the Duke and Duchess of York, Prince George and Prince Henry among the guests. As an impresario Dickie was spreading his wings.

His most important protégé was Cousin David, although the Prince of Wales would have been taken aback if anyone had said so. Since his marriage Dickie's attitude to his cousin had become almost parental. Having no troubles of his own, he listened the more attentively to the Prince's lamentations and, when he had heard them out, tried to convince him that married life would suit him and help him settle down. He jollied his cousin along as he had done on the tours, keeping his spirits up with trips to the British Empire Exhibition for rides on the Whip and the Giant Switchback. The Prince tried to look interested as they passed the stands; he was struck by a life-size model of himself, sculpted in Canadian butter, perfect, he thought, except that they had made his legs too fat.

Dickie had three months more in *Revenge* before starting the Signal Course at Portsmouth. Meanwhile Edwina ran faster and faster. She was at Wimbledon for the Ladies' semi-finals, Ascot for tea with the King and Queen, Cowes with the Vanderbilts and the Barings. In Paris she looked in on Mary and the Olympic Games. In one seven-day marathon she shot down to Southsea for the Duke and Duchess of Leeds' party on board *Aquitania*, with the Prince, Prince George, Dickie, Georgie, 'Buddy the drummer from Paris and a marvellous band'; observed the Spithead Naval Review from the deck of *Revenge*, dined on the Vanderbilts' yacht and watched the searchlight display from a motor launch; played tennis; returned to London; shopped; gave lunch to the King of Greece and Prince Andrew; whisked down to Broadlands for Molly's three-day Goodwood party, a non-stop cycle of tennis when fine, mah-jong when wet, with dancing and bridge after dinner; careered across country to Goodwood, Edwina at the wheel of the Rolls, racing Marjorie in the Bentley, and, one week later, whistled back up to London to go to the movies with Jeanie Norton and Hugh Molyneux, followed by supper at the Berkeley with Jeanie's husband Richard, her sister Kitty, Freddie Lonsdale the playwright and his wife, finishing the evening at the Brecknocks' party, where George Gershwin played and the Astaires danced.

Edwina's programme was planned like a military campaign. Weekend parties and formal dinners were arranged well in advance; careful hostesses spent days poring over lists of names to produce the right mixture of guests. So shrewdly balanced were these parties that the smallest alteration upset everything: 'Put it in your book', commanded Mrs Greville, Lady Cunard, Mrs Ashley and Mrs Vanderbilt. Woe betide the guest who tried to propose a change; Edwina and her friends marked the dates and kept their engagements from a mixture of duty, habit and fear. Where their own arrangements were concerned, the young people preferred to make decisions on the wing, leaving a run of days empty for an impulsive trip to Paris, keeping evenings free for a descent on a theatre or a cinema, or for raids on Oddenino's, the Embassy or the Quadrant. Edwina liked only two types of gathering: small parties, little lunches and suppers with three or four friends, or big receptions, huge dances and informal meals, where there was no danger of getting stuck beside a bore and from which she could escape when she wanted. Fancy dress was particularly useful (on one occasion Edwina and Jeanie Norton transformed themselves into white ostriches); only her friends knew whether she was there.

The sharp-tongued would have said that Edwina's whole life was a non-stop, sequential fancy-dress party: grey fox-fur with a rose-pink hat for the races, a white and orange silk suit under a blue coat for Cowes, white fox and a red hat for polo. By day she wore high heels and very short skirts, barely covering the knee, at night chiffon evening dresses, fur-trimmed 'cinema capes' and, in the South of France, loose satin pyjamas in dazzling colours. Edwina liked witty clothes: in 1923 she had marked the opening of Tutankhamun's tomb by appearing in a beaded dress embroidered with hieroglyphics and scarabs, and in 1924, when people were swooning over Michael Arlen's novel *The Green Hat*, she was seen about town in a green velvet cloche, the brim pinned back with diamond feathers. Keeping ahead of fashion took time and application. Edwina made three or four visits to Paris each spring and autumn, to fit shoes at Tétreau, hats at Reboux and dresses at Chanel, Vionnet and Patou. She also ordered clothes in London, squeezing in fittings between appointments with the manicurist, masseur, hairdresser and other acolytes who came regularly to Brook House. Their operations could be drastic. When heavy earrings were fashionable, Edwina had her lobes punctured with a device that was supposed to harden the exposed flesh, so that the ear could support the weight of miniature baskets of jewelled fruit. To stay slim, she ate little and exercised violently. Daily golf or tennis and two or three hours' dancing every night so flattened and straightened her figure that she could slip like a serpent into the narrowest dress, without recourse to an elasticated combination-corset. Beneath her clothes she wore nothing but thin chiffon or crêpe de Chine; however close-fitting, her clothes moved over her skin with no discontinuity.

Edwina was a perfectionist. A professional coach helped her improve her tennis, another worked on her golf. A little desultory strumming was popular at weekend parties, as the shadows lengthened between tea and dinner, so she took lessons on the ukelele, an unnecessary investment, since the so-called 'Hawaiian guitar' could produce only three or four simple chords. Training in voice production was also fashionable, the grandest coach being Miss Isobel English, who gave lessons in public speaking to ladies who wished to address drawing-room meetings. Like other well-connected married women, Edwina was invited to join committees, put together to raise money for deserving charities. She found the meetings tedious but dutifully played her part, getting up dinner parties at Brook House before the Marchioness of Carisbrooke's Ball for the Friends of the Poor, Lady Mond's Pompadour Ball in aid of the Infants' Hospital, Lady Tree's League of Mercy Ball and the Duchess of Norfolk's Ball in aid of the Mothercraft Training Society.

A stream of appeals came into Brook House, begging for Lady Louis' patronage: her name, her time, a subscription, or all three. Miss Underhill fielded these applications; it was Edwina, however, who saved the Dockland Settlements Flag Day by insisting that the organizers take out a Pluvius policy, which yielded five thousand pounds when a tenth of an inch of rain fell between breakfast and tea-time. When she was given responsibility Edwina enjoyed it. In 1922, for instance, she had become a trustee of the Cassel Hospital for Functional Nervous Disorders, founded in 1919 by her grandfather, and as the years passed she grew increasingly interested in the management of its affairs. As Sir Ernest had wished, the emphasis was on talking and listening therapy, rather than on drugs, the annual expenditure on pills being no more than a small sum for essentials like aspirin and cough mixture.

In general, however, Edwina thought sitting in conclave with 'old trouts' a self-indulgent waste of time. She was restless and easily bored. Both she and Dickie watched the clock, for opposing reasons. Dickie had too much to do; to save precious minutes, he designed special forms for concise reports and memoranda, practised quick reading and invented super-fast methods of dressing and undressing, with all-in-one undergarments and buttonless boots. Edwina had too little to occupy her good brain and tireless body, so she threw herself into hectic activity. Her frantic travels often ended abruptly. She tipped the two-seater Rolls into a ditch, was caught speeding at 34 miles an hour over a crossroads and prosecuted for dangerous driving. Edwina claimed that the car was too slow, sold it to Lady Alexandra Curzon ('Baba') and ordered a Hispano-Suiza. She decided they needed a fast motor launch like Bobby Casa Maury's latest acquisition, the *Jade*, and, once Dickie had tried it, so did he. The quickest solution was to buy the vessel from Bobby on the spot; the Mountbattens did so, rechristened it *Shadow I*, and engaged as coxswain an ex-torpedo-gunner who could double as an assistant chauffeur. They had made this purchase, Edwina thought, to celebrate Dickie's departure from *Revenge*, but for Dickie *Shadow I* was more of a consolation prize, for he was sad to leave his ship and his friends. After a rowdy farewell dinner he rushed away on leave before he could start to mope.

Polo at Deauville and Le Touquet and then, when autumn came, the Mountbattens sailed for New York with the Prince of Wales. They travelled in the *Berengaria*, one of the biggest ships afloat; Jeanie Norton shared their six-room suite, next to the Prince's quarters. Each morning Dickie had an electric bath and massage, while the Prince boxed with an ex-featherweight champion, and after exercise on the mechanical horse and the rowing machine the cousins plunged into the ship's swimming pool, a vast cave lined with marble columns and mock Pompeian mosaics. Dickie thought he was not enjoying himself as much as usual; he felt faint but decided it must be due to the weather. Edwina danced as long and as late as she did in London; the ship was a floating nightclub, where she and Jeanie entertained themselves much as in Mayfair, with bridge, poker and mah-jong parties, hilarious dinners at the Prince's table and hours of faultless performance on the dance-floor. Dickie felt worse and worse.

The Mountbattens were to stay at Port Washington on Long Island as the guests of Nell and Joshua Cosden, a new oil millionaire. From the moment they arrived things started to go wrong. Dickie was found to have tonsillitis and was put to bed. Edwina resented being left without an escort and sought sympathy from Lytle Hull, a good-looking American who was also staying in the house. While Dickie lay sweating upstairs, she aquaplaned behind fast motor boats, lunched under bright umbrellas on terraces by the water and danced at parties for the Prince. Dressed in only the thinnest evening clothes, for the nights were humid, she sped in streamlined launches across the Sound to Manhattan, staying until dawn at nightclubs in New York. 'Edwina appears to be having a good but hectic time,' Dickie nobly wrote in his diary. When he eventually managed to stagger up, it was for half-days only and, as he collapsed each afternoon, he could hear Edwina and her newest admirer, Harold Vanderbilt's friend from Harvard, Johnny Gaston, making plans on the telephone for the evening's parties.

By the end of the first week Dickie had summoned enough strength to accompany Edwina to the British Ambassador's dinner for the Prince but he could hardly bear the noise and dazzle of the nightclub to which she insisted on taking him afterwards. He could not warm to his wife's new friends; they were too familiar. His only pleasures were a little solitary golf on the Cosdens' private course, experiments with their movie projector and expeditions in a fifty-seven-mile-an-hour speedboat owned by Maurice Hekscher, one of the local polo-playing set. Edwina complained that Dickie was unsociable. Wanting to please her, he stayed up for a 'colossal party', given for the Prince and seven hundred guests by Mr Clarence McKay, in a reproduction eighteenth-century château, filled with tapestries and suits of armour. For those who felt jaded, there was a real-tennis court, a squash court and swimming pool, with Turkish baths and a professional masseur in attendance night and day. Edwina shone but Dickie's light burned dim. In an attempt to re-establish harmony, he moved from his invalid's quarters back into Edwina's bedroom. On their third night together a burglar got into the room and stole Edwina's diamond brooch, sapphires and an emerald ring. The jewels were insured but she was annoyed. Even while sleeping, Dickie could do nothing right.

The second week dragged on, rackety gatherings of Edwina's friends, interminable banquets in honour of the Prince. When Dickie declared that he could endure no more parties, Edwina accused him of being dull. They sat stony-faced through the Wells-Firpo prize-fight: 'No knockout', said Dickie's record, 'and Wells won on points'. So did Edwina. Dickie was dragged to another evening at the Colony, with Tommy Hitchcock, the polo player, and Johnny Gaston.

To cheer himself up, he went by himself to New York to buy the newest movie projector and choose films, finishing the day at Coney Island with a couple of Navy friends. This was more to Dickie's taste: a delicious dinner of hot dogs and ice cream sodas and spent the whole night on wonderful switchbacks and stunt places etc. like a glorified Wembley Amusement Park'. He returned home triumphant at two in the morning, to find that Edwina was dining with the Vincent Astors. Determined to report as soon as possible on his heavenly day, he sat up for her until she came in at six. She felt he was spying on her and was enraged.

The Mountbattens now took up an invitation from Mrs Pulitzer to stay with her at Manhasset and in new surroundings Edwina's temper cooled. Nada, Zia, the Duchess of Westminster and the Earl and Countess of Airlie were there as well and the larger party was less claustrophobic. For two days Edwina did only what her husband liked: aquaplaning off the Long Island shore, going to the *Ziegfeld Follies* and meeting Will Rogers afterwards for supper, admiring Dickie's projector and his collection of new movies. All the time, however, there was thunder in the air.

Edwina rewarded herself for being nice to Dickie by disappearing to New York for a flirtatious lunch with Lytle Hull. In four days' time the Mountbattens were going home, for the Signal Course was about to begin. Edwina announced that she intended to stay. There was another quarrel, which simmered all evening. Edwina had decided that she and Dickie should repay Lytle's hospitality with dinner, a play, dancing and supper at the Lido and El Fey. That night her husband wrote ruefully in his diary that entertaining 'Lyttle' (a revealing misspelling) had cost two hundred pounds.

Dickie rebelled. In the last two days of their holiday he would do as he liked. Edwina could join him or not, as she pleased. He shopped for toys at F. A. O. Schwarz and went again to the Coney Island fairground, and then, his confidence restored, he asked Edwina to listen to what he had to say. He knew that she wanted to see her friends, but could she not spend an evening alone with him for once? He had always warned her that the Navy must come first; that, and only that, was why he was leaving. Edwina melted. They dined together at the Colony, went to George White's *Scandals* and, since

175

they were not in evening dress, ignored the nightclubs and returned to East 73rd Street, the Pulitzers' house in New York. 'Early bed', Edwina noted, but the damage could not be repaired in a night.

Edwina had not been unfaithful to Dickie, not yet, but her restlessness and bad temper were not just symptoms of excessive energy and the desire to assert herself. Their marriage was not a success. Lonely and unhappy, she wanted reassurance, in bed and out of it and, although her husband adored her, he was clumsy and inexperienced. Edwina found it impossible to talk frankly to Dickie about her anxieties, for she feared that he would not take them seriously. She was also afraid that revealing her own insecurities might produce a torrent of embarrassing confessions from him. The fact that she believed in both these possibilities at once shows how confused she was.

Edwina did not know what was wrong and could not have explained it had she wished to, for she knew next to nothing of psychology and would not have thought it relevant to herself. This is not surprising; it was 1924, Edwina came from a conventional, unreflective family and, although the Mountbattens and their friends joked about 'complexes', they used the term to describe anything from passing fads to run-of-the-mill fantasies about boots and bicycles. It did not occur to a young woman who could not respond to an ardent husband that she should discuss her difficulties with a doctor. Instead, Edwina attacked Dickie, knowing, as unhappy people do, how to cause maximum pain. During their rows in America, she had discovered where he was most vulnerable. She accused him of not caring for her, of disliking her friends and belittling her tastes. How was Dickie to answer? If he argued with Edwina, she refused to believe him. This was too complicated; he was baffled and hurt. He apologized, agreed that he was a bore, a snob, too fond of uniforms, a hopeless dancer, a fusspot, a poor driver and, when someone else was driving, a bad navigator who made them late for dinner parties. Much of this was true but it was unfortunate that Dickie admitted it, for Edwina despised him all the more.

As a lover Dickie was unsatisfactory. He was enthusiastic but awkward, Edwina was tense. Unlike his father, who as a twenty-six-year-old bachelor had enjoyed a delightful affair with Mrs Lily Langtry, Dickie had married with no previous practice of love-making. At the beginning he had been nervous, which was natural, but after the

Mountbattens' three scratchy weeks in America it should have been obvious that things were going wrong. Dickie simply concluded that Edwina was over-tired and that he had been too demanding. Full of self-reproach, he sailed home on the *Homeric*. He was determined to cultivate the sort of skills Edwina seemed to like and, as a start, asked his fellow-passengers, Violet Westminster, Duff Cooper and Tony Pulitzer, to teach him to play bridge. Edwina's last-minute change of mind meant that Dickie had a large suite to himself but he tried not to resent the extravagance, working off his irritation in the gym: 'Amazed to find how unfit I was.'

Having got what she wanted, Edwina was contrite. For two or three days she was subdued, concentrating on duty visits to the Warburgs and her grandfather's other surviving friends. Her rowdier associates did not allow her a long retreat. Soon she was spending every night at the Alabam', the Mirador, El Fey, the Colony or the Werewolf and, when she and Jeanie decided to have an afternoon sleep in their rooms at the Ambassador Hotel, they were woken by Miller and Farrell's band, sent up by their friends to play in the sitting-room. When Edwina returned with Jeanie to the Cosdens' Long Island house, Lytle Hull and Johnny Gaston were there as well, sometimes together, more often separately. 'Row!!' Edwina wrote in her diary. 'Lytle went off to Boston early'; 'Awful muddle about everything and various rows!! I returned and stayed in bed. John went off to Boston'; 'I went to the cinema with Lytle'; 'John suddenly returned! Quiet evening! Talked!'; 'Row with Lytle. Dined at home. Made up row. Talked late'.

It is easy to guess what the rows were about. By remaining in America after Dickie had sailed, Edwina had emphasized her independence from her husband. Throughout her stay she had sought the attention of attractive, energetic men, with money and time to spare, protecting herself, she thought, by keeping several admirers in play simultaneously. This, she believed, showed that she was not available. Instead, for they were all vain, each man assumed that he had been singled out and, when Edwina refused him, accused her of trifling with his affections and seducing his friends. After a month of this, they were all exhausted.

Edwina had made a mistake. Bored by her marriage, she thought she had escaped to a place where she could behave as she wished. America was the New World, this the smartest, snappiest, most modern city in it. Because everyone she knew there liked new shows, new movies, new music and new people, she assumed that New York was less snobbish and philistine than London. People were generous, so she thought them open-minded. Edwina had not understood that, though new-minted, American society was respectable. For young, rich people, life was exciting but safe, like a children's party. Women were expected to behave with propriety; Edwina had exceeded the limits, encouraged by a crowd of admiring men. Now it seemed that she did not intend to deliver what she had promised – and her suitors, who looked foolish, were annoyed. Was Edwina wild or tame? She could not be both.

The Prince had made the same error on a larger scale. Some of his advisers thought that he was not always treated with sufficient respect by crowds and his critics and that his privacy was constantly invaded by the press. These views found their way into the London news-papers and were reprinted in America, where they were not warmly received. The American people were bewildered, said an editorial in *The World*. Was the Prince of Wales a serious public figure or a young man of fashion? He could not be both: 'In this country we specialize.' Consistency was expected of statesmen and party-goers alike: 'A President at a cabaret would be as unthinkable as Mr Valentino at a hearing of the Interstate Commerce Commission'. *The World* did not believe, though it repeated, some of the wilder stories that were circulating: that the Prince had lost his wallet, for example, while escorting an actress home in the middle of the night. Even so, the editor declared, by his choice of friends and diversions the Prince had managed to provoke an exhibition of social climbing 'which has added nothing to his prestige, nor to the prestige of royalty in general'.

The Prince and Edwina had misjudged their audience. The Prince had behaved like a playboy but expected to be treated as the heir to the throne. Edwina had flirted and then withdrawn, claiming to be shocked. Their hosts did not like their guests to blow hot and cold; these much-acclaimed visitors had failed the test.

It was time to go home. Edwina and Jeanie booked a suite on the *Aquitania*, Maurice Hekscher gave an all-night party, Lytle and Johnny, in the Cosdens' boat, escorted the liner out to sea. Weller groaned in her cabin, and 'dead beat and terribly depressed', Edwina made her way back to Dickie.

CHAPTER FOURTEEN

Infidelity

T he *Aquitania* came in to Southampton on 14 October. Dickie got leave from the Signal School, where he had begun the course two weeks before, changed out of uniform and, thus disguised, crept up to Edwina as she disembarked. This surprise fell flat: 'Dickie there to meet me', she wrote tersely in her diary.

Although Dickie was less stylish than Edwina's American admirers, he was reliable and devoted. Perhaps a little domesticity would put things right. Since their marriage the Mountbattens had lived in temporary lodgings, or with friends and relations; until recently, even Brook House had been shared with Mrs Cassel. What they needed, they thought, was a place of their own in the country and, just before their American trip, they found it. This was Adsdean in Sussex. It was not a beautiful house. Through a sea-mist, it looked like a cast-off wing of the Louvre; seen close, it was a jumble of ill-assorted wings. On the other hand, the park was large, with well-stocked woods and pleasant rides, and since Adsdean was near Chichester it could be reached easily from London, Broadlands, Portsmouth and Southampton, as the Mountbattens proved by timed experiments with the Rolls. Indeed, if all else failed, Dickie could get to the Signal School by sea.

Negotiations had been protracted and uncertain. Edwina and Dickie wanted to buy; the owners, Mr and Mrs Tennent, wished to let. The Mountbattens offered to rent; the Tennents decided to sell. Edwina and Dickie finally took the house and grounds on a long lease – argument continued for years over the status of the roads and the home farm – and, three days after Edwina returned from America, they moved in, with the servants, cars and ponies. On the next day Nannie brought the baby, who had spent the summer and autumn at Branksome and Wherwell, and that afternoon Mary and Marjorie arrived, closely followed by the ping-pong table and cinema apparatus. On the third day the Mountbattens welcomed their first guests:

the Casa Maurys, Poppy Baring and Prince George. Every weekend and on almost every weekday for the next fifteen years, when Edwina was at Adsdean, visitors were there too.

One habitué, at least for the first twelve months, was Mr Brittain Osborne, contractor and decorator, of Bond Street (address for telegrams: Adornista, London), whose team of workmen tidied up garrets and cellars, workshops and stables, divided the attics into maids' rooms, built quarters for the footmen, rewired, replumbed and reconstructed. Woodwork, walls, floors, furniture and hangings were renewed in the Pink, White, Yellow, Mauve and Blue Rooms, in the East Bedroom and the Best Bedroom (Peach), in the Day and Night Nurseries, Miss Ashley's Room and His Lordship's and Her Ladyship's rooms. Edwina wanted the house to look comfortable, harmonious and light. She slept in a bedroom of pink and silver, with crystal light-fittings and door furniture, and her bathroom was tiled with silvered mirror glass. Dickie required a special box-spring mattress, a lampshade painted with a Battle at Sea and a new down pillow made with feathers from his old one. He designed the lettering on the doorplates (BATHROOM) and specially printed endolithic labels (PLEASE SWITCH OFF THE LIGHT). He ordered a fire-escape and boiler and here and there installed a handy device combining a buzzer and flashing lamp, his own invention.

So many workmen went to and fro on their bicycles that Mr Tennent became suspicious and sent his wife to see how extensive the Mountbattens' alterations were. Agitated letters arrived; the landlords had understood that nothing was to be disturbed. When Dickie asked for permission to construct a nine-hole golf course, a hard tennis court and a polo ground, Mr Tennent was irate. After weeks of correspondence between solicitors, the Tennents at last agreed to everything, on the improbable condition that the property be restored to its original state when the Mountbattens gave up the lease.

The neighbours were agog. They heard about the decorations from the Bishop, who was asked to Adsdean for lunch, and they saw Lady Louis herself, a bird of paradise among doves, when she opened the Church bazaar. Edwina paid calls, hoping that people would be out but finding them hospitably at home: 'A terrible time. Quite exhausted.' Those who left cards in return generally found that Lady Louis was not there. For Dickie's sake she did receive a string of officers and their wives, who went home quite tamed, for even the

Infidelity

stiffest unbent when, after dinner, they were taught 'the Adsdean game', a mixture of table tennis and fives, in which players struck the ball with the flat of their hands, aiming for a corner pocket but frequently hitting a window: 'ruin to a billiard table', Marjorie observed. At weekends Dickie brought his fellow participants in the Signal Course to ride, shoot and play polo. After tea there were games of Progressive Ping Pong, while the less boisterous walked with Edwina or, if wet, practised the ukelele round the piano in the drawing-room. Edwina liked these lively officers, all younger than Dickie. Formal parties were another matter: 'Lunch with Dickie's Commander . . . awful'; dinner, 'Sticky'. When these invitations were issued, Edwina remembered that she did not like driving in the dark, that the roads were bad and policemen unkind: 'Dreadful fog'; 'Small car skidded into ditch'. Only the most persistent and skilful hostess could entrap Edwina; in her first two years at Adsdean she dined no more than six times at the houses of Dickie's senior colleagues.

People did not mind. They knew that Lady Louis' programme was full and that she was often away. This was true. Mary was now back from Paris and Edwina had to be in London to take her to dressmakers and chaperone her at parties, Molly being preoccupied with the search for a house in Westminster, for the Conservatives had got back into government in 1924 and Wilfrid was now Minister of Transport. He had to be near the House of Commons for late-night sittings and Molly wanted a headquarters from which to direct his political career. Mary was nervy and needed careful supervision. She looked confident: Edwina had taken her to have her red hair bobbed and permanently waved, guided her choice of clothes and equipped her with a motor car but, despite her sister's help, Mary found it difficult to make a splash. There was nothing new to say about the second Miss Ashley, for it had all been said about the first. Beside Lady Louis' Hispano-Suiza, her sister's Morris Cowley two-seater looked unremarkable; when Mary was presented at the first Court in 1925, her white dress only served as a foil for Edwina's gown of gold lamé. Three weeks later Edwina had six hundred people to a ball in Mary's honour, preceded by dinner for fifty. A cocktail bar was set up in the garden at Brook House, the dining-room was decorated with pink roses and mauve sweet peas and the ballroom stairs with spiky lupins, smelling faintly of pepper. Ambrose brought the band from the Embassy and the guests danced until five in the morning. It was hard to find Mary among the crowd; looking over the banisters, the housemaids could just see her, in a pale, floating dress, wisps of many-coloured chiffon falling round the hem. The newspapers said, meaning it as a compliment, that she looked almost as pretty as her elder sister.

Throughout June and July Edwina escorted Mary to dances and suppers, briefed her beforehand and compared notes with her next morning. Mary learnt to freeze unwanted admirers at twenty paces and, taken out by Edwina on Buttercup Day, how to sell flags for charity. Each weekend she travelled to another county and another house, accompanied by her maid. If she had no other invitation, she came to Adsdean. This programme continued until the first week of August, when Dickie and Edwina went over to Deauville for polo and Mary joined Wilfrid and Molly at Broadlands. Her visit was a disaster. Bobbie Cunningham-Reid was also staying in the house. He had often come to shoot; now he was there to fish. He was twenty-eight, tall and sleek, his perfect smile enhanced by the elegant line of his moustache. Bobbie looked pleased with himself, with reason – as one of the youngest officers in the Royal Flying Corps, he had shot down ten enemy aircraft in the First World War, for which he had received the Distinguished Flying Cross. Molly thought him a pet and some said that it was at her suggestion that Wilfrid had made Cunningham-Reid his Parliamentary Private Secretary, his eyes and ears in the House of Commons. The older and younger man got on well; Bobbie was ambitious and, keen to succeed in Parliament, listened respectfully to Wilfrid's stories of past political skirmishes. Those with sharp eyes considered him ingratiating.

To Molly's consternation and Wilfrid's surprise, Mary now announced that Bobbie was in love with her and she with him; worse, she had written a number of letters telling him so. There was a row. Mary was told that she was too young to know her own mind. Who could see into the heart of Cunningham-Reid? He might not be looking for a fortune – but as Mary's husband he would find one, for when she married she would receive the whole of the income from her share of Sir Ernest's estate. It was only three months since Mary had been launched; Mary's family did not wish her to be captured so early, brought down by a dare-devil like Cunningham-Reid.

Wilfrid tried to reason with Mary but botched it. She became hysterical. Molly sent for Edwina. By the time she got to Broadlands,

Infidelity

Mary had escaped to Brook House and, when Edwina reached Brook House, she found that Mary had fled to Adsdean. There Dickie comforted her until Edwina arrived, exhausted, at one o'clock in the morning. The next three days were occupied with interviews with Mary, with Wilfrid and Molly, and with Bobbie Cunningham-Reid. Mary, who remained at Adsdean, agreed to forget Bobbie and her plans for an early marriage; Bobbie undertook neither to see nor to correspond with Mary for the time being. Then, just as life was returning to normal for Dickie ('Work as usual - very interesting too, in connection with the short wave receiver') and Edwina ('Hugh came to lunch on his way to Beaulieu'), Mary broke down completely, wrecking the furniture in Dickie's bedroom, bursting into the drawing-room in her dressing-gown, lecturing Aunt Victoria, who had come to stay, and accusing an inoffensive guest of being a brain specialist in disguise. Edwina sent for her father but the doctor thought that if Mary saw Wilfrid she would lose what remained of her reason and he was hidden in the billiard room. Madness sharpened Mary's suspicions. She began to search the house, so Wilfrid was sent back to Broadlands. For three months Mary stayed at Adsdean, attended by four nurses working shifts, for she was too wild to be left alone. Five experts examined her, including an eminent psychoanalyst. 'Definitely not *dementia praecox*', Dickie noted in his diary: 'All attribute the blame largely where I do – curse him!' Nor did Dickie's opinion of Cunningham-Reid improve when Bobbie's mother arrived at Adsdean, uninvited, early one Sunday morning. Her son, she explained, possessed a wonderful magnetism. 'Alas', Dickie observed, 'we needed no telling'.

Edwina knew that her sister was highly strung – Mary had only managed to face her coming-out after a six-month regime of X-rays and injections – but she was shocked at the extent of her collapse. The remedy, she thought, was not to banish Cunningham-Reid or extract undertakings from Mary but to build up her confidence and hope that she would shake off her infatuation. With this in mind she looked for an attractive place where Mary could concentrate on getting better. By November she had found a suitable house at Blackwater, near Sunningdale, and arranged for Nurse Harrison to look after things there. When Mary was stronger, Edwina told Wilfrid, she could go abroad for several months, escorted by some suitable person who would keep Cunningham-Reid away. On this basis Wilfrid reluctantly agreed to release Mary from her promise not to communicate with Bobbie. Her rage abated. In late November Mary and her medical team left Adsdean.

Dickie's course at the Signal School had lasted nearly a year. It was comprehensive and difficult, with an examination every fortnight: Heliograph Orals, Coding, Valves, Procedure, Organization, Technical W/T . . . He did not find it easy – 'Signal Bosun's Exam, very stiff'; 'Theory A Paper, being very long some of us could not finish' – but he was conscientious: 'Worked up to 2 a.m. and am just about cooked'. After a day of polo he studied all night and, when he and Edwina were in London, Dickie would slip away to his books and charts while she went with her friends to a nightclub. If Edwina was at Brook House and Dickie was not required for parties there, he stayed in barracks at Portsmouth, sometimes keeping the spaniel with him for company. Often the only entry in his diary was 'Work as usual'. When the course ended in the late summer of 1925, Dickie, but no one else, was surprised when he came out top.

He still missed *Revenge* but, if he could not get back to his old ship, it should come to him. Mr Osborne was shown over Mountbatten's former cabin and, with the help of Mr Riggs, the electrician, invited to reproduce it at Brook House. The walls and ceiling of Dickie's bedroom were lined with cork and sprayed with white enamel, ducting was installed, as in a battleship, and the carpets removed. There was a regulation bunk, with brass rail, on top of regulation cupboards, and a folding wash-stand and other ship's furniture were made to order by ex-Servicemen. The windows were turned into two brass-bound portholes; a fan blew a stiff breeze into the room. The glass was replaced with *trompe l'oeil* views of the Grand Harbour at Valletta, in sunshine or, with the pressing of a switch, by moonlight. Against this painted background Dickie arranged his collection of cut-out ships, the Mediterranean Fleet at fifty feet to an inch, Edwina's birthday present to him. When darkness fell, or was induced to fall, the miniatures twinkled real Morse signals to each other, all along the line. If Dickie felt lonely, he could switch on a gadget that hummed soothingly like a ship's engines. There was another comforting presence: the hat, uniform and decorations of Dickie's father, displayed in a glass case, a First Sea Lord in full dress standing in the corner. Here Dickie slept in nautical austerity, while Edwina lay among swansdown and satin next door.

Infidelity

From September 1925, when he was posted to the Naval College at Greenwich, Dickie lived as much at Brook House as at Adsdean, rising at six to allow time for exercises, a plunge and shower – his bathroom was decorated with weeds, rocks and fishes, so that he might imagine himself deep-sea diving – before he breakfasted and rushed off to classes. Late-night parties, official engagements and polo had some-how to be fitted in to this routine. To help him do so, Dickie persuaded the Rolls-Royce coach builders to put a collapsible seat into a New Phantom, so that he could flit to work through what remained of the night, having first changed into pyjamas. His days were full: Physics, Intermediate Maths, Applied Mechanics, visits to valve factories, wireless transmitting and receiving stations, Radio House in London, 'where the Marconi Co. control everything' and, at the Astronomer Royal's invitation, to the Royal Observatory. He continued to invent – an experiment based on supersonic waves, a new central heating system for Adsdean; he was constantly adapting and refining. He polished up his French and German, learnt to dance the Charleston, worked at his polo. His latest mania was motor-boat racing. Compared with Maurice Hekscher's speedboat, *Shadow I* seemed slow, and early in 1925 Dickie ordered a fifty-five-miles-an-hour launch from an American yard, diplomatically explaining that this would allow British boatbuilders to see the most up-to-date American design. By the summer *Shadow II* had completed trials at Southampton; the engine was so clean and steady, the manufacturers said, that the helmsman and mechanic could safely wear evening clothes and silk hats while racing her. At the Hythe Regatta in July *Shadow II* came second in her class and at Bournemouth in August, to the Mountbattens' delight, she beat Claude Grahame-White's dashing *Gee Whiz*. In the autumn *Shadow I* was sold; the Mountbattens replaced her with a yacht, bought from Grahame-White for four thousand pounds. The sixty-six-ton *Shrimp* had three cabins and a large saloon; by the spring they had added a fourth cabin, a bathroom, a new deck-house, pantry and galley, a cook, a mechanic, a sofa and a gramophone.

Dickie's other passion was his baby daughter. He dressed her in his monkey jacket and photographed her, took her to see his ponies, flew his model aeroplane with her and brought her home a hedgehog he found in a lane at Adsdean. On her second birthday there was a tea party at Brook House. 'Ten children', Dickie noted; Edwina simply gave a list of her own friends. She remained detached from her

185

daughter. The child was twenty-two months old before Edwina referred to her in her diary as 'Patricia' rather than 'the baby'. She played with her occasionally and two or three times a year, when Nannie was away on holiday, Edwina lunched in the nursery. The infant was an ornament, with whom her mother was occasionally photographed for *Eve*, *Queen* and *The Lady*. In July 1925 they were seen together at Cowes, Patricia dressed in a tiny replica of her mother's dress and jacket.

It is true that Patricia was safer in the nursery, shielded from busybodies, journalists and kidnappers. She was also out of the way of family dramas, for Mary's breakdown was not the only crisis with which Edwina had to cope. In September 1925 Mrs Cassel died at Branksome Dene. Like Sir Ernest, she was taken to the cemetery at Kensal Green, and after the funeral a subdued gathering of friends and relations assembled at Brook House, where the lights were dimmed and the great mirrors reflected only the mourners' impenetrable black. 'She was such a dear to us both', said Dickie. Mrs Cassel's last present to him had been a firescreen, on which she had worked his coat of arms in *petit point*.

Further interruption came from Molly, who was building a mock Queen Anne house of pink and orange brick in Smith Street, a few hundred yards from the House of Commons. While Gayfere House was being finished, she stayed at Brook House, since she had to be in London to talk to carpenters, electricians and painters. Like Mrs Viveash and Mrs Maugham, she now went in for contrasting colours, uncarpeted floors and simplicity. In her new establishment Molly entertained for Wilfrid, now in his second year at the Ministry. His chief preoccupation was the passage through Parliament of the Electricity Bill; it was hard work and he would have preferred to stay in his office, supervising the classification and labelling of roads. Molly complained that he was overworked and, to persuade him to come home between tea and dinner, instituted 'husbands' parties', for men only, at which cocktails were served between five-thirty and a quarter to eight. Wilfrid was not in the inner circle of Ministers, but, in compensation, Molly sought to be the most advanced of political hostesses. She served cocktails before luncheon, learnt to tango, and wrote an article for the *Graphic* on 'Modes and Manners in the London Season'.

Molly strove to eclipse Edwina, as smoke might try to hide the moon. Mrs Ashley appeared in green lace and a gold sash; her stepdaughter wore black with diamond shoulder-straps and on each wrist a wide diamond bracelet with a diamond hook and eye. Molly had ostrich feathers, Edwina orchids made of amethysts. In London and, triumphantly, at Deauville, Lady Louis was proclaimed one of the six best-dressed women in the world. Her hair had been shingled early in 1925; she was sleek and elegant in summer ermine, in grey fox and apple-green silk. She wore neat suits from Chanel, double-breasted tweeds, a dark blue coat with a collar of red fox. Her innovations were instantly taken up: diamond slides in her hair in the evening, silver stockings and silver kid shoes, flowered chiffon frocks for dancing. She appeared at Deauville in one of the new rubberized silk bathing dresses, with a tightly knotted turban to keep her hair dry. Edwina adopted a fashion only if she thought it suited her. The Duchess of Peneranda had made it smart to sunbathe but when Edwina was not in the sea she covered herself up with one of Molyneux's chrysanthemum-patterned robes. In the evening, when other women wore black, she appeared in a petunia silk dress embroidered with crystals.

The world might have thought that Lady Louis lived her life in public. She was at all the brightest clubs, her current favourite being the Kit-Cat in the Haymarket, opened in the spring of 1925 in the presence of the Home Secretary. Four hundred people could squeeze on to the dance floor, Sophie Tucker sang and members could dine for fifteen and sixpence a head. A novel ventilation system made it possible to breathe. Artists from the supper clubs sometimes deigned to perform at home: George Gershwin came on from the Savoy to play 'Rhapsody in Blue' at Brook House; his song, 'The Man I Love', flopped in the United States until Edwina heard it and launched it in London. Layton and Johnstone sang at Lady Loughborough's dinner for Rudolf Valentino; 'Hutch', the ugly but dextrous black pianist, played in Marjorie's drawing-room. Stars like these disdained a fee, so their patrons gave them wrist-watches and cigarette cases, engraved with fulsome tributes: Paul Parnell of the Whitehall Band sported a pair of diamond cufflinks, a present from the Mountbattens, and, from the Prince of Wales, a diamond-studded watch fob with an ostrich feather crest and the royal motto 'Ich Dien'.

'Complete hecticness', Edwina wrote in her diary. She and Jeanie went to Mrs Fellowes' 'Night-time Day': breakfast at eight in the evening, followed by riding in the Row, luncheon at midnight, then tennis, ending with cocktails and dinner at the Savoy at seven o'clock in the morning. There was no time for sleep, as Edwina raced from one engagement to the next: 'The whole car skidded completely round . . . and crashed into a lorry on the way'; 'Smash with Hispano on way home. No one hurt'. No time either for discrimination: John Barrymore in *Hamlet*; 'Excellent'; the next night, *No, No Nanette*: 'Marvellous'. Dickie had his own aesthetic yardstick: 'Ibsen's play *The Doll's House* with Madge Talmadge in it. I had had it on the movies in *Revenge*'. He knew what he liked: *Ben Hur*; *The Lost World*; Sheila Loughborough's Egyptian magician; *The Gold Rush*; lunch with Constantinesco, inventor of the gearless car.

Dickie finished his course at Greenwich in the spring of 1926 and after Easter leave joined the battleship *Centurion* for a short spell with the Reserve Fleet. Since he was based at Portsmouth, he was able to come home to his ponies, his polo team and a new obsession: golf. For his birthday Edwina bought him a new set of clubs, including a Mammoth Niblick from Hamleys, the old ones being handed on to Thorogood, who practised keenly so that his master would have an expert partner. To make the game more challenging, Dickie occasionally wore a blindfold. When Edwina was out with her friends, he perfected his latest inventions: a wireless telegraphy history card, a valve buzzer circuit and a wireless tuning calculator. For company at Adsdean he had Nona Crichton's husband, Dick, who acted as the Mountbattens' agent, and Peter Murphy, who came on extended visits. Peter could talk about anything, said Andrew Yates, one of the Adsdean polo team, 'including the Virgin Birth, which he seemed to think had been a conjuring trick'. With Peter's help Dickie began work on a definitive handbook on polo, *Polo* by 'Marco'.

At weekends Edwina returned to Adsdean. The house was full. The Brecknocks came for short visits, the Casa Maurys for long ones, since Paula, when away from home, was susceptible to colds, flu and more exotic germs, and needed time both to develop and recover from her illnesses. Prince George appeared when he had leave from the Navy and the Prince of Wales descended in a light aeroplane. The Metcalfes drove down from London; Edwina had helped Fruity choose the ring when he got engaged to Lady Alexandra Curzon in 1925 and Dickie had been best man at their wedding. Georgie and Nada buzzed

Infidelity

over from St George, Sheila Loughborough brought 'Buffles' Mil-banke, 'the Boxing Baronet'. Jeanie Norton came with Lionel Portar-lington and his wife Winnie, a wealthy Australian, able, it was said, to live on the income of her income. Mary was absent. She was visiting various gentle Italian watering-places with Baroness von Buxhoevden, Aunt Victoria's old friend. To help the household operate efficiently, Dickie prepared a set of forms, issued each night to every guest, for completion in triplicate. One copy was retained, a second went to Dickie and the third to the staff. Guests indicated when they wished to be called in the morning (Dickie had designed an adjustable indicator, fixed to each bedroom door), ticked their preferred breakfast food and drink, listed the meals they intended to take that day. Was a car required, a horse, golf clubs or a boat? Were other friends expected and, if so, at what time? Would they be swimming, playing tennis, golf, or 'other'? Some visitors found this irksome.

The Mountbattens' stamina seemed inexhaustible, remarkably, since throughout the middle 1920s one or the other of them was generally ill or injured. Many of Dickie's wounds were self-inflicted, at golf, polo or in the laboratory: bruised cheeks, a damaged knee, electric shocks, a poisoned finger. He had conjunctivitis and sciatica and a selection of ailments left over from childhood: 'Was operated on for the 3rd time for tonsils and adenoids, this time I trust success-fully'. His flu, like his wife's, was seasonal. Edwina found it hard to shake off even little colds; although her frame was strong, her resistance was poor. Blood tests, X-rays and bismuth meals showed nothing significant but from the middle 'twenties to the early thirties' she suffered from toothache, neuralgia, intestinal cramp and, month after month, what her letters described as 'affairs in a flood'. She was prescribed massage, sleeping draughts and, for her eyes, beams, drops and exercises. Her nose was cocained and an infected toe cut off. She temporarily gave up smoking. Nothing helped, or not for long. 'Bad evening', 'still sunk'; on several occasions she fainted at dinner. She overtired herself, ate too little and strained her eyes because she thought spectacles disfiguring. Her days and nights were exhausting, being filled with trivia. There was also the strain of deceiving Dickie.

Edwina had dozens of admirers, 'ginks' they were called in the private slang of the Mountbatten circle. Dickie considered some of Edwina's friendships unwise but believed that they were innocent.

Most – but not all – of them were. Edwina's intimates fell into two categories. There were those who escorted her to supper parties and revues, when Dickie was unavailable. Edwina had a dozen such companions. Dickie did not, as a rule, dislike these men but he would have been surprised at some of the excursions they made with his wife. 'To queer places' with Aksel Wichfeld, after an evening at dubious dancing spots in Paris; 'a very spicy play' with Pierre Mérillon, a rich Swiss bachelor who, as people said, 'followed the seasons'; 'odd places' with Deering Davis; 'hectic night' with Antonio Portago, a sinuous South American. 'He danced a wonderful tango' but, Marjorie said, 'was otherwise quite useless'. Edwina made no secret of these expeditions. Dickie could have read all about them in her diaries, as the housemaids did, when they found them unlocked. Trouble did come not from here.

Dickie's real rivals were men like himself, good-looking, energetic and well-connected, with something he lacked, sexual assurance. Hugh Molyneux was one. His affair with Edwina began early in 1925; Dickie suspected nothing. In October 1925 Molyneux left England for India; a replacement was standing by. In July Edwina had been reintroduced to Laddie Sanford, whom she had first met at a party on Long Island the previous autumn. He had taken a house at Uxbridge for the summer and invited Edwina for lunch and a swim in his heated open-air pool. She took Fruity with her as a chaperone but by the end of the afternoon he had become redundant. The outcome of the visit was already obvious.

Sanford and his two sisters came from a family of wealthy carpet manufacturers, famous diplomats and celebrated horse-breeders. Laddie had plenty of money and could do as he liked, which was to hunt big game in Africa – his grandfather had worked with Stanley in the Congo – and supervise the horses that raced in the family colours of purple and gold. Sergeant Murphy, winner of the Grand National in 1923, came from Laddie's stable. Clean-living Englishmen found Laddie repellent. They called him a bounder and said he knew every *demi-mondaine* in London. They put up with him, however, for the sake of their wives, who thought him sweet: 'a nice, charming American', Edwina's contemporaries said later, 'a bit dim but a very good polo-player'. Laddie's current girlfriend was Doris Delavigne, who hunted amusing men. Edwina made her look shop-worn and insignificant and she was dropped. Telling everyone her heart was

Infidelity

broken, Miss Delavigne moved on to Lord Castlerosse, the stupefyingly fat gossip columnist on the *Express*, and married him.

By the end of July Laddie had been invited to Adsdean for the party to celebrate the Mountbattens' third wedding anniversary. Dickie did not like his guest but, as Sanford had been No. 1 in the Cambridge University Polo Team, he was a useful recruit for the Adsdean *équipe*. A month later Laddie was at Deauville, where, in navy-blue jacket, white trousers and two-tone brogues ('co-respondents' shoes') he was constantly at Edwina's side. Dickie was unperturbed even when it was reported, a fortnight later, that a client had asked a Bond Street jeweller to send several thousand pounds' worth of cigarette cases to Adsdean so that Lady Louis might select one.

Edwina had been distant but Dickie thought that she was ill. In mid-September he made a touching entry in his diary: 'Slept with Edwina!!' and, the next night, 'Slept in Edwina's room again'. 'Had dinner in bed with Dickie', was all Edwina wrote. His affection was more than she could bear. On the third night she rebuffed him. 'Edwina and I', Dickie noted, 'ever so nearly had a row'. He saw no warning signals, for he could not imagine that Edwina might be bored with him. Indeed, his most recent birthday present to his wife had been a portrait of himself, secretly commissioned from de Laszlo.

Edwina was careful to keep up appearances. She arranged Mary's house, moved furniture and pictures from Branksome Dene, which was to be sold, organized the Mount Vernon Hospital Ball, entertained Dickie's relations. She ensured that Adsdean and Brook House ran smoothly, that the servants did not quarrel and the guests were comfortable. Her surroundings were well ordered, her appearance perfect. Emotionally, however, Edwina was in disarray. She was increasingly irritated by Dickie, who, not being Laddie, did everything wrong. He was baffled and at the beginning of December confided in his cousin: 'Went to see David . . . He had a queer story about Edwina'. Dickie emerged from St James's Palace in a state of shock. The fog was so thick, he said, that he had better walk home in front of the car. In that way he could try to hide his misery from the driver. Dickie did not know how best to begin a discussion with Edwina. He did not want to injure her and he knew how easily she could find the words to hurt him. In fact there was no time to talk: she was dressing for Sheila Loughborough's dinner for Rudolf Valentino.

In the New Year Laddie returned to London and Edwina's gloom

191

lifted. He was at Brook House for lunch, for tea, for dinner. In the afternoon he and Edwina went to the cinema; at night he joined the Mountbattens at the theatre and accompanied them afterwards to the Kit-Cat. From there Dickie went home to bed; Edwina and Laddie moved on to eat kippers at Uncle's: 'Home 5 a.m.'. Dickie hated it, especially when Laddie sat at the other end of the table at Brook House, smiling smugly. Edwina's friends used to call on her in the morning and sit in her bedroom talking until it was time for her to dress. Laddie was the first to arrive. He looked so proprietorial that the others were embarrassed, especially when, as Dickie passed the door, Edwina called out, over the tea cups, that she was just in here with Laddie. Even when the Mountbattens were alone, Dickie was excluded. 'Darlingest', Edwina wrote in one evasive little note: 'So sorry I turned you out last night – I think it was the plague!' In London Edwina and Laddie went about openly together: 'To the 1st night of Cochran's new revue 1926. Quite good. After to the Embassy and talked'. To spare Dickie's feelings, Jeanie Norton said Edwina had spent the evening with her; by this time, however, he knew how things stood.

Jeanie was Edwina's closest woman friend. Like Edwina, she did as she pleased, but on less money. She and her husband Richard had sold their house in Westminster and moved to Great Cumberland Place, near Park Lane but on the wrong side of Marble Arch, and from here she went on weekdays to her office at the New Gallery Picture House in Regent Stret. For Jeanie had a job. This was unusual but people took it in their stride: had not Jeanie's mother, Lady Kinloch, the painter, opened a place in Chelsea where decorated furniture could be bought? The proprietors of the Picture House hoped to attract Mrs Norton's friends by showing movies that she thought they would like, starting with Ivor Novello in *The Rat* and, to follow, *Satan in Sables*. Jeanie's husband was a film producer and he had encouraged her to work at the New Gallery. Here she might catch the eye of a successful director, much as Diana Cooper had drawn that of Max Reinhardt, who had dressed her in Ospovat's beautiful clothes and put her in his theatrical spectacle, *The Miracle*, from which she had earned a large salary on two continents.

Jeanie was attractive: slim, long-legged, with wide-spaced eyes. Her smile was warmer and her short hair more curly than Edwina's but people said they looked alike. At times each might indeed have been

192

taken for the other, as they sat together on the sand at Deauville, in near-identical black bathing suits and smoked glasses, or in a dim-lit nightclub, as one or the other floated past, trailing essence of roses, in the arms of the Prince of Wales. They wore the same drop-waisted dresses, the same narrow satin gowns; Edwina was the one with the emerald and diamond chain, the Cartier bracelets and ring. Jeanie did not attract the attention of film or stage producers. She secured a bigger prize, the attention of Max Beaverbrook, owner of the *Daily Express*, Minister of Propaganda and Information in the last year of the First World War. By the end of 1925 Mrs Norton was at all Lord Beaverbrook's parties: in the White Room at the Savoy, with songs from Albert Coates and Sophie Tucker; at the *Daily Express* offices and the Kit-Cat Club. Now, had alibis been required, Edwina would have vouched for Jeanie. There was no need, for Richard had his own distractions.

The Beaverbrook/Norton/Mountbatten axis was strengthened in the spring of 1926, at the time of the General Strike. This had been foreseen for months. Coal exports had slumped, coal-owners had cut wages and miners' earnings were at subsistence level. By April 1926 discussions had got nowhere and when the miners threatened to stop work the employers locked them out. The Cabinet muddled the negotiations and the Trades Unions found themselves on strike. Dickie based himself at Adsdean, dashing back for polo practice between spells of duty at Portsmouth. He busied himself at the docks: 'Everything working like clockwork'. Edwina remained at Brook House. She rang up Dickie twice a day, to tell him that there was no public disorder and to assure herself that the telephone system was still working. The railways, docks and buses came to a standstill. As Minister of Transport, or of what little of it there was, Wilfrid fussed over contingency plans. The Navy moved mail, distributed petrol and brought convoys of food to London; undergraduates drove buses, ex-officers and excited businessmen worked the trains. Buffles Milbanke enrolled as a special constable and Mary's friend Barbara Cartland carried messages to parts of London she had never seen before. Astonished office-workers found themselves being ferried by Edwina, in the Hispano, and Ainsworth, Lady Louis' chauffeur, in the Rolls. Edwina had no strong opinions about the rights and wrongs of the Strike. Unlike Dickie, who blamed Communist agitators, she was simply anxious that London should not wind down and stop.

Edwina Mountbatten

Dickie was delighted that Edwina was doing her duty: 'You should hear me bragging about my wife to everyone I meet'. She was working from eleven to four in the YMCA canteen in Hyde Park, making tea and cooking sausages for volunteer lorry drivers. At each end of the day she and Jeanie sold the *Daily Express* and *Evening Standard* on the streets; the Beaverbrook presses were still running but the distributors would not deliver. After three days printing stopped. Jeanie and Edwina were rewarded with dinner at Ciro's and afterwards Beaverbrook and Castlerosse took them to St Bride's Street to exchange pleasantries with the pickets at the *Express* offices, where the firemen and telephonists had joined the strike. It did not occur to Edwina and Jeanie to think of themselves as blacklegs; when they met Beaverbrook's secretaries, who were standing in for the switchboard operators, they offered to help by working alternate shifts. Edwina had found canteen work exhausting; unused to standing for five hours in a steaming kitchen, she had staggered into Brook House at seven o'clock each night and gone straight to bed. The switchboard turned out to be worse. There were no little chats with Jeanie, just mechanical exchanges with disembodied voices. For five days she was on duty from 9 a.m. to midnight; 'The telephone never stopped and we nearly went mad'. In the middle of the day she had an hour off, useful for slipping home to see the hairdresser, have tea with Laddie or with the astounded Lytle Hull, who had inopportunely turned up in London. By the end of the week, too tired to move, Edwina and Jeanie simply stayed at the *Express* offices all day, dining there at midnight with Beaverbrook and Castlerosse and other members of the proprietor's court.

The strike was ten days old before the *Express* was on sale again. The presses were run by Beaverbrook's managers, trying to keep the oil off their oldest suits, and by printers who felt the stoppage had gone on long enough. Volunteers loaded bundles of newspapers and carried them to towns all over the country. Among these patriots was Ainsworth, in the Rolls, and Upton, in the Hispano-Suiza. Edwina and Jeanie were now doing an evening shift in the *Express* transport canteen. Edwina looked drawn and pale, with dark shadows under her eyes: 'Quite dead!' she wrote, on her Saturday morning off, 'stayed in bed till 11'. Doing the same routine job, day after day, was more killing than she had realized; like other volunteers, Edwina was learning what it took to keep the wheels turning. She was worn out, but she was also enjoying herself. In this oddly assorted team she could forget herself, for there was no time to be self-conscious when they all had work to do. 'I am *ordinately proud of you*', Dickie told her; she was so pleased to be working as hard as he was that she did not scold him for being patronizing. Edwina liked it when Laddie found her working at the switchboard; she enjoyed telling Lytle that she was too busy to have more than the briefest lunch with him. She had a job to do, she said.

Fortunately it was not for ever. One by one the men came back, although the coal strike dragged on for months. Some said afterwards that it had allowed professional people to experience for themselves the dreariness and exhaustion of the working man and woman's day, so that after 1926 the gulf between the classes was not so wide. Edwina did not moralize or reminisce. She had helped Max Beaverbrook when he was in a fix and that was that. She picked up her old life where she had left off: *They Knew What They Wanted* and *Easy Virtue* with Laddie, Mrs Corrigan's annual cabaret party, Eileen Sutherland's summer fancy-dress ball (Winnie Portarlington and Edwina went as gypsies), Emerald Cunard's party for the Prince of Wales. Laddie stayed in England all summer, basing himself at Esher Place, rented from the d'Abernons, but nearly every weekend he was at Adsdean. At the end of July, he and Edwina spent a day at Goodwood, while Dickie played polo. That evening all three returned to Adsdean. It was a clear summer evening. 'Hectic night', Edwina wrote afterwards, 'with a perfect moon'. Dickie was not so ecstatic. 'Bathed and went out in *Shadow*', he said flatly, 'which we got running after much trouble'.

At least Laddie was tactful enough to keep away from Cowes. Instead, another member of the Long Island set, Mary Elizabeth Altemus, came to stay with the Mountbattens on *Shrimp*. With her long legs, long hair, dark skin and high cheekbones, she looked like a Red Indian, which she partly was. Dickie liked Liz Altemus. She sailed on with the Mountbattens to Deauville, looking so lithe and brown as she dived from the side that Edwina decided to take up sunbathing after all. In the mornings she and Peter Murphy lay on the beach together and talked, Edwina in a swimsuit, Peter in baggy shorts, a straw hat protecting his bald head.

Dickie basked in this happy circle. Edwina was full of fun, as she had been in the first year of their marriage. On the way back from a polo match at Fleet in Hampshire, he heard her singing in the car. Perhaps she had got over her infatuation, for Laddie had returned to America. Dickie did not yet know that Edwina had a new admirer, Mike Wardell, manager of the *Evening Standard*, a good-looking, sociable member of the Beaverbrook circle, whom she had met at parties at the *Express*. That autumn, while Dickie worked at Portsmouth, Edwina stayed at Brook House during the week: 'Dined at the Ritz with Mike . . . after went to *Thy Name is Woman* and later to the Café de Paris'; 'Dined at home with Mike . . . to *Tip-Toes* and afterwards the Embassy and Little Club.' By the end of September their affair was in full swing: 'Very late and hectic'.

Dickie had no inkling of Edwina's latest attachment. He had other preoccupations, for in October he was to leave for Malta to take up a post as Assistant Fleet Wireless Officer with the Mediterranean Fleet. He stepped up his French and German lessons, tried out a Chrysler, the car he thought most suitable for the island, shopped for beds at Heals, sorted his books and prepared himself for the professional side of his new life by writing a paper on Valves. He also practised polo more assiduously than ever, for his new Commander-in-Chief, Sir Roger Keyes, was a keen supporter of the game, saying that it brought out all the qualities he looked for in an officer.

There was another, less pleasant distraction: the problem of Cunningham-Reid. Mary's year of purdah was over. Baroness von Buxhoevden had introduced her to people in Switzerland, Italy and France, but no one had supplanted Bobbie. Mary seemed perfectly sane; she had stayed at Adsdean and on *Shrimp* and there had been no hysteria. In early October she declared that she still wished to marry Bobbie. As she would be able to do what she wanted after her twenty-first birthday, in less than a year's time, Edwina and Dickie felt that there was little point in Wilfrid's continuing to object and very likely provoking Mary into another nervous breakdown. First, however, the family must be sure that Cunningham-Reid intended to make the marriage a success. For this, man-to-man discussions were required and, since Wilfrid could not bring himself to negotiate with Bobbie, Dickie acted as intermediary. The Mountbatten/ Cunningham-Reid conference took place on neutral territory, halfway between Gayfere House and Brook House, in the Burlington Arcade. The two men paced up and down, past the displays of rings and silk socks, and Dickie explained to Bobbie that, if he could show that he

had ten thousand pounds in the bank, the wedding could go ahead.

Three days later the Mountbattens took Mary to Broadlands to receive Wilfrid's reluctant consent. Molly was not there. The arrangements for the wedding, the reception and the preparation of Mary's trousseau were left to Edwina, who promised that for the next six months she would shuttle between Malta, London and Paris to be by her sister's side. Not that Edwina minded. She did not want to leave England, exchanging her friends' society for that of other officers' wives. Dickie had been looking forward to his new post. Not so now. 'Poor Dickie very depressed', Edwina wrote, having made him feel guilty. His attempts to please her misfired; for her birthday he gave her a brooch, designed by himself, in the form of a jewelled polo-player wearing the Adsdean colours. It started a fashion – but Dickie's gift reflected his own interests rather than Edwina's taste. Three weeks earlier he had given Jeanie a gold bracelet. Dickie treated her as a confidante – 'Jeanie and I rode until it was dark'; 'Heart to heart with Jeanie' – and this was his way of saying thank you. When Edwina saw the bracelet, did she know where it had come from?

Dickie bore Jeanie no grudge for introducing Edwina, via the *Express*, to Mike Wardell. By now he could not fail to see what was going on. Wardell was included in supper parties and visits to the theatre; he had stayed at Adsdean and Dickie had been taken to dine at his rival's house. The charitable view was that Edwina was showing off, the uncharitable that she sought to humiliate both men at once. Dickie went again to the Prince of Wales, and, comforted, resolved to let the affair run its course. It was hard to appear unconcerned, the more so because Edwina did not try to be discreet. There were no stories in the British press but the Mountbattens' friends and acquaintances talked among themselves. Edwina's behaviour was letting her husband down, damaging his name and jeopardizing his career. For every newspaper picture of Lady Louis, in cardigan and pearls, gazing thoughtfully into space, there was another of her walking on the golf course, the racecourse or the beach with a suave young man; for each report of her work for a charity ball, there was one of her presence at the opening of a new nightclub. She helped the needy but she also collected fines for speeding and danced the Charleston with Fred Astaire. Stories about Edwina's associates also damaged her. A disgruntled publicity agent maintained that the grand luncheon party Felix Warburg had given for the Mountbattens, while they were in

Edwina Mountbatten

New York on their honeymoon, had been intended to steer the British Government's financial business towards Mr Warburg's bank. Furthermore, it was alleged that the host had failed to pay the bill, including $154.95 for roses for Lady Louis. The story became the subject of a full-scale court case and, although it was untrue, it left an impression that the Mountbattens associated with the wrong sort of people.

Their departure for Malta was the opportunity for a new start. Dickie and Thorogood left first, just after Christmas, the polo ponies having been sent ahead by ship. Dickie was attached to HMS *Warspite* but between exercises at sea he was allowed to live ashore. He had found a house, Casa Medina, below the city walls of Valletta, an agreeable villa made up of four small houses, each with an identical front door giving on to the street. The place was quiet, with a garden and a flat roof for sunbathing and Dickie was sure Edwina would like it. While he waited for her to join him, he organized the servants, settled the ponies and worked out a routine for his work; this done, he wrote a long letter home, reflecting on the difficulties of the last twelve months.

Perhaps he had been insufficiently appreciative: '. . . I want you to know that no action however small of yours passes unnoticed by your spouse and that he is more grateful than he probably shows for the hundred and one little thoughtful acts by which you make life so very pleasant for him.' Without Edwina's help, he said, he would have no polo ponies and, by encouraging him to play, she had made a great difference in his life. Dickie might have chosen a better example. As he observed himself, he was gauche. He wished things were otherwise: 'If I could in any way alter my character or nature to be less selfish and more thoughtful I should be a very happy chap.' Edwina's barbs had pricked him: 'I should like to be able to wait until you have gone to sleep at night, sleep without snoring, steal out of bed without waking you up, sit up late and dance late with you, knock off making plans, writing chits and discussing servants. I should love to feel I really wasn't a snob and that I wasn't pompous and', he added unnecessarily, diminishing what had gone before, 'had a particularly ugly side to my anyhow hideous face'.

Edwina had said little but her unfaithfulness had made Dickie feel inadequate: 'I wish I could drive a car like Bobby Casa Maury, play the piano and talk culture like Peter, make enthusiastic remarks like

Infidelity

Ralph, play golf like Ronnie, shoot like Daddy, play polo like Jack. I wish I knew how to flirt with other women and especially with my wife. I wish I had sown many more wild oats in my youth' (was this their difficulty?) 'and could excite you more than I fear I do'.

Edwina had married Dickie for better or worse and he suspected that she might be regretting it: 'I wish I wasn't in the Navy and had to drag you out to Malta'. She had taken him for richer or poorer: 'I wish I had an equal share of the money so that I could give you far handsomer presents than I can really at present honestly manage'. She did not like to talk frankly, 'but I'm different from you in that I must unbottle my feelings to someone . . .' That person could only be Edwina. 'You happen to be my first, principle and truest friend', Dickie declared, forgetting his spelling. Edwina kept his letter. She did not reply.

CHAPTER FIFTEEN

Constant Dramas

On the day that Dickie wrote his apologia, Edwina was at Melton. Laddie Sanford was staying at a house nearby; he had reappeared in London just before Christmas and throughout January 1927 she saw him nearly every day, in London, at Melton, Newmarket and Newbury. Late nights and complicated train and car journeys in cold weather left them weak and miserable and eventually they collapsed with 'flu. Edwina's illness came at a moment of additional strain, Mike Wardell's return from a winter expedition to the South of France: 'Lunched with Mike and after went round to see Laddie . . . Mike came to dinner.'

At the end of the month, Mary's engagement was announced. With an heiress as his prospective bride, Bobbie Cunningham-Reid had not found it difficult to raise capital and Wilfrid was therefore obliged to fulfil his bargain. Edwina's departure for Malta was postponed again; she was helping Mary with her preparations. At last she set off, with Mary, who was filling in time before her marriage, and Peter Murphy, to smooth over any difficulties en route. Edwina's journey was not auspicious. She had a heavy cold, Mary and Peter fell ill in Rome, the train for Syracuse shook violently and the boat to Malta was filthy. The crossing took nine and a half hours and Dickie met them in pouring rain and a gale. 'Our house is completely bare', Edwina reported, 'no carpets down yet, or covers or curtains and so looks frightful and we shivered'. Between sneezes, she got things straight. Mary retired to bed and Peter decided that he would be more comfortable in the local hospital, to which he accordingly went. Edwina had been promised restorative winter sunshine but she might as well have stayed in England.

The weather improved, the house was made attractive and comfortable. Dickie fitted a new gramophone and amplifier; Edwina organized the planting of the garden. She disposed of duty calls – people she had to know but did not wish to see found her cards when they woke from their afternoon sleep – and had the Governor to dine. She looked up the wives of Dickie's more amusing colleagues and within a month the Mountbattens had formed their own like-minded court: Bez and Cecile McCoy, who lived next door; Michael Wentworth, Tony Simpson and Squeaker Morrison, Grisell and Eddie Hastings; the Curzon-Howes, Michael Hodges and his sister Betty; the Bowlbys, Teddy Heywood-Lonsdale and John Minter. Friends were pressed to come to stay. Marjorie and Jeanie, with Jeanie's children, arrived in April; Liz Altemus looked in on the way from America to England; Nada came for a month and the Yorks paid an official visit in *Renown*, with fireworks, a garden party, lunch with the Prime Minister, a dance at Admiralty House and two polo matches, for which Sir Roger Keyes persuaded the Duke to join his team.

It was not difficult for Edwina to look after her visitors. Although she had less room and fewer servants than at Brook House or Adsdean, she had more time to entertain her guests and herself. The weather was warm, so clothes and meals could be simple, the pace was slow, society easy and intimate and the amusements unpretentious: dances at the Sliema Club, supper at the Union Club, parties at Admiralty House and the Governor's Palace, polo. Edwina took her guests to the races to see her own horse, Messaoud, repeatedly fail to win. They visited the Old City and its surrounding villages and explored the bays, sands and rocky outcrops along the coast, picnicking, sunbathing and swimming in warm, clear water.

Shrimp lay in the harbour below the house. Without the yacht to take her away on dusty afternoons, Edwina would have felt shut in, for the island was small and the roads poor. Naval dinners, naval dances, naval ceremonies, the naval hierarchy – these oppressed her. Edwina could not settle to being a junior officer's wife. Dickie enjoyed it all: 'C in C took me aquaplaning in barge'; 'Polo War Game in the Ward Room'. He continued to adapt and invent, suggesting that lantern slides be used for night identification exercises, putting together an addendum to the Pocket Code, devising an electrode kite, 'which unfortunately carried away'. No one was more ambitious – but Dickie was so open about it that for the most part people forgave him. 'What an opportunity for anyone to earn an Albert Medal,' he wrote innocently in his diary, when a shipmate fell overboard and drowned in a calm sea. 'Wish I'd been on deck'.

Patricia was not brought out to Malta. Plans were too uncertain,

Edwina Mountbatten

Edwina said. The island was an excellent jumping-off point for southern Europe, Egypt and the Adriatic Coast and, when Dickie accompanied the Fleet on spring, summer and autumn cruises, lasting three weeks or more, Edwina wanted to travel with her friends. A month after she had arrived in Malta, she left, to shop in Paris with Mary and then to return to London, where Laddie was waiting.

Edwina was not completely irresponsible. Between outings with Laddie, the Brecknocks, Geordie Sutherland, the Casa Maurys, Jeanie and Kitty Kinloch, Jock Whitney and Liz and Johnny Altemus, she drank tea with Aunt Victoria, went shopping with Dickie's niece Dolla, and had lunch with her father. Wilfrid was cheerful, for Molly was away and he had been sitting in other people's drawing-rooms, where admiring ladies told him that he deserved a peerage and that he should be sent to run South Africa or be made Governor of Bombay. Such talk had trickled into the newspapers and, although nothing came of it, the rumours were flattering. Edwina also saw her daughter, noting these brief reunions in her diary, if only as an afterthought: 'Joined by Helen and Evelyn Fitzgerald at the Café de Paris and Night Light', one entry read: 'Very late bed. Patricia has whooping cough'.

From time to time Edwina also thought of Dickie, who was zig-zagging across the Mediterranean, mixing business with pleasure: 'A hard day's work. It blew hard which rather spoilt the Med Fleet's dance'. At the end of the spring cruise *Warspite* lay at Villefranche, on the coast of the South of France; here Dickie had arranged to meet Edwina and the Hispano. A wire explained that she and Liz had been delayed in Paris but not that they were there with Jock Whitney and Laddie. The two women eventually arrived, 'feeling like death', Edwina wrote in her diary, 'and utterly exhausted'. For a month Laddie had been pressing her to leave Dickie: 'Bad evening', she noted, after an argument in London; 'Awful evening', after another row in Paris. Edwina did not know what she wanted. She temporarily detached herself from Laddie and made the most of her interlude on the Mediterranean coast.

Edwina returned to Malta with two dozen pieces of luggage, brought back for her in *Warspite*. She hardly needed all her hats and dresses, for she stayed only three weeks. In early May she was back in London. Brook House was let to the Argentine Minister in London, but he and his family moved out, so that it could be used for the wedding. 'Mary very calm', Edwina thought, despite the introductory talk the married sister had given the bride the night before. The ceremony strained Mary's nerves but all was well and she managed to stride confidently down the steps of St Margaret's, the beaded fringes of her silver dress clinking as she went. Behind her tripped a band of attendants, including Marjorie's daughter, Mary Clementine, Jeanie Norton's Sarah, and Patricia. The flock was marshalled by Edwina and Jeanie, narrow-brimmed hats pulled down over their shingled heads, fur-collared summer coats clutched tight round their bodies, so that only their slender legs identified them. 'Tremendous crowds and great enthusiasm', Edwina reported. Dickie was not among the throng. He said that his work kept him in Malta, although, had he wanted leave, he could have got it. That particular week was not strenuous: 'Spent most of the morning making signals to fellows trying to get them to come and put their names down for polo'.

Dickie was implacable. He believed that Cunningham-Reid had tricked them all and, when the newspapers reported that the bride-groom's presents included a pair of guns from the Mountbattens, he wrote fiercely to Edwina: 'Is this true?' (It was not.) Perhaps the marriage would be a success. Anyhow, Edwina could not protect Mary all the time, however scatty she might be. At the last minute, as the Cunningham-Reids were leaving the reception, the sisters had a final word. Edwina's guess was right – Mary had forgotten a vital piece of equipment, her *douche*. Edwina smuggled it into the car and waved goodbye. For the time being she had done everything she could.

It was not only Mary's wedding that brought Edwina to London. Laddie Sanford was back with his polo team, the Hurricanes. He had taken Osterley for two months and at weekends stayed with Edwina at Adsdean, where they were chaperoned, in theory, by Jeanie and the usual crowd. They argued endlessly about the future; at the end of June, when Laddie returned to America, Edwina felt 'completely sunk'. Dickie was waiting for her, this time in Yugoslavia. 'Place quite lovely', Edwina observed but she felt languid and ill. She could not bring herself to talk freely to Dickie. To show she was sorry for being difficult, she bought him a new polo pony and tried to do little things he liked, cheering him on in the Aquatic Sports and agreeing to ride side-saddle, for the first time since their honeymoon. Dickie was equally miserable. Five years after their marriage, his life with Edwina had fallen away.

Edwina Mountbatten

Edwina was in a mess. Just before Mary's wedding, Hugh Molyneux had returned to London. People said that he had been fond of a Maharani, a liaison that had shocked both the British and the Indians, and that he needed comforting. Laddie was still away, so Edwina and Hugh consoled each other: 'danced . . . at the May Fair . . . Serious talk'. There was another complication: Mike Wardell. Laddie being in America, Edwina had agreed to join Max Beaverbrook's party at Deauville, on a yacht he had chartered, *Albion*. Jeanie, Mike and Valentine Castlerosse were Lord Beaverbrook's other guests. The days were wet and windy and the yacht, Edwina reported,' ground with an awful corkscrew motion'. Beaverbrook's wife was ill (she died in November) and he and Jeanie were on edge: 'Constant dramas', Edwina noted. Everything seemed unsteady. The more agreeable Mike Wardell became, the less Edwina liked it and after five days she fled, first to Paris and then to Brook House. Cables and telephone calls begged her to return and four days later she was back in *Albion*. The weather was better but the entertainment more depressing, for the Churchills had joined the party and to please Winston Lord Beaverbrook had arranged a tour of First World War battlefields, cemeteries and memorials. This melancholy pilgrimage brought Edwina and Mike together and, once they had returned to London, she found it difficult to shake him off: 'Lunch with Hugh at the Berkeley Grill . . . Had dinner on a tray and Mike came to see me'.

In mid-October Laddie arrived on the *Berengaria*. By now Edwina was almost hysterical. She looked thin and drawn. One night she would note 'long talk with Hugh', the next 'long talk with Mike'. She spoke of headaches and dizzy spells; her 'affairs', she told Dickie, were erratic and uncomfortable. The doctor thought she might be having trouble with her teeth, the dentist suggested that her eyes needed examination. Her friends thought her life was too nerve-racking. Marjorie described how a servant at Brook House had announced that he had shown Lord Molyneux to the morning-room and Mr Sanford to the library, 'but where should I put the other gentleman?'

Edwina dragged herself off to be X-rayed: 'Spent the day in awful state of nerves and misery'. The results came three days later. Further investigation was required. The year before Edwina had undergone 'a small operation to my inside', gynaecological trimming, performed by her obstetrician. There had been no secrecy about that surgery, which took place at Brook House in Dickie's dressing-room. This time she went to France. From the Ritz she sent Dickie a series of cables, encrypted with the help of the Pocket Code. Deciphered, they told him only that she was delayed in Paris for 'appendix treatment'. Edwina stayed five days in a nursing home: 'all sorts of unpleasant things but felt better on the whole'. Jeanie came over from London for a day and a night; when she left, Edwina said she felt like suicide. It sounds as if the operation was an abortion, illegal in England at that time. Whatever it was, she recovered quickly and, after three days in London, turned south to Malta. Dickie was overjoyed. Better still, this time Edwina brought Patricia.

The family was reunited – and reinforced with the arrival of Nada and Georgie, who was joining *Warspite* in the New Year. The Milford Havens had the house next-door, so that the two families were almost one. This was a happy time for Dickie. He took Patricia paddling and for rides in her pony-trap, at Christmas he decorated a tree and for her birthday he negotiated the purchase of a doll's house from neighbours whose daughter had grown up. He had house-keeping of his own to do, for Georgie's posting to *Warspite* meant that Dickie had to go elsewhere, and in mid-January he joined Sir Roger's flagship, *Queen Elizabeth*. Having arranged his cabin, Dickie turned his attention to the rest of the ship, his first move being to set up a committee to investigate the installation of a Frigidaire. This, and work on a series of wireless telegraphy lectures, still left time for pleasant excursions: round the island in *Shrimp*; to cocktails in Gordon Selfridge's yacht, moored in the harbour; to the Carnival, the races and the Governor's Palace with Aunt Victoria, who came out for a short holiday in February 1928. During Dickie's mother's visit the conversation became more serious. There was a limit to the amount of movie and polo talk Aunt Victoria would endure, so Edwina invited Professor Zammit, the archaeologist, to lunch and Maurice Baring, the man of letters.

When the Fleet began exercises in the Southern Mediterranean, Edwina and Nada arranged to go to Egypt to meet their husbands there. Edwina liked the dry heat, the monuments, the Cairo Museum. Her diary entries became long and detailed – four pages on Luxor – and she took dozens of photographs of bazaars, camels, 'our divine dragoman', and the Mena House Hotel, where her mother had stayed. The Cunningham-Reids were passing through Egypt on their way home from a ten-month honeymoon; Bobbie was nervous – but perhaps it was better that his first encounter with his new brother-in-law should take place on foreign soil. The meeting was perfectly executed. Dickie arrived in Alexandria just as the Cunningham-Reids were leaving and arranged to accompany Mary and Bobbie to their steamer to wave them off.

Apart from polo games – *Queen Elizabeth* against the Army – Dickie's time was largely his own. 'A perfect week', he said at the end, having explored the Great Pyramid (Edwina, being claustrophobic, stayed outside), watched a snake charmer and hired a native conjuror, who 'diddled Georgie and me out of £4!' The sisters-in-law had decided to take a boat up the Nile to Aswan and camp for three nights in the desert on the return journey. Sir Ernest would have been pleased by Edwina's opinion of the dam, 'an amazing and stupendous work', and gratified that, in spite of the heat, she made a noonday pilgrimage to the sugar factory he had started beside the Nile. 'Had our hair, nails etc done', Edwina noted, when they got to Cairo, 'as we are in a filthy state!!!' She was brown, bright-eyed and fit; 'My lovely Edwina', Dickie wrote, on the day she arrived in Malta; and, a week later, 'Edwina in black shorts very indecent but very sweet'.

He was sentimental and excited. Edwina, sadly, was not. She looked well but this, she told Dickie, was deceptive. Headaches, cramp, inconvenient and unpredictable floods all drove her back to the doctors. A course of X-rays was prescribed by a Parisian specialist, a restricted diet by an expert from Freiburg. She was told that on no account should she return to Malta, where the dust, or the water, or something, was undoubtedly doing her harm. Whatever the nature of Edwina's illness, it was not caused by loneliness or having too little to do. When Dickie came home in June on ten weeks' leave, he was simply built into the programme: '*This Year of Grace* and supper at the Savoy with Dickie, Laddie and Peter . . .' On Dickie's birthday Alice and Cecile were to join the Mountbattens on an expedition to Portsmouth. Edwina pleaded toothache and drove to London with Laddie. Dickie could not bear it. He began to feel ill himself. 'I have the feeling of a temperature and flue', he wrote, on his first day at home. Next came an attack of impetigo, a damaged knee. He sought comfort and advice from friends: 'Divine talk with Jeanie'. Lord Beaverbrook was annoyed.

Before his leave Dickie had been told that at the end of his tour in Malta, in a year's time, he was to return to the Signal School. This was the ideal time for the Mountbattens to enlarge their family. It was not difficult to start a conversation on the subject, for Mary was expecting a baby, and, when he had got over his 'flu, Dickie made his proposal. But was Edwina well enough? At the beginning of July, she went into a nursing home in Norfolk Square for what Dickie described in his diary as 'a sort of curettage'. A week later she was home but for ages, she said, it would be unwise to consider anything but the most chaste embraces. When she was better, she made Dickie take tremendous care: a first try in mid-August was followed by a visit to a doctor in Paris, a second effort, a week later, by a bismuth meal and three X-rays, prescribed by the same French doctor, who advised her to take things gently.

Two weeks after the second attempt, Edwina embarked in the *Leviathan* for America, with Peter Murphy as protector. For a fortnight she stayed with the Vanderbilts in New York and Newport, and then joined Laddie at the Sanfords' house on Long Island. At the beginning of October Edwina thought she might be pregnant, saw a doctor, who was guarded, and told Laddie. Now there was no question of leaving Dickie. For a week they argued: 'Nothing but rows and scenes'. A sudden loss of blood made Edwina uncertain. Was it a miscarriage, or some sort of haemorrhage? There were more quarrels.

Laddie did not know whether Edwina intended to stay or go. In the third week of October he asked for a decision. Overnight she made up her mind to go back to Dickie, told her maid to pack and early next morning arranged a passage home in the *Aquitania*. Laddie took Edwina down to the ship, staying on board until the last minute to see her off. 'Felt very gloomy and slightly ill', but as she got nearer home, she began to cheer up. 'Rather a riotous evening, full of practical jokes . . .' She consoled herself with the knowledge that she had done her duty by her husband, her daughter and what seemed increasingly likely to be, the child Dickie was hoping for: 'Really quite glad to be back.'

CHAPTER SIXTEEN

The Treaty

Back – but not to Malta. It was seven weeks before Edwina returned to Dickie. She was too proud to tell him that she was afraid. The London doctors could not decide whether she had already had an early miscarriage, was about to have a baby, or was merely experiencing some small internal maladjustment that would eventually right itself. 'Nothing to worry about', Edwina told Dickie, but she had many anxious conferences with Jeanie. The person to see was Dr Haig Ferguson, who had examined her when she was expecting Patricia, so Edwina took the night train to Edinburgh, learnt that the baby was due in May and got another sleeper back to London. With Patricia, her daughter's new 'Fairy Cycle', stacks of gramophone records and the Christmas puddings, Edwina set off for Malta. She arrived on 16 December, 'looking', Dickie noted adoringly, 'more divinely lovely than ever'.

A family Christmas, with stockings for Edwina and Patricia and a tree, was all very well and so was a family New Year ('Georgie dressed as a waiter was marvellous. Edwina wore pyjamas!') but after that there was nothing to do. Aunt Victoria felt seedy, Peter stayed in bed until after tea. Edwina won twelve shillings at the races; the Commander-in-Chief had a huge party at Admiralty House, amusing the guests with conjuring tricks after dinner. When the Fleet sailed on the January cruise, Edwina watched the destroyers and battleships making their way towards the horizon: 'Very fine sight', she wrote in her diary, and left with Nada and Peter to stay in Pierre Mérillon's house in Tunisia.

Dickie's tour of duty in Malta was coming to an end and at the end of June Casa Medina was to be given up. On the way home Edwina wanted to fit in one more holiday and, when Dickie left in mid-March for the Mediterranean and Atlantic Fleets' combined manoeuvres, she packed up their things, checked the inventory and took ship to Gibraltar. Here she said goodbye to Patricia and Nannie, who were going by sea to London. Ainsworth had brought the Hispano from England and Edwina and Harding, her maid, motored round to Algeciras, where Dickie, Georgie, Teddy Heywood-Lonsdale, Tom Hussey and Charles Lambe had now arrived. Edwina was keen to return to Africa and, when the officers got leave for five days, she and Dickie, Tom and Charles took the Hispano across the Straits to look at Moorish architecture. In Rabat they ran into Mrs Greville, who was appalled to see Edwina, seven and a half months pregnant, riding on a donkey. This was nothing. Their holiday over, the Mountbattens chartered a tug, leaving at four-thirty in the morning, to take them on the five-hour crossing to Gibraltar, so that Dickie could arrive in time for the Naval Review. When the Fleet sailed, Edwina and Ainsworth drove a hundred and sixty-five miles in the Hispano, with Harding in the back, over rocky hills to Ronda and on through the mountains to Malaga, where Edwina caught the train to Madrid: 'Terribly bumpy line and arrived feeling quite awful.' From here she caught an evening train to Barcelona, where Dickie, Charles Lambe and Charles Ellison were playing polo. The Mountbattens settled into the Ritz and began a week of gentle sightseeing. On 19 April Edwina woke at six, in such pain that Dickie got an English doctor, who was staying in the hotel. He rounded up a Spanish anaesthetist and an English nurse, for the baby was on its way. Dickie tried to telephone Queen Ena in Madrid. Alfonso answered and, saying, 'Leave everything to me', sent the Royal Guard, who attempted to arrest the doctor as he returned to the hotel with kit from the hospital. Dickie remained with Edwina for the first ten hours, after which she was given chloroform. Although the baby was five weeks early, she was quite well and strong. 'YOUR BABY SISTER HAS ARRIVED HERE', Dickie announced to Patricia, on headed writing-paper from the Ritz: 'I HAVE DRAWN HER PICTURE FOR YOU'.

Edwina stayed three weeks in her suite. Marjorie, who had been in Paris, leapt on to a train and arrived the day after the baby was born, so she was able to keep Dickie company, for he would have been disappointed if there had been no one to watch him play polo. Nannie came from London, with a supply of linen and baby clothes, hastily assembled by Miss Underhill's new assistant, Henrietta Treble. Peter was driven from Nice non-stop for twenty-four hours. He talked all the time to keep the chauffeur awake, which he was until they reached Barcelona, where the motor collided with a tram.

Edwina Mountbatten

The Mountbattens called the child Pamela, her other names, Carmen Louise, honouring, respectively, the Duchess of Peneranda and Dickie's younger sister. It took the baby's father some time to adjust. In the Ritz Dickie saw more of the baby than if she had been born at Brook House; he had also been closer to Edwina in her struggle. Things were found for him to do: he had seventy telegrams to answer and innumerable letters to write, he said proudly, as well as toasts to drink with his shipmates, anchored a few miles offshore.

Dickie returned to Malta to finish his duties; Edwina tottered to her feet and proceeded gingerly to Paris with Marjorie, Pamela and Nannie. There she soon revived, helped by flattering remarks from the team at Chanel, amazed that so soon after the baby's birth Lady Mountbatten was ready to be measured for models from the new collection. 'Baby flourishing', Edwina told Dickie, and sent half a dozen snapshots so that he could admire Pamela's nose, so like his own.

The infant's premature arrival had left Edwina with five weeks in hand. There was plenty to amuse her: Nada's new house, Lynden Manor, at Bray on the Thames, the Casa Maurys' aeroplane, *Toi et Moi*. There were meetings of the committee of 'Master's', the club at 7 Savile Row which Edwina and Baba Metcalfe had opened the previous winter as a counterpart to Buck's, the men's club next door. Captain Buckmaster, Buck's founder, had given the committee advice, as well as the remainder of his name, but he had not foreseen one flaw. Lady members did not like to lunch only with each other and male guests felt uncomfortable because they were not allowed to pay. Master's lasted only a year.

The club had not been opened as a challenge to the men; its founders had simply wanted an agreeable meeting-place of their own. Edwina was no campaigner. Her political opinions were conventional: she supported the Conservatives, her father's party, but she took no part in the 1929 election, unlike Molly, who kept an eye on Wilfrid's agent, and Mary, who helped organize Bobbie's campaign. From Blackpool Wilfrid had transferred himself to a constituency in the New Forest; Bobbie now moved to one in Southhampton, next door, using Adsdean as a base. Wilfrid kept his seat but his success was not enough to sweep in his son-in-law and Bobbie was defeated. Baldwin resigned, Labour took office and Wilfrid left the Ministry of Transport. Now he spent the mornings listening to women who told him he was wasted. Molly did not like it but, the crosser she became, the more Wilfrid kept away from home. This caused trouble later on.

Edwina heard the election results at a celebration given by Max Beaverbrook, who now invited her to come with him on a trip to Scandinavia and Russia, with Jeanie, Arnold Bennett, Mike Wardell and Venetia Stanley, Edwin Montagu's widow. They went in mid-August: 'A very funny party', Edwina wrote in a postcard to her father, 'but we are getting on top hole'. The SS *Arcadian* was the first passenger ship to visit Russia since the end of the Great War and the government did all it could to make these distinguished travellers welcome. Special railway carriages were laid on to transport Lord Beaverbrook and his entourage between Leningrad and Moscow and in the capital the party was looked after by the Foreign Minister, Maxim Litvinoff, and housed in his residence. Ivy Litvinoff, who was German, disliked Edwina's languid manner, 'like Isadora Duncan', she said in a letter to her sister, 'without the vitality'.

She was deceived. Edwina was never still. One night at the Embassy Club someone suggested that it would be fun to go to America (a waiter overheard and the news was in the papers next morning) and in late February 1930 Edwina, Marjorie and Brecky sailed for New York in the *Aquitania*. Edwina's account of the trip suggested that the Wall Street Crash, five months before, was over and forgotten. No one reading her diary would have known that speculators had been wiped out, farmers were in trouble, mills and factories at a standstill and unemployment rising. As Edwina hurtled from New York, via Chicago, to California and Mexico, from Beverly Hills, via New Orleans, to Florida, all the talk was of luxury and progress. At every stop she descended on smart department stores to buy gramophone records, jade sculpture, swimsuits and scarves; in each city she inspected modern architecture: the Chicago Opera House, the Bank of Manhattan Building, seventy storeys high, the Chrysler Building. 'Climbed all over the scaffolding', she noted, surely exaggerating, 'up on the 77th story'. Edwina thought everything marvellous.

Among her new friends were two admirers, Ronald Colman, the film star, now making *Raffles*, and Larry Gray, a friend of Douglas Fairbanks. Although Larry was good-looking, with fair hair, blue eyes and startlingly white teeth, his movie career had advanced slowly.

He outpaced Ronald Colman, however, in capturing Lady Louis. It was Larry who accompanied Edwina and the Brecknocks to William Randolph Hearst's 'ranch', San Simeon, a refuge two thousand feet up in the California mountains, at the end of a drive six miles long. A peculiar sort of ranch, it had elk, bison, giraffes, ostriches and deer, a private zoo in the garden, tennis courts, a golf course and an archery corner. If more courts and courses were required, they were added, overnight. When a visitor declared that the bathing pool was too small (she had been the first woman to swim the English Channel), Mr Hearst ordered another, lake-size. His residence consisted of several houses, assembled and furnished out of plunder from many quarters: 'entire Spanish churches', Edwina told Dickie, 'Italian villas, French chateaux and Greek Temples all thrown into one.' It was rumoured, Marjorie said, that somewhere on the premises was an entire English manor house, done up in packing cases.

Edwina's letter from San Simeon was one of few she wrote to Dickie, only five during a six-week trip. She did send cables, telling him where she was going, whether she had got there and when she was leaving, and once or twice she telephoned: 'Spoke to Hugh in the Midlands and Dickie at Adsdean . . . Beautifully clear and quite uncanny.' While Edwina travelled, Dickie concentrated on his work at the Signal School, driving there each day from Adsdean. He was Head of Wireless Instruction, a good teacher, for he took great trouble. He reformed the syllabus, set up a drawing-school to produce simple, standardized diagrams of every radio circuit, and oversaw the production of a catalogue of intelligible technical descriptions of every wireless-set used by the Royal Navy. When the Admiralty declared that coloured illustrations were unnecessary and expensive, Dickie bought a colour-printer and produced his own. His newest enthusiasm was aeroplanes. He had started lessons in 1929 and by February 1930 he was doing spins. A fortnight later he made his first solo flight. As the *Europa* came into Southampton, bringing Edwina home from America, Dickie circled overhead. Another week and he could have greeted her with figures of eight.

In Edwina's absence, Dickie had taken over day to day supervision of the Mountbattens' domestic affairs. Dick Crichton was in charge of the polo ponies and grooms, the yacht and her crew, the cars and gardens and their staffs, and repairs and improvements to the exterior of the house, leaving Miss Underhill and Miss Treble with responsi-

bility for running Brook House and Adsdean, correspondence, charities, the house accounts in both places and all the private accounts.
It was Dickie, too, who watched over Patricia, looking in on her for a
chat each morning, reading to her, taking her to the Natural History
Museum in London. He rode with her and when she came off her
pony, Rusty, and broke her arm, he carried her back to the house.
Dickie cabled news of the accident to Edwina, who was cross. He had
persuaded Patricia to try too difficult a ride, she said, and had then
failed to keep a close eye on her. This was unjust.

Edwina was the neglectful parent. In pictures of mother and daughter together, there was a space between them and, when Edwina put
an arm round Patricia's shoulders, she smiled not at her daughter but
for the camera. She was closer to Pamela. Resenting the easy friendship between Dickie and Patricia, Edwina wanted all her younger
child's affection. When Dickie returned to Adsdean from Malta in July
1929, he was excluded from the nursery: Nannie thought that Lord
Louis' visits disturbed the baby, or so Edwina said. Dickie was upset
but believed what he was told and stayed away. Edwina's albums
had no pictures of Dickie and Pamela together. Mother and daughter,
yes; father and daughter, no.

In those photographs Edwina looked pale and drawn. Abroad – in
Paris, Russia or America – she felt fit; at home she was always unwell.
Six weeks after Pamela's arrival, Edwina complained of swollen legs
and feet. To cure them, she had three weeks at the spa at Bagnoles
de l'Orne, seven hours west of Paris, for electric baths, massage,
douching and bed rest. In October she was at Ruthin Castle, a
sanatorium in Wales: 'Rests from 12–1 and 6–7 and bed at 10'.
The weather was freezing, the treatment rigorous: 'nasty drinks and
pummelling'. A trip to California with the Brecknocks kept Edwina
going for much of the following spring but one evening, when the
Wichfelds and Laddie were dining at Brook House, she collapsed.
Edwina told her guests she felt faint and sent them off to the theatre.
During the night her temperature rose and she started haemorrhaging.
After three increasingly anxious days Edwina's consultant concluded
that she had a severe internal infection, that there was a risk of
septicaemia, and that, without an operation, he might lose his patient.
Dickie's dressing-room was once more converted into a surgery. 'Most
unpleasant', was all Edwina said about it in her journal, 'but was
feeling so ill by that time I really didn't care.' Dickie raced up to

London, only to find that he was not allowed to see his wife, in case she thought he had been summoned to her deathbed.

Septicaemia was avoided but neuralgia and pernicious anaemia set in. Three weeks later Edwina was still in bed, thinking she would never recover. Finally the great pundit was summoned, Lord Dawson of Penn, who looked after the King: 'talked a lot of nonsense', Edwina declared, '. . . so I took matters into my own hands and sent to Paris for a doctor'. This was bold – Lord Dawson's patients did not argue – but, for all her spirit, Edwina found it hard not to despair. The French doctor gave her a transfusion and, to cleanse her blood, prescribed a diet of raw liver. 'Terrible', said Edwina, 'the entire day in tears.' Another month in bed, with electrical treatment, ray therapy and massage, and Edwina was able to stagger to the London Pavilion to receive the Prince of Wales at a charity performance, the Midnight Revue. The theatre was crammed with people who knew, or hoped to know, Lady Louis or the Prince. Lady Cunard took forty tickets – and was outdone by Mrs Corrigan, who had taken seventy-five. William Randolph Hearst was said to have paid two hundred pounds for his seat, plus a hundred for another for Marion Davies. People were there because everyone else was there, the men in white ties, the women in long dresses, summer furs and, for those who had come on from the last Court of the season, small tiaras. The show produced eleven thousand pounds. Edwina was a ghost, pale and insubstantial, in white silk, with white camellias and a diamond coronet. People knew she had been ill and admired her dedication. On that night the gossip writers treated her as semi-sanctified; Lady Mountbatten's illness had purified not just her blood but also her reputation.

It was autumn before Edwina rode again, Christmas before she was fully recovered. What were the illnesses that caused such dramatic collapse in an energetic, well-cared-for woman in her late twenties? It is tempting to think that, to draw attention to herself, Edwina was exaggerating her symptoms and making matters worse by trying drastic remedies. This may have been true, but she was certainly ill and often genuinely afraid. People thought that Lady Louis had inexhaustible reserves of energy. They did not see the entries in her diary: 'Quite exhausted'; 'Dead beat – Early bed'. Friends knew about her late mornings, for they sat upstairs, talking to her until noon, when she got up to dress. When Edwina was too tired to go out in

Adsdean

Nada, Georgie and Dickie

Dickie's mother, 'Aunt Victoria'

Peter Murphy, Edwina and Sophie Tucker

Larry Gray and Edwina

The Treaty

the evening, dinner was served in her bedroom, with Jeanie or Peter, Marjorie, Brecky, Hugh, Mike, Bobby or Paula to keep her company, and if she and Dickie had no other guests, they ordered supper to be sent upstairs on trays. Edwina was neither tireless nor immune to illness and pain. She wore herself out but, as long as she was interested in what she was doing, enthusiasm kept her going.

It was not only family life that left her unsatisfied. Edwina was ambitious: by the end of the 1920s she stood at the summit of society in London, Paris, Deauville, New York and Beverly Hills. It had not been a difficult climb. Her route had started at Sir Ernest's well-equipped base camp; dressmakers and shoemakers, hatters, hairdressers and manicurists, jewellers, florists and motor car manufacturers had supplied her kit; Dickie had given her an arm, the Prince of Wales and his brothers had encouraged her. Now she was at the top, the stylish, charming, ultra-sympathetic, exceedingly beautiful Lady Louis. But up here the air was thin and the mountains bare. So much arranging and frantic activity – and it had led to this? Dickie had a record of achievement in the Navy but Edwina's successes were lightweight and would be ephemeral. Illness was a symptom of frustration and discontent.

At the beginning of 1931 the interminable entertainment began again: 'lunched with the Aga Khan and the Begum at the Ritz . . . dined at the Brazilian Embassy . . . for a short time to the Kit Cat . . .' Edwina could not stand it. Rather than be ill again, she left London with Eileen Sutherland and Marjorie, on a cruise ship bound for the West Indies. As the *Samaria* sailed through the Caribbean, the days grew hotter, the sun brighter and Edwina increasingly bold. In Havana they joined up with Geordie Sutherland and Edwina's companion of the year before, Larry Gray. Geordie's private secretary, Gray Phillips, had a handsome nephew, Ted, who, with his cousin, Jack Evelyn, joined the party on its way to Mexico. Marjorie and Edwina knew the Phillips family – Ted, his father and brother had shot at Wherwell – and, since Ted had lived in South America and spoke Spanish, he was useful as well as decorative. This was a blow to Larry, who had hoped to have Edwina to himself. When the group posed for photographs on the steps of their rented house in Mexico City, Ted sat at the top, smiling broadly, dangling suede-shod feet, one arm round Edwina's shoulders. Larry, demoted, was at the bottom.

He hung on gamely for the next fortnight, staying close to Edwina on their expeditions to Indian villages, archaeological sites, pyramids, temples and floating gardens, but by the time they reached Los Angeles, he had almost given up. In the mornings Edwina rode with Ted, in the afternoons she swam with him in the ocean, before dinner they floated in the pool. Then Laddie appeared. It was difficult to ration the time so that no one felt aggrieved: 'Lunched in town with Larry very late having driven in with Ted at 90 miles an hour and been arrested on the way . . . Laddie came for dinner . . . to the Cotton Club and only got to bed very late.' Three months of sun, parties and irresponsibility – but when she came home Edwina had to face reality.

Dickie had received only four letters while his wife was away. Cables had come from every stop – 'Quite delicious here on the ocean and perfect weather as well' – and she had telephoned from America and on bad lines from Cuba and Mexico City. He had amused himself as best he could, taking photographs with a new camera, inventing an oval-headed polo stick, and at the beginning of February he had gone over to Darmstadt for a week, to celebrate the wedding of Alice's third daughter, Cecile, to Don, son of Uncle Ernest, the Grand Duke, and Aunt Onor. The family was there in full force. After the wedding some of the cousins stayed on, chatting in corners – 'made great friends with Olga (wife of Paul of Yugoslavia)' – and playing sardines in the dark. Dickie looked in at Wolfsgarten only on his last morning, on the way to the railway station. Nine years before, he and Edwina had come here on their honeymoon. They had run through the long grass in the orchard; now the trees were bare in the winter light. This family reunion had been important to Dickie. Edwina had chosen to miss the marriage of his Greek niece to his German cousin, disregarding his wishes and showing disrespect for his relations. It hurt.

At home one crisis followed another. Patricia came down with chicken pox and the doctors disagreed over her treatment. Pamela caught the illness from her sister and lay weak and despondent for days. Cunningham-Reid's name was entangled with that of an American woman, causing Mary to appear in hysterics at Brook House. Edwina was making her way across Cuba in a private Pullman. Not even Miss Underhill could reach her. There was worse to come. Marjorie had been shocked by Edwina's behaviour in the West Indies. The Brecknocks conferred, Brecky gritted his teeth and wrote to Dickie, telling him that Edwina was disgracing herself, the Mountbattens and the Cassels. For days Dickie wondered what he should do. At the end of a ghastly week he went to see Peter Murphy: 'Long and vital heart to heart'. That afternoon Edwina telephoned Brook House, on a bad and insecure line, via the switchboard at the Hotel Nacional in Havana. Whatever Dickie said left her unmoved. When the call was over, she changed, dined at the Sans Souci and went on to the Casino: 'Late bed again and getting quite ga-ga!' Dickie was devastated. Edwina had been vague. She had no idea when she would return. He now realized, years too late, that she was openly unfaithful and that she cared little for his dignity or her own. He ate a melancholy dinner at Brook House with Teddy Heywood-Lonsdale and together they drove down to Adsdean. It was as well that Dickie had some company. The entry in his diary was bleak: 'Worst night since Papa died.'

In the past, Dickie had discussed his marriage with one person only, the Prince of Wales. The Prince was away, so he first turned to Charlie Chaplin, who happened to be in England, and then poured out his woe to his mother, Peter, Teddy Heywood-Lonsdale and Jeanie Norton. These soundings taken, Dickie wrote to Edwina, care of the British Legation in Mexico City. His letter crossed with one she sent from Havana. It had been 'very pleasant' to hear his voice on the telephone, she wrote, her only reference to their recent conversation. If Dickie's letter ever got to Mexico, Edwina did not keep it with the rest of her correspondence. Nor, in her next letter, did she say that she had heard from him.

Now it was Edwina's turn for a shock. A week after she arrived in Mexico, the New York newspapers reported that she was seeking a divorce. The press had learnt that Lady Louis was on her way to Cuernavaca, a resort in the Andes used as a bolt-hole by Americans wanting to accelerate the qualifying period of separation from their spouses, and the gossip writers had drawn their own conclusions. Edwina knew she must cable Dickie before the story was published in London: 'Call me urgently tonight between eight and nine Mexican time'. At half past two in the morning Dickie telephoned. He had no more sleep that night. He told himself that the story was a fantasy, fabricated to sell newspapers. For months the popular press had been suggesting that Douglas Fairbanks and Mary Pickford were about to separate and that Edwina was the cause. This latest item presumably came from the same stable. Too ridiculous, Edwina assured Dickie, reinforcing her remarks on the telephone with another cable: 'Everyone treating whole thing as an enormous joke.' Dickie tried to think so too but the story was unsettling. It filtered into London and made him look a fool. Dickie was uncomfortable, his family embarrassed.

Things went from bad to worse. Worrying news came from Spain: 'Alfonso abdicated yesterday, or at all events', said Dickie, wanting to be precise, 'left Spain, in exile.' Pamela, having recovered from chicken pox, suddenly developed a temperature of a hundred and five. Dickie panicked: 'Got four doctors out from Portsmouth and a specialist . . . and a nurse from London'. Jeanie came to Adsdean and stayed as long as she could but when Pamela improved she returned to London, for Max Beaverbrook did not like her staying at Adsdean when Edwina was not there. Having induced Mrs Norton to be unfaithful to her husband, Beaverbrook suspected that he too was now deceived. He need not have worried. Edwina was the last person Jeanie would betray. Compassionate and honest, she helped Dickie face the truth. He admitted that he had allowed Edwina to intimidate him. He had let her wound him but now he was angry and would say so. Jeanie encouraged him to overcome his inhibitions: 'Complex vanished', he wrote firmly in his diary.

The Mountbattens' marriage could not be taken apart and reconstructed in a day. 'Heart to heart afternoon', Dickie reported, after collecting Edwina from the *Majestic*, but she seemed to take no notice and, after cocktails with Peter, Brecky and Mike Wardell, buzzed off to spend the evening with Laddie. Edwina did not want a painful discussion about intimate matters. Dickie insisted on pursuing the issue. 'Long arguments and nearly went mad', Edwina wrote. A talk with Jeanie made her realize that Dickie had endured enough. Contrite, she was all affection: 'Happiest night of my life,' Dickie recorded soaring from the depths to the zenith. For Edwina twenty-four hours of intimacy was enough. Three days in London, dancing at Ciro's with Laddie and at the Embassy with Hugh, and she left for Paris. That was the last straw.

On the night she returned to Brook House Dickie had it out with her: 'Nothing has ever caused me more pain', he told her afterwards. Hugh, Laddie, Mike, Ted – he asked about them all. Edwina was ashamed, Dickie surprised, for he discovered that he could stand up to his wife. A fortnight later he wrote Edwina a letter reviewing the events of that evening. The row had started as she was preparing for bed. They had better part, she had said at last, as she sat weeping in her bath. To Dickie's astonishment, he found that he was completely calm. Suddenly, he told her, he discovered 'you had lost that devastating ability to frighten me which only resulted in my being meek or rude.' He agreed that in the morning he should go. Afterwards he congratulated himself on having spoken 'quite naturally and friend-lily', a reaction that had chilled Edwina to the bone. It was she who had initiated a reconciliation. Dickie's bedroom door was shut. Edwina opened it, to return a book, she said, and the ice was broken.

That weekend the Mountbattens rode over the downs at Adsdean and discussed the future. They would stay together, with separate beds and, to some extent, separate lives. Edwina acknowledged that Dickie's work was important to him, promised not to complain when the Navy took him away and agreed to play her part when her presence was required. Dickie recognized Edwina's desire for something he could not supply. Neither of them knew what it was but they agreed that she could look for it elsewhere, as long as she behaved discreetly. People who did not know the Mountbattens believed that expediency held them together, that Dickie needed Edwina's money to support his career and way of living, while she liked his royal rank. This is naive. Dickie thought that hard work, not private wealth, was the key to success in his profession. Edwina's millions had bought polo ponies, servants and fast cars but, as he told her, she had also given him eight and half years' unhappiness. Edwina was not transfixed by Dickie's connections. She was proud and quite ready to make her own friends. Unfinished business kept the Mountbattens together. Dickie needed Edwina, emotionally if not physically. Though less dependent, she had not yet found a counter-attraction strong enough to pull her away.

'I should so like to have my mind put at rest', Dickie asked in his letter. Had Edwina's affairs with Hugh and Laddie been mere self-indulgence, or something more? He confessed that he would find it difficult to shake Laddie's hand – 'he has been the cause of pretty much all the unhappiness I have known' – but for Edwina's sake he would make the effort. Laddie could not be asked to Adsdean or Brook House but perhaps he and Dickie might meet on the polo ground? 'If you would like it,' Dickie suggested to Edwina. 'I'm sure the Bluejackets would be very proud to play against the Hurricanes'. Not, he added, 'their 32 goal side' but Laddie's second-class team, and only on a day off, when there were no important matches.

Edwina disliked being interrogated but this time she thought she should answer Dickie's questions. 'I suppose my affairs with Hugh and Laddie were what you would call serious,' she told him, adding diplomatically, 'but as they never in any way altered my affection and respect for you I don't myself think of them as such'. Dickie had all her admiration and all her friendship. As for his suggestion that he and Laddie should meet on the polo field: 'We'll discuss it tonight. You're a *very* sweet person and I love you very much.'

Dickie had his confrontation with Edwina in mid-May. She was wary and depressed for weeks; he forced himself to look forward. In early June he tried to summarize their discussions. 'I want you to be as great a friend to me as I am to you', he wrote, 'easy going and with no secrets.' For his own part he had little to confess. 'I have kissed and hugged 2 or 3 girls in the last 9 years'. The most interesting person he had met was 'the lovely Edwina Mountbatten . . . I find her quite different to the Edwina Ashley I knew, the girl I had idealised for 9 years: but I find her far more fun, far more sweet and can understand why all the world loves her'. Edwina was touched. 'No one could have been sweeter or more tolerant of me than you during the last years', she replied, 'and you'll never know how much your devotion and long sufferingness have meant to me. Now that we understand each other better and are such true friends I feel sure things will be so much easier and I feel so much happier about everything. I do too feel you're my best friend in all the world and a good deal more.'

So they made the best of it. Edwina would be a grateful wife; 'your restored but changed Dickie' a magnanimous husband. He, at least, kept his word.

CHAPTER SEVENTEEN

Various Trials

In four months, from February to May, Dickie had grown older and wiser. He now knew that Edwina could be humbled. His letters to her became more dignified, his attitude more mature. If she was selfish or angry, he did not allow himself to be humiliated but held his ground. He put small difficulties in perspective by thinking of the long term and rode out awkward moments by looking on their amusing side. Edwina did not like the new situation. There was no risk or excitement in affairs that were conducted with Dickie's permission and it was discomfiting to her lovers to know that they were observed by a complaisant husband. Her affair with Hugh came to an end; Laddie sailed home to America.

Dickie returned to Malta and waited for Edwina to join him. Week after week her departure was postponed, for she had found a new admirer, Bobby Sweeney, a good-looking young American golf champion who was a Rhodes Scholar at Oxford. Things had to be wound down at Brook House and Adsdean, Edwina told Dickie, and there was 'an awful political and financial crisis'. In late September Britain came off the Gold Standard and the value of the pound fell by more than a quarter. 'Things very gloomy', Edwina cabled. 'Doing everything possible.' That is, she raided the shops in Bond Street and Piccadilly, and went with Brecky to see *Smart Money* at the Regal.

Meanwhile Cousin Felix got to work on Edwina's affairs. Unless something were done, sixty per cent of her income would go in tax. 'I am to stay out of the country for financial reasons', Edwina wrote gloomily in her diary at the beginning of October. On her last morning in London she was called at eight, as if to the scaffold: 'Feeling like nothing on earth and terribly depressed . . . the gloom of leaving Brook House for good and most of my friends for about 2 years was awful.' For ten years Edwina had done as she liked; now the bills were coming in.

Edwina Mountbatten

'It was nice being at home for two years', Dickie told his mother, in his first letter to her from his new post as Fleet Wireless Officer in Malta: 'Such a help having you to go to and talk things over when times were difficult'. In future, he was sure, he and Edwina would be more settled. 'I feel she misses having no mother', wrote this most loving son, 'but she naturally feels she has done badly by you and has no right to expect any comfort or sympathy – which I think she needs.'

Aunt Victoria was cautious: 'Edwina is very dear and affectionate to me,' she told Dickie in reply, 'but I will not try and fish for her confidence as you know. Such things must come of themselves.' She added a line or two of advice, firmly set out in her upright italic hand. 'I think it were well, and you must not mind my saying it, if you let Edwina feel that you put trust in her business capacities (Dick C. declares they are very good) and leave many details to her to decide. The responsibility is good for her character and' – here was a tactful hint – 'you have done so much to cure yourself of over-conscientious worrying, that even on this particular financial position you must be able to put some responsibility on her shoulders, without feeling you are risking too much.' Dickie should learn to delegate, Edwina should be encouraged to work: it was a good prescription. The reorganization of the Mountbattens' finances was an ideal project.

For years Dickie had been the one who worried about Edwina's money and their joint expenditure. In the two years when he was at home, late 1929 to mid-1931, he had seen that, while expenses were mounting, Edwina's investment income was dropping. Substantially more also went in tax. Brook House was by far the greatest drain. In the twelve months from autumn 1930 to autumn 1931 nearly sixteen thousand pounds was eaten up in running costs alone. The scale of the operation was alarming: twenty-seven indoor and two outdoor servants were kept when the Mountbattens were in residence, fourteen indoor and three outdoor when they were away. It was not as if the place were particularly convenient. Brook House was a museum piece, difficult and expensive to maintain. Even Miss Underhill referred to it as a white elephant, rare but useless. Mary managed her Upper Brook Street house with much less expense and trouble; it had the latest gadgets and was modern and amusing, with a spot-lit squash court built over the garage and a cocktail bar in the cellar. Molly had moved to Wood Street, where she had gone in for glass tables,

222

bare walls and sequin curtains. Brook House looked – and was – old-fashioned.

In the late spring of 1931 the Mountbattens began to examine their living arrangements. They decided to be drastic. Cousin Felix estimated that the sale of Brook House and its contents could produce additional income, after tax, of seven and a half thousand pounds a year, plus a saving of a thousand or more on staff; Edwina asked her trustees to set a sale in motion. This was complicated. Since Sir Ernest's will expressly forbade the sale of Brook House and the dispersal of its treasures, lawyers were called in to establish exactly what Lady Louis could and could not do. The business took weeks; there was interminable correspondence between Edwina, the trustees and her solicitors, Redher and Higgs. (Telegraphic address, aptly: Ceaseless, London.) The sale was announced in October 1931.

An army of experts tramped through the house, drawing up inventories of pictures, furniture, books, china and glass. Edwina had decided not to ask for leave to sell some of the more valuable pieces – Maudie's Corot, for instance – not just because she expected objections from the lawyers but also because she liked these things. Instead, she thought of the Prince of Wales, who was looking for furnishings for Fort Belvedere. There, for the time being, Edwina sent her jade, the Van Dycks, Romneys and Raeburns. It was cheaper than storing them, 'and he's absolutely *thrilled*, like a child, and is going round in circles arranging where they are to go.' Everything she did not want to keep in storage was to be disposed of at a series of general and special auctions. It was an unfortunate time to sell: the library realized only £1803, the porcelain £12,000, the pictures £25,000. No one wanted the house. It stood empty for eighteen months and then the great mansion was pulled down and the ceilings, panelling and mantelpieces dispersed, except for one chunk of marble that eventually reappeared in the new Brook House as a dining-room table. For another residence arose on the foundations of the old: an eight-storey block of flats, the two upper floors an enormous penthouse looking over Hyde Park. This, by arrangement with the developers, was to be Edwina's new home. In a neatly executed step she had succeeded in continuing to fulfil Sir Ernest's wishes, for, although she no longer occupied the old Brook House, at least she lived on top of it.

Edwina Mountbatten

Edwina, Patricia and Pamela arrived in Malta in November 1931. 'Lovely having the old girl back', Dickie wrote in his diary that night. Her days and nights were now filled with the Navy: two Admirals and a Flag-Lieutenant to lunch; thirty officers and their wives for cocktails and Dickie's instructive polo films ('all got slightly tight'); an evening watching a play, written and performed for charity by the *Queen Elizabeth*'s midshipmen, with the Commander-in-Chief's daughters playing the female parts. ('Really quite good'.) Edwina tried to make the best of it. There was everything to help her do so: a pretty house and garden, good staff, and an excellent governess for the children, Miss Vick, who had looked after Freda Dudley Ward's girls. She spoke French, German and Italian, she was sensible and could take charge of the house when the Mountbattens were away. Malta was not a bad place for Edwina's exile. As part of the economy drive *Shrimp* had been sold to the son of Signor Puccini, the composer, but the Cunningham-Reids lent their yacht, *Lizard*, for trips round the bays and to Gozo. The summer was bright and hot and Edwina began to enjoy herself: 'Dance in the *Glorious* which was very well done with a series of sideshows and amusements and a cabaret all done by officers'; out in *Beagle* from five in the afternoon until half past midnight, watching night firing exercises. Although Dickie worked like a maniac, it was pleasant to be the wife of a popular, successful officer. At the end of June Admiral Chatfield and his wife asked Edwina to come with them in the Commander-in-Chief's yacht, *Bryony*, to Yugoslavia, where *Queen Elizabeth* was to call on the summer cruise. 'Lovely day at sea', Edwina wrote in her diary on the first morning. 'Stopped twice to bathe and tried diving.' Then the storm came. The next day she was on her way to London.

A month before, on 29 May, a Sunday newspaper, the *People*, had printed an article by an anonymous gossip columnist. The paragraph ran, in full:

> I am asked to reveal today the sequel to a scandal which has shaken society to the very depths. It concerns one of the leading hostesses in the country – a woman highly connected and immensely rich. Her association with a coloured man became so marked that they were the talk of the West End. Then one day the couple were caught in compromising circumstances. The sequel is that the society woman has been given hints to clear

out of England for a couple of years to let the affair blow over, and the hint comes from a quarter which cannot be ignored.

It was only a small squirt of poison, a mixture of snobbery, envy, racism and prurience. To those who knew her, and many who did not, the piece pointed to Edwina. Marjorie telephoned the Mountbattens, who thought the article best ignored. Meanwhile Aunt Victoria spoke to the King, who decided after thinking it over that the newspaper should be sued for libel. 'We don't want to add to the publicity', Dickie told his mother, in a letter written before they had seen the article or heard the King's views. Cables shot between England, *Queen Elizabeth*, now off the coast of Greece, and *Bryony*, sliding though the Adriatic Sea: 'Coded messages galore', Edwina wrote, amazed, 'and really nearly going mad'. When the Mountbattens heard what the King had to say, they had no choice but to come home. Norman Birkett was invited to act for Edwina; his first task was to request permission from the Treasury for her to return to England without jeopardizing her arrangements with the Revenue. Cousin Felix spent hours conferring in Birkett's chambers. Beneath the suffocating euphemism, the article seemed to imply that Edwina had been having an affair with Paul Robeson, the black American actor, and that the King and Queen had banished her from England. Was Edwina justified in suing? Legal procedure required that passers-by should be asked at random to whom they thought the article referred. If at least three said that it pointed to Lady Louis, her lawyers had a case. They did – and Edwina's counsel now declared that, unless the publishers of the *People* acknowledged that the piece was wrong, two million readers might believe the story.

Edwina thought the whole thing preposterous. She had seen Robeson in *Showboat* in 1928 and *Othello* in 1930 but she did not know him. Every guest who came to Brook House or Adsdean, every entertainer of significance who performed at her house, was mentioned in her daily diary; there, for her own records, was a note of every outing with every lover. Robeson's name did not appear. She believed that, having no substance, the story would die. Now she had to abandon her holiday. The Commander-in-Chief ordered up a couple of sea-planes, one to fetch Dickie to Yugoslavia, the other to bring his suitcases. Edwina was incredulous: 'all this because of an article referring to my association with a coloured man (Robeson) whom I have never met!!!!'

Edwina Mountbatten

To Trieste by steamer, to Paris by train, in a second-class sleeper in which there was hardly room for the Mountbattens, let alone eleven pieces of luggage. To London, where a party of supporters was waiting, a show of solidarity reinforced by Aunt Victoria's insistence that Dickie and Edwina stay not at an hotel but in her apartment at Kensington Palace. A conference with Cousin Felix, a conference with Sir Reginald Poole and Norman Birkett. Odhams Press, publishers of the *People*, had instructed Sir Patrick Hastings; he had advised them not to defend the case. Edwina wanted an apology, without damages, her advisers wanted it given in court. The more the libel was examined, the fouler it seemed to be. In Norman Birkett's words, 'it must be wholly, completely and finally destroyed.'

Two days after the Mountbattens got to London, the case was heard before Lord Hewart, the Lord Chief Justice. Every seat in the public gallery was taken. Mr Birkett denounced the infamy of the paragraph, Sir Patrick unreservedly apologized for the *People* and assured the Lord Chief Justice that the author of the piece had been dismissed. It was made clear that Lady Mountbatten lived abroad because her husband's work took her there. Nothing was said about tax. To remove any speck of doubt, the Mountbattens were cross-examined on oath, Dickie about his appointment in Malta, Edwina to confirm that she had never met the man alluded to in the story. That evening the Mountbattens gave a party at the Café de Paris for their friends. Bobbie said piously to Jeanie Norton that he was glad it was all over because being Edwina's brother-in-law had been 'a drawback' in the House of Commons. 'If you had not been her brother-in-law', Jeanie replied, 'you would not have been in the House of Commons.' The next day Aunt Victoria took the Mountbattens to lunch with the King and Queen at Buckingham Palace, Dickie in a morning coat he had hastily hired from Moss Bros. All the world could see that Edwina's name was cleared.

Or so they hoped. The action failed to kill the story, Lord Chief Justice, distinguished Counsel, agreed statements, formal apologies and all. For decades afterwards, even sensible people believed there must have been something in it, declaring that, if Lady Louis said she had never met Paul Robeson, she must have been lying. That is quite wrong. Edwina was not reticent about her men friends but for her to have committed perjury would have been out of character.

Her statement agreed, moreover, with an observation in the diaries of Paul Robeson's wife, Essie. 'It is most incredible', she wrote at the time of the London case, 'that people should be linking Paul's name with that of a famous titled English woman, since she is just about the one person in England we don't know.' Essie was well-briefed on the intricacies of her husband's private life and readily talked about her marriage and Paul's women friends in letters to her friends and in her diary, which was frank. If either of the Robesons had met Lady Mountbatten, Essie would not have written as she did.

Yet the rumour persisted, taking the oddest forms. One of Edwina's biographers assumed that, if Robeson was not her paramour, some other black man must have been. Edwina had given a silver cigarette-case, affectionately inscribed, to 'Hutch' the pianist, who had played at Brook House parties for nothing; it must have been him. This is piffle – but people wanted to believe that their prejudices were being violated and that the King and Queen, representing purity, had put a stop to it. The effects of the story were ineradicable for years.

Among the friends who gathered in London to support the Mountbattens was a new member of their circle, Yola Letellier. Yola was twenty-five, with freckles, slate-blue eyes, a heart-shaped face, long legs, a tiny waist and high-arched feet. She was pert, chic and amusing and talked non-stop in rapid French. Her aunt, who sang at the Opéra in Paris, had been a friend of the novelist Colette, and when the nineteen-year-old Yola Henriquet married the wealthy Henri Letellier, thirty years her senior, Colette had seen a story in it: *Gigi*. Colette's beautiful adolescent schoolgirl was modelled on Yola, her millionaire, with his four-seater de Dion-Bouton with collapsible hood, on Henri. In real life Letellier was not the heir to a sugar-factory but the proprietor of the mass circulation *Journal*, a creator of smart beach resorts and casinos and the owner of one of Deauville's best hotels. It was there that Dickie had first met Yola, in August 1928, when she had been married for less than two years. At the beginning of April 1932 he saw her again. The Mountbattens were spending a weekend with friends in Cannes and on the Saturday night they had all dined at the Casino. Dickie enjoyed himself and, when they got home, Edwina exploded. He had neglected her, she said, and danced with Yola, while she had to look after a lot of Admirals. Dickie thought this unfair, considering Edwina's past behaviour, and did not repent.

Edwina was used to Dickie's infatuations with pretty and amusing

227

girls who gave him admiration and attention. She made friends with his favourites – the latest was Admiral Fisher's daughter Ros – and let them see that she was glad her husband had charming women to keep him company. She never thought that she might lose him, although after the frank talks of the preceding summer she had made more of an effort to distract him if he seemed interested in anyone else. But that confrontation had left its mark; while Dickie was fond of his wife, she no longer excited him. Meeting Yola and finding that she thought him attractive began to restore his confidence. He could not wait to let Edwina know. 'Told her news', Dickie wrote in his diary, 'Amazing heart to heart.' Edwina was furious. Saying that she had to go to Paris for fittings, she set off to inspect her rival.

'Your girl is sweet', Edwina told Dickie, 'and I like her and we got on beautifully and are now gummed and I am lunching with her at her house on Tuesday!!!' He was delighted. 'Lovely letter from the old girl.' Edwina turned Yola, Dickie's discovery, into an ally. In the autumn she and Marjorie set off with Yola in the Hispano for Vienna and Budapest, driving in turns, to meet their new friend's set. On the way Yola gave them a comprehensive briefing on the members of her circle: Count Deym, the Liechtensteins, the Odelscalchis, Prince Dietrichstein, Anti Szapary, Etienne de Horthy, a troop of Austrians, Czechs, Poles and Hungarians. Edwina was enchanted. Yola's friends talked cleverly and danced well; the women were as handsome and intelligent as the men: 'Renaissance Bar, Kaiser Bar etc etc . . . To a musical comedy, Blüme von Hawaii . . .'

Dickie waited at home. From Vienna Edwina took off with Nada for a long trip to Persia and Iraq; she did not come back to Malta until mid-December. She was bored and sorry for herself; doctors diagnosed malaria, then jaundice. At the beginning of March Edwina was off again. Malta disagreed with her, she told Dickie. Something in the air or the water was making her ill. It was more than a year before she returned.

Edwina was not ill. She was desperately jealous of Dickie and Yola. She had wanted all her husband's attention for herself; now she wanted Yola's too. For a while she secured it. First she made her way to Paris to stay with the Letelliers at their house in Neuilly. Perhaps a French doctor could discover what was wrong. Within a week Edwina was swallowing bismuth and being measured by a surgeon, who nipped out her appendix and ordered her to eat nothing but consommé. The operation left her feeling low and to try to raise her spirits Yola sent for a hairdresser, a masseur, a manicurist, clothes from Patou's spring collection and a selection of hats from Suzy. In April she accompanied Edwina to Cannes, where Dickie's ship was lying off the coast. Now it was he who danced with his friends after dinner, Edwina who went up to bed. She said she was ill: 'a horrid day drinking Bismuth and having X-rays of my inside which is not by any means right yet'. That is, until Anti Szapary arrived from Tuscany. He took Edwina to Monte Carlo to see the Grand Prix, they had supper together and drove home to Cannes through the warm spring night. In the front of Edwina's diary Anti wrote his telephone number in Budapest. Next day Edwina and Yola turned east again. They had decided to try the Clinic Loew in Vienna: 'My inside is all wrong still and hers is too', Edwina told Dickie. The Clinic was near enough to Hungary for Edwina to hire an aeroplane to visit Anti at weekends.

Edwina and Yola remained in Vienna for two months – not that they liked the Clinic, for it was bare and the treatments unpleasant. 'Temperature at all hours', Edwina wrote in her journal, 'blood tests, tubes we have to swallow . . .' The doctors put them on a diet guaranteed to ruin their figures: thick soup, eggs, rusks, potatoes, minced meat and cocoa . . . 'C'est dégoutant', Yola wrote to Dickie. What was the matter with Edwina? At one time it would have been called *accidie*, the torpor produced by idleness, fasting and too much thinking about one's own physical and emotional state. In this case the condition was aggravated by Edwina's custom of taking violent purges to mortify her flesh and keep down her weight. It was, she said, amazing that she was still upright: 'My gall bladder, liver etc, don't work at all as they should, neither does my stomach or intestine.' Her nerves were affected and, unless something were done, 'I shall get completely neurasthenic in no time'. She was anaemic, thin and thoroughly run down. 'The doctors here say they can't *imagine* how any sensible medical man can have left me like this so long.'

At first Dickie was sympathetic: 'Poor sweet', he called Edwina, when he wrote about her in his diary. 'Yola is staying with her, the darling.' Edwina had told him that the experts had diagnosed a chronic illness, probably caused by a Mediterranean parasite, and that it was dangerous for her to come home. Dickie began to wonder. How could the doctors be sure that the infection was Maltese? Edwina might have got it in Persia. He wrote her a stiff letter. She should never have gone to this fashionable clinic, dragging Yola there. Vehement denials from Edwina: 'Obscure microbes and oddities' had been dis covered 'in her organs and blood supply', she said, of a type known to thrive in the Mediterranean, especially in Malta, 'much as I love it'. And she had not abducted anyone. On the contrary, it was Yola who had first thought of coming to Vienna for a diagnosis. Nor had Yola been forced to stay. The doctors had recommended that she needed treatment urgently, 'though not as urgently as for me.' Edwina and Yola moved on – to the Vienna Cottage Sanatorium, which had pine essence in the baths and a swimming pool with artificial waves: 'much healthier and fresher than we were before'. The treatment left the patients with aching limbs and swollen faces; 'Feeling *awful*', Edwina told Dickie, but in their photographs of picnics in the woods with Etienne and Anti she and Yola looked well and happy.

Dickie was having a difficult time. He had been promoted to Commander and in late June his appointment in Malta would come to an end. Packing up Casa Medina was a chore; perhaps they should keep part of the house for holidays? Edwina declared that this would be too expensive. To save money, she said, she and Yola had taken on an Austrian maid, rather than sending for their own. (Meanwhile Harding and her French counterpart waited at home, fully paid.) Trying to please, Dickie went painstakingly through the household accounts and, to Edwina's intense annoyance, asked the chef to cut down costs. This was a disaster. Monsieur Brinz, inherited from Mrs Bischoffsheim, was proud of his work and of himself. On one occasion Edwina had suggested that an untouched luncheon cake might be served a second time: Brinz stiffly agreed, producing it next day with *Gâteau d'hier* written on the menu. Now he protested to Lady Louis: he appreciated that times had changed but Lord Louis did not realize how much it cost to feed the staff. Edwina smoothed him down; Dickie apologized, so handsomely that Brinz agreed to prepare the food for a farewell cocktail party for two hundred and fifty people. Dickie closed the house, paid the bills and left for Paris, to meet Edwina and Yola.

Some of the Mountbattens' friends observed that it was intelligent of Edwina to be so kind to Yola. More observant people suspected that she was trying to prise apart her husband and his girlfriend. Dickie did not know what to think. Yola's birthday was near his own and he had suggested that they all celebrate together in Paris. Unsure of his ground, he wrote to Yola, saying that, if she wanted to have Edwina to herself at Neuilly, he would arrange to stay elsewhere. Edwina tore the letter up ('It was luckily brought into my room first'), warned Dickie not to be jealous and announced that she had already told Yola that she and Dickie would be staying in an hotel so as not to be a nuisance to the Letelliers. The Mountbattens came home and, to mark their return, gave a party at the Embassy and a dance at the Savoy. Yola was among the guests. She stayed at the Dorchester for a week but Dickie secured only one lunch with her. 'She came to see me', Edwina wrote in her diary. At least Dickie had something to look forward to; Yola had agreed to come to Adsdean for a week in July. The longed-for day arrived. A bath, tea, and Dickie was ready. Then Edwina telephoned from London. 'Yola can't come', Dickie wrote bleakly in his journal. Perhaps he would see her in the autumn, for he had arranged to take a four-month naval interpreter's course in France while his new ship was being got ready. Edwina did not object. She had to come to Paris for fittings and they could rent the apartment that belonged to Kay Norton, Jeanie's sister-in-law. It had a bright, airy studio for parties and they would be able to entertain all their friends.

Dickie signed on with his French teacher, Madame Callède, and Edwina arrived with her trunks and the Hispano. After three days Edwina announced that she and Yola were going back to Budapest to continue their cure. Dickie was cross and upset. Edwina tore up his letters, saying they were too hurtful to read. He felt sick and ill, probably, he thought, from eating too many cream cakes. ('I was poisoned too', Edwina retorted, 'and felt like *hell*.) A doctor was sent for: '*Il m'a donné un purgatif*'; Dickie noted, '*et m'a confiné au lit*'. He had decided that for the duration of the course he would write his diary and his letters in French, read only French books and see only French films. He worked hard. Many pages in his journal showed only '*Travail*', '*Déjeuner seul*', '*Travail*', '*Pluie*', and '*Diner seul.*'

At the beginning of September Madame Callède explained that she intended to take an autumn holiday and that lessons would be suspended. She was going to Orthez; this was no more than forty kilometres from Biarritz, where the Prince of Wales was staying with some friends. Dickie realized that with a little ingenuity he would be able to continue his studies and see his cousin. He therefore reserved

Edwina Mountbatten

rooms at the Palace Hotel in Biarritz and at the Belle Hôtesse in Orthez, hiring a twelve-cylinder Hispano in which to travel between them. What was he complaining about, Edwina asked sarcastically. While Dickie enjoyed himself, she and Yola were saving money; rather than staying at the best hotel in Budapest, the Dunapalota, they had taken rooms at a 'hideous and boring' Hotel-Sanatorium. What is more, on the road from France to Hungary they had shared rooms, although this had given them the reputation of being what Edwina called 'women susps.' She and Yola thought this amusing. 'I do hope you're not jealous', she said mischievously.

This was meant to irritate Dickie and it did. He did not interfere with Edwina's liaisons, he told her, and it was unfair of her to try to upset his relations with Yola. Edwina erupted. 'Dear Dickie', she wrote acidly, 'you needn't demand equal rights for men and women . . . I have never in any way tried to pinch her from you or I think tried to stop you seeing her if she wanted to, or you did'. Poor Dickie could do nothing against this barrage. 'If you get into that sort of mood', Edwina announced, 'think first before writing as it's asking for trouble.' It was fortunate, she said, 'that I'm sensible enough not to take your letter over-seriously' (which was exactly what she was doing) 'or it might have destroyed my friendship with Yola and my feelings for you. So don't do it again.'

Help was on its way, although neither of the Mountbattens knew it yet. Edwina's passion for Anti was wearing off. It was time to return to Dickie and to take Yola back to France. Edwina and Yola flew to Vienna, picked up the Hispano and motored at top speed to Biarritz, via Milan, Monte Carlo and Carcassonne. Edwina took the wheel, doing between two and three hundred miles a day. Just before Orthez she skidded on a slippery road and smashed into a stationary car: 'Hispano alright but other car not so good.' It was the last awkward twist. From now on the road was to be straighter and smoother.

At Biarritz Dickie and Henri were waiting. Edwina and Yola installed themselves in the Palace Hotel, bathed, dined and slept. The next day Dickie insisted on playing a polo match in a thunderstorm and Edwina nobly stood by to present the cups. At the game she met Ted Phillips' brother, Bunny.

CHAPTER EIGHTEEN

The Perfect Companion

Bunny Phillips was, as Edwina's friends noticed, Dickie with the volume turned down. Bunny was content to be a competent golfer, a good tennis player, a decent shot; Dickie practised madly with professional coaches. Bunny was a useful member of a polo team, Dickie so keen that he invented new equipment and codified the game. At the wheel, Bunny was reliable, Dickie, busy thinking up improvements to the car, accident-prone. Bunny piloted his partner safely round the dance-floor; Dickie concentrated so hard that he knocked Edwina's shins and once steered Yola into a table. Bunny was equable; Dickie competed against himself and everyone else.

All Edwina's lovers had a slight resemblance to her husband, who had become, in his thirties, strikingly good-looking. A diet recommended by Noel Coward had produced intriguing hollows beneath Dickie's high cheekbones, exercise and a clear conscience gave him bright eyes and a smooth brow. His nose, slightly aquiline, was strong, the chin just perceptibly cleft, the mouth asymmetrically wrinkled. His hair fell back in an artless wave. Dickie was almost too attractive. Bunny's looks did not disturb. With his square jaw, level brows and shining hair, the parting dead straight, he looked the very model of an officer in the Guards, which he was. Bunny was unusual in only two respects. One was that he spoke fluent Spanish; his mother came from South America and her family, the Bryces, had connections with the Grace Line, the South American and Caribbean shipping company. Bunny's other distinction was that he had an extremely long back and legs. He was called Bunny, rather than Harold, because as a child he had been dressed as a rabbit for a party. The name suited him, for he had a modest, friendly air, as if he were compensating for his excessive height. Presentable, well-mannered and safe, he was just what Edwina wanted.

When the Mountbattens returned to Paris, Bunny followed, slotting comfortably into their lives, a facilitator rather than a threat. Edwina, who had abducted Yola, now accused Dickie of trying to steal Bunny. Dickie protested that he was simply being welcoming but, to make sure that Bunny was clearly identified as her friend, rather than Dickie's, Edwina carried him off to Adsdean. Bunny was instantly at home. He praised Edwina's arrangements, petted the animals and the children. Pamela was hardly aware of the new visitor; Patricia was troubled. Her father did not eat his breakfast in her mother's boudoir, as Bunny did. Edwina noticed nothing. 'Peaceful dinner', she wrote in her diary, 'and lovely evening'. The peace was to last for years.

It took time for everyone to settle down. Edwina had 'Talks with Dickie', 'Talks with Bunny'; Dickie, still practising his French: '*Discussion avec Yola*'. Peter Murphy flew to Paris, ostensibly to see modern furniture for the new Brook House but chiefly to advise Edwina: 'Heart to heart with Peter'. Jeanie was staying with Max Beaverbrook at the Ritz and had a series of conferences with Edwina, Edwina and Bunny, Dickie, Dickie and Edwina, Dickie and Yola.

Meanwhile Edwina had begun to think about another expedition. Beside her bed she kept Blackie's Pocket Atlas, a fat little volume which she studied every night. All the world was there, page after page of coloured maps, and she wanted to explore it. There was nothing to hold her back. Dick Crichton looked after Adsdean; Nannie and Miss Vick took care of the children; Dickie had his work and Yola. The house in Malta had been given up for the time being and as yet the Mountbattens had no base of their own in London. The new Brook House was growing but it would be another two years before the penthouse blossomed at the top. These arguments were reinforced by Edwina's wish to be with Bunny Phillips. She had promised Dickie that she would not provoke gossip; where better to escape the press than the furthest corners of the world? So Edwina embarked on a great programme of travel and, once she had started, she could not stop. From early 1934 to mid-1936 she covered thousands of miles; in all that time she was in England for less than six months.

At the end of January 1934 she set off to South America with Bunny and, as chaperones, Marjorie and Jack Evelyn. 'Miss me a bit', Edwina told Dickie, in a pencilled note she left behind, 'as I shall certainly miss you a very great deal'. Not for long. 'Lovely day', she wrote, as the ship plugged towards Brazil, 'and a grand world!' Bunny was an ideal companion, unflappable and amenable, and Marjorie a good sport, ready, if necessary, to dance all night and ride all day. She helped smuggle cigarettes over the Argentine border, happily settled down on wet evenings to games of Russian Bank, bagatelle and Speculator, did not complain when Edwina disappeared 'to talk to Bunny' and, when she and Edwina shared a room, neither snored nor took more than her share of hanging space. Edwina had brought several thousand pounds' worth of jewellery with her, uninsured, which had to be eased through customs. Marjorie lent a hand. She was not embarrassed when Edwina 'flapped an eyelash', as the cousins called it, to induce directors of railway companies to offer private cars and ambassadors to provide diplomatic visas, but, when Edwina needed rescuing, Marjorie could be relied on to produce a reason for going home or moving on. Her own admirers were quickly despatched: 'My pipe', Marjorie explained in her diary of the trip, '. . . lit at the psychological moment, is one of the best antidotes to romance'. Jack Evelyn had come along not just because four was more comfortable a party than three but also to help put gossip writers off the scent. Marjorie found him tiresome – she did not share his fondness for practical jokes – but to Edwina and Bunny he was convenient. Jack knew this, but, being good-natured, did not mind. When the other three went off on strenuous expeditions, he stayed behind to organize a proper tea.

The centrepiece of the holiday was a ten-day stay at Nahuel Huapi in Argentina, a 27,000-acre ranch owned by the four Basualdo brothers and their uncle. Carlos Basualdo was married to Leonora Hughes, whom Edwina and Marjorie had first met in the mid-1920s, when she was the dancing partner of the famous 'Maurice', and the Basualdos were friends of the Prince of Wales and Noel Coward, who had visited them in 1931. Their estate was a paradise. The ranch encircled a dark blue lake, sixty miles long, studded with twenty wooded islands, enclosed on three sides by the snowy mountains of the Andes. Deep fjords cut into the peninsula, which was covered with fine cypresses: 'a mixture of Norway, Switzerland, Canada and the Lake District', Edwina wrote ecstatically, 'and then 100 per cent more lovely'. The house could not have been more splendidly equipped – 'marble bathrooms', Noel had reported, 'and glorious beds' – but the weather was unpredictable, especially out on the lake. Three years before, while the Prince of Wales was staying, it was said that a complete orchestra had gone to the bottom.

Edwina Mountbatten

One of the Basualdo brothers had just crossed the Andes on horse-back, a hard ride, he observed, but through magnificent country, sixty miles of jungle forest, lava fields and snow. Horses were obtained, a guide engaged and Edwina, Marjorie and Bunny set off. Two pack-horses carried bedding, spare jodhpurs and socks, Marjorie's blue leather cushion, a frying-pan, bread and a chunk of raw meat. Jack, who stayed behind, was charged with getting the heavy luggage to Chile by motor car, much more comfortable, he said, with lovelier scenery.

He was right. As the travellers crossed the Andes it poured with rain and the horses slid on the track. Since they had forgotten matches and whisky, they dined on bread and sardines. Without candles they could not play cards, so the only thing to do was to sleep, Edwina, Bunny, Marjorie and the guide together, jammed into a leaky tent with their wet ponchos and paraphernalia. By nightfall next day they reached Chile: 'Exhausted, frozen, covered in mud', Edwina wrote in her diary, 'but it was all grand!' On to Bolivia, Peru, Panama, Ecuador and Mexico, inspecting ruined temples, fortresses and villages, and also Katharine Hepburn, 'travelling incognito', Edwina noted: 'Disappointing looks'. On 2 May they got into New York. The city was noisy and humid and Edwina could not bear the thought of parting from Bunny. He and Jack were off to the Far East, via California. 'I shall envy them', she wrote wistfully in her diary, and turned her face to home.

'The old girl looking well and lovely', Dickie wrote in his diary on 15 May; 'Dined alone with her and saw photos'. Edwina had thought of him often, she said. In Peru she had bought him fine silver spurs and for his birthday she would give him the epidiascope he coveted. But Dickie knew that he now played second fiddle to Bunny. His role was to support his wife when she was at home and look after things while she was away. While Edwina dined at the Jockey Club in Buenos Aires, Dickie read to Patricia. As Edwina danced at Bahia in Santiago, Dickie hid Easter eggs in the garden at Adsdean; while she drank cocktails at the Strangers' Club in Panama, he entertained the children to a grown-up lunch, to celebrate Pamela's fifth birthday. Between lectures at the Tactical School at Portsmouth, flying practice and visits to the Prince of Wales at Fort Belvedere, Dickie discussed the electrical layout and lighting for the Brook House flat, conferred with architects, examined the accounts with Dick Crichton and Miss Underhill ('conference re future finances'), superintended Patricia's fat-free diet and chased items of luggage which Edwina sent home in advance. He was neither aggrieved nor unhappy. Three times he flew to Paris to see Yola and when he went out in London he allowed himself to have a good time: 'Joined Georgie and Nada at the Dorchester. Met a most amusing girl . . . who demanded to be kissed good night.' He had a new ship to interest him, *Daring*, one of the Navy's most up-to-date destroyers: '. . . even more marvellous than I imagined possible', Dickie told his mother. Before he took over, he sent for particulars of each member of the ship's company, copied the information on to a set of visiting cards and got Peter Murphy to shuffle the pack, call out names and test him. *Daring* had 140 officers and men. If Dickie could not instantly put a face to a name, he would find some pretext to talk, so that he should not forget the man again.

Daring was part of the First Destroyer Flotilla, Mediterranean Fleet. Dickie had asked Edwina whether it would be bad for her health to return to Malta but, as the alternative was the Home Fleet, she decided that she preferred a warm sea. 'Don't change any plans', she said confidently, once she had assured herself that Dickie would put her convenience first. The Mediterranean would be enjoyable: 'I'd come out in May for the two nice months, with the children.' She was in good spirits. 'Round the ship which looks a picture', she wrote proudly: 'Dickie's cabin too lovely'. She enjoyed the dances given by the various flotillas and found even the cocktail parties bearable. Malta now seemed the pleasantest place. Edwina tried a local dressmaker and a hairdresser in Sliema: 'Had the back of my head permanently waved in fear and trembling . . . but it turned out quite well'. The weather was gloriously hot, the water divinely blue. A champion swimmer gave her lessons and after four days she pleased Dickie by daring to dive from the side of *Lizard*.

When Peter Murphy came to stay, he was delighted to see this transformation. At the time of Edwina's escapades in Budapest their relations had been scratchy. She claimed that they had disagreed about politics; Peter was 'completely Soviet-minded', she complained to Dickie. In fact Peter had stayed away from the Mountbattens because he disapproved of Edwina's excursions with Yola and thought Dickie feeble for not protesting more strongly. Now Peter and Edwina made friends again. Peter explained that he had been suffering from toothache but that new teeth and a new job – he had opened a left-wing bookshop – had put him right. His visit to Malta overlapped with that of Noel Coward. They were an odd-looking pair, Peter plump and hairless except for his moustache, Noel, bronzed and skinny, dressed in abbreviated shorts and a hat he had bought from a Chinese coolie.

In late July Dickie left for the summer cruise and Edwina returned to London, snatching a day and a night in Paris en route, to see Yola and order autumn clothes. Then she disappeared, for on the voyage back from America at the end of May she had decided to join Bunny in the Far East. Six days travelling and Edwina was in Bangkok; Bunny was waiting, having come up from Saigon to find her. 'Meeting rest of party here tomorrow', Edwina noted, and, next day, 'Arrival of Crockers, Jack etc'. She was doctoring her diary; these sentences, squeezed in later and written with a different-coloured pencil, were added to make the record square with the fibs in her letters to Dickie. Jack Evelyn did not arrive for another two days, having tactfully left Bunny and Edwina for a private reunion. Then he joined them for twenty-four hours only, before flying home to England. He did not accompany Edwina and Bunny on their Far East tour, as Edwina implied. Nor did Mr and Mrs Harry Crocker, American friends with whom Edwina had stayed in Santa Monica.

From Bangkok Edwina and Bunny went by train and car to Angkor Wat to see the temples in the jungle. They bathed in the lake, watched Cambodian dancing in the market square, rode in a rickshaw, 'lovely in . . . the moonlight', and discussed the next stage of the trip. 'Various arguments . . .', Edwina told Dickie, 'the Crockers being even vaguer and madder than me . . .' They motored gently up to the coast and at Hanoi rented a Chinese junk for a three-day cruise. It was idyllic. By day they sailed among the islands, mooring at sunset among sampans with moth-like sails. They rowed and swam by moonlight in the phosphorescent sea, slept on deck and woke in the delicate misty dawn: 'Quite perfect'. They moved on to Bali and Java, flew to Singapore, and from there took a ship to Borneo and Sarawak. Edwina was blissfully happy. The Captain was charming, the sea smooth, their cabins luxurious and comfortable. Edwina read aloud to Bunny while he sorted photographs. He was loving and attentive. 'Worked back over my doings in the past years from childhood upwards', she wrote in her journal, 'and Bunny made a chart'.

At Kuching they were met by a guard of honour and a band. There was a rumour that Edwina was the Queen of England and a crowd had gathered: 'waving and shaking of hands etc till I really thought I was!' A night in Singapore ('Visited the Air Force Yachting Club and autographed the ceiling'), two days in Penang at the Runnymede Hotel and Edwina and Bunny were on their way home to Europe, via Bangkok, Calcutta, Jodhpur, Jask, Baghdad, Cairo, ('left Crockers . . .', Edwina wrote neatly in her diary) and Budapest: ('Saw Anti for a minute . . . awful evening for a time but lovely later'). At Amsterdam they parted and Edwina went on to Croydon. Dickie, who had been in Paris with Yola, got in half an hour before Edwina arrived.

Edwina now seemed to have the best of all words: an affectionate husband and a charming lover, a comfortable, well-organized existence at home and an adventurous life abroad. In London the penthouse was beginning to look as if it might soon be habitable. The Mountbattens' temporary London base was 29 Bryanston Court, a three-bedroom flat in a smart new block, where Jeanie Norton and Mrs Simpson, the Prince's friend, also had apartments. It was less bother than staying with Philip Sassoon, Edwina told Dickie, and at twenty guineas a week she thought they could afford it. Bunny was now part of the Mountbatten household, or would have been had the flat in Bryanston Court been big enough to fit him in. It was easier to put up Yola, who used Patricia's room when she came over in late September, easier still for everyone to nip over to Paris and stay with the Letelliers. Bunny, Edwina and Etienne de Horthy were all at the house in Neuilly in the second week of October; 'Dickie arrived over on the 8.30 plane', Edwina noted: 'Communal living!'

It was not harmonious. When Dickie paid attention to Yola, leaving Edwina to concentrate on Bunny, he was accused of neglect. If he showed an interest in what Bunny and Edwina were doing, he was told not to pry. Edwina's sunny moods suddenly gave way to scenes: 'Bad evening, tears and complications', she recorded, after a small misunderstanding over the use of the car. These days, however, her ill-temper did not last and afterwards she was prepared to apologize. Bunny was a good influence.

It was not surprising that Edwina showed signs of strain. She was living in cramped accommodation at a temporary address, her marriage was ramshackle and she was never in the same place for more than two days at a time. There were other tensions. The Cunningham-Reids were being difficult about the financial adjustments following the sale of the old Brook House. Mary had left the details to Bobbie, who claimed not to understand them and refused to sign the necessary papers. In the end Edwina turned the whole matter over to Cousin Felix.

Meanwhile, Molly and Wilfrid were going through a bad patch. Wilfrid felt out of place in his wife's house; his moustache, right-wing views and sporting stories did not harmonize with chrome and glass and artistic flower arrangements. He liked comfortable furniture and understanding women, who refilled his teacup, replenished his glass and listened to his opinions. Wilfrid now had time to spare; he had been made a peer – Lord Mount Temple – and no longer sat in the House of Commons. Instead, he had a favourite armchair in various drawing-rooms. Molly declared, puzzlingly, that if he would not stay with her, she would leave him. Wilfrid turned to Edwina. To his astonishment, his daughter backed her stepmother. At his age, Edwina told Wilfrid, he should settle down.

Dickie was not directly involved in these excitements. His turn was in October, when his brother Georgie came to him for advice. Three years before, in the summer of 1931, Nada had taken a short holiday in the South of France with three women friends, Consuelo Thaw, known as 'Tamar', her sister Gloria, and Wallis Simpson. At the time it did not seem strange. Cannes was fashionable, so much so that villas were in short supply. The cost of hotel rooms was astronomical and they had therefore decided to share, Wallis going in with Tamar, Nada with Gloria. Now, three years later, the holiday was the talk of New York. Gloria was a widow, sister-in-law of General Vanderbilt, on whose yacht Dickie and Edwina had first become acquainted in 1921. There had been one child of Gloria's marriage, 'Little Gloria', who was to inherit a large income when she came of age. Mrs Vanderbilt was said to be an unsuitable mother, who spent too much time in Europe, and the care and supervision of her daughter had been transferred to the girl's aunt, Gertrude Whitney. Gloria Vanderbilt wanted her back and in the battle over the child, and the child's inheritance, unpleasant things were said. A maid declared that she had seen Lady Milford Haven in Mrs Vanderbilt's bedroom, while they were staying on the French Riviera, and that the two women had been kissing. Respectable people, who neither lolled on their friends' eiderdowns nor indulged in extravagant displays of affection, reeled in amazement. Overnight Nada found herself branded a notorious lesbian. The Mountbattens drove over to Bray to confer with the Milford Havens. 'The family are certainly unlucky!!', Edwina observed in her diary.

Nada had always been uninhibited. She openly discussed subjects which others thought unmentionable even in private. She exaggerated and, as people expected of a sophisticated, half-Russian cosmopolitan, talked freely with no concessions to English modesty. The Milford Havens were considered odd. Georgie collected erotica and Nada made no secret of it. This prompted peculiar stories; that at Lynden Manor, for instance, the paintings on the walls concealed pornographic pictures. What the Milford Havens' own habits were, no one knew. That did not prevent people from speculating. Should Nada sue? After discussing the matter with Dickie, Edwina and Aunt Victoria, who took soundings at Buckingham Palace, the Milford Havens decided to do nothing.

There was a third reason why Edwina was unsettled: having moved ahead so fast, Dickie's career seemed to have shifted into reverse. 'Shock at Admiralty', he wrote in his diary on 6 September, just before Edwina's return. He was to be moved from *Daring*. All appeals failed. A fortnight later Dickie returned to his ship after a week's leave: 'Blow fell. We relieve 8th D.F. (China) boats'. The whole flotilla was to sail for Singapore in October, to take over duties on that station; there he was to exchange *Daring* for another, older destroyer. Dickie left for the Far East on 31 October, taking a piano, an accordion, and for company Peter Murphy and Andrew, Peter's pet tortoise. Edwina saw them off at Sheerness and went back to London to dine with Bunny at Quaglinos. Out of sight, out of mind; Dickie would have to look after himself. Next morning she and Bunny were off on their third long trip together, four months in the South Seas, returning via Java, New Zealand and Australia. To avoid comment in the press they had settled that Bunny should sail to New York in the *Bremen* while Edwina travelled to Canada in the *Empress of Britain*. They were to meet in a fortnight's time in California.

On 15 November Douglas Fairbanks met Edwina in Los Angeles and in the afternoon Bunny and Ted arrived from Mexico City. In New York Edwina had seen Mary Pickford, now living apart from her husband, who had offered her the use of 'Pickfair', so Edwina, Bunny and Ted installed themselves there. There would be no gossip, Edwina assured Dickie; Douglas was living elsewhere. She did not say that Ted and Bunny, her former and current lovers, were sharing the house where she and Dickie had spent part of their honeymoon. The Phillips brothers, she said, were still in Mexico City. To please Dickie, Edwina mentioned old friends in her letters home: Chaplin, the Astaires, with whom she dined at the Coconut Grove, Irving Thalberg and Norma Shearer 'asking tenderly after you'. She told him about the new acquaintances she made at Douglas's parties, the Clark Gables, for instance, and Loretta Young, people Dickie saw on *Daring*'s cinema screen, as he chugged through the Red Sea. Edwina might not be at his side, but at least she was in Hollywood, the next best place to be.

Edwina had said nothing to Dickie about her plan to explore the South Seas with Bunny but now she had to let him know roughly where she was going to be. 'Edwina telegraphed she has gone to Tahiti', Dickie wrote in his diary on 26 November; by then she was halfway there. As the RMS *Makura* steamed through a gap in the coral reef and entered the harbour at Papeete, Edwina worked on her alibi. In California, she said, some people called Tobin had invited her to come with them to the South Seas: 'I jumped at it'. Ted and Bunny had seen them all off at San Francisco and then returned to Ted's mysterious business in Mexico City. On the *Makura* Edwina and the Tobins had joined up with 'a charming couple called Robinson', who were planning to charter a copra boat and sail round the Marquesas and the other Society Islands, mapping and doing survey work. They would be away for the entire month of December, perhaps longer, and, as mail was infrequent and the cost of cabling extortionate, Dickie should not worry if there were no letters. Douglas Fairbanks might join her after Christmas, in a new six-hundred-ton yacht he wanted to try out, and he might bring the Phillips brothers with him. Even if this scheme did not come off, she would be well looked after. Mr Robinson was an experienced sailor; his was the smallest craft that had ever circled the globe and his book *Deep Water and Shoal* had been published in England, 'so get it'.

Edwina's letter was a mixture of fact and fiction. The Robinsons were real, the Tobins an invention. Douglas Fairbanks had indeed chartered a yacht and taken it to Tahiti but this was two years before, when he was filming *Robinson Crusoe*, and he showed no sign of doing so again. Ted Phillips had certainly returned to Mexico but his brother was on board *Makura* with Edwina. It was Bunny, not the Robinsons or the Tobins, who had arranged a month-long trip among the islands. Edwina believed she lied to spare Dickie's feelings. She was also protecting herself. Accepting these fictions allowed both the Mountbattens to avoid awkward questions. Edwina did not wish to face up to her own dishonesty; Dickie did not want to ask whether their marriage had a future. By pretending that Edwina's stories were true, they both saved face. Dickie was not deceived. It was better that Edwina should be with Bunny, rather than some man he did not know and might not like. If he was hurt, he tried not to show it. Edwina persuaded herself that she was being generous to both men, giving each of them part of her time and attention, committing herself to neither. If Dickie had questioned her about her fibs, she would have been outraged.

For three months Edwina and Bunny pottered through the South Seas, in a borrowed yacht, little fishing vessels, a schooner that took in copra. They ate sea snails, lobster and sea centipedes, adopted a tiny parrot, a puppy and two bluebirds, called on various Europeans who had settled on atolls here and there, swam, sunbathed and played the gramophone. Bunny speared fish and shot sharks with a revolver. 'I think the Pacific a perfect Paradise', Edwina declared, in the second of the two letters she sent Dickie between December 1934 and March 1935. ('There's only one boat a month so don't expect much literature'.) She returned to Malta at the end of April, after six months away.

Readjustment was not easy: at Casa Medina there was a mountain of letters to deal with and when Edwina tried to sunbathe on the roof she found herself covered in smuts. Aunt Victoria had been in Malta since mid-February and both Patricia and Pamela were there; to Edwina, used only to Bunny's company, the place seemed crowded. Casa Medina now housed not only the family but a small menagerie: a pair of chameleons Dickie had bought in Cairo for the children, two bushbabies, a dachshund Yola had given Pamela, and Rastus, a honey bear Edwina and Bunny had bought in Singapore the previous August, collected by Dickie on his way back from the Far East. 'Not feeling too well', Edwina complained, after her first full day at home. 'Only saw the children from afar'.

Dickie had returned to Malta two months before. He had made

the best of things and enjoyed his mission: polo in Ceylon, golf (Sunningdale rules) in Singapore, *Horse Feathers*, with the Marx Brothers, in an outdoor cinema in Aden. When the time came to turn round, Dickie found it hard to part with his ship. 'One of the most tragic days of my life', he wrote on 17 December, 'Today I handed over my beloved *Daring* . . . and took over the *Wishart*, 235 tons smaller, years older and not even so clean between decks. Cabin about half size'. Next morning Dickie took up his new command and by the afternoon he had persuaded himself that it had been a good move. He threw himself into realizing *Wishart*'s full potential. Scrubbing and painting improved her battered appearance, a carpenter and plumber set to work on Dickie's cabin, office and washroom. 'Our ship is named after the Almighty himself', he told the men, grasping at straws, 'to whom we pray daily: Our Father Wishart in Heaven . . .' They had met no one like this before, a Commander who knew everyone's name, kept chameleons and a bear in his cabin, produced a saxophone and asked for a jazz accompaniment to hymn-tunes on Sunday mornings. Greatly heartened, Dickie and the ship's company made their way home to Malta.

Edwina was amazed to see how much the children had grown. To Aunt Victoria, they recalled memories of their father as a small boy, fair, blue-eyed and bony. In her early years Patricia had been pale and listless and, fearing TB, Edwina had insisted that her nursery windows be fitted with special glass to enhance the sun's rays. Patricia's first governess, a Frenchwoman, thought her diet unsuitable; doctors inspected the child's ears, eyes, nose and throat, sounded her chest, sampled her blood, and recommended more fresh fruit and vegetables, little fat and good air. This prescription did no harm. Photographs of Patricia at the age of ten and eleven showed a tall, attractive girl, confident and happy, with a toothy smile. Pamela looked less at ease, as if she had too little sleep. She was prone to sudden fevers, ear and stomach aches, alarming her over-protective Nannie, whom she adored. Perhaps Pamela missed Edwina, who, like Maudie, was never there. Dickie was affectionate but guarded, for Edwina had ordered him not to upset Pamela and Nannie was vigilant. At Christmas Aunt Victoria had given the children stamp albums, so they could start a collection, and Patricia made sure that Pamela had her fair share from Edwina's letters. It did not help her sister understand where her mother had got to.

The Perfect Companion

Dickie was away from Malta for most of March and April. The Fleet was playing at war, chasing up and down the Mediterranean, alarming Spanish trawlermen. This year the practice was extra serious: Hitler, who had become Chancellor of Germany in January 1933, had announced that he intended to re-establish his country as a great power. Meanwhile the Italian army was skirmishing in North Africa, as part of Mussolini's plans for the conquest of Abyssinia. Dickie, steaming to Gibraltar, tried to sort out his views by reading John Strachey's book, *The Coming Struggle for Power*. This was unhelpful, being a case for Soviet planning, written by a disillusioned supporter of Sir Oswald Mosley, founder of the British Union of Fascists, but Dickie studied it conscientiously. It might come in useful if the country were taken over by the Left. Whatever happened, he and *Wishart* would be prepared. It was galling when, on the third day of the exercise, Dickie's ship was rammed and put out of action. Repairs would take days. 'Really miserable', Dickie wrote, as the First Destroyer Flotilla, with three hundred Gordon Highlanders and twenty-seven pipers, sailed for Alexandria without him.

'Lovely having the old girl back', Dickie said happily, when the Mountbattens were reunited in Malta in late April. 'Looking sweeter than ever'. Edwina did not stay long. 'Malta saps all our energy and ambition', she wrote in her diary, 'particularly in this weather and we all become completely gaga!' She wished she were back in the South Seas. In Malta the swimming and sunbathing were passable but social duties made her want to scream: 'a dinner bristling with the C-in-C and other Admirals and a dance of unbelievable tediousness!'; 'a party . . . quite good as parties go but the noise and heat terrifying and have come to the conclusion that all parties are hell!' She fled to Rome, and to Bunny. Yola joined them there and in May Edwina took her back to Malta. Peter Murphy was also staying and under his avuncular eye Edwina behaved herself. There were no scenes. It was a relief, none the less, when Yola's three weeks were up. 'Quite pleasant to have the house empty again', Edwina wrote happily in her diary, 'says the perfect hostess!!'

Her reward came in July. Dickie set off on a month's summer cruise, Edwina joined Yola and Bunny in Paris, and all three travelled down to the Riviera to meet Dickie when the flotilla came in. Here, a cheerful foursome, they celebrated the Mountbattens' thirteenth wedding anniversary. On each successive 18 July Dickie had given Edwina a piece of jewellery or an ornament, designed by himself, incorporating a Roman numeral. This year's present was a gold box; her gift to him a tiny stop-watch from Cartier.

At the end of the summer Dickie found himself alone again. Edwina had decided that Malta was unsafe for the children, for it looked as if there would be trouble in the Mediterranean, and at the end of July she put Patricia and Pamela, Nannie and Miss Vick on the train to Budapest. Hungary, Edwina thought, was the perfect refuge, being landlocked, inexpensive and governed by Etienne's uncle. While the children trundled along in the train, Edwina, Bunny and Yola drove eastwards in the Hispano. On the Brenner Pass they met thousands of Italian troops, 'quite interesting but . . . delayed us a bit'. A hundred kilometres from Budapest they found a pleasant hotel at Kekes, among pine woods up in the mountains: this, Edwina decided, was the right spot to instal the children, Nannie and Miss Vick. Having settled them in, she drove back, via Venice, to Rome, to collect Marjorie, who was coming out to Malta for a holiday.

In many ways life in Casa Medina proceeded as usual. Dickie and Bunny played polo, Edwina and her guests went greyhound racing and visited archaeological sites. They cruised round the island in *Cygnet*, a small boat the Mountbattens had bought in the South of France in July, to replace *Lizard*, which Mary and Bobbie had re-claimed. Dickie rehearsed for the Regatta, continuing his efforts even when he was ordered to take his sub-division to the South of France, to participate in the International Motor Boat Races. Here he saw the Prince of Wales, who was staying at Villa le Roc with Mrs Simpson. The Duke of Westminster had offered the Prince his yacht for a month's tour of the Dalmatian Coast and the Greek islands, 'avoiding however, the stormy part,' Mrs Simpson said in a letter to her Aunt Bessie. Could they not see that the skies were darkening and the wind rising? The Prince's cruise was cancelled, for by the third week of August, 'everyone and everything', Edwina wrote in her diary, was 'in a flap about the Italian Abyssinian question'.

'Dined with Stewart Perowne on his roof', she noted, 'and Wing Commander Jones played the piano to us after'. Anti-aircraft guns had been placed on the shore and booms stretched across the harbours. Air-raid shelters were constructed, instructions issued in case of emergency. 'The place is thick with barbed wire entanglements', Edwina told Wilfrid, 'and the ships at war stations, with warheads on their

Marjorie and Edwina

Yola, Edwina and Anti Szapary

Bunny Phillips

Yola Letellier

Edwina, Pamela and Patricia

torpedoes'. Two rooms in Casa Medina were made gas-proof. On 2 October general mobilization was declared in Italy and Mussolini broadcast to the nation. Within a week, Edwina was doing the same, having been asked by the Port Wireless Officer in Malta to read the London news bulletins, as counter-propaganda. 'Nearly died of fright when confronted with the microphones', Edwina wrote, not surprisingly, for they were enormous. Her nervousness soon disappeared and by the end of the month she casually fitted her trips to broadcasting headquarters, in the Governor's Palace, in between afternoon polo and cocktails. The weeks passed. It was becoming too cold to swim: at St Peter's Pool Edwina and Bunny watched Air Force manoeuvres instead. Blackouts were amusing at first ('searchlights looked lovely') but the novelty quickly wore off. Dickie was working; to pass the time Bunny practised polo and Edwina took cooking lessons from Brinz. The island seemed cramped, conversation repetitive. People came to dinner and quarrelled over rearmament until Edwina could bear no more.

She had done her bit and it was time to leave. Time, too, to extract the children from their mountain retreat. They had not heard from their mother for weeks. The weather had got colder and they needed warm clothing. Since none arrived, Nannie had kitted them out in scratchy pink flannel underclothes. The proprietor explained that the hotel was closing for the winter and asked Miss Vick to settle the bill. No money had been sent; another visitor said he had heard of Lady Louis and would lend what was required. Edwina had no idea where the children were, for she had lost the address. On the last day of November she and Yola set off to look for them.

Edwina's plan had been to send her daughters back to Malta but, while she was on her way to retrieve them, the crisis over Abyssinia grew worse. Arrangements were changed: Patricia, Pamela, Miss Vick and Nannie were despatched by train to Darmstadt to stay with Uncle Ernie. Dickie was diappointed. He had been looking forward to seeing the children. 'It is very sad and lonely in the house without you', he told Patricia, at the end of a ten-page letter, in which he recalled his own holidays at Darmstadt. Was Faix, the toy shop, still there? He told Patricia how to pronounce its name and where to look. She should explore the Schloss Museum, ('Do not forget to look for my old naval uniform which I wore in the war') and inquire after the old housekeeper at the New Palace: 'She was the daughter of Grandpapa's

247

first valet – an Italian with heavenly pointed whiskers'. Uncle Ernie was kind; he made up stories for the children, drew flowers for Pamela and helped Patricia write letters to her father in High German. Dickie was delighted to find that his daughter wrote more accurate German than himself. To polish up his grammar and his Gothic script, he engaged a tutor, and sent for the syllabus for the German naval interpreter's examination. Dickie was still working at his French, and at other people's, for he had put together a *French-English Naval Vocabulary*, existing manuals being worse than useless. Miss Underhill sent proof chapters for collection at various points on the Mediterranean shore, alerting Lord Louis with a signal that caused hilarity in the Fleet: 'French letter awaits you'. Dickie did not dare explain. Then he hit on the idea of asking Miss Underhill to encode her messages. She did her best but the result was worse. 'ORJUX awaits you', the cables said.

At Christmas Dickie was back in Malta: 'Had a bit of the servants' Xmas dinner on a tray'. It was five months before he saw Edwina or the children again. After leaving Patricia and Pamela at Darmstadt she had set off to China with Bunny. In Germany, she told Dickie, she had met 'some charming people called Ritter', who were going to Moscow on business and had invited her to accompany them: 'which would be most interesting as they know everything there is to know about the country and can show one around everywhere'. In jest, Edwina said, she had suggested that, if she went with them to Moscow, they should come with her on the Trans-Siberian Railway to China. 'To my surprise they seemed quite struck with the idea'. Did Dickie not agree that this was an excellent opportunity? Since the Ritters would be there to chaperone her ('I tell you all this as I like you to know and you're so understanding'), Bunny would be able to come with them: 'going out this way would be ideal from the point of view of no publicity as all thru' Russia and Siberia *no* advertisement of any kind is given to Tourists etc – it not being the policy of the Government and names are not even mentioned'. Dickie was growing accustomed to Edwina's fabrications. Knowing that she was lying allowed him to feel protective and superior. To tease her, he said that his German professor had met some Ritters at a party in London. Bunny marvelled at Edwina's reaction. 'They must be impostors', she exclaimed indignantly.

With Bunny, and a tortoise brought from Malta, Edwina proceeded via Manchuria, renamed Manchukuo by the Japanese, and dotted with concrete pillboxes, to Peking. The piercing wind and dry air were bad for her sinuses and by the end of the first week in February she felt dreadful. Edwina and Bunny decided to flee to a warmer climate, in a ship that was going from Shanghai to the Philippines. 'Your poor Ritters must have been fed up', Dickie observed, with tongue in cheek, 'being dragged off to Manila and Macassar'. Edwina's 'week or two in the Philippines' turned into seven weeks among the Celebes and the Moluccas, 'as happy as it is possible to be'. She and Bunny travelled on small cargo boats; one Captain demonstrated card tricks after dinner, another liked a game of shuffleboard. They called at Bali and Java, steamed back to Hong Kong and then on to Japan and back to America. In California Edwina returned to reality. The news from Europe was bad. A dock strike at San Francisco threatened to disrupt her onward journey, the sea was rough, the skies dull. Without a maid, she was obliged to do her own packing: 'Exhausted by the end of it'. At Southampton Dickie and Marjorie were waiting to welcome her. She had been out of England for almost two years.

CHAPTER NINETEEN

Lost Horizon

L ondon had changed. One addition was a square brick edifice at the top of Park Lane, the new Brook House, nearly ready for occupation. The façade had been designed by Lutyens, who had made the two top storeys different from the rest of the building by putting balconies on three sides and a circular window in the pediment. From Hyde Park the Mountbattens' penthouse looked like a ship, rising above the trees. It was reached by a private front door in Upper Brook Street, via a lift which took people straight up to the seventh floor in twelve seconds. This was the first of Dickie's special contrivances. The key that unlocked the street door also released the lift, which, in theory, then hurtled to ground level to await the awestruck visitor. 'I hear you have the fastest lift in Europe,' said Queen Mary and asked to see it. She and Dickie got in but the lift remembered an earlier instruction and to the Queen's astonishment hurtled past the welcoming party on the seventh floor, taking her almost to the roof.

The Mountbattens' new house had thirty rooms. On the top floor were Edwina's and Dickie's bedrooms, bathrooms, dressing-rooms and private sitting-rooms, giving on to the Park; two sets of rooms for visitors, looking south, and on the north side the maids' rooms and linen rooms. The floor below was largely taken up by the morning-room, drawing- and dining-rooms, all facing the Park, with folding doors that allowed them to be thrown open into a ballroom or a cinema with seats for a hundred and fifty. 'Quite a good place for entertaining', remarked Miss Underhill, who had been the first person to move in to new Brook House, as she had been the last to leave the old. On the south side was the children's wing, on the north the kitchen and the menservants' rooms. There were also two adjoining offices for Stella Underhill and her new deputy, Nancie Lees. All this the Mountbattens rented for £4200 a year.

Sir Ernest would have been pleased to see how much glass and marble had been installed in this small palace in the sky. The two floors of the penthouse were connected by a double curved staircase, all mirrors and polished chrome, and Dickie's illuminations were a tribute to the proprietor of the old Brook House. One touch and the roof and balcony were floodlit, a sight that brought gasps of amazement, and some criticism, from miles round. Dickie was largely responsible for the choice of plumbing ('Had bath at Brook House (VG) to test it') and Edwina saw to the decoration, with help from Nell Cosden, who was working with Victor Proetz, the New York decorator, and Reed Vreeland's startlingly fashionable wife, Diana. Rex Whistler was commissioned to paint Edwina's boudoir; four years earlier he had converted Philip Sassoon's dreary dining-room at Port Lympne into a *trompe l'oeil* tent of blue and white striped silk, framing walls displaying fantastic landscapes. Whistler first inspected Edwina's room in November 1936. It was spacious, seventeen feet by twenty-three, and he decided to divide each wall into small panels of different shapes and sizes. There were sixty of these, painted with fruit, flowers, cupids and goddesses, in grisaille against a background of delicate greyish blue. Broadlands was there, with Adsdean and the old Brook House. Dickie was shown on a polo pony and, reclining against a specially designed wall clock, fitted into a lunette, was a naked Venus, with Edwina's features, watched by Father Time. The murals looked fragile but they lasted longer than the walls. Whistler began by painting directly on to the plaster, but, seeing this, Edwina insisted that he start again, using canvas in portable frames. When war broke out two years later the panels were removed to Broadlands; not long afterwards a bomb came through the roof, wrecking all that remained.

Casa Medina had been given up at the end of April 1936, when Dickie joined the Naval Air department at the Admiralty. He was pleased with this post and not only because, as he observed to Edwina, 'compared to others it is a much more human division as regards leave and polo-playing'. As enthusiastic a pilot as he was a sailor, Dickie took to his new responsibilities like a duck to air. After two months' leave, he started his appointment, transferring himself at the same time into makeshift quarters at Brook House. At the Admiralty he advocated every sort of change. The Navy should use Typex enciphering machines, as the Royal Air Force did; new designs (his own) should be considered for the bridges of destroyers and (the King was roped in here) for naval full-dress uniform. He drew his superiors' attention to the 'Mountbatten Station Keeping Equipment', a contrivance to assist a line of ships to keep their distance when advancing abreast. Then there was a Swiss invention, the Oerlikon gun, whose rate of fire was superior to that of the Vickers weaponry favoured by the Gunnery School Experimental Department. Mountbatten's artful pressure played a large part in manoeuvring the Admiralty into ordering a large number of Oerlikons in May 1939. (In the Battle of Britain they were crucial.) Dickie's passion for innovation was not the only enthusiasm that spilled into his work. He was determined that the Navy's polo team should knock spots off its rivals from the other Services and that his superiors should know it: 'Great crowds', he wrote in his diary, after the Navy's handsome victory over the Royal Air Force on 10 June: '1st Lord, 2nd, 3rd and 4th Sea Lords'. His interest in the movies led him to push for a greater variety of films to be supplied to ships at sea and, as a first step, he arranged for Noel Coward to visit the Mediterranean and Home Fleets to find out what ordinary sailors preferred. Dickie knew what he liked himself: *Modern Times, Things to Come, Passport to Fame*; the men wanted George Formby and Jessie Matthews.

Edwina's preoccupations were more trivial: 'Major operation . . . on my ear lobes . . . reduced to mincemeat and then remodelled . . .' In August she followed Dickie into Brook House, sleeping in a guest room and giving impromptu dinner parties in his sitting-room. She murmured about headaches and neuralgia. Her days were filled with futile activity, she said, and at night she could not sleep.

The truth was that, having arranged matters so that she could do as she pleased, Edwina had made herself redundant. Adsdean was well-managed and the children little trouble. Patricia had now started school, Miss Faunce's in Queen's Gardens. Miss Vick left to look after a new set of charges, and her place in the schoolroom was taken by Mademoiselle Chevrier, a no-nonsense but affectionate Frenchwoman, who supervised Patricia's homework. (Edwina always called the new governess Mademoiselle Chévrier, insisting, despite her protestations, that there must be an accent on the 'e'.) Patricia flourished, for Miss Vick had taught her well and Dickie had set a good example, working as keenly at Patricia's books as she did herself. To encourage her to prepare neat letters and orderly files, he had bought her a small typewriter; secretarial skills, Dickie said, would be useful after the revolution of which left-wing people spoke. (He had been so impressed by G. D. H. Cole's articles on *The Decline of Capitalism* – 'which would affect us both' – that he had given his brother a subscription to the *New Statesman and Nation*.)

Edwina was bored and frustrated. Rain, fog and frost made her miserable. She longed for the Celebes, the Moluccas and the Iles Sous-le-Vent, the earthly paradise of Shangri-La, as it had been described in the best-selling novel, *The Lost Horizon*. Edwina had read this book on her first voyage to Tahiti in November 1934: 'excellent', she had written approvingly in her diary, 'quite fascinating'. The places she had explored with Bunny had been such another Eden, their travels together the most romantic journeys of Edwina's life. Some women who had time to spare went botanizing in the jungle or, like Laddie Sanford's sister, hunted rare game and sent their discoveries home to museums and learned societies. Edwina's mission, she decided, was to sail through tropical seas to islands unknown to fishermen and copra traders, even to the intrepid Mr Robinson, whose *Deep Water and Shoal* she had commended to Dickie. Here, at the edge of the world, Edwina and Bunny might, indeed very probably would, find heaven on earth.

By the autumn of 1936 Edwina's dream was taking solid shape. Bunny had commissioned the Tregaskie yard at Par to construct a three-masted schooner; he and Edwina called it *Lost Horizon*. She told her husband that Bunny had ordered a boat from a yard in Cornwall and that now and again they would be going to see how the work was getting on. Dickie was too tactful to suggest that he might come as well, which was fortunate, for he would have envied the smooth timbers and easy lines of Bunny's new toy, especially now that he had no boat of his own. *Shrimp* and *Cygnet* had gone, Edwina had said nothing about replacements and it was hard to make out a case while he was beached in an office in Whitehall.

In ordinary times Dickie would have been curious. Now, however, he had something more important on his mind: Cousin David's future. King George had died on 20 January; Mountbatten was the first to admit that he enjoyed his connection with his successor. Cousin David needed comfort and Dickie believed the King wanted him as a confidant. He was not entirely right. For the past two years that part had been played by Wallis Simpson. But to whom was the King to turn when it was about Mrs Simpson that he wished to talk?

Edwina Mountbatten

The Mountbattens had been close to the Prince for fifteen years. For the greater part of that time he had been attached to Freda Dudley Ward, whom Dickie and Edwina liked and respected. At the Fort they had seen the Prince construct something approximating to a home: Dickie had helped choose curtain fabric and, as well as pictures, Edwina had lent china (unsuitably placed, she thought, in a corner cupboard). Dickie was a regular visitor. He could drive to the Fort from Adsdean in just over an hour and in the early part of 1934, while he was in England, he looked in at least once a fortnight, generally staying for dinner and the night. In late March he found new fellow-guests: 'Simpson – 2 Americans'. By the autumn the Mountbattens were aware that Mrs Dudley Ward's place had been permanently usurped. When the Prince came to inspect the shell of the new Brook House in October 1934, it was Mrs Simpson who came with him; at the Embassy Club the Prince and Wallis sat all night together.

Mrs Simpson was now living at Bryanston Court, where, for a short time, the Mountbattens were her neighbours. Here the Prince came for supper with the Simpsons, dining on dishes meticulously presented, each portion of fish or bird being exactly the same size, by special arrangement with the supplier. Mrs Simpson had become a member of the Prince's circle but that did not make her one of the Mountbattens' friends. She was conventional and economical; they were original and rich. Mrs Simpson did not care for Lord Louis. She found him self-centred; he bombarded the Prince with memoranda and claimed that every one was urgent. Yet he did not trouble to learn how her own name was spelt; in his papers Dickie still referred to her as 'Wallace'. Socially ambitious herself, Mrs Simpson recognized careerism when she saw it. To eke out a small income and the handful of introductions she had brought to London, she had been obliged to manage and manipulate. She observed that Lord Louis also knew how to make a little go a long way: a word with the right person, a scrap of timely information. His resourcefulness was instinctive, hers conscious. That cannot have made Mrs Simpson comfortable. Then there was Lady Louis. She and Mrs Simpson presented themselves to the world in completely different ways. The newcomer's manner and appearance seemed contrived; Edwina was natural and assured. Next to her, Wallis was like a character in a play, costume fitted, lines learnt. Both women had neat, sleek heads – but Mrs Simpson, unlike Lady Louis, always looked as if she had just come from her hairdresser. Both were thin – but, unlike Edwina, Wallis seemed to calculate every morsel of her diet. This was a difficult time for Mrs Simpson. She found herself in a world where everyone knew everyone and each nuance mattered. Observant and imitative, she tried to get things right – but it was hard to appear relaxed at the same time. Being insecure, she was mortified when she muffed it, as she did when the new King took her to stay with the Mountbattens at Adsdean. This was in June 1936. Mrs Simpson brought a cold chicken from Fortnum and Mason, a gift which amused Edwina but did not go down well with Brinz.

At the end of September the Mountbattens travelled up to Scotland on the sleeper, to join the King at Balmoral. They saw the way in which Mrs Simpson announced the day's programme and shepherded everyone about, as if the place were her own. This was not new. At the Fort she had acted as hostess, greeting the King's guests when he was late, instructing the servants to replenish people's drinks. Some visitors had assumed that this was American practice, customary in houses where the host had no wife, or none at hand. Edwina and Marjorie knew better. At San Simeon, for example, Marion Davies did not dream of taking charge. 'I will ask Mr Hearst', she always said punctiliously. The Fort was the Prince's house, in which he could promote whomsoever he wished. Balmoral, on the other hand, was Queen Victoria's creation and Mrs Simpson a new arrival. Her appearance was as much out of place as her behaviour. In this eccentric retreat, upholstered in tartan, bursting with antlers, Mrs Simpson still managed to look odd. The King and his brother strode about in kilts, the others had brought old suits. Edwina wore tweeds and on her feet brogues of punched leather, with flaps. Wallis, in a smart narrow frock and high-heeled shoes, looked, as she stood on the lawn, as if she had been transported from Fifth Avenue. 'Poker after dinner', Dickie wrote in his journal on the first evening. 'We won'. This, in the game of country living, was not Mrs Simpson's only defeat.

On 30 September the Mountbattens journeyed overnight from Balmoral to London with the King; 'long and interesting talk', Dickie recorded, but during the next six weeks he seems to have had no other private conversation with his cousin. At the end of October Mrs Simpson and her husband were divorced. Throughout November there was much complicated manoeuvring among the King and his staff, the Prime Minister and the Cabinet. Lawyers gave opinions, archbishops offered advice. Mrs Simpson retreated to Cannes.

Edwina Mountbatten

Newspaper editors indicated that the British press could no longer hold back a story which had been discussed abroad for months: 'Papers full of David and Wallis', Dickie reported on 3 December spelling Mrs Simpson's name correctly for the first time. The tale was drawing to a moving but unsatisfactory close. 'George came to see us', Dickie wrote on 9 December: 'Sad news re David'. Next morning the King summoned Dickie to lunch at the Fort, where he found the three royal brothers and Walter Monckton, the King's legal adviser. In his diary Dickie gave only a brief account of the meeting. One sentence showed how jumpy and vulnerable his cousin had become: 'Home Secretary went in to see him and reduced him to tears when he said Wallis's English detectives must be taken away after abdication'.

'A day of gloom', Edwina wrote in her diary, 'very tragic. Bad evening.' She did not consider whether the King would have been a good, wise or happy monarch. To her he was a friend, obliged to choose between incompatible alternatives, forced to decide whether to repudiate the woman he loved or to throw over everything and everyone else. Edwina knew how painful it was to be faced with such a choice.

In his broadcast the Duke of Windsor had declared his allegiance to the new King. It was not a betrayal of their old friend when the Mountbattens did the same. 'Tea with Queen Mary at Marlborough House', Edwina reported on 9 February, 'and cocktails with the King and Queen at Piccadilly. (They only move to Buckingham Palace next week.)' Dickie could not help making comparisons: 'Levee. 1st of reign – longest I've known. 1 hr 25 min.' The Mountbattens attended the Kents' dinner party in honour of the King and Queen and later in the week the two little princesses came to tea at Brook House. 'Showed them Mickey Mouse films after', Edwina wrote in her diary, 'as we were trying out the cinema.'

The Mountbattens did not desert their former sovereign. 'Rang up George, David, Bertie and Yola', Dickie noted, at the beginning of March, and a week later he flew from Paris to Vienna to see the Duke, who was staying at Schloss Enzesfeld with Fruity Metcalfe, his only companion from the old days. 'Important talk with David,' Dickie wrote, 're possibility of returning.' This was moonshine. The Duke did not understand that he had burnt his boats and Dickie found it impossible to tell him so. 'Very sad saying goodbye, on both sides,' Dickie wrote. In the aeroplane on the way home he was sick.

Lost Horizon

Edwina was preoccupied with the troubles of her own family. On 2 December, just before the Abdication, Mary had asked her to call at 12 Upper Brook Street: 'Spent the afternoon . . . in deep discussion over her private affairs which could not be worse'. Bobbie Cunningham-Reid's chief asset had been his charm. At home, at least, he had ceased to exercise it and Mary wished to leave him forthwith. She and her maid moved next door, that is, into Brook House. Over dinner with Marjorie, Bunny and Mary's great friend Barbara Cartland (now Mrs McCorquodale), the Mountbattens and Mary considered what to do. Cousin Felix and Mary's solicitor arrived at the end of the meal: 'Cancelled Tauber film', Dickie wrote gloomily. Would Mary stay for weeks? Would she have a nervous breakdown, as she had done on her last long visit? Once again Dickie was pressed into service as go-between.

Edwina wanted blue sky and new faces, so in the New Year the Mountbattens took Patricia and Pamela to Switzerland, with Bunny, Yola and Mary. The snow was good, the sun hot and the holiday a success, in spite of illness and accidents: 'Pamela in bed with a temperature'; 'Mary with a bad eye all bound up'; 'Bun laid low with "Rheumatic wrenches"'. (Dickie had a different explanation: 'Bunny's back was bad', he noted in his journal, 'ricked while brushing his hair.')

A fortnight in Switzerland was, however, no substitute for several months in the tropics. Brook House was a comfortable and pleasant base but London was icy and the afternoons dark. Each day seemed to bring new dramas in Mary's legal battles with Bobbie. Dickie was absorbed in his work; even when they were in Switzerland he had dived into his books after dinner and one sunny afternoon he had disappeared to buy gear for technical drawing. The whole household coughed and wheezed. Pamela needed an operation to drain her ears, Edwina had neuralgia and a succession of streaming colds. This could not go on. Edwina declared that she must get away. *Lost Horizon* was nowhere near finished. At the beginning of February she had been brought round to Nicholson's yard in Southampton for completion, fitting-out and trials, but it would be another year before she was ready for the South Seas. Edwina had been to South America, dropped in on India, Australia and New Zealand, crossed Russia, visited China, Indo-China and Japan. That left Africa. To Africa she therefore went, with Bunny, Nada and Jack Evelyn.

Nigeria was cold, Bunny full of self-reproach. 'I have never done worse', he told Dickie, in his only message in eight weeks, 'than

257

suggest E. not taking her fur coat.' On to Nairobi, where the travellers hired an open Buick, with a Ford van for the luggage, and set off for a motor tour through Kenya, Uganda and the Belgian Congo. They first made their way to Happy Valley, where they ran into various expatriates they had hoped to miss, including the legendary Alice de Trafford, who had divorced one husband, married another, attempted to kill him and herself and, having lost him, turned to lovers instead. She now lived with a great many dogs and a pet eland. Edwina was more interested in the indigenous wild life: pink flamingoes and secretary birds, kingfishers and crocodiles on Lake Victoria, lions in the Congo. Who should turn up in the middle of the jungle but Molly's friend Rosita Forbes, on one of her expeditions? 'So altho' the place charming,' Edwina wrote in her diary, 'with little huts amusingly arranged . . . felt we must push on!'

In the middle of April she came home, having learnt as much about the Dark Continent as anyone could in two months. With her she brought several hundred photographs and a three-month-old lion cub, Sabi, whose mother had been shot for attacking a man near the river of that name in the Transvaal.

Edwina returned in time for Pamela's eighth birthday and the rehearsals for the Coronation, which was to take place on 12 May. Dickie had already fitted his special uniform. 'Rode with Georgie in Row to try our Coronation Procession Horses and Trousers'. In such a season it would have been impossible for Edwina to have been out of England. Everybody was entertaining everyone else. Throughout June and July she gave lunches and dinners at Brook House: for Osbert Sitwell, Mr and Mrs Hore-Belisha, Sir Alfred Beit, Jan Masaryk, the Channons. There was no spare minute, what with the first night of Noel's *Victoria Regina*, Emerald Cunard's concerts, dinner at Ciro's for Dickie's thirty-seventh birthday (Yola came over and stayed at the Savoy) and the Mountbattens' party for their fifteenth wedding anniversary. Dickie gave Edwina a bracelet of linked XVs, designed by himself, and Bunny helped them celebrate at Adsdean. At the end of June was an occasion Edwina had been forbidden to miss, the coming-out dance for the Wernhers' daughter, Gina. To Zia this was the most important event of Coronation Summer. Gina was attractive, with a sweet smile and beautiful manners, and, backed by the Wernhers' great wealth, she was to be steered out into London and the arms of a suitable husband. How fortunate that the Coronation had coincided with Gina's presentation to the world, for London teemed with appropriate suitors. The King, the Queen and the Duchess of Kent dined with the Wernhers before the ball; 'various other Royalties came in after', Edwina reported, 'very successful but rather cold'.

For Dickie, too, the celebration was well-timed, for that morning his appointment to Captain had been announced. 'Promoted at 37.0', Dickie exulted in his diary: 'Average age 42.5'. Edwina was pleased for Dickie and for them all. The Mountbattens nowadays felt more like a family, with Dickie doing well in his profession, Edwina presiding over Brook House, their own creation, Patricia at school and Pamela growing out of the nursery. Bunny spent nearly every weekend at Adsdean. The summer was hot, perfect for bathing, golf and croquet, although it was hard to manage the game when the lion cub kept interfering with the ball. Sabi was enchanting, like a large, floppy kitten. He did not destroy the furniture, tease the dogs, or savage the other exotic animals that were brought to pay their respects, Lord Moyne's gibbon, for instance, or the Heywood-Lonsdales' coatimundi. Emboldened, Bunny next imported a human being, Hassan, who had driven them in Kenya. He arrived in July and found London so cold that Yola and Edwina took him to Selfridge's to buy an overcoat: 'Caused quite a sensation', Edwina remarked.

These were happy months for the children. Dickie flew his model aeroplane, Edwina joined them in the kitchen for fudge and toffee-making. Their parents were not on edge; they quarrelled only three times, rows about polo and Edwina's refusal to go to parties where she might meet Laura Long, whom Dickie had unwisely praised as the best dancer in Europe. Wilfrid came to Adsdean for a long weekend. He had grown visibly older and seemed delighted to be told what to do: a little golf, a snooze after tea, a good dinner. Molly made a separate visit. It passed off smoothly, although she was observed scolding an urn of Jersey lilies, which had refused to grow symmetrically. Edwina had also made a truce with another figure from the past, Miss Cranston, her former chaperone, who called at Brook House to see the penthouse. She liked Rex Whistler's murals; he had not quite finished and fortunately Venus was as yet without Edwina's features.

At the beginning of August *Lost Horizon* was at last ready for sea trials. Bunny and Edwina had chosen a dinghy, cushions and a gramophone and on 11 August the schooner left Southampton on her maiden voyage, a little run across the Channel to Deauville. On board were Bunny, Edwina, Dickie, Patricia, a temporary crew, and Bunny's navigation instructor. Dickie and his entourage took up most of the space: he had dislocated his right shoulder playing polo and had therefore brought along the famous Mr Strong, to administer electrical treatment and massage, and Charles, his valet (Thorogood had moved to a grander post at Buckingham Palace), to help him dress and shave. Dickie sat like a potentate while the others did the work and at night slept soundly through the noise of foghorns that kept everyone else awake. His finest moment came when they reached Deauville. The yacht was not properly equipped, he pointed out, but with skilful navigation they might get her into port: 'Piloted ship in. Quite exciting as no helm indicator . . .'

In late August the Mountbattens left France for Germany. Aunt Victoria, who was staying at Wolfsgarten, had reported that Uncle Ernie was ill and wanted to see them. Dickie, Edwina and Patricia flew to Cologne, where the car waited to take them along the fast new autobahn to Darmstadt. The Mountbattens were apprehensive; Germany, which they both loved, was now an uncomfortable place. Hitler's rhetoric and behaviour were repellent; he seemed determined to lead his country into war. At least Wolfsgarten was unchanged. 'Place as delicious as ever', Edwina wrote in her diary. She and Dickie slept in the rooms they had occupied on their honeymoon, the first time since 1922 that they had been there together. 'Very sentimental', Dickie sighed, 'and E. very sweet.'

There were cheerful things to discuss; plans had to be made for the forthcoming wedding of Don's younger brother, Lu. The year before, he had met a Scottish girl, Margaret Geddes, when they were both studying modern painting and literature in South Germany. Lu was sensitive and intelligent, like his father, the Grand Duke, who had shocked his conservative neighbours by setting up an artists' colony at Wolfsgarten, decorating two of the rooms in *Jugendstil* and filling them with fine examples of contemporary furniture, china and glass. Margaret, who was known as Peg, was clever and energetic. Her father, Sir Auckland Geddes, was a Professor of Anatomy who had served as Minister of National Service in the Great War and had afterwards become President of the Board of Trade and then British Ambassador to the United States. He had disapproved of his daughter's wish to go to Germany, so she had written articles to earn the

fare herself. Although both sets of parents at first thought the proposed match unwise, Peg and Lu had won them round and the
wedding was to take place in London in the late autumn.

The Mountbattens' German holiday made a fitting end to a delightful summer. Pamela was starting boarding-school at Buckswood
Grange in Sussex; 'Very sad but charming little place', Edwina said,
getting its name wrong. 'Poor little mite', wrote Dickie. To distract
himself, he worked on his duo-tier gramophone attachment and
experimented with a dictaphone. September had been crisp and sunny
but, when the Mountbattens were held up by fog on the way home
to England, they knew that winter was on the way. It was time for
Lost Horizon to make for warmer waters. At the beginning of November
she put to sea. Bunny had completed his lessons in navigation and
Edwina joined him for a final rehearsal off Southampton: 'Sailed out
about 12.30 and swung the compasses . . . frightful mess on board,
stores and packages, but we managed to straighten out a lot.' The
plan was for Bunny to sail *Lost Horizon* to America and take her from
there to the Caribbean. The Mountbattens and Yola would meet him
in the West Indies, where Dickie had arranged to play in a polo
tournament. Since it seemed unwise for Bunny to set off alone with
an unknown crew, his mother had offered to accompany him as far
as the United States. On 5 November this unlikely party prepared to
depart. 'Turned very cold in the night', was the first, ominous entry
in Edwina's diary. 'More dramas . . . chiefly due to the Engineer's
Mate who we fear is a trouble maker and may have to be replaced
. . . the Cook Steward slightly tight last night and still feeling the
effects this morning'. It was too late to find replacements. At half past
twelve Edwina and Harold Phillips, Bunny's father, waved goodbye:
'Very sad and absolutely sunk in gloom.' Lunch on lobsters at the
Warsash Yacht Club cheered them up a little, the sun came out and,
from what they could see, *Lost Horizon* seemed to be making her way
safely into the open sea. Nine days later Bunny telephoned from
Lisbon. So far, so good.

Sad news had come from Germany. Uncle Ernie had died on 9
October and Lu and Peg's marriage was postponed until mid-
November. On the 15th the Mountbattens raced back from a shoot at
Wherwell to prepare for the arrival of the wedding guests. Aunt Onor
was to stay at Kensington Palace with Aunt Victoria, Don and Cecile
at Brook House with their two sons, Louis and Alexander, and their

Edwina Mountbatten

Nurse. The baby daughter, Johanna, remained at home in Germany. On the 16th the party set off with Lu's best man from Hesse on a Sabena flight from Frankfurt, via Ostend, to Croydon. Edwina motored up from Wherwell to Brook House to await them there; Dickie, who had spent the afternoon in Portsmouth, caught an early evening train back to town. 'Coming in to London', Edwina wrote in her diary, 'saw on posters there had been an air disaster and on later one "Prince and children killed".' At Ostend the pilot had tried to land in thick fog and a wing of the aeroplane had clipped a factory chimney. The machine had disintegrated. No one survived.

Aunt Victoria, Lu and Peg had been waiting at Croydon. They returned to Brook House and when Dickie arrived he found Edwina trying to comfort them. 'Terrible evening', she wrote, 'and Lu nearly out of his mind.' Peg's father was there, trying to help the grieving family to decide what to do. Sir Auckland suggested that the wedding had better take place immediately and next morning a small group of relations saw Lu and Peg married at St Peter's in Eaton Square. Dickie acted as best man; all, including the bride, wore black. While Edwina looked after Aunt Victoria, Dickie took Lu and Peg to the station to put them on the train to Ostend, where they took the coffins on board. That was their wedding journey. Dickie then returned to the Admiralty: 'Work. (Hard work.)'

On the following day there was a telephone call asking Dickie and Edwina to come straight away to Darmstadt. They collected Aunt Victoria and Cecile's fifteen-year-old brother, Philip, who was at school in Scotland, travelled all night and reached Darmstadt at six in the morning. Thirty members of the family had assembled to escort the coffins to the mausoleum. There beside the Grand Duke the bodies were placed: his wife, son, daughter-in-law, her unborn baby, the two grandsons. 'Too ghastly', Edwina wrote, 'one by one and quite endless . . .' The funeral took place four days later. When the Mountbattens returned to London, they were all exhausted. Edwina slept badly; the tragedy had sobered her.

In the middle of January 1938 the Mountbattens set off for America and the polo tournament. This was Dickie's first trip to New York since the ill-fated expedition in 1924. He enjoyed the voyage: Bozo the bush-baby came with them in the *Bremen*, Yola joined the ship at Cherbourg and Edwina, knowing she would soon see Bunny, did everything to please. On arrival, the Mountbattens were met by a representative of the Navy Department, with an official car, 'driven by bluejackets', Dickie said delightedly, 'and a siren!' The Mountbattens and their friends made a comfortable party, for four was better than two. After a happy week, they caught the train to Miami and in the morning took the Clipper to Jamaica. The next three weeks looked promising. *Lost Horizon* was in the bay; Admiral Meyrick's flagship, *York*, lay offshore and invitations to dances on board awaited the Mountbattens' party at their hotel, along with announcements of the cocktail parties and dinners that the Governor of the island and his wife were giving for the polo team. While Bunny examined *Lost Horizon* and Dickie the ponies, safely ferried from England, Edwina and Yola bathed in the pool and played a little golf.

The idyll lasted only twenty-four hours. On the last morning in January, while Dickie was visiting American destroyers in the bay, Edwina had a message asking her to telephone Nada: 'Terrible news of Georgie'. At the beginning of December Dickie's brother had slipped on a marble floor at Brook House; he said his thigh had given way. The bone was not broken and the doctors feared that something else was wrong. It was cancer. Nada asked her brother- and sister-in-law to return at once. For Edwina to disappear with Bunny in *Lost Horizon* was out of the question. By late February the Mountbattens were back at Brook House. Georgie was now in the Empire Nursing Home: 'as cheerful and charming as ever', Dickie wrote: 'He has no idea.' On 8 April he died with Aunt Victoria and Nada at his bedside: 'So peaceful in death', Dickie wrote, 'and so like Papa with his beard'. Edwina sat with Nada while Dickie walked in the Park with the children.

Meanwhile Bunny was making his way back to England in *Lost Horizon*. On 8 May, when he was nearly home, fire broke out on board. Bunny and the crew abandoned ship; luckily a Swedish vessel was passing by and picked them up. Dickie telephoned for Home Office permits so that the bedraggled sailors could be landed on the Isle of Wight, Edwina rounded up Harold and Mary Phillips, chartered a ferry boat, collected the adventurers and brought them home. The crew were installed in the YMCA at Portsmouth and Bunny and Edwina made for London. 'Thank God all safe', Edwina wrote in her diary – but *Lost Horizon* was at the bottom of the sea.

CHAPTER TWENTY

Mobilization

Perhaps it was just as well. Few expeditions could have been more foolhardy than an outing to the South Seas in a smart yacht, with an inexperienced captain and a ramshackle crew. It would have been astonishing if *Lost Horizon* had got there, a miracle if she had returned. The Pacific was not living up to its name: Japan had forced the Chinese government to flee and in 1936 had made a pact with Germany. Edwina and Bunny would have been pottering about on the edge of a whirlpool.

Better to remain at home, although all was not tranquil there. 'Everything looking pretty black', Edwina wrote in her journal on 12 March 1938. The Mountbattens did not want to be caught unawares. In the last week of that month Edwina attended a lecture on Air-Raid Precautions at her cousin Cuckoo Leith's house in London, topping it up next day with an Anti-Gas demonstration. In May Dickie had long talks with the King about the worsening international situation and when he was invited to act as captain of the English international polo team, due to play in America the following year, he declined. This was no time to ask the Admiralty for extra leave.

War was coming nearer. In mid-August Dickie went down to see Bunny and his regiment: 'Spent the next 5 hours witnessing 4th Guards Brigade manoeuvres, including a tank attack'. At Adsdean soldiers practised fighting in the park and, by the beginning of September there were hundreds of troops on the roads between Wherwell and Chichester. Dickie had left his Admiralty job at the end of 1937. He had been offered the command of a new destroyer, HMS *Kelly*, the first of a series of eight ships that were to make up the Fifth Destroyer Flotilla. *Kelly* was now being constructed at the Hawthorn Leslie yard on the Tyne and, while he waited, Dickie took a Senior Officers' Tactical Course at Portsmouth.

'Crisis with Germany over Czechoslovakia', Edwina wrote in her diary on 9 September. Four days earlier she had rewritten her will

264

and put her photograph albums in order. 'Listened to Hitler's speech', she noted on the 12th, 'which was most threatening and insulting and alarming'. This was the Führer's address to the Nazi Party at Nuremberg. An attack on Czechoslovakia seemed imminent. 'Chamberlain going to Germany to see Hitler', Edwina wrote on the 14th and, next day, 'listened to wireless news. Not very reassuring'. She had intended to have a week or two with Bunny in Yugoslavia before war closed the doors, but no one knew whether hostilities would be on or off. Edwina sat by the wireless: 'Chamberlain returned but no news yet'. She could not stand ambiguity and vacillation. Edwina decided to have her holiday; as she travelled east, at least she would be able to see for herself what was going on.

At Dubrovnik Edwina and Bunny settled into an hotel, where on the fourth day of their stay they had a cable from Dickie, advising them to return immediately. The Steamship Office knew nothing: 'decided to go to swim and sunbathe off the rocks and forget about it'. Chamberlain's talks with Hitler had been unsatisfactory. 'Got thru to Yola and Dickie', Edwina wrote on the morning of the 21st. 'News seemed better tho' at the expense of Czechoslovakia. France and England seem to be going to let her down but one feels anything to avert a war . . . Went out to swim at Lokrum. Too delicious for words'. Chamberlain flew back to Germany, received an offensive ultimatum from Hitler and returned to London to consult the Cabinet. Word filtered through to Kotor. 'Decided to motor up to Cetinje, the old capital of Montenegro, by the sensational motor mountain road . . . Told by our driver halfway up that he had learnt on the wireless last night European news much worse. France mobilizing, England calling out her Naval reserves etc etc. So became hysterical again!! But enjoyed lovely drive nevertheless and returned by Budra along the coast'. That evening Edwina and Bunny sailed back to Dubrovnik and began to make their way home.

This was not easy. Trains, aeroplanes and ships were packed with panicking people, scurrying north, south, west, anywhere as long as they could get away. In Turin the two frustrated travellers spent the afternoon at the cinema before boarding a sleeper to Paris. This was a nightmare: Edwina was used to having a compartment to herself, with a gramophone and her own silk sheets: 'Terrible crush and a second class upper berth with a Rumanian female below was all I could get'. Yola spent a frantic morning on the telephone and managed to reserve seats on a flight from France to England. In London there was frenzied activity. 'ARP precautions and trench digging going apace', Edwina noted, on her first day back in London, 'Hyde Park an astounding sight'. Dickie had been attending lectures on gun mounting, doing firing practice and trying on his gas mask. Patricia's school was moving out of London, so she and Mademoiselle Chevrier had been sent down to Adsdean, along with the pictures, silver and jade from Brook House. Edwina spent the morning seeing people from the Red Cross, 'with a view to turning Adsdean into a hospital . . . and running it as commandant myself'.

The confrontation was postponed. 'If at first you don't succeed', Chamberlain told the press, before another flight to Germany, 'try, try, try again'. At the Munich conference Britain and France agreed to the dismemberment of Czechoslovakia, and Chamberlain and Hitler to an exchange of signatures on a memorandum guaranteeing future consultation in times of difficulty and symbolizing the desire of their two countries never to go to war again. Edwina was sceptical: 'A let down of the Czechs and victory for Hitler as he has got most of the things he wanted . . .' For the time being, however, she was relieved, 'One feels peace at any cost! Played a little golf with Bunny . . .'

Ten days later Dickie joined the Royal Naval War College at Greenwich, where for the next five months he and his colleagues prepared themselves for the coming conflict by acting out a series of campaigns: 'Strategic game R52 – Started with me as C-in-C Red Sea'. He enjoyed it all: 'excellent lecture with nice tribute to Papa'. Edwina meanwhile embarked on her own preparations for war. First she joined Eileen Sutherland's Red Cross committee; next, she made an appointment to see Lady Reading, 're First Aid and ARP'. This was not Mrs Cassel's old friend, who had died in 1930, but the ex-Viceroy's second wife, his former private secretary in Delhi. Stella Reading, founder and head of the Women's Voluntary Service, was a formidable woman. She did not know Edwina well and disapproved of what she had heard. Lady Louis had better do some basic training before she offered her services as commandant of a hospital or chairman of a committee. Chastened, Edwina looked for ways to brief herself: 'An ARP lecture at Buckingham Palace, which the King, Queen and I and staff and servants attended'; 'Our first Red X lecture' (she had arranged a set of eight at Brook House) 'Marjorie and I and about 14 of the staff'. She signed up for the Red Cross examination ('Mrs Prentice, one of the head people . . . came and helped me over some points') and filled an exercise book with drawings of correctly bandaged limbs.

Edwina did not give up her pleasures: *Alexander's Ragtime Band* in the afternoon, *Dear Octopus* in the evening; Sibelius at the Queen's Hall, *Pygmalion*, the Motor Show, the Antique Dealers' Fair. In October 1938 she spent ten days in Hungary with Bunny and Yola, playing golf, shooting on the Regent's estate and dining at old-fashioned restaurants ('succulent food and a good Tzigane Band'), revisiting places where she had been happy and which she might not see again for years. In mid-November Bunny left for South America, to see to family business. Edwina was lonely, her neuralgia returned, her head ached. She tried a German doctor in Paris, a Greek doctor in London, a course of injections and a barium meal with scrambled eggs, followed by a series of X-rays. Her oculist scolded her for leaving off her spectacles and suggested she try the new lenses that covered the eyeballs. The apparatus was difficult to fit and painful to wear, the glass being thick and rigid, and at Christmas Edwina gave up the experiment. She did not expect her headaches to last much longer, for in mid-January Bunny was coming home and a month later they were going together to Batavia and New Guinea.

They arrived in Rangoon in late February 1939. 'I am very well and feel 100 percent better', Edwina announced. She had promised to send wires telling Dickie where she was, indicating that he direct his cables to MOUNTBATTEN only, 'as LADY MOUNTBATTEN brands me at once'. Not much of a disguise: on second thoughts, Edwina suggested tactlessly, messages had better be addressed to PHILLIPS. Few cables reached her. Dickie forgot his instructions and simply sent his wires POSTE RESTANTE, PACIFIC OCEAN. This was reasonable; from Burma Bunny and Edwina had moved on to Northern Sumatra and Batavia, where they hoped to find a vessel to take them to the islands in the Flores and Timor Seas, west of New Guinea. 'A blow here', Edwina told Dickie, 'as no boats seem to fit in . . .' She and Bunny therefore made a new plan. Robert Neville had spoken about the road that was being built between Burma and South West China, the supply route for the arms with which the Chinese were attempting to repel the Japanese. A trip up the Irrawaddy, along the Burma road and into China, as far as the old walled city of Yunnan-Fu, would, Edwina thought, 'be most interesting'. It was.

Edwina Mountbatten

The road, seven hundred miles of stony, precipitous track, could be travelled only by lorry, 'not more than 10 to 15 mph being possible for hours on end', Edwina told Dickie, 'bottom gear being used for long stretches'. The first three hundred miles on the Chinese side had been opened five weeks before, this part having been completed ('such as it is') in eight months. Thousands of labourers were working on the next stretch: 'nothing but the most primitive wooden implements . . . stone hand rollers, bamboo baskets for stone carrying and *everything* by hard labour'. Dynamite was used to shift great chunks of rock, leaving piles of boulders. Lurching and jolting, Edwina and Bunny climbed up and down and through the mountains, hoping not to meet oncoming traffic, for there was scarcely room to pass. 'At one point', Edwina noted in her diary, 'we were nearly pushed off road by recklessly descending lorry.' The two Europeans, enthroned upon a couple of basket chairs that had been packed into the lorry with the bedding, petrol cans, cooking pots, bullybeef and oil lamps, were not the sort of visitors to whom local Chinese officials were used. Edwina, the first woman to have travelled the length of the road, caused astonishment at the drivers' shelters where they spent the nights: 'Entertained by hornpiping sentries on duty. Difficulties in finding suitable lu lu sites'. Despite these discomforts, she enjoyed herself. The journey was worth it for the scenery alone: 'really magnificent, winding thru' wooded hills and over spurs of mountain . . . views for hundreds of miles . . .' This was pioneering work. Dickie had not been here, nor anyone they knew. Edwina kept her wits about her, noticing anything that a military strategist might find useful. 'Perhaps you should get this typed out for Robert . . . Aunt Victoria might be interested too'.

'Hope to have news of you all', Edwina wrote, as she and Bunny left for Indo-China, 'and depending on what I hear will make further plans'. Bunny thought he had better cable his regiment to ask whether he was wanted. No urgency, he was told, although a week earlier, on 21 March, Hitler had begun to threaten Poland. 'Old Chamberlain really seems to have had a shock', Edwina said in a letter from Java. 'But he *can't* be such a fool as to have believed those promises, surely, last September'. Her immediate difficulty was to decide whether to start for home or move on. At Batavia she had heard that a small ship was sailing almost immediately from Macassar in the Celebes to the islands in Dutch New Guinea, 'so cannot resist it as among the places are some I particularly wanted to go . . .' It would mean that Edwina would be away for Pamela's birthday, Easter and the children's holidays, 'but having come *all* the way out it seems a pity to miss it . . .' The voyage, she assured Dickie, 'food included', would cost only £50 a head and the news from Europe was so gloomy that she felt this might be her last chance. Another cable to Bunny's adjutant had produced the confident reply that he might safely stay away another month, 'so I gather', Edwina told Dickie, 'that there will be no war till May!!'

For three weeks she and Bunny sauntered among the islands of New Guinea, with a Dutch captain and crew and a varying mixture of fellow-voyagers: 'very nice little German . . . travelling Inspector for Singer Sewing Machines'; 'Mr Van Thiel, excellent on the guitar . . .' There was also a pair of wallabies, which Edwina decided to bring home to England, to replace Sabi, who had died in the Whale Island Zoo just before she left. 'What am I to feed them on?' she asked the native from whom she bought them. 'No problem at all. Just orchids.' At intervals Edwina and Bunny got fragments of increasingly gloomy news. 'Listened to the BBC wireless', she wrote in her diary on 4 April, 'which comes through very clear and heard that Chamberlain had at last taken a firm stand . . .' The Prime Minister had told the House of Commons that, if Poland's independence were threatened, Britain would be bound to support the Polish government. 'Let us hope that will make Hitler think twice', Edwina added stoutly, 'but why we could not have been firm and declared this policy ages ago I cannot imagine'.

When Edwina's aircraft touched down at Singapore on the way home at the end of April, she and Bunny bought newspapers for the first time for weeks. 'Not very enlightening', Edwina observed in her diary. She found it difficult to concentrate on current affairs; the long flight to Rangoon had given her a splitting headache and she was worried about the animals. At Bushira there was just time to take a taxi to the bazaar to look for spinach for them, at Athens she and Bunny fed them with plantains gathered on the Acropolis and, on the leg from Budapest to Leipzig ('an early lunch in the midst of Nazidom'), the wallabies shivered so much that Edwina had to cradle them on her lap. Bunny got off in Holland and on 4 May Edwina flew in to Croydon, sailing through customs and quarantine with no trouble. (Mountbatten had sent a line to the Minister of Agriculture, who was becoming used to it.) 'Dickie and the children and dogs all met me and we drove up to London . . . Quite exhausted'.

Past home-comings had been an anti-climax. Edwina would return, unwind and long to be off again. This time she had no desire to leave England or her family. She had come back in the first weeks of spring, when everything seemed delicate and precious. It was not warm enough for the wallabies to live outside and, until a heated enclosure could be built, Edwina made a home for them indoors: 'at the moment one in Dickie's bathroom and one in his Lulu. So afraid they will catch cold'. The news from Europe was no better – Hitler and Mussolini had announced a 'Pact of Steel' at the beginning of May – and throughout the spring and summer streams of refugees arrived in London. People Edwina had met on her travels wrote to ask for assistance for themselves or their relations: Leopold Neumann, owner of a dressmaking business in Vienna; Dr Tuttnauer, who practised face massage and needed a licence from the London County Council. Dickie wrote dozens of letters to the British authorities. Could a visa be obtained for Mr Wilhelm Kassel, whom the Mountbattens (that is, Edwina) had met in Switzerland, where he worked as a professional dancing partner? He came; Edwina tried unsuccessfully to get him a job at the Dorchester; he took up gardening and then joined the British Army. Dickie found it embarrassing to be constantly asking favours but to please Edwina he kept at it. She was moved by the dignified appeals that arrived each month, each week, each day, shocked by stories of discrimination and bullying. Hitherto she had given little thought to her own Jewish ancestry. Now she worked with the German-Jewish Aid Committee, the Federation of Czechoslovakian Jews and the Jewish Refugees' Committee to help people who were trying to escape from Hitler. She sent cheques to refugees who had nowhere else to turn; regular subsidies to people she had never met. Few people knew of these kindnesses.

In mid-June Bunny left for nine weeks' training at Pirbright; he had been appointed ADC to General Lloyd. Dickie was working with A. P. Cole, chief of destroyer design at the Admiralty, on the arrangement and fitting out of *Kelly*. The ship was the first of the new 'K' class, a fast and powerful vessel, armed with six 4.7-inch guns and two quintuple torpedo tubes. The Mountbatten Station Keeping Equipment was, of course, installed on the bridge and Dickie had managed to obtain for *Kelly* an odd-looking gadget, fitted to the foremast, a primitive contrivance taken from an experimental Swordfish aircraft. This, he explained, operated a sensory system, like a bat's, called 'radar'. For months Dickie fussed over his new ship. A mock-up of his cabin allowed him to work out how to store his gear, where to put bookshelves and the plug for his electric razor. No detail was neglected: there was to be a drying-room for towels, a ceremonial awning, a good selection of books and gramophone records, chosen by Edwina. The First Lieutenant-designate was instructed to make sure that nothing was overlooked: 'I am afraid', he replied to one of Mountbatten's letters, 'I have not been able to find any alternative storage for potatoes . . .' At the end of June Dickie took up his new command; in a fortnight *Kelly* would be ready for trials. Edwina still assumed that she and Dickie would be based in Malta. Within a month, however, her domestic arrangements were in disarray.

The immediate cause was not Hitler but Wilfrid. In late May, a fortnight after Edwina's return from the South Seas, her father had unexpectedly telephoned from Broadlands, asking her to come immediately to discuss what he called 'vital questions'. He wished to leave Molly and go off with a Frenchwoman. 'Found them all hysterical', Edwina wrote, and told Wilfrid he could certainly not abandon his wife at such a time. She was shocked to see how ill her father looked. Physicians came from London, said nothing could be done, and went away again. At the end of June the doctors announced that Wilfrid was sinking. He had Parkinson's disease and, being a not very robust seventy-one, could not be expected to last. He died on 3 July. 'Terribly sad losing Daddy', Edwina wrote in her diary, 'and really heartbroken but feel for his sake it was for the best as he could never have stood a long illness and invalidism'. Edwina did not sleep that night. Twice she went into Wilfrid's room, once with Molly, once alone. She had been fond of her weak, exasperating father, who had so often looked to her for help. Apart from the time when, bullied by Molly, he had agreed to send Edwina away to school, Wilfrid had always allowed her to do as she wished, never interfering nor uttering any reproach. His death was not a hard blow but it left a gap. On Wilfrid's death the ownership and management of the Broadlands estate passed to Edwina. Adsdean had to be given up, her late father's employees interviewed, appointments made with his tenants, Molly rehoused. The Cunningham-Reids' lawyer had been in touch before

Wilfrid was scarcely cold. How would the finances of Lady Louis' sister be affected? (Answer: hardly at all.)

All this became part of a general upheaval. 'Rumours rife as to the German occupation of Dantzig', Edwina noted at the end of June; it was clear that the predator could not be side-stepped for long. A blackout exercise was held over the south coast of England, lights being dimmed and warning sirens tried between eleven and four, and at Brook House Edwina started an ARP refresher course for her own and Marjorie's staff. Fire hoses, pumps and extinguishers were tested, experiments made with gas masks to see whether they leaked. The servants practised fire-drills and evacuation to the basement, curtains and blinds were inspected to ensure that no crack of light would attract the enemy. Edwina took her ARP examination and, having qualified, embarked on a Home Nursing course. She was not too busy for a holiday. In mid-August Bunny had arranged to take his Talbot to France to be serviced and Edwina decided to go with him. Their friends thought them insane. It was pointless, Edwina said, to hang about in England, waiting for war. Nothing might happen for months.

Edwina and Bunny dropped the Talbot in Paris, hired a rattletrap Peugeot and started down the valley of the Loire, visiting famous châteaux and staying at small hotels. 'News looks blacker than ever', Edwina noted on 23 August; Germany had signed a non-aggression pact with the Soviet Union. But when Bunny telephoned the porter at the Travellers' Club in Paris, to see whether any instructions had been left, there was no message. They trundled gently along the banks of the Loire to Saumur, Angers, Blois and Chinon: 'Established ourselves at Château Hotel, had baths etc and then called up Paris again'. Word had come; Bunny was to join General Lloyd immediately. At five o'clock next morning they were at Le Bourget, begging for seats on the mail delivery plane; by mid-morning they had reached Croydon. Bunny drove straight to Aldershot, Edwina to London: 'chaos already beginning'. Dickie had brought *Kelly* into Chatham; 'Decided to crash commission on Monday 28th', he wrote in his diary, '3 days instead of 3 weeks!' The entire ship's company worked day and night, storing, fuelling, ammunitioning. Only the cooks were excused duty when the time came to paint the ship, in a tender rose and lavender mixture, which, Dickie believed, most effectively camouflaged it against the sky. ('Mountbatten Pink', the Naval Stores

Department called it.) At half past three on the afternoon of the 28th *Kelly* put to sea.

Meanwhile, Edwina rushed hither and thither. The pictures, silver and jade, restored to Brook House after the Munich agreement, were now despatched to Broadlands. She drove Aunt Victoria down to Adsdean, lunched on *Kelly* with Dickie, dined in Guildford with Bunny, returned to London and listened to the wireless: 'Notes being exchanged between us and Hitler. Still very tense'. The WVS rang up to say that twenty-four children and two teachers were being evacuated from Wimbledon to Adsdean. 'News seems worse. Army mobilization.'

Decisions had to be taken quickly, although the emergency was inconvenient: 'Felt awful owing to affairs arriving a week early due to nerves I suppose!!' When bombs were expected, few places were as dangerous as a penthouse in Park Lane, so on 2 September Edwina moved into Kensington Palace with her team: her maid, Jessie Pallant, Miss Underhill, her assistant, Miss Lees, and Dorothy the housemaid. As fuel was rationed, the Rolls and Hispano were put away and Edwina bought herself an Austin Twelve. Miss Underhill organized the removal of the remaining furniture and fittings from Brook House, including the panels with the Whistler murals, not just for safe-keeping but also to reduce liability for rates and other payments, for, as Dickie had pointed out, taxes were sure to be increased and expenses must be cut down as far as possible.

The household had already shrunk, for the younger male staff at Adsdean and Broadlands – footmen, grooms and gardeners – had been called up. Frank Randell, the butler, and Brinz, the chef, re-mained; Dansie, the chauffeur, who had so often driven the Hispano across the Alps to meet Edwina in Venice, Vienna and Budapest, died of a heart attack shortly after war was declared. His place was taken by Xuereb, Dickie's Maltese manservant, who was not liable for conscription. It was a bad time to be losing strong young helpers, for Edwina had decided that she must begin the move from Adsdean to Broadlands, before bombs started dropping and while petrol was still available. 'Awful scenes and difficulties', she wrote, after lunch with Molly, who did not wish to move to her new house at Alresford.

After Wilfrid's death, Edwina had commissioned a thorough inspec-tion of her inheritance. Trees needed felling, cottages putting in order. The house was cold and damp, full of awkward passages leading to rooms too uncomfortable to use. There were few bathrooms and the kitchens and servants' rooms were a disgrace. If only architects and builders could be put to work at once – but in all this confusion no one could say what was allowed and, in any case, until Edwina's lawyers and accountants had gone through her father's papers, large sums could not be committed. Records had been kept by Wilfrid's agent, Commander North (one of the two handsomest men in Hampshire, people said, Colonel Ashley having been the other), but Dickie was shocked that there were no systems to show cumulative totals and help prevent duplication and waste. For instance, fifty-seven brushes of different types had been ordered from an ironmonger in London in May 1939, sixty copies each of *The Times* and the *Daily Express* delivered in the same month. Unravelling the costs of running Broadlands would take weeks.

War was declared on 3 September. *Kelly* had been instructed to remain at Portsmouth until further orders. Dickie, his officers and men spent another morning painting the hull, this time in the more orthodox style favoured by the Admiralty: 'Dark Grey', Dickie noted soberly, 'war colours'. He was calm, if apprehensive. 'It is only when one faces the prospect of death', he told Edwina, 'that one realizes how much one's loved ones mean'. In fact the early days of the war were, though tiring, rather tame. On the 3rd *Kelly* pottered about in the Channel, firing torpedoes at what might, or might not, be signs of the enemy. On the 4th she stayed in harbour ('got in some football for the men') and the following morning there was full calibre firing practice. A short submarine hunt came next, more firing and then a couple of days off. 'Met Mama, Patricia and Pamela and drove to Maiden Castle House. Picnic lunch . . . saw Bertie at Buck House. Dined with Edwina at Apéritif . . .' So ended the first week of the war.

A week later, after a trip to Cherbourg to extract the Duke and Duchess of Windsor from France, *Kelly* was joined by HMS *Kingston*, the second of the 'K' class destroyers in the Fifth Flotilla, of which Mountbatten was Captain. The ships were sturdy without but there were deficiencies within. 'Can you get my ski gloves?' Dickie asked Edwina. 'We get absolutely soaked at sea and ordinary leather ones get sopping wet'; 'I am running out of shirts. I think I gave you 15 to have washed – please get them sent back in small parcels (about 5 in each) c/o GPO London . . . There are no laundry facilities on board for shirts with stiff collars . . .' As *Kelly* and *Kingston* cruised up and down the Channel, Dickie thought of other commissions. 'I would be grateful if you could have about one good book per week sent me by post – mostly novels of all types . . . The books are intended chiefly for the officers'. Would Edwina make sure that Dickie's valuables were safely stored? Xuereb would bring a consignment to Broadlands: 'my valuable Purdey Guns . . . also a tin can of my full dress, unwanted clothes etc'. And, 'by the way, that leather despatch case with the ink triangle marked on it, which Yola gave me. If anything happens to me and you can't return the case to Yola, I would be grateful if the entire case could be destroyed as it is, after taking out the envelope marked DO NOT DESTROY . . .'

It was just like the old days. Their reunions were sweet: 'I can never tell you what fun it has been', Dickie told Edwina in late October, after her fourth visit in six weeks; '. . . it has taken the war to realize all that you do mean to me – so at all events I have Hitler to thank for that'. She gave him a small gold identification disc: ('I am wearing it round my neck now'), sent him a kitten, a scarf, ('knitted as you know by my own fair hands') and £150 to cover alterations to his bathroom on board *Kelly*. Small jealousies melted away, temporarily at least: 'Thank you so much darling for sending me Yola's letter. I am glad you didn't open it because I wouldn't ever open one of the Rabbit's to you although I regard him as a friend of mine'. Dickie adored Edwina from a distance; she sent clean clothes, comforting messages and tuck. (Or, as sailors call it, 'nutty'.) 'PS . . . I would like some plain hard white peppermints, like I bought in that little sweet shop with you and Yola – also another pot of honey like Mama sent me, please'. Loving letters took the place of physical proximity. 'We have had our ups and downs in our 17 years of married life', said Dickie, 'but I wouldn't marry anyone else if I had all my life to live over again – I can't say more.'

Edwina was now happily installed in her old home. 'The dogs are mad about Broadlands with all its rabbits', she wrote in her diary. She too found treasures to unearth: 'looked through things in the safe, including an old box of my mother's'. All day she moved furniture: 'matched up pairs of tables etc, some hidden behind others. Most lovely things . . .' At half-term the children came home from school, Pamela from Buckswood Grange, Patricia from St Giles, the Shaftesburys' house, where Miss Faunce, her staff and pupils had taken refuge. It was the children's first weekend at Broadlands since it had become their home. The autumn sun shone through uncurtained windows on to bare floors, leaves floated on Maudie's Japanese pool, for there were no gardeners to keep the water clear. No one knew what would happen next, so each day was a holiday. On Sunday, Guy Fawkes Day, Edwina produced fireworks and, since the authorities had forbidden their use outside, in case Roman Candles and Catherine Wheels attracted enemy aeroplanes, she and the girls let them off in the cellars and passages.

'Letters from Dickie from Scapa Flow', Edwina noted at the beginning of November. Not for long. As *Kelly* returned from a chase off the coast of Norway, she was hit by a huge wave and damaged on the starboard side and superstructure. One man was lost. *Kelly* plodded home for four days' repair work. Back to sea, another scrape ('the wind pushed us and we hit the 2 catamarans') and then *Kelly* returned to the Tyne for three weeks' boiler cleaning. Edwina went up to Newcastle to meet Dickie and bring him south for meetings at the Admiralty and a fortnight's leave. 'I do love Broadlands very much', he wrote afterwards, 'in fact I like it as much as I expected to dislike it and this is solely due to you – not only the lovely "home" atmosphere which you never fail to produce in any house – but also that you have so obviously wanted me to share it with you and have never minded my trying to help in the repairs and alterations. (I'm sorry about the food trolley, though!)' It was fortunate that Dickie approved of his new quarters, for he was to spend longer at Broadlands than he, or Edwina, had expected. Four days after his return to Newcastle, Mountbatten was ordered to take *Kelly* to the mouth of the Tyne to assist a burning tanker. A mine scraped along *Kelly*'s bottom and blew up under her stern. Miraculously, she did not sink but the damage was extensive. 'Had to dismantle all my cabin', Dickie noted sadly. There was one bright spot: Mike Wardell had chosen that day to come aboard. He returned to London shaken – and impressed. Repairs to *Kelly* would take at least two months. Most of the crew had already used up their free passes and spent their savings during the previous three weeks in dry dock, for they had expected to be at sea for Christmas. Edwina offered to pay the return fare for anyone who could otherwise not manage to get home; her thoughtfulness won the men's hearts. Dickie returned to Broadlands and there, for the next six weeks, he stayed.

Mobilization

Edwina was still looking for war work. She had suggested that Broadlands might be turned into a hospital but no one seemed to want it. In mid-October, when the dismantling of Adsdean was complete, she was ready to offer her services to her country. She started with the Women's Royal Naval Service. 'Very unsatisfactory and irritating interviews with Sir Archibald Carter re WRNS and then with Mrs Laughton Matthews . . .' For all her naval connections, Edwina got nowhere. The Women's Voluntary Service had no openings. At the Women's Auxiliary Air Force it was the same: 'an extraordinary interview with Lady Newall . . .' In late October Edwina called on Dame Helen Gwynne Vaughan, Head of the Women's Training Service. She was not encouraging. The ATS held out some hope and at the beginning of November Edwina was offered a commission, 'but I thought you would not be particularly keen on my joining the Army if I could help it!', she told her husband. In desperation she took up a suggestion of Dickie's and asked to see Lord Cromer, now Chairman of the Executive Committee that ran the Joint War Organization, established at the beginning of September by the Order of St John and the British Red Cross. Cromer thought that Edwina might be able to work as a mobile liaison officer between JWO headquarters and its medical mission to France, since she knew the country and its language and was willing to travel. Edwina was afraid that, by the time her application had been approved, it would be too late to send any civilians across the Channel: 'Everything is so slow in getting started'.

It is true that the outbreak of war had found many voluntary bodies at sixes and sevens. Having trundled comfortably along for years, they were suddenly inundated with applications and could not cope. In Edwina's case, however, the difficulty did not arise because her curriculum vitae got lost in the mail. On the contrary: her history was too well known. She disqualified herself because her reputation was that of a pleasure-lover, a woman who had kicked away the ladder up which, rung by rung, her conscientious upper-class contemporaries climbed to the top of charitable organizations. It was unfortunate, too, that she had been just too young for war service in 1914–1918; it looked as if, with no experience, she was proposing to parachute in at the top. In fact Edwina meant to do nothing of the sort. She said that she was prepared to work in the lowliest capacity – but who would believe her? Lady Mountbatten was, after all, semi-royal. Any organization that accepted her would have to put her on its committee at the very least. Not to do so would be improper – and a waste of a title that would enhance a letter-head. Better to send her elsewhere.

While Lord Cromer's committee deliberated, Edwina looked for something else to do. Lady Pound, wife of the First Sea Lord, was Chairman of the Depot for Knitted Garments for the Royal Navy: was there an opportunity here? Sir Dudley was invited to shoot at Broadlands in the New Year; Edwina was asked to join Betty Pound's committee. The Depot, in West Halkin Street, was already a sea of socks, hats, gloves and jerseys. 'They made a glorious muddle of it', Edwina told Dickie, in her first report, 'and poor Mrs Charles Larcom . . . who was the organizer retired to bed ill and exhausted yesterday, the day it was to open – unwisely I thought as they were nowhere near ready'. In such an emergency, who better to take over than the new recruit? 'I had to try and cope with it – surrounded by Lady Pound, Lady Backhouse, Loulou Forbes and all the pack flapping helplessly. They had already made so many mistakes it was hard and I can't think what will finally happen'. The old trouts were astonished to see Edwina in action. In a flash she identified bottlenecks, volunteers who were dim or confused, time-wasting procedures. Vigorous workers were put in charge of departments – receipt of garments, collection of wool, packing and posting, acknowledgement of cheques, accounting – and, where there were gaps, Edwina brought in her own lieutenants: her secretary, Miss Lees; Baroness von Buxhoevden and Mademoiselle Chevrier. By the end of November, Edwina, now Honorary Secretary, was attending meetings at the Admiralty with Lady Pound.

Lord Cromer had not forgotten their conversation. Edwina was now invited to join the committee of the Anglo-French Ambulance Corps and in early December she had separate interviews with, first, the Red Cross and then the Order of St John. It seemed to Edwina that liaison between these two bodies was more urgently needed than between England and France. Weeks went by, with no word about going abroad. This, however, was not the only way of crossing the Channel. 'To see Leslie Hore Belisha at the War Office', Edwina wrote in her diary at the beginning of December, 're a Concert Party I am getting up for France. Later to Basil Dean at Drury Lane and decided to make it an ENSA one'. A word to Ministers and officials, another to musical and theatrical friends, and within a week everything was fixed. Six days after Edwina had first thought of the idea, she was in Paris. 'To my amazement found Bunny with his camouflaged car . . . down on 48 hours leave to collect the Concert Party . . .!' Two nights with Yola, chic and lighthearted, late supper at Fouquets after the play, shopping for hats and shoes: 'so heavenly being over again'. The show was a success, two performances a day for four days, to audiences from the First and Second Divisions. The Duke of Gloucester looked in (he was liaison officer at GHQ) and Sir John Dill, the Corps Commander. 'All turns first class' – but Edwina was the star. 'They thanked me again and I said a few words from the box. Drank champagne with the company after . . .'

Edwina's work at the Depot had demonstrated that she was 'serious', her impromptu visit to France reminded people that she had good connections and could work fast. Lady Louis did not need committees – but at last they realized that they needed her. On 3 January 1940 she attended her first meeting of the Joint War Organization at the Kents' old house at 3 Belgrave Square, having been appointed by the St John Ambulance Brigade as Lady County President of the Nursing Division of London. Meanwhile at the Depot she had been welcomed on to the bridge as Vice-Chairman and Deputy to Lady Pound. Now Edwina discovered why Dickie was so fond of his official outfits. 'To a Red X St John Selection Board in uniform'; 'Lunch at the Mansion House . . . Went in uniform again'. She made the most of it. Her clothes were specially tailored, the skirt noticeably shorter than those worn by her colleagues, the jacket carefully fitted to skim her hips and give a neat line at the shoulders. Edwina's shoes were higher than other people's, her hat perched at a sharper angle. Black coat and skirt, black shoes, black stockings: the severity of the uniform set off Edwina's pale face, with its firm mouth, high cheekbones and enormous eyes. The younger women watched in admiration as Lady Louis swung through headquarters in a white cape, a cross between a film star and Florence Nightingale.

Dickie languished at Broadlands with 'flu and jaundice; Edwina was a dynamo. 'Work at the Depot trying chiefly to get wool by fair means or foul!', 'Signing endless Red X and St John appeal letters till I could hardly hold a pen!' Friends were roped in: 'My matinee in aid of the Red X and St John. King and Queen came and I sat in the box with them . . . (Final profit £3,200)'. Dickie's friends at Gaumont-British Films agreed that their cinemas could be used as collection points; the New Gallery Cinema, where Jeanie worked, became the organizing headquarters. When the railway companies seemed disinclined to carry parcels of wool and knitted goods for nothing, Edwina told the directors they ought to help the war effort and made them change their minds. People saw that she was articulate and able. She was asked to address the JWO Executive Committee; at first it was an ordeal but she soon acquired confidence, learning to pick out key issues, make her points crisply, and recognize when a subject was not worth pressing or an issue closed. She was invited to take the chair at meetings of the Lord Mayor's Appeal, which she did well, suppressing the wafflers, making sure people knew which items she considered important and which not, moving business along. In mid-April Edwina's responsibilities increased, when she also took on the presidency of the Hampshire Nursing Division of the Order of St John.

Minutes, agenda, correspondence, speeches, travelling arrangements, invitations: Miss Lees was swamped. Aunt Victoria's apartment at Kensington Palace was crowded with boxes and files and the telephone rang constantly. Edwina knew she must find a place of her own and at the beginning of March she took a small house in Charles Street, No. 33. Hitler notwithstanding, she also decided to go ahead with alterations and repairs at Broadlands. 'Building in or converting 7 new bathrooms', she reported in her diary, 'as well as putting in heating, mending roof and countless things which must be done and we definitely won't be able to do later owing to even less cash than now and rises of prices and lack of labour'.

It was difficult to be ill with builders in the house. By the beginning of February Dickie felt well enough to go out and, although he was still shaky, in the middle of the month he returned to *Kelly*. The repairs were finished and on 29 February she left Newcastle for Scapa Flow. 'Glorious night', Dickie wrote as the flotilla escorted the battle-cruiser *Hood* and the battleship *Valiant* into the open sea. A week later, as he arrived on the bridge one morning, there was a fearful thud. 'That', signalled HMS *Gurkha*, 'was not mine but me.' In the collision *Gurkha's* propeller had sliced thirty-five feet out of *Kelly's* upper deck. At Scapa a metal plate was riveted over the gash and Dickie was ordered to bring *Kelly* down to London for repairs and a refit. Back he came to Broadlands.

Mobilization

Six months before, Dickie had wondered when, if at all, he would be reunited with his family. Since the beginning of the war he had seen more of them than had generally been the case in peacetime.

The war had trickled along for months; in late April it suddenly engulfed everything in sight. 'Norwegian news awful', Edwina noted on 2 May, 'withdrawing all troops north of Narvik'. It was impossible to believe that France might be invaded. Bunny had just started ten days' leave and Edwina flew across the Channel to collect him: 'Paris looking too beautiful for words with all the chestnuts and laburnum and wisteria out'. Three days of shopping, dining and dancing with Yola, Henri and Yola's sister Henriette and then Edwina and Bunny returned to London; two days later he was recalled. On 10 May Germany invaded Holland, Belgium and Luxembourg. Edwina saw Bunny off at Heston: 'On to Broadlands. Ghastly day of bad news and worries. Gather Dickie been in all kinds of horrors'. Chamberlain resigned, Churchill became Prime Minister. Dickie did not know, for late on the previous night *Kelly* had been torpedoed. She was badly crippled, with a fifty-foot hole in her side and no power. Twenty-seven men were killed, many injured. Dickie asked for a tow. For ninety-one hours *Kelly* shuffled through the North Sea; she was rammed by an enemy torpedo-boat, attacked by German fighters. After the second terrifying night the tow rope broke. *Kelly* was now listing at five degrees and it looked as if she might capsize at any minute. Dickie discarded what weight he could spare (his work with Cole meant that he knew every plate and rivet in his ship) and evacuated all but six officers and twelve men. The sea was too rough to attach another tow line, so Dickie asked for tugs. German submarines were said to be nearby; it was a long wait. On 13 May *Kelly* reached the Tyne. She was cheered all the way up the river, for she was so badly damaged that it was amazing that Mountbatten had managed to save her. Reason had no part in Dickie's decision to struggle home. It was all instinct, the reaction of a captain who loved his ship and was determined not to lose her to the enemy. With courage and skill he had brought her back, more dead than alive, in an adventure better than any Hollywood film. The nation cheered, the Prime Minister was pleased, the Navy, with some exceptions at the top, applauded a gallant officer. 'Addressed troops for the last time', Dickie wrote, after saying farewell to his battered shipmates, for *Kelly* needed at least six months' repairs and the crew was to be dispersed. 'All volunteered to remain on or come to any other ship with me'. As soon as she could, Edwina caught the train to Newcastle. '. . . Poor old *Kelly* . . . Nothing remains of boiler or engine rooms and Wireless Control room. Bits and pieces of clothes and even men still strewn about . . . Amazing feat to have got her back, 300 miles'. A week after his ordeal had begun, Dickie returned to Broadlands once more.

'News appalling', Edwina wrote on 21 May. Holland had been overrun and the Germans were advancing into France. Bunny got back to Dover, 'very shattered after 2 weeks ceaseless nightmare and no sleep.' Edwina rushed down to meet him at St Margaret's Bay: 'Calais nearly gone now and one can see the flares and bombs exploding from here, 22 miles away'. Paris fell on 14 June. 'Too unbelievable', Edwina wrote in her journal, 'and makes one feel sick'. In late June the Park at Broadlands was taken over, with the farm and houses on the estate, as headquarters for the Fourth Division. 'Place teeming with Army lorries, tents etc . . . These troops making the most terrible mess of the place and I fear a perfect target of the house for Air Raids etc'. Bunny had joined the Coldstream Training Battalion at Pirbright; Dickie was at Immingham, at the mouth of the Humber. He worked long hours, interspersed with games of golf and evenings at the cinema. Edwina joined him for his fortieth birthday; they rode in an RAF flying boat to Hull, where the Commander of the Balloon Barrage gave them a celebratory dinner at the Station Hotel. No nightclubs now. 'Air Raid', Edwina noted, 'and sat up and watched a little'. Yola's birthday was three days later: 'her 35th', Dickie wrote wistfully in his diary. 'I wonder where she is . . .'

Edwina's work was more strenuous than Dickie's. She rushed between the Depot and St John headquarters: 'lectures on Types of Air Raid Wounds . . . Excellent and intensely interesting'. Between bandage practice and meetings to select applicants for nursing places with the Voluntary Aid Detachment, she searched for premises for a Centre for Intensive Nursing Training. Everything took ages: telephone calls were delayed until connections could be made, meetings interrupted by air-raid warnings, motor journeys complicated by the lack of road signs and place names, removed to frustrate a German invasion, expected at any time.

Mobilization

So far the Mountbattens had been spared. Now, in the summer of 1940, they faced a dreadful prospect. What would be their fate, and the children's, if the Germans crossed the Channel and invaded Britain? Edwina was Jewish by descent; so, therefore, were Patricia and Pamela. Dickie's genes were more to Hitler's liking but his close connection to the British royal family was a liability, quite apart from the fact that he was an enemy officer. The Nazis had a list of people who were to be exterminated and the Mountbattens assumed that their names were on it. If the Germans came, Edwina and her family might meet an unimaginably awful end. She and the children must prepare their escape. Some might think this cowardly; to Edwina, whose husband's relations had been thrown down wells or bombed to smithereens, it was common sense. At first Dickie was unenthusiastic – Edwina's scheme was extremely dangerous. She had made up her mind to buy a boat (three and a half thousand pounds should do it), hire a trustworthy skipper and one or two deck-hands, and sail from Salcombe in Devon via Madeira to the coast of Florida, a trip of just over three thousand miles. Dickie's reaction was characteristic. Other methods were impossible, so the best must be made of this one. With meticulous planning, judgement and imagination, it might work. His letters to Edwina in mid-June 1940 were like extracts from the *Boys' Own Paper*. To start with, he wrote, '. . . I send you A List of Charts, Publications and Instruments'. His own 'excellent little sextant' had been despatched from Newcastle; Edwina would find a compass and station pointer (sketch attached) in his bedroom at Charles Street. 'You had better tell the skipper to buy his own parallel rulers and dividers and provide pencils and rubbers etc. Otherwise get them from Henry Hughes and Son – I think in Fenchurch Street but they are in the telephone book. No need to get an expensive ruler for the trip!', he added cheerily. Dickie also sent his binoculars: 'Zeiss and still in first class order'. Next, Route Instructions: 'I have routed you with great care via neutral countries and so as to get the most satisfactory winds for your ocean trip . . . Nevertheless you must fill up with at the very least 5 weeks water supply at Madeira and will practically have to give up washing!' The voyage was beginning to sound like an adventure from *Swallows and Amazons*. 'I honestly believe that if you really study the Navigation Manual on your way over you will learn enough to be a real help to the skipper yourself and of course he can also brush up his knowledge if necessary'. It seemed to have slipped Dickie's mind that only an exceptionally experienced navigator would be familiar with the English Channel, the Bay of Biscay, the Atlantic, the Caribbean and the Gulf of Mexico.

It was vital to choose the right crew. 'Your skipper *must* be a bachelor or widower without dependants – a married man will never leave his wife at the last moment at such a time'. The same applied to the deck-hands. The loyal Xuereb, now the Mountbattens' chauffeur, should be taken along as engineer. 'He had better spend all next weekend on board and let him order *all* the spare parts he thinks might be needed if the Yacht broke down in an outlandish spot – you can call it the wilds of Cornwall to him'. When the time came for departure, a hundred pounds should be paid to the captain, with the promise of as much again on arrival, 'and the same sort of thing for the crew'. Meanwhile, Dickie might be killed in the attempt to defend Britain from the invader. Edwina should therefore take copies of essential documents: 'although I have not got much the will would help settle your claim'. Alternatively, Edwina and the children might be lost at sea, so perhaps Dickie should have a copy of her papers. This displeased Edwina, who considered it bad form to talk about money. It is not clear what Dickie expected an occupied Britain to be like. Everyday life might go on much as before. If he were left behind, he would need the registration number of the Vauxhall and 'a duplicate list of all my personal investments which I made into your marriage settlement'. To avoid problems later on, Edwina should settle all outstanding bills before her departure and make sure that the revolver and ammunition, which Dickie had given her in May, had all the proper licences. Edwina's property might disappear. Dickie had his diamond GCVO star 'and I would also like my platinum watch and pearl studs. I have nothing else of any value and bank notes may be worth nothing so without a few small pieces of jewellery I might not be able to start to join you if all had gone west'. What would happen to Broadlands? One day they might come back so they should go ahead with repairs and renovations: 'if all is well we shall certainly want the turbine dynamo'. Tin boxes of important documents – family papers, share certificates, wills and so forth – should be entrusted to Tiller, the head keeper ('open them in

Mobilization

Tiller's presence to show they contain *only* family papers and no money or jewellery'), and buried in a pre-determined spot in his garden. Burning and pillaging there might be but Edwina should still be business-like: 'get 2 copies of a written receipt from him – one for you and one for me – to enable us to recover them at leisure later on. Even a red government would hardly stop purely family documents being sent out, or photos'. Not that Dickie was sure what sort of a government would take over: 'Please leave the dogs at Broadlands . . . no one is going to oppress the working classes to the extent that they can't look after dogs'.

The moment drew near. The charts were purchased, a boat selected. France fell on 17 June; Dickie heard the news on the BBC and sent a line to Edwina. She hesitated. Looked at coolly, the plan was absurd. She thought again and decided to send Patricia and Pamela to America, with Marjorie's son David and his Swedish governess. (No permit could be got for Mademoiselle Chevrier, since Britain did not recognize the new French government.) They were to travel as evacuees and, once in America, Patricia and Pamela could stay with Mrs Vanderbilt. Dickie got a night's leave to return to Broadlands to say goodbye; Edwina took the children to buy warm clothes and have their hair cut, dashing to the Bank of England in the middle to ask for permission from the Governor, Montagu Norman, to send money to America for their upkeep. (It was refused.) 'Too sad and all in tears', Edwina wrote in her journal. It seemed right to send the children away, although when she learnt that the King and Queen were keeping the princesses at home, she wondered whether she had been precipitate.

Her own escape was forgotten. Edwina had pulled herself together in the nick of time.

CHAPTER TWENTY-ONE

The Warrior and the Healer

E dwina's letters to the children were meant to reassure: 'We're certainly in the front line now', she wrote in mid-September 1940. 'But don't worry and I promise to take all the care I can! I am getting pretty nippy!!!! at dodging what I don't want to come into contact with!!' That is, the falling masonry, charred timber and splintered glass that was left behind each morning after the German bombers' raids. The new St John Training Centre had opened just in time. A month before the start of the Blitz, twenty-five volunteers enrolled for the new two-week Intensive First Aid Course. Edwina was among them. From nine in the morning until six at night the students learnt about the effects of machine-gun fire, burns, blast and lacerations caused by flying missiles. Lady Louis' participation secured publicity for the course. The *Tatler* had a page of pictures: 'Mrs Gardner is attending to Mrs Wilkinson's supposedly broken ankle, and on the left Mrs Evans and Mrs Moeran are struggling with an unruly bandage.' Eyes shining, hair gleaming, in every photograph Edwina drew the eye. Applications poured in and within a month similar training centres were starting everywhere.

Edwina found the course exhausting. No wonder. Other students did not dine at the Ritz and eat their supper at the Café de Paris. But where were the casualties? So far, Edwina's knowledge was all theoretical. Longing to practise her new skills, she enrolled at the Westminster Hospital for a month's training on the wards. She began her apprenticeship on 4 September. It was messier, harder, humbler work than she had expected. All morning she worked in the Soldiers' Surgical Ward: 'Carried stuff round and died of heat and fatigue and Bed Pans! but enjoyed it a lot . . . Dinner in bed.' On the third morning she was allowed to watch an operation: 'made me feel very sick . . .' As she finished her first week, the Blitz began. No time now for queasiness. 'Terrible Air Raid injuries . . . Awful lacerations and fractures due to Plate Glass, head and chest and arms.' She did not flinch during amptutations: 'very interesting but horrible . . .'

It was not terror but exhaustion that made Edwina unsteady on her feet: 'Explosions, whistling bombs etc . . . never stopped till 6 a.m. Worst night I have spent (in Basement) on Camp Bed!! House shaking to pieces.' Three bombs fell in Eaton Square, just missing the Depot and the Training Centre. Their neighbours were not so lucky: 'Buckingham Palace hit for 2nd time this week.' Kensington Palace was knocked about (fortunately Aunt Victoria was staying with Nada) and at Brook House a bomb crashed through the roof, down the staircase and into the lower floor of the penthouse. 'A lot of damage', Edwina wrote in her diary, and, looking on the bright side, 'Can get out of rent temporarily anyway which is something.' She felt increasingly insecure at Charles Street. The walls shook, the gas went on and off, windows shivered in their frames. When a time-bomb was discovered outside, Jessie, the housekeeper, and Monroe, the parlourmaid, were evacuated and the furniture removed. Edwina booked herself into Claridge's. In November she moved into 15 Chester Street. 'Not falling to pieces *quite* so much', Edwina told Patricia and Pamela. 'Altho' the tiles and windows have already been blown out several times . . .' She arranged for the basement to be strengthened and here she slept during the worst raids. The reinforcement was largely psychological for, as she discovered afterwards, if the house had received a direct hit, her refuge would either have caved in or been blown up with the rest.

Broadlands had already received a battering. Throughout the summer Germany had attacked south-east England with fleets of bombers escorted by fighters. In late August a Messerschmitt had crashed in front of the home farm; eight bombs fell on the Park in a single night. Southampton had been badly damaged. Edwina and Aunt Victoria drove down to see what was left of the docks and found that the cold storage place had gone up in flames, instantly roasting all the Mountbattens' game. In September, when enemy aeroplanes were ordered to concentrate on London, Broadlands became relatively peaceful. 'Gloriously quiet night', Edwina wrote on Friday the 13th, 'with only occasional German machines and odd bombs and Anti Aircraft fire'.

Unlike Edwina, Dickie had time to brood. His job at Immingham was undemanding. Bunny was stationed nearby and throughout July and August the two men played golf together and spent occasional evenings at the cinema. They liked the same sort of thing; on the Mountbattens' eighteenth wedding anniversary Dickie and Bunny celebrated together with a trip to Grimsby to see *Top Hat*. In early October Mountbatten's flotilla was ordered south to Plymouth. 'You will laugh at this address,' Dickie told Edwina, in his first letter from Devonport, 'and remark: "The old sybarite always falls on his feet".' He and his staff had been put in the local Library but, when Admiral Dunbar Nasmith heard that Dickie was sleeping on a camp bed, he immediately asked him to Admiralty House '. . . and he and Lady Nasmith both told me to invite you to come and stay as soon as and whenever you like.' Edwina did not join her husband. She was organizing the move from Charles Street to Chester Street, working for another Red Cross and St John Flag Day, inspecting Rest Centres in Islington and the East End, keeping up morale with a visit to the Craven A cigarette factory in the Hampstead Road. She was too busy to get away to Devon – but she did manage a long weekend with the Angleseys at Plas Newydd. 'Beautiful wild grounds and gardens', Edwina wrote in her diary, but the chief attraction was Bunny, who was now stationed nearby.

Edwina did not feel that she was neglecting Dickie. It was hardly worth going to Devonport to meet him when he might be ordered to sea at any moment. During October and November he was engaged on various operations in the Channel. While searching for German destroyers in French waters, the flotilla was mistakenly attacked by two British bombers, one of which was lost, and at the end of November *Javelin* was hit by German torpedoes. Forty-six men were killed and the ship's bow and stern blown off. Charitable people said that Mountbatten's manoeuvres had been correct, if slow. The general conclusion was that he had erred. 'We have heard about Daddy's adventure', Pamela wrote from New York in a letter to 'Darlingest Mummy'. The girls were happy to think that their father was a hero. First *Kelly*, now *Javelin*. '. . . Exactly like last time', Patricia observed. 'It really is extraordinary that of all the Flotilla it should have been you.' She was not the only one to notice the coincidence. Some of Mountbatten's colleagues resented the fact that his accidents brought him so much popular admiration. Others thought his ingenuity and daring might be put to better use.

Edwina was happier than she had been for years, for she liked her work and knew that she did it well. There was little point in being anxious about Dickie, since she did not know what he had been doing until afterwards. Bunny was close by. He had spent much of November convalescing at Broadlands (Edwina had brought him there to have his appendix removed), along with Peter Murphy, swathed in bandages after a motor accident. Aunt Victoria refused to be intimidated by the Blitz, although she could sometimes be persuaded to come to Broadlands to keep Edwina company at weekends. Molly appeared to have settled into her house at Alresford. Edwina called on her once a month and, since petrol was strictly rationed, her stepmother could hardly ask for more frequent visits. And there was no need, at least for the time being, to worry about Mary. Her divorce from Cunningham-Reid had been painful, but at the end of August 1940 she had announced her engagement to Captain Laurie Gardner, son of Sir Ernest Gardner, a Conservative Member of Parliament. They were married at the beginning of September. As for the children, Edwina had never fretted about them and she did not intend to do so now. From the moment that Patricia and Pamela arrived in America, the Mountbattens' friends had rallied round. The Pells took them to the National Horse Show ('Not half as good as the one at Olympia', Patricia said loyally). Mrs Vanderbilt carried them off to her place at Newport. The Fifth Avenue house was being 'autumn cleaned', so all the furniture came too. At the end of the holidays, 'Aunt Grace' disappeared to Hot Springs for her own programme of restoration and renovation, leaving the children in the care of an English governess, Miss Pugh. This was not a success. Patricia and Pamela wanted Mademoiselle Chevrier and, when their parents read their weekly letters, they agreed that 'Zelle must be got to America as soon as possible.

For it now dawned upon the Mountbattens that their daughters had jumped out of the frying-pan into the fire. Two attractive, innocent, near-royal evacuees, thrown on the mercy of the American people, were just what gossip columnists wanted. Snobs pounced: 'Hardly had we sat down to lunch than she began talking about "dear King George" and all the others . . .' Unfamiliar people telephoned with invitations. 'Nearly everyone we meet knows you,' Patricia told her parents, '. . . they all love you and say you are the best looking pair they ever met – here! here!' The children were not sure whom to trust. One stranger they met at lunch claimed to have saved Aunt Alice from drowning: 'What a coincidence', Patricia said politely. At home there were occasional treats – visits to the circus, the zoo, children's concerts and the pantomime – but now the sisters were taken out every day. In one week on Long Island they saw *Ghost Breakers* three times. At Adsdean and Broadlands they had all they needed and wanted – ponies, dogs, bicycles, a caravan – but the children of these wealthy American families were loaded with possessions. 'Synthia who is 16 . . . had a sweet tiny little car which she drives herself,' Pamela wrote, 'though the chauffeur has to go with her.' Bad examples presented themselves on all sides. One zealous hostess fitted out the children with complete summer wardrobes, 'millions of things', Patricia told her parents. 'Of course,' she explained, 'I didn't like the idea at all and was very embarrassed, but what could you do, she just insisted . . .'

This was frightful. Dickie and Edwina thought they had taken care of everything. Patricia had been asked to make sure that at Mrs Vanderbilt's they had their own bills for telephone calls and laundry, and the Mountbattens had 'an arrangement' with Nell Cosden, who looked after the children's clothes, Pamela's pocket money and Patricia's allowance. As the Treasury had not allowed Edwina to open a bank account in America, John Schiff, Jacob's grandson, had agreed to deal with large bills for school and medical fees. (The Mountbattens insisted on depositing equivalent sums in an account in London, to repay him after the war.) Edwina explained this to Patricia. 'Darling now all is arranged about the money . . . so don't accept any more . . .*please*!! It is very kind and generous and meant only to help but we don't want to be in debt to more people than necessary . . .' She was sorry if she had not thought sufficiently far ahead. 'Of course you must have winter things, coats etc when necessary and new dresses occasionally. You get lovely cheap little ready mades at Bonwit Tellers and Maceys etc and there are wonderful shoe shops . . . You should be able to manage quite well with 'Zelle's help on fairly little.' For Mademoiselle Chevrier was on her way. 'Thank you *so* much for sending her', Patricia wrote with relief, 'it makes all the difference.'

'All I am doing is dreary work', Edwina told 'Darlingest P & P'. At the beginning of October she had gone to see the makeshift shelters and rest centres in the Underground. At each station there was a First Aid Post, staffed by workers from St John and the Red Cross. Their hours were long – some shifts went from six in the evening until eight o'clock next morning – and the conditions dreadful. These sanctuaries were crowded and insanitary, ill-lit and poorly ventilated. There was no clear procedure for distributing blankets and other necessities to the desperate people who sought refuge there. No one knew who was supposed to be in charge. Edwina was horrified. She came home 'quite ga ga', she told the girls, 'with the most terrible fogs and atmospheres and niffinesses.' Her colleagues at the JWO agreed that something must be done and made Edwina responsible for all St John volunteers working in Rest Centres, Shelters and First Aid Posts. Her first action was to ask to see Ellen Wilkinson, the Home Office Minister, and Florence Horsburgh at the Ministry of Health. Within days the Government had appointed someone to take specific charge of shelters. But this was not a job for a politician, sitting at a desk. It required a catalyst, someone who would tour the shelters regularly, encourage the volunteers, keep up standards, nag until funds and equipment were provided to help people who were homeless, frightened and ill. Whoever took on the task needed a sharp eye, a good memory, access to powerful people and the ability to make an urgent case succinctly and persuasively. Edwina stepped in. She had time and energy, the charm and natural authority to go anywhere and talk to anyone, a presence that commanded respect and attention. Above all, she had stamina.

As night fell, she set off in her little car, sensing her way through the blackout, on a round of inspections, planned so that she visited each shelter at least once every two weeks. Holborn, Covent Garden and Bermondsey one night, Aldwych, Bond Street, Oxford Circus and Piccadilly the next. Controllers, councillors and Medical Officers discovered that Lady Louis saw everything and forgot nothing. She spoke quietly but her questions were penetrating; she worked quickly but no corner was uninspected. She went everywhere: to the shelters at Courage's Brewery, Swan and Edgar's department store, Selfridge's, the Midland Bank, St Martin's Crypt. She was at Bethnal Green, Liverpool Street, Deptford, Stepney, Moorgate, Hackney: 'Got completely lost and only returned at 5 a.m.' She turned up in Battersea, St Pancras, Chelsea, West Ham, the City, driving through smoking streets, jolting over the rubble, flashing her emergency pass at anyone who tried to stop her. Danger? She ignored it. When air-raid sirens went, Edwina leapt into her car and set off. There she was, beside the bomb craters, among the burnt-out ruins, her pale face, with its huge eyes, instantly recognizable. And later, in the Underground, she could be seen making her way between the rows of beds, 'stacked like apple trays', said Daphne Heald, who went with her. Everyone knew Lady Louis.

Edwina made the most of her celebrity. 'Started a tour with Godfrey Winn (journalist) . . . Sick Bay and Old People's Home in Chelsea and First Aid Post at the Adelphi . . .' She talked about shelters to the King and Queen, the Kents, the Minister of Health. She stood no nonsense from patronizing or unhelpful people, however highly placed. Sir John Anderson was one she scorned. Now Lord President, he had been Home Secretary for six months in the middle of 1940, and Edwina considered him responsible for the disgusting state into which the shelters had been allowed to fall. 'A terror', she called him in her diary, 'and the real Oppressor of Bengal.'

'Don't you know there's a war on?' people said, when others were demanding or impatient, but the fact that they were working for an heroic cause did not make Edwina's colleagues into saints. 'Ceaseless worries and dramas', she wrote in her journal after a sticky morning at the office. She was careful not to have favourites. People took turns in coming with her to the shelters and, when she needed briefing before a meeting with local officials or at a ministry, she made sure that she got it first-hand from the workers, however junior, on the spot. Younger women in her team were reverent and adoring: Lady Louis managed to be effective, frivolous, self-sacrificing and glamorous, all at once. In the middle of a sixteen-hour day she skipped in to Elizabeth Arden for a facial or a manicure; she lunched at the Mirabelle, dined at Claridge's, and, after a tour of Underground shelters with Prince George, had supper with him at the Savoy. War, she maintained, was no excuse for being drab. St John insignia must be highly polished, stocking seams straight, hems level. Edwina's permanent wave was always in good order. She took sandwiches to Arden's and, while her hair fizzed, worked through a stack of files and correspondence. Edwina was the most striking woman at any gathering. She had discarded her white cape (it looked too theatrical and attracted the dirt) but her black coat and skirt accentuated her slim figure. She wore little jewellery: a plain ring and cuff links of enamel and gold – her wedding anniversary present from Dickie. For her anniversary present, in July 1940, Edwina chose lovely things: 'Shopping (jewels) in the lunch hour and I think I made a good investment or rather 2. Ring and earrings, Boucheron.' Hitler should not be allowed to drive all the elegance from her life 'Bought some flowers,' Edwina wrote in January 1941, 'costing as much as pearls.'

Senior colleagues respected her. Lady Louis worked, that was the main thing. Her mornings were spent organizing the Nursing Flying Squad, interviewing prospective VADs and looking for full-time workers for Medical Aid Posts, and in the afternoons she went round to the Knitted Garments Depot. The older women found Edwina Mountbatten more modest and conscientious than they had expected, and more likeable. She remembered people's names, their most recent illnesses, their anniversaries; she wrote charming thank you letters and had an endearingly soft spot for animals. One morning in January 1941 she had come heartbroken to the office: 'Day marred by death of baby wallaby'. It had emerged from its mother's pouch and died of cold. Edwina's colleagues knew that the indomitable, competent Lady Louis was as human as anyone else. She mislaid her spectacles, lost her way in the dark, suffered from car sickness, twisted her fingers and repeatedly looked at her watch before she had to make a speech. She worked on when others would have stopped: 'Very mouldy all day with slight temperature and aches and throat.' No one thought Edwina's promotion too rapid when in early January 1941 she moved up another rank, to Lady District Officer and Acting Lady Deputy District Superintendent, only two places from the top of the tree.

The first half of 1941 was a time of increasing privation and difficulty. At the end of June Edwina took Bunny and a group of friends to *Rise Above It*, the musical comedy revue with Hermione Gingold and Hermione Baddeley. 'Quite good' was all she said in her diary but 'We must rise above it' soon became for Edwina, as for many others, an all-purpose exhortation. There was a good deal to surmount. Destruction by air-raids, losses at sea, German military successes. By early summer Edwina was exhausted. The ill tidings distressed her, she was worn out by shelter work, earache, toothache and neuralgia. There were family troubles. 'Marjorie to lunch,' Edwina reported at the end of January, 'with startling news of her divorce from Brecky.' In mid-February there was another shock: 'Mary wants to finish the whole thing as it's not a success.' Once more Cousin Felix was called in to arrange the terms of a divorce. His services were also required by the Mountbattens. 'Owing to new Budget with Income Tax at 10/-

and Super Tax at 19/6, we are in a pickle', Edwina wrote in her diary in mid-April, 'and will be reduced to below £5000 a year spendable income!!!' It was not easy to see how they could save. The Rolls had been disposed of long since, the Remount people had requisitioned the fitter polo ponies and the oldest had been put out to grass. Dickie suggested small economies: 'I have given 3 binoculars . . . to *sell* to the Ministry of Supply', he told Edwina, '. . . the proceeds to be used to help in our various charities which we can't otherwise afford any longer'. He also sent home his Leica photographic enlarger: 'Bunny could show you how to use it and save pounds'. Lavish entertainment was impossible. Prices of restaurant meals were fixed and Edwina now had no time or energy for nightclubs. She was at Broadlands, having an early night after a meeting to discuss the District Nursing Service, when the Café de Paris was hit in early March. Forty people were killed and many injured.

Clothing and food were rationed: 'I am amused to hear you are all chewing raw carrots for your complexion,' Edwina told Patricia, 'while we are eating carrots in every form for nourishing purposes according to the Ministry of Food's order!! Also potatoes and oatmeal! Certain things are impossible to get and many extremely difficult but one is already used to doing without' (here she sounded as patriotic as the Queen) 'and we are probably all the better for the lack of them' (there she spoke like Nannie). In mid-May two large plots at Broadlands were taken over by a local market gardener, who agreed to supply the Mountbattens with fresh vegetables and fruit, the cost to be deducted from his rent. 'We are keeping 2 glass houses and a few farms ourselves,' Edwina told Dickie, 'and the end 'Yew Hedge' garden for the moment . . .' A man and a boy remained to look after these; on summer weekends Edwina did a little therapeutic weeding. Mr Yeats, who had saved Edwina and Mary from submersion in the Test, dealt with the rest of the Park, with a lad to help him, and Mrs Lankester supervised the housekeeping, with the help of Lightfoot, the only maid. There were fewer rooms to clean, dust and polish, for the Ministry of Health had started work on converting Broadlands into an annexe of the Southampton General Hospital. Furniture was stored in the dining-room and cellars, Edwina's sitting-room was used for meals. The garden door became the front door, the brushing-room the kitchen, and the butler's bedroom an eating and sitting-room for the now depleted staff. The Mountbattens retained seven bedrooms for themselves, the children, Aunt Victoria and their guests, and on the upper floor they kept sleeping quarters for the staff. 'All the rest will be theirs,' Edwina told Dickie. 'It'll be a *terrible* work! and I am taking a week's leave to cope with it . . .' The Head Room became an operating theatre, the Secretary's room was converted into what Edwina cheerily described as a 'Sluice lulu!!' She was pleased that the house was being used in this way. It was better than having billets or a transit camp, and 'the Hospital people . . . Doctors, Matron etc are charming and all are *so* grateful and relieved.'

At the end of April 1941 the Fifth Flotilla was sent south to help the Mediterranean Fleet. The invasion of Greece had given the Germans air superiority in the central Mediterranean and Malta was under heavy attack. As *Kelly* docked, seventy German bombers came over. 'I can't of course say very much, because of the censorship', Dickie told Edwina, 'but you can imagine my emotions . . . the bright blue sky, the brilliant sunshine, the warm sea are as lovely as ever and it seems incredible to think of the death and destruction that come at night.' Most of the population took refuge in underground caves and shelters and Mountbatten decided that half his officers and men should join them there each night that *Kelly* was in port. He did not include himself, for he could not bear to think that his ship might be hit while he slept safely ashore. 'All of us have had many narrow shaves', he told Robert Neville '. . . I won't pretend it's fun.' When *Kelly* left Malta, it was for Crete.

Dickie knew that there was a good chance that *Kelly* might be sunk. He was right to be pessimistic. The Germans were attacking Crete with high-level bombers, British air cover was minimal and British battleships had been temporarily withdrawn. At dawn on 23 May *Kashmir* was hit, then *Kelly*. Within thirty seconds she capsized, all guns firing, every man at action stations. 'I felt I ought to be the last to leave the ship,' Dickie told Patricia, 'and I left it a bit late because the bridge turned over on top of me'. When he surfaced, after a struggle, he jettisoned his heavy tin hat. This was an error, for the Germans were machine-gunning the bodies in the water. Having helped the weak and injured to what rafts and floats there were, Dickie called for three cheers as *Kelly* went down.

That morning Edwina heard from the Admiralty that *Kelly* had been lost. Peter Murphy took her out to lunch at Claridge's while they waited for news and in the afternoon she learnt that Dickie was still in one piece. *Kipling* had appeared on the horizon, dodged the bombers and scooped up the survivors from *Kashmir* and *Kelly*. 'Once again all right', Dickie cabled Edwina, when *Kipling* reached Alexandria, 'but this time heartbroken.' *Kelly* had been in one scrap after another, he said in a farewell address to his crew. 'Now she lies in fifteen hundred fathoms and with her half our shipmates.' Until this last adventure, skilful handling had always brought *Kelly* home. Dickie's men had sailed with him willingly; if they saw his deficiencies, they did not care, for he was a natural leader, strong, open and courageous. Devoted to *Kelly* and her company, he had inspired the same love and trust in himself. Fifty years after *Kelly* vanished beneath the waves, those who served in her still met to honour her memory.

On 18 June Dickie came home, having travelled, via Africa, under the pointless alias of Mr Lewis Mountain. At home the air-raids were as bad as ever. 'Plymouth very badly hit again', Edwina had noted in her diary at the end of April: '. . . 5th time in 9 nights.' By day Broadlands looked the most peaceful place on earth – in the late spring a great sweep of daffodils appeared in the Park and at the beginning of June Bunny caught his first salmon in the Test – but it was too close to the south coast to be safe. On 21 June, Dickie's first weekend at home, there was a heavy raid. Dickie, Edwina, Bunny, and Peter were up until four in the morning, helping to put out fires started by the incendiaries that had fallen on the roof. More than two dozen high explosive bombs had also been dropped, destroying farm buildings and battering the cottages. 'Poor Broadlands itself . . . badly shaken up,' Edwina told Patricia and Pamela, '. . . However it all might have been worse . . .'

After his hammering in the Mediterranean, Dickie was glad to walk through the woods and ride across the fields. He was touched when Edwina asked him to take over the direction of the estate; she had also decided to leave Broadlands to him in her will. 'Now I look upon it', he said, 'as every bit as much my home as yours.' Edwina was sympathetic and kind, less irritable than at any time in the Mountbattens' married life. When Dickie was at home she found time to ride and walk with him and in London she allowed him to persuade her to go to the cinema. 'Quite a change and I think it does one good sometimes', she said in a letter to Patricia, although the films were generally more to Dickie's taste than her own. She spent an occasional night away from the shelters and, to amuse Dickie, went with him to dine and dance. 'I am always bucked when you are so sweet and nice about inviting friends like Angie Laycock', he told her gratefully. (This was Freda Dudley Ward's daughter, on whom Dickie had a sentimental crush). 'I loved dancing with you darling,' he added, so that Edwina should not feel jealous. 'In fact', he observed, 'our steps fit better than at any time since Delhi, just as our lives seem to dovetail more perfectly.'

This was true. Day and night they had both been exposed to danger, Dickie at sea, Edwina as she steered her way through the battered streets. Like her husband, Edwina expected fearlessness and dedication from her staff; like the sailors on *Kelly*, Edwina's team gave all their energy and devotion. She had found that, like Dickie, she could lead. Like Dickie, too, she could get things done, for she too had influence and useful connections. Ministers and civil servants saw her, listened to her, delivered what she asked. Requests from Lady Louis did not moulder at the bottom of the pile, for if there were delays an inquiry would come from the top, even perhaps, from the Prime Minister himself. Like Dickie, Edwina did not confine herself to official channels. Whom you knew, people said, was more important than what you knew, but in Edwina's case, as in Dickie's, her success was not simply due to the fact that she had well-placed friends and acquaintances. Those whom she approached believed that she knew what she was talking about. They were right. Both the Mountbattens understood the need for full and precise briefing. Before Dickie brought a new idea to the Admiralty, he spent hours looking into it, analysing the arguments for and against. When Edwina wanted to make a case at the Home Office, the Ministries of Health, Labour and Food, she consulted professional experts and volunteers with first-hand experience. Her representations were heard because she knew her stuff. Indeed, having listened to all sides, she was usually better informed than anyone else.

Sharing more, the Mountbattens had become more affectionate. Edwina now knew what it was to sit all night over reports and correspondence. She admired Dickie's application and copied him by sticking at her paperwork for as long as he did – longer even. Dickie did not smile at these self-imposed endurance tests. He was touched to see how determined Edwina was; glad, too, that she was using her intelligence and administrative skill on something that was, at last, worthwhile. His mother was particularly pleased. 'Your parents are learning the hard lessons of carrying out their present duties', she told Patricia, 'with the world around them changing and death . . . visible and present daily . . .'

By now, too, some of the tension had gone out of the Mountbattens' marriage. Dickie knew that Edwina understood that he had no great interest in sex; he spoke of it as if it were a mixture of psychology and hydraulics. He liked attractive women, but he was sentimental rather than passionate. Dickie was also aware, for Bunny had told him, that Edwina found love-making tedious. It was not sexual frustration or an insatiable appetite that had driven her affairs in the 'twenties and 'thirties but the desire to assert herself. With reason. Dickie was a maddening husband. He wanted his wife's complete and constant attention. He had no sense of proportion: all his worries, from the shortcomings of the Admiralty to the whereabouts of a missing tooth-brush, were of equal importance to him, and, he believed, to Edwina as well. He was garrulous, unable to distinguish between the confidences of marriage and secrets that could be told to other people. Immature – but affectionate, generous, inventive and brave – Dickie had all the characteristics of a delightful, exasperating twelve-year-old boy. Edwina had her own agenda and mothering her husband was not on it. She wanted freedom to find out who she was and what she could do and resented it when Dickie ate into her time and intruded on her privacy. In the Mountbattens' early years together Edwina had no defence against such incursions, no job, no more than a superficial interest in her children, music, painting, literature, gardening. She could not fend off her husband with the excuse that she had too much to do. Some women would have sought refuge in religion. Edwina was too literal for that. For others, illness would have offered an escape; she tried that and did not like it.

Rather than taking refuge in God or headaches, Edwina had turned to Hugh and Laddie, Mike, Larry and Ted, with other flirtations in between. That part of her life, at least, was sacrosanct, for Dickie had not dared to question her. Then, after nine years of marriage, he had asked for an explanation. It had been little help to either of them. Dickie had remained as possessive as before, Edwina as self-protective. Her efforts to enlarge her independence began to take a different form: after a short spell of invalidism, in which she enlisted Yola, she had gone in for travel. Bunny, whom she met in the autumn of 1933, was an ideal companion. Dickie dealt with this development by making up his mind to like his wife's lover. 'The fact that I encourage the Rabbit', he told Edwina in April 1941, 'is not that I don't care but that I love you so very much that I want you to be happy and I like him better than all your friends and have no doubt that he is *au fond* nicer than me'. Edwina was not altogether pleased. Having mapped out a part of her life she thought she could call her own, she had seen Dickie annex it. When she protested, Dickie observed jovially that he refused to go in for what he called 'rabbital rivalry'. In her work Edwina had at last found something of her own. There she was in charge, success or failure her responsibility. Friends said that Edwina worked long and late as a way of competing with Dickie. They were right – but there was another reason. Taking on an ever-growing burden was a way of ensuring that everything else took second place.

In the autumn of 1941 Dickie was given command of the aircraft carrier *Illustrious*. She had been badly damaged in the Mediterranean but had got away through the Suez Canal to the United States, where she was now under repair at a yard in Norfolk, Virginia. The Admiralty wanted Mountbatten to go over to America to take up his new post; as repairs would take until the end of the year at least, he was looking forward to several months with Patricia and Pamela. Unfortunately Edwina chose this moment to announce that it was time to bring the children back to England. Dickie believed that for the present they should stay in America, Edwina accused him of being selfish and, when he consulted Robert Neville and Bunny, of lobbying for support. It was quite wrong, she said, for one parent (Dickie) to be reunited with the girls, rather than the other (herself). This was the sort of illogical reasoning with which Dickie had to cope when Edwina worked herself into a jealous state. By now he knew that the only way to defuse the argument was by diverting her attention. 'I am so anxious that we should *both* be able to be with them', he told Edwina. 'Can you not get a mission when I go over? I shall be there 3 or 4 months I expect.'

Dickie's suggestion was shrewd and timely. Edwina believed that the sooner America could be persuaded to enter the war the better. For months support had been pouring in to Britain from the United States. Voluntary organizations worked to raise money, collect, pack and ship supplies: in May 1941, for instance, Edwina had taken delivery of several mobile X-ray units, a gift to Hampshire from New Hampshire, and each week she received bundles of clothing and other essentials to help re-equip people who had been bombed out of their houses. A group of American Red Cross nurses had been sent to London and in July the International Commissioner came over to see the work they and their British colleagues were doing. Edwina and Angela Limerick, Deputy Chairman of the Joint War Organization, gave him dinner, spoke vividly of difficulties and shortages and indicated how the American Red Cross might help. It was obvious that the JWO needed all the support that could be given and that, if a mission were to be sent to the United States, no representatives would be more eloquent than these two.

Edwina could not make up her mind. She did not want to leave a job that was interesting and useful; in her absence, who would go down to the shelters? Paperwork would pile up, she would miss a whole string of meetings. First she was pulled one way, then the other. If she went with Dickie, she would be deserting Bunny. If she stayed behind, she would forgo the opportunity to see the children. It was this, in the end, that tipped the scale. During Patricia and Pamela's absence in America, Edwina had become closer to her daughters. She found it easier to express her feelings on paper than face to face; being busy, she had more to say. In the past she had often believed, unjustly, that she had to prise the girls away from their father, who had no difficulty in showing them affection and keeping them amused. Now that Patricia and Pamela were far away from both parents, she no longer felt at a disadvantage.

Edwina knew from the children's letters that they missed her. Dickie had proposed that one week Patricia should write to him and Pamela to Edwina, the next week the other way round. Each parent sent a weekly letter addressed to both the girls. The system worked well. Edwina wrote regularly and at length. Her letters were not as long as those she received, however, for each week the children sent at least half a dozen foolscap pages apiece. Pamela's letters were written in a small, upright hand, very like her father's, and ingeniously illustrated. She was precise, giving the age of every child she met, the height of each pony she rode, the exact layout of the houses in which she stayed. 'We went to a place where they make and roll bandages for the Red Cross. All the children sat at one table, Patricia and I, Peggy, Polly, Priscilla and a girl called Flora, who was eleven. If her name had been Plora all our names would have begun with *P*. We made 170 nose bandages just the six of us . . .'

The Warrior and the Healer

Patricia was more reflective. Most of the burden of negotiating with Mrs Vanderbilt fell on her shoulders. 'We are not going to stay with Mrs Warburg quite yet, as Aunt Grace would like us to stay on here and keep her company . . . I wrote to Mrs Warburg, explaining everything . . .' It was often difficult to work out local protocol. America was supposed to be classless but, according to Mrs Vanderbilt, a great many people were 'not suitable'. Edwina suspected anti-semitism. When another visit to the Warburgs was put off, she wrote fiercely to Patricia. 'I think the Vanderbilt set point of view about people like them *preposterous* and I thoroughly disapprove. And I know you will too . . . They are a very decent, loyal and charming family and so are the Schiffs and just as good as any Vanderbilt!!!' Edwina was furious. 'People really are amazing and very disillusioning at times and if this war does away with all that social snobbery it will have achieved one good thing anyway.'

Mademoiselle Chevrier was a godsend. She made sure that the girls were not paraded at smart lunch and supper parties and taught them how to wash, mend and iron their own clothes to reduce the laundry bills. Patricia and Pamela said afterwards that their guardian dragooned them into doing their weekly letters but they wrote so sparklingly that it is hard to think they saw it as a chore. There was so much to describe: tobogganing in New Jersey; being registered as aliens and finger-printed at the Post Office; Pamela's first cocktail ('it was called a sirop de grenadine . . . not a cocktail at all, but a kind of little drink made with fruit juices . . .'). Patricia wanted her mother's advice on matters too personal to discuss with Mrs Vanderbilt or even with 'Zelle. Edwina remembered how lonely she herself had been at sixteen, unable to confide in Molly, too shy to consult Marjorie's mother. 'I feel so miserable', she told Patricia, '. . . being so far away and quite unable to discuss any little worries or problems you may be having. It is just at your sort of age one wants it and it's so difficult to work out things for oneself sometimes.'

At least Edwina was not anxious about the children's education. Foxcroft, the fashionable school suggested by Mrs Vanderbilt's daughter Grace, had been firmly turned down in favour of Miss Hewitt's establishment on 79th Street. The headmistress was English and the school unpretentious. Indeed, Patricia assured her parents, it was said to be 'rather like Miss Faunce's, in fact she knows her.' Mademoiselle Chevrier had inspected the curriculum, 'which sounds just right . . .'

Edwina Mountbatten

Edwina did not agree. She was happy for Pamela to take the standard subjects offered in the lower school but she did not want Patricia to waste time learning futile accomplishments that would be of no value in the post-war world. She should take a Business Course, 'particularly keep up your Typing and I want you to learn either Shorthand or better still Speedwriting which is simpler . . . It's also called SHORTSCRIPT. Then Book Keeping; Card Indexing; Double Entries etc'. These were subjects Edwina wished she had mastered herself. She was not over-ambitious. 'I am less interested in your being very competent in dealing with Banking, Taxation, Stocks and Bonds etc but of course it is very useful to know something of all of these.' Patricia should not be tempted to drop German for Spanish, which she could learn when she left school. 'Whoever wins the war there will still be many million Germans in the world and the language will always be useful and you know some already.' Modern English Literature, Current Events and History of Art were important. And, emphatically, *'Don't omit to keep up your Geography.'*

Miss Hewitt's was not like Patricia's school in London. The girls sat on the tables and called the headmistress 'Miss Hew'. Patricia was scandalized: 'Fauncey would faint.' There were no rules, 'so discipline is not what it could be'. However, she said, charitably, 'I think they behave very well, considering they're over here.' Patricia felt rather a fish out of water. She and Enid Paget, the other English girl in her year, blushed when the mistress scolded their classmates for going to the drugstore in the lunch hour, trying on lipstick and powder there, 'smoking like volcanoes *and* flirting with the bartenders!!! . . . Can you imagine it!' It was hard to mix unobtrusively with the rest. The press had printed various ingratiating paragraphs about what it called 'Great Britain's pre-eminent young refugees.' It was thought amazing that the Mountbatten girls should attend 'routine classes', more so that they should walk to them. 'They were seen the other day', gushed the *New York World*, 'weaving their way democratically through the noon day traffic at Madison Ave, and 54th St, unchaperoned.' Coverage of this sort made life awkward. On Patricia's first day 'a giantess came up to me and asked: "Are you Patricia Mountbatten?" so I said yes, and she said "I am Mimi McAdoo, my grandfather used to be Senator for California, of course he isn't now."'

Sometimes, Patricia told her mother, she felt like a ginger beer bottle whose cork was about to fly off. Fortunately 'Zelle managed to keep the girls away from Junior League dances, 'benefits' for Britain's War Effort and suchlike. (She had cleverly explained to Mrs Vanderbilt that the Mountbatten children were constitutionally debarred from these, because of their relationship to the royal family.) Patricia tried to make the best of their situation. She could not hide the fact that she and Pamela were homesick. One letter described a reconnoitring expedition to the docks. A policeman, on the lookout for saboteurs, had warned Mademoiselle Chevrier and her charges to keep away from the liners berthed alongside. 'I wish we could have got on one of the ships and gone home to you all', Patricia wrote wistfully, 'even as stowaways.'

At the beginning of August Edwina decided that she would go with Dickie and on the 15th the Mountbattens set off, he with his tin helmet, she with five dazzling necklaces, seven rings, six bracelets, assorted earclips and brooches, and the gold and enamel links Dickie had given her to wear with her uniform. Edwina needed her jewellery; at every stop life became less austere. 'Dazed by brilliant lights,' she wrote in her diary, when they landed in Lisbon: 'copious food including butter, fruit and meat!!' On the 18th they were in the Azores, on the morning of the 19th in Bermuda and that evening Dickie and Edwina were reunited with the children and 'Zelle in an apartment, borrowed from Mr and Mrs Dresselhuys, at the Plaza Hotel on Fifth Avenue. Fourteen months, three thousand miles and another world. 'Very warm in New York,' Edwina wrote in her diary, 'and excess of food, lights and general waste and frivolity rather upsetting.' The gaieties she had once enjoyed horrified her now: 'Their disregard of cost and extravagance quite shocks one . . . and one is out of tune with such shallowness and appalling high rate of living.' In a day or two she began to acclimatize. It was delightful to shop at well-stocked department stores, to spend a leisurely hour with the hairdresser and manicurist. There was no danger that Edwina might be more than momentarily seduced. A long weekend at Newport revived all her dislike of snobbery and greed, 'kind and hospitable tho' the people seem to be and anxious to give one a good time.'

Now that they had seen the children, the Mountbattens were anxious to get down to work. Dickie flew to Norfolk to see how *Illustrious* was getting on, Edwina called at the Washington headquarters of British War Relief, Bundles for Britain and the American Red Cross. When she saw the tour that had been planned for her, she was aghast. It was not so much the distance she was expected to cover, although this was bad enough. Three long trips – to Chicago and the north-west, California, and the east coast – would be killing. What frightened her was the list of important-sounding societies she had been invited to address. Her initiation took place at a meeting of the Newport Chapter of the Red Cross. It was the first time Edwina had delivered a lecture to a large gathering of strangers and she was nervous. All day, at cocktails, during lunch, watching afternoon tennis, her hands shook and her head ached. She felt more at ease when she got into her uniform and, once she had stood up and begun, she found to her astonishment that her voice was steady and her mind alert. Here, and in her next appearance at Southampton, on Long Island, Edwina could hardly fail, for her audiences were largely composed of enthusiastic and admiring women, Anglophiles all. The real test came when she spoke to the Executive Board of British War Relief, eighteen earnest businessmen, meeting at the Chase National Bank in New York. Having succeeded there, Edwina became less apprehensive. She never relaxed completely – unlike Dickie, she was not a natural speaker – but she discovered that by telling a story simply and directly she could hold her audience. Dickie made Edwina learn her speeches by heart, as he did himself; at their first rehearsal she watched in horror when he tore up the draft she had written out. He could not teach her all his tricks: how to catch the eye of an attentive listener, first in one part of the room, then in another, how to project her voice and use rhetorical devices – pauses, emphasis, repetition. Techniques like these needed years of practice. It did not matter. Edwina's large, myopic gaze, focusing nowhere, seemed to take in everyone at once. Her slender form, severely clad in black and white, held every eye; her crisp, clean delivery required no elaboration, for her story was dramatic enough by itself. All she had to do was to describe everyday conditions in wartime Britain. It was spell-binding.

Day after day, Edwina explained what life at home was like. In St Louis she addressed Junior Red Cross members at local schools, the County branch, a unit made up of Greek immigrants, a lunch for seven hundred people; 'by then I was a rag.' Meetings in Chicago, Minneapolis, St Paul, Milwaukee, lunch with six hundred women in Detroit, a visit to the Packard plant to see marine engines being built, cocktails and dinner at the Country Club: 'All seemed rather drunk but very sweet otherwise.' After a week she was exhausted. Meanwhile Dickie played with the children, looked in on the Sperry laboratories and the Curtiss-Wright aeroplane plant, saw a little polo and a Marx Brothers film and gave the Overseas Press Club a fifty-minute talk on the war in Europe, more effective than hours of spouting by politicians. As Edwina flew in to Washington, he left on the transcontinental stratocruiser for Honolulu, where the Commander-in-Chief of the United States Pacific Fleet had invited him to visit the Pearl Harbor Yard and Naval Base. Bad weather delayed manoeuvres; Dickie filled in time with a lecture on the Battle of Crete, which he gave first to an audience of six hundred Army officers and then to a thousand from the Navy. At half past four on a wet, windy, pitch-black morning, he joined a visiting British destroyer squadron in a mock onslaught on Pearl Harbor. ('I flew plane'.) Dickie was not impressed by what he saw. He asked his hosts why their aeroplanes were drawn up in lines on the airfield: 'If you're attacked, you'll lose them all'.

Edwina's reception in Washington was overwhelming: 'Bands, Representatives of State Department etc and crowds round the platform in the street.' It was the same in Philadelphia: 'Interviews and photos. Lunch of about 1000 . . . Shook hands and talked to hundreds.' From there she returned to New York. Carola Rothschild, a family friend, had presented Patricia with funds for a ten-day trip across the country and on 26 September she set off with Edwina for California. When they reached San Francisco Patricia began to see how hard her mother worked. Lunch with the presidents of every voluntary committee; visits to the local headquarters of the Red Cross and British War Relief; an address to hundreds of volunteers, whom Edwina afterwards met at tea; cocktails at one house; dinner at another; coffee with the bigwigs of the *San Francisco Chronicle*, a performance of *The Forbidden City*; bed at two-thirty in the morning. The following day was the same, plus an afternoon trip down the coast to see redwood trees and orange groves. In Los Angeles the whirlwind began again: a huge Red Cross rally, dinner with film producers and stars, late bed. Next morning Edwina sat by the pool, fitting in radio broadcasts between swims. Patricia was impressed.

It would have been a pity if her holiday had been entirely filled with rallies and receptions. Things looked up when Dickie flew in from Honolulu. During Edwina's visit to the Los Angeles Red Cross, father and daughter toured the Warner Studios; while Edwina sat by the pool, discussing War Relief with a local organizer, Dickie and Patricia swam in it. Edwina was not all earnestness: 'Spencer Tracey and Edward Arnold and Robert Taylor lunched . . . very nice.' But pleasure made her feel unsettled; it was shrewd of the Fairbankses to include a group of War Relief workers in the dance they gave in the Mountbattens' honour. Dickie was delighted to find that half a dozen British Naval officers had been invited too, although that, for him, was not the chief attraction. 'Sat next to Norma Shearer', he wrote happily in his diary. 'Danced a lot with Rita Hayworth.' The next leg of Edwina's tour took her to the north-east to speak in various cities, ending with a huge Red Cross luncheon at the Waldorf Hotel in New York. Lady Limerick was there, in the middle of her own trip, and she and Edwina were able to compare notes. It was clear to both of them that many people they had met were surprised, even shamed, by America's continued neutrality. Edwina said as much to the President when she and Dickie stayed with the Roosevelts at the White House.

The Mountbattens were now based at Mrs Vanderbilt's mansion at 640 Fifth Avenue. Edwina made an effort to see Patricia and Pamela; indeed, they spent more time with her than they had done at home. 'To the Rodeo' she wrote in her diary. 'Visited Miss Hewitt's . . . then had Ice Cream . . . all went to see *A Yank in the RAF.*' Edwina was determined to fit in all she could. After a day in Boston, for instance, she flew back to New York in the evening, 'more dead than alive', changed, dined and went out with Dickie, Nell Cosden and Victor Proetz to *Hellzapoppin'*, ending with supper at a boogie-woogie club downtown. At half past midnight she boarded a train for Boston, where she was to start a tour of towns in New Hampshire; 'so tired I could cry.'

Edwina believed that she should be seen at her husband's side. On their first trip to America together in 1924, Dickie had been left to his own devices while she tore around in fast cars and motor yachts. Now the Mountbattens performed as a pair, he in his white uniform, she in her black, the warrior and the healer. Onlookers saw a happy, affectionate couple, each supporting the other. Those who did not know them assumed that they had a perfect marriage. One admirer wrote to Edwina to say that she had seen them in a train, sitting among their luggage, '. . . at ease, not smoking or fidgeting, and seeming so much in harmony . . .' (It was a mirage; on that day they had not yet left England.) Thousands of people believed this fairy tale. One was Dickie. At last his marriage seemed to have become the partnership he had always wanted. 'I personally feel closer to you now,' he told Edwina, 'than at any time during the previous ten or twelve years.' This was in a letter written in mid-October 1941. 'I have been so immensely proud of the really wonderful show you have put up here and know that all the family – not only Mama but the King and Queen and George etc – will all be equally proud of all you have done when I tell them.' The awkward 'I personally' is revealing. Dickie knew he could not speak for Edwina. She played her part marvellously – but she remained aloof. Two months' touring was demanding enough; living up to her role as her husband's inseparable companion was a strain. She was saved by a message from London.

Dickie had expected to stay in the United States until November, when he was to sail home with *Illustrious*. On 7 October, word came that he was to go straight away to the British Embassy in Washington. He was required in London at once. The Prime Minister had decided that Mountbatten was the man to revive Combined Operations, the mixed air-naval-military raiding and landing force, of which he had great hopes. Dickie went back to New York to talk things over with Edwina. He did not want to give up *Illustrious* but Churchill had sent for him and he could not refuse. He left New York on 21 October. For the first time in his life, he told Edwina, he was apprehensive about a new job. 'What do I know of soldiering? I wish I had my dear old *Illustrious*. I know I'd have done marvels with her!!!' At least Dickie was still able to smile at himself. His medals and orders had been packed in his trunk, instead of the suitcase he had with him. If the ship bringing them home were torpedoed, they would go to the bottom. 'I brought them all over . . . as I was told decorations were worn at the White House and you know I can never resist my lovely ribbons etc!!!' Urgent wires were despatched to Edwina, asking her to retrieve them. '*What* a laugh you can have at my expense . . .'

On 23 October Dickie reached Lisbon, where he spent the night at the British Naval Attaché's house, 58 Rua Sacramenta A Lapa. Edwina would see, he said ruefully, that it was 'a Rabbital address . . .' For at that very moment, as Dickie wound his way back to England, Bunny was setting off for America to take up an intelligence job with William Stephenson at British Security Co-ordination headquarters in New York. One of Dickie's last acts before leaving had been to arrange a passage for Bunny in a battleship that was sailing to Bermuda. He was not sure why he went to such trouble. 'We should dislike each other but somehow I can't help having a genuine fundamental affection for the old Rabbit.'

Edwina's work in the United States was done. Thousands had heard her speak, hundreds had shaken her hand. Her words had been printed in newspapers, journals and magazines, her photographs, in uniform and out of it, had appeared in every publication, from mimeographed parish newsheets to American *Vogue*. She was drained. Now she did everything for which there had been no time before: lunch with Salvador Dali, who had painted her portrait five years before, shopping with 'Zelle and Patricia, a meal at the Automat ('Excellent for 1.20 for two'). She took 'Zelle and the children to Radio City to see Fred Astaire's new film, *You'll Never Get Rich*, and watched ice-skating on the rink in front of the Rockefeller Center. One morning the four of them caught a bus and went exploring. They lunched in a small town fifty miles from New York and swung along the homeward road together until the bus caught up with them. The children never forgot this happy time. Their mother was relaxed and amusing; she seemed to prefer dining upstairs to going out with her friends. This was true. Edwina was tired of being on parade.

A cable came from Dickie, saying that he had arrived safely in London, and, in the same hour, there was another from Bermuda, to tell Edwina that Bunny would be in New York at lunch-time. The children fell back into second place. A little holiday with discreet friends in South Carolina, a day or two at Hot Springs (risky, for Mrs Vanderbilt was there for her cure), and Edwina and Bunny returned to New York. They did not dare go about alone together. Patricia and Pamela were their chaperones at *How Green is My Valley*, 'Zelle and the children escorted them to *Weekend in Havana* at the Roxy. Dickie had asked Edwina to be discreet; her behaviour was irreproachable. On her last evening in New York, when she and Bunny wanted to be by themselves, she scrambled eggs for them both at his flat in the Beverley. Late that night she caught the train to Canada.

One last effort and the tour would be over. 'Excepting for leaving the children and the Rabbit,' Edwina told Dickie, 'I long for good old London and Broadlands and the dogs.' ('It will be lovely seeing you again', she added considerately.) She had a heavy programme, made worse by her hosts' habit of slotting in extra engagements as she went along. When Edwina got to Toronto, she learnt that before her first official appointment, a St John Inspection at Hamilton, she was to visit a Canadian minesweeper and meet the local War Savings Campaign Committee. She collapsed into bed at two in the morning. Next day she had five inspections, with as many speeches, and then a dinner party, 'Caught the train to Ottawa at 1 a.m. Nearly dead!!!' She had been given two rest days – but these were not without stress. Queen Mary's sister-in-law, Princess Alice, Countess of Athlone, had invited Edwina to stay at Government House and she knew that she had to be on her best behaviour. 'The Family', certainly the womenfolk, watched keenly. Her Excellency told Queen Mary that they had all found Edwina improved: 'I think that she is a hard worker and clever, tho' one always feels that she has a hard streak in her character. But she certainly charmed everyone here and was more than nice with all the Old Trouts. This war has brought out a lot of good in all kinds of people one imagined merely butterflies and selfish ones at that.' Princess Alice was not the only one with a critical eye. 'The Athlones are very charming as usual', Edwina reported to Dickie, '. . . all seems very pre-war down to the 6 course meals and plentiful footmen!!'

The Canadian tour was the worst yet. Edwina covered enormous distances, in freezing weather, backwards and forwards across different time zones. From Ottawa she flew sixteen hundred miles to Winnipeg. Seven engagements in twenty-four hours, a bumpy journey to Toronto, landing at three o'clock in the morning, three hours' rest, an eight o'clock start for Montreal . . . by this time she could have given her speeches in her sleep. In Quebec, her hosts asked her to deliver her remarks in French as well as English. When Edwina returned to New York, she could hardly stand.

She had applied for a passage to England at the end of November, on a Clipper that was going via Bermuda and the Azores; now that her mission was finished, she told the British Minister, people at home might think she was staying away from the war. Permission to travel was given and arrangements made, not just for Edwina but for Pamela as well. The Mountbattens had agreed to compromise on the question of bringing the girls home. Patricia had only half a year to go before her final examinations at Miss Hewitt's but Pamela was at a stage where she could easily move back into her English school. She was bored and irritable, for she did not like being cooped up at 640 Fifth Avenue. Bad weather delayed the flight. Edwina was jumpy. 'Dined with B. at the Mayan Restaurant. Back after to 640 to talk. Very sad and depressed.' At three o'clock in the morning of 26 November she made herself go to bed, rising two and half hours later to leave for the airport. Patricia and 'Zelle came to La Guardia to say goodbye. The journey home was long, with a five-day pause in the middle while Edwina waited in Lisbon for a 'priority connection'. At last, on 1 December, she secured a place on a flight to Bristol, leaving Pamela at the British Embassy until a passage could be got for her.

In London Edwina found pea-soup fog, bone-chilling damp, and Dickie, spilling over with pride and enthusiasm. Everyone he met had told him what a success his wife's tour had been. They were right. Those who had heard Edwina could not fail to understand what Britain was up against. Her mission could not have been better timed. On 7 December Japan attacked the American Fleet at Pearl Harbor. A week after Edwina came home, the United States entered the war.

CHAPTER TWENTY-TWO

The Bombshell

Five months earlier, Edwina had been shocked at the contrast between England and America. When she came home, it was even harder to adjust. Dim lights struggled feebly against the fog that seeped in on dark December evenings. Derelict houses were boarded up; there were gaps where buildings had once stood. Weariness and misery lowered Edwina's resistance: as soon as she returned she developed a streaming cold. She missed Bunny. He had asked her to look out his spare uniform; she wanted to send his favourite soap and tobacco in the parcel. 'Shops empty of goods', she wrote despairingly, '. . . No paper or boxes and very little choice'.

Edwina turned back to the piles of letters, draft reports, minutes of missed committee meetings. It was impossible to relax at home: 'Endless Christmas cards etc', 'Molly Mt. T . . . full of the usual moans'. One bad day followed another. First came the Japanese attack on Manila, Honolulu and Malaya. Angie Laycock's husband, Bob, was reported missing. On 9 December Dickie retired to bed with 'flu; Edwina spent a gloomy evening with Pamela McKenna, visiting Courtauld's underground shelter. On the following morning *Repulse* and the *Prince of Wales* were sunk by Japanese bombers. Six hundred men were lost. There was no cheer at the end of the year: 'News bad . . . Hong Kong taken by the filthy Japs after a heroic struggle'. The second wallaby died at Broadlands.

Edwina survived by living from day to day, sustained by occasional pleasures: Pamela's return from Lisbon in mid-December; Noel Coward's birthday party; walks with the dogs at Broadlands; a visit to Windsor with Dickie's nephew, Philip. The two princesses dressed up in the costumes they had worn for *Cinderella*, the family Christmas pantomime. Dickie got better. Nothing could squash him for long. Bob Laycock reappeared, safe and well. *Kelly* also had a sort of resurrection. Mountbatten had told her story to Noel Coward, who turned it into a film. Dickie could not have been more pleased. The script? Here were his own speeches to the crew. Problems with the Admiralty? He wheeled Noel in to see the First Lord and the Minister of Information. The cast? When Noel was stuck for plausible-looking extras, Dickie rounded up off-duty sailors from Portsmouth and convalescent patients from the naval hospital.

Dickie did not pine for *Illustrious*. 'You will note that I have developed my usual enthusiasm about this job,' he told Edwina in mid-November. He had been catapulted into the post of Adviser to the Chiefs of Staff of the three Services, with responsibility for the key aspects of Combined Operations: administration, planning, intelligence, training and communications. Commodore Mountbatten, as Dickie now became, surveyed his empire and wondered how to describe himself: 'SCPRPNR', he wrote in the back of his diary, or, perhaps, 'SCRP' or, possibly, 'PRSC'. None would do. He settled on 'CPC: Chief Planner, Coordinator of Cover, Security, Public Relations, Political Warfare, Records'. What did Churchill have in mind? '*Don't* be too influenced by the person who originated the idea of the job', Edwina had urged Dickie in a letter from America, 'and keep to the principles you discussed here'.

Dickie wanted a clear directive from No. 10. He got it. He was instructed to mount a series of raids on the coast of Occupied Europe, attacking with ever-increasing force, building up to his principal task, the preparation of a full-scale invasion. Young, keen and daring, Mountbatten was just the man for the job, more so, certainly, than his predecessor, Sir Roger Keyes, his former Commander-in-Chief, now aged seventy. Replacing Sir Roger was not easy. He had been unimaginative but he was well loved. Not by all, for he had antagonized the Chiefs of Staff, who were suspicious of an organization that trespassed across Service boundaries and poached on their ground. At least Sir Roger had experience and seniority; Mountbatten lacked both. Dickie knew that he walked on eggshells. As he told Patricia, 'I seem constantly to be attending meetings with people I never in my life expected to sit at the same table with on duty' (off duty was a different matter, as the First Sea Lord, who had shot at Broadlands, understood) 'or taking the Chair at other meetings at which I always seem to be the youngest person in the room'. Needing friends, he imported his own. Ran Antrim joined the staff, Peter Murphy promised to help with propaganda, Harold Wernher took over procurement and Bobby Casa Maury was enlisted as head of intelligence. Robert

The Bombshell

Neville was unable to leave the Admiralty but Tom Hussey was already at Combined Operations, working on the experimental side. With these familiar faces round him, Dickie felt more secure. One offer of help was not taken up, Beaverbrook's suggestion that he should act as Mountbatten's patron in Whitehall. Dickie indicated that he preferred to fight his own battles. This did not go down well.

He worked hard; 'till 1 a.m. at office', 'With PM 11–12.30'. Long hours did not bother him, for this was fun. 'Inspected No 4 Commando & saw street fighting; . . . No 9 Commando . . . PT & wallscaling & attack . . .'; 'No 3 Commando . . . cliffscaling and wire crossing & boat pulling . . .' He watched smoke demonstrations and beach operations, examined assault ships and raiding craft. Within two months of taking over he had organized a small raid at Vaagso, off the Norwegian coast, the first operation jointly planned and executed by all three Services. 'Very successful', Edwina wrote in her diary, 'Dickie's 1st venture'. It could have been the title of a story for boys.

Edwina's work was less glamorous but equally taxing. Each day she and Nancie Lees dealt with countless reports that came in from hospitals, first aid posts and emergency centres across the country. Could the JWO find volunteers, medical equipment, clothing, bedding? Requests arrived from troops abroad and ships at sea. One crisis followed another. Lady Pound fell ill, so Edwina had complete charge of the Depot. At St John the President was taken to hospital and Edwina was asked to do her work as well. The staff at the JWO tried and failed to divert the flow of paper that streamed into the office. Half the night she sat reading, propped up against her pillows; each morning she arrived with a stack of draft comments and replies. She insisted on receiving people; to get rid of timewasters, she had a bellpush installed beneath the edge of her desk, so that an assistant could be summoned, with a pile of papers urgently needing Lady Louis' signature. Callers who had outstayed their welcome found themselves apologizing and making for the door. 'I seem to take on more and more things and to get caught in all sorts of horrors', she told Patricia. 'Friday night Robert and I went to a Red X and Aid for Russia Dance at the Polygon Hotel at Southampton!! during which proceeding I had to Auction (thru' a Microphone!) a box of Russian cigarettes presented by the Russian Ambassador. I rooked someone for £5-10-0-. Pretty good . . . And then I had to make a speech so it was hardly an evening of fun and laughter . . .'

Edwina Mountbatten

Few days were free from worry. The Mountbattens had always been hospitable and, although the scale of their entertaining was reduced, small parties were still held at Chester Street during the week. Seven or eight to dinner was not uncommon. Feeding everyone was a struggle. Edwina begged Patricia for cheese and 'anything sweet!' At Broadlands, Edwina told her, 'I've had to fall back on a tinned ham, (2 years old) to feed 6 guests. *Delicious* & better than a fresh one'. The house was freezing: 'We ran out of coke this week', Edwina reported in early February, 'so had no heating and no hot water. Our permit got held up and the weather was then so bad the horse-van could not deliver'. Getting to and from Broadlands became increasingly difficult. 'We are being cut off our Basic Petrol Ration', she wrote in March, '4 gallons a month . . . Quite right . . . everything is being tightened up beyond all measure.'

At weekends Edwina got down to Broadlands by train, taking a suitcase full of paperwork. Once there, she and Dickie tried to keep some time free for walks, a ride and letter-writing, but it was almost impossible. The first patients were now arriving from the Southampton General Hospital and as a rule Edwina spent at least half a day visiting the wards. Friends and relations squeezed into the Mountbattens' quarters: Aunt Victoria, Dickie's nephews, David and Philip, Peter Murphy, Paula Long, Robert Neville. 'We've got no Parlourmaid and no Kitchenmaid', Edwina told Patricia, 'and only a girl of 15 . . . so you can imagine the chaos'. Reinforcements appeared at Easter: 'a wonderful steward called Topliss . . . like a stage one; very keen but inclined to do fantastic things, never having been ashore in service at all'. The new arrival was surprised that the house in Chester Street was so cramped. When Pamela came to London for half-term, she and her dachshund shared a bedroom with Edwina and the Sealyhams, Mizzen and Jib; Philip slept on a camp bed in the drawing-room.

As the months passed, life became still harder. 'We're to be rationed for light and heating (on points)', Edwina told Patricia at the end of April. 'Enormous taxes are now put on Entertainment, Tobacco, Beer, Whisky etc and no one can put lace on undies, or pleats or more than 2 buttons on skirts!! I think we'll rise above it!!' Soap was rationed and it took hours to track down a bathing cap and a belt for Pamela's Girl Guide uniform. 'If any one thought of sending me 6 lipsticks', Edwina suggested to Patricia, 'Dorothy Gray Colour Brass Band I should be enchanted . . .' Other things too: 'a doz. little imitation blonde tortoiseshell hair combs or medium colour! Unprocurable here! Also some very fine black silk stockings (9½) either very fine *real* black or a fine gun metal colour. Nylon *and* ordinary, and a few ordinary *sun burn* colour ones'. Not all of these were for herself. Mizzen attacked all male dogs, ruining their owners' stockings.

Patricia was now eighteen. Her coming-out could not have been more different from her mother's. She took off with 'Zelle on a trip to Colorado by Greyhound bus, 'only $53 return and the best way of really seeing the country'. Mrs Vanderbilt was reduced to telling everyone how enterprising she thought they were. Edwina was pleased: 'just the sort of trip I would have loved . . . and after the war we must do some together!!' Picnics with students at the School of Mining in Denver were more fun than smart dances with the inarticulate heirs to East Coast fortunes. 'Did you lose your heart?' Edwina asked. 'I expect so, temporarily anyway!!' She was not inviting confidences and Patricia knew that it would be pointless to offer them. Edwina did not want to talk about emotions. She was too busy for reflection, too detached to give anything but practical advice. When Patricia went to Washington to dine and spend a night at the White House, her mother said nothing about the sort of welcome she could expect, observing only that Patricia should be sure to address her host as 'Mr President' and the formidable Eleanor as 'Mrs Roosevelt': 'I feel like Daddy giving you these instructions'.

Edwina's letters may have been superficial but at least they were frequent, and a note scribbled while she sat under the hair-drier at Elizabeth Arden was better than nothing at all. She wrote faithfully once a week, although the post generally arrived late and in the wrong order, for, rather than use the ordinary mail, which was held up by the censor, Dickie preferred to employ friends and acquaintances as couriers. The grander the messengers, the longer the delivery seemed to take: 'Daddy's special snails', Edwina called these postmen. Emissaries constantly came and went, now that America had entered the war. 'A fair amount of excitement here of course', Patricia reported, '. . . but nothing seems to have changed so far'. Air-raid alarms were tried out in New York but no bombs fell. In the spring of 1942 Patricia came home to join the WRNS, flying back with a detachment of American servicemen. At Paddington her parents were waiting on the platform. With a shriek of joy she threw herself into their arms.

Edwina Mountbatten

It was half a year since Patricia had seen her mother. Her father was less of a stranger, for they had spent a day together only three weeks before, while he was on a mission to America for the Prime Minister. Dickie had completely justified Churchill's confidence in his appointment. He had reorganized the structure of Combined Operations, streamlined procedures and brought training methods up to date. He invented new departments, labelled with new combinations of initials. Ingenious people were enlisted: J. D. Bernal, the crystallographer, and Solly Zuckerman, the biologist. Geoffrey Pyke was working on 'Habbakuk', a project to assemble a giant aircraft-carrier out of reinforced ice, 'Pykrete'. Nothing was too outrageous, although some innovations came to nothing, like the suggestion that lightweight body armour could be made by lining waistcoats with cellophane. Other inquiries turned out to be important: a major study on night vision, Zuckerman's work on anti-seasickness drugs, and on suitable ration packs for commandos. The team's most important contribution was a general one. The members of Mountbatten's brains trust taught their colleagues to ask precise questions and look for exact answers. How many bombs were needed to knock out an artillery battery? What sort of weapons caused the most casualties? Some said that Dickie had brought together a crew of subversives. (Evelyn Waugh lunched with Mountbatten, Bernal and Pyke and thought the place 'a nest of Communists'.) They were right. Orthodoxy was undermined, loose thinking jumped upon.

Dickie's greatest triumph was to mix the skills and resources of all three Services. Two operations pleased the Prime Minister: the capture of a German radar installation at Bruneval and the destruction of the dry dock at St Nazaire. In early March Churchill invited Mountbatten to lunch at Downing Street and announced that he was to be promoted from Chief Planner to Chief. He was to sit as fourth Chief of Staff and attend all meetings of the Chiefs of Staff Committee, as a full member, whenever major issues were on the agenda. To reflect the mixed nature of his responsibilities, he was to have the acting ranks of Vice-Admiral, Lieutenant-General and Air Marshal. The other Chiefs were not pleased. It was seven weeks before the new appointment was announced. Edwina was proud of Dickie's 'Triphibious Command', as she put it, although, trying to ensure that he did not become too pompous, she overdid her teasing. 'General Goering will be put into the shade', she said in a letter to Patricia, 'by his manifold ranks, uniforms and decorations and dramatic and theatrical position'. In fact, Dickie assured his daughter, he had not yet dared to kit himself out in an Army or Air Force uniform: 'I am at present too shy and plead insufficient coupons'. As for popular adulation, he knew the other Chiefs of Staff would not like it. 'Edwina and I went to the Albert Hall Pageant', he wrote in his diary in the week that his appointment was announced. 'Luckily Xuereb went wrong and we arrived late and went to the wrong box and thus escaped Mr Robertson's scheme of giving me a special public welcome'.

There was plenty of publicity to come. In the late summer Noel Coward had finished *In Which We Serve*, or, as Dickie always called it, 'the *Kelly* film'. On 27 September the Mountbattens took Patricia to the preview and the launching party at the Savoy. Dickie was thrilled. In the next three weeks he saw it twice more, once at a private performance for the King, the Queen and the Roosevelts in the Buckingham Palace air-raid shelter, once at a special showing at Combined Operations headquarters. Mike Wardell was there, reliving his own stomach-churning trip on board *Kelly*. One shot was of particular interest to him and the proprietor of his newspaper, the moment when a copy of the *Daily Express* for 1 September 1939 was shown floating in the sea. Its headline: THERE WILL BE NO WAR THIS YEAR. Beaverbrook was furious. This made him all the more suspicious of Mountbatten.

The 'stunt' at the Albert Hall was as much in Edwina's honour as in Dickie's, for her civil defence work in London was well known. At the beginning of July she was appointed to the highest post a woman could hold in the St John Ambulance Brigade: Superintendent in Chief of the Nursing Division. In addition to her duties in the Joint War Organization, the mobile units, rest centres, first aid and medical aid posts in the shelters, she was now responsible for organizing and supervising sixty thousand adult volunteers and ten thousand cadets. In the second half of 1942 she travelled constantly, visiting convalescent homes, blood transfusion centres, hospitals and ARP posts, seeing where volunteers and equipment were needed and ensuring that they were being properly used. She opened bazaars, presided at auctions, looked in at sales and exhibitions in aid of Wings for Victory, the Penny a Week Fund for Prisoners' Parcels, War Savings Committees and Salvage Weeks. She became expert at inspecting a Guard of Honour, murmuring the right words as she moved along the line, admiring medals, straightening insignia. She took the salute at Parades of Representatives of Voluntary Organizations, standing for hours, often in rain or a cold wind, as the ranks of nursing and ambulance staff filed past the reviewing stand. She sometimes thought she would not last the day. Visits to large towns and cities generally included a Civic Dance and, when she left, it was to drive miles to stay with people who were running local voluntary organizations and had advice to give or requests to pass on. Late into the night Edwina sat up in bed, drafting letters of thanks and making notes to remind herself of things she had promised to do: enquire about someone's missing son, speed up supplies for a hospital, suggest a name for inclusion in the Honours List.

Birmingham, Bristol, Weymouth, North and South Shields, Maidstone, Leicester, Newcastle, Chippenham, Hull, Beverley, Bridlington, Whitley Bay, York, Doncaster, Sheffield, Leeds, Bradford, Blackpool, Preston, Lytham St Anne's – all this in late 1942, plus five area conferences in Hampshire. There was so much to do at the office that Edwina was kept in London until the last minute. Dark, cold trains, jolting and noise made everything worse. After September 1942 the railway companies ceased to reserve seats in compartments. Nancie Lees was horrified, for she knew that, if necessary, Lady Louis would stand up all the way. Resourceful local officials came to the rescue. A seat was always kept.

By October Edwina was exhausted. Her only holiday had been a day or two at Broadlands with Bunny, who had come home briefly in mid-June. He was now working with Colonel Donovan, who was organizing American Intelligence at the Office of Strategic Services. (One of Bunny's first tasks had been to organize the opening of the locks on the safe at the German Embassy in Washington. There was nothing inside, except a set of keys to the safe at the British Embassy.) Edwina did not know how long it would be before she saw him again.

Two months later she had a bad blow. Her old friend Prince George, the Duke of Kent, had left his job at the Admiralty at the beginning of the war and now represented the RAF on ambassadorial missions for the King. In mid-August he had come to Broadlands for a night or two while he carried out a programme of local inspections. 'I loved my stay', he wrote afterwards, '. . . sorry about the chips on your door post!' On the 25th a flying boat in which the Duke was travelling flew into dense mist, crashed into the top of a Scottish hillside, slid

The Bombshell

down a slope and burst into flames. His family was devastated.

August had been a dreadful month. In the early hours of the 19th Combined Operations had launched a raid on Dieppe, after weeks of argument over tactics and support. In the short term it was a failure: a thousand men were killed, two thousand prisoners taken. Many of the dead and wounded were Canadians; Lord Beaverbrook, their fellow countryman, did not forget this. Intelligence had been lamentable and support from the RAF was cancelled at the last minute. Important lessons were learnt, at a high price. The next big operation, the Anglo-American invasion of North-West Africa in November 1942 (Operation Torch), was a success, another step forward toward the goal the Prime Minister had set, the invasion of Continental Europe.

Dieppe apart, for Dickie, 1942 had been a successful year, full of exciting schemes and bursts of achievement. Now he looked forward to a family holiday. Aunt Victoria, Robert Neville and Edwina's friend Esmé Howard-Johnson were to join the Mountbattens at Broadlands, the Laycocks and Bobby Casa Maury had been invited to a post-Christmas party at Chester Street. For Edwina it was all too much. Her tours had used up all her energy. In November and December she had spent many nights in London on duty at JWO headquarters, watching for incendiaries. Shopping for Christmas gifts and supplies had been another nightmare. General Marshall had brought a ham from America; Edwina was so anxious not to lose sight of it on the journey from London to Romsey that she left her suitcase on the train, with all the presents and her diary for 1942. 'Dined late at home', Dickie wrote in his journal on 29 December, 'row'. He did not realize what a strain Edwina's year had been. Recognition came when she received the CBE in the New Year Honours List. The euphoria lasted half a day. Then Edwina returned to the treadmill.

The first five months of 1943 were harder than any she had ever known. Friday 26 February was a typical London day. Edwina began by taking the chair at a meeting at Gas Industries House to discuss the Health Department Training Course for civil defence workers. 'Then rushed to an Overseas Selection Board and then 2 appointments . . . including one with General Hood, DGMS.' After lunch at Chester Street (the Chetwodes, the Harrimans, David Margesson and Mollie Buccleuch), Edwina went round to her office. At least she had no evening engagements: 'dined up in my room . . . exhausted'.

Dickie was worn out as well. In London he worked an eighteen-hour day and on top of this he tried to make a weekly trip to inspect stations under his command. In one two-day tour he gave sixteen speeches, 'nearly as much as Mummy seems to do', he told Patricia. The Prime Minister often summoned him late at night. 'Drove fast to Chequers', Dickie noted in his diary, '. . . Talked till 03.45'. A year of pressure had eaten away his resistance. At the beginning of April 1943, in the middle of a lecture to the staff course at Camberley, he began to feel feverish and weak. By evening he had a temperature of a hundred and three. He was taken to Broadlands and put to bed, with Aunt Victoria and Edwina in attendance, and a Surgeon Captain, who diagnosed pneumonia. After ten days he staggered up for an hour or so but it was another two weeks before he returned shakily to work.

This was just after Easter. Edwina had taken a week's leave, badly needed, and forced herself to refuse nearly all local meetings. The lawns were bright with daffodils and the flowering shrubs smelt sharp in the hot sun. 'The place looking lovely', Edwina wrote in her journal, although everything was untidy. Trees blown down in the spring gales still lay on the ground, desultory attempts at weeding could not keep the flowerbeds clear. In mid-April 'Zelle came home from America, in time for Pamela's fourteenth birthday, which they celebrated with a trip to the cinema in Southampton. Since there was no petrol, this was a lengthy outing. When the film finished, they waited for three and a half hours until Commander North could come to take them home.

A month back at work and Edwina was ragged again. 'Felt terrible all day', she wrote in her diary at the end of May, '. . . worked hard all the same . . .' Short breaks at Broadlands kept her going. She pottered in the walled garden and sat in the sun, chatting to Patricia, home on twelve hours' leave from HMS *Pendragon*. Each day Edwina walked to the farm to see the latest acquisition, two Suffolk Punches, magnificent chestnuts with enormous hooves. It was Robert Neville's idea that she should breed draught horses. When the war ended, he said, petrol would still be rationed, probably for ever. Since the great animals gave Edwina so much pleasure, Dickie and Patricia did not tell her that Robert was talking nonsense.

Broadlands was a solace but Edwina longed to travel. Dickie had got away to Casablanca at the beginning of the year, for a conference on the Allies' future strategy. 'Here I am', he wrote tactlessly, 'sitting by my verandah, a blue sky overhead & the sun streaming in'. Edwina had asked him to bring her some Chanel No. 5; alas, the troops had got there first and emptied all the shops. Edwina felt trapped and hated it. When the St John Ambulance Organization asked her to go to Northern Ireland, she jumped at the chance. Her tour followed the usual pattern: visits to hospitals, civil defence posts, Harland and Wolff's shipyard, seamen's clubs and the Red Cross, inspections, demonstrations, rallies and a pageant. On the seventh day she set off on an adventure of her own: a reconnoitring expedition to Classiebawn Castle, where, thirty-five years before, she had played on the beach and looked for shrimps in the pools. Wilfrid had closed the house in 1922, when Sligo became part of the new Republic of Ireland. He had never returned. The place now belonged to Edwina and, before she left England, she had asked for permission to travel to Eire to see it. For twenty years the only occupants had been mice and spiders. Edwina wandered through the house, across creaking floors, into deserted rooms. When evening came, she went down to the village and in the morning she turned back to England. Twenty-four hours and five changes of transport later, she was in London. Her excursion might have been a dream.

There was no time for nostalgia. Edwina's diary was full: a three-day trip to the West Riding in late June, inspections in the Midlands and East Anglia, Lincolnshire, Devon and Somerset. She had to make a speech in Trafalgar Square to mark the London Salvage Drive, visit the Seamen's Hospital at Greenwich, attend the Salute to China Rally at the Albert Hall, Mrs Churchill's Aid to Russia meetings and the Allied Nations Summer Fair. Nowadays her idea of a treat was high tea with boiled eggs, an early evening film, a small snack at Quaglino's, and no papers to deal with before morning.

From June to October she was happy, for shortly after her return from Ireland Edwina heard that Bunny was coming home. He arrived in London on 23 June and made his way to Chester Street. It was Dickie's forty-third birthday. 'We all three and Peter went to see *Sweet and Low*', Edwina wrote contentedly, 'and dined at home after'. For the next month she worked less hard, stopping at six o'clock to go to the theatre with Bunny. At weekends they went down to Broadlands. Bunny fished, Edwina read and gardened. 'Quiet evening', she wrote in her journal: 'Lovely and peaceful with Bun'.

For a good part of that time Dickie was away. 'Off on an overseas trip', Edwina wrote circumspectly in her diary, for she was breaking rules by mentioning his absence at all. He was in the Mediterranean, to observe the invasion of Sicily, Operation Husky. Three weeks after Dickie got home, he was off again, to a grand strategic conference with Churchill, Roosevelt and their Chiefs of Staff. 'Here we are in Canada', Dickie announced in his first letter from Quebec. He and his team were housed in Château Frontenac, a vast, mock-baronial hotel owned by the Canadian Pacific Railway. 'The food is wonderful', Dickie reported to Edwina, 'and we are all over-eating'. When Bunny turned up on a mission for Sir William Stephenson, Dickie made him an honorary member of the Combined Operations staff and put him in a bedroom temporarily vacated by Professor Bernal. 'I think he is enjoying being in the midst of this weird party', Dickie observed, 'and it is lovely having him as I can discuss my terrific problems with him . . .'

It was fortunate that Dickie had a confidant at his elbow. 'Such a fantastically staggering thing has happened', he wrote on 28 August, '. . . I hardly know how to tell you'. With the agreement of their Chiefs of Staff, the Prime Minister and the President had asked Dickie to go as Supreme Allied Commander to South-East Asia: 'that is pretty well everything west of Saigon'. Dickie had been anxious to return to sea; that hope was now dashed but there were compensations. 'It is the first time in history that a naval officer has been given supreme command over land and air forces', he explained, and (an after-thought, in different coloured ink), 'It will mean another stripe'. When he had recovered from his surprise, Dickie inquired about terms and conditions. 'I understand that the British and American Naval, Military and Air Commanders in Chief will be placed under my orders as well as all the Chinese forces in my new theatre'. Edwina smelt trouble. 'You must be having a fascinating time', she wrote to Dickie, as he set off to Washington to discuss his new job, 'but for God's sake do something about the political set-up, otherwise all is useless'. She was right. It took almost a year to sort out the structure of South-East Asia Command, twelve months in which time and energy were wasted in internal argument.

Dickie knew his task would not be easy. As well as leading the fight against the Japanese, he would have to cope with the Commanders-in-Chief of the Allied Land Forces and Allied Air Forces, with Auchinleck, Commander-in-Chief in India, Wavell, the Viceroy, Generalissimo Chiang Kai-shek, the Chinese head of state, and General

The Bombshell

Stilwell, 'Vinegar Joe', Commander of Chinese troops in Burma and Assam. 'The more I think of this job the more it frightens me', Dickie told Edwina. He would need her more than ever. 'I've got so used to leaning on you and hearing your brutally frank but well deserved criticisms! But above all you have been such a help with all the people I have to deal with'. It would be marvellous if she could take over the organization of St John Ambulance in India. 'Wouldn't it be romantic to live together in the place we got engaged?' 'PS', he added tactfully: 'Please don't think I underestimate the importance of your job. I am just being a very selfish husband who'd like to have his wife with him!' Edwina did not intend to join her husband in South-East Asia. She was happy to help him prepare. People Dickie needed to see were invited to lunch at Chester Street: the Wavells; General Wingate, who had been running expeditions behind the lines in Burma; Dr Wellington Koo, the Chinese Ambassador in London. At weekends Edwina entertained Dickie's future colleagues at Broadlands: General Pownall, who was to be the Supreme Commander's Chief of Staff, and General Wedemeyer, his American deputy. But it was unthinkable that she should abandon her own work.

Edwina did not come to Northolt to say goodbye. She remained at home with Bunny. This was his last weekend at Broadlands, for he was going out to South-East Asia too, to do intelligence work for Pownall. 'It will be grand having the Rabbit to help', Dickie had observed enthusiastically, 'even at rather a distance on someone else's staff'. Grand for him but not for Edwina, although Dickie had sportingly assured her that letters for Bunny could always be sent in the Supreme Commander's bag. Bunny left in mid-October. The next two months were difficult. Air-raids had begun again. The weather was icy, afternoons dark. In London shops closed at four o'clock. First Edwina felt cold and shivery, then hot and feverish. She retired to bed, doped herself and woke up with 'flu. She refused to go on sick leave.

Every day she was on parade at some official gathering; between meetings she was working with Irving Berlin on a fund-raising show at the London Palladium, *This Is The Army*, in aid of British Service charities. He had also given St John all the rights in *My British Buddy*, a composition he sang himself, movingly if not tunefully. This caused complications. The publishers objected and, when they were overruled, declared that paper rationing prevented them from printing copies. Edwina protested; if necessary, she said, she would ask the Prime Minister to release extra supplies. She won.

A procession of visitors looked in at Chester Street for lunch, tea, drinks or supper. Wedemeyer, Somerville, General Macleod, Commander de Coustabadie, Irving Asher, Admiral Jerram, Admiral Holland, General Grimsdale – all knew they were welcome to drop in when they were in London. They brought letters from Dickie, the latest instalment of his diary, presents for the family ('a cigarette lighter made by a prisoner of war, 3 little Dog padlocks from Agra with an amusing patent key'). He urged his colleagues to call, for he wanted to know what Edwina thought of them. She was not always encouraging. 'I also saw Sir Horace Seymour', she wrote, after one visit. 'He said very nice things about you tho' I thought him slightly gaga and permanently dazed. It may however have been his "off-day".' She did not hesitate to pass on compliments. '. . . You've put new energy and hope into all those serving and working in your part of the world', she said, in a letter sent at the end of December. 'I hear it on all sides which is very nice . . .' No more waspish remarks, written by a wife who felt jealous and excluded. Now that Edwina had achieved a reputation for herself, she could admit that she was proud of her husband.

She told Dickie little about her own struggles. When Italy declared war on Germany in mid-October, Edwina helped set up an Italian Relief Unit, although its efforts were hampered by the fact that the enemy still controlled Rome and two-thirds of the country. The Allied invasion of Sicily and the South meant more work for the Joint War Organization's Wounded and Missing Department and for the office that assisted returning prisoners of war. Edwina also continued her regional tours. At the beginning of December, only half-recovered from 'flu, she began a two-day marathon in Lancashire ('Engine breakdown and arrived 2 hours late. Hull Police car took me to Rowley . . .') and two days later she was in Worcestershire, coming back exhausted to Broadlands at the end of a difficult week. As the year drew to a close, the generator at Broadlands began to pack up. 'The hell of a time with the water, light and heating', Edwina said afterwards. 'One could hardly see at night or operate in the theatre or keep warm'. She did not tell Dickie about it until the cause was discovered and the problem solved.

There was no point in worrying Dickie with what Edwina called

The Bombshell

'Sagas'. Instead, she gave him family news. Aunt Victoria and Baroness von Buxhoevden had arrived for Christmas; they had required military permits to come through an encampment of American troops in the Park. Peter Murphy joined the family for the holidays, Marjorie and David came by train from Wherwell. Every letter had a sentence about Patricia, who was now based at HMS *Tormentor* at Warsash. She was working hard and looking well, with plenty of beaux. Edwina was encouraging but did not pry; her letters to Dickie indicated that his adored elder daughter was popular and happy but that so far there was no danger that she would lose her heart.

'I feel that frequent and full letters are the only way that family life & love can be kept alive', Dickie declared. He was so keen for his family to know exactly what he was doing that he scattered copies of his SEAC diary like leaves. The account was frank. He had tried to strike a balance, he said. 'If I don't make it fairly full and honest, it will be of no interest. If it is too indiscreet and any one of you quotes it you'll get me shot!' Edwina implored Dickie not to send sensitive material to Patricia and Pamela, who had nowhere safe to keep it: 'It would get *all* concerned into trouble if anything happened and is not fair. Also please remember that Aunt V. is terribly indiscreet these days and quite forgets the things she should *not* mention'. Dickie admitted that Edwina was right, although his solution only made the problem worse. In future, he said, he would keep two diaries, one secret, the other extra-secret. Edwina had to keep track of both.

Dickie wanted to tell Edwina all his difficulties and worries. There were many, for his plans were constantly frustrated. He had proposed an operation to cut Japanese communications in eastern Burma; the Chiefs of Staff replied that this was premature. He was denied the troops and matériel he needed. When he asked for a five-fold increase in the number of parachutes manufactured in India, he was informed that this would divert cloth from the civilian market, as well as upsetting the economy. He wanted to improve the railway, with the help of American experts, so that greater tonnages of supplies could be carried to China and to British forces in Burma; this was opposed by the Indian Government on the grounds that American methods would not work and, if they did, would be inflationary. Refusing to be intimidated by economists' arguments, Dickie asked Peter Murphy to consult experts at home, all sworn to secrecy. Peter spoke to Maynard Keynes and Professor Harold Laski and recommended that

Dickie should leave well alone. No progress was made on parachutes but, with the help of Churchill, who worked on the Viceroy, it was at least agreed that American engineers should be brought in to manage the railway.

Morale was a major problem. Mountbatten's troops thought of themselves as the Forgotten Army. Forgotten? Their Commander told them that no one had even heard of them. Together, they would change that. They were perfectly able to defeat the Japanese, he declared, to fight during the monsoon, to beat malaria and dysentery. Mountbatten put heart into an army that had been abject and defeatist. He travelled whenever he could, often at great risk, calling at outposts, inspecting hospitals, visiting the front line. He told the men that reinforcements and supplies were on their way; he mentioned conversations with the Prime Minister and the King. Those who heard him understood at once that their Commander had support from the highest quarters and that he would not be slow to mobilize it.

The Mountbattens were glad to see the end of 1943. On 31 December Dickie lay in bed in Delhi, recovering from 'flu and thinking over the frustrations of the last few months. 'Am going to fight hard with what's left', he wrote defiantly in his diary. Edwina saw the New Year in with mulled wine at the Buists': 'Awful night only getting to bed at 2.30 a.m. and then having poor Mizzie with a choking fit . . .' It was a distressing beginning. The next twelve months were worse.

'Everything here is *very* grim', Edwina told Dickie in mid-April, 'and more depressing than I can say. People overtired and terribly over-worked'. Tempers were short and meetings difficult: '. . . my first Women's Advisory Committee . . . all day from 11.30 till 6'; 'the VAD Standing Committee which was a trial'. It was a relief to leave London on tours of inspection. In late February Edwina spent three days in Liverpool, staying for two nights with Hugh Sefton, formerly Hugh Molyneux, and his wife, Foxie Gwynne, at Croxteth. 'Can you beat that!!' Edwina asked Dickie, 'First time I have been there. Better late than never!!' The house was icy, she said sweetly. 'I don't think I should have made a very good chatelaine!!' In mid-April she had two long days in Cumberland, returning shattered on a train that left Carlisle at half past one in the morning. A month later she was in Lancashire and Derbyshire, at the beginning of July she spent two days in the Isle of Man. Requests poured into the office: could Lady Louis visit Civil Defence posts at the Croydon Engineering Works, attend meetings at the Ministry of Health to discuss post-war policy, speak at ceremonies to 'Salute the Soldier'? 'I hate doing these extra things', Edwina told Dickie in early March, 'but it's almost impossible to refuse to do *any*'.

This alone would have been a heavy load. There was also the family to look after. In the early summer Germany began sending pilotless V-weapons over London and other large cities. Aunt Victoria was no longer safe at Kensington Palace but she could not come to Broadlands, for the Park was full of troops waiting to cross the Channel and new regulations had come into force, preventing 'inessential movement' in and out of restricted areas. Appeals to the Home Office and the War Office got nowhere. Edwina confided in the Queen, who invited Dickie's mother to come to Windsor. Aunt Victoria was grateful to Edwina for arranging the move. 'You are indeed a true daughter to me, my dear', she told her. 'The K & Q are most friendly . . . We have lunch, tea and dinner together and the rest of the time I can do as I like so that I have not the unpleasant feeling of being in anybody's way. I have not lived in the castle for years and enjoy going about the grounds. The alterations', she declared, having thought about it, 'are mostly real improvements'.

Managing Broadlands was an increasing struggle. Menus were repetitious and boring, although Irving Berlin enlivened the store cupboard with a present of Coca-Cola and tinned pineapple. Brinz saved sugar and margarine to make a cake for Patricia's twentieth birthday and Edwina proudly took it over to Hamble. One sadness was the death of Mrs Lankester, who had been taken into Broadlands Annexe for an operation and had collapsed just as Edwina thought she was beginning to recover. Her loss left a huge gap in the staff: 'I can't think what we shall do as she was the only person who knew where anything was . . .' There were others on whom Edwina had to keep an eye: Nurse Harrison, who was in Bournemouth, under the flight path of the pilotless bombs; Molly, who did not understand that on Friday nights, after a killing week in London, the last thing Edwina wanted was to drop in for a drink at Alresford. Then there was Mary. She had decided to marry again and, as before, looked to Edwina to steer her through. For her new husband, Mary had selected Lord Delamere, whose family owned thousands of acres near Lake Naivasha in Kenya. Edwina held Mary's hand protectively at the Caxton Hall Registry Office and after the ceremony gave her a wedding breakfast at Chester Street. This time Mary really appeared to be settled. She adored Tom Delamere, who seemed affectionate and reliable. Moreover, unlike his two predecessors, he had ample funds of his own.

The wedding was one bright spot in a lonely and difficult year. Now and again Edwina was cheered by some new experience: General Eisenhower had her to dinner ('full of charm and tremendous vitality . . . it was nice of him to ask me in the middle of all his headaches'); the Prime Minister invited her to see the underground War Rooms, to which the War Cabinet retired when it was too risky to remain in No. 10. 'Winston very sweetly told Colville his secretary to take me to the Map Room', Edwina told Dickie, 'and show me all your areas and give me a rough idea of the operations . . . *what* country and what a vast area'. On one of the SEAC charts she traced the old Burma road from Lashio to Kunming: 'it helps in picturing the enormous mountains and denseness of jungle, the hell of an area to fight in'. Her greatest boost was the news of the Allied invasion of Normandy, which began on 6 June, an effort that owed a great deal to plans and equipment devised by Dickie and his team at Combined Operations. Now he received a congratulatory cable, sent jointly by Churchill, General Marshall, Field Marshal Smuts and the Chiefs of Staff. What pleased him most, however, was Edwina's praise.

At last things were moving, in Europe at any rate. In Dickie's part of the world progress was almost imperceptible. His letters showed how desperate he was. At the beginning of 1944 his planners devised a scheme to attack the Japanese from the south. In February it was rejected. Churchill was keen but refused to overrule the Chiefs of Staff, who were not. Their American counterparts also opposed the plan, in part because they had been got at by a second team which Stilwell had disloyally sent to Washington to undermine Mountbatten's case. Dickie felt abandoned on all sides. He was desperately lonely. If Edwina would not come out, perhaps Patricia could be transferred to SEAC? He wrote to Sybil Cholmondeley, a Chief Officer in the WRNS, who spoke to Edwina. She was angry, shocked to think that Dickie should appear to be seeking favours. The Prime Minister had been criticized by people who said special arrangements had been made for his daughter: 'Patricia would be the first to be filled with horror if she thought anything was being done that could be thought to come into that category'. The first thing, Edwina said, was to see if Patricia could be persuaded to try for an officer's commission. 'These days', she complained, forgetting her own frivolous youth, 'girls have no drive or ambition'.

Fortunately Dickie had Bunny to confide in. Since the two men got on so well, Edwina had suggested that her husband might speed up her lover's correspondence: '. . . please put B.'s letters *in* your envelope just with Edwina on wherever possible as I feel it's safer'. Peter Murphy had also come to SEAC for a short visit, insinuated into Dickie's staff as a representative of the Political Intelligence Department of the Foreign Office. He installed himself in Mountbatten's headquarters, 'full of groans at how awful India is', Dickie reported. 'The fact that he lies in his very beautiful garden getting sunburnt & is stuffing himself with eggs and bananas he seems to discount!' Peter was not the only person to dislike what Dickie called the 'social and political atmosphere' of Delhi. Ceylon had been suggested as an alternative and in mid-February Peter and Bunny went off to have a look at it. The island was the loveliest place in the world, they said; two months later SEAC headquarters moved to Kandy.

In early February the Japanese had invaded Assam, hoping to cut communications between the Fourteenth Army and Stilwell's Chinese forces and to establish a foothold from which to move further into India. In three weeks' hard fighting the British held their ground, eventually repelling the enemy and killing more than half the invading force. 'You can imagine what a load it is off my mind to have our first big battle', Dickie told Edwina. A fortnight later he had a setback. He was driving along a jungle track when the front wheel of his Jeep pushed aside a sharp bamboo, which sprang back and hit his left eye. To save his sight, his eyes were bandaged and he was forbidden to read, write or travel until his wound was healed. This was bad news. The Japanese were besieging the garrison at Imphal, key to an important railhead and supply depot near the Indian-Burmese border. The relief operation was being co-ordinated at General Slim's headquarters and Dickie wanted to be on the spot. After five days, half-blind and in great pain, he insisted on returning to work.

Dickie tried to reassure Edwina. There was no long-term damage, he told her, and meanwhile a secretary typed his letters and his reading was done for him by a team of friends. She could tell at once that he was in low spirits. Dickie was worried about his eye and desperately anxious about Imphal. He was about to lose Peter, who had to return to London. Some of Mountbatten's colleagues thought him a menace but Dickie had found him a grand help. 'He is a great social success . . .', Dickie added, 'and is lunching with the Wavells today in a Guards tie!' Bunny was going back to Washington. 'The Rabbit and I parted very nearly in tears', Dickie told Edwina; '. . . we used to ride together every evening when I could get away & used to talk & talk & talk. I always thought I'd get to like him very much once I really knew him & when he was with us you will agree that I didn't get much chance of seeing him alone!!' Before Bunny left, Edwina sent him, care of Mountbatten, a grateful letter and a vial of bath oil. Bunny was such a sweet person, she declared in a covering letter addressed to Dickie, 'and has I think an exceptionally good brain'. Her husband did not go quite as far as this. 'I must say he has a fine straightforward character', he replied judiciously, 'and I can quite understand why you are so fond of him . . . You might send me a bottle of bath essence one day!!'

'I wish it were permissible to have wives out', Dickie sighed, in a letter to Edwina in early May. 'I could and would unload a lot on you – but I'd probably only seem irritable again, which I'd hate to do with you. It isn't overwork – I do far less hours than in London – it's just a constant strain'. Edwina knew that Dickie was having a difficult time. 'My hair has gone visibly greyer', he told her, 'my middle-aged spread is increasing, I get tired fairly easily . . .' He still slept well but unremitting stress had taken all the pleasure out of his job. 'Any fun there was in having a large house, many ADCs and servants, aeroplanes, special trains, motor cars and horses, I really had as a youngster, thanks to you, darling; & so it's poor compensation for the hellish constant strain of it all'. Now that Bunny and Peter had gone, he had few people with whom he could relax. 'I am surrounded by the staff & just talk shop'.

He had all Edwina's sympathy. 'People really don't know (even the Press) whether we are attacking in Burma or defending in India!' she said. 'The High Ups do, but not the man in the street and none of the terrific Geographical obstacles have ever been made clear.' She tried to keep Dickie's spirits up by reminding him of his good fortune in having such a loyal team. 'Now *nice* Bourne is'; 'Your nice General Wheeler called in to see me last night . . . full of your praises and he seems another great supporter and I should think a very able man as well. You certainly are particularly lucky with your US colleagues . . .' General Pownall, Mountbatten's Chief of Staff, was, Edwina thought, 'a real pearl . . . so sound and understanding and I should think extremely evenly balanced'. Admiral Fraser, who succeeded Somerville as Naval Commander-in-Chief in September 1944, she considered charming 'and I should think a great asset to your command. He appeared so well balanced and very unconventional and broadminded and with a grand sense of humour. He said he remembered you as the best Sub he ever had and so felt you are probably an equally good Supreme Commander'. All this helped. So did Edwina's assurances that the Prime Minister understood what Dickie was trying to achieve. 'You certainly have Winston at the back of you', she wrote, when Dickie was at his lowest point, 'and he is tremendously loyal and appreciative, which means a lot'.

She also gave practical assistance. As soon as he arrived in the East, Mountbatten had made a point of inspecting as many military hospitals as he could. His report was alarming. Facilities were often dreadful, staff in pathetically short supply. He had begged the War Office for seven hundred nurses; none was sent. By the beginning of 1944 he was frantic. Could Edwina do anything? 'I realize what a monumental task I am asking you to undertake', he told her, but this was the sort of challenge she liked. He should send her an official signal and when it came she would speak to the Matron of the Queen Alexandra's Nursing Corps. Trained nurses and welfare workers were in short supply but she would tell the St John organization in India to offer Lady Wavell all the people they could spare and she would also have a word with Colonel Sleeman at the Red Cross. As soon as Dickie's cable arrived, Edwina got to work. The Minister of Health and his wife were invited to lunch at Chester Street; this led to a long conference at the India Office, where Edwina put her case. By the end of January she was able to tell Dickie that this department would support his request. She warned him not to expect too much too soon. 'Our fight will be with the War Office'. There were endless difficulties, until Edwina had a word with Churchill. All objections were removed. Medical aid for SEAC was to be furnished at once and a senior adviser appointed to co-ordinate it. The stately minuet began once more.

In mid-March it was agreed that Major-General Telfer Smollett would be appointed as Red Cross and St John Commissioner and sent out, 'by *our* people', Edwina said firmly, not the Red Cross. Dickie had now been waiting for more than four months for his nurses and Edwina was beginning to think that the only way to get things moving would be for her to go out to India herself, see what was required and come back with a plan of action. Lady Limerick had just left on a similar tour in North Africa and Italy. 'If you get *our* people plus Lady Wavell and the Chinese to invite me for a few weeks', Edwina told Dickie, 'I might be able to do a little good . . .' No sooner had she made up her mind to arrange a trip than the Government declared a general ban on 'journeys by wives who wish to join their husbands abroad'. This was awkward. When Dickie had asked about bringing Patricia out, Edwina had said sternly that they must do nothing that might provoke criticism, however unjust. Now she was caught by the same argument. Dickie warned her that people would say that she was getting round the ban and coming to join him. Better to leave it for a few months. Edwina was furious. All she wanted was to be allowed to do a duty tour, in her own right. For the time being she agreed to wait.

'You know how much I want you to come out', Dickie assured her. He was sick of his irascible colleagues. 'The older they get the more hysterical they become', he told Edwina. 'These old men drive me *nuts*!!' His family was never out of his mind for long. On 10 February he sent Edwina a telegram from Delhi: 'Loving thoughts from scene of our engagement twenty-two years ago'. She was amazed: 'How clever of you to remember the date!' In mid-July it began to look as if he might be able to come home on leave. The relieving force had broken through at Imphal and on 10 July the enemy had ordered a general retreat. 'It is the most important defeat the Japs have ever suffered in their military career', Dickie said proudly. This was the moment to come to London to ask for more resources. Dickie decided to return at the beginning of August, bringing Noel Coward, who was just finishing a SEAC tour, and a small staff. He would not be able to stay long but he needed at least a week for meetings with Churchill, Eden and Beaverbrook. Above all, he longed to talk to Edwina. 'I can't tell you how much I'm looking forward to seeing my old girl again!'

There had already been one long-awaited reunion. A month before Dickie's return, Bunny came back to London, after an absence of eight and a half months. His letters had been infrequent and imprecise: 'I don't at all understand what the Rabbit's movements mean', Edwina

The Bombshell

had told Dickie at Easter. In mid-April she heard that Bunny was in Australia, 'but nothing further . . .' A month later he cabled to tell her he was in New York, 'saying he may be seeing us soon-ish.' Then he sent a wire to say that he would not be leaving America 'for some time'. Edwina was puzzled. '. . . I don't even know what his future plans or job are to be . . .' Some vagueness was understandable, since Bunny was in Intelligence, but Dickie's work was secret too and he always managed to let his family know what he was up to. Edwina chased Dickie to find out whether her letters and presents had been delivered. Was Bunny all right – or had his feelings changed?

Edwina herself had been less than frank. 'Dined with Murrows . . .', she had noted in her diary in mid-January 1944, 'picking up Bill Paley just returned from USA!!!' Colonel Paley was attached to Eisenhower's staff. He was a brilliant publicist, who had just launched an American radio station to broadcast to the occupied countries. This was Paley's special field; at home he had made a great success of the Columbia Broadcasting System. An attractive and gregarious man, he had a crowd of well-connected women friends in London, who were flattered when he remembered to bring luxuries from America: orange and lemon concentrate for Nancy Tree, Guerlain perfume for Mrs Laurence Olivier, four pairs of stockings for Mrs Randolph Churchill – and for Edwina all these (the perfume was Chanel) plus half a dozen lipsticks. She was his particular favourite. From February 1944 to the end of June, Edwina and Bill Paley spent most of their free time together. Dickie was well aware of their friendship but Edwina did not tell him that Paley came with her to Broadlands on spring and summer weekends. 'Bill & I did lawn scything and walked and sunbathed. Too delicious.'

Bunny knew. On the evening of his return to London, Edwina was pledged to dine with the Murrows as Paley's guest at Claridge's. As time went on it became clear to Bunny that he could hardly get her to himself. He was staying at Chester Street but Edwina's secretaries and colleagues were forever rushing in and out – and it seemed to Edwina, too, that Bunny was evasive. Perhaps things would settle down when they got to Broadlands. Bunny fished, Edwina lay in the sun. Pamela had come home for the summer holidays, Patricia and her current admirer arrived on twenty-four hours' leave. Peaceful Saturdays and Sundays – but things were not quite right. Edwina was tired and ill; Bunny caught no fish (that, admittedly, was not unusual).

Edwina Mountbatten

It was understandable that they should have moved apart. For months they had been living in different worlds.

Dickie returned on 4 August. It was difficult to fit everyone into 15 Chester Street, impossible to give both Bunny and Dickie the attention each deserved. Dickie was overjoyed to be home. He wanted to see his mother, Peter Murphy, the Laycocks, the King and Queen; Edwina was swept off to Buckingham Palace for dinner and Chequers for a night. ('Winston in grand form', she noted. 'Croquet and cinema . . .'). Dickie was determined to have one long weekend at Broadlands. On Saturday, while he rode with Patricia and Pamela, Edwina and Bunny drove the pony trap and sunbathed. 'A really glorious day with strong sun'; too strong, she said, for she did not sleep that night and next day her head was pounding. Bunny returned to London on Sunday, Dickie on Monday morning. Edwina, unusually, decided to remain in the country for an extra day. She had to be in town on the Tuesday, to give lunch to Mrs Churchill and Robert Morgenthau, the US Secretary of the Treasury, and take them on a tour of shelters and first aid posts, but she looked as if she should have been in bed. Her face was swollen, her eyes blotchy. She said she had run into a wasp. That night she forced herself to write in her diary the news Bunny had given her at the weekend. He was engaged to be married, to Nada's niece, Harold and Zia's daughter Gina.

CHAPTER TWENTY-THREE

Edwina Inspects

In the morning Edwina found a note from Dickie. He had seen Gina and Nada at the Hungaria the night before: 'They told me of the engagement, of which Nada said you knew. My darling sweet – what a shock for you all the same'. Dickie was almost as stunned as his wife. Recent conversations with Bunny had persuaded him that he should not stand in Edwina's way if she and her lover wished to marry: 'I had intended over the weekend to offer to make it easy for you . . . somehow the remarks you made to me stopped me from pursuing a heart-to-heart, but my one idea was to help you in any way I could . . .'

Three times that day – at breakfast, mid-morning and in the early evening – Bunny came to Chester Street to explain. Edwina could not take in what he was saying; nor could Dickie, when Bunny looked in on him after dinner. To steady herself, Edwina fixed her thoughts on work. On the following day she went back to the shelters: 'Arrived in Battersea shortly after Bomb had dropped. Bad incident'. Dickie was in France, visiting Eisenhower and Montgomery. The Third Army had reached the Seine, north-west and south-east of Paris. 'Great victory won today', Dickie wrote in his diary. 'German army finished'. In London that night he worked until 3 a.m., taking an hour off in the middle so that he and Edwina, two wraiths, could look in at the Hungaria for a drink with the engaged couple.

Dickie had intended to return to Ceylon at the end of the week but, not liking to leave Edwina, he put off his departure. On Friday the Mountbattens drove down to Broadlands. It poured with rain. Edwina took the dogs for damp and melancholy walks along the river bank: 'One of the most miserable days I have ever spent'. Dickie and Patricia were afraid that she might throw herself in among the weeds. Two days later Edwina took Dickie to Northolt for the first stage of his journey back to Ceylon. From Gibraltar he sent a long and tender letter. She still had a bad patch to go through, he knew. The worst time would be the week of Bunny and Gina's marriage. 'After that they will presumably live a year or two in Washington & when you next meet I feel the difficulties will have disappeared & you will find a new firm and lasting friendship based on your 11 years' happiness . . . Come out & visit SEAC soon & stay with me in the King's Pavilion – it will take your mind off all this & be lovely for me'. She was not to mope. 'Get among cheery friends – Bill Paley & others – & don't let your mind dwell constantly on this as you will end up by running to get under a flying bomb!!!' Dickie was serious. 'Don't take avoidable risks in London . . . I admire your courage in staying – but let it be tempered with reason'. The letter was signed 'Your unchanging but devoted old Dickie' – an echo of the 'restored but changed Dickie' who had written so magnanimously in 1931.

Edwina was moved. 'I can never tell you how touched I've been at all your sweetness and understanding', she replied. '. . . I wouldn't want things changed now as far as Bunny & I are concerned even if they could be'. Not only, she said, because the crisis had helped her to appreciate Dickie's kindness and sensitivity but also, rationalizing furiously, 'because I know it is all for the best and hard though it is bound to be temporarily to readjust one's ideas and one's life, I have always felt that Bunny needed so much his own little home and Family, and if I wouldn't give it him, it was so important for him to find someone sweet like Gina who would'. She was telling the truth. A month before Bunny's return to England, Edwina had stayed with the Wernhers after a St John & Red Cross rally in Leicester and she and Gina had travelled back to London together on the train. Edwina did not know that, during Bunny's last visit to England, he had met Gina by chance in Park Lane. He saw that she had grown up into an attractive and capable young woman. Greatly daring, for all the family knew about Bunny's connection with Edwina, Gina had sent Bunny her photograph at Christmas and a correspondence had begun. As they sat in the train, Edwina had suddenly said to Gina, 'You know, you ought to marry Bunny'. Had she guessed? If so, it now did little to cushion the shock.

Disbelief, anger, guilt and, finally, resignation. 'Much as I adore him', Edwina told Dickie, 'I really don't think somehow that a permanent partnership between us would have worked – certainly less now than ever before . . . I was really only unhappy because of his muddled frame of mind and hysteria which increased mine! But I am now much more reasonable and convinced that Gina and he will be *really* happy and that it is perfect from every point of view. And very largely so because it has in a way brought me closer to you than ever before and made me realize how immensely lucky I am to have the affection and loyalty of someone as sweet and unique as you'. She would do her best to look forward. 'I shall not be gloomy and silly I promise you – I have my ups and downs!! but the latter are on the ascendant – and even though as you say there will be another trying time when Bunny comes over next I think I can now cope with that too!' She missed Dickie. 'It was wonderful to have you holding my hand just at the bad time . . . I have an angelic family and such marvellous friends and what more *can* one want?'

Dickie had urged Edwina to lean on people who cared for her. Bill Paley took her out ('angelic and helped a lot'), Noel came to lunch and dried her tears when she told him what had happened. Patricia wanted to be of use – but what was she to do? Her mother had told her on the telephone about Bunny's forthcoming marriage but neither she nor Patricia had known how to continue the conversation. Edwina had never confided in her daughters and Patricia was not sure whether she wished to do so. Now she turned to her father. Dickie advised her to write a letter. '. . . I'm practically grown-up now', Patricia explained, 'and I understand a lot of things you don't think I understand. And so I just can't help knowing exactly how you are feeling at the moment. You're a funny sort of person', she went on, emboldened, 'and you don't like being sympathised with in physical or mental affliction and I admire you tremendously for it. But somehow I hoped that by telling you this it might help a little; it's nice to know someone understands . . .'

Discreet, protective, brief. Patricia's letter could not have been better. Edwina, so proud and inhibited, understood at last that, although Patricia was devoted to her father, this did not mean that she had no love and admiration to spare. A daughter could be friends with both her parents. Patricia promised to spend the following weekend at Broadlands: 'Please try and come down early', she told Edwina. 'I think it will do you good'. An embrace, a long walk arm-in-arm, 'the first really heart to heart I have ever had with Mummy', Patricia told her father. 'Rather amazing after twenty years'. They had discussed Bunny, 'quite naturally . . . and how she felt over it, and about you, and your ups and downs but fundamental fondness and understanding of each other . . . she was quite a different person this weekend – almost her old self. I don't think I have ever seen anyone changed so much as that first weekend do you? It sort of stabbed me every time I looked at her and one felt so powerless . . .' Patricia had not overlooked her father. She was glad he had got back safely: 'I hated thinking of you returning in the complicated emotional state you were in'.

Edwina survived. 'Coming to slowly!' she wrote in her diary in late August. For days, however, nothing seemed quite real, and not only in Edwina's private life. 'The French marched the Germans out of Paris', she wrote in her diary on 23 August; 'Hardly credible'. Next day she and Mademoiselle Chevrier toasted the beginning of the liberation of Paris. A Medical Civilian Relief Unit left for France on 31 August and ten days later Edwina went over herself, to see what additional help was needed. The visit could not fail to raise her spirits. Eisenhower sent his own converted bomber to bring her from Heston, lent her a staff car and driver and put her up at the Twenty-First Army headquarters near Bayeux. 'He said charming things about you', Edwina told Dickie, 'and was the most thoughtful & delightful host. This included sending his own personal DRs to meet us about 6 miles from his villa who preceded us thru' the little towns with sirens full on which speeded up our progress considerably altho' I felt very embarrassed and disapproving in principle!'

She was accompanied by Joe Weld, who worked in Mountbatten's SEAC Rear Link in London. 'I really don't know what I would have done without him. Motoring in France in the operational areas is no joke. Bridges are blown up, roads and fields mined, German and Allied tanks, lorries and all types of vehicles are lying abandoned or burnt and overturned all along the roads . . .' Edwina and Colonel Weld struggled through, with one bad moment, when their heavy American car teetered on the edge of a flimsy improvised pontoon. Edwina was too exhilarated to be nervous. It was wonderful to be on French soil again, to see the Mulberry landing-stage as she flew over the coast, and watch the first hospital ship sail out of the newly opened harbour at Dieppe. Trim and crisp in her new khaki battle-dress, Edwina flashed through the tented hospitals at Bayeux and Caen. She inspected Ambulance Columns and Red Cross stores, visited welfare workers and the Civilian Relief Unit. Her admiration soared for what she called 'the *real* French . . . their spirit and courage is marvellous'.

Edwina Inspects

Each day the Allies moved further into Holland and Belgium; between the pages of her diary Edwina kept the maps, cut from the newspapers, showing the progress of the advance. No one was more proud – or more aware of the cost. The country was devastated. Caen had been wrecked, surrounding villages shelled and bombed. Falaise was flattened, Rouen badly damaged, the road to Paris battered and ugly, bridges blown up and verges disfigured. At Caen there were 'hundreds of wounded, British, USA, Germans, Poles, Czechs, French, Belgian, most of them just in from the Antwerp areas'. To save civilization, lives and landscapes had been destroyed. Wherever she looked, she saw a massive clearing-up job waiting to be done. 'Arrived in Paris with a lump in my throat', Edwina told Dickie. The suburbs were in a bad state but when she reached the centre of the city she was amazed to find that it had hardly been touched. Peter Murphy's flat was in good order, the Ritz unmarked. Here, as in the old days, Edwina stayed. 'Of course complete lack of fuel, transport, soap, coffee, milk etc . . .' She dined frugally at her hotel with Bill Paley and, on her second night, shared Diana and Duff Cooper's rations at the Embassy. Others ate more lavishly. 'Black market (started by the Germans) rampant in Paris I believe, tho' de Gaulle has already reduced it a great deal'.

How had Yola fared? Dickie had last had word of her in 1941, when out of the blue he had received a cable from her sister, saying little but sending love. Three years had passed since then. Yola was said to be staying somewhere near Beauvais, fifty miles from Paris, so Edwina set off in Eisenhower's car to find her. The huge American automobile drew up at the house, Yola's poodle rushed forward, mad with excitement. One by one the family came out into the garden: Henri, Yola, her mother and sister, 'all quite unchanged, and as enchanting as ever', Edwina told Dickie, 'and just as ridiculous!' Had Edwina kept her vow, Yola wanted to know at once. When the war started they had promised each other that they would neither eat chocolate nor paint their nails until hostilities were over. After Dunkirk Edwina had broken her pledge, saying that it did not seem to be doing much good – but she did not tell Yola, only murmuring that in England there was hardly any chocolate or nail polish to be had. Yola confessed that she had succumbed – not that life in Paris had been easy. Villa Maillot had been requisitioned by the Germans and she and Henri had been squeezed into three rooms upstairs. The winters had been so cold that she had been obliged to wear her full-length ermine coat in bed. Undaunted, the Letelliers and their friends had continued to give little parties, *salons* in the Métro, for instance, where it was warm, at which they served cakes of soya flour from the best tea room in Paris. 'And the Marché Noir has helped a lot I think!' Edwina murmured to Dickie, overlooking the fact that she disapproved of it. 'Anyway it was *lovely* to see Yola again . . . I asked her for a letter for you . . .'

In mid-October Edwina returned to Paris. The late summer sun made patterns through the chestnut leaves. At Boucheron the manager produced a pair of earrings, ordered in 1939; Bill Paley gave her lunch at the Ritz. It might have been a dream, in which everything was in its place, but wrong. The Vendôme, where Edwina stayed, had been requisitioned by the British Army; at the Embassy Duff and Diana Cooper had only a fortnight's fuel and no hope of getting any more; bicycles, the chief form of transport, were painted bright pink, green and blue; there were no taxis. Edwina and Yola took a brougham home to the Villa Maillot after dining with the Gérards. '. . . An antediluvian horse and coachman', Edwina told Dickie, 'which walked the whole way out to Neuilly and took us over an hour. Each time the driver flicked his whip, Yola put her head out of the window and screamed, *'Ne fouettez pas le pauvre cheval!'* The journey cost twelve hundred francs; Yola said that was cheap.

Edwina was under exceptional strain. She was trying to deal with the needs of the homeless and hungry in newly-liberated Europe, prisoners of war awaiting repatriation, wounded and convalescent servicemen, and at the same time her attention had to be given to trifles, the annual Christmas card nightmare, for instance. Another nagging headache was produced by Bunny's farewell present, an early Biro ballpoint pen. This had been one of his most precious possessions; now he bequeathed it to Dickie. It would write without refilling, he told him, 'for hundreds of miles'. Unfortunately the ink had just run out and, as the pen was not yet on general sale, Dickie commissioned Edwina to track down the inventor and ask for a refill – this at a time when she did not wish to think of Bunny and when she already had more than enough to do. Edwina did not complain. Keeping Dickie happy was part of the war effort. 'You really go through continuous hell and disappointments', she told him in a sympathetic letter, after he had been told to postpone an attack on

Rangoon. No one had a more helpful representative in London. At the funeral of Princess Beatrice, Dickie's mother's aunt, Edwina said a word or two about his problems. '. . . The King was full of your own difficulties and the lack of support they gave you'.

It was in Kandy, however, that Dickie wanted her. At last it began to look as if Edwina would be allowed to go out to SEAC as the official representative of the Joint War Organization, with Nancie Lees as Staff Officer. By the end of October everything was agreed. Edwina was to go to India, Ceylon, Burma and Chungking, to inspect hospitals, casualty clearing stations, welfare centres and arrangements for allocating staff and distributing supplies. 'My medical staff are all sincerely delighted', Dickie told her. 'Their view is that the mere fact you are coming will put all the hospitals on their toes'. He wanted her to see everything: 'I had quite a time persuading the Generals that you were tough enough to go up to the Casualty Clearing Stations and live rough!' In the twenty-five years since Edwina's first trip to India he had learnt a good deal about her determination and stamina. In the old days he had recommended that she bring dark glasses and riding habits; now his letters discussed bed rolls and camp beds, insect repellent and mosquito boots. ('I personally wear black half-wellingtons with blue trousers and brown sambhur skin boots in Khaki.') In his eagerness to assist, Dickie went almost too far. 'I have learnt quite a lot about these hospital visits', he said enthusiastically, 'and will dictate a series of notes and hints which may help you, including phrases in Urdu, Ghurkali, Swahili, Chinyanja and Chinese!'

Edwina did not need lessons in how to assess a hospital. If Dickie wanted to make himself useful he could have a look at her programme. Her hosts had suggested that she visit one establishment each day. By starting early and working late, Edwina said firmly, it was perfectly possible to fit in two. They had proposed regular rest days. Edwina preferred to work long stretches, with a two- or three-day break at the end of a fortnight. She had been asked to look at recreation centres. She thought it more important to see the arrangements made for troops who were going on leave. 'I myself have heard awful reports of these from the families of your men and there is no doubt it's psychologically mad to start men off going on leave with complete lack of any amenities. Many of them in the past have preferred *not* to go on leave at all because of these Transit Camps'. Edwina suspected that the authorities would want her to visit only the better hospitals and welfare centres. 'Please *try* and arrange that this is not the case', she said briskly. It was particularly important to keep a free quarter of an hour here and there: 'so I can ask unexpectedly to see another ward or something else they have *not arranged* for me to see. That is the only way one can compare the real picture with the window-dressing. And it can be done quite innocently and spontaneously . . . it's of tremendous value.'

'You and Miss Lees will be my guests from the time you leave England until you return', Dickie told Edwina. His own aeroplane, 'the beloved *Sister Anne*' would carry them from London; Sergeant Coulson, Royal Marines, 'who went with me to Casablanca and Quebec . . .', would act as Steward and look after them. Squadron Leader Donald Erskine Crum, 'my charming Air ADC', would accompany the flight and see to arrangements en route: 'Donald has orders to settle all bills, including food in the aircraft, hotel bills etc'. *Sister Anne* was not only comfortable and efficient – she had Pratt and Whitney engines and long-range fuel tanks – but also capacious: 'You and Miss Lees can share 500lbs of luggage provided it is small and compact'.

Six months earlier Edwina would have been irritated by Dickie's solicitude but now it was exactly what she needed. Exhausted, lonely, tense with cold, she spent the last afternoon of 1944 packing, sorting papers and worrying about Jib, her sickly Sealyham. 'Did not wait up to see the New Year in', she wrote in her diary. 'Delighted to see the end of the old one!!' India was waiting, with its hot sun, strong light and bright colours; Edwina had new people to meet and an important job to do. Weary-eyed, after a night seeing to last-minute paperwork and mourning for Jibbie ('put to sleep . . . really heartbroken'), she climbed into *Sister Anne* at five o'clock on the morning of 5 January. She was away for more than three months.

From the outset it turned out to be the hardest trip she had ever made. Even the Supreme Commander could not instruct the elements. The aeroplane battled against winds so strong that the pilot decided to break the first day's flight at Gibraltar; Nancie was green with nausea and Edwina had splitting neuralgia. The delay reduced their stop in Malta to half a day and a night: Edwina inspected Bighi Naval Hospital by flashlight at 10 p.m. There was time, however, to call on old friends. 'Everyone cried on my shoulders', Edwina told Patricia and Pamela, 'and then revived themselves and me with neat whisky . . .', thankfully, for the wind cut like a knife. To Cairo, where Edwina inspected JWO Civilian Relief Teams, now embarking for Greece, on to Baghdad to see the RAF hospital, and then *Sister Anne* took off for the last leg of the journey, the overnight flight to India. Edwina had one of two lower bunks, 'with my feet resting on General Telfer Smollett's head'. The aeroplane was icy and, when they landed, the passengers were numb. After lunch at Government House in Karachi, Edwina insisted that they sit and work in the garden, although the sky was overcast. The weather was cold and she shivered. So did poor Nancie. Working with Lady Louis had always been an endurance test but already the tour was proving tougher than she had expected, and they were still miles from the front line and the jungle. After a noisy, bumpy night flight other people might have gone to bed but, when the letters and reports were done, Edwina wanted to see the Merchant Navy Hostel and the YMCA.

Edwina and Miss Lees had now been joined by Major Bryan Hunter, whom Dickie had seconded to them as escorting officer. Major Hunter was looking forward to the assignment. He had brought his golf clubs and squash racquet, in the hope that he could get in the occasional game. There was no time for play. Edwina whistled round Karachi at a tremendous pace, inspecting medical and welfare establishments, with Nancie and Major Hunter frantically taking notes in her wake. Each night they put together a report of that day's work, listing action points and ensuring that they were followed through. Letters of thanks had to be written, cables sent to people at home, deficiencies of drugs and equipment inquired into. Edwina asked to see places that were not in her programme; every evening Nancie and Major Hunter toiled to build in these extra visits. Edwina was shocked by what she found. If all hospitals were like these, no wonder the troops complained. Her task was even more urgent than she had imagined.

From Karachi Edwina and her team proceeded to Delhi. Here she found Sergeant Watson of Hawes and Curtis, waiting to measure her for bush shirts, and a message to say that the Supreme Commander was expected the following day. Dickie was on his way north to the front; what was more natural than that he should pause in Delhi? 'Conducted to the Viceroy's House', Edwina told Patricia and Pamela, 'which is immense with *endless* marble floored corridors and rooms so huge one is exhausted walking to one's bath and Lulu next door. Not my cup of tea at all . . . All rather stately and pompous . . .' No dances and garden parties now. 'Visited Rear Link HQ where discussions were held with General King regarding welfare questions in India and South East Asia . . . with General Hance, Director of Medical Services India . . .' There were long talks with Lady Wavell about Red Cross work, with Sir Edward Benthall, Transport ('bad'), Sir Patrick Spens, Chief Justice ('good'), and General Wilson, Director Medical Services, India Command.

Dickie took off for the front, Edwina returned to Delhi, for a morning of talks before she left in *Sister Anne* for three days in Lucknow. The file of reports grew thicker. '*Indian Military Hospital*: special beds, now manufactured in India, needed for pneumonia cases. *British Military Hospital*: air conditioning plant burnt out in operating theatre; shortage of books in recreation rooms, no map of Burma Campaign, most recent *Picture Post* more than six months old; acute lack of electric light bulbs, night nursing done by torchlight; shortage of wire gauze for doors; no lockers in Indian troops' wards; one ward over-crowded; latrines needed flushing and disinfecting; windows dirty (responsibility of Public Works department).'

On, via Cawnpore to Secunderabad: 'Dead beat. Much hotter'. Here, Edwina told Patricia and Pamela, a marvellous hospital city had been built. Wards and operating theatres were first-class but no one had inspected the kitchens. The locally made electric stoves were useless, more cooks were needed. Nurses explained that it was difficult to provide an appropriate diet for patients with jaw and facial injuries: 'Ice Cream freezers should be an ordnance issue. No jellies were obtainable'. The welfare side was a mess. Letters to patients went astray. Ants had eaten the binding of books sent from England, there being no copper sulphate in the glue. Patients complained that they were made to wear ill-fitting suits when they were taken out to entertainments that were supposed to raise morale. The Army boots chafed the long un-British feet of Indian and African troops. All this was reported. Edwina missed nothing. Four hospitals in two days – and a lightning visit to see Red Cross depots and stores in the New and Old Jails, the RAMC Convalescent Unit and an exhibition of Muscle and Skin Control. ('Certain Natives stick skewers and swords into themselves', Edwina noted punctiliously in her diary.)

To Madras to inspect the Joint War Charities Supply Depot, review a parade of six hundred St John members, visit the British hospital

Edwina Inspects

('. . . no refrigerators . . . coir matting dart boards supplied by Indian Red Cross no good . . . lighting over the operating table extremely inadequate . . .'), tour the Indian hospital ('no fans . . . flies from nearby sewage farm . . . insufficient transport for essential needs'). Signals flashed back to Delhi, Kandy, London. Edwina's hosts had been asked not to put on receptions in the evening, a time reserved for meetings with volunteers, medical officers and other key people. Her only excursion at night was to a dance for patients from a British military hospital in Bangalore and, since the event had been arranged as part of their physiotherapy, it was hardly a diversion. The people Edwina wanted to see were too busy to indulge in small talk at dinner parties. In her diary she made a note of the most interesting people she met: the architects and engineers who had built the hospital town at Jalahalli from converted *basha* huts, a physiotherapist who had introduced patients to leather work, the inventor who had devised a soft boot that could be worn over a plaster cast, an ingenious salvage worker who had converted motor car seats into comfortable armchairs for a recreation room. Neurosurgeons, psychiatrists, hospital sisters, transport managers and store-keepers . . . these people did not dine at Government House.

It sometimes took a day or two before Edwina's hosts understood that she really did not wish to be entertained. In Bombay, for instance, Sir John and Lady Colville began by taking her to the cinema to see *This Happy Breed* and the next night there was a dinner at Government House, 'for a mere 44!' Edwina hardly broke her stride: five hospitals, visits to WRNS quarters, an ambulance train and a hospital ship, thirty-six hours in Poona examining eye, ear, nose and throat wards, blood plasma centres, artificial limb fitting, and a hospital for West African troops. Back to Bombay for a three-day break with Dickie: 'Supposed to be Rest Days', Edwina wrote in her diary, 'but did not quite materialize!!' She wanted to dictate reports, write letters, see Basil Dean and other ENSA people about shows for the troops; Dickie ordered her to have a holiday. They compromised and went together to look at the rebuilding of the docks.

This was at the end of January 1945. The second stage of Edwina's tour was to last nearly a month, taking in north-east India, the Burma coast and, if there were no battles in the way, a trip to the front. She began with an unannounced visit to the British Military Hospital at Jhansi; 'a comfortable atmosphere', she reported, although neither

345

the Officer in Charge nor the Matron knew the names of the senior medical staff and the Commanding Officer for the district was, she thought, 'not exactly a ball of fire'. Having shaken the authorities throughout the military hospital service, for word soon got round that Lady Louis had departed from her programme, Edwina flew north to Comilla, near the mouth of the Ganges. Miss Lees and Major Hunter started another file: *'Dental Centre* . . . new material for setting not being used; *Diet Kitchens* fitted with Primus stoves . . . inclined to explode; plenty of DDT but kerosene to dissolve it is short . . .; a home-made operating lamp . . . the surgeon maintained that . . . a first class modern light would not be justified, because it would be bulky and in any event, might break during transit; this of course, is nonsense'.

To Dacca by ambulance train, travelling overnight; three days there to see six hospitals ('Ward had iron bedsteads but had hessian straps instead of spring, and this collects bugs') and two Convalescent Units. ('Before men are passed out they have to carry out a ten-mile route march and a five-mile cross-country run'). On the first night Edwina watched the ENSA show in an officers' ward, on the next she was at a dance for the men. 'I took my hat off to her', wrote Joyce Grenfell, one of the entertainers, in her wartime journal. 'She looks chic and attractive and never stops working'. At Chittagong Edwina dutifully took a rest day at an Army holiday camp, before moving on to Cox's Bazaar and Akyab. 'Left by Jeep . . . but owning to miscalculation over Spring Tide after a few miles came to deep water . . . had to wade across with all clothes on head – luckily got another Jeep on other side . . . stuck again further along but eventually travelled by 3 ton lorry . . .'

By now Edwina was able to draw general lessons from her visits. The JWO had asked her to look at the personnel side. She reported that in every establishment the nursing staff was under strength; that there were marked disparities between the pay and conditions of British nurses and their Indian colleagues; that members of Queen Alexandra's Indian Medical Nursing Service felt that periods of service abroad were too long and complained that 'going to parties is in many cases an order'. She had been invited to examine hospitals; in doing so she had acquired a knowledge of air-conditioning, sterilization, lighting and electricity generation, the equipping and running of canteens, fly-proofing, water-supply and sanitation. Doctors in one place heard from her about techniques that were practised elsewhere; overworked staff, trying to do too much with too little, were assured that their difficulties were not unique and that she would do her best to see they were addressed. Edwina, Miss Lees and Major Hunter forgot nothing: patients needed sewing kits and boiled sweets; light metal camp beds were required; West African troops had no postage concessions; procedure for dealing with blind patients was sometimes confused; only one Dakota was available for evacuation at Akyab; a Private in the 10th Gloucesters had received no mail for three months ('Write to Welfare, Eastern Command').

By 17 February they had reached Calcutta. 'Met by Lady Rutherford the Governor's wife and others and drove off to the Club for coffee etc'. Within the Club it was dark and cool. A fan turned slowly above each member's armchair. Did the Secretary not know that in local hospitals there was no more than one fan to a ward? Edwina left with funds for forty. Two days later Dickie returned from his tour of forward areas, eager to hear how she was getting on. 'I am so proud of the grand job you are doing', he had told her in a letter from SEAC headquarters, 'and get such a kick out of hearing your praises being sung by everybody that matters'. 'Supposedly a Rest Day', Edwina wrote again in her diary on the 21st, 'but as usual found endless interviews, correspondence and engagements piled up'. Dickie took her for an afternoon drive through the town and coaxed her into dining at the 300 but that was all. Edwina was unstoppable.

On 24 February she set off for the front. That night she stayed at General Slim's camp, the headquarters of the Fourteenth Army. In the next ten days she flew from one camp to another: Sadaung ('lunched with General Monty Stopford who came out of nearby Battle to see me'), Shwebo, Sinthe ('Visited operating theatre where saw grenade shattered jaw being operated on'). On the 27th Edwina crossed the Irrawaddy. Now she was only a few miles behind the front line: 'the Jungle still littered with live mines and shells and very revolting stench of rotting bodies all around!' At Bahe Edwina and Nancie slept in tents made of parachute silk (the Thirty-Sixth Division was entirely supported from the air so there was plenty of it) and hung their stockings out to dry on the guy ropes. Edwina liked the danger. 'Drove out to forward areas to within 500 yds of Jap positions with stench and debris of yesterday's fighting . . . Drove wildly with General Festing and saw most advanced Posts. Live shells and booby

Traps still strewn around. Drove all along Trails – troops so surprised to see a woman and me' (she meant 'let alone me') 'they nearly died!!'

Myitkyina, Ledo, Duma: by 5 March Edwina was in North Assam, her headquarters a bungalow on a tea estate. Two days later she flew over the mountains to China, with Dickie and a party of generals. Edwina was to spend a week touring medical establishments, Dickie had two days of talks. While the warriors discussed strategy she fitted in a hospital, an orphanage, a university and the Institute of Health. Dickie and his party left on the morning of 10 March. Now Edwina, Miss Lees and Major Hunter could start work in earnest. On the 12th they flew to Kunming; 'Visited Delousing Station . . . Chinese Military Hospital . . . Research and Epidemic Bureau . . . Blood Bank . . . Friends Ambulance Unit'. After a bumpy flight over the mountains to Paoshan to see Red Cross Field Ambulance Units and American Field Hospitals, Edwina, Nancie, Major Hunter and assorted Chinese and American generals set off by Jeep down the Burma Road to Mengshi. 'Surface execrable in parts and as narrow and dangerous as ever', Edwina wrote in her diary. 'From mountain tops 8,000 ft corkscrewing down . . . and up again'. While the others gritted their teeth, Edwina airily pointed out that parts of the track had been widened since 1939. It was, she said, 'a great thrill'.

The Chinese tour was almost over, to Edwina's relief. She knew some of the places she had seen were showpieces and it was difficult to press her hosts to take her behind the scenes. Too much time was taken up by speeches of welcome and farewell, elaborate lunches and sixteen-course dinners. Everywhere there had been presentations: two dozen umbrellas, a pair of shoes and a hat, made by crippled soldiers; a photograph (of himself) from the Governor of Kunming and a jade ring from his wife; flowers, paintings, lengths of silk. The Generalissimo gave Edwina musical instruments and a Ming vase; Major Hunter and Miss Lees each got four pounds of tea. Edwina's two assistants had been able to catch up on lost sleep, note-taking and typing being for the moment assigned to a military interpreter who understood Chinese. There was a price to pay. 'Very badly done', Edwina scribbled on the top of the draft report. 'No method. No names of places after dates. Many names missing. ACTION IN BIG LETTERS ALWAYS'. It took Miss Lees and Major Hunter hours to fill in the missing information.

It was not surprising that Edwina was testy. They had all begun to

Edwina Inspects

droop. On 18 March her party was due to return to Calcutta, where at last they might draw breath. To Major Hunter's consternation, Edwina declared that she wished to travel south from Dimapur on a leave train, third class, to see what conditions were like. Nancie and General Fung could come in *Sister Anne*; she and Major Hunter would meet them at Pandu. No wonder the soldiers had complained. 'The trains are definitely filthy', Edwina informed Patricia and Pamela, 'with no light whatsoever, no washing facilities or lus, just an occasional slit in the floor! and very few refreshment facilities of any kind. And as the journeys are endless I am not surprised the troops get pretty fed up . . .' Major Hunter brought a cushion; Edwina told him he could make himself comfortable if he wished, but she intended to travel exactly as the men did. She spent the night in the luggage rack. 'Tousled, dirty and bleary-eyed', Edwina wrote in her diary: 'Got some wishy washy tea by walking back up the line at 7 a.m. about ¼ mile and some army issue biscuits'. Major Hunter thought it was hell.

Two days later Edwina was on her way to Ceylon: 'Good trip and tried to work but very tired'. She had spent much of the previous forty-eight hours briefing Red Cross people and seeing the Press. Dickie had implored her to keep some time free for a holiday in Kandy but Edwina could not get herself off the treadmill. On her first morning at King's Pavilion he took her riding; 'a glorious mountain road on delightful ponies. I then did a quick change and started off on a Hospital round'. Dickie was working, Edwina protested, so she must be allowed to do so too. Only on the third day, while he was away in Burma, did she admit to Peter Murphy that she was too exhausted to function efficiently. Knowing it was hopeless to expect her to lie on a long chair in the porch, Peter sensibly put Edwina in a Jeep and took her on a tour of the country north of Kandy. Even here it was impossible to stop her overdoing it: '. . . Fantastic rock formations 400 ft high 1500 years old . . . Fine figures on frescoes and incredible ruins of Palaces etc right on top only reached by terrifying climb on face of rock with narrow iron protection. Very tired and hot'.

Edwina would not slow down. Dickie insisted that she remain in Ceylon for at least two and a half weeks, to give herself time to unwind. She agreed – and promptly took on more. Twice Dickie captured her for a two-day break at Dimbula, the tea planter's bungalow he had taken in the hills. There she worked through a pile of reports and correspondence. She could not sleep and her ears ached; she armed herself with pills and carried on. A two-day visit to hospitals in Colombo, a day in Trincomalee and Jaffna, back to Colombo, speeches, interviews and official entertaining in Kandy – by the time Edwina left Ceylon on 9 April she had seen hospitals, convalescent depots, cafeterias and clubs, hospital ships, dental surgeries, YMCAs and the Hospital Supplies Association, addressed the WRNS, Welfare and Canteen workers and VADs, inspected parades of St John and Red Cross representatives and tasted the beer at the Royal Stag, in the Services Holiday Camp run by the NAAFI. She had spoken to hundreds of patients, the last one being Major Hunter, who had collapsed.

Four days of meetings and press conferences in Delhi and then the Mountbattens flew off for a brief holiday, thirty-six hours in Bikaner as guests of their old friend the Maharajah. Edwina thought it perfect. There was no tiger-hunting here, for the lands round the Shooting Palace had been turned into an animal sanctuary. Their host did not display Rolls-Royces, gold and jewels; his proudest purchase was the equipment in local military hospitals. The Maharajah and his guests dined in a lush garden, beautifully lighted, and on the last day he gave a farewell lunch in Edwina's honour. She liked the clear notes of the Indian music that played in the background, tinkling, like ice in a glass, against the murmur of conversation. The afternoon was hot – a hundred and two degrees – and she was very weary. Dickie took her up to Karachi in his second-best aeroplane, a York, and saw her off at five next morning. In two days she was home.

It was mid-April. Broadlands seemed liked heaven. Aunt Victoria was there and Pamela was back from St Giles for Easter. Patricia arrived for ten days' leave. She had survived a stiff course and was now Third Officer Mountbatten, smart in her new uniform. Having passed out top of the cypher class, she had been posted to the C-in-C Nore's unit at Chatham, where she worked in a tunnel a hundred feet below ground. 'Not as bad as it sounds', Patricia assured her mother, who hated being shut up, 'as it is well-lit and air-conditioned'. Edwina was pleased: 'Proud Mama feels all puffed out'. Chatham was a sought-after station, being near enough to London to allow an occasional fling in town. 'We'll have a real riot somehow when I return', Edwina had promised, for she had been in Burma on Patricia's twenty-first birthday, 'miserable thinking of you with none of us to celebrate'. Well-meant, but all Edwina managed when she got home was a family outing to *Gay Rosalinda* with dinner at Pastoria afterwards. 'Work piled high . . .', she wrote on her first day back in the office.

For a month Edwina hardly stopped. Her first task was to report to the Joint War Organization. It was not difficult to galvanize them, once they heard her describe what she had seen: hospitals desperate for staff, equipment and drugs, welfare organizations short of the most basic supplies. Tackling Ministers was more difficult. Edwina spent hours at the War Office, the Ministry of Health, the India Office: 'all waffling around still and achieving very little', she told Dickie, 'but I hope to do a good deal of prodding and pushing . . .' The War Office agreed to send out more VADs and trained nurses but would not do so until formal requests came from the India Office; the India Office insisted that medical workers travelling to South-East Asia should not be parted from their luggage, obliging them to go by sea, which took weeks; objections were made to Mountbatten's proposal that his staff should include an officer responsible for the co-ordination of medical and relief work.

Edwina turned to Ismay, who advised her to write to the Prime Minister. 'He says it's quite useless trying to talk to him nowadays', she informed Dickie, 'as he won't listen to *anyone* and only wants to hear his own voice! but he will read 2 sheets of paper at the most!' Edwina and Ismay drafted a flattering letter, keeping it to one and a half sheets and its requests to the minimum. Churchill invited Edwina to lunch and made sympathetic noises but nothing happened. She kept up pressure from all directions: 'I saw the King and Queen yesterday and told them about my trip . . .'; 'half an hour with Mr Bevin last night who was extraordinarily understanding and cooperative . . .' The Viceroy and General Auchinleck sent letters of support; so did Lady Wavell, now one of Edwina's warmest admirers. According to Dickie, the Vicereine had declared that Lady Louis was 'an asset to the Empire'.

It was on Dickie, however, that Edwina had made the greatest impression. He was so proud that, without stopping to think whether he might be embarrassing her, or anyone else, he had written about her work to the whole family, including the King. Whatever Edwina had recommended must be done. She had urged Dickie to go himself to see civil relief work in Burma; within two days of her departure for

Edwina Mountbatten

England he set off. Edwina had given her husband a complete set of her own notes, so that he could see whether her suggestions and recommendations had been taken up. 'On the whole', he wrote in his war diary, 'I found they had, but I think it shook my Civil Affairs people considerably to find that I knew exactly what deficiencies to look for . . .'

In every way Edwina had exceeded Dickie's expectations. 'I fear I was very indiscreet in the way I discussed secret stuff with you – many a man has been broken for less!! – but really it was only on those matters on which I wanted the comfort and support I could now get from you and no one else'. She had been patient and understanding. 'I hope you didn't mind my mentioning about my girl friends – it was only to show you that they never have meant to me what the Rabbit meant to you and so can never come between us, provided', he added cheerfully, 'you no longer make difficulties about my seeing them, within reason, as you were apt to do in the old days!' Patronizing though Dickie's tributes were, he meant well and Edwina took them in good part. It helped that she had seen the size of the task that faced him: 'I am so very proud of all you have achieved', she wrote after she had returned home, 'and the unbelievable obstacles and disappointments you have overcome . . . I know how hard it has been'. He had been such good company; 'this new relationship has made me very happy'. Dickie agreed. He did not remind Edwina (had he noticed?) that this was the fourth time they had rebuilt their marriage.

Edwina was speaking truthfully when she told Dickie how devoted she was, how much she relied on him and admired him. It was a pity that her feelings were so shut in; only in times of high emotion could she forget herself and give Dickie the approval he craved. One such moment came at the beginning of May, just before the start of the monsoon, when General Slim and the Fourteenth Army marched into Rangoon. The Japanese surrendered on 3 May. Victory in Burma was assured. 'Really magnificent and we are all overjoyed', Edwina told Dickie. She had already sent a telegram of congratulation, 'prized', he declared, 'above the 3 dozen I got from all the Prime Ministers, Governors, Generals and Admirals all over the world'.

This news coincided with the rumour that the war in Europe was over. Hitler had killed himself on 30 April, on 2 May the Russians took Berlin, and in Italy, on the same day, the Germans capitulated.

Edwina Inspects

On 7 May Germany surrendered. What had become of Dickie's scattered relations? Alexander Geddes, who worked at the War Office, had been in Germany for the surrender and had managed to see his sister and brother-in-law, Peg and Lu. Although many of the surrounding towns and villages had been destroyed, Wolfsgarten was intact. The castle at Darmstadt was in ruins, the buildings and some of the coffins at the Rosenhohe destroyed. Much of Wolfsgarten had been converted into a civilian hospital; Lu and Peg lived in part of a wing, with twenty-five dependents. Other friends and relations were thought to be making their way from the East, now occupied by the Russians, but there was no way of knowing who would arrive until the moment when the handcarts appeared at the gate.

Piecing together the patchwork took months. Many friends and members of the family were dead; others had been arrested by the Americans or the Germans. Fear and mistrust had governed them all. Throughout the war Lu and Peg would not have a wireless set in the house; only when they were alone in the open air did they dare discuss what they really felt. In March 1944 Hitler had dismissed former ruling Princes from the Army, fearing that they might be a focus of disaffection, and for the remainder of the war Lu and Peg had lived under house arrest at Wolfsgarten. There had been frightening moments, especially towards the end, when the local Gestapo bosses panicked as the Americans moved in. Now people were beginning to breathe freely again.

'It has been a week of tremendous happenings', Edwina told Dickie, when Germany's surrender was announced, 'but I personally did no celebrating whatsoever'. In South-East Asia the war continued; now, Edwina thought, Dickie would at last be able to secure the resources he needed. Two days' public holiday was declared to mark Victory in Europe; Edwina and her colleagues were too busy to take time off. On 17 May she left on a tour of Italy, Greece and the Middle East, to see hospitals and convalescent depots for sick and wounded troops. Europe was full of refugees: 'I've seen hundreds of Repatriated Prisoners of War, both our own and Empire ones and others of all Nationalities', Edwina reported to Dickie, in a pencilled letter scribbled late at night. 'Then the Displaced and Stateless People who are pouring into Austria and Italy from all sides and are a frightful problem. You get 40 or 50 nationalities in one camp sometimes . . .' On 10 June she returned to London, bringing her colleague Muriel Watson, who was coming home after a long spell of work in the Near East with St John, and Mrs Hoppe, a Red Cross worker from Kenya, who had been out of England for nine years. By the time they reached Northolt, Edwina had discovered that, having been away so long, her new acquaintance had nowhere to go. She took her back to Chester Street for the night; years afterwards Mrs Hoppe remembered the perfection of the crisp linen sheets. Edwina also slid gratefully into bed: 'More dead than alive'.

CHAPTER TWENTY-FOUR

Deliverance

Within hours, Edwina was ready to return to work. Someone
suggested a Red Cross inspection in General MacArthur's
forward area, north of Australia, west of the Philippines; she
wanted to go at once but the authorities dithered. She was not the
only one to be frustrated. For weeks Dickie had been trying to arrange
a meeting in London to see Churchill and the Chiefs of Staff, to discuss
his plans to invade Malaya. He had been repeatedly put off. 'The
Election has disrupted everything here', Edwina told him. 'They are
all behaving like Fishwives and private schoolboys . . .' Polling was
to take place on 4 July but it would take three weeks to collect and
count the votes. By the 24th, therefore, the Prime Minister would
be turning his attention to future strategy. Ismay pencilled in an
appointment on that day. Since Churchill was to be in Potsdam for
talks with Truman and Stalin, Mountbatten could join the party there
and travel back to London with the Prime Minister. On the way to
Germany Dickie arranged to stop in France to see Yola. Edwina
was alarmed. Paris was all eyes and ears, Neuilly full of watchful
neighbours. Dickie promised to be careful. He would stay with Duff
Cooper at the Embassy and, if he took Yola out, they would go 'to
some tiny little non-black market place'. In that case, Edwina replied,
she would not try to dissuade him – and perhaps he could bring her
some scent. 'It's the only cheap thing in France. COTY, corner of Place
Vendôme and rue de la Paix. AMBRE ANTIQUE and CHYPRE . . .'

Dickie returned to London on 25 July. 'Election results tomorrow'.
Peter Murphy had predicted that the Conservatives would lose and,
although she was fond of Churchill, Edwina hoped Peter was right.
On the 26th she was as jumpy as a cat: 'Worked . . . shopped violently
. . . looked at a revolting house. Tea with the King and Queen'. Then
the news came: 'Overwhelming Victory for the Socialists. Winston
out, Attlee new Prime Minister. Labour gained 390 seats . . . Election
result stunned everyone, even the Labourites. I am delighted'.

Edwina Mountbatten

For ten days Dickie and Edwina rested at Broadlands. The grass was long, the river glittered in the sun. Pamela had left St Giles, Patricia had a fortnight's leave. There was a week of reunions: with Aunt Victoria, Alice and Louise, Marjorie and Cousin Anna. The Mountbattens spent a night at Windsor with the King and Queen; three days later they drank tea with Queen Mary. Everyone was affectionate and good-tempered. Dickie had indicated that while he was in London he would like to see his women friends and to his surprise Edwina made no difficulties. 'The sweetest change', he told her, 'is the way you have conquered what we *all* thought was an unreasoning jealousy . . . You can feel easy in your mind that there is real safety in numbers & that I won't do anything silly'.

Poor Dickie. Even his compliments were clumsy. If Edwina minded, she did not show it. She had more important matters to think about. It was now certain that within weeks she would be going out to the Pacific to inspect hospitals, rest camps and travelling arrangements for the troops. Suddenly, in the space of a few days, everything changed. On 6 August an atomic bomb was dropped on Hiroshima, three days later another on Nagasaki. Edwina said nothing in her diary. Like most people, she knew little about this new weapon, more terrible than all the deadly instruments deployed in the last six years of war. A bomb of immense destructive power had been used against a cruel and fanatical enemy; its importance lay in the fact that it had brought hostilities to an end. At lunch time on 9 August Dickie brought word that Japan had capitulated.

Mountbatten was to leave for Ceylon in three days' time, a victor now. His last hours in England were frantic: meetings with the SEAC planning staff and Ronald Brockman, his Naval Secretary and right-hand man in Kandy; a lunch party at Chester Street for Ernest Bevin, the new Foreign Secretary, and his wife (a borrowed table turned up in a horse-drawn van, after the guests had arrived); discussions with Clement Attlee, the new Prime Minister; talks with Ismay; an interview with Ed Murrow. He left London on 12 August, missing the celebrations for Victory over Japan. This time Edwina felt able to take part and on the 19th she, Patricia and Pamela were among the royal party at the Thanksgiving Service in St Paul's. Before the war, Edwina would have wanted to skip away afterwards to something more amusing. Now she rode with the procession. Thirty-six hours later, at two o'clock in the morning, she left for SEAC. Even she could not have hoped for a more dangerous and difficult job.

South-East Asia Command covered more than one and a half million square miles. In the jungles, mountains and islands were at least half a million Japanese, officers and men, many of whom did not yet know that their country had been defeated. A hundred and twenty-eight million people lived in the countries which the enemy had overrun – Malaya, Sumatra, Borneo, Java, the Philippines, New Guinea, the Celebes, Singapore, Cambodia, Thailand, large parts of China and Burma. They had suffered greatly. More piteous still were the prisoners of war and civil internees, more than a hundred and twenty thousand, who had managed to survive in dozens of unspeakably dreadful camps. These captives had to be sought out and brought home. The task was urgent. Some prisoners had been incarcerated since Japan had first entered the war, three and a half years before. Men, women and children had been treated abominably. Worn and wasted, clad in rags, they had been forced to work in the steaming heat. No medicine, no news, nowhere but filthy corners in which to try to wash and sleep. This much had been established from Intelligence reports; no one knew how many people were in each camp and in what condition. Someone had to find out straightaway, so that doctors and nurses could be sent in and transport organized. Mountbatten could not do all this and at the same time supervise the transition from military to civil government in a dozen different territories. There was only one person to whom he believed he could delegate the rescue operation: Edwina.

She arrived in Kandy on 23 August. Until the Japanese had formally signed the surrender document in Tokyo, no military landings were to take place, on General MacArthur's orders. Dickie's reoccupying forces waited at sea, the relief teams stood by. At least the delay gave time for the rescue to be planned and co-ordinated. During the next twelve days Mountbatten's team, of whom Edwina was one, considered every aspect of RAPWI, the scheme for the Recovery of Allied Prisoners of War and Internees. A transport directorate was established, to assemble a fleet of hospital ships to bring food and supplies to the occupied areas and take off people who were fit to travel by sea. This was Operation Mastiff. The Royal Air Force and the Royal Auxiliary Air Force waited with Dakotas and light aircraft; their first task would be to find the camps and shower them with leaflets (Operation Birdcage), telling the prisoners and their tormentors that Japan had surrendered. Supplies were to be dropped in remote areas and people parachuted in to take charge of the camps and organize their evacuation. Discussions with the British, Indian and Australian Red Cross produced teams of nurses and VADs, who were to stand by until they could be flown in. Medical supplies and equipment were got ready, welfare officers instructed to prepare and pack stocks of bedding, clothes, washing things and cigarettes.

In Kandy Dickie hurried things along. Edwina flew to India to whip up the Red Cross at a meeting chaired in Simla by Lady Wavell. From there she went to Delhi, to stay at Viceroy's House as the guest of Sir John and Lady Colville, who were standing in for the Wavells. With her was Elizabeth Ward, a young, lively FANY, who had been working in SEAC after a spell at the Special Operations Executive, and had now been assigned as Staff Officer to Lady Louis. Edwina's hosts were anxious to entertain her; how was she to remind people that she had come out here to work? When it was time to go down to dinner, Elizabeth, in her best uniform, went to collect Edwina, whom she found in evening clothes, with jewels. Elizabeth was on the point of rushing back to change when she saw Lady Louis slipping out of her dress. Of course it must be uniform when they were here on duty. For the next three months, it was.

On 2 September the surrender was signed in Tokyo. Now the Allied forces could move in, clear any pockets of Japanese resistance, find the camps, remove their commanders and make these fearful places safe for the relief teams to enter. This would take days, prolonging the suffering of the internees and prisoners of war, many of whom might die before help arrived. Edwina was determined to set off at once. She left next day, with two sympathetic and reliable St John colleagues who had arrived the week before, Beatrice Girouard, Assistant Superintendent, and Marjorie Miller, County Nursing Officer for Suffolk. They were accompanied by General Tyndall, General Thompson, the Director of Medical Services for SEAC, and Major Abhey Singh, one of Dickie's ADCs.

The first stop was Rangoon, the clearing centre to which newly liberated men, women and children were already being flown in from Bangkok, Malaya and Burma. Edwina toured hospitals and transit camps, talking to hundreds of British, Australian and Dutch ex-prisoners: 'Grim stories and unbelievable what they have been through . . .' She took names, addresses and messages; when night

Deliverance

fell, she asked for a hurricane lamp and carried on. Many of the prisoners had been brought to Rangoon from Siam. There, next morning, Edwina went. She had asked for a casualty clearing unit to be flown in but the generals had explained that the place was still too dangerous for women and the nurses had been ordered to stay behind. A hundred and fifty thousand fully armed Japanese were said to be at large in the country, the port of Bangkok was mined, the airfield damaged. General Slim, the Commander-in-Chief, was anxious about Edwina's safety. She took no notice. At the airfield Edwina and Mrs Girouard found an enormous gathering of local RAPWI people, who were receiving newly-released men and ushering them into the Dakotas for transport to Rangoon. The ex-prisoners were in an appalling state. One young soldier had worked for three and a half years on the Burma-Siam railway, surviving on starvation rations of a pound of rice a day. 'Lady Louis was the first white lady I saw', he said afterwards . . . 'I had no idea who I was talking to'.

A deputation of officials, in full court dress, also waited at the airport, sent by the Regent, who had insisted that Edwina should be his guest. This was awkward. Some said that he had organized the local resistance movement, keeping in touch with SEAC via a radio set hidden in his palace, but the British maintained that his government had collaborated with the Japanese. To cover their embarrassment – and minimize demands for compensation – his people now tried to make a good impression on the Supreme Commander's wife. 'Regent gave a banquet for us at Palace', Edwina wrote in her diary. There were seventeen courses, followed by speeches. She was then allowed to escape, in a blue Rolls-Royce, to the Civil Hospital. On the following morning, the Regent and his wife called after breakfast to ask whether Edwina had slept well and to tell her that an escort had been arranged to take her to the camp at Nakhom Pathon. Her outriders turned out to be a detachment of local police and soldiers and a group of armed Japanese staff officers. Edwina's hosts meant well. So did Yanagida, the Japanese commander of the camp, who was waiting, in full dress uniform with sword, to welcome Lady Louis at the main gate. That was too much. Edwina stopped her driver and refused to proceed until Yanagida had been removed. This so-called 'hospital camp' had operated without drugs, surgical or medical supplies. Doctors and medical personnel, prisoners themselves, had improvised their equipment from pieces of wood, bamboo, old bits of tin, glass, 'anything that could be found lying about', Edwina wrote in her official report, 'or obtained secretly from the native populations outside'. Anaesthetics and drugs had been extracted from shrubs and herbs, artificial limbs constructed out of scrap. Nearly twenty thousand prisoners had died there in 1942 and 1943, during the construction of the Burma-Siam railway. The camp was crammed with sick men, suffering from TB, malnutrition, gangrene and dysentery. Edwina knelt beside them and explained that they were going home. She climbed on to the wooden platforms which served as communal beds and told a crowd of scarecrows what fine men they were. They tried to carry her on their shoulders but, too weak to do so, cracked out a cheer instead. No one who was there ever forgot that visit.

Other camps were as bad. At Nakom Nyak Edwina found Harold Cassel, Cousin Felix's son, who had been missing since 1942. His hair had turned completely white. Only days before he and his fellow-prisoners had been ordered by their guards to open up the caves in the rocks above the camp. There they were to be shut up and left to die. Allied victory had nearly come too late. When the Japanese commander learnt that his government had surrendered, conditions improved. Half-starved prisoners were given pork and beans; slowly they began to revive. Before she visited the camp, Edwina had heard that some of the men were making up for lost time by raping the village women. This would not do. She was sure, she told them, that they would uphold the honourable traditions of the British Army. The hint was understood and the raping ceased.

At Tamuang Edwina saw five thousand prisoners, British, Dutch, Australian and American. Supplies had not yet been dropped; those who had clothes at all wore the remains of what had once been shorts. 'Do you wish me to be frank?' Edwina inquired, when someone asked what her first impressions were. Her answer: 'Well, you ALL smell!' Direct, unaffected, good-humoured and kind, in an instant she reassured them that one day life would return to normal. She distributed boiled sweets and cigarettes ('REAL Players Virginia!' the men said admiringly); she asked the authorities to ensure that relief parcels included packets of condoms, to kit out those who might want to celebrate their freedom in a brothel.

Edwina left Mrs Girouard and Miss Miller to supervise the evacuation of the Siamese camps and on 9 September flew on to her next stop. 'Magnificent sight seeing the British Navy assembled off Port

Deliverance

Swettenham and Penang', she wrote in her diary, 'and in full possession of Singapore'. Among the vessels were the hospital ships, waiting to take scores of prisoners and internees for treatment in India and Australia. Edwina went aboard each one. It was hot and exhausting. The *Amarapoora* was typical: an ancient steamer with only a few fans to stir the air in the crowded wards. Edwina stayed below for three hours, giving each of six hundred patients a word or a smile.

Singapore was a mess. Buildings were overgrown, roads cracked and torn. Power and water supplies were fitful, where they worked at all. Two hundred high-ranking officials were staying at Government House – 'the bigwigs', Edwina called them – but they slept on the floor and dined on baked beans. Dickie joined Edwina there when he arrived on 11 September for the surrender ceremony. His flagship, HMS *Sussex*, was loaded with supplies, desperately needed for the inmates of the camps that spilt all over the island, thirty of them, containing altogether more than thirty-five thousand prisoners and internees. In the forty-eight hours before Dickie got to Singapore, Edwina toured two of the worst, Sime Road Civilian Internee Camp and Changi Gaol. Four a half thousand men, women and children were crowded into Sime Road; at Changi there were twelve thousand British, Australian and Dutch prisoners of war. They were stunned when they saw Edwina. Many of the men were wrecks – torture had been common – but she was astonished by their resilience and resource. Prisoners had managed to keep diaries, even to build and hide three illicit radio receivers, on which they had listened to the BBC. Workshops had been set up; 'every kind of supply was turned out', Edwina said in her report, 'from spectacle frames and shoes to musical instruments'. One bold inmate, Harry Chumbley, of the Royal Army Ordnance Corps, asked Edwina for her autograph. For paper he offered a Japanese ten-dollar note, for a pen a piece of bamboo, for ink blood drawn from his finger. She signed.

The surrender ceremony took place on the morning of 12 September. Edwina watched as the Japanese generals were marched up, one by one, disarmed, between a double row of British and Indian guards, and made to hand over their swords to their opposite numbers, right down the line of command. Mountbatten had devised this piece of theatre. In another age and in other circumstances the performance might have seemed melodramatic, even vindictive. Dickie was determined to crush all respect for Japanese militarism; humiliation, he believed, would drive the victors' message home. To those who looked on, the ceremony was a mark of atonement for all they had suffered. Edwina watched from the balcony of the Municipal Buildings, with a small group of Chinese and Malayan St John volunteers, who had made their way again and again into the Sime Road camp to do what they could, at enormous risk to themselves. She had asked Dr Robert MacGregor, Director of Medical Services in Malaya and a St John Commissioner before the war, whether she could meet the ambulance men and women of Singapore. He could not promise much, for his people were scattered, telephones did not work and there was no transport. The wind carried the word and on the afternoon of 13 September fifteen hundred volunteers from the St John Medical Auxiliary Service assembled in the grounds of Government House; European, Chinese, Indian, Malayan, almost every one bearing a St John badge or button, the only scrap of uniform they had dared to retain during the Japanese occupation. 'Wonderful welcome', Edwina wrote in her diary. The honour, they thought, was theirs.

The Mountbattens had barely three and a half days together in Singapore. During that time they worked non-stop. At Kranji, a camp in the south of the island, they saw two thousand men, at Simbawang seven hundred more. They went to Neeson camp, Seletar, MacArthur, Serangoon Road, River Valley Road. Those who met Edwina did not forget her. Bill Griffiths, an airman, had lost his sight and hands in Java, when his captors had forced him to defuse a bomb. Edwina stopped by his bed in the Alexandra Hospital in Singapore to tell him that she would herself ensure that he received all the assistance he needed from the military and medical authorities at home. She did as she promised – but it was her words that carried Mr Griffiths through the next anxious weeks. At Singapore General Hospital she met a patient who had first worked on the Burma-Siam railway and had then been moved to Changi. Too dazed to take in what she said, he none the less remembered her kindly smile – and a glimpse of sunburnt waist between her khaki battledress jacket and skirt.

In less desperate days, one other visit would have attracted more attention. On the afternoon of 13 September Edwina and Elizabeth Ward drove with Dr MacGregor to the Leper Hospital. In a moment Edwina was with patients, shaking their hands, touching their arms, stroking their foreheads. Visitors were rare; it was remarkable to find

Deliverance

one who did not flinch. Edwina's actions were instinctive; she did not stop to think that at the same time they were symbolic.

She did not waste a moment. After lunching with Dickie in HMS *Sussex*, she spent the afternoon in the bowels of the ship, thanking the cooks and bakers who were working round the clock to provide rations for the camps. There she met Commander Hok, who was directing the Royal Navy's efforts to get supplies into Changi and elsewhere. He was an immediate ally. Like Edwina, he understood that, as well as food, clothes and soap, the ex-prisoners and internees needed magazines, books, playing cards, mending kits and toys for the children; he had found it difficult to get others to agree. Lady Louis asked him to send cables off at once, with her authority.

Journalists covering the surrender were invited for drinks, ex-prisoners of war brought back to Government House for supper. Years afterwards, they remembered how intently the Mountbattens listened to their stories. One afternoon, between meetings with Dickie's planners, he and Edwina called at Raffles Hotel to see the Bakers, who had been brought from Java, where Mr Baker had been imprisoned in one camp, his wife and three small children in another. Shortly after the surrender he had managed to get through to Tjidang in Batavia, where he found his family. When the Mountbattens arrived, Dickie took the boys on his knees, Edwina the little girl. For half an hour Dickie questioned the parents (Baker was in Intelligence) and, as they described what they had endured, the colour drained from Edwina's face. Mr Baker never forgot the horror in her eyes.

The first fortnight of her mission had been harrowing. The next stage was worse. On 15 September Edwina, Major Abhey Singh, General Thompson and Group Captain Hill took off in *Sister Anne* for Sumatra. There were at least twenty camps on the island, all dreadful. Pakan Baroe, Edwina's base, was in low-lying, swampy country. Many prisoners had died of malaria, starvation, exhaustion and disease. At Padang hundreds of civilians had been interned in two enormous camps, men in one, women and children in the other. 'Although only ½ mile apart', Edwina noted in her diary, 'families have been allowed no communication at all . . . Men had to make coffins and often found later through Chinese collaborators that it was their own wife who had died'. Palembang was vile. At the rear of the camp, by the edge of the jungle, Edwina saw the makeshift cemetery: 'little crosses and shallow graves dug by P of W too weak themselves to stand at times'. One ex-prisoner, a British naval officer, saw her smooth the ground with her foot. The dry soil crumbled, revealing a bone. Takahashi, a Japanese lieutenant who was standing nearby, murmured something. An apology? An excuse? Edwina rounded on him. She said only one word: 'Pigi' (Go). It was an order. He slunk away. None of those men saw him again.

These prisoners and internees had been cut off for years. On a slip of paper, stuck in the front of her diary, Edwina had made a note of things to tell them about civilian life: 'Rations adequate but little variety. Coupons. Queues'. She explained that there was a Labour Government and described its programme: '1. Repatriation. 2. Housing. 3. State Medical Service. 4. Education. 5. Social Insurance Scheme'. And now she would see that they were taken home.

It was not easy. There were no Allied troops in Sumatra and the Navy had not yet arrived. Coasts and beaches were heavily mined and the rescuers depended on the Japanese, still armed, to guide them through the jungle and up the rivers to the camps. At the small Chinese hotel in which Edwina stayed at Pakan Baroe she was guarded by a few ex-prisoners of war with rifles but no ammunition. 'Wonderful position', she observed wryly. 'Luckily the Japs doing as they are told on the whole so far'. Edwina and her team pored over maps and codebooks until two o'clock each morning and, under their direction, a handful of people from 'E Group' and Mastiff Control organized the evacuation of seventeen thousand prisoners and internees. Airstrips were improvised so that Dakotas could be flown in, Liberator bombers brought supplies. In the most inaccessible places, Red Cross workers came in by parachute. It was difficult to decide what to do first, for everything had to be done at once. Edwina would not admit that anything was impossible. If air and motor transport could not be got to a camp, she herself ordered the Japanese to help evacuate its inmates by river. Thousands of prisoners were taken in small boats or on bamboo rafts through the creeks and swamps and transferred at the river's mouth to landing craft brought from Singapore. Edwina had suggested this procedure. It was risky but it worked.

As she moved from camp to camp, Edwina looked for people who had been reported missing. An office had been established in Singapore to collect information; she carried its lists wherever she went. Many people were traced in this way, the most miraculous discovery being that of the Bull family. The father, a former Supreme

Deliverance

Court judge in Singapore, had been interned in the Sime Road camp; his wife had managed to escape with their children, one an infant, in a ship that was then bombed and sunk by the Japanese. In Sumatra Edwina found Mrs Bull and the baby, who had been picked up from a raft, and in an orphanage in Batavia the children. They had been cast up on the coast of Java. On 26 September she flew them back to Singapore in *Sister Anne*.

After a day in Singapore Edwina left on 20 September for French Indo-China. Her party now included Captain Marriott, of the Argyll and Sutherland Highlanders, an ex-prisoner of war who had joined her team in Sumatra. Conditions in the camps in the south of the country were comparatively good. Large numbers of French ex-prisoners had already been issued with military and naval uniform, internees at Mytho had been housed in decent barracks and the hospitals were well organized. The politics of the place were complex. Three days before Edwina's arrival the Communist Viet Minh had proclaimed the independence of the Republic of Vietnam; on 21 September, while she was in Saigon, General Gracey, her host at Government House, put the whole of Southern Indo-China under martial law. British policy, as declared by Mountbatten, was that the French should be left to fight their own battles with the Viet Minh, while British and Indian troops dealt only with the Japanese. General Gracey believed that unless he acted quickly Southern Indo-China would fall apart and, the day after Edwina's departure, ignoring instructions, he supported a French *coup d'état* in Saigon. Although Dickie was not sure whether Gracey's judgement had been correct, he defended him before the Chiefs of Staff. Some said that Mountbatten had been got at by the French, others that he simply decided that Gracey had acted in good faith. It did not occur to people to think that Edwina might have had some influence. She respected Gracey and approved of his efforts to keep order and assist those who were working in local camps and hospitals. Furthermore, she was impressed by the French people she met, ex-prisoners themselves, who were getting on with reorganizing and rehabilitation. To Dickie, his wife's opinion mattered.

When she had travelled in this part of the world before the war, Edwina had not asked about its politics and no one had bothered to tell her. The French had been in charge in Indo-China, the Dutch in the Netherlands East Indies; during the war they had been ousted by

365

the Japanese and now they wanted their countries back. These days Edwina was more interested; she was also better informed. Better, often, than Dickie's staff, for during her tours of the camps she talked at length to prisoners of war, among them intelligence officers who had gathered information from their own networks and drawn their own conclusions. Furthermore, in working with local people to undo the damage caused by the Japanese, Edwina and her advisers learnt about their loyalties and aspirations. Four days in Java, for instance, told her more about Dr Soekarno's Indonesian independence movement than Dickie's intelligence sources had discovered in many weeks. One person to whom she listened was Laurens van der Post, who had been imprisoned in Java for two years; another was Colonel C. W. Maisy, whom she sent to Singapore to speak to Dickie. Edwina was also given a paper prepared by a mysterious Captain Lambert, a British prisoner of war, who had been ordered by the Japanese to work in the Department of Information. There he had gathered a great deal of intelligence about the strength and extent of Indonesian opposition to the Dutch. Edwina showed Dickie Captain Lambert's report. Dutch critics later alleged that Mountbatten had encouraged the nationalists (he had certainly urged the Dutch to talk to Soekarno) and some maintained that this had been at Lady Mountbatten's instigation. Hers was not the only influence but it was certainly important.

Edwina's immediate concern was to do what she could for the British, Australian and Dutch captives in camps and hospitals in Java. She was particularly disturbed by the conditions in which she found the women and children: 'overcrowding, no sanitation, flies everywhere'. At Semarang she met women who had been beaten, abused and forced to work as coolies. The young girls had been taken away, all boys of ten and over removed to the men's camp. 'We had only the little chaps', one mother said sadly to Edwina. Children as young as five had been put to hauling timber. Hundreds had died. It was astonishing that so many had survived. Twelve thousand women and children were packed into Semarang; Edwina decided that they must be evacuated at once. British Army drivers took them to the airfield, RAF officers organized landings and take-offs: all these men had only just been freed themselves. At times Japanese pilots and their aircraft had to be used for communication flights. Captain Malcolm Syms, newly liberated from Bicycle Camp, Batavia, and now in charge

Deliverance

of transporting evacuees from the camps to the waiting Dakotas, remembered meeting Lady Louis at the airfield. He offered to take her luggage over to her Jeep; 'She smiled and said that her husband always made her carry her own bag'. In these circumstances Edwina did not look for special treatment.

She returned to headquarters in Singapore for three days; then she and Elizabeth left for Borneo, Labuan and Moratai. At one of the Australian hospitals Edwina met Bombardier Maxham and Private Bottsoil, survivors of a forced march through mountains and jungle. Twelve hundred British and Australian prisoners had started out; all but six had perished. In these islands the rescue operation was well under way. The Australian and American Red Cross had established recovery camps and arrangements had been made to evacuate men who were fit to travel. Tented hospitals perched on the cliffs above the sea. After a month of horrors, it was heaven. Edwina and Elizabeth swam in crystalline seas and went canoeing on water as still as a mirror. But it was impossible to forget what they had seen and heard. Although they were exhausted, they could not rest. 'Are you asleep?', Edwina whispered to Elizabeth in their hut on the beach. 'No. Are you?' They had worked well together. Elizabeth was quick-witted and efficient; like Edwina, she seemed tireless. She was also tactful, which was vital, for Edwina was exacting. She relied heavily on Elizabeth but, when they appeared together in public, Lady Louis was the star. Their relations were always correct: Edwina neither sought nor gave confidences. Living side by side in the jungle, however, they acquired an affection for one another. They shared everything, including the sickly 'Carnation' scent, produced by a local shopkeeper, in which they washed when there was no water for a bath. Their experiences had often been terrifying: each knew what the other was thinking as they were driven off into the jungle to search for camps, their only companions a Japanese driver and a Japanese guide.

Those grim days were behind them now. In the Philippines, Edwina's next stop, the Australian and American Red Cross had taken charge of the recovery and repatriation of prisoners of war from Formosa, Korea and Japan. Four thousand British and Indian men and women were awaiting evacuation. They did not expect to leave for days, weeks even, for the ships were full and they had heard that priority had been given to getting American servicemen home from the Pacific. One British Army engineer, newly arrived from Okinawa, summoned enough courage to ask Edwina whether he might be home for Christmas. She assured him that she would do her best, and she did. Ten years later Edwina met him at a flower show in England. When he mentioned Manila, she exclaimed, 'Of course, you're the chap who was afraid he wouldn't be home for Christmas!' It was not surprising that he had remembered the conversation but he was astounded that she had done so too.

From Manila Edwina and her team flew to Hong Kong. ('Airborne at 9.30. Had an extraordinary meal about 10 of warm fried chicken, given us by the Americans, tea and marmalade . . .') The internment camp here had been emptied and the reception camp for evacuees in transit was in good order. Hong Kong had been badly damaged; people had been so short of firewood that anything that would burn had been taken for fuel. The inhabitants had paid a high price for their release and now they intended to celebrate: 'First a Service March & Fly Past, with wreaths laid on the Memorial. Then a Chinese Gala and drinking party, followed by a Chinese Victory Procession, with drums, dancers, acrobats, music, effigies . . . in the evening a marvellous firework and searchlight show'. The festivities marked the end of Edwina's tour. She returned to Singapore, arriving five minutes after Dickie flew in from Rangoon. Neither had expected to see the other and during the next forty-eight hours they scarcely did. Mountbatten was embroiled in talks with the Dutch over the crisis in the Netherlands East Indies, Edwina caught up in meetings: 'Hellish evening . . . Ceaseless interviews. Bed at 2 a.m.'.

Dickie's plan was to return to Kandy and work from there. He wanted Edwina to rest and he was looking forward to seeing Patricia, who was on her way from England. She had now been transferred to SEAC Rear Link in Delhi and was to take up her post there in a fortnight's time, at the beginning of November. Her arrival could not have been better timed. Not because Dickie was lonely – he had Peter Murphy and Teddy Heywood-Lonsdale to keep him company, as well as Edwina – but because Patricia's visit obliged Edwina to lift her eyes from her work. For two weeks she took a holiday – apart from report-writing sessions with Elizabeth, press briefings and a three-day visit to see Telfer Smollett in India and inspect hospitals and POW Convalescent Depots at Bangalore and Jallahalli. The rest of her time was devoted to Patricia. They drove, shopped, looked at temples and in the evening Dickie, Edwina and Patricia dined with friends and went to parties: the Planners' dance, cocktails with the RAF, the Wren ratings dance. Twice the Mountbattens took Patricia for a long weekend at the bungalow in the hills. 'Brilliant sun and clear skies', Edwina wrote in her diary. 'Log fires at night as we are 5000 ft . . . glorious dinner and laughed a good deal'. She was tired but not scratchy, for she had done a good job and she knew it.

On 13 November Edwina and Dickie returned to Singapore. She was pleased with what she found. Ninety thousand prisoners of war and internees had been removed from the camps; nearly seventy thousand were on their way home. Not all the news was good. Horrifying stories were coming in from Java, where the Dutch and the nationalists were now at war. Edwina sympathized with the independence movement but she was appalled by the reports from camps in Middle and East Java, where Dutch prisoners were still interned. The day after her arrival in Singapore, she flew to Batavia. 'Everyone fully armed and atmosphere tense with suspicion and fear.' Edwina went to the Indonesian hospital, to talk to people she believed to be influential, and spoke at length to the Dutch Red Cross, the British Commander, General Christison, and the Political Adviser, Mr Dening, from the Foreign Office in London, urging them to renew their efforts to clear the camps. She had worked until the last minute of her stay and could do no more.

On 25 November Edwina started for home. She was tearful when she said goodbye. 'I've loved my time out here', she told Dickie, 'and I am so glad you really feel it all went off well . . .' In a letter she left for him to read after she had gone, she spoke of the happy times they had enjoyed in Ceylon and India and of the great day of the surrender ceremony. 'I feel so proud at the way you have coped and are still coping with everything . . .' It was true.

And Dickie? He had mentioned Edwina in despatches in his official report to the War Office; his staff thought she deserved a greater honour but he could hardly recommend her himself. His private tribute came in a letter that was delivered on 28 November, Edwina's birthday. 'If you weren't my wife', he wrote, 'I'd offer you permanent employment in a very high rank on my staff and I know of no other woman I'd say that to!' It was the highest praise he could give.

CHAPTER TWENTY-FIVE

Diminuendo

E dwina was now forty-four. Exposure to the sun had wrinkled the fine skin on her face but her hair had not faded nor her eyes dulled. When she stood at ease her spine curved and she seemed to sway back, in a nineteen-twenties posture, but she still walked with the erect carriage she had learnt at Miss Potts'. She was very thin; under her clothes she wore only an insubstantial pair of cami-knickers. Alterations to her clothes meant that they still hung perfectly but much of her once smart wardrobe now seemed dated. In uniform, however, she looked wonderful.

New clothes were not the only items in short supply. Fuel and many foods were still rationed. Edwina kept the menu from one of her nights with Dickie in the York – four courses, including lobster mayonnaise and steak – 'roughing it in SEAC', she observed. 'Can you somehow have some *sugar* and *butter* or any *cooking fat* sent me each month from somewhere?' A case of oranges at Christmas was a godsend. A greater problem was that she had nowhere to live in London. Her tenancy of 15 Chester Street had come to an end while she was on her tour, the lease of the Brook House apartment had been taken over by Stewart & Lloyd's, so for the time being she moved into the Dorchester Hotel. After the rigours of the past few months, ostentatiousness and luxury made her uncomfortable. By mid-December Edwina was sick of the place. In January the house next door became available and on the 15th she moved into 16 Chester Street. 'Had food with Pammy on trays out of a tin as Aga wouldn't work. No fuel so not surprising. Cold intense.' Chairs, tables and chests of drawers came from Broadlands. There were no able-bodied men to shift things, so Edwina and Nancie did it themselves: '. . . lay flat on my tummy diving under mountains of furniture and then . . . heaved it out of windows and doors ready for London!' It had been a hard year. Edwina's reward came on 1 January 1946, when, to her astonishment, Justina Nasmith telephoned before breakfast to

370

congratulate her on the award of the DCVO, announced in the New Year's Honours List that morning. 'It was a *complete* surprise', Edwina told Dickie, 'as I had *no* notification at all. I believe the K and Q did it themselves . . .'

But how was Dickie to be thanked for his war work? Early in December 1945 he had heard that he was to receive a barony. This would not do. The new rank would give him a seat in the House of Lords but, in terms of precedence, his present status as the son of a Marquess and a member of the royal family put him higher. There were frantic consultations with Ronnie Brockman, Peter Murphy and General Browning, Dickie's Chief of Staff. A telegram shot off to the First Lord, to be shown to Churchill, with copies for Aunt Victoria, Edwina and the King. Dickie was thinking not only of himself but of SEAC. He knew that Montgomery and Alexander were to have viscountcies; giving Mountbatten a lesser honour than his colleagues would reflect both on his men and his command. He summarized his case in two briefing papers for Edwina, 'so couched that you could show them (one at a time of course) to the King – saying that they were not intended by me for his eyes.' Dickie's covering letter discussed his own honour for three pages, before – 'How typical of me . . .' – he remembered to congratulate her on her DCVO. In mid-February Edwina called at the Palace. Quiet pressure did the trick. Dickie was offered a viscountcy and took it 'in the National Interest, subject to minor conditions, such as continuing to call myself Lord Louis Mountbatten.' Edwina thought this 'about right'.

Half her time was taken up with lobbying. There were long negotiations over the award of a Civil Defence medal to volunteers in the Joint War Organization and with the Secretary of the Honours Committee at 10 Downing Street. She also checked the St John Ambulance lists. At her suggestion, the Maharajah of Jodhpur, Major Abhey Singh, General Thompson and General Denning were all admitted to the Venerable Order and Edwina also recommended both Bill and Aileen Slim, citing Dickie in support: 'Hope this was OK!!'

Nor had she forgotten those she had left behind. Within a week of getting home, Edwina had called on the Foreign Secretary, the Secretaries of State for War, India and the Colonies, and Mr and Mrs Attlee. Her mission was twofold. First, she wanted to report on the efforts of the professional and voluntary workers in RAPWI and to give the latest news on the progress of the repatriation programme.

Second, she and Dickie thought it vital for Ministers to have a first-hand account of the difficulties facing the Supreme Commander as he tried to restore order in the newly-liberated territories. The decisions Mountbatten had to take were urgent and far-reaching and the complexities of South-East Asian politics were not understood by people at home. There were complaints from old hands who deplored Mountbatten's failure to crack down on local nationalist movements: he was accused of being at best naive, at worst the tool of international Communism. Some said he was manipulated by Peter Murphy, others by his wife. Peter's briefing on post-surrender policy had certainly stressed that the nationalists' demands could not be ignored and, after her visits to French Indo-China, Malaya and Java, Edwina had said the same. By upbringing and temperament Dickie was a forward-looking liberal; indeed, when Lawson, Secretary of State for War, visited the Supreme Commander in Singapore in September 1945, Mountbatten had assured him that he was a Socialist himself. Moreover, as the man on the spot, charged with restoring and maintaining stability, he did not want a series of civil wars in country after country, not least because he had little with which to wage them. He reminded his critics that freedom was, after all, the principle for which the war had been fought; this argument cut little ice with traditionalists.

The Mountbattens hoped that the new Labour Government would be less hidebound. They were disappointed. 'They frankly appeared to have little idea of either the geography or military implications or feeling of the peoples', Edwina told Dickie, after she had discussed the situation in the Netherlands East Indies with Attlee, Bevin and their colleagues. 'I spoke very frankly altho' of course stressing it was only my private opinion but based on personal contacts with all sides . . . Java is considered very little here, it's so remote and people are much more interested in getting an extra pair of shoes out of Stafford Cripps and an extra oz of sugar out of Ben Smith . . . The Opposition and Winston are behaving shamefully and childishly and I shd. think greatly strengthening the hand of the Gvt, who are *not* having an easy time with anyone.' Edwina did not give up. She conferred with representatives of the Indonesian nationalist movement, brought to her by Tom Driberg, the Labour MP, who had visited SEAC on behalf of *Reynold's News*. 'Makes a lot of sense', Edwina assured Dickie, 'and was most helpful'. Driberg arranged for her to see Philip Noel-Baker, Minister of State at the Foreign Office, 'with whom he says I shall have to be patient and calm but firm and factual', Edwina told Dickie, 'as he's completely woolly-headed and ignorant and largely misinformed'. The Foreign Secretary made her fume: 'Bevin is behaving like the *Worst Conservative Diehard* and as Anthony (Eden) said to me a day or two ago even he is surprised at how much more reactionary he is than even he (Anthony) would have dared to be!!' Although some Ministers and officials must have thought Lady Louis a nuisance, none could ignore her. Edwina's reputation stood too high. She knew her facts, indeed, she was better informed than the authorities in Whitehall. Ministers quailed. Between the two of them, the Mountbattens knew more than enough about South-East Asia.

Edwina had now decided to return to SEAC at the end of February, to see that the last stages of repatriation were going according to plan and to look at civilian relief work in Indo-China, Malaya and the Dutch East Indies. This would also allow her to join Dickie for the Victory celebrations in Delhi in the first week of March. He pressed her to leave time for a holiday: various Indian princes had invited the Mountbattens to stay and the King and ex-Regent of Siam wanted them for an informal visit to Bangkok. The Australians had asked Dickie for an official tour and he suggested that they make it a joint one. From there they could go on to New Zealand: 'Above all I want a couple of days Big Game fishing. It is Blue Marlin, isn't it?' 'Striped Marlin or Swordfish', Edwina said firmly, having been there before with Bunny. A triumphal progress was the last thing she wanted but she was ready to support Dickie, on condition that she could put a visit to good use by arranging to inspect St John and Red Cross units in Australia and New Zealand. But could she afford the fare? Dickie would be carried by Transport Command; non-Service passengers had to buy a ticket. With income tax, and super-tax at nineteen and sixpence in the pound, the Mountbattens' finances were tight. 'If the worst comes to the worst', Dickie declared, 'the Red Cross will have to pay. I could make a 7-year Covenant . . . to pay them back'. Luckily a helpful Air Marshal secured a free passage, 'for Civil Relief and Welfare', and the problem was overcome.

Edwina left England on 25 February. A fortnight in India, five days in Siam and then she got back to work. In Saigon she saw the RAPWI people, who were still clearing internment camps, and when she reached Singapore on 17 March she dived straightaway into a huge International Red Cross conference. Important visitors were arriving hourly. One was Lord Killearn, sent out as Special Commissioner for South-East Asia, another Pandit Nehru, who came from Delhi to look into the conditions of the Indian minority in Malaya. Some of Mountbatten's staff warned him that Nehru's visit might provoke trouble. Although the Viceroy had not objected to the Indian leader's tour, the Governor-General in Burma had refused to receive him and Dickie was advised that he should do the same. Dickie refused to cold-shoulder this interesting visitor. Indeed, when he discovered that one of the staff had officiously ruled that no transport should be laid on for him, Dickie ensured that his own official car was standing by. From Government House Mountbatten and Nehru drove together to the YMCA, a sight which so bewitched the crowds that even anti-British demonstrators cheered. There Edwina was waiting with a group of Indian welfare workers but, as she came forward to greet the visitor, a mob of Nehru's admirers surged into the building and swept her aside. Edwina and Nehru were introduced as she emerged from beneath a table; then – and later – they had no time to be nervous with each other.

Next morning Edwina left for Java, where a RAPWI team was still in place. Field ambulance services were operating at Bandung in the western part of the island; these and the casualty clearing stations were well-run but it was distressing to see the condition of the Indonesians, driven by civil war from their villages and towns. The native people were sick and starving, their children covered in sores. The Dutch, once prosperous, were in a sorry state. Those who had suffered in camps run by the Japanese wept as they described their situation now. Having survived the war, they said piteously, they would now die of the peace, for with little food and no money they could not get home. Edwina sought out representatives of the British, Swiss, Indian, Chinese and Indonesian Red Cross and helped them draw up a collaborative programme but, as she told Dickie, until the two sides settled their differences, conditions would not improve. She could do little more, for she could not be seen to be interfering in local politics. It was difficult not to overstep the mark, especially when Edwina found herself seated between Dr Van Mook, the Dutch representative, and Mr Sjahrir, the new Indonesian Prime Minister, at a dinner in her honour. 'I hopped from one to another to show no favouritism'.

On the morning of 23 March the Mountbattens took off for their

Edwina

Sorting knitted garments

Visiting a hospital

The Mountbatten family

Talking to the troops

Diminuendo

Australian tour in Dickie's York – *Sister Anne* had crashed on an island off the Japanese coast two months before – arriving in Canberra twenty-four hours later. Edwina was amazed: 'In 1935 it took me 4 days.' When Dickie had first visited Australia, twenty-five years before, it was as assistant stage manager to his cousin, the Prince of Wales. This time he was the star. In Melbourne cheering crowds lined the route from the airport, in Sydney the Mountbattens' car was surrounded by enthusiastic well-wishers. Dickie loved it, despite the 'hot-making' compliments from his fans ('She's a beaut but he's more of a beaut'). The Mountbattens were top of the bill – and Dickie was delighted to share the stage with Edwina. 'Terribly hectic and tiring', she thought, as she sat through the speeches and civic presentations. It was embarrassing to hear herself praised so fulsomely, half a dozen times a day. Standing for hours in a reception line made her feet ache, shaking hundreds of hands left her fingers swollen and her wrist sore. Nevertheless she found to her surprise that she was enjoying herself. People were direct and informal: she did not have to struggle to put them at their ease. Letters and telegrams poured in from people she had met in hospitals, welfare centres and prison camps, thanking her, welcoming her, sending good wishes. She floated, exhausted, on a sea of gratitude and affection.

In New Zealand it was the same. By now Edwina had got into her stride. At every stop she inspected units of St John, each evening there was a civic gathering. She was having a marvellous time, talking to medical students, arranging hospital visits, receiving deputations from St John, while Dickie met the Cabinet and caught up with various generals. His programme completed, it was time to set off in search of striped marlin. Alas, the visitors were out of luck. Edwina gazed at the sea: 'Ate a lot and talked and read.' It was the first time for years that she had spoken of opening a book.

Dickie flew back to Singapore, leaving Edwina free to concentrate on her tour: six days of visits to hospitals, vocational training centres, convalescent homes, workshops for the old and disabled. She passed through country she had last seen with Bunny in 1935; these days, however, descriptions of natural wonders took only a few lines in her diary. The rest was filled with the names of doctors, nurses and occupational therapists, notes about hospital conditions and types of treatment, a record of her engagements and the distances she had travelled. 'Dead beat', she wrote on 13 April, '. . . 22 speeches in NZ

375

in 12 days.' Back to Australia and Tasmania for two and a half weeks of eighteen-hour days. The big receptions were a nightmare. It was impossible to hear what people were saying and after two or three hours of handshaking Edwina could hardly distinguish one face from another. She was sustained by reunions with old friends: doctors, nurses, Red Cross and St John volunteers, whom she had first met on her tour of SEAC hospitals and the camps, people with whom she had worked in RAPWI, ex-prisoners and internees whom she had last seen in Malaya, Thailand, Java and Sumatra. She wanted to know how they were and what they had been doing; Edwina was interested in individuals, not in performing before a throng. Yet she could not fail to be touched by the applause that greeted her wherever she went. In Hobart the townsfolk stood on their doorsteps and sang 'For She's a Jolly Good Fellow', in Brisbane they came out in their pyjamas at six in the morning. She was thrilled to be asked to march in the procession to the Cenotaph with 'the Diggers', veterans of the Great War: 'the *only woman* who had ever been invited to march in Dawn Service Contingents . . . the March which was at a fast pace and downhill over Tramways etc taxed my control and energy considerably especially as I have not marched since I was a Girl Guide!!'

Edwina got back to Singapore on 4 May. After six weeks' travel it was a joy to be able to unpack. Re-pack, rather, for three days later the Mountbattens took off for the Himalayas with Patricia and John Brabourne, Dickie's ADC. 'A short holiday in Kashmir or possibly Nepal would be heaven', Edwina had told Dickie at the beginning of the year. He had arranged both. They returned to Singapore on 20 May, in time for the swearing-in of the new Governor-General, Malcolm McDonald. The Supreme Command had been wound up. The Mountbattens' last week was taken up with parties; at one a baby elephant was brought in, carrying a howdah with 'Farewell to Supremo' spelt out in light-bulbs. Edwina worked till the end: 'Visited Union Jack Club run by WVS' she wrote on 20 May, the last day, 'and then looked in at Sime Road Camp to settle some points, then did more dictation' – this before the Mountbattens' farewell cocktail party for four hundred people – '. . . then 2 solid hours signing and writing . . .' At eleven o'clock that night Edwina, Dickie and Patricia left Malaya for home.

What were the Mountbattens to do with themselves? People murmured about an important job for Dickie: the Duke of Gloucester suggested that his cousin should succeed him as Governor-General of Australia, Lord Kemsley believed he would make a good Prime Minister, the King thought he should become some sort of Chief of Staff to the Minister of Defence. The Maharajah of Bikaner, an old friend, begged him to come to India as Viceroy when Wavell retired. Dickie was flattered but, he told Edwina, 'I really want to go back to the Navy, as you know, and don't like the idea of governing . . .' This was true. 'It made me feel so homesick dining on board ship again', he had written in his diary after an evening in HMS *Cumberland* in late 1945. Now he asked the First Lord, A. V. Alexander, whether there was a chance that he could go back to sea. Commander of an aircraft-carrier squadron? An appointment in the Mediterranean? The Admiralty said they would let him know. Edwina began to make tentative inquiries about houses in Malta and meanwhile Dickie, now a Rear-Admiral, set about enjoying seven months' unused leave.

It was fun to be a hero. A guard of honour awaited the Mountbattens as they passed through France on their way home; three days after their return to England Dickie drove through London in the Victory Parade, followed by lunch with the Prime Minister and the Service Chiefs. Oxford gave him an honorary degree; so did Cambridge, plus the Freedom of the City and an honorary fellowship of his old college. He was presented with the Freedom of the City of London and, with Edwina, the Freedom of the Borough of Romsey. (In return Dickie presented the Mayor and Corporation with a captured Japanese field gun on wheels. Expecting something smaller, they had set aside a place to hang it on the wall.) He became President of the Royal Life-Saving Society, Commodore of the Royal Thames Yacht Club, an honorary member of a string of livery companies. The Shipwrights made him a Warden, the Grocers gave him a silver sabre. He laid a foundation stone in Bournemouth, attended the State Opening of Parliament. ('Rather fine', Edwina wrote in her diary, 'but a lot of fuss about nothing as it only lasts 12 minutes.') At the beginning of December Dickie was admitted to the Order of the Garter. 'Everyone very thrilled', Edwina said, and as her Christmas present ordered a Garter Star for him, in diamonds. Less fuss was made of her achievements. The American Red Cross presented Lady Louis with the Silver Distinguished Service medal, the Belgian Red Cross gave her the Gold Medal for War Services. That was all. People showed their respect by asking Edwina's advice: 'a long meeting with the M of H re the Hospital Car Service . . .'; 'rushed off early to attend an LCC Emergency Nursing Scheme Meeting . . .' There were other signs of recognition: 'Tennis finals at Wimbledon . . . Sat next to Queen Mary. Tea with her and party in Royal Box after'. Edwina was now considered serious and respectable. She was invited to Lambeth Palace for discussions with the Archbishop of Canterbury; the Bishop of Singapore looked in at Chester Street to talk about welfare arrangements in Malaya. Praise did not go to Edwina's head. Now she no longer had a major job to do, she felt diminished. She spent her days coping with routine duties and a ragbag of useful but undramatic engagements. Instead of devoting herself to her work, she was obliged to fit it in between receptions in Dickie's honour and, increasingly, entertainments of the sort that had lapsed during the war: 'State dinner for Queen Wilhelmina . . . Well done but rather long after', 'Dined with Emerald Cunard at Dorchester'.

It was odd to be able to take time off, to have restful weekends at Broadlands, gossiping with Paula, Peter and Yola. Dickie practised swordplay with his kukri in the Park, in the evening they played cards and pencil and paper games. John Brabourne, Dickie's ADC in SEAC, often came to stay. The Mountbattens liked him and Edwina thought he would make a charming son-in-law. '. . . Good news', she wrote in her diary on 16 July. 'Patricia has definitely said yes!' Discussions with John's mother, Lady Brabourne, sessions with his trustees, an interview with the Archbishop of Canterbury, who agreed to take the wedding service, consultations with Molyneux, who was to make Patricia's dress, and Constance Spry, who was in charge of the flowers: 'Everyone getting very overworked and rather cross', Edwina wrote on 17 October, 'and Operation Wedding closing in upon us.' Dickie was in his element, orchestrating traffic arrangements, monitoring the invitation list, drafting speeches. Six hundred people attended a reception in the local hall, three hundred and seventy relations and intimate friends celebrated in the house. Ten days later the Mountbattens were at St Margaret's, Westminster, for the marriage of Myra Wernher, Gina's sister. 'Not a patch on our wedding!!', Edwina said happily, like many a bride's mother.

It seemed centuries since her parting from Bunny. People said that Edwina had become a different person, that she was obsessed with work, inaccessible to her old friends. Some complained that, when they spoke of the amusing times before the war, Edwina looked severe

Diminuendo

or, worse, claimed not to know what they were talking about. It was true that these days she had no time for what she regarded as idle pleasure. Absorbed in preparations for the next appointment, the next committee, the next inspection, she was too busy for reminiscence and hardly took in what her friends were saying. She was lonely, none the less. Marjorie worked closely with Edwina at St John but, when they met outside the office, they discussed what went on within it. Jeanie Norton had died in the spring of 1945, Yola was in Paris, Nada caught up with family affairs. Edwina had outgrown her pre-war women friends; Paula was her only confidante, partly because she had little to do and could come round at short notice. Then Edwina found Malcolm Sargent.

She had met him first in January 1941, when he conducted the London Philharmonic in a performance at the Albert Hall. The orchestra had just finished a British tour of ten cities, 'the Blitz tour', afternoon and evening concerts of classical music, played between bombing raids. The symphonies of Beethoven, Schubert, Tchaikovsky and Dvorak went down beautifully, for with the war had come a hunger for music that was eloquent and uplifting. Sargent had become a star. He worked like a demon; as principal conductor of the Liverpool Philharmonic Orchestra he gave more than eighty concerts a year. In mid-1941 he joined the BBC's 'Brains Trust', as one of a panel of guests who extemporized answers to listeners' questions. ('How does a fly land on the ceiling?', 'What are the five attributes of a full and happy life?') Among women listeners Sargent was said to be the programme's most popular contributor. Girls queued up outside the stage door for his autograph, adoring audiences cried, 'Malcolm! Malcolm!' At the Albert Hall he conducted by Royal Command, leading a choir of two thousand in *Jerusalem*, reinforced by the voices of the audience, five thousand strong, including those of the King, the Queen and the courtiers in the Royal Box. Sargent was as well-known as Lady Louis Mountbatten and had as devoted a following. He was stylish, successful and unhappy.

'Then at 2.30 went to a lovely concert, the Messiah, conducted by Malcolm Sargent at the Albert Hall', Edwina wrote in her diary on 5 January 1946. 'Dined after at the Savoy Grill.' This was eight weeks after her return from the RAPWI tour. Messages were still coming in to congratulate her on her DCVO, announced a few days before, but she was in low spirits. She was staying at the Dorchester, full of frivolous people, and on the previous day she had gone to the funeral of Sir Roger Keyes, Dickie's Commander-in-Chief in Malta so long ago. London seemed small and cold. After her work in South-East Asia, it was difficult to readjust to the everyday world and she felt deflated. Sargent understood. Each day he rose to the heights and fell to the depths. In the darkened concert hall he stood under a sharply focused spotlight, orchestra, choir and audience at his command. When he took off his tail coat and white tie, he was a slight, worn man with thinning hair. He lived in a rented basement flat in Kensington, a piano squeezed into his bedroom, his music kept in a windowless box-room where his son, Peter, slept when he came home on leave. Young women flocked to see him but his own daughter, Pamela, had died in 1944 at the age of eighteen, after years of suffering from the after-effects of polio. Sargent's wife had asked for a divorce. The music he conducted was sublime, his private life unsatisfying and incomplete.

Edwina rescued him. Sargent talked easily to well-connected ladies; here was one whose conversation was not trite. A week after the Albert Hall performance in 1946, Edwina was in Manchester, seeing the Radium Treatment Rooms at the Christie Hospital. 'Then drove to Liverpool . . . looked in at Malcolm Sargent's Youth Concert. Delightful.' In the mornings she watched him rehearse at the Philharmonic Hall, in the afternoons she was in the audience. 'Beethoven, Elgar. Quite beautiful. Talked a lot and had a delicious dinner and we both came down to London on the night train'.

Sargent introduced her to his son, who was in the RAF; Edwina thought that Peter, at twenty, would be a friend for Pamela, now nearly seventeen. (Pamela did not agree.) Sargent dined at Chester Street and Edwina went to every performance he conducted: ('Elgar's The Kingdom. Lovely'). It was not just Elgar that made Edwina sentimental. Like Sargent, she felt she knew the people who came to hear his concerts; she had met them in shelters and hospitals, he had taken his musicians to play to them in munitions factories and canteens. Together they had helped to win the war. For Edwina, these concerts were a sort of musical communion.

Edwina said nothing about her new friend in her letters to her husband, but, when Dickie returned from Singapore in June 1946, the two men were introduced. 'Malcolm came round for drinks', Edwina wrote in her diary at the end of the Mountbattens' first full day in

Diminuendo

London. Dickie was not bowled over. He was not keen on music, except for marches, fanfares and songs from revues, and he thought Sargent smooth. Aunt Victoria called him 'The Bandmaster'. The Sargent magic also failed to work on Pamela. Edwina's infatuation was embarrassing; when Sargent came for drinks or dinner, they had to have champagne, since that was what he liked. Edwina sparkled; the rest of the family glumly drank it down. She brought cream and eggs every week from Broadlands, to build up Sargent's strength, and pressed for official recognition for his services to music. As a result, he was knighted in the 1947 Birthday Honours. She found a spacious flat for him at 9 Royal Albert Hall Mansions, overlooking the Park, saw to its decoration and provided furniture and pictures from the store at Broadlands. Now Sargent had a music room, dining-room, drawing-room and a business-room large enough to house three secretaries. A manservant was found to look after Sir Malcolm and his wardrobe. Edwina's sympathy, imagination and application to detail had given Sargent exactly what he needed; he was surprised and overwhelmed.

She was not there to see him move into his new quarters. In the New Year Dickie began a Senior Officers' Technical Course at Portsmouth, in preparation for a post with the Mediterranean Fleet. Edwina found a house in Malta and began negotiations with its owner. Then, on 18 December, while she and Dickie were frantically signing Christmas cards, they were interrupted by a call from Downing Street. 'PM sent for me and staggered me', Dickie wrote in his diary; Edwina: 'Bombshell from PM'.

CHAPTER TWENTY-SIX

The Last Vicereine

'Possible new horror job' was all Edwina said in her diary. What Dickie had been offered was the Viceroyalty of India. 'Bit of a shock for him, you know', Attlee said in his memoirs, when he described his interview with Mountbatten. It was.

The new Viceroy was to be the last. For thirty years British and Indian leaders had been discussing independence. Now its time had come. The war had been a catalyst. In 1939 the Indian National Congress Party had withdrawn its representatives from the eleven British/Indian provincial governments, declaring that they wanted no part in hostilities between the imperial powers. This was serious, more so when Japan entered the war and Burma was overrun. Even Churchill, who had spoken loudest against Indian independence, grudgingly conceded that a placatory move must be made and the Lord Privy Seal, Stafford Cripps, had been sent out to find a formula for agreement. Cripps had committed the British Government to a policy of complete independence for India, inside or outside the Commonwealth, as she preferred. His mission got no further. The Congress Party wanted freedom now, the British would not grant it until Japan had been defeated. Indian leaders called for a campaign of civil disobedience; the principal rebels, including Gandhi, were put in jail. Wavell, a good and honourable man, did his best to break the deadlock but got nowhere. It was impossible to satisfy everyone. The Hindu leaders wanted a united India, the Muslim League demanded what amounted to a separate state. As the Japanese were gradually beaten back, Churchill and his supporters began to have second thoughts. The Viceroy was in despair. Downing Street and the India Office tied his hands: Mountbatten was amazed when Wavell told him he had been forbidden to have an informal talk with Gandhi. (Dickie, who was craftier, would have spoken first and told London afterwards.)

Two steps forward, one step back, so the parties danced their careful minuet. When Attlee succeeded Churchill in July 1945, there was another forward shuffle. In March 1946 a Cabinet Mission arrived in Delhi, charged with devising a scheme for a federal India. Division in the sub-continent was now deeper than ever; in recent provincial elections the Congress Party had carried the areas that were mainly Hindu, the League had triumphed in Muslim localities. After days of bargaining, discussion came to a halt and the Mission returned to London, leaving Wavell to pick up the pieces. In mid-August the Muslim League called for a 'Direct Action Day', which lit the fuse. In Calcutta more than twenty thousand people died or were badly hurt in three days of rioting between the communities; there were fierce confrontations in Bihar and East Bengal; the Punjab was a tinderbox. Hindu and Muslim continued to work alongside one another in the services that held India together – the bureaucracy, the railway and telegraph companies, the police and the army – but as people began to panic it looked as if these too might disintegrate. 'I have only one solution', Wavell admitted to Mountbatten. He called it Operation Madhouse: British withdrawal from India, province by province, beginning with women and children, then male civilians, then the army. The only other solution, he told the Cabinet, was to reinforce the Indian Army with four or five British divisions and face the prospect of continuing to rule the sub-continent for another fifteen years. The Government refused to contemplate either course. Wavell was instructed to re-open negotiations.

Even the most experienced advisers were pessimistic. George Abell, the Viceroy's wise and subtle Private Secretary, told the Cabinet that in his view there was only a ten per cent chance of getting the Indian leaders to agree on an acceptable scheme. The Prime Minister saw that Wavell had shot his bolt. The job needed someone new, with imagination, verve and persistence. 'We are trying to avoid an ignominious scuttle', he assured the Foreign Secretary. 'But a scuttle it will be if things are allowed to drift.' Attlee looked for another Viceroy and, not surprisingly, hit on Dickie. He was lively and exciting, Attlee said afterwards in his memoirs. 'He had an extraordinary facility for getting on with all kinds of people. He was also blessed with a very unusual wife'.

Would a less unusual wife have leapt at the chance of becoming Vicereine to the last Viceroy? Edwina was unenthusiastic. She wanted to press on with post-war relief work in Britain and Europe: 'Marjorie to lunch', she wrote sadly in mid-February 1947, while discussions about the Viceroyalty were going on, '. . . she leaves for a Tour of Austria and Italy on Sunday and I should have gone too had it not been for this Indian saga!!' She had also been looking forward to a more settled private life. During the week, while Dickie was in Portsmouth, Edwina intended to concentrate on work and her own friends ('a lovely concert of Malcolm's at the RAH . . .') and at week-ends to start straightening things out at Broadlands. She wanted to reorganize the household at Chester Street; Classiebawn Castle needed her attention. If the Mountbattens went to India, Edwina would have to set aside all thoughts of trips to Ireland – or anywhere else.

Months before, when Dickie had mentioned the Maharajah of Bikaner's suggestion that he should succeed Wavell as Viceroy, he had assured Edwina that he did not want the job. 'If it ever became unavoidable', he had added, 'I know that you would make the world's ideal Vicereine!' Edwina hated the idea. She did not want an official existence, hedged about by protocol, with every act observed. Private life in England was not easy – 'Coal and light and fuel crisis acute', she noted in February 1947, 'and all transport affected and 7 foot snow drifts in places and blizzards over whole country' – but at least it *was* private. Edwina could not bear the thought of being on display all the time. She felt unwell – it was the onset of the menopause – and after long consultations with Paula she arranged to go into hospital at the end of February for a partial hysterectomy. She was anxious and irritable. It is not surprising that she wanted to stay at home.

Edwina did not think only of herself. The 'horror job' would be dreadfully difficult; even Dickie might fail. Other members of the family were equally alarmed. 'Damn! Damn! Damn!' said Dickie's mother, who never swore, when she heard the news. Aunt Victoria believed that the politicians wanted her son to do the work they dared not do themselves and she thought it would be a miracle if he came home professionally and physically unscathed. Would she ever see him again? Aunt Victoria was eighty-three and, although she was still bright and vigorous, there had been one or two scares. At the beginning of the New Year she had felt a sudden pain in her right arm; 'Normal Arterio Sclerosis and nothing serious', Dickie noted in his diary. But it was a worry.

Dickie had not expected the job and he did not want it. Why take on a task even more hopeless than the one he had been given in South-East Asia? There, after interminable struggles, he had succeeded, with little help from his masters at home. In India the situation was deteriorating rapidly; were the politicians and officials in London ready to give the Viceroy the backing he required? It had not been easy to persuade the Admiralty that an ex-Supreme Commander should go back to sea. What would the Sea Lords' reaction be when they learnt that he was off again, to one of the grandest shore-based posts of all? As an ex-Viceroy, it would be even harder to convince them that he wanted no more than to be a simple Admiral.

Dickie had always been ready to do his duty but this time he was determined to refuse the Prime Minister's offer. 'Discussed PM's plan with Peter, Charles Lambe and Philip till all hours', Edwina wrote in her diary. The Mountbattens talked again to Stafford and Isobel Cripps. If it would help, Cripps declared, he would accompany Dickie to India and serve under him there, a generous offer, but embarrassing, for, if Dickie were to do the job at all, he wanted a fresh start. 'No progress regarding India', Edwina wrote, 'in fact if anything we seem to be going backwards'.

Every question, every reply drew Dickie further in. The Prime Minister was asked to associate himself with the First Lord and the First Sea Lord in guaranteeing Mountbatten's return to the Navy – this was agreed. Dickie tried another argument. If the Government were serious about independence, they would be prepared to set a firm date for the transfer of power. The Cabinet had in fact talked on and off about a deadline but the Prime Minister was opposed to committing the Government to a precise date which might prove practically and politically difficult. Now Attlee suggested the second half of 1948. More letters went to and fro. 'Peter crosser and more tired than ever', Edwina wrote. Dickie asked whether 'the second half of 1948' meant 'the end of the first six months', that is, June 1948. 'At home all day', Edwina noted on 17 February, 'but continuous conferences and Long Distance calls!!'

The time-limit was agreed. On 20 February Mountbatten's appointment as Viceroy was announced to both Houses of Parliament, in a statement on the Government's policy for India. 'Badly done', Edwina thought, 'and much criticism and suspicion about Wavell's treatment and future of India expressed'. (Wavell had been told about the prospective changes only a week before.) Churchill was incensed. In public he condemned the Government for embarking on 'Operation Scuttle'; in private he criticized Mountbatten for taking on the job. 'Everyone very nice about D. personally of course', Edwina noted. '. . . We dined at home and went to the Odeon'.

Dickie and Edwina were to leave in a month's time. Packing was the last thing Edwina wanted to think about as she waited to go into hospital at the end of February. 'Anaesthetics wonderful now', she wrote in her diary, 'and one knows and feels nothing after injection. But very uncomfortable'. She was shaky for days but there was no time to lose. Edwina had to look for clothes for herself and Pamela, who was coming to Delhi with her parents; in post-war London there was little available. Lady Wavell sent Edwina various useful tips. 'I found a tiara superfluous during the war . . . but have worn it several times this winter. Nice gloves are difficult to get here . . . Enid, Connaught Place, is the best dressmaker.' Edwina's seamstress came to the rescue, altering old garments and running up new ones. Formal clothes were needed for receptions and dinners: 'A non-stop day of work, shopping, including Hat-buying!! and fittings . . .' The most important sessions were to try the dress Edwina was to wear at the new Viceroy's first public engagement in Delhi, the Swearing-In Ceremony. She chose a gown of ivory brocade, cut so that the fabric caught the light. Its extreme simplicity set off her decorations, the Conspicuous Service Medal, the Grand Cross of the Order of St John, the Crown of India . . . 'Dickie and I had Gala photos taken', Edwina noted on 14 March, '. . . complete with Orders, decorations and Jewels and Tiara, Separate and Joint. Feeling awful still'. A rush of goodbyes to the family, the final weekend at Broadlands, a farewell cocktail party at the RAC: 'About 700 people . . . wonderful mixture. Duke of Gloucester, Queen Ena, Marina, Red X, St John, including caretakers at my office . . .' The last day was a nightmare: 'Packing in a frenzy and all nearly demented. People looking in to say goodbye making things worse'. On the morning of 19 March the Mountbattens set off in the York, for Dickie had stipulated that as Viceroy he should have the use of his SEAC aeroplane. When they landed in Malta for a night-stop, Edwina went for a nostalgic drive, 'to see house we might have lived in, but for India'.

The Mountbattens arrived in Delhi on 22 March, the Wavells left next day. 'Looked round Viceroy's House to get our bearings'. This was not Viceregal Lodge, where Edwina had stayed in 1921, but the great edifice in New Delhi, designed by Lutyens. The place was vast, the staff enormous. A fortnight later Edwina was still inspecting rooms. Lady Wavell had told her what she could expect. 'Glass: Ample. China: Ample. Electro-plate: Ample, though not attractive. There is also some Gold and Silver Plate'. There were too many small flower vases; large ones were needed for the huge reception rooms. The Wavells had not thought it right to redecorate Viceroy's House during the war and Eugenie Wavell was afraid Edwina would think it a mess. 'The South-East wing, after the Naval Staff left, was turned into a BOR's Leave Camp. It now looks awful . . .' New curtains and covers were needed but spare pieces were short lengths only and of little use. 'I wrote to Lenygan and Morant for samples of chintz but I am told they are not available. Since 1943 there have been so many more important things to do . . .' Lady Wavell had a point. 'I always thought the Viceroy's House looked beautifully kept . . .', Edwina had replied tactfully, '. . . and for the short time we are to be there it would be quite unjustifiable to take on any real redecorating or renovating'. Once she began to explore, however, she decided that a major spring-clean could not wait. The place was a mixture of splendour and shabbiness. Behind handsome doors were state rooms hung with cobwebs; the Viceroy's study was painted a depressing green. The new Vicereine looked into everything: the timing, composition and cost of meals, the state of the servants' quarters, the condition of the linen and plate, the management of the gardens and the stables. The Comptroller of the Household was amazed.

The Mountbattens intended their Viceroyalty to be an instrument of change. To help them, they had a team of trusted friends. Dickie had made it clear to Attlee that he meant to choose his own advisers and graft them on to the existing staff in Delhi. Four new posts were created in Viceroy's House: Pug Ismay became Chief of Staff; Sir Eric Miéville, former Assistant Private Secretary to the King, was to act as the Viceroy's Principal Secretary; Alan Campbell-Johnson and Vernon Erskine-Crum, who had worked with Mountbatten in SEAC, were appointed, respectively, Press Attaché and Conference Secretary. The Secretariat was headed by Ronald Brockman, Dickie's Naval Secretary since 1943, with George Nicholls, who had been in Combined Operations, as his deputy. Peter Howes, who thought he was on his way to Malta as Mountbatten's Flag Lieutenant, found himself in Delhi instead, as Senior ADC; George Abell, who was preparing to go home, learnt after his initial briefing meeting with Mountbatten that the new Viceroy had asked him to stay on. Edwina had also brought out two of her closest colleagues, Muriel Watson as Personal Assistant and Elizabeth Ward as Personal Secretary. Peter Murphy was installed as chief confidant and prop.

It was clear from the beginning that the Mountbattens' regime was going to be different. For the first, and indeed the last, time, photographers and film cameramen were invited to take pictures of the Swearing-In Ceremony, from a temporary platform designed by Dickie himself and erected high up in the dome of Durbar Hall. Mountbatten told his staff that he proposed to abandon precedent and deliver a brief address. Another surprise: journalists assigned to cover the ceremony were handed a neatly printed press release, prepared by Campbell-Johnson. The Viceroy-designate and his staff knew the importance of first impressions.

One innovation followed another. Edwina had consulted Stella Reading, who had worked at Viceregal Lodge in the 1920s. Lady Reading, observant and shrewd, set out her thoughts in a memorandum. The invitation list, she told Edwina, was of the utmost importance. People lobbied and conspired to be included: 'and the misinterpretation attached to the intrigue is even worse than the intrigue itself'. Edwina examined the records and insisted on a new beginning. 'The invitation list has . . . rather gone by the board', she told Patricia triumphantly, '. . . it was previously mostly based on who had written their names in "the Book", or who hadn't, certainly as far as Indians were concerned. Now we invite those we want to see who are really making some contribution to the problems of India, high and low alike'. The Mountbattens could not always please themselves. 'On big pompous occasions of course', Edwina wrote, 'all the *right* people come with the gold plate out and God Savers and all the Panoply but we have tried to unbend and become more approachable and human . . .' At Edwina's suggestion the Court Circular was reworded: 'We now don't see, receive or interview people according to their social or official status but receive everyone and we don't honour people with invitations and with our august presences but invite and attend. With the changing times and delicate feelings existing it's so much better and all that was so out of date for India . . .' After all, Edwina observed, 'it's not by words or pompous notices that one keeps up the prestige of the Crown and one's country but I think by behaviour and example'.

It was not easy to overturn habit and routine. Although the Viceroy and Vicereine were no longer treated like gods, they were still regarded by their retinue as the embodiment of the majesty of the King-Emperor and his Queen. The very doorhandles in Viceroy's House were modelled in the shape of lions couchants, wearing imperial crowns. The Mountbattens fought against protection and protocol. Dickie insisted on riding with Pamela, with only a single bodyguard, at half-past six each morning, Edwina asked for lunch to be served informally beside the swimming pool. 'No ADCs or staff eating with us except when we have guests', she informed Patricia, 'and sometimes if we want to talk business, like with the Spens, Jinnahs etc not even then! . . .' The Comptroller was not sure who was more troublesome, Her Excellency, who was so unconventional, or His Excellency, who did whatever he pleased – at least, until Her Excellency intervened: 'I have had to dissuade Daddy from driving the Jeep when he thinks it would be fun . . .'

Dickie had appointed six ADCs, three British, three Indian. Hitherto only the Chief of Staff had included Indians in his entourage; 'strange', Edwina observed to Patricia. 'It would seem to be a necessity and elementarily sound.' The staff was advised to be less self-important and more professional; as Lady Reading had pointed out to Edwina, 'the focal point of most troubles in Vice-Regal circles is the ADCs' Room'. Here people waited to go in to see the Viceroy. Inevitably they overheard bits and pieces of conversation and discussions on the telephone: Viceroy's House was full of rumour. To counteract it, Dickie encouraged his staff to be open and straightforward. So that his key advisers always knew what the Viceroy was doing, saying and thinking, Dickie kept notes of every meeting, circulated a daily summary and had an informal discussion with his team each morning. People continued to gossip and conspire but, by making themselves accessible, the Mountbattens made sure that rumours did not last long.

The house and gardens were opened more often and to a greater variety of visitors than before. The Mountbattens' first week in India coincided with the Asian Relations Conference, which had been meeting at the Red Fort in Old Delhi. Edwina and Dickie gave a garden party for conference delegates, members of the Legislative

Edwina Mountbatten

Assembly and senior officials in Delhi – seven hundred guests in all. 'I think Viceroy's House and grounds are now looked on more as a *part* of India than as a British stronghold', Edwina told Patricia in late April. Of all her Indian guests, 'I don't think more than 6 had ever been here before and yet they had all been prominent in some form of public life for many years! I admit a number had been in prison for nationalist convictions or offences and for a time were out of circulation but they were around long before and have been released for over one or two years now.' On the day after Edwina wrote that letter, the Mountbattens gave a party for six hundred people from the staff of the Viceregal estate.

Other British women in positions of influence and authority had made Indian friends, worked with Indian women and invited them to their houses. Edwina was not the first. As Vicereine, however, she was the grandest; self-conscious, snobbish memsahibs could not fail to notice. There was a multitude of these. Stella Reading thought their influence pernicious. She particularized. They criticized local customs without understanding their origin, she said, talked critically about religion, lecturing great philosophers, touted for money for their favourite charities. They wanted to know as little as possible about India and Indians. Edwina, however, had come to learn. 'I must see for myself', she said to Muriel and Elizabeth, and she did.

Although she was not remote, on formal occasions Edwina could be as grand as any of her predecessors – grander even. When she made an entrance, with or without fanfares, no one forgot that she was Vicereine. Back straight, head high, she moved proudly down the marble stairs, slowly she proceeded through the long rooms. Some thought her distant, not knowing that without her glasses she could hardly see them. Others mistook her reserve for *ennui*. Edwina was often tired – her days began early – and her feet and head ached. 'I just have not had one *second* free', she wrote at the end of her first four weeks in Delhi, 'and have been so dead beat that I just felt I couldn't get down to writing. Last weekend I meant to and then found I had 600 letters to sign in 24 hours so my few hours in the watches of the night had to be devoted to that and it's such a short quick signature too!!!' (This was ironical: each letter had to be signed 'Edwina Mountbatten of Burma'.) The temperature was 106 degrees and climbing fast: 'I still tell Pammy it's the same cool weather and she's standing up to it wonderfully so far'. Pamela was having an interesting and amusing time – on her eighteenth birthday the family held a small dance by the pool – and, as for Dickie, Edwina reported that he was 'enjoying it all *madly*, thank God'. Not so Edwina. 'I pretend to', she confided to Patricia, 'and that it's a great adventure, which it is, and I love the work and my Indians and a lot of the interest, but how I long for lovely Broadlands and sweet little Chester Street and the cosy and simple life. Even ringing a bell and no-one answering!!!' Eugenie Wavell had sent Edwina a list of the personal servants who would look after her everyday needs: her bearer, *durzi, chaprassi* and *khidmatgar*. Edwina never found herself alone. Everything was too imposing, too theatrical. She wanted privacy and peace: 'My neuralgia has been *frightful* but I still hope for the best – makes life however even more difficult'. The Sealyham, her closest companion, was also ill at ease: 'My Mizzie is standing up to everything fairly well – really hates India – no good smells – hot etc etc. He can't be stripped properly as no-one can do it and so has been rather badly shorn in layers with scissors by the local vet and does not look his best, poor sweet!!!'

Work was a comfort. Before she left England, Edwina had inquired about the activities of voluntary and missionary societies in India. Her friend Agatha Harrison had told her about the work of the Indian Conciliation Group, Grace Lankester, another colleague, provided an introduction to the Women's India Conference. Isobel Cripps gave Edwina the names of a number of influential Indian women, Stella Reading urged her to revive the local Women's Voluntary Service. The day after the Swearing-In, Edwina got cracking. The first name on her list was that of her mother's old friend, Mrs Sarojini Naidu, a celebrated poet and campaigner for independence and now a member of Congress. She was ill and could not keep her appointment – but there were plenty of others. '. . . Received Mrs Pandit, Nehru's sister, very interesting and attractive, Health Minister for UP, Cabinet Minis-ter, and then Shreemati Kamala Devi, Socialist Social Worker'. Next day Edwina met the leaders of the YWCA, the WVS, Delhi Welfare, and Mrs Clubwala, the kingpin of social work in Madras. Between meetings with the household and her staff, she saw the head of the Red Cross; Lady Rama Rao, the President of the All-India Women's Conference; Miss Wilson of the Lady Minto Nurses; the heads of the Nursing Association and the Human Rights Commission; and Dr Ambedkar, who came on behalf of the lowly Scheduled Castes, 'the untouchables'. Grace Lankester and Agatha Harrison had recommended an early meeting with Horace Alexander, the Quaker, who was close to Gandhi and had known his friend C. F. Andrews. Ten days after her arrival in India, Edwina spent half a morning with him.

In her first three weeks as Vicereine, Edwina visited the Indian and British military hospitals, the Victoria Zenana hospital, the Rajputana Rifles Welfare Centre, the Irwin Hospital and the College of Nursing. One of her happiest discoveries was Lady Irwin College, 'the Domestic Science College with students from all over India and from all religions and political views. Very heartening show'. Edwina's days now began as they had done in London: 'Have arranged early routine of my own personal work, talks with D. and Pammy at breakfast at 9 and Staff Meeting of Muriel, Elizabeth and Mr Bannerjee' (her secretary) 'at 10 . . .' Each morning she received visitors. Some calls were purely ceremonial, most were appointments with people who could tell her what she could do for India. Within a month she had made friends with four of the country's most able people: Mrs Naidu; Mrs Pandit; Miss Maniben Patel, the daughter and confidante of Sardar Vallabhbhai Patel, Member of the Executive Council with responsibility for Home Affairs, Information and Broadcasting; and Rajkumari Amrit Kaur, Gandhi's friend and personal secretary. Like Edwina, these women were busy, but they saw that she was genuinely interested in what they were doing. Primed with questions, Edwina spent the afternoons on reconnaissance: 'with Pamela, Muriel and Elizabeth to the Food and Nutrition Exhibition'; 'visited the Viceroy's Dispensary to deal with all estate people, who number over 4000!'. Edwina was finding her feet – and so was her daughter. Before she left London, the Quakers had supplied Pamela with a list of progressive young people, whom she now sought out. This was not easy, for they were often in gaol.

Edwina did not keep her discoveries to herself. Stella Reading had told her that she had been shocked to find how little the Viceroy was kept in touch with opinion among people outside his own circle. Edwina summarized her conversations and sent reports to Dickie: 'To His Excellency, From Her Excellency'. Lady Reading had also suggested that Edwina issue an occasional newsletter to selected friends at home. Just as Dickie had circulated copies of his wartime diaries among his family and friends, so Edwina now sent regular bulletins to Patricia, Dickie's sister Louise, Lady Brabourne, her colleagues at St John and the Red Cross and, wisely, to Aunt Victoria, who could be relied on to show them to the King and Queen.

Edwina did not pull her punches. Much of the trouble between Hindu, Muslim and Sikh was, she declared, 'artificially engineered and is the result of previous policies, missed opportunities and mistakes made on all sides'. It was quite clear, she said 'that India's problem is largely economic and social, far more than religious or political . . .' Improvements were urgently needed in general living conditions, standards of education, employment and health. She pointed to the facts: ninety-two per cent of the population was illiterate; twenty in a thousand women died in childbirth; a hundred and sixty-two in every thousand babies died in the first weeks of life; four hundred and thirty children in a thousand died before the age of five. The medical profession was scandalously ill-paid: a fully qualified State Registered Nurse received the equivalent of seven pounds four-pence a month. For a population of four hundred million, there were fewer nurses than in London. A major obstacle to recruitment was the reluctance of ordinary Indian women to take on professional or voluntary work. Nursing was considered menial – understandably, given the levels of pay and the poor standard of accommodation in hospitals – and purdah kept many Moslem women at home. Edwina intended to help her new friends change all this.

She started with those whom she expected to give a lead. A fortnight after the Mountbattens' arrival in Delhi, Dickie called a meeting of the British Residents in the Indian States; between an official luncheon and a State dinner, Edwina gave a tea party for the wives, at which she induced them to talk about welfare and medical services in India. Some knew next to nothing. Four days later the provincial Governors arrived for consultations with the Viceroy. This time, Edwina decided, the wives would have a conference of their own. Having briefed two or three of the livelier ones before breakfast, she gathered them all together for a seven-hour session. 'Interesting day', she wrote in her diary that night. 'Lack of knowledge and parochial viewpoint and Anti-Indian feeling of many appalling even now'. At lunch-time she introduced the Governors' wives to the Members of the Executive Council who looked after Industry and Health; on the second day they met the Members for Food and Public Works, together with senior officers of the medical and nursing services, civil and military, representatives of the Red Cross, St John Ambulance, the Guides, the

Edwina Mountbatten

WVS, and the YWCA. It was the first time such a meeting had taken place. Led by the Vicereine, a brisk and incisive chairman, the conference identified ways in which existing organizations could co-operate and extend their scope, needs which were not being met, overlaps which could be eliminated. This meeting, Edwina declared, was just a beginning. Another would be held in two or three months' time, to bring in all the Indian-sponsored welfare organizations. 'Dead beat', she wrote when the conference was over. The participants felt as if they had been swept up in a tornado.

Some missed the point. Her Excellency was befriending the wives, they said, to make it easier for His Excellency to influence the husbands. This was not Edwina's principal motive, although it was certainly the case that, by involving the womenfolk in her endeavours, Edwina encouraged them to face the implications of the transfer of power. They were apprehensive but at least they now looked forward. It is also true that Edwina's conversations with leading Indian women were a help to Dickie in his negotiations with their husbands, fathers and brothers: '. . . Attended a Private Party given by Begum Liaquat Ali Khan to enable me to meet the Ladies of the Muslim League. A fantastic evening'; '. . . Mrs Aruna Asaf Ali . . . she was always wildly anti-British, working underground in last years and refused to see me at first but we made firm friends I think, however, and I liked her'. The hardest to unfreeze was Miss Fatima Jinnah, sister of the President of the All-India Muslim League. 'Fascinating evening. Two very clever and queer people', Edwina noted, after the Jinnahs had dined at Viceroy's House on 6 April. 'I rather liked them but found them fanatical on their Pakistan and quite impracticable'. Little by little – 'Miss Jinnah came to tea', 'dinner for Mr and Miss Jinnah . . .' – Edwina tried to thaw out her new acquaintance. It was difficult. When Edwina said how pleasing it was that at Lady Irwin College an overwhelmingly Hindu class had elected a Muslim as head girl, Miss Jinnah replied ominously, 'We have not been able to start our propaganda in that college yet'. Like her brother, Miss Jinnah was proud, intense and awkward. 'My God, he was cold', Dickie remarked after his first interview with the Muslim leader. Jinnah did not find it easy to relax. Photographers had assembled in the garden to take pictures of the meeting and Jinnah, expecting that Edwina would stand between himself and Dickie, had prepared an appropriate remark. 'A rose between two thorns!' he exclaimed gallantly – too late, for he found that he was in the middle himself, with a Mountbatten on either side.

With Nehru there were no such difficulties. Charming and culti-vated, he was never at a loss for the right phrase or gesture. He was fit and trim – he practised yoga – and unlike Jinnah, who was gaunt and sickly, with bad teeth, Nehru was good-looking. In the buttonhole of his homespun tunic he always wore a freshly plucked rose. No gaucheness or inhibition here. Nehru had not forgotten the Mountbat-tens' welcome in Singapore in 1947. He brought his daughter, Indira, and Krishna Menon, his friend and colleague, to lunch at Viceroy's House; he looked in regularly to confer with Dickie; his sister, Mrs Pandit, quickly became Edwina's ally and supporter.

Gandhi made the deepest impression. Slight, bent, clad in hand-spun dhoti and shawl, the Mahatma seemed a fragile figure; his strength showed in his bright eyes. His first meeting with Mountbatten was at the end of March. Dickie asked Edwina to help him make Gandhi feel welcome, for Viceroy's House represented everything he opposed. Tea was brought – Gandhi ate curds of goatsmilk, from the tin bowl he had used in prison – and for an hour and a quarter the Mountbattens sat with their visitor in the garden and encouraged him to reminisce. Gandhi was acute and unpredict-able and, before they moved on to business, Dickie wanted to win his trust. Edwina listened. Seventy-seven years' observation had made Gandhi a shrewd judge of character; he had heard about the work Edwina had done since the beginning of the war and he knew that she had spoken to Agatha Harrison, Grace Lankester and others who understood what he was trying to do. As the Mountbattens led their visitor into Dickie's study, Gandhi put his left hand on Edwina's shoulder, leaning on her to steady himself. One photographer caught the moment, all who saw the picture understood the meaning of the gesture. Lady Louis had Gandhi's blessing. And Dickie? 'I felt completely at home with him', the Mahatma said afterwards to Horace Alexander. 'I talked to him as if I were talking to Charlie Andrews'. When Edwina herself saw Horace Alexander three days later, she said straight out, 'Of course we think that Gandhi and his friends are absolutely right. We must try to fit in with what they want us to do'.

But what did India want? Jinnah insisted on an independent Pakis-tan, Nehru was not prepared to contemplate a divided India. The Nawabs, Rajahs and Maharajahs, rulers of the Princely States, did not wish to relinquish their special status. Sikh leaders insisted that the Punjab be divided; there were demands for the partition of Bengal. When Mountbatten alluded to future links with the Commonwealth, Nehru was pessimistic, Jinnah ominously non-committal. Gandhi was completely opposed to any sort of partition. Rather than accept the division of India, he declared, Congress should be prepared to agree to government by the Muslim League. When Mountbatten asked what he would recommend, Gandhi advised him to invite Jinnah to form an interim central government. Dickie was startled. (Others less so, for this kite had been flown before.) The suggestion, the Viceroy told his staff, was 'undoubtedly mad'. Even so, it should not be dismissed out of hand. The Congress leaders rejected Gandhi's scheme. Mountbatten was disappointed. Gandhi withdrew to Bihar and took no further part in constitutional discussions. The Mahatma's silence made negotiations easier but, without his support and approval, the decisions made by the Viceroy and the party leaders lacked legitimacy.

Mountbatten and his staff recognized that independence without partition was impossible. The leaders of the Congress Party knew it too. They had thought so for weeks, even before the new Viceroy's arrival; their discussions with Mountbatten, in ones and twos and threes, had been part of the process by which they acknowledged it. In his morning meetings with the staff, Dickie had suggested various types of constitution for an independent India: an alliance, like the League of Nations (unpromising), a union, like the Union of Soviet Republics (window-dressing), a federation, like the relationship between Washington and the American States (tricky). Whatever solution was adopted – and Mountbatten believed that firm decision was required rather than interminable negotiation – the Government in London had to move quickly. On 17 April Mountbatten told the Secretary of State for India that there must be no delay if civil war were to be averted.

By the end of the month a Plan had been drafted. It provided for partition, with Bengal and the Punjab being left to choose autonomy, union with either India or Pakistan, or further division, part of a province going one way, part the other. The fate of the Princely States was not spelt out but it looked as if they would be permitted to decide their future for themselves. Mountbatten had discussed the draft scheme with the leaders of the various parties – it is not clear in how much depth and detail – and he and his staff believed that in principle they had accepted it. On 3 May Ismay and Abell took the Plan to London.

The days grew hotter, the factions more suspicious. Sir Frederick Burrows, Governor of Bengal, was afraid that Communist agitators would provoke a breakdown of law and order in his province. Sir Evan Jenkins, Governor of the Punjab, was beset by rivalry between Muslims and non-Muslims, Sikhs and Hindu Jats. In Lahore there was danger of civil war. In Bihar the authorities were nervous: there a mere fifty European officials managed a population of forty million. In the troubled areas of East Bengal twenty-five million Hindus lived alongside as many Muslims. The situation was disturbing in the North West Frontier Province, which was on the brink of a revolt. The Governor, Sir Olaf Caroe, wanted an election; the pro-Congress Prime Minister did not; the leaders of the Muslim League were all in gaol. The tribesmen in the Khyber were anti-Hindu and if the British left India they wanted their lands to be a separate enclave. Mountbatten decided to fly north to see things for himself, taking Edwina and Pamela with him. They arrived in Peshawar to find that an enormous crowd of Muslim League supporters had assembled less than a mile from the town; they were threatening to march on Government House to place their grievances before the Viceroy. The only way to deflect them, Sir Olaf suggested, was for the Viceroy to go to the place where the demonstrators had collected. Dickie decided to go, Edwina refused to stay behind. From a railway embankment the Mountbattens looked down over wave on wave of more than seventy thousand angry people, bristling with knives, chanting 'Pakistan Zindabad', brandishing illegal green and white flags. Two figures stood on the raised earth above the fields, Dickie and Edwina, silhouetted against the sky. Anyone could have picked them off with a bullet or a bomb. They waited, Viceroy and Vicereine, simply dressed in bush shirts – luckily the fabric was a greenish-brown, near enough to the Muslim League colours. They raised their arms to greet the demonstrators. Silence, and then the staff heard cheers and shouts. Twenty minutes later, Dickie and Edwina clambered cheerfully down the embankment into their car and the thousands melted away.

After talks in Rawalpindi, Dickie and Pamela returned to Delhi, leaving Edwina, who wished to inspect the areas of worst disturbance in the North West Frontier Province and the Punjab. 'It was such a sad Tour', she wrote, 'the devastation is like the Blitz at its worst – whole areas completely destroyed and burnt out wilfully and the killed, maimed and homeless and penniless as a result really tragic. In those 2 Provinces largely Hindu and Sikh victims but also a good proportion of Muslims so it all seems so senseless and yet nothing seems to stop them . . .' In four days she and Muriel covered fifteen hundred miles by air and travelled long distances over uneven tracks by car, Jeep and on foot. They managed to reach every destination but one, Multan, the last place on Edwina's itinerary. A dust-storm made it impossible to find the landing-field, although the pilot tried repeatedly, dropping down to less than three hundred feet. Muriel eventually persuaded Edwina to call off the attempt. A fortnight later she tried again, fitting in a visit by starting from Delhi at half past five in the morning.

Sympathy was not enough. Edwina wanted to find out what had been going on. The people in charge were in an impossible position. How were they to advise these unfortunates, when no one knew what the future of the North West Frontier Province or the Punjab was to be? Present policy was to encourage refugees to return to their homes or, if those were uninhabitable, to stay with friends, relations or their own religious fraternity. This was unrealistic. The refugees were terrified and their fear infectious. Damage to property would take weeks to repair. Cries for vengeance were accompanied by demands for compensation; no one knew whence it would come. Everyone was waiting to know what would be decided in Delhi and London. Meanwhile, Edwina pointed out, the hospitals lacked equipment and supplies; more camps were required to ease over-crowding; the refugees needed advice on hygiene; municipal commit-tees were struggling to provide better drainage and clean water. These deficiencies were bound to lead to epidemics; without occupation for the refugees, there would be further disturbances. It was to all this that Edwina addressed herself.

'The real hot weather . . . is still ahead of us', she wrote in her newsletter at the end of April. In Delhi it was now a hundred and seven degrees. 'Work proceeds *non stop*', she told Patricia, 'and we've all been feeling pretty mouldy, Daddy included, so we're off to Simla tomorrow'. On 6 May the Mountbattens and Pamela left in the Viceregal Dakota for Ambala, where they transferred to Dickie's new open-topped Buick for the three-hour, five-thousand-foot climb up the twisting road to Simla. 'House hideous', Edwina wrote in her diary. 'Bogus English Baronial, Hollywood's idea of Viceregal Lodge'. After dinner they looked for entertainment. 'Tried to have cinema but it did not work'. Rather than sit in the cavernous rooms, all chocolate-brown paint and varnished wood, Edwina remained in the garden among the roses and rhododendrons. There she worked with Muriel and Elizabeth and, when her letters and reports were done, lay in the sun until her skin was toasted. Dickie kept to his study. With its curved wall of windows and pale-green painted walls, it was one of the few light and airy rooms in the house. He was overwhelmed with papers.

As well as his own staff, Dickie had brought with him V. P. Menon, the friend and confidant of Sardar Patel, Member of the Executive Council with responsibility for Information and Home Affairs. Patel was a skilful politician, who knew how to manipulate the Congress Party. Menon had taken part in earlier negotiations over independence in 1945 and 1946; on his advice Mountbatten considered various alternatives to the draft Plan, to accommodate possible objections from Jinnah. With Nehru, who arrived on the third day, the Mountbattens and Pamela drove to the Retreat at Mashobra, the Viceroy's weekend house. The place lay at the end of a rickshaw path through the Viceregal orchards: 'Quite glorious and completely remote'. It was a happy expedition; Nehru scrambled over the terraces, insisting that the party try a new technique of walking backwards up the slopes, easier on the lungs, he said, and less taxing for the leg-muscles. Edwina made an effort to join in the fun: 'awful neuralgia and sickness and felt like death'. She carried on: an evening at the local races with the staff, a lunch party for the Governor of the Punjab, 'a dinner with various Rajahs, small ones . . . did a good deal of work'.

Dickie was having a difficult time. His talks with Nehru had begun promisingly, so much so that he decided to show him the latest version of the draft Plan, with the minor amendments the Cabinet had requested when they saw it in London. To Mountbatten's consternation, Nehru rejected the changes altogether. The Plan must be altered, to make it plain that India, as understood by himself and his supporters, was the successor of British India, and that Pakistan, as envisaged by the Muslim League, was seceding from it. 'Non-stop conferences and headaches have started again', Edwina wrote in her diary. Mountbatten and Miéville set about drafting telegrams to Abell and Ismay in London, Campbell-Johnson prepared another com-muniqué. Within half a day Dickie had made the best of this unexpec-ted blow. His staff, he said, had advised him not to show the draft to Nehru but, on a hunch, he had done so. How fortunate it was. They would all have looked foolish if they had presented the Plan for Nehru's signature and then he had turned it down. Moreover, the Viceroy said, his talks with Nehru had helped him take negotiations further. When Mountbatten had first arrived in Simla, four days earlier, he and V. P. Menon had talked about the future relationship between Britain and India and, with Menon's encouragement, Mountbatten and his staff had begun to think out a procedure by which India might join the British Commonwealth, with a form of words that left out any objectionable references to 'Empire' and 'King-Emperor'. Menon had long favoured this idea and so, on bal-ance, had Sardar Patel. Nehru disagreed. Now, after his outburst over the draft, he became more flexible. Menon suggested that, if both India and Pakistan accepted Commonwealth membership, the unity of the sub-continent would in a sense be preserved and, indeed, it would become far more difficult for Bengal, the North West Frontier Province or other states to opt out of the new India. Furthermore, if India chose 'Dominion Status', independence might be granted more quickly. Nehru was inclined to agree.

Discussions went on all day. Edwina was not present at the meetings but, at meals and during walks in the garden between sessions, she heard how the negotiations were getting on. V. P. Menon told his daughter afterwards that Lady Louis' conversations with Nehru played a significant part in helping him to make up his mind to go for Commonwealth membership. By the time Nehru left on the Sunday evening, a new formula had been agreed. Mountbatten sent a telegram to Ismay in London: the aim was a transfer of power, with Dominion Status for both India and Pakistan. If the Plan were to succeed, Mountbatten declared, independence must be granted not in 1948 but in 1947.

Two days later the Mountbattens returned to Delhi. This was on 14 May. When he was once more installed in the capital (no light undertaking – three hundred and thirty people were required to move the Viceroy by road and rail from Simla), Mountbatten learnt that the Cabinet wanted to see him to discuss the revised Plan, not surpris-ingly, since it was so different from the one they had been asked to approve ten days before. Rather than receive a ministerial mission in Delhi, which might add to the confusion, Dickie offered to fly to London. He intended to leave on 18 May. This was just long enough for him to discuss the new draft with Jinnah, who refused to sign anything but indicated his assent in principle, and for Mountbatten to get Nehru's general agreement, in writing. The Viceroy wanted no more misunderstandings.

The Mountbattens arrived at Northolt on 19 May. They stayed at Buckingham Palace: 'So cold we are nearly dying of it and sitting in inadequate thin suits and a pathetic Fur Coat'. The days were packed: work at the office ('too strange being back again so soon!'); meetings with Lady Reading, Agatha Harrison, Grace Lankester and Lord Listowel, the new Secretary of State for India ('young and energetic', Edwina told Patricia approvingly); appointments with dressmakers and doctors; lunches for the family and with Malcolm Sargent (Dickie dined with his mother and sister). With the King, the Queen and the two princesses, the Mountbattens went to *Bless the Bride*. Nothing could have been more appropriate. 'Saw Elizabeth re Philip', Dickie noted in his diary next day and, the day after, 'Philip and I talked re Lilibet'. Princess Elizabeth was almost twenty-one, Dickie's nephew twenty-six. 'He has now got engaged to Lili-beth', Edwina wrote happily in her diary. (She could never spell it right.)

'Nice being back', Dickie wrote cheerfully in his Delhi diary. A day visiting local riot areas with Edwina, a day spent in staff meetings to report on the talks in London (the Cabinet had approved the Plan, the Opposition leadership had agreed in principle not to obstruct the necessary legislation) and then Mountbatten hurled himself into a last round of negotiations. Discussions started on 2 June. 'First meeting 10.00 with 7 leaders'. All but Jinnah seemed prepared to back the Plan. 'Saw Jinnah alone 12–12.30 . . .' Mountbatten's visitor remained unforthcoming. 'Saw Gandhi 12.30–13.45.' Dickie was anxious that the Mahatma's conscience might tell him to speak against the Plan, wrecking it altogether in an effort to prevent the vivisection of the sub-continent. He braced himself for a difficult discussion. As the meeting began, Gandhi gave the Viceroy a note written on the back of an envelope: 'I am sorry I can't speak . . . I know you don't want me to break my silence. There are one or two things I must talk about but not today . . .' The Viceroy was impressed. Although Gandhi's vow allowed him to interrupt his Monday silence to speak on matters of urgent importance, he had decided not to intervene.

At midnight Jinnah returned and stayed until one. Without the concurrence of the full Muslim League Council, he told Mountbatten, he had no authority to support the Plan. In that case, said Dickie, exasperated, he would speak for the Muslim League himself, on the assumption that, when the Council did meet, it would ratify the agreement. He had one request. The seven party leaders were meeting again in the morning. Mountbatten intended to tell them that Mr Jinnah had given him satisfactory assurances; would the Muslim leader at least nod his head in acquiescence? Jinnah only bowed impassively.

June 3rd: '. . . staff meeting bedroom 08.15. Krishna Menon 09.20. Nehru 09.30. Meeting with 7 leaders 10.00. Steered through OK. 2 Dominions accepted'. Mountbatten told Patricia that these had been the worst hours of his life. 'Broadcast to world at 7.0'. On the morning of 4 June the Viceroy gave a news conference to three hundred journalists. It was a brilliant performance. The Indians had wanted independence and had made partition inevitable. It was for them to make it work. And the date? 'How long will His Excellency stay as His Excellency . . .?' someone asked. The answer was a surprise, 'I think', the Viceroy replied, considering for a moment, 'the transfer could be about the 15th of August'. The remark was made so casually that it was not reported in the summary of the proceedings that was wired to London. The Prime Minister's Private Secretary observed that it would be a squeeze to get the Bill through Parliament in time; Attlee, notoriously terse, said simply: 'Accept Viceroy's proposal'.

Dickie had one task more that day. He had heard that the Mahatma was likely to criticize the Plan at his evening Prayer Meeting; he therefore invited him to call at Viceroy's House beforehand. Surely, Dickie said, what he had announced had not been a Mountbatten but a Gandhi Plan, for in it he had tried to embody all the Mahatma had urged: non-coercion, self-determination, the earliest possible date for British withdrawal, a friendly attitude to Dominion status. Gandhi knew that Mountbatten was sincere. 'The Viceroy has no hand in it', he told the Prayer Meeting. 'In fact he is as opposed to division as Congress itself but if both of us – Hindus and Muslims – cannot agree on anything else, then the Viceroy is left with no choice'.

'Played the gramophone', Edwina wrote at the end of this momentous day, 'and talked after'. There were seventy-two days to go until 15 August. Years before, when Dickie had set out with the Prince of Wales on the Far East tour, he had counted down on his Tear-Off Calendar the days that remained until his reunion with Edwina. Now he got the Viceregal Press to print another, with large numbers and huge letters: 'Seventy Days left to Prepare for the Transfer of Power'; 'Sixty-nine Days left . . .'; 'Sixty-eight . . .'

'Of course no one is completely satisfied', Edwina wrote to Patricia, 'and we're still sitting on lesser volcanos.' Neither Congress nor the Muslim League had considered the difficulties before them. The Viceroy's gesture was a signal that they should cease arguing about the past and address themselves to the future. The police, the army, the judiciary and the civil service had to be taken apart, every post being reallocated to one or the other of the two new countries. Financial transfers had to be unravelled, assets redistributed. Every sort of detail had to be negotiated. There were rows over buildings, furniture, motor cars and flags. While these arguments took place, day after day, government had to be carried on.

Mountbatten's position was delicate. Nehru and Jinnah, their colleagues, the Congress and the League watched like hawks for any sign of favouritism. To be useful, he had to remain impartial. Edwina played her part. From London she brought a mother-of-pearl box for Rajkumari Amrit Kaur and another for Miss Fatima Jinnah. Her Excellency's greatest triumph came on 4 July: 'Mrs Pandit, Mrs Matthai and Miss Jinnah to tea, the first time the latter and Mrs Pandit have spoken for 3 years! . . . Very tiring but very successful. Mrs Matthai, Indian Christian, helped a lot'. While Dickie listened patiently to arguments about revenues, troops and boundaries, Edwina encouraged people who were trying to improve health, housing and education, regardless of communal differences. Pamela played an important part. She was working in a free medical clinic and dispensary for poor outpatients from Delhi and the surrounding countryside. It opened six mornings a week, receiving some two hundred patients a day, and twice a week a Red Cross car took volunteer staff to outlying villages, to see people too ill or too impoverished to come to the capital.

Work became more of an effort every day. Dickie, Edwina and Pamela rode early, while it was still cool, but by midday the thermometer was near to bursting. Throughout the month the average temperature at night was ninety-three degrees, a hundred and ten by day. The Mountbattens escaped to Simla only once, for five days in mid-June, but thundery weather made Edwina groggy and Pamela, who was worn out, had a fever from a badly infected leg. They staggered into the garden while Dickie soldiered on.

One of the Viceroy's immediate worries was the future of the Princely States, the five hundred and sixty-five territories, of varying size, wealth and importance, that were responsible not to the Government in Delhi but directly to the British Crown. What was to happen to them? Mountbatten did not wish to leave the Princes to negotiate for themselves after Independence. If they were offered good terms, he said, they might be prevailed upon to join the new India. V. P. Menon suggested a formula: the rulers should transfer to Delhi responsibility for defence, foreign affairs and communications; the Government should agree to protect their remaining rights and leave their private revenues alone. Nehru and Patel accepted these conditions on the understanding that all, or almost all, the Hindu states could thereby be persuaded to accede to India. Menon emphasized that Mountbatten's help would be crucial; the Princes would trust a Viceroy, particularly one who was the King's cousin. Mountbatten said he would see what he could do. One by one the rulers came to Viceroy's House. 'Maharajah and Maharani of Gwalior to lunch', Edwina noted and, two days later, 'His Highness of Jodhpur'. (He had upset V. P. Menon by threatening to shoot him with a pistol hidden inside a fountain pen.)

It took all Dickie's energy and ingenuity to coax and bully the rulers into accepting Patel's terms. The two who gave the most difficulty were the Nizam of Hyderabad and the Maharajah of Kashmir. The Nizam was a Muslim, his state, India's largest (it was the size of France and had a population of sixteen million), mainly Hindu. The Nizam was being manipulated by a powerful Muslim faction, in close touch with Jinnah, and refused to travel to Delhi, and Mountbatten was warned that, if he went to Hyderabad, he would not be given audience. In successive messages, Mountbatten explained that, if the Nizam did not accede, he might lose both his state and his throne, warnings that had no perceptible effect. Sir Walter Monckton, the Nizam's legal adviser, tried to negotiate an agreement on his client's behalf, but he and Menon did not hit it off and Sir Walter was reduced to drafting testy letters of complaint to London. The Indian leaders reluctantly agreed to give the Nizam two months more to make up his mind and Mountbatten offered his services as an intermediary in the future. The day of reckoning was thus put off.

In Kashmir, on the other hand, a Hindu dynasty ruled a largely Muslim state. The Maharajah could not bring himself to believe that the British were actually leaving India, and refused to consider joining up with anyone or anywhere. Matters were complicated by the fact that Nehru himself had close and sentimental ties with Kashmir, for it was from here that his family came. Dickie decided that he had better visit the Maharajah at home. 'Flew up to Kashmir arr. 11.30', Edwina wrote on 18 June, at the end of the Mountbattens' six days in Simla. 'Met by H. H. and Her H. at hideous Palace'. The visit started on the wrong note: in the middle of the first banquet Dickie accidentally knocked a bell under the table, alerting the servants, who rushed in to clear the plates and glasses. The band struck up 'God Save the King', the guests scrambled to their feet, the heir-apparent giggled, the Mountbattens smiled, their host looked stony. Dickie had been hoping for a private talk but no time had been set aside for this in the programme the Maharajah had arranged. He took his guests on an all-day fishing trip, he packed them into a Jeep to hunt bear. Dickie did not shoot; he had given it up, with polo, for the duration of the war and thought that, as Viceroy, he should continue to refrain. The visitors were taken to an exhibition of carpet-making, papier-mâché work, embroidery and woodcarving, and encouraged to go shopping. There were splendid dinners and a garden party, at which Dickie invested Their Highnesses with various decorations; the Maharajah took the medals and ribbons but not the hints about a little chat. One day remained. 'H. H. laid low with cholic!' Edwina reported disbelievingly, '. . . we set off on another fishing expedition . . . Back very late for dinner, good-byes etc etc'. Dickie at least managed to corner the Prime Minister, who assured him that the Maharajah would give the issue of accession 'serious consideration'. Weeks later, he was still considering.

'Twenty-one Days to Prepare for the Transfer of Power . . .' On 25 July the Chamber of Princes assembled in Delhi, twenty-five rulers and seventy-four representatives of the lesser states. Resplendent in his orders and decorations, the Viceroy addressed the gathering. More talks in the Viceroy's study; the stragglers signed. By the end of July Dickie had shepherded nearly all his flock safely into the fold.

Edwina Mountbatten

Edwina was engaged on diplomatic negotiations of her own. The most useful thing she could do, she believed, was to persuade the leaders of medical and social welfare organizations in the sub-continent to work together, so that, when the British left, a well-knit team of experienced people would be ready to take over. Throughout June and July she called on the leaders of voluntary associations and professional bodies, introduced members of one committee to those of another, pored over pages of smudgy documents to find out who did what. She spent hours discussing arrangements for Indian authorities and Indian charitable organizations to manage their in-heritance of buildings, staff and income. '. . . Saw Mr Newman, Architect to Gvt of India for Hospitals'; '. . . a long morning with discussions of high policy regarding the Dufferin Fund'. One cause was close to her heart, the passage of the Nursing Council Bill, intended to establish and maintain standards of nursing care. A measure had been drafted but had languished in the Legislature since 1943; Edwina was determined to get it through. For weeks she briefed supporters, lobbied those who wavered, with shrewd advice from her allies: Maniben Patel, Rajkumari Amrit Kaur. At the last minute it looked as if the Bill might fail; Edwina appealed to Nehru. Two days later, legislation was approved.

The clock ticked on. It was still very hot. Edwina wore the thinnest cotton dresses; her hair was flat and limp. 'Most of our air conditioners have given out and burst into flames!', she told Patricia, 'and sparks fly in every sense and in every direction in consequence!' She slept without air conditioning; Dickie depended on it. In his study in Viceroy's House – now painted pale green like the one at Simla – he had the machines at full blast, 'so cold', Edwina observed, 'that we have to put fur coats on to enter and one sees poor Mr Gandhi sadly pulling his rags around him!! altho' I insist on it being turned off just before he arrives. Other Indians arrive in sweaters! I think the acceptance of the *Plan* has been largely due to the leaders being got at in such arctic conditions that they were ossified. A very good technique!!'

'Nineteen Days . . .' At the end of June the provincial assemblies of Bengal and the Punjab had voted for partition: each province had to be divided, villages, cantonments, fields, going here to India, there to Pakistan. In Bengal the tension was frightening, in Punjab worse. Sikhs, Hindus and Muslims advanced conflicting claims to each piece

The Vicereine

With the Maharajah of Bikaner

With Gandhi

With Nehru

of land, each village track. A Punjab Boundary Force was formed to maintain a unified military command throughout the area; it could do little to prevent determined Sikh leaders from threatening violence and Muslim leaders from answering in kind. Already there was arson and murder. The Governors-designate of East and West Punjab declared that, if the militants were arrested, there would be worse violence. Everyone was afraid.

Who was to determine how the two provinces should be divided and where the boundaries should be? After much deliberation, it was decided that ultimate responsibility should be given to one man. This was the distinguished lawyer, Sir Cyril Radcliffe, who was now appointed Chairman of an independent Boundary Commission. Radcliffe arrived in Delhi on 8 July and began work at once. He and Dickie ostentatiously avoided one another, so that people could not say that either had influenced the other's judgement. Radcliffe stayed not with the Mountbattens but in a separate house on the Viceregal estate, where he sat among his maps and files, and Mountbatten announced that he did not wish to be told how Radcliffe was getting on. Even so, Congress and the League remained suspicious. Small issues blew up out of all proportion.

Dickie and Edwina were under phenomenal strain. On top of everything else, there were normal Viceregal duties: opening exhibitions, receiving callers, attending official dinners and receptions, writing, interminably, letters of sympathy, congratulation and thanks. However tired she was, Edwina was a punctilious correspondent. One waspish Delhi resident observed that, as Lady Louis left a party, her bearer would arrive with a grateful message for her hostess. Foreign governments were already appointing ambassadors to India and sending them to Delhi to get their bearings before the transfer of power. In ten days the Mountbattens received representatives from America, China, Holland, France and Belgium; all had to be welcomed and entertained. There were official and informal celebrations: on 12 June the Viceroy and Vicereine had eighty-seven people to a State dinner for the King's Birthday. On 18 July Dickie and Edwina celebrated their silver wedding anniversary: the staff presented them with an inscribed salver, the family with a cigarette box. Gandhi sent Edwina a sweet letter, addressed to his 'dear sister'. Ninety-five people dined: 'Nehru, Jinnah and the whole Cabinet, a number of the Princes and all our Staff, even the stenographers and my Indian

Secretary Mr Bannerjee who had *never* had a meal with his masters *ever*!' Official photographs showed a happy couple but the Mount-battens' marriage was as tense as it had always been. Edwina's meno-pause made her difficult to live with. Each night when Dickie went up to kiss her before returning to his pile of work he had to endure tearful scenes and recriminations for things he was totally unconscious of having done, offensive remarks he did not know he had made.

It was an effort to appear cool and serene. Everyone was overworked and on edge; Viceroy and Vicereine knew that at all costs they must seem controlled and calm. Dickie often looked tired. Sometimes Edwina could hardly stand it. 'We had the Jinnahs to dinner', she wrote in her diary on 25 July, 'he in an unbearable mood and quite hopeless. He has already become a megalomaniac and a pathological case so God help Pakistan'. Jinnah had monopolized the conversation, insisting that everyone listen to a series of long and unfunny jokes, and, instead of waiting for the Viceroy and Vicereine to leave the room first at the end of dinner, as was customary, the Jinnahs walked out at the same time as Their Excellencies. In normal times Edwina would not have been fussed; now she was almost as irritated as Dickie. 'Nehru and Indira and her husband and Mrs Pandit to dinner', she wrote next day. 'All quite charming and a joy after last night!!'

There was another worry. Mountbatten had believed that, after independence, he would be asked to stay on as Governor-General of both India and Pakistan. The discussions over Dominion Status had strengthened this impression, although on this subject, admittedly, Jinnah had given nothing away. At the beginning of July he at last came clean. 'What I thought would happen funnily enough', Edwina told Patricia,' and which neither Daddy nor any of his staff EVER contemplated has occurred, and Mr Jinnah himself wants to be Governor General of Pakistan (highly confidential of course)'. Some stratospheric appointment might be available for Dickie – Jinnah suggested that he become Chairman of the Joint Defence Committee – but that was all. Jinnah could not be moved. When Mountbatten explained that a Governor-General's powers were minute, a Prime Minister's very great. Jinnah smugly replied: 'In my position it is I who will give the advice and others will act on it'.

India wanted Mountbatten, Pakistan did not. 'Serious Staff Meeting re future GG', he wrote in his diary on 4 July. 'Worrying day'. That night, after a dinner for American Independence Day, he discussed the matter with Edwina. 'It's a complete nightmare', she wrote, 'and having come out to do and succeeded in doing a completely *impartial* job one dreads the thought of him, thru' a series of unexpected and possibly unpredictable events, being finally thrown into the one camp and having to go over to one side.' She had long ago made up her mind that in August they should go home. The staff, with the exception of Brockman, believed that they should stay. Mountbatten decided to seek advice and on 7 July Ismay and Campbell-Johnson set off for London. 'All going round in circles', Edwina wrote in her diary that night, 'tempers short and heat intense.'

Downing Street, Buckingham Palace, Chartwell: after each stop on his round, Ismay cabled Delhi. 'More heartburns and discussions', Edwina wrote on 9 July. 'Overwhelming opinion however that we should stay and the King, PM, Opposition, as well as all here including Mr Jinnah urged D. to accept. Also to take on Chairmanship of Joint Defence Council. Decided therefore no alternative. Many misgivings. Morally, logically as well as personally feel it's wrong but that D. has been faced with such a position that he cannot refuse.' On 10 July it was announced that Mountbatten was to become India's first Governor-General, Jinnah Pakistan's. It would be at least another year before Edwina could return to England.

'Two Days to Prepare for the Transfer of Power . . .' 'A hectic morning of work and interviews', Edwina wrote on 13 August, 'an early lunch before leaving to fly to Karachi.' The Mountbattens were going to Pakistan to bring greetings from the King and their own good wishes on the eve of the country's transition to Dominion status. Jinnah was not at the airport to meet them but among those who were was Colonel Birnie, the Military Secretary, with news of a plot to assassinate the Muslim leader during the State procession the following day. If Mountbatten were ready to carry on with the programme, so was his host. Dickie and Edwina agreed that arrangements should not be altered. A State dinner, a reception for fifteen hundred of the leading citizens of Pakistan ('sweet drinks', Campbell-Johnson reported, 'and soft music played by a band of bearded warriors in kilts') and then, on the morning of 14 August, Dickie and Edwina drove to the Assembly in an open Rolls-Royce, lent by a Maharajah. Here, after some preliminary argument about precedence, for the Viceroyalty still had fourteen hours to run, Mountbatten addressed the Members, Jinnah delivered an address, and, according to the sharp-eyed Campbell-Johnson, Edwina sympathetically pressed Miss Jinnah's hand. This was no time for frostiness, especially since they might all be blown up on the way back to Government House. The little party climbed into their open cars, Mountbatten and Jinnah first, next Edwina and Miss Jinnah, then Pamela and Begum Liaquat Ali Khan, the Prime Minister's wife. The crowds were docile. 'Thank God I have brought you back alive', Jinnah told Mountbatten, as their car turned in through the gates. Dickie thought privately that he might have said the same. At five in the afternoon the Mountbattens said goodbye. For the first time Edwina thought that Miss Jinnah showed a little emotion.

And now India. When the Viceroy had selected 15 August for the transfer of power, the astrologers were aghast. Nothing could be more inauspicious. Fortunately, however, the final minutes of 14 August were acceptable. Dickie and Edwina returned from Karachi at five o'clock in the afternoon. 'Hard work at once', Edwina noted, refusing to lose a second. That night Nehru addressed the Legislative Assembly: 'At the stroke of the midnight hour when the world sleeps, India will awake to life and freedom'. While the Prime Minister gave his address, the Mountbattens waited at what would shortly no longer be Viceroy's House. They dined ('Film: Bob Hope, *My Favourite Brunette*'). With Campbell-Johnson's help, Dickie tidied his desk. Journalists and photographers assembled. Still they waited. At twenty minutes past midnight Nehru arrived, with his colleague Rajendra Prasad, President of the Constituent Assembly. No one seemed to know what to do. Nehru propped himself against Mountbatten's desk, Prasad murmured something, forgot his lines, was prompted by his Prime Minister. They had come to say that the Constituent Assembly had assumed its new responsibilities and to confirm their invitation to Mountbatten to be India's first Governor-General. Nehru then presented Mountbatten with a large envelope, containing, he said, the names of the Ministers whom he was to swear in later that morning. When the visitors had gone, Dickie opened the packet. So great had been the excitement that whoever prepared the envelope had forgotten to put anything inside.

No time for sleep. At half past eight the Mountbattens proceeded to the Durbar Hall for the Swearing-In, their second in five months. They made their way to the golden thrones, Dickie in full dress, Edwina in gold brocade, and, as they sat down, a flash bulb exploded.

The Last Vicereine

The audience shivered – was it a bomb? Neither Dickie nor Edwina moved an eyelid. Out into the sun for the State drive to the Council Chamber. The crowds were enormous but police and soldiers managed to make an opening and the Mountbattens, decorations, jewels and all, were ushered, almost lifted, into the building. Before they left, Dickie ordered the guard of honour, four hundred men, to leave their arms inside the chamber and try to move the spectators back. Nehru climbed to the roof of the building to signal to the masses to make way; only then could the Mountbattens escape to their coach. People pressed forward to shake hands; from every side there were cries of 'Mountbatten Ki Jai', 'Lady Mountbatten Ki Jai'.

In the late afternoon came the great event of the day, the unfurling of the Indian flag near the war memorial in Princes Park. On Mountbatten's instructions, all British flags had been quietly put away; the Independence ceremonies were not a wake but a celebration. Thirty thousand people were expected at the ceremony, three hundred thousand came, some said more than half a million. Escorted by the mounted Bodyguard, Dickie and Edwina drove at snail's pace to the parade ground. Nothing could be seen of the grandstand, for the crowd had invaded the reserved places, clinging to the backs, arms and seats, six people to a chair. The wives of some of Dickie's staff were trapped between the stands and the dais, until people cried encouragingly, 'Make way for the memsahibs!'; Mrs Campbell-Johnson took refuge in the BBC recording van, in which Wynford Vaughan Thomas was feverishly making one of the most excited outside broadcasts of his life. Elizabeth Ward lost her sandals, Pamela was engulfed, until Nehru fought his way through the crowd to rescue her. Dickie and Edwina could not move, for their coach had stuck some twenty-five yards from the flagstaff. Nehru managed to reach them but the vehicle and its occupants could get no further. Edwina could see a row of brightly coloured turbans where the troops were attempting to muster. After hurried consultations with Nehru and the Commandant of the Bodyguard, Mountbatten decided that the only thing to do was to ignore the rest of the programme and give orders to hoist the flag and fire the salute. The flag broke, saffron, green and white, and at that moment a rainbow appeared in the sky.

A State banquet, speeches and at a quarter past nine the Mountbattens received three thousand guests in the State drawing-rooms and reception rooms of Government House. The Moghul gardens were

411

illuminated with coloured lights, the night air was soft and cool. At two o'clock in the morning the last visitors trickled home. For once, Edwina broke off that night's diary entry in mid-sentence. Although she found it difficult to tell him so, she was overjoyed by her husband's success. Dickie saw it and was grateful. It was, he said, a joint achievement. 'I've written to thank so many people for their help in finding the right solution for India', he told her, in a letter written on 18 August, 'but so far I've not written to the person who helped me most . . . Thank you, my pet, with all my heart.'

CHAPTER TWENTY-SEVEN

Torn Apart

Power had been transferred; this was the time to which they had looked forward. No one had foreseen the horror that now befell them all. On 16 August Mountbatten had presented the new leaders – Nehru and Sardar Patel, Baldev Singh for the Sikhs, and Liaquat Ali Khan, the Prime Minister of Pakistan – with Sir Cyril Radcliffe's recommendations. They had been ready on 13 August – there had been whispering about the details – but Mountbatten had deliberately delayed their release until after Independence. Disappointment was inevitable; why mar the celebrations?

All parties were indignant. Mountbatten left the leaders to digest Sir Cyril's report; in the afternoon they came to what was now Government House to discuss their objections. They had promised to accept the new boundaries, and, though they found the Award distasteful, the politicians kept their bargain. Meanwhile, their followers took matters into their own hands. In the last days before Independence, there had been increasing violence in the Punjab, inflamed by rumours of atrocities by Sikhs, Muslims and Hindus and stories of attacks by one community against another. On the afternoon of the 16th Auchinleck reported that civil war had broken out. Nehru and Liaquat Ali Khan decided to go together to the Punjab to see things for themselves and make decisions on the spot. What they found was horrifying.

The next three months were dreadful. In villages and towns people set upon one another. Shops and houses were destroyed, mosques and temples burnt. Women were raped and abducted, children killed, whole families slaughtered. Fear drove people from their homes; they fled with carts and bundles, Hindus to India, Muslims to Pakistan. On 26 August Edwina left for a three-day tour of East and West Punjab with Rajkumari Amrit Kaur, now Minister of Health. At Ambala they saw fifteen thousand people in a Muslim squatters' camp, 'right out in open, hardly any food or even water and no sanitation'. The Hindu and Sikh camps at Lahore were ghastly. At the Civil Hospital in Sialkot disinfectants and drugs were unavailable; dressings had been made from paper and leaves. 'Drove then across country on oily roads (having been up to our knees in mud all day owing to monsoon) to Gudjranwala with small military escort . . . Hindus and Sikhs housed in schools in terrible distress . . .' Together the two women drew up lists of what was needed. Rajkumari Amrit Kaur gave instructions, Edwina mobilized teams of volunteers. 'Drove to Air Field with Dickie and Panditji to talk business re Refugees . . . ' she noted on her return to Delhi. The two men were flying to Lahore for a meeting of the Joint Defence Council, to discuss the future of the Punjab Boundary Force. Fifty-five thousand troops had tried to control the slaughter; they could do little. For a week Mountbatten had defended the Force against its critics, trying to forestall those who demanded that it be broken into separate national contingents. At the meeting in Lahore he was obliged to accept that, since both governments appeared to have lost confidence in the Force, it was only prudent to disband it altogether. Its winding-up brought an end to Mountbatten's own executive responsibilities. He was only Governor-General of India now ('funny', he wrote in that day's diary entry, 'seeing ladies curtseying to [Jinnah] and not me – but quite right') and it was constitutionally incorrect for him to intervene in daily administrative or operational duties. To emphasize the change, he decided to retreat to the mountains for ten days' rest with Edwina and Pamela. The two new governments must tackle their difficulties themselves.

'Lazed in bed all morning', Dickie reported in his diary; while he drowsed, Edwina inspected the grounds with the gardener and dictated Red Cross reports to Mr Bannerjee. Hot sun broke through the mist, the trees made sharp shadows on the lawns. Edwina tried to unwind – a luncheon party for Auchinleck and Compton Mackenzie, *The Razor's Edge* after dinner – but it was impossible to forget what was happening on the plains below. On the morning of the third day the Mountbattens learnt that there had been an attack on one of the trains travelling from Simla to Delhi. Sarah Ismay had been on board, with her fiancé, Flight Lieutenant Beaumont, one of the ADCs. A hundred Muslims had been on the train; all had been butchered, except for Beaumont's bearer, whom they had hidden beneath the seat. That evening a message came from Delhi to say that the son of the Household Treasurer had been stabbed. The Treasurer and his wife insisted on leaving Simla to attend the boy's funeral. Next day the Mountbattens heard that their train had been attacked by a huge mob of Sikhs and Hindus. 'Both were killed', Edwina wrote, 'as were all other Muslims on train . . . this madness gets worse each day'. Violence had broken out in Delhi; hundreds of refugees were making their way to the capital. She could not bear to be doing nothing. That night Edwina told Dickie she had to return.

She did not go back alone. On 4 September V. P. Menon telephoned to ask for the Governor-General's help. On the 5th the Mountbattens drove down to the plain. While Dickie discussed the next move with his staff, Edwina made arrangements to protect the families of the Muslim retainers who worked at Government House. Five thousand more people were brought inside the compound. It was difficult to feed everyone, for supplies were getting low, as smallholders abandoned their farms and distributors their shops. Edwina gave instructions that everyone who lived and worked in Government House was now on strict rations. 'Pammy . . . has become quite keen on SPAM', Edwina wrote. 'The ADCs are mad with rage at me as they think food can be spirited out of the skies or else that Gvt House must have been so *brim* full with supplies that we could continue on full rations for weeks.'

Dickie immediately set up an Emergency Committee. One aspect of its work remained secret, the fact that at Nehru's request the Governor-General had agreed to take the chair. The last thing Mountbatten wanted people to think was that the ex-Viceroy still directed India's affairs. Like the staff at Combined Operations, in SEAC and Viceroy's House, the Committee met daily, first thing in the morning. All members were encouraged to speak freely, allude to any problem, air any view. From these discussions, rather than a preconceived plan, priorities were established. To help his team work efficiently, Mountbatten set up a small Military Emergency Staff, under the leadership of General Peter Rees, who had run the Punjab Boundary Force until its dissolution. A Map Room was fitted out in Government House, as specified by Dickie: maps of such a size posted here, desks and telephones sited there, information exhibited this way in graphs, that way in charts. Pamela was attached to General Rees as his personal assistant. Papers submitted to and emanating from the Emergency Committee were copied to Edwina, now Chairman of the Relief Committee, which saw to medical supplies, food, clothing, shelter and water for the refugees in the hundred-odd camps that had appeared in the large cities and beside the main roads, north, south, east and west, along which the refugees were fleeing. Edwina sent for representatives of all the relevant voluntary organizations and set up her own co-ordinating body, the United Council for Relief and Welfare. For the next two months she and Rajkumari Amrit Kaur worked eighteen hours a day.

'Bodies lying around on roads everywhere'; the ADCs escorting Her Excellency found themselves heaving corpses into the car for delivery to the nearest mortuary. Fires burnt in the city, at night fanatics attacked the hospitals. Edwina asked for protection for staff and patients; the Governor-General's Bodyguard, reinforced by a company of Gurkhas, was assigned to hospital duty. On 9 September Campbell-Johnson and Martin Gilliatt, Deputy Military Secretary, drove out on a tour of inspection. They were challenged, their driver was shot dead, a bullet grazed Gilliatt's ear. 'I hope you are not worrying about us', Edwina told Patricia on the 12th. 'We are still alive and going strong and the situation is in hand . . .'

As Chairman of the United Council, she was now called in to sessions of the Emergency Committee. Each morning, after Dickie's meeting, Edwina went out to see camps and hospitals. The Muslim women in their refuge on the Ridge wanted guards to protect them while they made bread, the Irwin Hospital was under fire from Sten guns and mortars, Minto nurses had to be ferried to the makeshift shelter at Humayun's Tomb. Sixteen thousand refugees had been moved there from the Ridge; at Purana Quila, another huge camp, there were already fifty thousand, among them, it was reported, a group of enraged Muslims with a cache of arms. Torrential rain was falling now: 'Visited the Jama Masjid which unofficially is housing 5,000 Refugees. Filth and conditions indescribable'. Edwina battled through the mud, one day taking Muriel, the next Elizabeth. They had all had cholera injections, for there was great danger of infection. On 21 September the rain stopped for a day. 'A perfectly glorious morning early and we took a party consisting of Panditji, the Patels, Amrit etc and flew over the Refugee columns going West and East. A tragic sight . . . mile after mile . . . walking, in bullock carts, tongas, trucks . . .' Each morning the Emergency Committee saw the lines on the maps. This was what they represented: streams of people, old and young, moving through bare country. At one point the Mountbattens' party flew over two columns somnambulistically passing each other in opposite directions, one of Sikhs, one of Muslims, too dazed or too weary to notice, let alone attack, each other. That morning Edwina must have seen more than half a million refugees.

In Delhi itself there was now less violence but the homeless were in a piteous state. 'Downpours of rain still so heavy that everything seems flooded', Edwina wrote on 25 September, '. . . lights, telephones, bells etc are all cut off.' Cholera had broken out at Purana Quila. Edwina had set up a Finance Sub-Committee, run by a group of prominent Indians, to handle funds coming in from the Red Cross, St John, the YMCA and other sources. It was difficult to pack more committees into the timetable. 'Another full day of hideous meetings and conferences', she wrote on 29 September. When she had a spare hour, she flew off to see the work in the camps and to encourage her team of volunteers, many of them Indian women, like Bimla Thapar and Amrit's niece, Jaya Dalip Singh, who had given up her social life and was working night and day. Once a week at least Edwina talked to Gandhi, who had returned to Delhi after achieving a near-miracle in Calcutta. The authorities there had braced themselves for riots but the Mahatma had asked for calm and reinforced his appeal with a fast, so humbling the communities that Hindus and Muslims ceased their attacks on one another. He had sent trusted disciples to railway stations and crossing points, instructing them to hold prayer meetings at the slightest sign of trouble. The discipline these followers had learnt from Gandhi showed them how to control the crowds; there were astonishing scenes of reconciliation.

Not everywhere. In East Punjab violence continued unabated. The expulsion of Muslims from other states had swollen the numbers in the refugee columns and in some places people had died of starvation. Edwina's Council despatched volunteers and supplies to the Punjab; quantities of cholera and other vaccines went to the camps; food and clothing were sent in. Volunteers from the Friends, St John Ambulance and other organizations worked under the direction of able and experienced people: Richard Symonds, for instance, stationed on the Pakistan side, who reported to the Indian Government, and Horace Alexander, on the Indian side, who reported to the Pakistan Government. As the frenzy died down in Delhi, Edwina felt able to go to see the situation for herself. On 6 October she left with Muriel Watson for Jullundur, where Sir Chandulal Trivedi, the Governor, now had his headquarters and the Refugee Commissioner was based. Amritsar, where she spent the next night, was riot-ravaged. Here, in the middle of a conference with administrative officials and the military, Edwina heard that a message had come through to Delhi to say that Patricia had had a son. 'I gathered that I was a Grandmama and that you were both flourishing and that Daddy was at the Chief's House playing Roulette! Very 1947!! Women work and men play!' Edwina was ecstatic. 'So exciting having all the details . . .', she wrote later. '. . . How punctual it was and well-arranged. Perfect Staff work in every way.'

Edwina's letter to Patricia was sent on 1 November, three weeks after the baby arrived. There had been no time for even a note: although the Emergency Committee was now meeting only twice a week, the Mountbattens were overwhelmed. 'Bad news from Kashmir', Edwina wrote on 24 October. Tribesmen from the North West Frontier Province were making their way into Kashmir and by the morning of the 25th some five thousand men were nearing the capital, Srinagar. It was clear that Pakistan was behind this provocation; army lorries had been used to convey the raiders along the Rawalpindi road. The Maharajah of Kashmir had signed a standstill agreement three days before the transfer of power; there had been no further developments. If India had tried to hurry him up, Pakistan would have been able to allege that Kashmir was being interfered with. Now the Maharajah asked India for help. Mountbatten advised Nehru against sending troops into a neutral state; they should be despatched only if the Maharajah offered to accede to India and promised, as soon as order was restored, to hold a referendum or an election to confirm his decision. That, Dickie believed, would answer the accusation that India had forced the Maharajah's hand. V. P. Menon was sent to Kashmir to discuss the position. He returned on the 26th. The Maharajah, completely unnerved, had left Srinagar with his wife and son. Only one squadron of cavalry stood by to defend the town. On 27 October the Indian Government flew in three hundred and thirty men of the First Sikh Battalion to block the invasion. The raiders – and Pakistan – were taken by surprise. On that same day, Edwina had arranged to leave for a tour of camps in West Punjab. A border war was not going to stop her. 'I am not sure whether I am supposed to arrest you', said the local Commander, who met her aeroplane, 'but for the time being come and have some lunch'. On the 28th, the worst day of the Kashmir crisis, Edwina was at Dera Ghazikhan: 'Very remote. No communications except our Army wireless. No rail, telephone or proper light'. When her party reached Multan, she learnt that the Maharajah of Kashmir had signed a letter of accession to India and agreed to a referendum.

Kashmir was not Dickie's only headache. The Nizam of Hyderabad had now used up the extra two months he had been given to make up his mind on the question of accession. Negotiators had gone to and fro between Delhi and Hyderabad; now it looked as if Hyderabad was manoeuvring to join up with Pakistan. 'It's just one damn thing after another', Edwina said despairingly.

One immediate issue was whether or not Their Excellencies should fly home for the wedding of Princess Elizabeth and their nephew Philip on 20 November. The Mountbattens had intended to be there; it was a family, as well as a royal, occasion and Pamela was to be a bridesmaid. Now they were not sure whether they should leave India at all. On 1 November Dickie flew to Lahore for a day to try to persuade Jinnah to discuss the situation in Kashmir. For a week negotiations continued, interspersed with discussions on the problem of Hyderabad. Between meetings of the Defence Committee, receptions and interviews, Dickie found time for exercise, rest and recuperation; 'Pammy and I rode. Massage'. Nothing seemed to worry him for long. Edwina did not relax. She worked even while she sunbathed, dictating in the garden, studying reports by the pool. Nehru and Gandhi urged the Mountbattens to go to London for the wedding. (The Mahatma asked Edwina to take his present, a piece of handspun cloth.) 'Endless changes about departure for England,' she wrote in her diary on 8 November. 'To be or not to be Time??!!' That day, Dickie had succeeded in getting the leaders of both India and Pakistan to start work on a detailed formula for the settlement of the Kashmir dispute. The Mountbattens left Delhi at dawn on the 10th.

Dickie's diary logged their movements: 'Wedding. London. Pamela left 09.04 to join bridesmaids . . . Procession into (& out of) Westminster Abbey'. They returned on the 24th. Edwina was reeling. 'Thanks for being so sweet and understanding during these days in England', she told Dickie, in a note sent to his room when they got back to Government House. He had been heroic, claiming that he did not mind when Sargent came down for one of their only two nights at Broadlands. Now he was too busy to quarrel. This upset Edwina.

419

Did Dickie not care about her feelings? Worn out, nervy, she was impossible to please. One friend soothed her: 'Called on Gandhi at Banghy Colony, had tea and saw him spin'. In the Mahatma's simple quarters Edwina at last sat still. She went to him now, in her first free moment after coming home.

In an effort to draw back from day-to-day involvement in administrative affairs, Dickie had decided that it was time to wind up the Emergency Committee. On 28 November it met for the last time. Responsibility for the refugees was handed over to the Indian Government and to Edwina's United Council for Relief and Welfare. The Cabinet had declared that the thousands of Hindus who had fled to East Punjab should remain there, for if they were forced to migrate tension would be spread in other states. Many refugees preferred to stay, complaining, none the less, that the lands they had left behind were more fertile and more extensive than those they were now allocated. The boldest demanded compensation. Among the refugees was a large number of discontented Sikhs; if they began to demonstrate, the cycle of violence might start again. To minimize the risk of protest, Edwina insisted that camps be clean and well managed, refugees' questions dealt with and their fears assuaged, and occupation found for the hundreds of new arrivals. The United Council supervised this.

Throughout December and January Edwina travelled through the Punjab. In Delhi she oversaw the Missing Persons Office, set up to trace people who had been separated from their families, and worked with the Ministry of Health and the voluntary agencies to assist those who had lost limbs, their sight or speech. 'Amrit Kaur and I flew off at 7', Edwina noted on 18 January 1948, 'and spent the day at Jullundur and Amritsar with Refugees and sick . . . Conditions much better and camp arrangements excellent. Dead beat on return'. No wonder. There was never a minute's rest. Dickie had announced that he intended to visit every Province and principal state before his time in India came to an end. Few Viceroys had managed this in a five-year term of office; the Mountbattens had six months. Fitting in the tours was not easy; their hosts wanted to lay on lavish entertainment, lasting days. Furthermore, Dickie and Edwina had thought that by this time they would have fewer official duties and had told would-be visitors that the winter of 1947–8 would be the best time to come to Delhi. They wanted to see John and Patricia, Dickie was looking

Torn Apart

forward to a visit from Yola, Edwina had invited Paula, Kay Norton, Marjorie and Malcolm Sargent. Edwina's guests said they were perfectly happy to amuse themselves, but a programme had to be arranged. 'Kaysie and Yola are here', Edwina reported to Patricia on 7 December, 'and although I fear I've hardly set eyes on them I *think* they're enjoying themselves and certainly they've *never* drawn breath'.

Some of these commitments could be combined. Kay and Yola accompanied the Mountbattens to Jaipur in mid-December for the Maharajah's Silver Jubilee. Polo featured prominently in the celebrations; Dickie, still a non-player, umpired instead. Yola had brought a fur coat in case India was cold; a picnic lunch and duck shoot gave her an opportunity to huddle charmingly within it. 'Darling', Edwina asked Patricia, 'do you think you could call Nancie up and arrange to bring out, duly insured, I fear, on your arm my Sable coat, also the Silver Fox one, as I think I shall need them both'. Patricia and John arrived on 18 December, in time for a post-Christmas visit to Gwalior: Bunny and Gina Phillips came on 1 January and joined the Mountbattens on a trip to Bikaner. At each place Dickie and Edwina were given gifts and honours. After the transfer of power he had received an earldom; there was almost no room on his uniform for further decorations. Edwina had been awarded the GBE at the end of 1947 and in January 1948 the Chinese Order of the Brilliant Star. Dickie believed that she laughed at this flummery. Edwina certainly thought titles, medals and ribbons a bore but she was proud of the service they honoured: 'Well deserved for Daddy and I am delighted for him . . . I agree with you that Earl Mountbatten of Burma is *much* nicer and it's agreed that it should be that now'.

Edwina had not slowed her pace. Between polo and the state banquet at Jaipur she fitted in a visit to the local hospital, at Gwalior she whistled round schools, medical and welfare organizations, at Bikaner she squeezed in a couple of hospitals between a semi-state dinner and a military tournament. The Mountbattens' guests hardly saw them. In Delhi, Edwina managed only one long talk with Yola, for her days were taken up with meetings. It was not at home, in Government House, that she stopped to reflect. Her oasis was at Gandhi's side. He sat at his spinning-wheel, listening, saying little. The simplicity of his remarks put even the most tangled problems into perspective. On 12 January, the Mahatma came to see Mountbatten, to tell him that he was about to undertake a fast, which he would end

421

only when he was satisfied that the communities were reconciled. All India watched. The days passed, the frail old man grew weaker. On 17 January the Mountbattens called to see Gandhi; his body was fading away but his wits remained keen and his will was as strong as ever. The Cabinet had established an inter-communal Peace Committee; reports from Gandhi's disciples persuaded him that its efforts were sincere. On the morning of 18 January he broke his fast.

On the 23rd Dickie and Edwina left Delhi for a four-day trip to Bhopal and Nagpur. From there they proceeded to Madras to stay with the Governor and his wife, Sir Archibald and Lady Nye. 'Non stop day and killing', Edwina wrote on the 28th. Dickie returned to Delhi on 30 January. Edwina remained, for she had arranged to spend a day at the Christian Medical College at Vellore. When she returned to Madras that evening she heard that, at five o'clock, Gandhi had been shot during his Prayer Meeting. Edwina felt numb. She reached Delhi by late morning. The Mahatma's body had been placed on a carriage draped with the Congress flag and covered with flowers; an immense crowd followed it along the six-mile route from Birla House, where the assassination had occurred, to the Raj Ghat, the open space by the banks of the Jumna, where the cremation was to take place. So great was the throng at the burning-ground that the Mountbattens and those round them were in danger of being pushed into the flames. Thinking quickly, Dickie ordered everyone to sit down; the Governor-General, his family and his staff seated themselves in the dust. It was also an act of homage. The Mahatma's body was placed on the pyre, people pressed forward to throw flower petals, the fire was kindled. As the crowd cried, 'Gandhi is immortal', Dickie rose, surveyed the vast assembly and, saying 'We must go now', led his party away.

CHAPTER TWENTY-EIGHT

Breaking Her Silence

Edwina did not turn to Dickie in her grief. For weeks their relations had been strained; at one point during Yola's visit they had all had what Dickie described as 'a three-cornered row', so miserable that Yola had offered to go home. Peter Murphy was a help; he had returned to England in late June 1947 but had come back to Delhi at the end of the year to stay at Government House. In mid-January he sent a letter to Edwina's room. He had been talking to Dickie, fresh from a particularly bitter quarrel. Edwina was in a dreadful state, Dickie said unhappily; he could do nothing right. Peter was trying to straighten out the tangle.

What I feel is wrong somehow between you and Dickie is that you have gradually come to feel that his attitude is a measure of his feelings towards *you* – whereas actually, of course, it's just a sign of bloody bad manners!! . . . The moment you showed Dickie that you felt he was not behaving as if he was fond of you and pleased to be with you, he became self conscious about it and felt that something he did quite inadvertently (like glancing at his watch, or ringing up and making a plan without consulting you) might be the signal for you to *say* (in so many words), 'It's quite clear from what you've just done that your heart isn't really in what we are saying and doing together, but that you are really filling in time until you go and do something you *really* want to do'! . . . Poor old Dickie's become rattled: he is now in the state of feeling that he *must* try not to do silly little things which are habits and second nature to him . . . and *you* must try, Edwina dear, to be patient with him . . . It distresses me so that you ever imagine that you are not a very great deep love in his life. I have been his confidant off and on for 25 years: you know that. What it seems you *don't* know is the unfailing affection and loyalty that he feels for you and that he has spoken of so freely to me.

Edwina Mountbatten

There has never been a *moment* in the past, Edwina – *however* difficult things may have appeared and in circumstances when 99 men out of a 100 would have felt they no longer had any responsibility – that Dickie didn't put *your* happiness first. I think if you look into your heart and honestly remember how good a *friend* he had been to you, you will realise that what I say is true . . . *Do* do that, Edwinski: his manner won't change all at once!

Edwina had no time to consider Peter's letter. On the day she received it she and Dickie left Delhi for Bhopal, Nagpur and Madras and, when she returned, Gandhi's death overshadowed everything. She worked all the harder, relentlessly inspecting refugee camps and hospitals and concentrating on the work of her committees. Angela Limerick came from England to see the work that Red Cross volunteers were doing and to discuss lines of command with Edwina: '. . . All very difficult!!' The United Council for Relief and Welfare took up many hours: 'Presided at a Finance Sub-Committee . . . followed by an Executive, non-stop talks and interviews and work.' The Council had been asked to take on the job of recovering and repatriating women who had been abducted from their homes in the frenzied days after partition, daughters, sisters and wives who now found themselves living far away from their own towns and villages, often in religious communities quite different from their own. The women were ashamed of what had happened to them: some preferred their new lives but their families demanded that they be sent back. Tracing them was difficult, persuading them to go home was harrowing.

Throughout February and March Edwina denied herself even a minute to reflect. She was fully stretched. On top of their usual work she and Dickie had to fit in visits to India's States and Provinces to say their last farewells. Kanpur: 'D. inspected Home Guard while I went to Infectious Diseases Hospital . . .'; Benares; Calcutta; Cuttack; Puri; Assam; Kapurthala (by mistake the Maharajah proposed a toast to Lord and Lady Willingdon, Viceroy and Vicereine in the nineteen-thirties); Travancore; Cochin; Udaipur; Mysore; Ootacamund: 'Perfectly lovely, . . . golf at the most beautiful course . . .' Everywhere there were dinners and receptions, with speeches, dancing and presentations. Although Edwina loved the country through which they travelled, she found the visits exhausting. She insisted on packing extra engagements into her itinerary: a TB Sanatorium and the Welsh

Mission hospital at Shillong, three hospitals in Mysore, and, at the end of the Mountbattens' stay at 'Ooty', a three-day tour of medical and welfare establishments in South India. 'Off with Her Ex. on the wild rush', wrote James Scott, in attendance as ADC, after another dawn start.

There was no rest. In Delhi Dickie and Edwina had an interminable programme: 'the Czech Ambassador to present credentials . . .'; 'final match of Delhi Women's Hockey league . . .'; 'Pammy and I attended the 20th Kennel Club of India Championship Dog Show.' Dickie conferred degrees at the University of Delhi, Edwina spoke at Convocation at Lady Irwin College, they both attended 'an enjoyable though not very good' snake and conjuring performance for the staff. In mid-February they shot up to Dehra Dun, in mid-March to Burma and from there to Calcutta, circling over Mandalay and the sites of SEAC's wartime battles. The Mountbattens' aides were worn out; only experience and professionalism got Edwina through. Driving along twisting tracks made her feel sick, flying in unpressurized aircraft brought on her neuralgia. The mountain roads were vertiginous, the landing strips primitive. At Dehra Dun cars were lined up so that the Mountbattens' aircraft could take off by the light of the headlamps. The ADCs who accompanied Lady Louis sometimes thought her smiles forced, her remarks conventional. No wonder: she was sleep-walking through the flower shows and exhibitions of arts and crafts.

Dickie was full of beans, busily drafting *aides-mémoires* on India's relations with the Commonwealth; the future of the Princely States; the need for Cabinet Ministers to take regular holidays; the urgency of an oil exploration programme; the necessity, if government were to be carried on efficiently, for senior public servants to have air-conditioning in their bedrooms. Mountbatten saw his role as that of an elder statesman. He held the ring at meetings between Nehru and Liaquat Ali Khan; the Kashmir issue had been referred to the United Nations, drafts and discussion papers on the future of Hyderabad wafted back and forth between the Nizam and the Cabinet in Delhi.

Unlike Edwina, Dickie could forget his in-tray: 'Lovely early morning ride with Patricia . . . Governors' photo group before lunch.' He knew how to conserve his energy: Jim Scott noticed His Excellency's knack of unobtrusively nodding off during other people's speeches and of waking up just in time to reply. When guests were staying in the house, Dickie made sure they were entertained after dinner –

425

'Teapot Game', 'the Adsdean Game', 'Peter played' – and as a rule the evening ended with a film: *The Shape of Things to Come*, *Perils of Pauline* and, once Bunny had gone home, *Lost Horizon*. In times of crisis, Dickie distracted himself by working on his 'Relationship Tables', tracing and delineating the interlocking branches of his family tree according to an ingenious coding system he had devised himself. A combination of genealogy, history and algebra, it was a perfect tranquillizer.

Edwina had no such solace. Articles in the *New Statesman* and *Reynold's News* were her night-time reading; she told Lady Nye that when she could not sleep she played the Enigma Variations on the gramophone. Pills gave her some respite from insomnia and pain: Nembutal for sleeplessness, Optalidon for her blinding headaches. The sun made her dizzy; 'Heat in open car was terrific!' Edwina reported, after a drive of a hundred miles through the villages north of Trivandrum. There was hardly time for a consoling talk with Paula on the discomforts of the menopause. One good gossip and Edwina was off on a tour of maternity and child welfare centres in Delhi. A fortnight later she had a morning free to sit by the pool and talk to her guests: 'Saw a little of the house party for once!!', she wrote on 25 February. This was Edwina's first opportunity for a proper conversation with Marjorie, who had arrived weeks before. She left on 3 April, taking a hundred and twenty-eight pounds of excess baggage and fourteen pieces of hand luggage.

Malcolm Sargent now arrived on a roundabout journey to a music festival in Turkey. Edwina and Dickie had decided to have two days off at Mashobra with Pamela and Patricia (John had returned to England) and Paula and Malcolm came with them. There, at least, Edwina hoped to be able to have a peaceful time with her guests. By the time they reached the Retreat, Paula had developed a fever and Malcolm was suffering from dysentery. Patricia caught a chill but her mother was too busy to sympathize. Back in Delhi, Paula languished on a day-bed, ice packs round her head; Sargent tottered round the garden. The doctor declared that the maestro was too weak to fly to Ankara, Edwina insisted that he cancel his programme and stay another ten days. '. . . Lucky to have had him for so long', she said afterwards, but she had managed to set aside only one evening for a quiet talk.

Edwina's visitors saw only one side of her life in Delhi. 'Dinner of

426

85', she wrote in her diary on 1 April, 'followed by Indian Music and Dancing . . . Excellent as usual and Malcolm fascinated.' He had not known the days when food was rationed and the grounds packed with refugees. Next day the Mountbattens took Sargent to the Inter-Service Tattoo. 'We drove in state from Bikaner House', Edwina noted, 'performance magnificent against background of Purana Quila and forked lightning'. It was at Purana Quila, only a few months before, that temporary shelter had been found for thousands of Muslims, too terrified to remain on the streets of Delhi. It would have taken weeks for Edwina to explain all this to her guests and, even then, they would have only just begun to discover what India had come to mean to her.

One person seemed to understand. On the day Sargent left for London, Edwina called on Pandit Nehru at 17 York Road. '. . . Delightful gossip with Jawaharlal at his house', she wrote that night; until now her diary had not referred to him by his first name. The day had been hot – nearly a hundred and seven degrees – but Nehru's verandah was cool and peaceful. It was not unusual for Edwina to drop in at the Prime Minister's house. Since Partition they had worked together on relief and welfare policy and by now they were good friends. A fortnight after Independence day Edwina suddenly realized how fond of Nehru she had become. This was in September 1947. She had called on Amrit Kaur to discuss the riots in Delhi and late at night they heard that the Prime Minister had gone out to investigate and had disappeared. Amrit and Edwina searched the dark streets and found him standing by the roadside, calming a crowd of angry men armed with knives. 'Brought him back!', Edwina wrote triumphantly in her diary. She had liked Nehru's recklessness; he liked being rescued.

Four months later Gandhi was assassinated. Unable to say what she felt, Edwina had written Nehru a letter, trying to comfort him – as she had once tried to comfort Dickie after his father's death. Formality dropped away – but then Edwina's friends had come to stay and the Mountbattens had set off on their tours. Now, in early summer, Edwina and Nehru at last had time to themselves. She returned to Government House soothed and refreshed.

She longed to continue their conversation but her programme was as full as ever. The thermometer was climbing. By 8 May it was a hundred and twelve degrees. Edwina suggested to Dickie that they invite Nehru to the Retreat: 'getting you to Mashobra to talk naturally and informally had become an obsession', she told him afterwards. Nehru accepted at once. He was weary and full of self-doubt. In a note to Edwina, confirming that he was coming, he spoke of needing someone 'to talk to me sanely and confidently, as you can do so well.' He had been badly shaken by the loss of Gandhi; Delhi politics depressed him. '. . . I am in some danger of losing faith in myself and in the work I do . . . What has happened, is happening, to the values we cherished? Where are our brave ideals?' A few days in the mountains would restore him. Paula went off to the airport and that afternoon Dickie and Edwina, Pamela and Nehru left for Mashobra.

They drove up the last part of the road to Simla, in a bright red open-topped Talbot, Dickie at the wheel. The air grew cooler and Edwina's spirits rose. Next morning she and Nehru climbed through the orchards along the terraced hillsides; in the early evening, while Dickie worked on his family tree, Edwina, Pamela and Nehru walked among the old wooden houses in Simla, a cheerful crowd straggling along behind them, '. . . his admirers', Edwina said proudly. Each day was more blissful than the one before: 'Snow peaked mountains, clear and bright and brilliant skies. Drove small car and two jeeps . . . along the Tibet road . . . Picnic lunch . . .' After tea on Sunday Edwina went to her sitting-room to write letters. Nehru came to look for her, moved towards her and upset the inkstand. They were too busy mopping up to be abashed. At supper the conversation was gay. Dickie told amusing stories – he did it well – and got them all to play pencil and paper games. 'A perfect evening,' Edwina wrote in her diary, and, when the others had left, '. . . a fascinating heart to heart with J. N.'

Her reserve had vanished. She talked about herself; Nehru was thoughtful and attentive. Their early lives could not have been more different – for her a patchy schooling, marriage, twenty years' frivolity, for him an English education at Harrow and Cambridge, rebellion, confinement in British prisons – but, as they spoke, Edwina felt that Nehru understood everything about her. Early in the morning they met in the garden, late in the day they sat together. Nehru's holiday was nearly over. Next morning Edwina rose at half past six to say goodbye. She sent a letter after him. 'I hated seeing you drive away this morning . . . you have left me with a strange sense of peace and happiness. Perhaps I have brought you the same?' Edwina's letter crossed with one from Delhi. 'Life is a dreary business', Nehru wrote, 'and when a bright patch comes it rather takes one's breath away . . .' Joy was mixed with sadness, for now, he said bleakly, 'the surrounding shadows seem darker.'

'Feeling exhausted and terrible', Edwina wrote two days later. She was restless and prickly: 'both D. and I felt awful.' They remained in Simla for a week. Dickie piloted the open-topped car down to the plains, 'hotter and hotter till Kalka where we stewed at 106 degrees.' When would Edwina see Nehru? She asked him to dinner; he came, bringing Krishna Menon. Dickie and Pamela went on to the YWCA Ball; Edwina stayed at home, talking late. She worked until half past two in the morning, for when Nehru and Krishna left her, she could not sleep.

No sooner were they reunited than she was torn away. When they were together, Edwina was exhilarated. She forgot fatigue and illness, the past and the future. Nehru was troubled. 'What did you tell me and what did I say to you . . .?', he asked, in a letter written after one of their late-night conversations at Government House. 'The more one talks, the more there is to say and there is so much that it is difficult to put into words. I have a feeling that I did not say the right thing or did not put it in the right way'. They must take care not to forget their responsibilities to other people. Edwina was alarmed: 'The thought of any reservations . . . between us rather frightens me'.

Rajagopalachari, Governor of Bengal, was to succeed Dickie as Head of State. His arrival in Delhi told Edwina that their time in India was almost over. The Mountbattens had been there for nearly fifteen months; in a fortnight they would be gone. Edwina had not wanted to come. Now she hated the thought of going home. 'The heat increases', she wrote on 6 June, '. . . the hot wind has commenced and scorching dust storms are upon us. But I love Delhi even like this and India and the Indians and my heart aches at the thought of leaving them so soon.'

The time slipped away: 8 June: the Governor of East Punjab and Lady Trivedi came to stay and say goodbye; 9 June: the Indian and Foreign Press gave a farewell party; 10 June: for the last time the Mountbattens gave a dinner for the King's Birthday. A year before Dickie had been counting down the days. Now Edwina did the same. On the 11th she and Nehru found time for a long, uninterrupted talk.

Edwina Mountbatten

At five in the morning he collected her from Government House, by five-forty they were flying east to Bareilly in the United Provinces. Edwina wanted to say goodbye to her mother's old friend, Sarojini Naidu, now Governor of that region, who was at her summer residence, Naini Tal. The car lurched along the winding road but Edwina did not mind. She and Nehru walked in the gardens and floated on a boat on the lake. 'Talked with Naidu family, who are all enchanting'; Edwina liked Padmaja, the elder daughter, 'the little elf' of whom Sarojini had spoken to Maudie, fifty years before.

At dawn next morning Edwina and Nehru went out to ride in the mountains, picking their way up stony, narrow tracks. They looked back along the path. As they came back to earth, they talked about the future. 'This was the only promise we ever made', Edwina wrote to Nehru afterwards, 'on the road to Naini Tal – that nothing we did or felt would ever be allowed to come between you and your work or me and mine – because that would spoil everything.'

'Edwina and PM back 7.0', Dickie wrote in his diary. 'Immediate Hyderabad Talks . . . More talks after dinner. Worked till 1.30am.' The Nizam was in the grip of a gang of bloodthirsty fanatics, who terrorized the local Hindu population and spoke of war against India. How long could negotiations go on? Nehru and Mountbatten felt they must consult Sardar Patel, who was at Dehra Dun. On the day after her return from Naini Tal, Edwina set off with Dickie, Amrit and Nehru on the five-hour flight to the north. Amrit sat with Dickie; Edwina with Nehru. Weeks later she remembered their drive down through the hills to the airfield: 'the long and fascinating talk we had . . . including our views on religion and spiritual values . . . I felt a little sick after coming fast along part of the road where it was twisty but I rose above it, so enchanted . . .'

Seven days to prepare for departure . . . now Nehru could not face the prospect. Would Edwina not remain to carry on her work with the refugees? She reminded him that he had told her to be practical. 'And so it will be and it has to be', he said sadly. 'How wise and right you are, but wisdom brings little satisfaction. A feeling of acute malaise is creeping over me, and horror seizes me when I look at a picture in my mind of your shaking thousands of hands on the night of the 20th and saying your final goodbye . . . Dickie and you cannot bypass your fate, just as I cannot bypass mine. So you will shake hands with a few thousands of persons . . . I shall wander away . . .'

Breaking Her Silence

Monday 14 June: a six-hour flight to Baroda for the Mountbattens to say goodbye to the Maharajah; Tuesday 15th: a last journey to the camps at Panipat and Kurukshetra, where thirty thousand people were still housed. It was 115 degrees; as Edwina stood in the blazing sun, a vast crowd of refugees pressed round her to say goodbye. Wednesday: Edwina's final meeting on the rescue and repatriation of abducted women; the presentation of an address by the municipal council; the Mountbattens' farewell reception for the Personal Staff; Amrit's last party . . . Edwina was confused and dizzy, Dickie struggled against an attack of dysentery. He wanted above everything to tidy up the last loose ends; Kashmir was still a stalemate, Hyderabad a muddle. Walter Monckton, sent to the Nizam with yet another draft agreement, telegraphed the one word: 'Lost'. The talks were broken off.

'Broken off . . .' Edwina felt as if she were being ripped apart. 'A Farewell Party for clerical staff . . . we dined with Jawaha and his family . . . sat in the garden with full moon. Sadder and sadder.' More farewells: 'Our Household Domestic Indoor and Outdoor Staff Party. Huge success. Conjurors, Band, dancers. Many women attended, lots out of Purdah for the first time.' Edwina's example had done much to encourage Indian women. She had worked hard for India; as she said in her farewell message, broadcast throughout the sub-continent, there was so much still to do. Saturday 20th: 'Dickie, Pammy and I drove to Old Delhi in Rolls and then transferred to open car. Thru' Chandi Chowk, poorest and busiest part, route packed with friendly and cheering crowds . . .' The last time the King's representative had travelled down this thoroughfare had been thirty-seven years before, when Lord Hardinge had driven there as Viceroy and there had been an attempt on his life.

June 20th was the Mountbattens' last night in India. The Cabinet gave a banquet in their honour. When Nehru and Dickie spoke, Edwina could not restrain her tears. Nehru was too upset to take in a word of her farewell speech. Seven thousand people came to the reception. 'To bed 05.00', Dickie noted, '. . . called again 05.45!' Edwina did not sleep. 'Night spent in attempting to round up, write and work.' They said goodbye to the servants and the staff, Dickie inspected the guard of honour, pictures were taken. Rajagopalachari and Nehru drove with them to the airfield at Palam. 'Three guards of honour', Dickie reported afterwards, 'all Cabinet and Corps Diploma-

431

tique . . . Fighter Escort, 33 Gun Salute. Tears all round. Left 08.20.' It was the most miserable day of Edwina's life.

Early that morning Nehru had come to Government House to say goodbye. Edwina had given him one of her greatest treasures, a small eighteenth-century French box of enamel and gold. She also presented him with an emerald ring. If he needed money, for he gave away all his own, he should sell it. Nehru was a romantic but even he found this fanciful. More baffling still was Edwina's last gift, the silver St Christopher medallion Maudie had once given Wilfrid. Edwina sent it from the airfield, just before the York took off for England. 'What do you want me to do with it?' Nehru asked, amazed. 'Am I supposed to wear it round my neck? Heaven forbid.' Other packages had been delivered from Government House, two photographs of Dickie and Edwina and a silver box, suitably engraved. 'For your private ear', Nehru said confidentially to Edwina, 'I might tell you . . . that the spelling of my name was all wrong!' He did not mind: '. . . In a way I like this mistake . . .' The inscription would remind him of Dickie, '. . . who has thus far failed to grasp completely how my name should be written or pronounced.'

And Nehru's farewell gift to Edwina? An ancient coin, which she attached to a bracelet, a box of ripe mangoes, brought from Lucknow, and a copy of his autobiography to read on the way home. 'India has given me many things,' she had told him, and the most precious had been bestowed on her at the very end. Nehru had shown her how to speak about her feelings. She thanked him with all her heart. 'It makes me so happy and still slightly incredulous that you should talk to me and write as you do and I want to do the same . . . I have never felt in my life that I wanted to, or could, to anyone, till now.'

'Very sad and lost', Edwina wrote in her diary as she travelled home. In Malta, where they stopped en route, she said goodbye to Mizzen, her Sealyham, who had been with her at Adsdean and throughout the war. The dog was old. In quarantine he would pine and, having consulted Nehru, Edwina had decided to have Mizzen put down. She felt utterly bereft. Edwina's friends gathered round: 'Talked with Paula early', 'Saw 'Zelle', 'Looked in at Marjorie's to see the Schiffs', 'Lunch at home with Kaysie . . . Malcolm fetched me at 7 and we went to see Larry Olivier in *Hamlet*'. She caught up with the family: 'Early lunch with Aunt Victoria', 'Molly Mount Temple to tea.' Dickie's nephew, Prince Philip (now Duke of Edinburgh), came to

Breaking Her Silence

Broadlands: 'uproarious evening of imitations, mad games etc.' Entertaining everyone was a strain. 'All Dickie's family, Germans, Greeks etc are descending on me from the far corners of the earth', Edwina told Nehru. 'They will have to sleep in dormitories in the only 4 spare bedrooms I have got or go into the Hospital as patients to qualify for beds.' There was hardly a servant in the place; 'I will have to cook and scrub as well'. This - and the visitors' 'vast appetites' – was an exaggeration but it was true that shortages of food and fuel made housekeeping difficult. Many goods were still rationed: 'points and coupons and food and servants are one enormous headache.'

Broadlands was Edwina's consolation. 'It has a character quite of its own', she told Nehru. She loved the view of the river from her bedroom windows, the walk through the trees and across the fields, the smell of new-cut grass. The place needed attention, for only the most urgent repairs and maintenance had been done during the war. 'I have resorted to very hard work as a possible solution to the present situation', she told Nehru at the beginning of July, '. . . it has helped although it is really only a drug.' She tried to sort out her papers but it was not easy to do so at 16 Chester Street, with people constantly coming and going. Compared with the vast spaces of Government House, the place was 'a sardine tin, out of which we and all our belongings are literally bulging! I am sitting on the floor in the bathroom, the only corner.' In mid-August Edwina and Dickie took Pamela, Patricia and John to Classiebawn Castle for five days. 'A lot of work has been done', she told Nehru, 'repairs, light installed, bath, cooker etc . . . the place quite transformed.' It was not yet habitable, however, so they stayed at the inn in the village. It had one bath with only cold running water, and, when Dickie saw what emerged from the taps, he declared that he would wash elsewhere. Edwina liked the simplicity of everything. Her letters to Nehru were ecstatic: 'Scrambled over the rocks and dabbled in the pools. Back by the beach of white sand . . . brilliant sun and sapphire and multi-emerald coloured seas and countryside with its white-washed thatched cottages . . . we shrimped off the rocks and sat about in shorts sunbathing . . .' Edwina ate fried sole, in Dublin she feasted on lobster. 'Bought sweets, sheets, linen and underclothes, all without coupons!' Ireland, Edwina told Nehru, was like India, beautiful and pitiable.

Simple food, fresh air and exercise brought Edwina back to life. Not for long. In London she felt permanently tired, at Broadlands she was miserable. 'Feeling quite awful,' she noted at the beginning of August, '. . . general exhaustion and depression, I think.' Small things upset her – 'Domestic dramas which are becoming increasingly boring. Cook versus Charles!' – and she worried about the state of the world. Attlee had given a dinner for the Mountbattens at Downing Street; ministers and their wives were kind but Edwina thought them insular. 'Life is lonely and empty and unreal', she told Nehru. The Buckingham Palace garden party was 'a waste of time . . . but Dickie insists'. In mid-September the Mountbattens took Pamela to stay with Yola and her sister in the South of France. 'I somehow seem to have grown out of all this,' Edwina told Nehru, 'the people, the life, even the scenery.' She was shocked by the black market; the meals, she said sternly, were much too plentiful. People chattered all the time about trivia. It was difficult to find time and a place to concentrate on her daily letter to Nehru: 'nothing to write on anywhere – a peculiarity of all French houses – and I am precariously balanced on the edge of my bed writing on my knee.'

She was homesick for India. Dinner with an Indian students' society in London was more fun than the most splendid party, an evening watching Indian dancing better than the plays or concerts she had once enjoyed. On weekdays Edwina went across the Park to her office, hoping to find letters from India, sent over from the Residence by Krishna Menon, now High Commissioner in London. When they came, her heart was light. On days when there was no letter she was cast down; sometimes, able to wait no longer, she telephoned. The calls were hardly private. Her 'clear exciting voice', Nehru said, had come through with the help of half a dozen operators: 'Delhi, Bombay, Poona . . . indeed once or twice they repeated your words to me.' On paper Nehru and Edwina could speak more intimately; even so, there was a risk that letters might go astray. They were sent to and from London in the diplomatic bag, each letter in a double cover. At first Edwina marked the inner envelope 'For the Prime Minister'; later, on reflection, she changed this to 'For Himself', as she did on envelopes for Dickie, numbering the letters so that Nehru would know if there were gaps. She was anxious in case they might go missing: 'I have awful thoughts of lost letters being read by Communists or stenographers'.

'I write to you in a very restrained manner', Nehru told Edwina. Not so. His letters were all she could desire. He had walked alone through the Mountbattens' former quarters at Government House. Dickie's swords and trophies had been removed from his study and the place was empty. Edwina's things had also been taken away but he still felt her presence, 'a fragrance on the air'. Where was she? Seeking her, he had read her letters a second time and a third: 'I lose myself in dreamland, which is very unbecoming in a PM. But then I am only incidentally a PM . . .' Work overwhelmed him; he sought refuge in poetry, myths and legends, fairy tales. The French Ambassador had asked him to dine and see Cocteau's film *La Belle et La Bête*. 'I liked it and it soothed me . . . the cares that infest the day folded their tents like the Arabs and as silently stole away.' Nehru was living his own fairy tale, he said, the story of a battle between convention and chemistry. 'Chemistry won, more or less.'

More or less. India came first. 'I am convinced that we have to function in our respective orbits', he told Edwina, 'or else either or both of us will lose our roots and feel terribly unhappy.' His responsibilities were heavy, his office often a burden; Edwina had lightened the load: 'You came and unlocked the doors and windows.' To her he could write freely; his letters were poems, his own and those of other people: Yeats, Swinburne, Euripides, Auden, Joyce, Blake, the Song of Solomon. Dickie's correspondence had never been like this. Nehru loved words. Edwina was his inspiration, writing to her his solace. At two in the morning, when he had finished his official papers, he would begin his daily letter; already light-headed, he grew dizzy. From Kashmir he sent her a gift, not shawls or silver but a piece of Indian birch bark: 'In olden times it was used in place of paper for writing manuscripts.'

He realized that people were beginning to notice; his women friends guessed why he was distracted. One was Colleen Nye, wife of the Governor of Madras, who had known Nehru for years. Something had changed him. 'Edwina?', she asked. Nehru nodded and turned away. Another was Padmaja. Aeons ago, when she was eighteen, Nehru had written her a long series of affectionate letters and she believed she still occupied a corner of his heart. Now Padmaja had come to Delhi to help arrange Nehru's new house. She asked him what was the matter, answering her own question by saying that she knew all about it. When Nehru found a photograph of Edwina dashed to the ground, he knew who was responsible.

It was not only heartache that troubled him. At the beginning of

435

Edwina Mountbatten

August 1948 Pakistan announced that her troops would be sent into Kashmir. India waited. The blow came but it fell on Pakistan. Jinnah had been ailing long before the transfer of power; on 11 September he died. '. . . What a poor lonely figure he has been', Nehru wrote to Edwina, 'living a starved life of isolation, lacking friendship and affection.' Some said that, if negotiations over independence had taken longer, there might have been no need for partition. Before the shape of the new India had been agreed, Jinnah would have gone for ever. If the thought crossed Nehru's mind, he did not say so. Nor did Edwina, nor Dickie. They had been swept along by the events and moods of the time, as they had perceived them. Jinnah had been a clever and cunning negotiator, but he was not the only one. Dealing with his supporters might be even more difficult now they were without a leader. Nehru saw trouble ahead.

There was no time to look back. Kashmir was quiet but there were disturbances in Hyderabad. The issue of accession had been referred to the United Nations, India and Pakistan being warned not to interfere, but at the beginning of August an aeroplane that had crashed on its way to Hyderabad from Karachi was found to be carrying guns and ammunition. On 13 September Indian troops moved into the State. Three days later everything was over. The Nizam's forces surrendered, his ministers resigned, the pro-Muslim paramilitaries were banned. Dickie disapproved of the invasion, knowing that in Britain India would be regarded as the aggressor. He wrote to Nehru and Rajagopalachari to tell them so. Edwina disagreed. 'Right is right and wrong is wrong', she said loyally. Fortunately Nehru would soon be able to explain things himself, for he had arranged to come to England in early October for a conference of Dominion Prime Ministers, before going on to a meeting of the United Nations General Assembly in Paris. The prospect had sustained Edwina for months. Nehru was nervous, but he persuaded himself that his fears were chiefly about his clothes. 'I shall look thoroughly disreputable in my Charlie Chaplin attire', he wrote anxiously in late July. For the past twenty-eight years he had worn only handspun, handwoven garments. 'Abroad I relax this rule', but, as it was impractical to invest in a new wardrobe for such a short visit, he would have to rely on 'some ancient relics'. Edwina was more concerned with logistics. Where would they meet? 'Like you I don't like the idea of a crowd although I want the earliest glimpse . . .' When would he come to

Breaking Her Silence

Broadlands? How long could he stay? Whom would he like to bring? Stafford Cripps had hinted to Krishna Menon that the Mountbattens might think of asking Ernest Bevin to Broadlands for a day: 'I was *very* firm.' Edwina wanted her guest to have a quiet time: Cripps and Krishna Menon were the only politicians to be invited, to luncheon only. Nehru's sister, Mrs Pandit, and two of her daughters, Tara and Lekha, were asked to stay.

'At midnight Jawaha came in to see us on his way from the airfield,' Edwina wrote in her diary on 6 October: 'Too lovely'. She had stayed up late with Dickie and Pamela, in the hope that he would look in on his way to Claridge's, just round the corner. A long talk had to wait until the following afternoon, when Edwina drove Nehru down to Broadlands. She had asked Dickie to give them a little time to themselves. This was awkward; he was spending the day in Plymouth and could have come conveniently to Romsey from there. To please Edwina, however, he returned to London on the night train and motored down with Pamela next day. 'How many chaperones do you require!', Edwina had asked Nehru. She did not expect an answer. For weeks she had thought about this visit; now Nehru was here, she was too excited to believe it. She was in his hands and she would be guided by him.

Edwina's moodiness was not new but Dickie was puzzled by the intensity of these cycles of elation and despair. He could see that she admired Nehru. So did he. He thought of him as a friend, a younger colleague. (Although Nehru was twelve years older, in Dickie's eyes he was a novice in the art of governing.) The correspondence between Edwina and Nehru was certainly voluminous but Dickie took that in his stride. He knew that Nehru was talkative and confiding; the two men discussed politics, to Edwina Nehru wrote philosophy. That was all. Dickie did not ask himself whether he could trust Nehru. The question did not occur to him.

He could indeed rely upon his friend. On paper Nehru had been carried away; his relationship with Edwina had been shaped by their letters. Words, words – and, as he said, there were still a thousand ideas to discuss. Nehru was relieved to find that their reunion was as marvellous as their correspondence had led them to expect. At Broadlands he and Edwina poured out their feelings in talk – in the drawing-room, by the river, at dinner, in the garden. They laughed and wept; Nehru pressed Edwina's hands, took her arm, hugged her,

437

as he liked to when he was moved. And more? Those who knew them well thought not. The family's quarters at Broadlands were small, servants ever-present. More important, Nehru respected Dickie. He would have considered it disloyal, ill-mannered and wrong to deceive his friend. Edwina? To all her lovers she had given only the shell of herself. In exposing her doubts and hopes, she had entrusted herself to Nehru in a way that was more profound than a mere physical embrace. Nothing must be allowed to degrade this precious relationship.

'A heavenly weekend', Edwina wrote ecstatically. When they returned to London she raced through her work: 'Jawaha picked me up and we went to Epstein's studio', 'I took Jawaha to see *Medea* . . .' It was wonderful to be able to telephone Nehru, to see him every day – at the Lord Mayor's banquet, at a left-wing reception at the King's Hall, at the dinner for the Dominion Premiers at Buckingham Palace. ('You are being much better fed and looked after here than you were in Delhi', Edwina wrote on the back of the menu, sending it across to Nehru, 'but you always had your full ration of affection and admiration'.) She knew they would soon be parted. Nehru was moving on to Paris, Edwina to Malta; Dickie had been appointed Commander of the First Cruiser Squadron, Mediterranean Fleet, and his leave was up. One last weekend at Broadlands ('we made Jawaha play Racing Demon! Such fun!') and on 25 October they said goodbye. Nehru came to Northolt next morning to see them off. Edwina wore dark glasses to hide her tears.

'It is extraordinary being back here again, enveloped by the Navy', Edwina told Nehru, 'and in a comparatively JUNIOR position . . . very levelling and educative!! D. tells me in the *Malta* precedence list as a Rear Admiral and wife we come about 15th . . .!!' In the Naval hierarchy Dickie ranked third. The Commander-in-Chief, Arthur Power, had served under him in South-East Asia and sometimes forgot the new arrangements and called Mountbatten 'Sir'. Edwina calmed the women down. She took particular trouble with Lady Power, newly married and shy, who found herself gently steered into the leading role. 'I am being a very conventional Naval wife', Edwina reported to Nehru, 'entertaining and calling and keeping my place'. That was true. At meetings of the Malta Council of St John it was the Governor-General's wife who presided; on the Council of the District Nurses Association Edwina sat as an ordinary member, dutifully attending interminable sessions to discuss arrangements for the Christmas Ball. Being inconspicuous was not always easy. When a son was born to Prince Philip and Princess Elizabeth in mid-November, the Mountbattens were showered with messages: 'Everyone in a state of high excitement about "the baby" and sweetly enthusiastic and congratulatory'. People would keep asking Edwina to take the chair at councils and committees and, although she constantly refused invitations to run things, she could not say no to everything.

Large-scale philanthropic work was impossible. Edwina had no office, and for assistance depended on Pamela and an occasional part-time secretary. There was little space in which to work, for the house Edwina had selected, Villa Guardamangia, was in a dreadful state, and while it was being made habitable the Mountbattens lived in the Hotel Phoenicia. Dealing with workmen was a nightmare: 'Villa going backwards', she told Nehru at the beginning of December. To cheer herself up she bought plants for the garden and 'enchanting goldfish with lazy, swishy tails, 18 at 4d each.' At Christmas she was still tearing round the island in search of lamps and furniture; just as everything was finished the kitchen wall collapsed. They moved in on 29 December: 'gassed by paint and cold intense!' The garden had been tidied – in desperation Edwina had planted bougainvillaea round an unshiftable statue of Mercury, six feet high and wearing a bowler hat – and the house transformed. 'The best decorating job of your life', Dickie told Edwina in a New Year letter, thanking her for her sweetness and patience during their first two and a half months in Malta.

He was generous. Edwina had been restless and abrupt. 'One feels one's brain and even one's energy shrinking to fit the tiny island', she told Nehru. She missed trees and green spaces. Each day Edwina waited for letters from India. 'Why these fusses and spacings and rationings!!' she demanded, after a week without post. Nehru was working twenty hours a day; somehow he managed to write three or four times a week, even while he was travelling. 'Am I to start numbering these letters again?' he asked anxiously, in a note from the Hotel George V in Paris. '. . . I am still between two worlds and these letters are forlorn fragments, rooted in neither . . .' Nehru returned to Delhi to find a packet of letters from Edwina and a birthday message from her husband. Dickie still muddled the spelling of Nehru's first name and now got his age wrong. 'Why add to my years?' Nehru said wryly to Edwina, '59 is bad enough.'

At the beginning of January 1949 Dickie left on the winter cruise and Edwina returned to England. Even here she was unsettled. She spent a night at Sandringham ('quite the ugliest house I have ever seen . . .'), with Philip, Elizabeth and the baby. Everyone was friendly but, Edwina told Nehru, 'I always feel most bogus in this kind of circle.' Without Dickie it was even more of an effort to join in an evening of 'ridiculous games' and a gangster film. 'I always feel I am about to say something which will surprise and shock them most terribly! So a good deal of restraint has to be exercised . . .' Rushing round London, calling on relations, running errands for Dickie – Edwina's programme was as frantic as ever. In mid-January she joined her husband for the Squadron's official visit to Greece. While Dickie received generals and admirals and talked to his cousins, Edwina toured refugee camps and met the local representatives of the Save the Children Fund, for three years of civil war had left thousands homeless and destitute. She returned to Broadlands for a few days' peace and solitude but the house was cold and the woods were hung with dank fog. Back in Malta the weather was no bettter: 'Violent gales, torrential rain and icy cold.' Only one thing kept Edwina going, the promise of a reunion with Nehru.

She was returning to India in mid-February. 'Do you remember the calendar Dickie put up?' Nehru had asked. In his mind's eye, he said, he now had one of his own. Edwina did not want her visit to cause malicious gossip. Pamela accompanied her and their programme had at its centre a tour of refugee camps and hospitals. Edwina had accepted an invitation to stay at Government House in Delhi as the guest of Rajagopalachari; 'I shall get a pair of binoculars and look at you from a distance', Nehru told her. He wanted Edwina and Pamela to come to him; when 'Rajaji' anxiously asked him whether he thought Government House might have too many poignant memories for Lady Louis to be comfortable there, Nehru agreed that she would be happier in a house that had not once been her own. Three days after Edwina and Pamela arrived, the Governor-General took himself off to Jaipur and his guests moved to the Prime Minister's residence.

In five weeks Edwina wrote only one letter to Dickie. 'The picture is not complete without you', she declared, but she was too busy and too happy to miss him. There were parties, receptions – one, given by the Governor-General ('Seems so natural to be curtseying to him!'), for fifteen hundred of her old friends – and a succession of reunions: with the United Council for Relief and Welfare, the workers at refugee camps outside Delhi, with Rajkumari Amrit Kaur, Mridula Sarabhai and the Trivedis. Edwina was ceaselessly on the move: two days in East Punjab, three in Calcutta, twenty-four hours in Allahabad, the Prime Minister's home town, to help him open a new wing at the local hospital. There, at five in the morning, Nehru came into Edwina's room to tell her that Sarojini Naidu had died during the night. They flew to Lucknow for the funeral. 'Incredible scenes', Edwina wrote in her diary. 'Thousands of people streaming in to pay their last respects.' Back to Delhi to visit refugee resettlement projects at the Chattapur Collective Farm, to see the new Harijan Colony, the Maternity and Welfare Centre for the families of the Governor-General's Bodyguard, the Government House Primary School. The students at Lady Irwin College asked Edwina to their gymnastic display, the garage staff at Government House gave a tea party.

The best part of the day was before breakfast, when Edwina and Nehru met in the garden. They had promised each other a holiday, four days in Orissa, so that Nehru could show Edwina the temple of Konarak and take her swimming at Puri on the Bay of Bengal. They were not alone – Pamela, Indira, Nehru's niece Rita and his sister Betty accompanied them. Edwina and Nehru walked on the white sand in the moonlight and swam in the waves at sunrise. Nehru discoursed on Indian history, local legends, his life in prison; Edwina felt she could listen for ever. The words swam in her head, not surprisingly, for she had a temperature of a hundred and three. The doctor thought it was malaria and when they got her back to Delhi she was advised to postpone her return to England. It was almost blissful to be ill: 'Jawaha too wonderful . . .'

Six days later, on 21 March, Edwina and Pamela took off from Delhi. From the airport Edwina sent a last letter to Nehru: 'A huge tear just about to drop'. The Prime Minister walked in his garden: 'The house was lighted up, except for one wing . . . your rooms down below and mine on the first floor. The darkness stood out, a sign of a light that had gone, of life stealing away and leaving an emptiness behind.' Next day, to console his master, Nehru's cook produced *Poussin Contesse Mountbatten* and *crème brûlée*, one of Lady Louis' favourite puddings. Anthony Eden was in Delhi and came to the Prime Minister's House for lunch. Nehru had no appetite.

Edwina Mountbatten

Edwina could not settle. She was quarrelsome, bristling with accusations that Dickie had slighted or ignored her. He did not know how to reply. At least the Navy appreciated him but when, in announcing his promotion to Vice-Admiral, he said as much, there was a scene. Dickie left for Cyprus, where the Squadron was to make an official visit. From *Liverpool* he wrote a letter, headed, appropriately, 'At Sea'.

> . . . After nearly 27 years together it is not very surprising that we sometimes get on each other's nerves but although we have both had flare-ups in the past I have never known them to really get me down. And yet when we had that row in the boat yesterday . . . I became so violently unhappy that I really felt physically sick and, greedy as I usually am, I could eat no lunch and, talkative as I usually am, I could find nothing to say.
>
> Let me begin by criticizing myself: I am terribly self-centred and rather conceited and full of the vainglory of uniforms and decorations. As a young man I had religious scruples about doing more than kiss a woman until one was married. I often wonder if you realize how little I knew about marriage before we married . . .
>
> You suggested it might be better not to come to Cyprus yesterday, and I very nearly agreed – I felt we had got on each other's nerves to such a point where a long rest from each other was the only hope. I was utterly miserable last night and it was pure misery that made me blurt out the news of my promotion in that gauche and thoughtless way . . .

But the faults were not only on one side. Edwina had said things that were hurtful and untrue. For instance, she had agreed that, while she and Pamela were in India, Dickie should invite Patricia to Malta. Jealous of the affection between father and daughter, Edwina launched into the vilest accusations, declaring that Dickie was trying to conspire against her. He was shocked to the core.

> I don't need to tell you that your most devoted and loyal friend, who adores you in her shy and reserved way more than one could normally guess, is Patricia. Pammy adores you too – and perhaps because of me gets on better with you; but I am pretty sure that if the only way of saving your life were to sacrifice her own Patricia would just beat Pammy to it. You know very well,

darling, that nothing I could do could turn Patricia against you. In fact no one (except possibly yourself) could ever affect her very deep and loyal and loving feelings for you. So do please believe me when I say that the one thing I've always worked for is complete family love and friendship . . .

Edwina's jealousy was unreasonable.

As for Yola, we are all such friends that it is fun being together – but there are times when it is fun being alone. Just as you wept with disappointment when circumstances meant that I was going to be home the first evening that you and Jawahar were going to be together, I sometimes also feel I'd like to be alone with Yola . . . I never minded your seeing Malcolm and Jawahar alone, as you know . . .

Until the moment when they had said goodbye, he too had thought it best that they should not meet in Cyprus.

But then the old old miracle happened. You pressed my hand and caught my eye and gave me that divine smile which I like to think you give to no one else and which I can assure you I get from no one else and I kissed the back of your hair and the old heart fluttered in the same ridiculous way in which it has fluttered for 28 years, ever since I first met you at that divine dance of the Vanderbilts, and I realised that if you came to Cyprus in that mood, my mood would meet you more than half way and we could have a wonderfully happy time . . .

Edwina's reply was all he could desire, although it was only a cable seven words long: 'So looking forward to Cyprus dear Vice-Admiral'.

Dickie's chief failing was that he was not Nehru. Malta, however pleasant, was not India. Edwina tried to persuade herself that she had readjusted. She had not. '. . . Darkest despair and thoroughly rebellious,' she confessed to Nehru. 'Late last night in the privacy of my room I indulged not in a few tears but in a good cry.' She thought she wanted solitude. Left alone, she felt excluded. When the Squadron visited ports in the Mediterranean and Adriatic, Edwina insisted on accompanying Dickie. While he met naval and military colleagues, she looked at hospitals, museums, gardens, churches, palaces and fortifications. It pleased her to preside over official dinners, where she could display her skill at mixing unlikely groups of guests – politicians who had not spoken to each other for years, people who had fought on opposite sides in the war. All this made Edwina glad that she had come. Then there would be a day of tedious receptions in Dickie's honour, or a dull party, and she felt trapped.

It was not that Edwina wanted to be the centre of attention. When Princess Elizabeth came to Malta for a month in December 1949 (Prince Philip had joined the Mediterranean Fleet in October) and Edwina was eclipsed, she did not mind, although it was a nuisance to have to give up her own quarters and move in to Dickie's bedroom. (He was banished to another.) 'I feel as though I was in Piccadilly Circus', she told Nehru. 'There is so much noise of every kind! Dickie tells me he never noticed it!' Domestic complications apart, Edwina enjoyed looking after her visitor. 'It's lovely seeing her so radiant and leading a more or less human and normal existence for once.' Princess Elizabeth visited hospitals and destroyers, drove in state and unveiled plaques; Edwina happily took second place. She was delighted when her guest asked if she could prolong her visit and stay for Christmas, sorry to lose her. 'Lilibeth has left with a tear in her eyes and a lump in her throat', Edwina told Nehru. '. . . Putting her into the Viking when she left was I thought rather like putting a bird back into a very small cage and I felt sad and nearly tearful myself!' Being shut in by convention and protocol, having to follow a pre-arranged programme, finding herself timetabled, organized, categorized – Edwina could think of no worse fate.

As long as she could make her own decisions, she was relaxed and happy. Losing control made her angry – with Malta, with the Navy and with Dickie. There were other constraints. The Mountbattens' expenditure constantly outran their means. Their joint annual income before tax came to a hundred and thirteen thousand pounds, but a large part of Edwina's share went to various charities, covenants and annuities. Before the war these charges, together with income tax and super-tax, had left the Mountbattens with a net income of some forty thousand pounds a year. Increased taxation now reduced it by nine-tenths. Dickie reviewed the domestic accounts. In London they had a tiny staff, at Broadlands a few more, plus the farm and estate people. No scope there for economy – but Dickie's Mediterranean appointment also obliged them to keep a third establishment in Malta. Dickie looked through the books with Ronald Brockman, who had run his office in Delhi. He pointed out that at Villa Guardamangia the

Breaking Her Silence

Mountbattens employed a staff of nineteen: a butler, a housekeeper, two housemaids, two charwomen and (shared with the ship in harbour) six stewards, three cooks, two Marine drivers, a Marine valet and a coxswain. This for a family of three, with one or two occasional guests. Dickie's verdict: 'We are not too grossly overstaffed'.

Small economies were practicable: '. . . Quite like the old days', Edwina wrote in her diary after a morning in Paris with Pamela, 'looking at Callot's clothes and Suzy's hats and ordering a few . . .' Now, however, she selected two rather than twenty. Savings could be made on large outlays. 'The Standard Motor Company have now agreed to give us a new Vanguard for the old one free of charge when we get back', Dickie reported to Edwina in late February 1950, as his Mediterranean appointment came to an end. But drastic measures were required to tackle the underlying problem. Edwina's income was derived from a trust, established under the terms of her grandfather's will. Certain statutory restraints, intended to protect heiresses against predatory husbands, not only denied her access to the capital sum but also prevented her from enjoying some of the interest it earned. In the spring of 1947 the Mountbattens and Cousin Felix considered whether these restrictions might somehow be set aside. Sir Felix consulted Walter Monckton, who advised the Mountbattens to apply to the High Court, as and when additional funds were required. They were outraged. 'Edwina and I cannot sufficiently express our absolute horror at the prospect of going through life making a series of annual appeals . . .', Dickie wrote from Delhi. 'Honestly, Cousin Felix, Edwina and I cannot carry on like this . . . Broadlands is hopelessly mortgaged and we are in a thoroughly unsound financial position. Although I know the Courts are not in the least interested in a testator's feelings, I should imagine that Sir Ernest Cassel would be turning in his grave . . .'

There was another course, to lodge a Petition in the House of Lords to bring in a Personal Bill to apply specifically to Edwina's case. The 1948 Budget, which introduced a capital levy, strengthened the Mountbattens' resolve to press ahead. The Petition was lodged and certified and the Mountbatten Estate Bill sent to a House of Lords Committee. In the winter of 1948 it made its way through all the necessary stages in the Lords. Then everything stopped. 'Some people are being *bloody* of course', Edwina told Dickie in a letter from London, '. . . you will probably have seen certain cuttings already . . .' In the

Daily Express Beaverbrook enjoyed an anti-Mountbatten campaign, in the Commons some Labour Members indicated, not unreasonably, that if the law were to be amended, it should not be changed only on behalf of those who could afford the expense of a Personal Bill. The Leader of the House was disinclined to set aside parliamentary time for legislation that Government supporters disliked. The Chancellor of the Exchequer had indicated that the passage of the Bill would deprive the Treasury of a very large sum. In early summer 1949 a solution was found. Edwina withdrew her Bill and the Government introduced its own, the Married Women (Removal of Restraint) Bill, a measure of general application. It was mid-December before it passed all its stages and received Royal Assent. Four more years' negotiating with the Public Trustees and at last Dickie and Edwina were in funds again.

Money was not Edwina's only worry. Mary was not in a good state: Kenya, Lord Delamere's home, did not agree with her. Her fine, pale skin burnt easily in the sun and she was intimidated by the hard, experienced women who were her neighbours in the 'White Highlands'. She came home to England in April 1949 and in October she collapsed. Edwina took her sister to the London Clinic for an operation; after it, Mary's mind gave way. 'No danger to life', Edwina told Nehru, 'but physically and mentally she is a very sick woman.'

'Fate or the bad fairies always see to it that one does not become too favoured and spoilt and secure', Edwina observed to Nehru, 'A good thing I suppose!' She revived when he came to England in the spring for a meeting of Commonwealth Prime Ministers. Two weekends were kept free for Broadlands. Edwina was intoxicated by the early spring: 'double cherries etc azaleas starting and beeches just about to burst out. Woods a mass of bluebells and primroses and pink ragwort.' For Nehru it was all unreal: the sharp, insistent English April, Edwina's adoration. Another parting: Nehru left for Switzerland, the Mountbattens for Malta. He was back at the beginning of October, on his way to America with Indira, returning four weeks later on his way home. Three days later he was gone again.

What were they to each other? Edwina thought of Nehru as a poet but he was also a politician, bold and far-seeing, constantly putting his ideas and his person to the test, offering himself to the vast crowds that flocked to hear him. Edwina was his safety-net. Policemen and soldiers guarded him, a reminder of how vulnerable he was. People badgered him all the time, yet he was alone. Millions thought him all-powerful but the problems he faced could not be solved by one man in one lifetime. His countrymen seemed to forget that he was only a human being. Nehru was comforted because Edwina cared for him.

He liked to mesmerize. It pleased him to manage a crowd – how much more difficult to hold one individual in thrall. He was vain: the rose, the spotless linen . . . He made an effort to keep trim and fit. 'PS' he wrote, 'I am having a daily swim'. From time to time he thought of giving up smoking; 'I don't want to be smug. But always at the back of my mind is the thought that I am slipping away, getting soft . . .'

Nehru could not work unceasingly. It was pleasant to have an intelligent woman friend in whom he could confide. It delighted him to be of service, to bring Edwina sugar from America (in Britain it was rationed). She asked him to send *petits-suisses* from Switzerland; when his hosts warned him that soft cheese would not travel and presented him with Gruyère, he packed that off instead. He brought Edwina mangoes from India, cigarettes from Egypt; he sent her the chocolates he had been given by the Arab League. To Nehru it was an ideal relationship. No great adjustments need be made; this was not a marriage, with its infringements and compromises. He had been a widower for many years and liked his privacy.

The correspondence between Edwina and Nehru was rhapsodic but chaste, alluding only in general terms to the physical passion they denied themselves. In January 1949, for instance, Nehru sent Edwina a new book of photographs of the erotic sculpture on the Temple of the Sun in Orissa. 'I must say they took my breath away for an instant', he told her. 'They were strong meat. And then my mind wandered and tried to picture to itself the society in which these sculptures were made. Obviously no one could have put them there on the walls of a sacred temple if there was any thought of impiety or of any passion or lust attached to them. It was presumably about a dispassionate and objective rendering of life. There was no sense of shame or of hiding anything . . . The old Indians wrote amazingly detailed books about the sex business, treating it quite calmly and dispassionately. There is no attempt at what is called sex appeal . . .'

Edwina took up the cue. 'I am so intrigued about the Sun Temple

Sculptures', she replied. 'I never feel worried and shocked at something which is natural and frank and factual. It is only vulgarity and
subterfuge which disgusts and bores me. That is why I dislike vulgar
stories and cheap books and films based on crude sex appeal. I am
even rather disgusted by them and I know in consequence am thought
sometimes to be rather boringly prudish!' Edwina had indicated that
she had once had romantic friendships; Nehru had observed indul-
gently that he wished he had known 'her other selves'. She was at
pains to explain that her attitude was 'primarily mystical'. 'I think I
am not interested in sex as sex', she continued. 'There must be so
much more to it, beauty of spirit and form and in its conception.
But I think you and I are in the minority! Yet another treasured
bond.'

'I feel you understand as no one else has ever done', Edwina wrote
gratefully to Nehru. They were fellow-creatures. She had always felt
herself to be a foreigner; indeed, she assured him, she was hardly
English at all. Edwina had found her identity: she belonged to India.
He sent her his photograph; she exclaimed that they were beginning
to look alike. This was absurd.

Edwina's devotion was not surprising. In Nehru Edwina had found
a man she could love, respect and trust. Her grandfather had been
too remote, her father too weak. Dickie was an enthusiastic boy,
Bunny too tame. Nehru's love was worth having, for he was wise,
subtle and clever. He treated her as an equal, unlike Dickie, who
believed that he did so, but failed to get the balance right, either
deferring too much or being inadvertently patronizing. Edwina
wanted her opinions to be taken seriously; she liked to feel that she
was contributing to a discussion. With Nehru she could talk about
everything – Berlin, Malaya, Korea, China, the Cold War, the likely
outcome of an election. She spoke about these things to Dickie, to
Peter Murphy and, for that matter, to the Prime Minister and the
Chancellor of the Exchequer, but, although they knew she was
intelligent and experienced, she sensed that they considered her
an amateur. The men she met in London and Malta were always
giving women the benefit of their views; Nehru did not con-
descend.

He was gallant and graceful, never trampling on her feelings, able
to express the finest shades of emotion with delicacy. Edwina had
been afraid of love. She could accept it from strangers – refugees,

prisoners of war, sick adults, starving children – but she withdrew from the embrace of her family and friends. Nehru changed her. She learnt not just how to give but to receive. He respected, stimulated and needed her, he taught her that she needed him.

CHAPTER TWENTY-NINE

Poetry and Philosophy

'You have brought me all I was yearning for,' Edwina told Nehru in May 1949, 'happiness, balance, misery even! but we know the reason (and we would not change it) and there is infinitely more power and purpose to life . . .' She was bound to Dickie and he to the Navy: Edwina squared up to her duty and made the best of it. This was not always easy.

In May 1950 Dickie's term with the First Cruiser Squadron came to an end. Rung by rung he was climbing up the professional ladder. Now he was appointed to the Board of the Admiralty as Fourth Sea Lord, in charge of supplies and pay. It was considered an uninteresting post. 'What can one do to help the country in looking after stores, clothes and oil fuel?' Dickie lamented to Patricia. 'And Pay would only help if one had a free hand.' Within days of taking up his new job, he had answered his own question. In his first month he inspected the five main naval depots, called at every office in the Victualling and Stores Department, looked over torpedo workshops and typing pools. Dickie had admired the methodical way in which Edwina had investigated medical and welfare arrangements in SEAC; now he applied the same principles. Warehouses were emptied of unusable and obsolete equipment, surpluses identified and eliminated. House-keeping on this scale was fun. Furthermore, Dickie told his son-in-law, 'As 4th Sea Lord I have such an unimportant job that no one could possibly feel jealous or think I was trying to throw my weight about.' He tried to be inconspicuous but there were times when he did not hesitate to go to the top. 'Victory over Pay!', Dickie wrote in his diary, after a confrontation with Emanuel Shinwell, Minister of Defence, and Hugh Gaitskell, Minister of State at the Treasury. Considering the extent of Mountbatten's acquaintance and the depth of his experience, he managed to irritate his colleagues remarkably little.

Outside the office he was less inhibited. At the start of the Festival of Britain in May 1951 the Mountbattens drove in the royal procession to St Paul's Cathedral for the opening service and went with the King and Queen to hear the inaugural concert at the Festival Hall. (Ismay got stuck for forty minutes in one of the foolproof lifts.) For Edwina a little of the Family went a long way: 'All in good but childish spirits', she told Nehru in a letter from Sandringham in January 1951, 'the youngest of the party being Queen Mary . . . who was kicking Charles' balloons around the room last night.' She did not share their taste for silly games, practical jokes with apple-pie beds and disguises. Shooting made her shudder; she could not bear to touch the feathers of the dead pheasants and partridges. Royal residences were colder and less comfortable than her own (Broadlands, unusually, had carpeted bathrooms) and the thick crested writing-paper was too heavy for airletters. The formal side of Court life made her more impatient than ever. 'A week of the Dutch State visit and State Banquet etc.', Edwina told Nehru in November 1950. Attlee was on his way to Washington to discuss the Korean War; at such a time, she observed, 'the pomp and ceremony and gold plate and brilliant uniforms seemed particularly unreal.'

Edwina was irritated by the parochialism of British society, by the insularity of its leaders. In July 1951 she flew back to London from Cornwall in a small aeroplane: the country looked heavenly, she told Nehru, 'serene and peaceful and solid . . . I suddenly felt *exasperated* at it'. Britain was so small compared with India's vast deserts, towering mountain ranges and endless plains. Nehru was struggling to bring his people into the twentieth century; at home, Edwina said, things were going backwards to the nineteenth. In October 1951 the Conservatives were returned to office; Edwina was not impressed. 'The new Cabinet all with vast fortunes and incomes and fleets of private cars and chauffeurs have patriotically cut their salaries and their transport. We have all swallowed hard and tried to clap!' She considered that important jobs had gone to the wrong people: 'Poor Walter Monckton went in to Winston hoping he was going to be offered the Attorney General and came out with Labour! Oliver Lyttelton's appointment to Colonies I don't like at all . . . Still no Minister for Education or Health. So it appears that Health, Education and Social Services do not interest the new Government. But the people feel somewhat differently!' At the Lord Mayor's Banquet, where Churchill was to make his first public statement since the Election, Edwina sat between Lord Woolton, the new Lord President, and the Speaker of the House of Commons, 'Shakes' Morrison. She was horrified by the Prime Minister's speech, 'extolling the virtues of the USA', she told Nehru disbelievingly, 'linking them all with that most valuable asset the Atom Bomb!!' Her neighbours agreed. 'A most unfortunate reference', they whispered consolingly. 'But no one can control him!'

The best of the old world was going. On 24 September Aunt Victoria died at Kensington Palace. Dickie's mother was eighty-seven; while she was at Broadlands in the summer her heart had started giving trouble. She had insisted on returning to London: 'It is better to die at home', she said firmly. On 28 September there was a family funeral service at the Chapel Royal and then the coffin was taken to Portsmouth, where a frigate carried it across to the Isle of Wight, so that Victoria could be buried next to her husband. Edwina was as bereft as Dickie. From the beginning she had liked and respected her mother-in-law; she was proud to have won her affection and admiration. Aunt Victoria had understood her intelligent, restless daughter-in-law; she had influenced her too. From the time of her marriage, Edwina had followed her mother-in-law's example and kept a daily diary. A fortnight after the funeral, she put it away for ever.

Edwina made herself look forward. It helped when Broadlands was restored to her. The hospital moved out at the end of 1949, rooms were reclaimed, furniture unstacked, the boxes from India opened. For the first time since 1913, the happy period before she and Mary had been sent away to school, Edwina took full possession of the house, the gardens and the woods. In August 1951 she and Dickie gave a huge party, 'a terrific success', she told Nehru. The house, the orangery and the dairy were illuminated, floodlights shone on the curves of the river. 'The Mayor and Mayoress of Romsey, present and past, Conservative, Labour and Liberal, a brewer, railwayman, farmer, the doctors and the curate and St Johnites, all mixed up with Princess Lilibeth and Margaret and Philip and . . . the Government and Opposition . . . all the Services and many nationalities . . . and the Stage and Screen.' Ambrose brought two bands; five hundred and fifty guests danced all night, some until half-past five in the morning. The party was given for Pamela, now twenty-one; to Edwina it also celebrated the renaissance of her house.

Another childhood paradise had been returned to her the year before, when she stayed at Classiebawn Castle, for the first time since she was fourteen. 'I felt I should make a tremendous effort to maintain it', Edwina told Nehru, 'scraped together odd bits of furniture and furnishings and sent over the Broadlands electrician to wire up the house and get local help to instal bathrooms, a good water supply and modernise the whole place . . . Our drawing room carpet is one I questioned years ago being good enough for our old Servants' Hall in London and I am overcome now at its excellent quality! How times change!' Living arrangements in London had also been sorted out. The Mountbattens did not renew their lease of the Brook House apartment and early in 1950 16 Chester Street was sold. In May Dickie and Edwina moved into 2 Wilton Crescent, a good-sized house south of Hyde Park. A small flat, with a door connecting it to the house, was carved out of the mews behind, a refuge for Dickie, purchased and furnished with his share of his mother's estate. To Wilton Crescent came many of the treasures Edwina had kept when her grandfather's house had been demolished and the contents sold; when the Duke of Windsor looked in for a drink in February 1952, he recognized the pictures as the ones he had borrowed in the 'thirties.

Two years after she took charge of the new house, Edwina had to leave it. In May 1952 Dickie became Commander-in-Chief of the Mediterranean Fleet; Wilton Crescent was let and the Mountbattens returned to Malta. Dickie was on top of the world, for this was one of the two most important commands in the Royal Navy. The British controlled both ends of the Mediterranean; round its shores were friendly countries and pleasant harbours. The Commander-in-Chief could deploy a large aircraft carrier, three cruisers, three squadrons of destroyers and three of frigates, a submarine squadron, a school of mine-sweepers and amphibious warfare ships, and a host of smaller vessels. There was one disadvantage. With the top job went an official establishment, Admiralty House, an old building in the middle of Valletta. It was not a patch on Villa Guardamangia: 'absolutely no view at all', Edwina complained to Nehru, 'not an inch of garden and the racket day and night is deafening – endless clanging peals of church bells and hooting cars and heavy lorries changing gear, chattering and screaming voices, wirelesses.' An empty bombsite opposite her bedroom window was used by workmen to chisel blocks of stone. The house had large rooms for entertaining but in summer they were oppressive: 'utterly *airless*, only two ceiling fans and no air conditioning.' Edwina tried to make the best of it. At least, she said, Malta was nearer than London to India.

There was some compensation in having the use of the Commander-in-Chief's frigate, *Surprise*, for official visits. The Mountbattens' first major excursion was to Yugoslavia. 'I do not want their Regime any more than I want the Soviet one', Edwina told Nehru, 'but I do want to know their leaders and people and the progress they are making – good or bad – from my own eyes and not thru' biased propaganda.' In Dickie's flagship, *Glasgow*, the Mountbattens entertained a mixture of ex-Fascists, Communists and Monarchists; Edwina was particularly impressed by the women, many of whom had fought in the Resistance. One, who had lost half a foot and whose face was slashed with scars, was reputed to have strangled seven Germans, 'with her own hands.' Edwina was bowled over by Tito: 'fine physique, good looks and vital personality . . . a kind and simple side . . . very well read . . .' The Marshal had insisted that Lady Louis be invited to lunch ('a non-woman affair') at his villa on the island of Brioni, so Edwina was predisposed to like him. She came away convinced of the virtues of Titoism.

They called on the Greeks, descended on Cyprus, looked in on the Lebanon and Israel. *Surprise* had room for guests: Malcolm Sargent accompanied them on a cruise from Naples to Algiers in the autumn of 1952. Gracie Fields came aboard to sing to the sailors from the quarterdeck of the largest ship: 'She lives in Capri now', Edwina told Nehru, 'and has recently married the Italian man who came to see to her electrical supplies. Most convenient especially as he seemed very charming and nice . . .' In November Dickie and Edwina paid an official visit to Rome, which included a private luncheon at Castel Gandolfo with Pope Pius XII, '. . . a remarkably fine looking man with a sensitive and very beautiful head', Edwina declared, 'and you feel his goodness flowing out of him. I kept on feeling, very illogically, I suppose, what a pity it was that he is a Roman Catholic . . .'

Dickie's days were not filled only with official calls, underwater fishing, polo and regattas. He regularly took a squadron out to sea and enjoyed leading the Fleet on manoeuvres. His chief task was to follow political and strategic issues in the Mediterranean, to keep the Fleet in a state of readiness and oversee its deployment. Throughout the summer and autumn of 1952 much of his time was given to dealing with his American colleague, Admiral Carney, Commander-in-Chief,

Poetry and Philosophy

Mediterranean, in the North Atlantic Treaty Organization. Some suggested that, since Carney represented NATO, he should be given supreme command over the whole Mediterranean. The British disagreed. Difficulties multiplied. In the winter of 1952 it was at last decided that a separate NATO Command should control all Allied naval forces in the Mediterranean and all air forces concerned with maritime war, under a new Commander, CINCAFMED. Who was to be appointed? Mountbatten, now an Admiral, had experience in leading a combined force and in running an international command. 'We've got it', he triumphantly told his staff when the decision was announced.

'I am afraid this will mean a big Allied set-up in Malta', Dickie told Robert Neville, 'and will be a great bore for me and a lot of extra work.' His duties were almost doubled but he was delighted to be in charge. Mountbatten's first directive announced that in mid-March 1953 an integrated naval/air headquarters would be opened in Malta; his team was led by admirals from Italy, France, Greece, the United States and Turkey. So many flags fluttered from the front of the NATO building in Malta that to British residents it was known as Selfridge's.

The new appointment also gave Dickie more reason – not that he thought he required any – for discussing policy with important people. A stream of grandees passed though Malta, among them the British Foreign Secretary, Anthony Eden. On their travels the Mountbattens dropped in on various Heads of State. 'An intimate little party for 80', Edwina wrote to Nehru from Morocco in May 1953. 'I sat next to the Grand Vizier to the Sultan who is 107 and has held his post, like the Prime Minister, for 50 years.' That summer Dickie and Edwina went to Greece, in October 1953 they were in the Canal Zone, in November in Ethiopia, where the Emperor presented Edwina with a monkey, 'with long white moustaches . . . very sentimental and sweet and appears to adore me already.' (The monkey, that is.) The visitors had prepared for their stay by reading *Black Mischief*. The officers were amused when Evelyn Waugh's novel came to life – they had been asked to walk backwards when leaving the Emperor's presence – but Edwina defended her hosts. The Ethiopians, she told Nehru, not meaning to be condescending, had 'all the natural charm and manners of an uncivilized country.'

Dickie now learnt that the Admiralty wanted him to remain in Malta until the end of 1954, seven months later than Edwina had expected.

Edwina Mountbatten

'We feel resigned though frustrated . . .', she told Nehru, for she had endured more than enough of supra-national bureaucracy. A high-level visit from the North Atlantic Council in July 1954 was almost too much: fourteen ambassadors, led by Pug Ismay, a dinner party of thirty-four, followed by a reception for ninety-two. 'Great success', said Dickie's diary; Edwina's report to Nehru was less enthusiastic. 'The gentleman from Ireland had never been further south than Paris so he nearly *died* of heat . . . The gentleman from Denmark kept saying how exciting it was to be in the TROPICS. Dickie took them all to sea in *Surprise* to see a Fleet Review . . . This was much enjoyed by the "NATO boys", although even though the sea was glassy they all took sea-sick precautions before embarking . . .' Maltese politics got her down: Dom Mintoff, leader of the Maltese Labour Party, had concocted a scheme for unification with Britain and drawn Dickie into supporting the idea. Mintoff had then gone to London to discuss it with influential people, among them Lord Beaverbrook. When he learnt that Mountbatten was a backer, Beaverbrook lost interest in the plan and it expired. To Edwina, who was worrying about the atomic bomb, the Korean War, insurgency in Malaya and Kenya and trouble in the Middle East, all this was an irrelevance.

There was so much to do at home: schemes for a volunteer car service for hospital patients and a 'housewives mutual help service'; a plan to demolish the unattractive 'bachelors' wing' at Broadlands, clear out the coal cellar, rearrange the kitchens, restore the plaster ceilings and cornices. Edwina wanted to see more of Patricia, John and their young family and of Pamela, who had left Malta the year before. 'Probably a very good plan for her', Edwina had said to Dickie, 'though sad for us . . . But quite understandable. Malta is very small and narrow . . .'

They were all growing up and growing old. In the last few months of 1952, white hairs had appeared on Edwina's head and, she told Nehru, 'my already lined and weatherbeaten face is like a spider's web as far as I can see.' This reflection had been prompted by a reunion with the Churchills, who had borrowed Beaverbrook's villa in the South of France and invited the Mountbattens to dinner. On this occasion, at least, the Prime Minister seemed to have mellowed. Other old friends had gone for ever. In the spring of 1952, three weeks after the Mountbattens' visit to Sandringham, news came of the King's death. 'A real shock', Edwina had written to Nehru. 'How fit we had found him shooting and walking in spite of intense cold and arctic winds. Poor little Lilibeth. It is a tragic homecoming . . .' She and Prince Philip had left Britain the week before on the first stage of a tour to Kenya, Ceylon, Australia and New Zealand, taking Pamela as lady-in-waiting. The Mountbattens went to the airport to meet the sorrowing party. That afternoon, 8 February, Edwina suddenly started to haemorrhage and in the evening she went into hospital. Surgeons found nothing malignant and three days later she appeared, looking fragile, in Westminster Hall, where the body of the late King, her old friend Prince Bertie, had been brought to lie in state. The coffin was taken to Windsor, in a ceremony resembling the funeral of the late King's father, George V, who had died only sixteen years before.

Queen Mary died little more than a year later. The Mountbattens travelled from Malta for the lying-in-state and the funeral: 'the most varied Royalties . . .', Edwina told Nehru, 'Queens Juliana and Frederica of Greece, Ex-King Umberto of Italy, who I had not seen for 20 years or more and who until he came up to me and greeted me warmly I had taken to be one of the new Court officials!! The King of the Belgians very pathetic and lost and on the defensive, the Grand Duke of Luxembourg and a few Hannoverians . . .' Seventeen months after that, in July 1954, Edwina heard that her stepmother had died. The Mountbattens were in Florence, celebrating Dickie's fiftieth birthday with Patricia, John, Pamela, the Brockmans and Malcolm Sargent, and Edwina was disinclined to break off her holiday for Molly's funeral. At the last moment she repented. It was just as well. When she got to Broadlands she found a full-scale row. In her will Molly had expressed a special wish to be buried with Wilfrid and Maudie in the family vault in Romsey Cemetery. 'You can imagine how high feeling was running', Edwina told Nehru, 'and how much smoothing all round had to be done!' Mary, meanwhile, was in the middle of another nervous breakdown.

Complicating everything was the fact that Dickie had no idea what he would be asked to do next. 'No news of any new appointments', Edwina told Nehru in August 1954. 'I believe there is a battle Royal raging as to who is to be the next First Sea Lord. Dickie's name is of course frequently mentioned and continuously attacked in the *Express*!! but there are others "in the running" and many in high places who would like Dickie sent elsewhere . . . One would like to know *sometime* so as to plan one's life!'

The Admirals were not sure whether they wanted Mountbatten. He had already had his share of senior jobs and it did not help that he had made no secret of his wish for the post which his father had been obliged to resign. Admiral Cunningham declared that, though Mountbatten had great gifts, he lacked judgement. 'I am sure you will be able to help, dear Pug', Edwina wrote sweetly to Ismay. 'It would be heartbreaking if Dickie's remarkable personality and outstanding ability was to be wasted in these next *vital* years in a Back Yard.' Jim Thomas, First Lord of the Admiralty, urged the professionals to be sensible. The Navy had done worse than the other Services in recent reviews of defence policy; what they needed at the Admiralty was not a clever sailor but a man who could steer his way through political shoals. In mid-September 1954 Dickie heard that the Admiralty would support him. 'But it may take some weeks still before he hears anything definite', Edwina told Nehru, 'and we are prepared for anything.' She was right to be cautious. In his youth Churchill had been First Lord himself; now, at the end of his career, it pleased him to tease the Admirals. In the third week of October the invitation finally arrived.

'Today we start a Farewell tour', Edwina told Nehru in November, 'Rome, Algiers, Naples, Athens, Ankara, Cairo and Fayed, only one night in each place and a ghastly programme at every stop. And the work and engagements and goodbye parties here are *unceasing* . . .' On 10 December the Mountbattens left Malta for the last time. '. . . Thousands of people thronging the old Fortifications and Bastions . . . the Gun Salutes and cheering ships' companies and the strains of "Will Ye No Come Back Again?" and "They Are Jolly Good Fellows"!' ('He's a Jolly Good Fellow', according to Dickie's diary.) 'Most unofficial and unauthorized but very touching – the screaming of the sirens of the Malta tugs and small ships and Dickie being pulled off in a boat to *Surprise* by Admirals of five different nations.' (Dickie said six.) 'We thought they would all explode as some were fat and breathless anyway!' When the time came for the Mountbattens to leave the officers and men of *Surprise*, everyone was in tears.

Dickie had achieved his ambition. 'First day as First Sea Lord', he wrote in his diary on 18 April 1955. 'Thrill to sit under Papa's picture.' Of all his colleagues, however, he was least disposed to looking back.

Poetry and Philosophy

Like all maturing organizations the department had ossified. The wheels of the machine turned, administering for adminstration's sake. Mountbatten believed that the Admiralty was there to serve the Navy, not the other way round. From now on all correspondence was to be answered within a week. Over the years policy had been made incrementally: a cut here, a little expansion there, in accordance with current financial targets. No one had asked the fundamental question: What was the Navy for? Mountbatten was determined to do so. A Way Ahead Committee was set up; during the next two years its members inspected, reported on and reorganized the Navy's entire administrative and logistical structure. Manning and recruitment were studied, measures taken to make a naval career attractive to ambitious people. In one of his regular newsletters, Mountbatten called for official encouragement for spare-time activities, 'such as sailing, mountaineering, pot-holing, canoeing, underwater fishing etc, which do so much to strengthen character and leadership . . .' He looked at the size and shape of the country's sea-going resources: the Reserve Fleet was pruned, existing construction programmes re-examined. Guided missile carrying destroyers were to be one arm of the Navy, the other a fleet that could carry men and equipment for use at sea, on land or in the air, wherever they were needed, Mountbatten's 'Triphibious Command' recreated and reshaped. This last objective took years to achieve.

Dickie loved his work. Edwina did not. 'Of course I function continuously and I suppose do a little good', she told Nehru, '. . . but Dickie's present job looms so large that I dare do and say nothing "without due thought" which is frightful and almost suffocates me.' She felt 'low and discouraged, like an animal in a trap'. Her houses were a solace. 'The sun has shone so fiercely', Edwina wrote from Broadlands in August 1955, 'one could imagine oneself in India.' In September the Mountbattens took Paula Long to Classiebawn Castle. Edwina walked for miles along the beaches, climbing over the dunes. The hedges were full of wild fuchsia, thunderstorms wonderfully dramatic. The house in Wilton Crescent had been retrieved from the Mountbattens' tenants; it was a convenient and comfortable base but Edwina hated the yellow smog that blanketed the city in the winter. Something seemed to be wrong with Britain: there were strikes by railwaymen, dockers, miners, seamen, transport workers and printers. Newspapers failed to appear. '. . . The wireless gives some news', Edwina told Nehru, 'but appears to concentrate now mainly on SPORT, ENTERTAINMENT AND DR BILLY GRAHAM . . . as a NATION we are utterly lost and helpless! One cannot wrap up the "Fish" in the *New Statesman* or even the *Manchester Guardian . . .'*

Edwina did not think the politicians could put things right. The Government was out of touch, she said, the Opposition in disarray. 'Poor Clem so mishandled Nye Bevan that he tied himself in knots', she reported to Nehru, after Bevan had challenged Attlee, as well as Churchill, on British support for the hydrogen bomb. As for the trade unions, 'We are in a jam at the moment and I fear a lot of innocent people will suffer. The good humour of the ordinary British citizen and their calmness is a tremendous asset but they are inwardly very angry altho' sympathetic to many of the demands.' Meanwhile the Prime Minister's heirs apparent had no idea when he would leave office, if at all. Churchill, now over eighty, enjoyed keeping his Ministers – and everyone else – in suspense. 'It looks *really* now as though Winston is on the way out', Edwina told Nehru in March 1955, 'but he still refuses to make any announcement and indeed makes very silly little digs at the Press . . .' On 5 April the Prime Minister resigned, in the middle of the newspaper strike. 'Rather tragic that Winston should go at such a moment, without the blaze of headlines', Edwina observed, 'but I suppose in a way it fitted with the general pattern. We all felt rather black and sad, however, when the inevitable finally occurred . . .'

Churchill's successor was Anthony Eden. No one was surprised; he had long been waiting in the wings. The Mountbattens had seen Eden regularly during the past three and half years. He had come to Broadlands, called on them in Malta, lunched and dined with them in London. He listened courteously to Edwina when she lobbied him about relief work in Berlin, Korea and elsewhere and while she tried to explain why, in her opinion, the Government was pursuing the wrong line in Malaya, Kenya, the Middle East and the United Nations. The Foreign Office did not change its line: Edwina suspected that Eden had either misunderstood her arguments or failed to press them home. When Nehru was in England, Edwina arranged for Eden to meet him at Broadlands and she had urged the Foreign Secretary to make an official visit to Delhi. The Edens went in February 1955 and stayed at Prime Minister's House. ('I want to know where they slept', Edwina asked enviously, 'in my room, I assume, and the one next door. *Lucky* people.') Nehru thought his guest was finding it difficult to cope with the complexities of post-war foreign policy. 'Eden seemed very confused', he told Edwina after a discussion on Indo-China. Illness had worn Eden down, years of waiting for Churchill had diluted his authority. 'So nice and charming but so weak', was Edwina's view.

The new Prime Minister's great test came in the summer of 1956, when General Nasser nationalized the Suez Canal Company. British and French reaction was immediate and hostile. Eden, who had resigned from the Government in 1938 rather than appease Hitler and Mussolini, warned his colleagues that Nasser was another dictator whom it was necessary to deter. 'The Suez crisis becomes more and more complex', Edwina told Nehru on 6 August, 'and Dickie is never off the telephone to Anthony. The latter Dickie says is trying to remain sane and calm and fair. But what with our own hysterical idiots and the French madmen . . . one almost despairs.'

Mountbatten did his best to deflect the Prime Minister from military action. Departing from all the rules, he wrote directly to Eden; when that appeal failed, he asked the First Lord to convey to the Prime Minister his protest 'at the use of my Service'. He could do no more. As an officer Mountbatten served the Crown. It was the Government's responsibility to formulate policy, his duty to obey instructions. 'The Service' meant serving, for better or worse; the same obligation applied to the First Sea Lord as to his officers and men. Dickie had worked hard to prove that, despite his royal connections, the Supreme Command, his Viceroyalty, he was a loyal officer, going where he was sent, doing what he was told. The First Lord of the Admiralty ordered Mountbatten to remain at his post; he did. Dickie was 'in a quite ghastly position', Edwina told Nehru. 'His job is to carry out orders.' Then the Government yielded to international, particularly to American, pressure and called off the action. On 9 November it was announced that the Prime Minister was suffering from 'nervous exhaustion', two days later he left the country for three weeks' rest in Jamaica. On 9 January 1957 Eden announced his resignation from the premiership; he also gave up his parliamentary seat. 'Anthony's end was something of a tragedy', Edwina told Nehru, '. . . much as I differed from him politically I feel sad.'

At its height the Suez crisis seemed to illustrate the influence of individuals – Nasser, Eden, Eisenhower – on the course of world affairs. Nehru wondered whether in the long run politicians made much difference. 'There is a sense of unreality about it all', he told Edwina, in a letter from a Conference of Commonwealth Foreign Ministers in Colombo in January 1950: 'a vast mass of human beings, impelled by elemental urges . . . people seem to be unaware of this and imagine that they can deal with them in some superior governmental way.' Speculative, fatalistic, conscious of the limits of his own power – it was not surprising that Nehru took this view. Edwina was not so sure. She had spent years trying to deal with the misery and confusion caused by political and military leaders who were misguided, deluded, in some cases plainly wicked. In her eyes, the fact that people believed in promoting a particular cause or ideology did not make them any less responsible for the consequences. 'Why does it always seem easier for the leaders of Communist and Fascist movements to get released and carry on their dangerous and insidious activities than any other category of offender?', she wrote desperately to Nehru in late 1949, after listening to discussions about the Amnesty Bill in France. 'It is the same in every country and it terrifies me. I am always haunted by the endless war memorials in every town and village of the British Isles and a sense of horrible guilt creeps over me, because one feels so powerless and so apprehensive that all these sacrifices seem to have been in vain.'

Edwina was an idealist. Left to themselves, she believed, lions would lie down with lambs. She took her politics from well-meaning editorials in the *New Statesman*; she was influenced by her association with people who could be unselfish to the point of saintliness. On her travels for the Save the Children Fund, the Red Cross and St John Ambulance, Edwina saw the victims of wars and revolutions. The more she learnt, the more convinced she was that politicians did not know what they were doing. In early 1950, for instance, she was in Malaya, where terrorism had flared up again. On her return to London, Edwina asked to see Griffiths, Secretary of State for the Colonies. She told Nehru that she had spoken bluntly. 'Malcolm MacDonald is the only one who even begins to see the problem realistically and does not make himself believe that the troubles in the Federation are merely due to Moscow or a few discontented Chinese. It is fast becoming a nationalist movement and we must offer some alternative pretty fast . . .' An enlightened civil administrator was needed in Malaya, she declared, not a military dictator. (The Government had appointed a British General as Head of Anti-Bandit Operations.) Griffiths listened politely; there was no change.

Edwina was sickened by British and American Cold War rhetoric. Nehru had given her his views: 'The problem is not Communism,' he told her in January 1950. 'The problem is there in varying degrees all over the world. Communism offers a solution. That solution, though partly right, is not adequate and, in some respects, is very wrong, that is, in so far as it is based on hatred and violence and the suppression of the individual . . . Merely to shout and curse at Communism is not to find a solution.' People Edwina knew accused her of being 'pink'; at a party in June 1950 she was seated next to Hewlett Johnson, 'the Red Dean of Canterbury'. 'Riveting, I thought, charming and extremely balanced! Perhaps Protocol and Precedence etc thought I was the best person to put next to such a "hideous Communist" . . . Very progressive views and says so . . . Wasted in the Church!'

In 1951 she went to West and East Africa. Edwina thought Britain's post-war colonial policy was all wrong. The British Army officers who entertained her in Nigeria tried to please by asking how they could obtain *Polo* by Marco for their clubs in Lagos and Kaduna. Edwina was not impressed. Kenya was no better. 'Some unbelievably boring British who should be firmly removed', she told Nehru, 'and sent to Cheltenham to retire painlessly.' Here, of all places, Britain needed enlightened representatives. When Edwina came home, she arranged to see the Prime Minister and the Secretary of State for Commonwealth Relations. 'There will be some plain speaking!!' she said bravely. Nehru did not hold out much hope. 'You might have produced some slight effect on Clem Attlee', he observed, 'but it is sheer optimisim to believe that Gordon-Walker can be influenced in this way.'

Edwina did not give up. In March 1952, on her way to look at relief work in Japan, South Korea and North Borneo, she returned to Malaya. There she saw General Sir Gerald Templer, who had been sent out as High Commissioner. '. . . Amazed me with his ignorance of the problem and his completely mad approach to it', she reported to Nehru. 'I told him quite plainly that, if those were his intentions, in a few months he would be packing his bags for the UK as what structure there was would entirely collapse.' On her return Edwina went to see the Foreign Secretary. She also told him what she thought about Korea. 'He was *furious*, rather like Oliver Lyttelton and Kenya!'

Edwina Mountbatten

For she had also expressed her disapproval of British policy there. 'I despair of what they are doing . . .', she lamented to Nehru. 'Most of my African colleagues – even reactionary ones – appear to be in gaol . . .'

Year in, year out, Edwina travelled on relief work. In 1953 she was at the site of the earthquake in the Ionian Isles, in 1954 in the Malayan jungle. The following year she inspected Red Cross, St John and Save the Children teams in Burma and Korea, in 1956 she flew to Vienna to see what could be done for the refugees who were pouring in from Hungary. Between these expeditions she travelled to America and Canada (twenty-five speeches in seventeen days) and to New Zealand, to drum up support for the United Nations Childrens' Emergency Fund. Wherever she went Edwina saw the results of dilatoriness and obscurantism. Cyprus was another example. Relations between the Greek and Turkish communities were so bad that the island had become an armed fortress. The Governor rode in an armoured car: '3 bombs in his bed', Edwina told Nehru, '. . . If only we had acted years ago with vision and intelligence . . . the old, old story . . .' All over the world colonial peoples were clamouring for self-government. Desperate Governors begged Lady Louis to come out to organize relief work in countries where order had collapsed; in places that were still relatively stable the authorities invited her to visit their territories to assess what could be done to vaccinate children, improve nutrition, establish educational and medical services. Local political leaders might decline to negotiate with 'imperialists' or with each other but in her St John uniform Edwina could see anyone, go everywhere.

Her outlook was progressive, her purpose humanitarian. She was as dedicated to her mission as the patriots or freedom fighters were to their own. '. . . This tour has been so testing and overwhelming', Edwina told Dickie, after five weeks in the West Indies, the Bahamas, British Honduras and British Guiana early in 1958. 'I had to carry on with bad laryngitis again and feeling ghastly . . . We've had, as well as the small Hurricane, torrential rains, Earth tremors . . . weather the worst in 50 years!' The files kept by Edwina's secretaries in the nineteen-fifties were full of letters thanking pilots, navigators and drivers for their valiant work in thunder, fog, duststorms and turbulence. Although Edwina complained to Dickie and Nehru that she was presented with impossible schedules, packed tight with engagements, she tried to fulfil every request. If the aeroplane in which she travelled had to be diverted or floods or riots prevented her from reaching a hospital, camp or school where she was expected, a letter would go off immediately to her disappointed hosts, apologizing and asking when she might be allowed to try again. No journey was too daunting, no distance too great.

Edwina's critics suggested that she had become an ostentatious do-gooder, so fanatical about helping the sick and dispossessed that she had no time or patience for her old friends. This was unfair. Edwina was not an easy person to live with – not because she was consumed by the importance of her mission but because she was a perfectionist, who exacted the same standards and performance from other people as from herself. It is true that she was proud of her wide and varied acquaintance, her knowledge of every part of the world, the fact that she was known everywhere. She deserved to be. At a gathering at Lancaster House in London in June 1951, she told Nehru, she had joined a conversation 'rather brazenly, without introduction'. A West Indian had asked her what country she was representing. 'But of course', announced someone who recognized her, 'You belong to us *all!*' Edwina was delighted, more so when one of 'a delicious group of Indians' declared firmly: 'She may be a World Citizen but she's *ours* primarily.'

In many respects Edwina was indeed better informed than Secretaries of State for Foreign Affairs, the Colonies, Commonwealth Relations, men who were generally either new to the job or the prisoners of their own and their officials' prejudices. Edwina had formed her own views over many years. She compared notes with Dickie and she was also influenced by Nehru, whose letters offered a steady supply of information and opinion. (He was not infallible. Ho Chi Minh, the Communist President of North Vietnam, struck him as 'one of the most likeable men I have come across. He gives one the impression of integrity, goodwill and peace.') Discussions with Nehru, Dickie, their colleagues and the Mountbattens' friends, together with her own experience – all this gave Edwina an unparalleled vantage point. She was considered left-wing; in fact she was a peace-loving, romantic democrat. Her myopia was more pronounced when she looked east toward the Urals; westward, her eyes were sharp. Edwina was constantly irritated by what she considered the rabid anti-Communism of the Americans. When she mentioned in her diary, in April 1949, that she had spent an evening seeing 'lengthy and questionable films' with Dickie's shipmates, she was referring not to anything sexually suggestive but to *The Iron Curtain*, an American film about a Soviet spy ring. The Sunday service on an American destroyer was full of references to the hydrogen bomb, Edwina told Nehru in May 1957; 'Poor old God gets brought into everything nowadays.'

These views did Edwina no good. People felt that she was not entitled to have opinions, still less critical ones, and that she should certainly refrain from voicing them. Cabinet Ministers were alarmed. Amateurs themselves, frantically trying to master their portfolios, they disliked being unsettled, particularly by a woman. Matters were made worse by the fact that Lady Louis was so insistently progressive. When the then Lord Altrincham published an article in the *National and English Review* in 1957, criticizing some aspects of the Court and the monarchy, he was publicly berated. Not by Edwina. The article, she told Nehru, was 'admittedly in very bad taste and exaggerated in many ways', but it was 'basically sound and even constructive.' She had no time for snobs or bigots. Racial conflict in England in 1958 was, she said, 'a terrible shock to me and I think to the nation as a whole.' Here she was optimistic. Edwina's failure to discriminate was notable. Rosita Forbes had asked her whether a certain person was black or white. 'No idea', Edwina replied. It was true. She was not afraid to be out of step. The United Nations, she said, was 'a racket'; NATO 'had everything wrong with it' – this from the wife of the First Sea Lord.

People talked. The most vicious attacks began in 1952, three weeks after the death of the King. Dickie was used to being sniped at, particularly by the Beaverbrook press, but he was astonished at what hit him now. 'Four different people have come to me in the last 2 or 3 days', he wrote to Edwina on 28 February (she was in Delhi), 'to say that London is buzzing with rumours and talk in the clubs etc that I was to be offered an immediate post abroad so as to remove us from being able to influence Lilibet through Philip. My own influence was viewed with apprehension but there was also the view that I would be passing on extreme left-wing views from you! Of course you always tell me that I am very right wing and reactionary compared to you – so that you may not be altogether surprised at this. However last night an incident occurred which I find so upsetting that I felt I must sit down and tell you all about it right away.' The Deputy

Director of Naval Intelligence had brought Mountbatten 'a very hot TOP SECRET' letter from the Foreign Office to the Admiralty, saying that in Washington a certain Mr Ulius Louis Amoss, proprietor of a newsletter known as *International Services of Information*, had come to the British Mission to say that he had learnt that Mountbatten was 'deeply involved with the Communist Party'. The British Minister in Washington had observed that it was curious that Amoss had not begun by taking his information to the State Department or the FBI. If, as seemed likely, the story were published, the Embassy would declare the allegation to be completely baseless; in England the Admiralty would take appropriate action and inform the Palace.

'You can imagine the hornet's nest this has stirred up', Dickie wrote. President Eisenhower had just indicated that he would accept Mountbatten as the Allied Naval Commander in Chief for the Mediterranean. Would the American Chiefs of Staff now object? The First Lord of the Admiralty, the First Sea Lord and others had discussed the matter with Dickie: 'Everyone has been most sympathetic and friendly and anxious to help in any way possible.' Edwina was indignant. 'You always stress the point about *my* politics!! but I can assure you that whatever *I* may think your attitude is and whether we agree or not, *I* have endless worryings about *your* links with people such as Peter and supposedly Communist sympathizers from many who appear to think I am Right Wing compared to you!! The only difference between us is that I don't tell you about these remarks because they come from circles not in touch with you and I hit them for six. The criticism is not only one sided however I can assure you . . .' Dickie had advised Edwina to take particular care on her visit to UN and American forces in South Korea. 'The Americans may be watching you a bit . . . for signs of anti-American (Pro-Communist) tendencies – but you know that already. Beware however of the Press . . .' Her reply was tart. 'You may rest assured that I shall confine myself entirely to Medical and Relief matters – I am not interested in any others as there is nothing one can do anyway to stop people murdering each other unnecessarily because of Politicians!'

There was a lull. In 1953, as the country was preparing for the Coronation, the stories started again. Unpleasant insinuations were made in the Beaverbrook press. The Mountbattens believed that their every move was watched: when Edwina wanted a valuable necklace reset, she decided to have the work done in Paris to avoid unkind

467

remarks. Dickie wondered whether counter-allegations should be planted; Peter thought it unwise. Edwina agreed, 'chiefly', she told Dickie, 'because any reference only draws more attention to the Vendetta and even somewhat suggests that Max's campaign is more damaging than it really is'.

Then, in the early summer, there was a major row. On 1 June, the day before the Coronation, Prime Ministers were received for lunch at Buckingham Palace. The Mountbattens were there, and Nehru, who had come to London for the celebrations. At the reception Edwina found herself standing next to Oliver Lyttelton, the Colonial Secretary. After making what Edwina considered disparaging remarks about Malta, India and Malaya, Lyttelton asked to be introduced to Nehru. The conversation was disastrous. Somehow they found themselves discussing terrorism in Kenya, a topic on which the Colonial Secretary was feeling touchy. Allegations of brutality by British police and military officers had just been brought to his attention and an investigation was under way. Edwina did not know this. When she murmured something about 'the perpetuation of violence, bitterness and hatred', Lyttelton exploded. Edwina managed to change the subject but she was horrified. She was so angry and upset that, unusually, she wrote a memorandum of the conversation when she got home.

Dickie next heard, 'through a more than reliable source', Edwina told Nehru, that Lyttelton had reported the whole matter to the Prime Minister and the Cabinet, saying that Lady Louis had declared that British police and troops were worse than Mau Mau terrorists, that she had a reputation for being anti-British ('not Anti-American', she observed to Nehru, 'You will smile!') and left-wing. Dickie's informant also told him that, for these reasons, it had been thought unwise for Lady Louis to accompany her husband in *Surprise* on his forthcoming official visit to Turkey. Sure enough, a letter then came to Mountbatten from the First Lord, saying that *Surprise* should stay behind. The danger of press criticism was given as an excuse. The Mountbattens were taken aback. The President of Turkey had invited them both as his guests and Edwina was to carry out an official programme of visits to hospitals, universities and other institutions, as well as attending formal naval functions.

Edwina wrote a blistering letter to Lyttelton, attaching the relevant part of her memorandum of the Buckingham Palace conversation. She was disgusted, she told Nehru. 'Turkey is serious but not the end of the world. My reputation and the campaign against me is not all-important. Dickie's is!' If her support for the National Health Service meant that she was left-wing, she declared, 'Who isn't!' If she was considered anti-British because she believed in racial equality, she was certainly guilty and proud of it. 'But it's pretty disillusioning that Individuals are persecuted and penalised because of their views – and that through the back door!' She might as well be living in a police state, she said bitterly, 'in fact one might be behind the Iron Curtain!!' How could she fight something like this, she asked, 'especially where most of the Campaign is carried on behind Closed Doors and underground?' Not by exchanging letters with the Colonial Secretary, that was clear. Edwina did some sapping and mining. She showed the correspondence, including Nehru's recollections of the incident, not just to the First Lord but also to the Foreign Secretary. Five days later Dickie received a signal from the Admiralty saying that there were no objections to Lady Louis accompanying him to Turkey in *Surprise*.

Successful, unconventional, close to royalty, supposedly rich – the Mountbattens were an ideal target. Dickie became so exasperated by repeated innuendo in the press that he considered a libel action. Again, he was advised against it. In 1954 he thought about protesting to the Press Council; Peter Murphy persuaded him to do nothing. Edwina tried to be careful: on her visit to India that spring her tickets were booked in the name of Mrs Ashley. Once she got to India, the rumours began. Edwina, Nehru and Dickie ignored them. There was speculation about the nature of the relationship between Lady Louis and the Prime Minister of India, but it would have been indecorous, as well as pointless, to try to answer it. Edwina and Nehru had decided long ago that they would take gossip in their stride.

What Edwina found intolerable, however, were stories about her politics. They were generally wrong and in any case she thought them intrusive. A particularly searing episode occurred during her visit to India in February 1957. It was a difficult time. There had been further argument in the United Nations Security Council over the status of Kashmir, which had formally acceded to India on 26 January. Britain and the United States objected, in India there was talk of leaving the Commonwealth. 'There has been a lot of publicity about your visit', Dickie warned Edwina in a letter written on 29 January, 'not all of it very kind.' In a report on demonstrations in Pakistan, at which effigies of Nehru had been set alight, the BBC had mentioned that Lady Louis had appeared at the Republic Day Parade in Delhi with Nehru and Marshal Zhukov, the Russian Defence Minister. Stories implied that Edwina was pro-Soviet, anti-British.

When she saw what the press was saying, Edwina was incensed. She had taken scrupulous care to avoid all official functions. 'Naturally I was at the Republic Day Parade,' she told Dickie, 'with Malcolm MacDonald and the Heads of 60 other countries and a million people from all over the world. I did not even drive with J. in Madras or Poona or elsewhere and was always miles behind . . . I do not see what other anti-Max (Press) precautions one could have taken.' She was distressed that Dickie's name should have been dragged in, determined to face down her critics. Dickie had told Edwina that the new First Lord, Lord Hailsham, had advised him to shield her from the press on her return to England. She would let him do no such thing. 'To try and avoid them and make arrangements to keep them away if they (as they usually do) wish to see me can only lead to suspicion and criticism and looks like running away from them. The advice you have been given is I fear not pshicologically or practically sound . . .' She agreed, however, that it would be helpful to accept an invitation to watch the forthcoming England-France Rugby International from the Royal Box, for, as Dickie pointed out 'it's pretty full with the PM and Cabinet Ministers etc.'

What upset Edwina most was that, in seeking to injure her, the critics attacked her beloved India. Her adopted country was as much her home as Broadlands; every year, from 1950 to 1960, she went to Delhi. She stopped in India on her way south, west and east to places she was visiting for St John and the Red Cross; when her tours took her to the Far East, she called there on the way out and the way back. Her visits, Nehru told her, were the pivot upon which everything else revolved. Edwina stayed at Prime Minister's House, with Indira or Mrs Pandit as chaperone. From there she and Nehru went off to see hydro-electric projects, universities, temples, the new city of Chandigarh. They did not go alone; their only time together was on quiet walks before breakfast in the garden or during an occasional evening stroll before the sun went down.

At home she longed for India. From Wilton Crescent, Villa Guardamangia, Admiralty House, Broadlands, scores of letters came, sympathizing with Nehru's worries over Kashmir and Tibet, taking up the points he made about his Cabinet colleagues, enquiring about the countless natural disasters his country suffered: drought, earthquakes, cyclones, floods, famine. She gave her views only when Nehru asked for them; the ex-Viceroy was less circumspect. 'It was improper of him to write', Nehru murmured to Edwina, when her husband asked him to intervene in a disciplinary case. 'Dickie seems to think that I can behave like a Grand Moghul or a Supremo and override rules and regulations . . .' Nehru thought Edwina's judgement easily as good as her husband's, sometimes better. 'Your mind is acute and masculine in its approach to business', he told her, 'or, at any rate, that is the way men put it.' Edwina was a useful as well as a sympathetic confidante. Almost too sympathetic; her analysis was skewed by her unshakeable belief that all Nehru said and did must be right. She was touchingly proud of her Indian connections. 'A delicious curry party in the destroyer *Rana*', Edwina reported to Nehru from Malta in December 1949: 'Of course I could eat and enjoy it hotter than anyone else!' Her assertions were sometimes ridiculous, that the world's best kippers, for instance, were served at the Indian High Commission in Ceylon.

'My watch still keeps India time', Edwina told Nehru, in a letter written on the flight from Bombay to London in April 1951. In Cairo, where the aircraft stopped to refuel, she found one of Nehru's handkerchiefs in her grey wool overcoat pocket: 'that cheered me'. Edwina clung to every reminder of the country she loved and the man she adored. India and Nehru, Nehru and India: in her mind and her heart they were intertwined. His letters were her lifeline; his gifts fragments of another world: pressed flowers from Kashmir, dried ferns from Sikkim, saffron, tea, orchids, mangoes, a sandalwood box, a crocodile skin (shot by a Maharajah). In return Edwina sent heather from Classiebawn Castle and 'gentians and alpenstocks' (she meant 'edelweiss') gathered in the Swiss Alps. Nehru was enchanted. Overworked, lonely, often uncertain, he looked to Edwina for companionship and support. In the summer of 1954 he talked of giving up the premiership, of retiring to the mountains. He was tired, bored with politics and politicians, afraid, he said, of losing his grip: '. . . I would probably come back in a better mood some time later'. If only he could discuss it all with Edwina. She had become as indispensable to Nehru as he was to her.

471

Edwina Mountbatten

Nehru did not resign. Instead, he took himself to Mashobra for a rest: 'Six years ago, almost to the day . . . the air and the rooms and the corridors are full of whispers of the past. I have lived here for five days in this atmosphere, getting rather mixed up with what has been and what is.' Whenever he could, he came to England, eight times between 1950 and 1957. His visits were short, for he was either tied up in meetings at Downing Street or Chequers or hurrying on to official engagements in Europe or America. But he always left at least one weekend for Broadlands. It was there, one summer evening, that Mrs Travis, the Mountbattens' archivist, saw them across the fields as she made her way home – Pandit Nehru and Lady Louis, silhouetted against the sky. They seemed so much at ease that she felt it right to wish them well. Mrs Travis waved, together, they returned her salute. No two people could have looked more in harmony.

CHAPTER THIRTY

Leave-taking

As time passed, the relationship between Edwina and Nehru became less fevered. 'Ten years!', Nehru wrote on 12 March 1957. He had been looking through his papers. 'I came across your letters, neatly placed in separate bundles in large envelopes. For each year there was a big and sometimes rather fat envelope. The first one was for 1948 and though this was for six months only it was far the fattest. The next one, for 1949, was also a heavy one but smaller . . . Progressively these annual envelopes became thinner, representing fewer letters. And of course my letters to you during these years followed the same pattern.' Why was this? 'Had the poetry turned into prose?' Nehru did not think so. 'But nine years ago there was the novelty of a new and wonderful discovery which moved me to the depths and possessed me. That novelty could not last in that way, for we adapt ourselves even to surprises and wonders. Indeed, it was wonderful enough for us, living far from each other and meeting infrequently, to continue the experience, that deep feeling which itself is so full of wonder and which gives a certain fulness to life. My life has been full enough in many ways and I have been absorbed in and have passionately pursued the love of India and her people and sought to give them such service as I could. But you came to add to it and not to come in its way. And so I am infinitely thankful . . .'

As Nehru said, the packages told their own story. At first Nehru and Edwina had written to each other every day. A year later they were writing once a week, by 1954 once a fortnight. Now, ten years on, Edwina's letters came at three-week intervals. The falling-off was greater on Nehru's side. He tried but the volume of his work made correspondence difficult. 'You tell me that you waited day after day . . . and there was no letter', he wrote contritely in February 1955, 'except the brief and rather formal one from the office of Air India International from Geneva . . . I am so sorry . . . I shall now try to send a letter once a week, writing on Sunday usually or perhaps

Monday. So long as I am in Delhi this can be done more or less regularly, but when I travel it might be more difficult to keep to this timetable . . .' A week later: 'This is my Sunday letter!' Then: 'I have missed Sunday and am writing to you on Tuesday.' Edwina did not reproach him. In mid-March 1955 a madman had hurled himself at the Prime Minister's car and tried to stab him. When Edwina heard the news, her heart stood still. Nehru thrust the man away: 'There was no danger . . .', he assured her. Intermittent letters were better than an everlasting silence. 'Ten years . . .', Edwina wrote in March 1957, '. . . monumental in their history and so powerful in the effects on our personal lives. All the incidents you mention and the strange course of events . . . I seem steeped in them.' His letter had touched her deeply.

In 1958 Nehru again began to talk of resignation. Edwina instructed him to have a holiday and in late May he set off with Indira for a month's trek in the Kulu Valley. His doctors had forbidden him to climb higher than seven or eight thousand feet. He ignored them, he told Edwina triumphantly, '. . . up to thirteen thousand five hundred!' He had spoken of getting away from everything. 'Tell me whether I should continue to write to you or *not*?' Edwina asked. 'I shall well understand if you say "not a note for the next months".' Her question took his breath away. 'What have I said, written or done to deserve this?' Nehru replied. 'I am hurt at the suggestion. And how do you think I would fare if months passed without a letter from you? . . . Have you realized what your letters mean to me?' Edwina was relieved. Never ceasing to marvel at what had happened, she could not believe that her letters were so important.

Dickie could not fail to see the attachment between Nehru and Edwina. He asked no questions. Whatever the situation was, tact and understanding would see them through. Until the dénouement, Dickie was determined to behave naturally. He sent Nehru encouraging letters, full of political tips; when Edwina went to Delhi, he wrote ahead, begging her host to see she got some rest. Nehru replied in a kindly way, never failing to take an interest in his friend's enthusiasms; flying saucers, cosmology, computers. 'Dickie once spoke to me about a memory machine', Nehru told Edwina, 'and I have been recently reading about it . . . I confess I disliked the look and the thought of it.'

Leave-taking

Dickie did not expect Edwina to confide in him. He only wished he knew how to make her happy. Their relations were harmonious for ninety-nine per cent of the time but then there would be an explosion over some trivial incident: a row when Edwina's canaries were alarmed by a gun salute on *Surprise*, an argument over the merits of a certain journalist. Depression and loneliness impelled Edwina to lash out; she then looked for evidence to justify her outburst. These battles generally ended with an announcement from Edwina that she intended to leave Dickie; in the early and middle nineteen-fifties she spoke constantly of divorce. 'I've never attempted to stop you or hold you and I never shall', Dickie declared. 'I don't want you to stay against your will. I'm not that selfish . . .' This was true. Dickie had told Patricia and Pamela that the great advantage of his having the mews flat was that he would have somewhere to go if Edwina asked him to leave Wilton Crescent and Broadlands.

Edwina and Dickie did not part. They were inextricably bound together, not just by their children and grandchildren, their friends, shared history and possessions, but by ties that were harder to break than these. Knowing people suggested that the Mountbattens stayed together because Edwina valued her husband's royal connections and because he needed her money. This showed how ignorant they were. From the beginning Dickie had been bewitched by his 'divine Edwina', beautiful, vivacious, intelligent and forthright. That magic remained. He could not cure her tormented heart but he could help and comfort her; he believed she needed him as much as he needed her. Adoration, excitement and a sense of responsibility held Dickie to Edwina; affection, duty and gratitude tied her to him.

Once, and once only, Edwina revealed her feelings. This was in February 1952, just after her haemorrhage. She thought she might be dying and before she was taken into the operating theatre she handed Dickie an envelope. He took it away to open when he was alone. 'I have been thinking about all those letters I have from Jawaha', Edwina wrote, 'and what should be done with them . . .' She had originally intended to leave them to Paula Long (this shows how Edwina's heart could overrule her head, for Paula hardly possessed a cupboard, let alone a safe) but she had changed her mind. 'I would like you to have them for your life time', she told Dickie. 'You will realize that they are a mixture of typical Jawaha letters, full of interest and facts and really historic documents. Some of them have no "personal" remarks at all. Others are love letters in a sense, though you yourself will realize the strange relationship – most of it spiritual – which exists between us. J. has obviously meant a very great deal in my life in these last years and I think I in his. Our meetings have been rare and always fleeting but I think I understand him, and perhaps he me, as well as any human beings *can* ever understand each other. Particularly when two like us are generally thousands of miles apart and in such different lives and circumstances!!' She told Dickie where the letters were kept and asked him to read them. He might want to publish various passages: '. . . as having been written to you and me or, even better possibly as though written to nobody, just a sort of diary. It seems selfish otherwise for this wealth of material, with his own reflections and attitudes and actions, never to see the light of day at all . . .'

So far Edwina's letter had been chiefly about herself and Nehru, but it was written as a tribute to Dickie, a testament to her feelings for him. At the end Edwina said so, if obliquely. 'It is rather wonderful that my affection and respect and gratitude and *love* for you are really so great that I feel you would understand and not in any way be hurt, rather the contrary. We understand each other so well although so often we seem to differ and to be miles apart . . . My admiration and my devotion to you are very great. I think you know that. I have had a very full and a very happy life on the whole – all thanks to you! Bless you and with my lasting love . . .'

Dickie said little. He was too dazed with happiness at hearing, later that day, that Edwina was going to be all right. It was a year before he gave her his considered reaction, in a letter to Delhi, where she was resting after another illness. This was in February 1953. Whatever were to happen to either of them, he told Edwina, he would treasure her letter. 'I'm glad you realize that I know and have always under-stood the very special relationship between Jawaha and you – made the easier by my fondness and admiration for him and by the remark-ably lucky fact that among my many defects God did not add jealousy in any degree or form . . . Only my desire for your happiness exists. That is why I've always made your visits to each other easy and been faintly hurt when at times (such as in 1951) you didn't take me into your confidence right away.' He had been reading her letter and thinking over the history of their marriage. 'Considering how deeply fond we are of each other and how proud and admiring I certainly

Leave-taking

am of all your wonderful achievements, I cannot but be sad and worried that we should have had so many differences.' He could not understand it. She had no need to feel envious or injured. 'I know I'm selfish and difficult but that doesn't change my deep and profound love for you . . . You have been my mainstay, my inspiration and my true companion for far more than half my life . . .'

Edwina could not speak to Dickie about her feelings for him but no wife worked harder to help her husband succeed, in small ways ('you so cheerfully put up with that foul swell on Sunday') and in large. When Lord Selkirk, the new First Lord of the Admiralty, visited Delhi in September 1958, Edwina asked Nehru to put in a good word. 'He is pleasant and intelligent . . . but thinks he knows everything and deliberately disregards Dickie's advice . . . Please give D. a pat on the back.' The new Minister of Defence, Duncan Sandys, was invited to dine at Wilton Crescent and to shoot at Broadlands. Within weeks he had been won round to Dickie's idea of what a post-Suez Navy should look like. In May 1958 the Prime Minister offered Mountbatten the post of Chief of the Defence Staff, the head of a new and powerful central organization, directly responsible to the Minister of Defence and independent of the three Chiefs of Staff. Edwina was delighted. 'I think at heart Dickie loves Politics', she told Nehru, 'though he would *never* admit it!!' To help things along, the Macmillans and the Sandys were asked to Broadlands for a weekend in November. 'Can't you see our little party', Edwina asked Nehru, '. . . Dickie trying (very unsubtly !!) to get what he can out of the PM and Minister of Defence!! And I chatting madly about nonsenses as though I knew nothing about all the machinations!! And watching Lady Dorothy doing her embroidery! What *extraordinary* things one does . . .'

These days Edwina did not complain. She was calm and sweet-tempered, smiling through ministerial dinners, official visits, State occasions. The storms seemed to be over. Yola came to stay at Broadlands and, although Edwina watched every move she and Dickie made, there were no scenes. She was kind and considerate, even meek. Dickie was astonished to find her sitting in the hall waiting quietly until he was ready. This was a new Edwina. When she was abroad, he missed her more than ever. His life was incomplete without her. 'The house is very lonely without you', he wrote in 1959, when she had set off on some tour of inspection. 'I shall hate passing your door in a few minutes when I go to bed, without looking in.' His birthday present that year – she was 58 – was a handsome wrought-iron gate for Broadlands, her monogram on one side, his on the other. It closed an epoch and opened another; the years of difficulty were over and the journey ahead promised to be peaceful and companionable.

The family flourished. Patricia, with four children now, was happily established in Kent, John was making a name for himelf as a film producer. In mid-November 1959 Pamela became engaged to David Hicks, an interior designer. 'He is very charming and I like him so much', Edwina told Nehru in an excited letter, '. . . just older than she, works hard and seriously, is artistic and gifted . . .' They were married in Romsey on 13 January 1960. 'Snowed hard all day and dislocated traffic', Dickie noted in his diary, but the staff struggled in to Broadlands and, although some of the family missed the lunch party, everyone reached the Abbey in time. The bride was dressed in white satin, edged with white mink, falling behind her in a shining river; 'hardly room for me in the car' wrote her happy father. John Brabourne was best man, the Duke of Edinburgh proposed the health of the bride. Nine hundred guests came to Broadlands afterwards, three hundred and fifty gathered in the local hall. 'You and Daddy did a typically marvellous job,' Patricia wrote to her mother afterwards, '. . . But I know how exhausting it all is . . .'

Edwina was extremely tired. She had always driven herself hard and in the last few years the strain had begun to tell. After her operation in 1952 she had set off for a strenuous tour in South Korea; on her return home she had cracked a rib. She developed a high fever in Petra and contracted a throat infection in Algeria. That winter she had bad 'flu. 'India will set me up', she assured Dickie. After three weeks there, taking 'Metatone', she felt 'less worm-like'. In 1956 and 1957 she had a series of infections: 'voiceless again', 'a roaring throat', 'bad laryngitis', bad tooth. She took 'Multivites' to boost her vitamin intake. Optalidon for her neuralgia, Nembutal to help her sleep. In 1956 her doctor, Wilkes Harvey, warned her that she had mild angina and that if she did not slow down she would be dead in three years. Edwina took no notice. Two years later, in the autumn of 1958, a swelling appeared on her face, a growth in the parotid gland which was surgically removed. For a time Edwina's face sagged at one side, as if she had had a stroke, an educative experience, she told Nehru

Leave-taking

afterwards (she said nothing about her operation at the time), for people stared at her lopsided cheek and drooping eye. To prove to herself that she did not mind, she flew to Paris to display her face to Yola, who was aghast. Getting over the operation took weeks. Then in January 1959 Edwina caught chickenpox from a grandchild. To convalesce, she went off to Delhi, coming back apparently restored. At the end of June, however, Edwina told Nehru that she was 'not so good.'

Edwina admitted that she was doing too much. In October she went with Dickie on a twelve-day tour of defence establishments in the United States, 'a killer', she confessed to Nehru; on the day after their return, she had five major engagements, the next day four. 'Quite happy, though rather breathless', she reported at the end of 1959. After Pamela's wedding, she promised to come to India for a rest, before beginning a tour of Malaya and Borneo that even she thought daunting. Before she left, she saw Dr Wilkes Harvey and Dr McManus. They warned her not to overtax herself, for her angina was worse. Without care, she was told, she had only months to live.

Six non-stop days in Cyprus, a difficult flight to Bombay, on to Delhi: 'Of *course* my arrival coincided with President Voroshilov's official State Visit and of course I was photographed being introduced to him', Edwina told Dickie, '. . . So the *Express* etc will have great fun . . .' Edwina left India on 5 February, scribbling a long letter to Dickie before her departure, full of news about his sister Alice, who was in Delhi, and instructions for the packing and storage of Pamela's wedding dress and veil. 'I am off at 5.30 am . . .'

On 18 February, after a fortnight in Malaya, Edwina arrived in North Borneo. She was met at Jesselton Airport by the Acting Governor, Mr Turner and his wife, and by the local Commissioner General of the St John Ambulance Brigade, Dr Blaauw, and his headquarters officer, Miss Checkley, who was stationed in North Borneo for a year. It was hot and humid; Edwina changed into a fresh uniform before alighting from the aircraft but, by the time she got out of the car at the Turners' residence, her skirt was saturated. The next day, the 19th, was a rest day; Edwina asked if she could spend it at Kota Belud, a jungle training area for the Army. On the way home she was in good spirits and, although she said she felt a little unwell, she would not allow Miss Checkley to call a doctor. That night, on the way back from a

479

dinner in her honour, she stumbled, steadying herself by catching a railing. She slept little and, when she woke, she had splitting neuralgia.

Edwina agreed to see Dr Blaauw in the morning. He thought she might be starting 'flu or malaria but she insisted on carrying out her programme. At midday Mrs Turner persuaded her to rest in her room; when Edwina heard that her hosts had cancelled a luncheon that had been arranged for her, she observed that this seemed 'rather drastic'. In the late afternoon, after inspecting a St John Parade, shaking hands with everyone (except the Police Band, who were encumbered with their instruments), presenting certificates and watching first-aid demonstrations, Edwina's head was bursting. She decided to return to the Residence, skipping a tea party. Dr Blaauw came again. In the evening a reception was being held at the Residence; the Turners suggested that Edwina take things gently. Miss Checkley and a maid supported her downstairs but she insisted on entering the drawing-room unaided. At nine she withdrew, apologizing for not having taken a more active part, and collapsed. In the morning, Edwina was due to leave for Singapore.

At half past seven Irene Checkley went to Edwina's room to call her. There was no reply. She had died in her sleep. The doctors said her heart had given out at about half past two in the morning. That evening, Sunday 21 February, her coffin, covered with a St John Ambulance flag, was placed in the aircraft to begin the long journey home. With it, among the wreaths, were the orchids that had been sent to the Jesselton Show. Mr Turner had opened the boxes himself: 'I intended to ask her to do so', he said sadly in his report to Dickie, 'as she so clearly knew much more about flowers than I did.' Miss Checkley brought Edwina's possessions. Beside the bed she had seen a pile of papers and, thinking that Lady Louis' correspondence was not for other eyes, she put them in her own suitcase. Once home, she consulted Marjorie Brecknock, who had come to the airport to receive the coffin. They were Nehru's letters, Edwina's nightly reading. Marjorie told Miss Checkley that she should not be shy about handing them over to Lord Louis. Dickie gave them to Pamela to look through.

He had heard the news in a daze. 'To sleep 01.30. Telephone direct from Ministry woke me at 03.20 for call from Governor of Borneo. Failed to get through, though 03.40 telegram from him saying that

Leave-taking

Edwina had died peacefully in her sleep.' Dickie was devastated. 'TRAGEDY', he wrote at the top of the page in his daily diary; conscientiously he tried to set down what had happened, in writing that shuddered over the page. His family stayed with him, Elizabeth Ward, now Mrs Collins, tried to comfort him as she struggled with messages and telegrams. 'Fantastic BBC TV and Newspaper coverage', Dickie noted bravely. 'Hundreds of telegrams and letters from Presidents, Kings, Prime Ministers, Ambassadors, C-in-Cs and organizations, and touching ones from friends and humble folk.' He did not glory in it. Dickie was moved and proud – but what was the use of tributes when Edwina was not there to receive them? Monday and Tuesday were ghastly. Dickie tried to work. 'Attended Defence Committee meeting', he wrote on the 24th '. . . Dealt with Blue Streak and NATO . . . then PM let me leave.' At half past nine that evening Edwina's body was brought to Broadlands. Commander North had asked the staff to come to the house if they wished; everyone was there, lined up, waiting. What were they to do? He fell back on naval discipline. 'Off caps', he ordered, as the car turned into the drive. Edwina's dog, Snippet, ran out to greet her mistress. That was the worst of all.

The coffin was taken to Romsey Abbey and placed before the altar. Thirteen hours it remained there, fifty-two men of the house and estate standing guard in turn. Dickie had encouraged the staff to come to say their own farewell. Those who did saw him standing there, not trying to hide his tears.

Thirty years before, on a wet afternoon when she had nothing to do, Edwina had written to Dickie. She had been thinking about her death, she said, and had decided that to be interred in Romsey Cemetery would be bad for her claustrophobia. Could she be buried 'in a sack at sea'? This request was repeated in her will. On 25 February the family took her body to Portsmouth, where the coffin was piped aboard a frigate. They went aboard, the ship and its escort made for the open sea. There the Archbishop of Canterbury read the burial service and Edwina was committed to the waves. The ship that carried her was *Wakeful*; she, who had been so restless, went at last to her long sleep. From *Trishul*, an Indian frigate sent by Nehru, his wreath of marigolds was cast upon the sea. There it rose and fell, until it too was overcome.

Edwina Mountbatten

That winter Dickie went through the Christmas list alone. On the hundreds of cards he sent to his colleagues, he wrote this message:

> For thirty-eight years my wife and I sent Christmas cards together. I am sure that you will understand that I would like this to be the last one.

Acknowledgements

Truth is stranger than fiction. It is also elusive. This book could not have been written without first-class sources; every fact and judgement in it is drawn from the private and published papers of its chief characters and from the recollections of people who knew and worked with them.

Much of this material comes from the Broadlands Archive, which holds the letters written by Sir Ernest Cassel, his family and friends, Maudie and Wilfrid Ashley's correspondence, letters from and to Mrs Cassel, Edwina's sister Mary, her stepmother, Dickie's mother, brother and sisters. There are packets of letters from friends and relations, among them many from the Prince of Wales, the Duke of York, the Duke of Kent, Marjorie Brecknock, Peter Murphy, Robert Neville, and Yola Letellier. Forty-one years of correspondence between the Mountbattens has been preserved, everything from pencilled notes about appointments to Dickie's memoranda of important events: the cruise on the Vanderbilts' yacht, the near-parting in 1931 and so on. The Mountbattens' daily diaries are there, and shelves of photograph albums, tape-recordings and cans of film. All the accounts and correspondence relating to Adsdean, Brook House and 2 Wilton Crescent have been kept, and the papers concerning the running of Broadlands while the Mountbattens lived there. Several files deal with the management of Viceroy's House in 1947–8. Other boxes contain the letters sent by Patricia and Pamela to their parents and those they received from them; one bulky file holds the letters the children wrote from America during the war. Their drawings and school reports have been retained, and the magazine Patricia composed at Adsdean. There are cabinets full of correspondence with lawyers, solicitors, accountants, insurers, builders, decorators, furriers, jewellers, dressmakers, travel companies, veterinary surgeons and hotel proprietors. Staff reports are carefully filed, wage-sheets attached. Letters asking for subscriptions have been kept, with replies from Miss Underhill and her successors. Copies of Edwina's reports for St John Ambulance and the Red Cross are to be found in the Archive, with her own notes, and records of all her tours during and after the war. Here, too, are the hundreds of letters Edwina and Pandit Nehru wrote to each other between 1947 and 1960.

I am immensely grateful to the trustees for allowing me to see and use this material. All references, unless otherwise specified, are to this one archive. I have not given notes referring to specific files, letters and diary entries; almost every sentence draws upon at least one document, often several. Since these family papers remain closed, more detailed annotation would anyhow be unhelpful. All quotations retain the grammar and punctuation of the originals and also the spelling – Edwina's, especially, is often erratic.

One quotation, on page 309, is taken from the Royal Archives at Windsor (RA GV CC53/962). With the gracious permission of Her Majesty the Queen I have been able to make use of this material.

My greatest debt is to Edwina's daughters, the Countess Mountbatten of Burma and Lady Pamela Hicks. They invited me to write this book, lent me their papers, photographs and other memorabilia, directed me to people who had known their parents, opened doors that would otherwise have remained closed. No biographer can have hoped for more trust. Every discussion was frank; no pressure was applied. I have also had the good fortune to see Dickie and Edwina Mountbatten through the eyes of their sons-in-law, Lord Brabourne and David Hicks. I am very grateful for their help and encouragement.

My thanks are also due to Mr Rajiv Gandhi, who made it possible for me to see Edwina's letters to his grandfather, Pandit Nehru, and who allowed me to include quotations from their correspondence.

Many of the Mountbattens' relations, friends and colleagues have been ready to talk to me; others have brought valuable material to my attention. I would like to thank the following people: Dr and Mrs P.C. Alexander; Dr Anandalakshmy; Lord Annan; Lady Lettice Ashley-Cooper; Lieutenant-Colonel Sir Frederick Burnaby-Atkins and Mrs Burnaby-Atkins; Mrs Paul Barnard; John Barratt; Mr and Mrs Birch; Mrs de Bono; Sir Ronald Brockman; Mrs Brown; Dame Anne Bryans; Brenda Bury; Mrs David Butters; the Hon. Mrs Angus Campbell; Alan Campbell-Johnson; Miss Barbara Cartland; Sir Roger Cary; Sir Harold Cassel; Dr Amela Chaudhury; Miss Anne Chisholm; Mrs Irene

Acknowledgements

Christodoulides (formerly Miss Irene Checkley); Mrs Charles Collins (formerly Miss Elizabeth Ward); Ms Jane Cushman; Miss Sylvia Darley; Michael Davie; Miss Dido Davies; Mrs Rita Dhar; T.J. Everard; Roy Faibish; Douglas Fairbanks Jr.; Mrs Field (formerly Miss Nancie Lees); George Fischer; Sir Denis Forman; Mrs Esme Fowke; Mrs E.M.J. Flux-Dundas; Sir Martin Gilliatt; Jenny Gillies; Sir David Goodall; John Grigg; Brodrick Haldane; Vinit Haksar; John Hanson; Albrecht Hassmann; Stephen Hearst; H.R.H. Princess Margaret of Hesse; Lady Heald; Mrs E. Heywood-Lonsdale; Mrs Hinde; Commander Hok; Henry Hollman; Miss Ann Hopkin; Mrs David Horsburgh; Dr Kenneth Hutchin; Lady Margaret Illingworth; Mrs Philip Ironside (formerly Miss Henrietta Treble); Ian Jack; Maohu Jain; Mrs Peter Jones; Major General Sir James Lunt; Mr and Mrs Ian Macintosh; the Hon. Mrs George Marten; Lady Alexandra Metcalfe; General and Mrs Misra; Mrs Naintara; B.K. Nehru; Sir Robert Neville; Bernard Ostry; Lieutenant Commander Robert de Pass; Mr and Mrs Jehangir Patel; Ms Patricia S. Patterson; Mrs Harold Phillips; Emma Pilkington; Mrs Josefine Pugh; Sir Frank Roberts; Paul Robeson Jr.; Andrew Robinson; Kenneth Rose; Mr and Mrs Jerome Rubin; Madame Jacques Ruillier (formerly Madame Henri Letellier); Sir James Scott; Miss Marjorie Sykes; Viscountess Slim; Mr and Mrs Ram Subramanian; Dr David Soltau; Richard Symonds; Mrs Jaya Thadani; Mrs Bimla Thapar; Filios Theodorou; Michael Thornton; Dr W.G. Tillman; Raleigh Trevelyan; Sir Charles Troughton; James Tuckey; Mark Tully; Lady Urquhart; Sir Robert and Lady Wade-Gery; Mrs Gladys Walford; Miss Muriel Watson; Mrs David Weekes; Mrs and Mrs Rocky Wilkins; Captain Andrew Yates; Mrs Yeats; Salvo Vassallo; Philip Ziegler.

Some of those with whom I talked have died during the writing of this book: Horace Alexander; Sir George Abell; Marjorie, Countess of Brecknock; Jeanne, Lady Camoys; Miss Hermione Cassel; Sybil, Marchioness of Cholmondeley; Lady Nye; William Paley; Mrs Vijaya Lakshmi Pandit; the Duke of Portland; Mrs Harold Saxton. I will remember them with gratitude.

I would also like to thank Harold Payne, editor of the newsletter that is circulated to those who were prisoners of war in the Far East, and those readers who wrote to me: Howard Baker; F.J. Baxter; J.B. Bayes; Harold Chumbley; F. Cox; R.G. Davis; S. Evans; J.L. Francis; W. Griffiths; A.W.W. Hammond; A.W. Harrington; C.W. Holtham; Ronald Killick; R. Laird; Neville Milston; William Percy; Charles

Robson; F.F. Shuttle; Ray Stubbs; Captain M.H. Syms; James Thompson; L.S. Toseland; J. Walsh; F.G. Wren. Many nursing and welfare officers were kind enough to give me their recollections of their work with Edwina during and after the war. Among those whom I would like to thank are: Mrs J.A. Crewe; Miss M.J. Downing; Miss C.J. Ensor; Mrs F. Jerram; Mrs P. Kenny.

I am also indebted to the librarians and archivists who have helped me find my way through a mass of material; Oliver Everett, Librarian of the Royal Archives, and his staff; Miss Julia Findlater, Deputy Curator of the Museum and Library of the Order of St John; Miss Karen Jefferson, Curator of the Robeson Collection; Miss S. Goldthorpe, Director, the Order of St John and the British Red Cross Society; Miss Patricia Want, Librarian at the Royal College of Obstetricians and Gynaecologists; Miss Jackie Kavanagh at the B.B.C. Written Archives Centre, and the staff of the B.B.C. Sound Archive; Mrs S. Bailey, Librarian of Wadham College, Oxford; the Librarian at the Oxford High School for Girls; the staff of the Public Record Office, the Imperial War Museum, the London Library and the Institute of Advanced Studies in the Humanities at Edinburgh University. I would like to give my warmest thanks to Dr Christopher Woolgar, Director of the Hartley Library at the University of Southampton, and to Mrs Mollie Travis and Mrs Molly Chalk, the archivists at Broadlands, on whom I have depended completely.

Douglas Matthews, Librarian of the London Library, has compiled the index to this book, Carol O'Brien and her staff at Collins have edited it, and it has been typed – several times – by Lois Price, Felicity Smith, Marnie Matthews, Becci Morris and, the final draft, by Malcolm Butler's team at Words-worth. I am very grateful to them all.

Index

NOTE: Ranks and titles are generally the highest mentioned in the text.

Abell, George, 383, 388, 397, 399
Abyssinia, 245–6
Admiralty: Dickie as 1st Sea Lord at, 458–9
Adsdean, Sussex (house), 179–81, 188, 191, 266, 271
Afghanistan, 119
Africa: Edwina visits, 257–8
Aga Khan, 215
Ainsworth (chauffeur), 193–4, 209
Airlie, David Ogilvy, 7th or 11th Earl, and Alexandra, Countess of, 175
Alde House, Aldeburgh, 72–4
Alexander, Prince of Hesse, 261–2
Alexander, A. V., 377
Alexander, Horace, 392, 395, 417
Alexandra, Queen of Edward VII, 44–5, 96, 132–3
Alfonso XIII, King of Spain, 138, 209, 218
Alice, Princess of Greece (Dickie's sister), 99, 128, 152, 155, 356, 479
Alice, Princess of Hesse (Queen Victoria's granddaughter), 67
Ali Khan, Liaquat, 413, 425
Ali Khan, Begum Liaquat, 394, 410
Alma-Tadema, Sir Lawrence, 52
Altemus, John, 202
Altemus, Mary Elizabeth, 195, 201–2
Altrincham, John Grigg, 2nd Baron, 466
Ambedkar, Dr B.-R., 391
Ambrose (band leader), 452
Amoss, Ulius Louis, 467
Anderson, Sir John, 292
Andrew, Prince of Greece, 152
Andrews, C. F., 392, 395
Antrim, Randal McDonnell, 8th Earl of, 312
Argentina, 235
Arnold, Edward, 306
Asaf Ali, Aruna, 394
Asher, Irving, 324

Ashley, Lady Alice, 11–12, 41, 64
Ashley, Evelyn (Edwina's grandfather), 11–12, 16, 30
Ashley, Harry (Edwina's uncle), 64, 66
Ashley, Mary (Edwina's sister) see Delamere, Mary, Lady
Ashley, Maudie (Amalia Mary Maud; née Cassel; Edwina's mother): birth and childhood, 4–6; coming out and social life, 8–10; appearance, 8; health, 11; meets Wilfrid, 11–12; engagement and marriage, 12–16, 19, 34; and birth of Edwina, 17–19; at Broadlands, 18; at Brook House, 20; entertaining, 21, 28–9; second pregnancy and birth of Mary, 23–4; relations with Edwina, 26, 29–33; declining health, 27, 36–41, 45–8; in Egypt and Biarritz, 27–9, 33, 37, 43; financial management, 33–4; returns to Broadlands, 43, 46; death and will, 48–50
Ashley, Molly see Mount Temple, Muriel, Lady
Ashley, Wilfrid (Edwina's father) see Mount Temple, Wilfrid William Ashley, Baron
Ashley-Cooper, Lady Dorothy, 25
Ashley-Cooper, Lady Mary, 25, 131
Asian Relations Conference, 1946, 389
Asquith, Herbert Henry, 1st Earl of Oxford and Asquith, 132
Astaire, Adele, 162, 170, 242
Astaire, Fred, 162, 170, 197, 242, 308
Astor, Vincent, 175
Athlone, Princess Alice, Countess of, 309
atomic bombs, 356
Attlee, Clement (later 1st Earl): as Prime Minister, 355–6, 372, 383; appoints Dickie Viceroy, 382, 385; and Indian independence, 383, 402; entertains

Attlee, Clement – *cont.*
Mountbattens, 434; and Korean War, 451; and Bevan, 460
Atwood, Miss (governess), 58, 60–63, 65–6, 70
Auchinleck, General Sir Claude, 322, 413–14
Australia, 88, 373, 375–6

Backhouse, Lady, 278
Baddeley, Hermione, 293
Baker, Sir Benjamin, 20
Baker family (Singapore), 363
Baldwin, Stanley (*later* 1st Earl), 210
Balfour, Arthur James (*later* 1st Earl), 21, 24
Ballin, Albert, 42–3, 51, 53, 55
Balmoral, 255
Bankhead, Tallulah, 159
Bannerjee (Edwina's secretary), 392, 408, 414
Baring, Maurice, 205
Baring, Helen ('Poppy'), 85, 100, 180
Barker, Edith, 70
Barrymore, John, 188
Basualdo brothers, 235–6
Basualdo, Carlos and Leonora (*née* Hughes), 235
Battenberg, Prince Louis of *see* Milford Haven, Admiral of the Fleet Prince Louis, 1st Marquess of
Bayham, David Pratt, Viscount, 285, 325
Beatrice, Princess, 341
Beauchamp, Dr, 38
Beaumont, Sarah (*née* Ismay), 414
Beaumont, Flight-Lieutenant Wentworth Hubert Charles, 414
Beaverbrook, William Maxwell Aitken, 1st Baron: at Monte Carlo, 86; and Jean Norton, 193, 204, 211, 218, 234; in General Strike, 194–5; Edwina joins on yacht, 204; trip to Scandinavia and Russia, 211; offers help to Dickie at Combined Operations, 313; and film *In Which We Serve*, 317; and Dieppe raid, 319; meets Dickie as SEAC commander, 332; anti-Mountbatten campaign, 446, 467–8, 470; meets Mintoff, 456
Becht, Sophie, 139

Beit, Sir Alfred, 10, 258
Bengal: 1947 partition, 406
Bennett, Arnold, 211
Benson, E. F., 52
Benson, Rosalind, 65
Benthall, Sir Edward, 344
Berlin, Irving, 323, 327
Bernal, J. D., 316, 322
Bevan, Aneurin, 460
Bevin, Ernest, 351, 356, 372–3, 437
Biarritz, 28, 32, 42, 231–2
Bikaner (India), 350
Bikaner, Maharajah of, 377, 384
Birdcage, Operation, 357
Birkett, Norman, 225–6
Bischoffsheim, Louis, 3, 40
Bischoffsheim, Mrs Louis, 8–9, 18–19, 24–5, 35, 37, 40–42, 63, 128
Blaauw, Dr R. H., 479–80
Bonde, Baron and Baroness, 77
Borneo, North, 479–80
Bottsoil, Private, 367
Boscawen, Pamela, 114, 120
Bournemouth, 51–2 *see also* Branksome Dene
Brabourne, Doreen, Lady, 392
Brabourne, John Ulick, 7th Baron (Patricia's husband), 376, 378, 420–21, 426, 433, 456, 478
Brabourne, Patricia Edwina Victoria, Lady (*later* Countess Mountbatten of Burma; Edwina's elder daughter): birth, 165–7; christened, 168; Edwina's relations with, 169, 185–6, 202, 213; Dickie's devotion to, 168–9, 185, 213, 237, 442–3; at Adsdean, 179; at Mary's wedding, 203; taken to Malta, 205, 208, 224; breaks arm, 213; chicken-pox, 216; and Bunny Phillips, 234; diet, 237; appearance, 244; in Budapest, 246; in Darmstadt, 247–8; schooling, 252, 275; school evacuated, 266; in New York during war, 285, 289–90, 301–3, 309, 315; wartime letters from Edwina, 286–7, 290–91, 296, 314–15; and Dickie's wartime activities, 288; parents visit in New York, 299–300, 303, 308–10; travels with mother in USA, 305–6; and rationing at home, 314; return to

Index

England and service in WRNS, 315–16, 320, 325, 328, 350; home leaves, 333–4, 350–51, 356; and Edwina's reaction to Bunny's engagement, 335, 337; and Edwina's trip to SEAC, 343–4, 349; at victory thanksgiving, 356; joins SEAC Rear Link in India, 368–9; holiday in Himalayas, 376; marriage, 378; letters from Edwina in India, 389–90, 392, 398, 401, 403, 406, 408, 416, 418, 421; son born, 418; visit to India, 420–21, 425–6; visits Classiebawn, 433; visits father in Malta, 442; family, 456, 478

Branksome Dene, Bournemouth, 51, 97, 155–7

Brecknock, John Charles Henry Platt, Earl of ('Brecky'): engagement and marriage, 74, 85; friendship with Edwina, 106; and night life, 154, 157, 221; visits USA, 212; and Edwina's illness, 215; divorce, 293

Brecknock, Marjorie, Countess of (née Jenkins; Edwina's cousin): friendship with Edwina, 25–6, 34–5, 38, 42, 54, 63, 65–6, 72, 106, 202; and Molly, 58; visits Edwina at school, 70; joins Edwina on trip to continent, 74–9; marriage, 85; and Edwina's independence, 87; and Edwina's engagement, 99; joins Edwina in Paris, 125; wedding present for Edwina, 132; and night life, 154, 157, 161; and Edwina's babies, 165, 167, 209–10; visits Adsdean, 179, 181, 188; visits Malta, 201, 246; in USA, 211; and Edwina's illness, 215; on West Indies cruise, 215; and People libel case, 225; accompanies Edwina to Vienna and Budapest, 228; in South America with Edwina, 234–6; and Edwina's return to England, 249; divorce, 293; visits Broadlands, 325, 356; works with St John, 379; tour of Austria and Italy, 383–4; visit to India, 421, 426; and Edwina's return from India, 432; meets Edwina's coffin, 480

Brinz, Monsieur (chef), 230, 247, 255, 273

Broadbent, Sir William, 11, 23

Broadlands, Hampshire: described, 17; Wilfrid occupies, 30, 48; Maudie at, 43, 46–7; Edwina at, after mother's death, 52; Molly redecorates, 56; Mountbattens honeymoon at, 134, 136; Edwina inherits, 271, 273; Edwina sends Brook House valuables to, 273; Edwina moves to, 273–7; maintenance and management, 274, 327; Dickie at, in wartime, 279, 280–82, 334; alterations and repairs, 280, 456; taken over by army, 282; and German air raids, 287, 296; as market garden, 294; as hospital annexe, 294–5, 314; Edwina bequeaths to Dickie, 296; Edwina's weekends at, 378; Edwina at, on return from India, 433; Nehru visits, 437–8, 446, 472; staff and finances, 444–5; restored to Edwina, 452

Brockman, Ronald, 356, 371, 387, 444

Brook House, Park Lane (London): Cassel buys and improves, 19–20; Edwina at, 80–82, 85, 87; servants and organisation, 80–82; in Cassel's will, 97; Mountbattens occupy, 136, 164–5; let, 160, 202; altered for Edwina's baby, 164; Dickie's mock-up of cabin at, 184–5; running costs, 222; sale and demolition, 223; Edwina reoccupies penthouse, 223, 250–51; rebuilt, 250–51; bombed, 251, 287; valuables sent to Broadlands, 273; apartment leased, 370; Mountbattens' lease lapses, 453

Browning, Lt.-General Sir Frederick ('Boy'), 371

Bruneval (France), 316

Bryanston Court (London), 239, 254

Buccleuch, Vreda Esther Mary, Duchess of ('Mollie'), 319

Buchanan, Miss, 77

Buckmaster, Captain, 210

Buckswood Grange school, Sussex, 261, 275

Budapest, 226, 231–2, 246

Bull family (internees), 364–5

Burma, 267–8, 328, 347, 351–2
Burma-Siam railway, 360
Burrows, Sir Frederick, 397
Buxhoevden, Baroness von, 139, 189, 196, 278, 325

Caernarvon, Henry Herbert, 6th Earl of, and Catherine, Countess of (*formerly* Lord and Lady Porchester), 131
Café de Paris (London), 294
Callède, Madame (French teacher), 231
Campbell-Bannerman, Sir Henry, 21
Campbell-Johnson, Alan, 387–8, 400, 409–10, 416
Campbell-Johnson, Mrs Alan, 411
Canada, 308–9, 322
Carey Evans *see* Evans
Carney, Admiral Robert B., 454–5
Caroe, Sir Olaf, 397
Carter, Sir Archibald, 277
Cartland, Barbara (Mrs McCorquodale), 193, 257
Casablanca, 320
Casa Maury, Bobby, Marquis de, 168, 173, 180, 188, 202, 215, 312
Casa Maury, Paula, Marquise de *see* Long, Paula
Casement, Sir Roger, 64
Cassel Hospital for Functional Nervous Disorders, 172
Cassel, Amalia (Sir Ernest's mother), 1, 4
Cassel, Annette (*née* Maxwell; Sir Ernest's wife), 4, 17
Cassel, Sir Ernest (Edwina's grandfather): character and background, 1–2; business career and interests, 2–4, 6–8, 10, 19, 36; settles in England, 4; marriage, 4; Catholicism, 4; relations with daughter, 4–5; social position, 7–8; relations with Edward VII, 7–8, 19, 24, 28, 31, 43–4; country house, 10; knighthood, 10; and Maudie's engagement and marriage, 13–14, 16–17; made PC, 19; buys and improves Brook House, 19; Swiss property, 22, 54; and Edwina as child, 23, 26, 35; and Maudie's second pregnancy, 24; and Maudie's health, 27, 36, 39–40; visits Egypt

and Biarritz, 27–8; and Maudie's finances, 30–31; and rearmament against German threat, 42–3, 51, 54; and death of Edward VII, 44–5; and Maudie's death, 50; charitable gifts and benefactions, 50–51, 87; buys properties, 51–2; capacity to listen, 52; on *Ypyranga* cruise, 53–4; and outbreak of Great War, 55; and Wilfrid's second marriage, 56; attacked in war, 58–9; and amputation of Edwina's toe, 63; and Edwina's visit to Moulton Paddocks, 66; fondness for Edwina, 70, 78; and Edwina's tour of continent, 74–6, 78–9; and Edwina's coming out, 75, 83–5; life at Brook House, 80–82, 85, 87; visits Riviera, 85–8; death and funeral, 94–6; will, 96–8
Cassel, Sir Felix: childhood with mother, 4–5; relations with Edwina as child, 25, 35, 63; marriage, 57; and Sir Ernest's death, 94; in Sir Ernest's will, 97; Wilhelmina entertains, 106; looks after Edwina's financial interests, 112, 221, 293, 445; and Mountbattens' marriage settlement, 129; and Brook House, 164, 223, 240; and birth of Patricia, 165, 167; and *People* libel action, 225–6; and Mary's divorce, 257
Cassel, Harold, 350
Cassel, Helen, Lady (Sir Felix's wife), 57, 63, 106
Cassel, Jacob (Sir Ernest's father), 1–2, 4
Cassel, Josefine, 57
Cassel, Joseph, 2
Cassel, Loeb Benedict, 2
Cassel, Max (Sir Ernest's brother), 2, 4
Cassel, Wilhelmina (Schoenbrunn; Sir Ernest's sister; 'Auntie-Grannie'; Mrs Cassel), 2, 4; looks after Maudie, 8–9; and Maudie's marriage, 16; as grandmother to Edwina, 18; and Edwina's childhood, 25, 35; visits Maudie in Egypt, 37–8; gives pocket money to Edwina, 46; and Maudie's death, 50; in Bournemouth, 51, 82, 106; finds governess for Edwina, 53; in

Index

Switzerland, 54–5; looks after children in war, 58; and amputation of Edwina's toe, 63; visits Edwina at school 70; and Edwina's visit to Rome, 79; and Sir Ernest's death, 94, 96; inheritance from Sir Ernest, 96–7; allowance to Edwina, 98; and Edwina's engagement, 99–100, 112, 113, 123; and Edwina's visit to India, 106, 110, 112; pays for Edwina's wedding, 130; wedding present to Edwina, 132; Christmas present to Edwina, 153; and Brook House expenses, 160, 164; death, 186

Castlerosse, Doris, Viscountess (née Delavigne), 190–91

Castlerosse, Valentine, Viscount, 191, 194, 204

Cecile, Princess (Dickie's niece), 131, 155, 216, 261–2

Centurion, HMS, 188

Ceylon, 329, 349–50

Chaliapin, Fedor, 149

Chamberlain, Neville, 265–6, 268–9, 281

Chanak crisis, 142

Changi Gaol, Singapore, 361, 363

Channon, Sir Henry ('Chips'), 258

Chaplin, Charlie, 146–8, 217, 242

Charles, Prince of Wales, 439–40

Charles Street (London), 280

Chatfield, Admiral Sir Ernle, 142, 224

Chattopadhyay, Sarojini *see* Naidu, Sarojini

Checkley, Irene, 479–80

Chester Street (London), 314, 319, 354, 370, 384, 433, 453

Chetwode, Field-Marshal Philip W., 1st Baron, 319

Chevrier, Mademoiselle ('Zelle'): as governess to Patricia, 252, 266, 278, 285; in USA with Patricia and Pamela, 290, 301–3, 308; returns to England, 315, 320; and liberation of Paris, 338; and Edwina's return from India, 432

Chiang Kai-shek, 322

China, 248–9, 267–8, 348

Chinnery-Haldane, Marjorie, 68

Cholmondeley, Sybil, Marchioness of, 83, 328

Christie, Agatha, 169

Chumbley, Harry, 361

Churchill, Clementine (Lady), 86

Churchill, John Strange (Jack), 10

Churchill, Lord Randolph, 10

Churchill, Mrs Randolph (Hon. Pamela), 333

Churchill, (Sir) Winston Leonard Spencer: Cassel employs, 10; and Maudie's pregnancy, 17; in Biarritz with Cassel, 42–3; at Broadlands, 45; as First Lord of the Admiralty, 51; and Great War, 55; joins Cassel on Riviera, 86; becomes wartime Prime Minister (1940), 281; appoints Dickie to head Combined Operations, 307, 312; appoints Dickie a Chief of Staff, 316; at Quebec Conference, 322; and Dickie's SEAC command, 326, 328, 331–2, 355; invites Edwina to War Rooms, 328; Edwina visits, 334; Edwina reports to after SEAC tour, 351; loses 1945 election, 355; and Indian independence, 382, 386; 1951 government, 451; Mountbattens visit in France, 456; resigns, 460

Clark, Dr Jackson, 62

Classiebawn Castle (Ireland), 321, 384, 433, 453, 459

Clubwala, Mrs Mary (Mrs Clubwala Jadhav), 391

Cochran, C. B., 159

Cooper, Gladys, 104

Coates, Albert, 193

Coats, Audrey *see* James, Audrey

Coats, Betty, 89

Coats, Dudley, 89

Coats, Mabel, 89

Cole, A. P., 270, 281

Cole, G. D. H., 253

Colette, 227

Colman, Ronald, 211–12

Colville, Sir John (Jock), 328

Colville, Sir John (*later* 1st Baron Clydesmuir), and Agnes Anne, Lady, 345, 358

Combined Operations, 307, 312, 316

Congress Party (India), 382–3, 396, 399, 403, 407

Connaught, Prince Arthur, Duke of, 136

Constantine, King of Greece, 152
Coogan, Jackie, 147
Cooper, A. Duff, 177, 339–40
Cooper, Lady Diana, 192, 339–40
Coronation, 1936, 258
Corrigan, Mrs Laura, 128, 195, 214
Cosden, Joshua, 173–4, 177
Cosden, Nell, 173–4, 177, 251, 306
Cotton, Arthur, 124, 132
Coulson, Sergeant (Royal Marines), 342
Countiss, Mrs (of Chicago), 146
Coustabadie, Commander de, 324
Coward, Noel, 233, 235, 238, 252, 258, 311–12, 317, 332, 337
Cranston, Jane, 75–8, 86, 259
Crete, 295
Crichton, Nona, 136
Crichton, Richard, 188, 212, 234, 236
Cripps, Isobel, Lady, 385, 391
Cripps, Sir Stafford, 382, 385, 437
Crocker, Mr & Mrs Harry, 238
Cromer, Rowland Thomas Baring, 2nd Earl of, 112, 114, 277–8
Crum, Squadron Leader Donald Erskine, 342
Cugnoni, Elena, 77, 79
Cullum, Nurse, 54–5
Cunard, Emerald (Maud Alice), Lady, 128, 132, 157–8, 171, 195, 214, 258, 378
Cunningham, Admiral of the Fleet Andrew, Baron, 458
Cunningham-Reid, Robert (Bobbie): in Cowes, 162; and Mary, 182–4, 196–7; engagement and marriage to Mary, 200, 203; in Egypt, 205–6; political activities, 210; infidelity, 216; lends yacht to Mountbattens, 224, 246; and Edwina's libel action against *People*, 226; and Brook House sale, 240; divorce, 257, 289
Curzon, Lady Alexandra *see* Metcalfe, Lady Alexandra
Curzon, Cynthia, 70
Curzon, Richard, 90, 92
Curzon-Howe family, 201
Cygnet (boat), 246
Cyprus, 464
Czechoslovakia, 265–6

Dali, Salvador, 308
Dansie (chauffeur), 273
Daring, HMS, 237, 241, 244
Darmstadt, 139, 260, 262, 353
Davidson, Colin, 85, 92
Davies, Marion, 214, 255
Davis, Deering, 190
Dawson of Penn, Bertrand Edward, Viscount, 214
Dean, Basil, 278, 345
Delamere, Mary, Lady (Ruth Mary Clarice; *née* Ashley; Edwina's sister): born, 24–5; character, 35; relations with mother, 29; childhood with Edwina, 34, 41, 46, 53; life after mother's death, 52, 54; appendicitis, 54; and stepmother, 55, 57–8, 60; sent to school, 60–61, 63; at The Links school with Edwina, 66–71; dependence on Edwina, 72–3; in Sir Ernest's will, 97–8; meets Dickie, 129; as Edwina's bridesmaid, 131; Edwina visits at Heathfield, 157; in Scotland, 162–3; at finishing school in Paris, 163, 170; visits Adsdean, 179, 182; return to England, 181–2; and Cunningham-Reid, 182–4, 196–7; breakdown, 183, 186; visits Italy, 189; engagement and marriage to Cunningham-Reid, 200, 202–3; in Malta, 200; in Egypt, 205–6; pregnancy, 207; political activities, 210; and husband's infidelity, 216; her house, 222; and Brook House sale, 240; divorce, 257, 289; and father's death, 271–2; second marriage and divorce, 289, 293; third marriage, 327–8; collapse after return from Kenya, 446
Delamere, Thomas Cholmondeley, 4th Baron, 327–8
de Laszlo, Sir Philip, 11–12, 157, 191
Demarest, Charlotte, 149
de Mille, Cecil B., 146
Denning, Lt.-General Sir Reginald, 371
Depot for Knitted Garments for the Royal Navy, 278–9, 282, 293, 313
de Rothschild, Aline, 83
de Rothschild, Baron Ferdinand, 10
de Rothschild, Baron Meyer, 10

Index

de Rothschild, Nathan, 10
de Trafford, Alice, 258
de Trafford, Violet, 32
Devéria, Laura, 53–5, 57–8, 157
Devi, Shreemati Kamala, 391
Devonshire, Spencer Compton
  Cavendish, 8th Duke of, 24
Dieppe, 319
Dill, General Sir John, 279
Donovan, Colonel William, 318
Dorothy (housemaid), 273
Douglas-Pennant, Eileen, 72
Dresselhuys, Mrs, 157
Driberg, Tom, 372
du Buisson, Peggy, 72
Dudley Ward, Freda, 88, 105–6, 127, 132,
  159, 224, 254
Dunrobin (Scotland), 93, 142–3
Duse, Eleonora, 21
Dutch East Indies, 366, 369, 372–3

Eden, Anthony (later 1st Earl of Avon),
  332, 373, 441, 455, 460–61
Edward VII, King (formerly Prince of
  Wales): friendship with Sir Ernest
  Cassel, 7–8, 24, 28, 31, 43–4; at
  Maudie's wedding, 16–17; succeeds
  to throne, 18–19; as Edwina's
  godfather, 18; in Biarritz, 28, 42–3;
  decline and death, 43–4; gives
  present to Sir Ernest, 96–7
Edward VIII, King see Windsor, Edward,
  Duke of
Egypt, 27–8, 31–3, 37, 205–6
Eisenhower, General Dwight D., 328,
  335, 338, 461, 467
Elizabeth II, Queen (formerly Princess),
  401, 419, 439–40, 444, 452, 457
Elizabeth, Queen of George VI (née
  Bowes-Lyon; then Duchess of
  York): at Bisham Abbey, 88;
  engagement and marriage, 157–8,
  160; at Fairbanks film, 170; in
  Malta, 201; accession, 256; Dickie
  visits, 334; Edwina sees after SEAC
  tour, 351; Mountbattens visit, 356,
  401
Ellison, Charles, 209
Eltzbacher, J. W., 2
Embassy Club (London), 153

Emergency Committee (India), 415–16,
  418, 420
Ena, Queen of Spain, 138, 209, 386
English, Isobel, 172
Epstein, Sir Jacob, 438
Erskine-Crum, Brigadier Vernon, 387
Ethiopia, 455; see also Abyssinia
Evans, Olwen Carey (Lady), 107
Evans, Colonel (Sir) Thomas John Carey,
  109, 117
Evelyn, Jack, 215, 234–6, 238
Everett, Henry, 34, 38, 65
Everett, Jack, 63, 65
Everett, Robert, 34, 38, 63, 65

Fairbanks, Douglas, 144, 146–7, 169–70,
  217, 241–2, 306
Falmouth, Margaret Florence Lucy,
  Viscountess, 114, 120
Far East: Edwina tours, 238–9
Faunce, Miss (headmistress), 252, 275, 301
Fellowes, Daisy, 187
Ferguson, Dr Haig, 208
Fermoy, Edmund Maurice Roche, 4th
  Baron, 104
Festing, General Sir Francis W., 347
Festival of Britain, 1951, 450–1
Fields, Gracie, 454
Fisher, Admiral of the Fleet Sir John
  Arbuthnot (later 1st Baron), 21, 43
Fisher, Ros, 228
Fitzgerald, Helen & Evelyn, 202
Forbes, Rosita, 57, 258, 466
Forbes-Sempill, Molly see Mount Temple,
  Muriel, Lady
Foster, Joan, 65
France: 1940 defeat, 285; liberation
  (1944–5), 338–9
Franklen, Syssyllt, 68, 71–4, 78–9, 159
Franz Ferdinand, Archduke of
  Austro-Hungary, 55
Fraser, Admiral Bruce Austin (later Baron
  Fraser of North Cape), 331
Frederica, Queen of Greece, 457
Fritze, Nurse, 54
Fung, General 349

Gaba (German teacher), 68
Gable, Clark, 242
Gaitskell, Hugh, 450

493

Gandhi, Indira, 395, 408, 441, 446, 470, 474

Gandhi, Mohandas Karamchand (Mahatma): and Lord Reading, 118; jailed, 382; and Dickie's viceroyalty, 392; meets Mountbattens, 395; opposes partition, 396; and independence plan, 401–2, 406; and Dickie's air conditioning, 406; congratulatory letter to Edwina, 407; and communal violence, 417; and Princess Elizabeth's wedding, 419; calms Edwina, 420–21; fast, 421–2; assassinated, 422, 424, 427

Gardner, Captain Laurie, 289

Gaston, John, 174–5, 177–8

Gaulle, Charles de, 339

Gayfere House, Smith Street (London), 186

Geddes, Alexander, 353

Geddes, Sir Auckland, 260, 262

Geddes, Sir Eric, 141

Geddes, Margaret see Hesse, Margaret, Princess of

Gellibrand, Paula see Long, Paula

General Elections: 1929, 210–11; 1945, 355; 1951, 451

General Strike, 1926, 193–5

George V, King, 44, 113–14, 123, 127, 152, 225–6, 253

George VI, King (formerly Duke of York; 'Prince Bertie'): at Brook House, 85; at Bisham Abbey, 88; at Jutland, 89; studies at Cambridge, 90; at Dunrobin, 93, 142; and Edwina's wedding, 119; sees Edwina before marriage, 125; and night life, 153, 157; engagement and marriage, 157–8, 160; at Fairbanks film, 170; in Malta, 201; accession, 256; Dickie visits, 334; Edwina sees after SEAC tour, 351; Mountbattens visit, 356, 401; and Dickie's post-war career, 377; death, 456–7

George, Prince see Kent, Prince George, Duke of

Germany: wartime advances in west, 281; military defeat and surrender, 335, 338, 352–3

Gershwin, George, 159, 170, 187

Gilliatt, (Sir) Martin, 416

Gingold, Hermione, 293

Girouard, Beatrice, 358–60

Glasgow, HMS, 454

Gloucester, Prince Henry, Duke of, 85, 90, 170, 279, 376, 386

Glyn, Elinor, 16

Godfrey (butler at Brook House), 94

Goldschmidt, Julius, 3, 36

Gordon Walker, Patrick, 463

Gracey, Major-General Sir Douglas, 365

Grafton Galleries (club), 153

Graham-White, Claude, 185

Gray, Larry, 211–12, 215

Greenwich: Naval College, 185, 188; R. N. War College, 266

Grenfell, Joyce, 346

Greville, Mrs Ronald: social life, 24, 84, 100; in India, 93, 98, 110, 112; entertains Mountbattens, 128; wedding present for Mountbattens, 132; and Edwina's social life, 171; and Edwina's pregnancy, 209

Griffith, D. W., 147

Griffiths, James, 462–3

Griffiths, William, 362

Grigg, John see Altrincham, John Grigg, 2nd Baron

Grimsdale, Major General G. E., 324

Grove, The, Stanmore, 25–6, 34, 63

Gubbay, Hannah, 161

Gurkha, HMS, 280

Gwalior, Maharajah and Maharani of, 404

Hailsham, Quintin McGarel Hogg, 2nd Viscount (later Baron), 470

Haldane, Richard Burdon, Viscount, 51

Hall-Walker, Rosemary, 65

Hammond, Paul, 91, 104, 145, 162

Hance, General James Bennett, 344

Harding (Edwina's maid), 209, 230

Harding, Warren G., 149

Hardinge of Penshurst, Charles, 1st Baron, 431

Hare Park, Newmarket, 97

Harriman, Averell, 319

Harris, Mrs (Edwina's nurse), 22

Harrison, Agatha, 391, 395, 401

Harrison, Ellen, 49, 132, 134, 183, 327

·Index

Harvey, Dr Wilkes, 478–9
Hassan (driver), 259
Hastings, Grisell & Eddie, 201
Hastings, Sir Patrick, 226
Hay, Captain, 104
Hayworth, Rita, 306
Heald, Daphne, 292
Hearst, William Randolph, 212, 214, 255
Hekscher, Maurice, 174, 178, 185
Helena, Princess, 161
Henry, Prince see Gloucester, Prince Henry, Duke of
Hepburn, Katherine, 236
Hermon, Richard, 85
Hervey, Mrs, 73–4
Hesse (Germany), 2, 101–2, 139–40; family die in air crash, 262
Hesse, Eleanore (of Somslich), Grand Duchess of ('Onor'), 139–40; killed, 261–2
Hesse, Ernest Louis, Grand Duke of, 139–40, 247, 260–61
Hesse, George Donatus, Grand Duke of ('Don'), 139–40, 260–61; killed, 262
Hesse, Margaret, Princess of (née Geddes; 'Peg'), 260–62, 353
Hewart, Gordon, 1st Baron, 226
Hewitt (headmistress, New York), 301–2
Heywood-Lonsdale, Teddy, 201, 209, 217, 368
Hicks, David (Pamela's husband), 478
Hicks, Lady Pamela Carmen Louise (née Mountbatten; Edwina's younger daughter): born 209–10; relations with mother, 213, 244, 442; health, 216, 218, 244; in Malta, 224, 439; birthdays, 236, 258; in Budapest, 246; in Darmstadt, 247–8; childhood, 259; schooling, 261, 275; evacuated to New York, 285, 289–90, 301–3; wartime letters from Edwina, 286–7, 290–91, 296; parents visit in New York, 299–300, 303, 308; returns to England, 309–11, 333–4; and Edwina's trip to SEAC, 343–4, 349; at Broadlands, 350, 356; at victory thanksgiving, 356; and Sargents, 380–81; with parents in India, 386, 390, 392, 397, 399, 403–4, 414–15, 419, 425–6, 428, 431; at Princess

Elizabeth's wedding, 419; visits Classiebawn, 433; accompanies Edwina on 1949 visit to India, 440–41; 21st birthday party, 452; leaves Malta, 456; accompanies Princess Elizabeth and Prince Philip on tour, 457; marriage, 478; reads Edwina's letters from Nehru, 480
Hill, Group Captain, 363
Hilton, James: The Lost Horizon, 253
Himalayas, 376
Hiroshima, 356
Hirsch, Baron Moritz de, 2–4
Hiscock (Dickie's valet), 112, 116
Hitchcock, Tommy, 175
Hitler, Adolf, 245, 265–6, 268–9, 270, 352
Ho Chi Minh, 465
Hodges, Betty and Michael, 201
Hok, Commander, 363
Holland, Henry, 17
Holland, Vice-Admiral Sir Ian, 324
Hollywood, 146–8
Hong Kong, 368
Hood, General (Sir) Alexander, 319
Hoppe, Mrs (Red Cross worker), 354
Hore-Belisha, Cynthia (later Lady), 258, 278
Hore-Belisha, Leslie (later Baron), 258
Horsburgh, Florence, 291
Horthy, Etienne de, 228, 230, 239
Howard, Henry, 104
Howard Johnson, Esmé, 319
Howes, Howard (florist), 133
Howes, Peter, 387
Hull, Lytle, 174–5, 177–8, 194–5
Hungary, 226, 231–2, 246, 267
Hunter, Major Bryan, 343, 346–50
Husky, Operation, 322
Hussey, Tom, 209, 313
Hutchinson, Leslie ('Hutch'), 187, 227
Hyderabad (India), 404–5, 419, 425, 430–31, 436

Illustrious, HMS, 299, 303, 307
Imphal, 329–30, 332
India: Dickie visits with Prince of Wales, 102–5; Edwina visits Dickie in, 106–11, 114, 116–20; Edwina inspects wartime hospitals in, 343–7, 349–50; Dickie offered Viceroyalty,

India – *cont.*
382–6; independence movement in, 382–3, 385, 395–6; Mountbattens take up Viceroyalty, 386–7; Viceregal style and routine in, 388–92; political and social situation, 392; proposed partition, 395–400; proposed membership of Commonwealth, 400; transfer of power, 401–3, 410–13; princely states, 404–5, 425; boundaries, 413; communal violence and disorder, 413–20; Mountbattens' tours in, 420–22, 424–5, 430–31; Mountbattens leave, 431–3; Edwina revisits (1949), 440–41; damaged in press attacks on Edwina, 470; Edwina's obsession with, 471

Indo-China, French, 365, 372–3

Indonesia, 366, 369; *see also* Dutch East Indies

International Services of Information, 467

In Which We Serve (film), 317

Ismay, General Hastings Lionel, Baron ('Pug'), 351, 355–6, 387, 397, 400, 451, 456, 458

Italy: and Abyssinia, 245–7; declares war on Germany, 324

James, Audrey, 85, 88, 90, 100, 109, 140, 159

Japan: Dickie visits, 126; as pre-war threat, 264; wartime campaigns, 310–11, 328–30, 332, 352; capitulates, 356–8; prisoners of war and refugees, 357–61; surrender ceremony, 361–2

Japhet, Saemy, 52

Java, 369, 373, 374

Javelin, HMS, 288

Jenkins, Anna (Wilhelmina's daughter): born, 4–5; marriage, 25; and Edwina's childhood, 35; visits Maudie in Egypt, 37, 41; as Sir Ernest Cassel's hostess in London, 51; finds governess for Edwina, 53; at Villa Cassel, 54; visits Edwina at school 70; in London, 82; and Edwina's coming out, 83; and Sir Ernest's death, 94; inheritance, 97; at Edwina's wedding, 134; at birth of Patricia, 165; and victory procession, 356

Jenkins, Colonel Atherton Edward (Teddy), 25, 58, 70, 75–7, 128

Jenkins, Sir Evan, 397

Jenny, Mademoiselle, 52, 54

Jerram, Rear-Admiral Sir Rowland, 324

Jinnah, Fatima, 394, 403, 410

Jinnah, Mahomed Ali: calls for partition at independence, 389, 394–6, 399, 401–3; and Hyderabad, 404; Mountbattens entertain, 407–8; as Governor-General of Pakistan, 408–9, 414; and Dickie's post-independence position, 408–9; and establishment of Pakistan, 410; death, 436

Jodhpur, Maharajah of, 371, 404

Joel, Commander, 159

Johanna, Princess of Hesse, 262

Johnson, Hewlett, Dean of Canterbury, 463

Joint Defence Council (India), 408–9

Joint War Organization, 277, 279–80, 291, 300, 313, 324, 341, 346, 351, 371

Jolliffe, William, 85

Joshua, Mrs, 84, 86, 128

Joshua, Nell, 86

Juliana, Queen of the Netherlands, 457

Kashmir, 418–19, 425, 431, 436, 469

Kashmir, HMS, 295–6

Kashmir, Maharajah of, 404–5, 418–19

Kassel, Wilhelm, 270

Kaur, Rajkumari Amrit, 392, 403, 406, 413–14, 416, 420, 427, 430–31, 441

Kelly, HMS: Dickie offered command of, 264; Dickie fits out and takes over, 270–74, 280; at outbreak of war, 274–5; damaged at sea, 276, 280; torpedoed and saved, 281–2; in Mediterranean, 295; sunk off Crete, 295–6; film of, 311–12

Kemsley, James Gomer Berry, 1st Viscount, 377

Kent, Prince George, Duke of, 158, 160, 167, 170, 180, 188, 292; killed, 318–19

Kent, Princess Marina, Duchess of, 386

Kent, William, 17

Index

Kenya, 468
Keppel, Alice, 21, 24, 28, 42, 44–5, 63
Kern, Jerome, 144
Keyes, Admiral Sir Roger, 196, 205, 312, 380
Keynes, John Maynard, Baron, 325
Killearn, Miles Lampson, 1st Baron, 374
King, General, 344
Kingston, HMS, 274–5
Kinloch, Kitty (Jennie Norton's sister), 202
Kipling, HMS, 296
Kitchener, Field Marshal Horatio Herbert, 1st Earl, 64
Koo, Dr Wellington, 323
Krishna Menon, V. K., 395, 429–30, 434, 437

Laking, Sir Guy, 52
Lambe, Charles, 209, 385
Lambert, Captain, 366
Langtry, Lily, 176
Lankester, Mrs (housekeeper), 80, 94; death, 327
Lankester, Grace, 391, 395, 401
Larcom, Mrs Charles, 278
Lascelles, John, 85
Laski, Harold, 325
Law, Andrew Bonar, 142
Lawson, John James, 372
Laycock, Angela, 297, 334
Laycock, Robert, 311, 334
Layton and Johnstone (entertainers), 187
Lees, Nancy, 250, 273, 278, 280, 313, 318; on SEAC tour, 341–3, 346–9
Leigh, Vivien (Mrs Laurence Olivier), 333
Leopold, King of the Belgians, 86
Lettellier, Henri, 227, 231, 281, 340
Letellier, Yola: friendship with Mountbattens, 227–31, 234, 237–9, 246–7, 256–8, 261, 275; accompanies Mountbattens to USA, 262–3; and Edwina's post-war return to England, 265–6; in wartime France, 279, 281–2, 340; Edwina sees after liberation, 339–40; Dickie visits in Paris, 355; at Broadlands, 378, 477; visit to India, 421, 423; sees Edwina's face after operation, 479

Limerick, Angela, Countess of, 300, 306, 332, 424
Lindsay, Lady Margaret, 68, 71, 80, 103, 128, 157, 162, 165
Links, The (school), 66–72
Listowel, William Hare, 5th Earl of, 401
Litvinoff, Ivy & Maxim, 211
Lizard (yacht), 224, 237
Lloyd, General Cyril, 270, 272
Lloyd George, David (*later* 1st Earl), 51, 142
Long, Laura, 259
Long, Rev. Lawrence, 132
Long, Paula (*née* Gellibrand; then Marquesa de Casa Maury): friendship with Edwina, 168, 180, 188, 215, 378–9, 384; at Broadlands, 314; visit to India, 421, 426, 428; and Edwina's return from India, 432; at Classiebawn, 459; and Edwina's letters from Nehru, 475
Lonsdale, Frederick, 170
Lost Horizon (schooner), 253, 257, 259–61, 263; sinks, 263–4
Loughborough, Sheila, Lady (*later* Milbanke), 189, 191
Louis, Prince of Hesse, 139–40, 260–62, 353
Lovatelli, Conte & Contessa, 77
Lutyens, Sir Edwin, 114, 250, 387
Luynes, Duc & Duchesse de, 76
Lynden Manor, Bray, 210
Lyttelton, Oliver (*later* 1st Viscount Chandos), 451, 463, 468

McCoy, Bez & Cecile, 201
MacDonald, Malcolm, 376, 462, 470
MacGowan (butler), 159–60, 164
MacGregor, Dr Robert, 362
McKay, Clarence, 174
McKenna, Pamela, 311
Mackenzie, Sir Compton, 414
Mackgill, Sir George, 59
Maclean, Mrs, 148
Macleod, General M. W. M., 324
McManus, Dr, 479
Macmillan, Harold and Lady Dorothy, 477
Maiden Castle House, Dorset, 160, 163
Maisy, Colonel C. W., 366
Makura, RMS, 242–3

Malaspira, Constance, 77, 79
Malaspira, Folco, 77, 79
Malaya, 373–4, 376, 462
Malmesbury family, 65
Malta: Mountbattens stay in, 196,
    198–203, 205–6, 208, 224, 228, 230,
    237–8, 243–6, 248; war preparations,
    246–7; during war, 295;
    Mountbattens return to (1948),
    438–40, 444–5; Dickie as C. in C. in,
    453–5; NATO command in, 455–6;
    politics in, 456; Mountbattens' final
    departure from, 458
Manzi-Fe, Galeazzo, 77, 79
Margaret Rose, Princess, 452
Margarita, Princess (Dickie's niece), 131,
    155, 157
Margesson, David, 319
Marjoribanks, Dudley Coutts, 19
Marriott, Captain, 365
Marshall, General George, 319
Martin (chauffeur), 158–60
Mary, Queen of George V, 123, 130, 250,
    256, 309, 356, 451; death, 457
Mary, Princess, 88, 128, 130
Masaryk, Jan, 258
Master's club, Savile Row (London), 210
Mastiff, Operation, 357
Matthai, Mrs, 403
Maxham, Bombardier, 367
May, Monsieur, 76
Melba, Dame Nellie, 156
Menon, V. K. Krishna see Krishna
    Menon, V. K.
Menon, Vapal Pangunni, 399–400, 404,
    415, 418
Mérillon, Pierre, 190, 208
Messervy, Frank, 105
Metcalfe, Lady Alexandra (née Curzon;
    'Baba'), 173, 188, 210
Metcalfe, Captain E. D. ('Fruity'): in
    India, 108; injured, 119; meets
    Mountbattens in England, 128;
    Mountbattens entertain, 136; night
    life and social round, 153–4, 157,
    161; marriage, 188; with Duke of
    Windsor, 256
Meyrick, Admiral Sir Sidney Julius, 263
Michael, Grand Duke of Russia, 132
Miéville, Sir Eric, 387, 399

Milbanke, Sir John Charles Peniston
    ('Buffles'; 'The Boxing Baronet'),
    189, 193
Milford Haven, David Mountbatten, 3rd
    Marquess of, 314
Milford Haven, George Mountbatten,
    2nd Marquess of (Dickie's elder
    brother): relations with Dickie, 89,
    98–9; meets Edwina, 98–9; title, 102;
    friendship with Edwina, 104; Mrs
    Cassel entertains, 106; and Dickie's
    engagement, 113; in Paris, 141; and
    night life, 154; visits Adsdean, 188;
    in Malta, 205; and Nada's relations
    with Gloria Vanderbilt, 240–41;
    collects erotica, 241; death from
    cancer, 263
Milford Haven, Admiral of the Fleet
    Prince Louis Mountbatten, 1st
    Marquess of (formerly Battenberg;
    Dickie's father): and outbreak of
    Great War, 55; resigns, 59; meets
    Edwina, 92; as guest of Dudley
    Pound, 93; death, 93; financial
    position, 100–101; naval career,
    101–2; affair with Lillie Langtry, 176
Milford Haven, Nada, Marchioness of
    (George's wife), 90; meets Edwina,
    98–9; friendship with Edwina, 104;
    Mrs Cassel entertains, 106;
    chaperones Edwina, 125, 127; in
    Paris with Mountbattens, 141; and
    night life, 154; joins Edwina at Brook
    House for birth of baby, 165; visits
    Riviera with Edwina, 167; in USA,
    175; visits Adsdean, 188; in Malta,
    201, 205; visits Tunisia, 208; relations
    with Gloria Vanderbilt, 240–41;
    character and manner, 241; and
    husband's death, 263; and Bunny
    Phillips' engagement, 334–5
Milford Haven, Victoria, Dowager
    Marchioness of (formerly Princess
    Victoria of Hesse): relations with
    Dickie, 99–103; advice to Dickie on
    Edwina's trip to India, 108–9; and
    Dickie's engagement to Edwina,
    113–14; gives Edwina ruby, 128;
    wedding present for Mountbattens,
    132; apartments at Kensington

Index

Palace, 152, 157; Edwina visits, 157; visits Brook House, 165; and Edwina's baby, 165, 167; relations with Edwina, 202; in Malta, 205; correspondence with Mountbattens, 222; and *People* libel on Edwina, 225–6; and Mountbatten children, 244; and Prince Louis of Hesse's wedding, 261–2; and Edwina's war work, 280; in war, 287, 289; visits Broadlands, 314, 319, 325, 350, 356; stays at Windsor, 327; mocks Sargent, 381; opposes Dickie's Viceroyalty, 384; letters from Edwina in India, 393; death, 452

Miller, Marjorie, 358, 360

Minart, Minette (governess), 28, 37, 39, 41–2, 46–8, 50, 52

Minter, John, 201

Mintoff, Dom, 456

Miscattelli, Marchese, 77

Molyneux, Hugh *see* Sefton, Hugh Molyneux, 7th Earl of

Molyneux (dressmaker), 378

Monckton, Sir Walter (*later* Viscount), 256, 404, 431, 445, 451

Mond family, 64

Mond, Mary, 64–5

Monte Carlo, 85–6

Montgomery, General Bernard Law (*later* Viscount), 335

Morgenthau, Robert, 334

Morrison, 'Squeaker', 201

Morrison, William ('Shakes'), 452

Mosley, Sir Oswald, 245

Mott, Captain, 77, 79

Moulton Paddocks, near Newmarket, 10, 31, 66, 97, 128–9

Mountbatten of Burma, Edwina Cynthia Annette, Countess (*née* Ashley): born, 18–19; childhood, 22–6, 29, 35, 39; relations with Sir Ernest, 26; relations with parents, 26, 29–34; pets, 26, 61–2, 65; in Biarritz, 28–9, 42; and savings account, 31; character as child, 34–5, 41, 52–3; and mother's illness, 37–8, 41–2, 45–6, 48; education and languages, 41, 52, 72; pocket money, 46; 9th birthday, 47; and mother's death,

48, 52–3; on *Ypyranga* cruise, 53–4; taught by Laura Devéria, 53–4; relations with stepmother, 55, 57–8; and Mary's absence at school, 60–61; eyesight, 61, 83, 149, 157, 267; hunting, 61; orderliness, 62; appearance, 62, 82, 116, 370; toe amputated, 62–3; takes interest in Great War, 64; attends The Links school, 67–72; lacrosse-playing, 69; at Domestic Science College, 72–4; post-war tour to continent, 74–9; at Brook House as grandfather's companion, 80–2, 85, 87; coming out and social round, 83–8; first meetings with Dickie, 88–92; on *Venetia* cruise, 91–2; and grandfather's death, 94–5; inheritance, 97–8; visits Dickie's family, 98–9; Dickie proposes to, 99–100; and Dickie's tour of India with Prince of Wales, 102–6; travels to and in India, 106–11, 114, 116–20; engagement, 112–14, 123; return to England, 114–15, 120, 122; and Dickie's finances, 115; gives Rolls Royce to Dickie, 115–17, 132; risk-taking, 117; on North-West Frontier, 119; plans Paris honeymoon, 122, 124–5; wedding preparations, 125, 130–33; routine of reunions with Dickie, 127–8; driving and motor cars, 129, 153; wedding and honeymoon, 133–9; first trip to USA, 143–50; in Hollywood film, 147–8; night life, 153–4; home comforts, 154; and Dickie's absences on duty, 155, 157; de Laszlo's portrait of, 157; motor accidents, 158, 173, 188; pregnancy, 161–5; restless social life, 161–3, 170–73, 187–8; moves to Brook House, 164–5; and birth of daughter (Patricia), 165; visits Riviera, 167–8; relations with Patricia, 169, 185–6, 202, 213; dress and style, 171–2, 187, 279, 292–3, 370, 386; charitable activities, 172–3; accompanies Prince of Wales to USA, 173–7; jewellery stolen, 174; difficulties of marriage,

Edwina Mountbatten

Mountbatten of Burma, Edwina – *cont.*
176–7, 191, 198–9, 203, 216–19, 239;
lives at Adsdean, 179–80, 188;
ailments and illnesses, 189, 206–8,
213–15,
228–30, 252, 267, 293, 391, 478;
liaisons and affairs, 189–92, 196–7,
200, 202–4, 207, 215–20, 228, 232,
233–4, 298; activities in General
Strike, 193–5; with Dickie in Malta,
198, 200–3, 208; surgical operations,
204–5, 207, 213–14, 228, 384, 386;
visits Egypt, 205–6; with Peter
Murphy in USA, 207; returns to
Dickie, 207–8; second daughter
(Pamela), 207–10; opens Master's
club, 210; political views, 210,
459–70; visits Russia with
Beaverbrook, 211; 1930 trip to USA,
211; relations with Pamela, 213, 244,
443; West Indies cruise, 215–17;
reconciliation with Dickie, 219–21;
and financial slump, 221–2; and
disposal of Brook House, 223; 1931
return to Malta, 224; and libel action
against *People*, 224–6; and Dickie's
women friends, 228, 231; trips to
Vienna, Budapest and Persia,
228–32; begins affair with Bunny
Phillips, 233–9; travels with Bunny,
234–9, 241–3, 248–9, 253, 257–8,
267–9; boredom and discontent in
England, 252–3, 257; and Abdication
crisis, 256; and wartime
preparations, 264–5, 272; in
Yugoslavia, 265; Red Cross training,
266–7; travels Burma Road, 267–8;
settles in England (1939), 270; aids
European refugees, 270; and father's
death, 271; moves to Broadlands,
273–5; seeks and finds war work,
277–9, 282; works for St John
Ambulance, 280, 282, 286, 291–3,
313; plans wartime escape from
England, 283–5; hospital training,
286–7; inspects air raid shelters,
290–92; wartime finances and
economies, 293–4; and Dickie's
home leave, 296–7; improved
relations with Dickie, 296–9, 306–7;
leadership and influence, 297;
attitude to sex, 298; wartime visit to
USA, 299–301, 303–8;
speechmaking, 304, 309, 313, 375;
Dali's portrait of, 308; tours Canada,
308–9; returns to England, 310–11;
wartime entertaining, 313;
Superintendent of St John
Ambulance, 317–18; strain and
exhaustion, 319; awarded CBE, 319;
working tours, 321, 326; encourages
Dickie in SEAC, 330–31; helps with
medical aid for SEAC, 331–2; and
Bunny's engagement, 334–8; in
liberated France, 338–40; inspection
tour of SEAC, 341–50; return to
England from SEAC, 350–51;
growing devotion to Dickie, 352;
tours Italy, Greece and Middle East,
353; in victory procession, 356; and
relief work with prisoners in S. E.
Asia, 357–69; and Asian nationalist
movements, 366, 369, 372–3;
awarded DCVO, 371; returns to Asia
and Australia, 373–6; honours, 377;
new seriousness of purpose, 378–9;
and Sargent, 379–81, 384, 401, 419,
421, 426–7; as Vicereine of India,
383–6; hysterectomy, 384, 386;
arrival in Delhi, 386–7; style and
routine in India, 388–94, 407; on
political and social situation in India,
393, 398; visits N. W. Frontier
Province, 397–8; and Indian
independence plans, 400, 402–6; and
Indian welfare organizations, 403,
406; silver wedding, 407–8; renewed
marriage strains, 408, 419–20, 423,
442–4, 475–8; at transfer of power in
India, 410–12; post-independence
duties and activities, 414, 420, 424,
426; and communal violence in
India, 415–18; in Kashmir, 418–19; at
Princess Elizabeth's wedding, 419;
tours in India, 420–22, 424–5,
430–31; and Gandhi, 420–21;
awarded GBE, 421; difficulty in
relaxing, 426; relations with Nehru,
427–32, 436–8, 446–9, 469–73; leaves
India, 431–3; correspondence with

Index

Nehru, 433–5, 438–40, 442, 444, 446, 450–66, 473, 475–8; meets Nehru in England, 438, 446–7; 1948 return to Malta, 439–40, 443–4; visits Nehru in India, 440–42; financial situation, 444–5; petitions for Mountbatten Estate Bill, 445–6; and post-war politics, 451–2; diary, 452; in Malta with Dickie as C. in C., 453–6; signs of ageing, 456; travels for relief work, 463–5; press criticisms of, 466–70; later travels, 478–9; face affected by operation, 478–9; decline and death, 478–81; buried at sea, 481

Mountbatten of Burma, Admiral of the Fleet Louis, 1st Earl ('Dickie'; i.e. Albert Nicholas Louis Francis): and father's resignation, 59–60; first meetings with Edwina, 88–93; naval training and service in Great War, 89–90; at Cambridge, 90; on *Venetia* with Edwina, 90–92; and father's death, 93–5; and Cassel's death, 95–6; family, 98–9, 101–2; proposes to Edwina, 99–100; financial position, 101, 115–16; tour of India with Prince of Wales, 102–6, 108, 114–15, 122–3, 126; punctiliousness, 103; and Edwina's visit to India, 106–11; engagement, 112–14, 123; receives Rolls Royce from Edwina, 115–17, 132; feelings for Edwina, 116; wedding, 119–20, 123, 127, 129–35; names, 120; business investment, 123–4; return to England, 127–8; routine of reunions, 127–8; made KCVO, 129; honeymoon trip, 134–41; and naval economies, 141–2; shooting, 143; first trip to USA, 143–50; in Hollywood film, 147–8; speech at Navy League, Washington, 148; joins HMS *Revenge*, 151–2, 155–6, 158–60, 162–3; night life, 153–4; and birth of daughter Patricia, 165–6; devotion to Patricia, 168–9, 185, 213, 236, 442; on naval signals course, 170, 179, 184; self-discipline, 173; motor launches and yachts, 173, 185; accompanies Prince of Wales to USA, 173–6; tonsillitis, 174; difficulties of marriage, 176–7, 191, 198–9, 203, 216–19; at Adsdean, 179; at Greenwich Naval College, 185, 188; inventions, 188–9, 201; serves on *Centurion*, 188; golf, 188; ailments and injuries, 189, 206; and Edwina's amours and affairs, 190–92, 217–20; de Laszlo's portrait of, 191; and General Strike, 193–5; posted to Malta, 196, 198, 200–3, 205–6; apologetic letter to Edwina, 198–9; and birth of second daughter (Pamela), 209–10; as instructor at Signals School, 212; flying, 212; and Edwina's behaviour in West Indies, 216–19, 239; reconciliation with Edwina, 219–21; return to Malta, 224, 230; and *People* libel case, 226; relations with Yola Letellier, 227–8, 230–2, 239; and Edwina's illness, 229–30; promoted Commander, 230; attempts economies, 230, 294; takes interpreter's course, 231; appearance, 233; and Bunny Phillips, 233–4, 236–7, 242–3, 298–9, 307–8, 330; commands HMS *Daring*, 237, 241; posted to Far East, 241; commands HMS *Wishart*, 244; and inter-war tensions, 245, 264; improves languages, 248; and new Brook House, 250–1; joins Naval Air Department, 251; innovations at Admiralty, 251–2; left-wing influences on, 252–3; and Prince of Wales in abdication crisis, 253–5; 37th birthday, 258; promoted Captain, 259; sails on *Lost Horizon*, 259; offered command of HMS *Kelly*, 264; on tactical course, 264; at R. N. War College, Greenwich, 266; takes over *Kelly*, 270–3; and management of Broadlands, 274; at outbreak of war, 274; brings torpedoed *Kelly* to Tyne, 281; and Edwina's proposed escape from England, 283–5; sees Bunny in war, 287–8; commands flotilla, 288; and sinking of *Kelly* 295–6; Edwina bequeathes Broadlands to, 296; improved

501

Mountbatten of Burma, Louis – *cont.* ·
relations with Edwina, 296–8, 306–7,
352; attitude to sex, 298; wartime
visit to USA, 299–300, 303–7;
speechmaking, 304–5; heads
Combined Operations, 307, 312–13,
316; made a Chief of Staff, 316–17;
overwork and exhaustion, 319–20;
pneumonia, 320; at Casablanca
conference, 320; as Supreme
Commander, S. E. Asia, 322–3,
325–6, 328–31, 353, 355; distributes
SEAC diary, 325; and Normandy
invasion, 328; injures eye, 329; visit
to England from SEAC, 332, 334;
and Bunny's engagement, 335–6;
and Edwina's tour of SEAC, 341–2,
345, 347, 349, 351–2; women friends,
352, 356; 1945 visit to England,
355–6; and Japanese surrender
ceremony, 361–3; and French
Indo-China, 365; and Dutch East
Indies, 368; praises Edwina for relief
work in S. E. Asia, 369; viscountcy,
371; and local nationalist
movements, 371–2; post-war visit to
India and Australia, 373–5; post-war
career, 377; made Rear Admiral, 377;
civil honours, 377; KG, 377; and
Patricia's wedding, 378; begins
Senior Officers' Technical Course,
381; offered Viceroyalty of India,
382–6; takes up appointment as
Viceroy, 386–7; aides and staff,
387–8; regime and style as Viceroy,
388–90, 393; kept informed by
Edwina, 392; negotiates Indian
independence and partition,
395–407; visits N. W. Frontier
Province, 397; and London talks,
401; and Princely States, 404–5; and
air-conditioning, 406; silver
wedding, 407; renewed strains in
marriage, 408, 420, 423, 442–4;
post-independence position as
Governor-General, 408–10, 425; and
transfer of power in India, 409–12;
and Indian communal violence,
413–15; chairs Emergency
Committee, 415; at wedding of
Princess Elizabeth, 419; tours of
India, 420–2, 424–5, 430–1; Earldom,
421; interest in genealogy, 426; and
Nehru, 429–30, 437–8, 474–6; leaves
India, 431–2; commands
Mediterranean 1st Cruiser
Squadron, 438, 444–5; promoted
Vice-Admiral, 442; financial
situation, 444–5; as 4th Sea Lord,
450; made C. in C. Mediterranean
Fleet, 453–5; heads NATO command
in Mediterranean, 455, 467; 50th
birthday, 457; as 1st Sea Lord,
458–9; opposes Suez action, 461; and
Edwina's relief tours, 464; press
attacks on, 466–9; unsettled
relationship with Edwina, 475–8;
and Edwina's death, 480–2;
French-English Naval Vocabulary, 248;
Polo (by 'Marco'), 188
Mountbatten, Princess Louise (Dickie's
sister): meets Edwina, 99; Mrs
Cassel entertains, 128; Dickie buys
furs for, 140; at Kensington Palace,
152; at Dickie's departure to join
HMS *Revenge*, 155; sees Edwina
during Dickie's absence, 157;
Dickie's daughter named for, 210; at
Broadlands, 356; and Dickie's
Viceroyalty in India, 392
Mountbatten, Pamela (Edwina's
daughter) *see* Hicks, Lady Pamela
Mountbatten, Patricia (Edwina's
daughter) *see* Brabourne, Patricia
Edwina Victoria, Lady
Mount Temple of Lee, Muriel, Lady
(*formerly* Forbes-Semphill; *née*
Spencer; Wilfrid's second wife;
'Molly'): marriage to Wilfrid, 55–6,
60; manner, 56–7; relations with
Edwina and Mary, 57–8, 60–61, 72;
fishing, 63; sends Edwina away to
school, 64–6; visits Edwina at
school, 70; in Monte Carlo, 86; and
Edwina's engagement, 114; invited
to Buckingham Palace, 128; and
Edwina's honeymoon, 134; and
Mountbattens' return from USA,
151; visits Branksome, 153; unwell in
Monte Carlo, 167; and Edwina's

Index

social life, 171; and
Cunningham-Reid, 182; builds
London house, 186; entertaining,
186–7; political activities, 210–11;
Wood Street house, 222, 240;
tensions of marriage, 240; visits
Adsdean, 259; and death of Wilfrid,
271; moves to Alresford, 273, 289;
complaints, 311; and Edwina's war
work, 327; and Edwina's return from
India, 432; death, 457

Mount Temple of Lee, Wilfrid William
Ashley, Baron (Edwina's father):
meets Maudie, 11–12; engagement
and marriage to Maudie, 12–16, 19,
25, 34; and Brook House, 19–20;
ambitions, 21–2, 202; wins Blackpool
seat, 23; relations with Edwina, 23,
26, 29–30, 32–4; visits Egypt, 27–8;
finances, 30–31, 34, 48; and
Maudie's ill-health, 37–8, 40–41, 43,
45; retains seat in 1910 elections, 40,
47; takes Edwina to Cleethorpes, 47;
and Maudie's death and will, 48–50;
second marriage (to Molly), 55–7,
60; in Great War, 58, 60–61; and
hostility to Cassel in war, 59;
fishing, 63; and Edwina's schooling,
65; in Monte Carlo, 86; and Cassel's
death, 94; cuts allowance to Edwina,
98; hears of Edwina's attachment to
Dickie, 106; and Edwina's
engagement, 113–15, 117, 123; meets
Dickie, 128; and Edwina's marriage
settlement, 129; and Edwina's
wedding and honeymoon, 130, 132,
134; holds political office, 142, 186,
210; visits Branksome, 153; and
Edwina's baby, 167; relations with
daughter Mary, 182–3, 196; in
General Strike, 193; wins New
Forest constituency, 210; loses office,
210–11; peerage, 240; deterioration
of marriage, 240; visits Adsdean,
259; marriage breakdown, 271;
death, 271, 274

Munich agreement, 1938, 266

Murphy, Peter: friendship with
Mountbattens, 89–90, 140, 154,
160–61, 188, 195, 200, 206–9, 215,

237; Dickie confides in, 217; Edwina
confides in, 234; political views, 237;
in Malta, 237–8, 245; accompanies
Dickie to Far East, 241; motor
accident, 289; with Edwina in war,
295–6, 321; helps Dickie at
Combined Operations, 312; visits
Broadlands, 314, 325, 378; helps
Dickie at SEAC, 325; joins Dickie's
staff, 329–30; Paris flat, 339; and
Edwina's SEAC tour, 349; on 1945
election, 355; with Dickie in Ceylon,
368; and Dickie's viscountcy, 371;
accused of influencing Dickie, 372;
and Dickie's offer of Viceroyalty,
385; in India with Dickie, 388; helps
Mountbattens' marriage, 423; and
public criticism of Dickie, 467–9

Murrow, Ed, 333, 356

Muslim League (India/Pakistan), 382–3,
396, 399, 402, 407

Mussolini, Benito, 245, 247, 270

Nagasaki, 356

Naidu, Padmaja, 23, 430, 435

Naidu, Sarojini (née Chattopadhyay), 9,
21, 23, 391–2, 430; death, 441

Nasmith, Justina, Lady, 370

Nasmith, Admiral Sir Martin Eric
Dunbar-, 288

Nasser, Gamal Abdel, 461

Navy League (USA), 148

Nehru, Jawaharlal (Pandit): visits
Malaya, 374; character, 395; and
Indian independence negotiations,
396, 399–400, 403; and princely
states, 404; and Hyderabad
question, 405; Mountbattens
entertain, 407–8; and transfer of
power in India, 410–11; and
communal violence, 413–14, 416;
and Kashmir troubles, 418; and
Princess Elizabeth's wedding, 419;
Dickie arbitrates for, 425; relations
with Edwina, 427–31, 435–8, 443,
446–9, 469–74; and Mountbattens'
departure from India, 432;
correspondence with Edwina,
433–5, 438–40, 442, 444, 446, 450–66,
473–8; and occupation of Kashmir,

Nehru, Jawaharlal (Pandit) – *cont.*
    436; at Dominion Prime Ministers'
    conference, 436; sees Edwina in
    England, 437–8, 446–7, 472; Edwina
    visits in India, 440–41; Eden meets,
    460–1; questions influence of
    individuals, 462; on Communism,
    463; Lyttelton meets, 468;
    assassination atttempt on, 474;
    mountain holiday, 474
Neumann, Leopold, 270
Neville, General Sir Robert, 267, 295,
    299, 312–14, 319–20, 455
Newall, Olive, Lady, 277
New Guinea, 268
New York: Edwina visits, 173–8; Patricia
    and Pamela evacuated to, 285,
    289–90, 301–3, 309, 315
New Zealand, 373, 375
Nice and Friendly (film), 147, 153
Nicholls, George, 387
Nielson, Eulalia, 145, 148
Nielson, Lieut. Frederick, USN, 145
Nisbit, Miss (nurse), 164–5, 167
Noel-Baker, Philip, 372
Normandy invasion, 1944, 328
North, Commander William, 274, 320, 481
North Atlantic Treaty Organisation
    (NATO), 455–6
Northcliffe, Alfred Harmsworth,
    Viscount 86
North West Frontier Province (India),
    397–8
Norton, Jeanie: friendship with Edwina,
    170–71, 173, 177–8, 187, 192–3, 202;
    way of life, 192–3; relations with
    Beaverbrook 193, 204, 211, 218; in
    General Strike, 194; friendship with
    Dickie, 197; visits Malta, 201; at
    Mary's wedding, 203; and Edwina's
    illness and pregnancy, 208, 215;
    Dickie confides in, 217–18; rebukes
    Cunningham-Reid, 226; and
    Edwina's relations with Bunny
    Phillips, 234; London flat, 239; at
    New Gallery Cinema, 280; death,
    379
Norton, Kay (Kaysie), 231, 421, 432
Norton, Richard, 170, 192–3
Norton, Sarah, 203

Nye, Sir Archibald, 422
Nye, Colleen, Lady, 422, 426, 435

Olga, Princess of Yugoslavia, 216
Olivier, Laurence, 432; *see also* Leigh,
    Vivien
Ollard, Nurse, 54
Osborne, Brittain, 180, 184
Ozanne, Madame, 163

Paget, Enid, 302
Pakenham, Dermot, 21, 34
Pakenham, Joan, 34, 131
Pakistan: proposed as separate state,
    394–5, 397, 399; and Commonwealth
    membership, 400; Dominion status,
    409; at transfer of power, 410; and
    violence in Punjab, 417; and
    Kashmir dispute, 418–19, 436
Paley, Colonel William, 333, 336–7,
    339–40
Pallant, Jessie, 273
Pandit, Lekha and Tara (Mrs Pandit's
    daughters), 437
Pandit, Vijaya Lakshmi, 391–2, 395, 403,
    408, 437, 470
Paris: Mountbattens honeymoon in, 122,
    124, 136–7, 139, 141; liberated, 338;
    Edwina visits, 339–40; Dickie visits,
    355
Parnell, Paul, 187
Passant, Jessie, 94
Patel, Maniben, 392, 406
Patel, Sardar Vallabhbhai, 392, 399–400,
    404, 413, 416, 430
Patricia, Princess, 27
Pearl Harbor, 305, 310
Pell, Mrs & Mrs Stephen H. P., 145, 289
Peneranda, Carmen, Duchess of, 210
People (newspaper), 224, 226
Perowne, Stewart, 246
Philip, Prince, Duke of Edinburgh:
    Edwina visits Windsor with, 311;
    and Dickie's offer of Viceroyalty,
    385; engagement and marriage, 401,
    419; visits Broadlands, 432–3, 452;
    son born, 439–40; joins
    Mediterranean Fleet, 444; at
    Pamela's wedding, 478
Philippines, 249, 367

Index

Phillips, 'Bunny' (Harold): relations with Edwina, 232, 233–4, 238, 245–6, 259, 298–9, 311; world travels with Edwina, 234–9, 241–3, 248–9, 253, 257–8, 267–9; in Malta, 246–7; builds and sails *Lost Horizon*, 253, 259–61, 263; in Switzerland, 257; in USA, 262–3; and preparations for war, 264, 270, 272; in Yugoslavia and Hungary, 265, 267; French holiday with Edwina before outbreak of war, 272; serves in France, 279, 281; evacuated to England, 282; sees Dickie in war, 287–8; appendix removed, 289; at Broadlands, 296, 318; Dickie's attitude to, 298–9, 308; intelligence post in USA, 307–8, 309, 311; home leave, 321; in Quebec, 322; serves in S. E. Asia, 323, 329; returns to Washington, 330; secret movements, 332–3; in England, 332–4; engagement to Gina Wernher, 334–7; gives ballpoint to Dickie, 340; visits India, 426
Phillips, Gina (*née* Wernher), 258, 334–7, 421
Phillips, Gray, 215
Phillips, Harold (Bunny's father), 261, 263
Phillips, Mary, 263
Phillips, Ted, 215–16, 241–2
Pickford, Mary, 144, 146–7, 169, 217, 241
Pilcher, Nigel, 22
Pius XII, Pope, 454
Poce, Signora, 77
Poland, 268–9
Porchester, Lord *see* Caernarvon, Henry Herbert, 6th Earl of
Portago, Antonio, 190
Portarlington, Lionel Dawson-Damer, 6th Earl of, and Winnifreda, Countess of, 189, 195
Potts, Jane (headmistress), 67–9, 71–3
Pound, Admiral Sir Dudley, 93, 278
Pound, Elizabeth, Lady, 278–9, 313
Powell, Miss (manicurist), 157
Power, Admiral Sir Arthur, 438
Power, Margaret Joyce, Lady, 438
Pownall, Lt.-General Sir Henry, 323, 331
Prasad, Rajendra, 410

Pratt, Lady Mary Clementine, 203
Prince of Wales, HMS, 311
Proetz, Victor, 251, 306
Pugh, Miss (governess), 289
Pulitzer, Mrs, 168, 175
Pulitzer, Tony, 177
Punjab., 406–7, 413–14, 417, 420
Punjab Boundary Force, 407, 414–15
Pyke, Geoffrey, 316

Quebec, 322
Queen Elizabeth, HMS, 205–6, 224–5
Quicke, Violet, 68

Radcliffe, Sir Cyril, 407, 413
Rajagopalachari, Chakravarti, 429, 431, 436, 440
Rama Rao, Lady, 391
Randell, Frank, 273
Rangoon, 352, 358–9
Rasdill (chauffeur), 129, 137, 139
Rawlinson of Trent, General Seymour Rawlinson, 1st Baron, 120
Reading, Alice Edith, Countess of (*later* Marchioness), 112–13, 116–18, 266
Reading, Rufus Isaacs, Baron (*later* 1st Marquess of), 58–9, 93, 112–14, 117–20
Reading, Stella, Marchioness of, 266, 388–92, 401
Recovery of Allied Prisoners of War and Internees (RAPWI), 357, 371, 373–4
Red Cross, 278–9, 288
Redher and Higgs (solicitors), 223
Reed (violin teacher), 69
Rees, General Peter, 415
Rees, Rosemary, 65
Reid, Sir James, 44
Reinhardt, Max, 192
Reiss, Nancy, 68
Renshaw, Lady Winifred, 90
Repeating Gramophone Company, 123–4
Repulse, HMS, 311
Revenge, HMS, 151–2, 155–6, 158–60, 162–3
Rhys, Charles, 85
Riggs (electrician), 184
Robertson, (Sir) Johnston Forbes, 21, 52
Robeson, Essie, 227

Robeson, Paul, 225–7
Robinson (Edwina's alibi), 242–3, 253
Rogers, Will, 175
Rome, 76–9
Roosevelt, Eleanor, 315
Roosevelt, Franklin Delano, 306, 315, 322
Rose, Joseph, the elder, 17
Rosenheim, Mrs, 86
Rothschild, Carola, 305
Rothschild see also de Rothschild
Rotsmann, Georgina von, 139
Russia (USSR), 211
Ruth, Babe, 144
Rutherford, Audrey, Lady, 347

Saadi Bey, Richid, 11, 86
St John, Order of: in war, 277–9; Edwina
    works with, 280, 282, 286, 288, 291,
    313; Edwina made Superintendent
    in Chief of Nursing division, 317;
    Edwina's post-war work with, 379
St Nazaire, 316
Samuel (music teacher), 68–9
Sandringham, Norfolk, 440, 451
Sandys, Duncan, 477
Sanford, Laddie, 190–2, 194–6, 200,
    202–4, 206–7, 213, 216, 218–21
Sarabhai, Mridula, 441
Sargent, Sir Malcolm: friendship with
    Edwina, 379–81, 384, 401, 419, 443,
    457; visit to India, 421, 426–7; and
    Edwina's return from India, 432; on
    Surprise cruise, 454
Sargent, Pamela & Peter (Sir Malcolm's
    children), 380
Sassoon, Sir Edward, 83
Sassoon, Sir Philip, 83, 128, 160–61, 167,
    239, 251
Schiff, Frieda, 6, 88
Schiff, Jacob, 6, 85–6
Schiff, John, 290
Scott, James, 425
Sefton, Hugh Molyneux, 7th Earl of, 125,
    162, 170, 190, 204, 215, 218–21, 326
Sefton, Josephine, Countess of (née
    Gwynne; 'Foxie'), 326
Selfridge, Gordon, 205
Selkirk, George Douglas-Hamilton, 10th
    Earl of, 477
Seymour, Sir Horace, 324

Shadow I (motor launch), 173, 185
Shadow II (motor launch), 185, 195
Shaftesbury, Constance Sibell, Countess
    of, 18
Shearer, Norma, 242, 306
Shinwell, Emanuel, 450
Shrimp (yacht), 185, 201, 205; sold, 224,
    263
Siam (later Thailand), 359–61
Sicily: invasion and campaign in, 322,
    324
Sime Road Camp, Singapore, 361, 375
Simla (India), 398–9, 404
Simon, Sir John, 86
Simpson, Tony, 201
Simpson, Mrs Wallis see Windsor, Wallis,
    Duchess of
Simson, Dr H. J. F., 161, 165
Singapore, 361–3, 365
Singh, Major Abhey, 358, 363, 371
Singh, Baldev, 413
Singh, Jaya Dalip, 417
Sitwell, (Sir) Osbert, 258
Six Mile Bottom, near Newmarket, 51, 97
Sjahrir, Soetan, 374
Sleeman, Colonel Sir James Lewis, 331
Slim, Aileen, Lady, 371
Slim, General Sir William, 329, 347, 352,
    359, 371
Sloane-Stanley, Diana, 65, 68
Sloane-Stanley, Lavender, 65
Smith, Charles (Dickie's valet), 260
Smollett, Major-General Telfer, 331, 343,
    368
Soekarno, Ahmed, 366
Somerville, Admiral Sir James, 324, 331
Sondes, Emma Beatrice, Countess, 127
Sophie, Princess ('Tiny'; Dickie's niece),
    131, 155
South America, 234–6
South-East Asia Command (SEAC):
    Dickie heads, 322, 325, 328–31;
    medical aid, 331–2; Edwina visits,
    341–8; refugees and released
    prisoners of war in, 357–69, 373; and
    nationalist politics, 366, 372–3
South Seas: Edwina in, 242–3
Spain: Mountbattens' honeymoon in,
    137–8
Spens, Sir Patrick, 344, 389

Index

Speyer, Sir Edgar, 59
Spry, Constance, 378
Stanley, Venetia (Montagu), 211
Steed, Wickham, 21
Stephenson, Sir William, 307, 322
Stilwell, General Joseph, 323, 329
Stonor, Sir Harry, 85–6
Stopford, General Monty, 347
Strachey, John: *The Coming Struggle for Power*, 245
Strong (electrical therapist), 260
Strong, Mrs (of British School in Rome), 77–9
Stuart, James, 85
Sturt, Lois, 65
Suez crisis, 1956, 461
Sumatra, 364–5
Surprise (yacht), 454, 456
Sutherland, Eileen, Duchess of, 93, 158, 195, 215, 266
Sutherland, George Sutherland-Leveson-Gower, 5th Duke of, 95, 104, 132, 158, 202, 215
Sweeney, Bobby, 221
Switzerland, 22, 54–5, 257
Symonds, Richard, 417
Syms, Captain Malcolm, 366
Szapary, Anti, 228–30, 232

Tahiti, 242
Takahashi, Lieutenant, 364
Talbot, Commander, 152
Talmadge, Madge, 188
Talmadge, Norma, 159
Taylor, Robert, 306
Teano, Vittoria Colonna, Princess, 21
Templer, General Sir Gerald, 463
Tennent, Mr & Mrs (of Adsdean), 179–80
Thalberg, Irving, 242
Thapar, Bimla, 417
Thaw, Consuelo ('Tamar'), 240
Theodora, Princess (Dickie's niece; 'Dolla'), 131, 155, 157, 202
Thomas, James (*later* 1st Viscount Cilcennin), 458
Thompson, Colonel Robert M., 145–8
Thompson, General Sir Treffry Owen, 358, 363, 371
Thorogood (valet), 129, 139, 147, 151, 159–60, 188, 198, 260

Tiller (head keeper at Broadlands), 284–5
Tirpitz, Admiral Alfred von, 43, 55
Tito, Josip Broz, 454
Topliss (steward), 314
Torch, Operation, 319
Tor Royal, near Plymouth, 124
Tracey, Spencer, 306
Tracy, Hanbury, 10
Treble, Henrietta, 209, 212
Tree, Beerbohm,. 52
Tree, Nancy, 333
Trivedi, Sir Chandulal, 417, 441
Trivedi, Kusum, Lady, 429, 441
Tucker (butler), 164
Tucker, Sophie, 187, 193
Turner, Evelyn, 479–80
Turner, Robert Noel, 479–80
Turner, Mrs (housekeeper), 61
Tuttnauer, Dr, 270
Tweedmouth, Edward Marjoribanks, 2nd Baron, 19
Tyndall, Major-General William Ernest, 358

Umberto, King of Italy, 457
Underhill, Stella: runs Brook House, 80–82, 87, 94–5, 136, 157, 164, 212, 236; on Brook House as white elephant, 222; sends proofs to Dickie, 248; in new Brook House, 250; moves to Kensington Palace, 273
United Council for Relief and Welfare (India), 416, 420, 424
United States of America: Mountbattens' first visit, 143–50; Prince of Wales visits with Mountbattens, 173–4; Edwina visits (1930), 207, 211–12; Mountbattens' 1938 trip to, 262–3; Patricia and Pamela evacuated to, 285, 299–303; Mountbattens make wartime visit to, 299–300, 303–8; enters war, 310; Dickie's mission to, 316

Vaagso (Norway), 313
Valentino, Rudolf, 187, 191
Vanderbilt, Gloria, 240–41
Vanderbilt, Gloria (daughter), 240
Vanderbilt, Grace: social life, 84–5, 89,

Vanderbilt, Grace – *cont.*
91–2, 99; entertains Mountbattens, 128; in New York, 149–50; midshipmen meet, 160; at Brook House, 160–61; and Edwina's social life, 171; entertains Pamela and Patricia in New York during war, 289–90, 301, 303, 315; Mountbattens stay with, 306

Vanderbilt, Harold, 174

van der Post, (Sir) Laurens, 366

Van Mook Dr H. J., 374

Vaughan, Dame Helen Gwynne, 277

Vaughan Thomas, Wynford, 411

Vick, Miss (governess), 224, 246–7, 252

Victoria, Princess, 44

Vienna, 228–30

Villa Cassel (Switzerland), 22, 54, 97

Villa des Cèdres (Riviera), 87, 91

Voroshilov, Marshal Klement E., 479

Vreeland, Diana, 251

Wallace, Lucy, 16

Warburg, Felix, 145, 151, 197–8

Warburg, Mrs Felix, 301

Ward, Elizabeth: on SEAC tour with Edwina, 358, 362, 367–8; in India, 388, 390, 392, 399, 416; at transfer of power in India, 411; and Edwina's death, 481

Wardell, Michael, 196–7, 200, 204, 211, 215, 218, 276, 317

Warspite, HMS, 198, 202, 205

Watson, Sergeant (of Hawes & Curtis), 343

Watson, Muriel, 353, 388, 390, 392, 398–9, 416–17

Waugh, Evelyn, 316; *Black Mischief*, 455

Wavell, Field Marshal Archibald, Earl, 322, 351, 382–5

Wavell, Eugenie, Countess, 331–2, 344, 351, 358, 386–7

Way Ahead Committee (Admiralty), 459

Wedemeyer, General Albert C., 323–4

Weld, Colonel Sir Joseph, 338

Weller (Edwina's maid), 80, 107, 112, 116, 124, 137, 139, 151, 160, 178

Wentworth, Michael, 201

Wernher, Gina *see* Phillips, Gina

Wernher, Harold, 98, 125, 128, 132, 312

Wernher, Sir Julius, 10, 75, 98

Wernher, Myra, 378

Wernher, Lady Zia, 75, 98, 125, 128, 132, 175, 258

West Indies, 215–16

Westminster, Violet, Duchess of, 175, 177

Wherwell Priory, 25, 42, 47

Whistler, Rex, 251, 259

White, George, 175

Whiteman, Paul, 145, 150, 160

Whitney, Gertrude, 240

Whitney, John Hay (Jock), 202

Wichfeld, Aksel and Mabel, 190, 213

Wilhelmina, Queen of the Netherlands, 378

Wilkinson, Ellen, 291

Willingdon, Freeman Freeman-Thomas, 1st Marquess of, 114

Wilmer, Dr (oculist), 148

Wilson, Mrs (of Lady Minto Nurses), 391

Wilson, Major-General Sir Gordon, 344

Wilson, Field Marshal Sir Henry, 128

Wilson, Randolph, 85

Wilton Crescent (London), 453, 459

Windsor, Edward, Duke of (*formerly* Prince of Wales; *then* King Edward VIII): Dickie accompanies to Australia, 88, 375; relations with Dickie, 91; tours India and Japan, 92–3, 98–9, 102–6, 110–11, 113, 126–7; and Edwina's wedding, 119; offers Tor Royal (house) to Dickie, 124; Mountbattens entertain, 136; and night life, 153–4, 157; codeword to Freda Dudley Ward, 159; and birth of Patricia, 167; at Fairbanks film, 170; in USA with Mountbattens, 173–4, 178; visits Adsdean, 188; on Edwina's amours, 191; at theatrical charity performance, 214; and difficulties of Dickie's marriage, 217; receives pictures and china from Brook House, 223; at Biarritz, 231; friendship with Basualdos, 235; relations with Mrs Simpson, 246, 253, 255–6; succession and abdication crisis, 253–6; returns from

Index

France in war, 274; visits Wilton
Crescent, 453
Windsor, Wallis, Duchess of (*formerly*
Simpson), 239–40, 246, 253–6, 274
Wingate, General Orde, 323
Winn, Godfrey, 292
Wishart, HMS, 244–5
Wolfsgarten, 353
Woodard, Miss (children's nurse), 164,
167–8
Woolton, Frederick J., 1st Earl, 451
Worsfold (groom), 61–2
Wyatt, Thomas, 19

Xuereb (chauffeur), 273, 275, 284, 317

Yamamoto, Colonel, 126
Yanagida (Japanese camp commander), 359
Yates, Andrew, 188
Young, Loretta, 242
Ypyranga (ship), 53
Yugoslavia, 265, 454

Zammit, Sir Themistocles, 205
Zhukov, Marshal Georgi K., 470
Zichy, Count, 149
Zuckerman, Solly, Baron, 316

THE UNIVERSITY OF WINCHESTER

Martial Rose Library
Tel: 01962 827306

To be returned on or before the day marked above, subject to recall.